OCA Java SE 7 Programmer I
Certification Guide

OCA Java SE 7 Programmer I Certification Guide

PREPARE FOR THE 1Z0-803 EXAM

MALA GUPTA

MANNING
SHELTER ISLAND

For online information and ordering of this and other Manning books, please visit
www.manning.com. The publisher offers discounts on this book when ordered in quantity.
For more information, please contact

Special Sales Department
Manning Publications Co.
20 Baldwin Road
PO Box 261
Shelter Island, NY 11964
Email: orders@manning.com

 Manning Publications Co.   Development editor: Cynthia Kane
20 Baldwin Road   Technical editor: Brent Watson
PO Box 261   Technical proofreader: Jeanne Boyarsky
Shelter Island, NY 11964   Copyeditors: Tara Walsh, Bob Herbstman,
                                                  Nancy Wolfe Kotary
                                  Proofreader: Andy Carroll
                                   Typesetter: Dennis Dalinnik
                                  Illustrator: Martin Murtonen
                               Cover designer: Marija Tudor

ISBN: 9781617291043
Printed in the United States of America
  6 7 8 9 10 – MAL – 19 18 17 16 15 14

To my pillar of strength, my best friend,
and my husband, Dheeraj Prakash

brief contents

Introduction   1

1 ■ Java basics   13

2 ■ Working with Java data types   69

3 ■ Methods and encapsulation   110

4 ■ String, StringBuilder, Arrays, and ArrayList   174

5 ■ Flow control   243

6 ■ Working with inheritance   295

7 ■ Exception handling   348

8 ■ Full mock exam   405

contents

foreword xvii
preface xix
acknowledgments xxi
about this book xxiii
about the author xxx
about the cover illustration xxxi

Introduction   1

1   Disclaimer   2

2   Introduction to OCA Java SE 7 Programmer
    certification   2

*The importance of OCA Java SE 7 Programmer certification   2
Comparing OCA Java exam versions   3 ▪ Comparing the OCA
Java SE 7 Programmer I (1Z0-803) and OCP Java SE 7
Programmer II (1Z0-804) exams   4 ▪ Complete exam objectives,
mapped to book chapters, and readiness checklist   4*

3   FAQs   8

FAQs on exam preparation   8 ▪ FAQs on taking the exam   10

4   The testing engine used in the exam   12

1   *Java basics*   13

1.1   The structure of a Java class and source code file   14

Structure of a Java class   15 ▪ Structure and components of a Java source code file   21

1.2   Executable Java applications   25

Executable Java classes versus nonexecutable Java classes   25 Main method   26

1.3   Java packages   29

The need for packages   29 ▪ Defining classes in a package using the package statement   30 ▪ Using simple names with import statements   32 ▪ Using packaged classes without using the import statement   34 ▪ Importing a single member versus all members of a package   35 ▪ Can you recursively import subpackages?   35 ▪ Importing classes from the default package   36 ▪ Static imports   36

1.4   Java access modifiers   37

Access modifiers   37 ▪ Public access modifier   39 Protected access modifier   40 ▪ Default access (package access)   42 Private access modifier   45

1.5   Nonaccess modifiers   47

Abstract modifier   48 ▪ Final modifier   49 ▪ Static modifier   51

1.6   Summary   54

1.7   Review notes   55

1.8   Sample exam questions   58

1.9   Answers to sample exam questions   62

2   *Working with Java data types*   69

2.1   Primitive variables   70

Category: Boolean   72 ▪ Category: Numeric   73 Category: Character   78 ▪ Confusion with the names of the primitive data types   79

2.2   Identifiers   80

Valid and invalid identifiers   81

2.3   Object reference variables   82

What are object reference variables?   82 ▪ Differentiating between object reference variables and primitive variables   84

2.4 Operators 85

Assignment operators 87 • Arithmetic operators 89
Relational operators 92 • Logical operators 94
Operator precedence 96

2.5 Summary 98

2.6 Review notes 98

2.7 Sample exam questions 101

2.8 Answers to sample exam questions 104

3 **Methods and encapsulation 110**

3.1 Scope of variables 112

Local variables 112 • Method parameters 114
Instance variables 115 • Class variables 116
Overlapping variable scopes 117

3.2 Object's life cycle 120

An object is born 120 • Object is accessible 122
Object is inaccessible 123

3.3 Create methods with arguments and return values 124

Return type of a method 125 • Method parameters 127
Return statement 130

3.4 Create an overloaded method 132

Argument list 133 • Return type 135 • Access modifier 135

3.5 Constructors of a class 136

User-defined constructors 137 • Default constructor 140
Overloaded constructors 142

3.6 Accessing object fields 145

What is an object field? 145 • Read and write object fields 145
Calling methods on objects 148

3.7 Apply encapsulation principles to a class 150

Need for encapsulation 150 • Apply encapsulation 151

3.8 Passing objects and primitives to methods 153

Passing primitives to methods 153 • Passing object references
to methods 155

3.9 Summary 158

3.10 Review notes 158

3.11   Sample exam questions   162

3.12   Answers to sample exam questions   166

4   *String, StringBuilder, Arrays, and ArrayList*   174

4.1   Welcome to the world of the String class   175

*Creating String objects   176 ▪ The class String is immutable   179
Methods of the class String   182 ▪ String objects
and operators   186 ▪ Determining equality of Strings   187*

4.2   Mutable strings: StringBuilder   189

*The StringBuilder class is mutable   190
Creating StringBuilder objects   190 ▪ Methods of class
StringBuilder   192 ▪ A quick note on the class StringBuffer   197*

4.3   Arrays   197

*What is an array?   197 ▪ Array declaration   199
Array allocation   200 ▪ Array initialization   201
Combining array declaration, allocation, and initialization   203
Asymmetrical multidimensional arrays   204 ▪ Arrays of type
interface, abstract class, and class Object   205 ▪ Members of
an array   206*

4.4   ArrayList   206

*Creating an ArrayList   207 ▪ Adding elements to
an ArrayList   209 ▪ Accessing elements of an ArrayList   211
Modifying the elements of an ArrayList   212 ▪ Deleting the
elements of an ArrayList   213 ▪ Other methods of ArrayList   215*

4.5   Comparing objects for equality   221

*The method equals in the class java.lang.Object   221
Comparing objects of a user-defined class   221 ▪ Incorrect method
signature of the equals method   223 ▪ Contract of the
equals method   224*

4.6   Summary   225

4.7   Review notes   227

4.8   Sample exam questions   232

4.9   Answers to sample exam questions   236

5   *Flow control*   243

5.1   The if and if-else constructs   245

*The if construct and its flavors   245 ▪ Missing else blocks   248
Implications of the presence and absence of { } in*

if-else constructs 249 ▪ *Appropriate versus inappropriate expressions passed as arguments to an if statement 251 Nested if constructs 252*

5.2 The switch statement 254

Create and use a switch statement 254 ▪ *Comparing a switch statement with multiple if-else constructs 254* ▪ *Arguments passed to a switch statement 257* ▪ *Values passed to the label case of a switch statement 258* ▪ *Use of break statements within a switch statement 259*

5.3 The for loop 260

Initialization block 262 ▪ *Termination condition 263 The update clause 263* ▪ *Nested for loop 264*

5.4 The enhanced for loop 265

Limitations of the enhanced for loop 268 ▪ *Nested enhanced for loop 269*

5.5 The while and do-while loops 270

The while loop 271 ▪ *The do-while loop 272 While and do-while block, expression, and nesting rules 274*

5.6 Comparing loop constructs 274

Comparing do-while and while loops 274 ▪ *Comparing for and enhanced for loops 275* ▪ *Comparing for and while loops 276*

5.7 Loop statements: break and continue 276

The break statement 276 ▪ *The continue statement 278 Labeled statements 279*

5.8 Summary 280

5.9 Review notes 280

5.10 Sample exam questions 283

5.11 Answers to sample exam questions 287

6 *Working with inheritance 295*

6.1 Inheritance with classes 296

Need to inherit classes 296 ▪ *A derived class contains within it an object of its base class 300* ▪ *Which base class members are inherited by a derived class? 301* ▪ *Which base class members aren't inherited by a derived class? 301* ▪ *Derived classes can define additional properties and behavior 301* ▪ *Abstract base class versus concrete base class 302*

6.2   Use interfaces   304

Properties of members of an Interface   307 ▪ Why a class can't extend multiple classes   308 ▪ Implementing multiple interfaces   308

6.3   Reference variable and object types   310

Using a variable of the derived class to access its own object   311 Using a variable of the base class to access an object of a derived class   312 ▪ Using a variable of an implemented interface to access a derived class object   312 ▪ The need for accessing an object using the variables of its base class or implemented interfaces   313

6.4   Casting   316

How to cast a variable to another type   316 Need for casting   318

6.5   Use this and super to access objects and constructors   319

Object reference: this   319 ▪ Object reference: super   321

6.6   Polymorphism   324

Polymorphism with classes   324 ▪ Binding of variables and methods at compile time and runtime   329 Polymorphism with interfaces   330

6.7   Summary   333

6.8   Review notes   334

6.9   Sample exam questions   336

6.10   Answers to sample exam questions   340

7 *Exception handling*   *348*

7.1   Exceptions in Java   349

A taste of exceptions   349 ▪ Why handle exceptions separately?   352 ▪ Do exceptions offer any other benefits?   353

7.2   What happens when an exception is thrown?   354

Creating try-catch-finally blocks   356 ▪ Will a finally block execute even if the catch block defines a return statement?   361 What happens if both a catch and a finally block define return statements?   362 ▪ What happens if a finally block modifies the value returned from a catch block?   363 ▪ Does the order of the exceptions caught in the catch blocks matter?   364 ▪ Can I rethrow an exception or the error I catch?   366 ▪ Can I declare my methods to throw a checked exception, instead of handling it?   367

I can create nested loops, so can I create nested try-catch blocks too? 367

7.3 Categories of exceptions 369

Identifying exception categories 369 ▪ *Checked exceptions* 370
Runtime exceptions (also known as unchecked exceptions) 371
Errors 372

7.4 Common exception classes and categories 374

*ArrayIndexOutOfBoundsException and
IndexOutOfBoundsException* 375 ▪ *ClassCastException* 376
IllegalArgumentException 378 ▪ *IllegalStateException* 378
NullPointerException 379 ▪ *NumberFormatException* 382
ExceptionInInitializerError 384 ▪ *StackOverflowError* 386
NoClassDefFoundError 386 ▪ *OutOfMemoryError* 387

7.5 Summary 387

7.6 Review notes 388

7.7 Sample exam questions 393

7.8 Answers to sample exam questions 397

8 *Full mock exam* 405

8.1 Mock exam 405

8.2 Answers to mock exam questions 439

appendix *Answers to Twist in the Tale exercises* 502

index 519

foreword

Taking the OCA Java Programmer I exam is a bit like taking a driving test. First you learn the basics, like where the brakes are. Then you start driving, and then you get ready to take the driving test to get your license. The written test includes things everyone should know, things that you'll never use after the road test, and some things that are tricky edge cases. While the programmer exam cares about breaks more than brakes, it certainly likes edge cases!

Consider Mala Gupta your driving instructor to get you ready for the programmer exam. Mala points out what you'll need to know when programming in the real world—on your first job.

And consider this book your driver's manual. It gives you the rules of the road of Java, plus the gotchas that show up on that pesky written test. But don't worry, it is much more fun to read this book than the driver's manual. Just like the driver's manual won't teach you everything about driving, this book won't teach you everything there is to know about Java. If you haven't yet, read an intro to a Java book first. Start with a book like *Head First Java* or *Thinking in Java* and then come back to this book to study for the exam.

As the technical proofreader of this book, I got to see it evolve and get better as Mala worked on it. Through the conversations we had on little things, I learned that Mala knows her stuff and is a great teacher of Java. While I've only technical proofread a handful of books, I've posted reviews of over 150 technical books on Amazon, which makes it easy to spot a book that isn't clear or helpful. I'm happy to say that Mala's explanations are all very clear, and the pointers are great.

I also got to read Mala's posts in the certification forums at coderanch.com. She's been sharing updates about the exam as it comes out and posting fairly regularly for over a year. As a senior moderator at coderanch.com, it is great to see an author sharing her wisdom. It's also nice to see the similarity in writing style between the forum posts and the book. This shows the book is readable and written in an easy-to-understand, casual style.

I particularly liked the diagrams, flow charts, and cartoons in this book. And, of course, the annotated code examples I've come to expect from any Manning book. Each chapter ends with sample mock exam questions and there is a full mock exam at the end. This gives you good practice in getting ready for the exam. Wrong answers are well explained so you don't make the same mistakes over and over.

My favorite part of the book is the "Twist in the Tale" exercises. Mala gives a number of examples of how making a seemingly minor change to the code can have major consequences. These exercises develop your attention to detail so you are more observant for the mock exam questions and the exam itself.

I had already passed the OCA Java Programmer exam with a score of 98% before reading this book. If I hadn't, the questions would have prepared me for the exam. Studying from this book will give you the skills and confidence you need to become an Oracle Certified Associate Java Programmer. Happy coding and good luck on the exam!

JEANNE BOYARSKY
SENIOR DEVELOPER & MODERATOR
CODERANCH

preface

Java programmer certifications are designed to tell would-be employers whether you really know your stuff, and cracking the OCA Java SE 7 Programmer Certification is not an easy task. Thorough preparation is crucial if you want to pass the exam the first time with a score that you can be proud of. You need to know Java inside and out, and you need to understand the certification process so that you're ready for the challenging questions you'll face in the exam.

This book is a comprehensive guide to the 1Z0-803 exam. You'll explore a wide range of important Java topics as you systematically learn how to pass the certification exam. Each chapter starts with a list of the exam objectives covered in that chapter. Throughout the book you'll find sample questions and exercises designed to reinforce key concepts and prepare you for what you'll see in the real exam, along with numerous tips, notes, and visual aids.

Unlike many other exam guides, this book provides multiple ways to digest important techniques and concepts, including comic conversations, analogies, pictorial representations, flowcharts, UML diagrams, and, naturally, lots of well-commented code. The book also gives insight into typical exam question mistakes and guides you in avoiding traps and pitfalls. It provides

- 100% coverage of exam topics, all mapped to chapter and section numbers
- Hands-on coding exercises, including particularly challenging ones that throw in a twist

- Instruction on what's happening behind the scenes using the actual code from the Java API source
- Mastery of both the concepts and the exam

This book is written for developers with a working knowledge of Java. My hope is that the book will deepen your knowledge, prepare you well for the exam, and that you will pass it with flying colors!

acknowledgments

First and foremost, I thank Dheeraj Prakash—my pillar of strength, my best friend and my husband. This book wouldn't exist without his efforts. His constant guidance, encouragement, and love kept me going. He helped me to get started with this book and got me over the goal line.

My sincere gratitude to Marjan Bace, publisher at Manning, for giving me the opportunity to author this book. The Manning team has been wonderful—Scott Meyers ensured that it was worth it for Manning to have a book on this subject. Cynthia Kane, my development editor, played a major role in shaping the organization of individual chapters and the overall book. It has been a real pleasure to work with her. Copyeditors Tara Walsh, Bob Herbstman, and Nancy Wolfe Kotary not only applied their magic to sentence and language constructions but also supplemented their editing with valuable suggestions on technical content.

Technical Editor Brent Watson did a brilliant job of reviewing the complete book contents in a limited time, catching even the smallest errors in the book. Technical Proofreader Jeanne Boyarsky was outstanding and an amazing person to work with. She was very quick at reviewing the book, with an eye for detail. Proofreader Andy Carroll was extremely capable and talented. He reviewed the final manuscript with great precision.

The technical reviewers on this book did an awesome job of reviewing the contents and sharing their valuable feedback and comments: Roel De Nijs, Ivan Todorovic, Michael Piscatello, Javier Valverde, Anayonkar Shivalkar, Kyle Smith, Niklas Rosencrantz, Ashwin Mhatre, Janki Shah, Dmitriy Andrushko, Nitesh Nandwana, and Priyanka Manchanda. I would also like to thank Ozren Harlovic, Review Editor, for managing the whole review process and meticulously funneling the feedback to make this book better.

Martin Murtonen did an outstanding job of converting the black and white hand-drawn illustrations into glorious images. It was amazing to scrutinize the page proofs. I thank Dennis Dalinnik for adjusting the images in the final page proofs, which was a lot of work. Janet Vail and Mary Piergies were awesome in their expertise at turning all text, code, and images into publishable form. I am also grateful to Candace Gillhoolley and Nermina Miller for their efforts in promoting the book.

I thank the MEAP readers for buying the book while it was being developed and for their suggestions, corrections, and encouragement: Samuel Prette, David C., Diego Poggioli, Baptize, Jayagopi Jagadeesan, David Vonka, Joel Rainey, Steve Breese, and Jörgen Persson.

I would also like to thank my former colleagues Harry Mantheakis, Paul Rosenthal, and Selvan Rajan, whose names I use in coding examples throughout the book. I have always looked up to them.

I thank my nine-year-old daughter, Shreya, an artist, who often advised me on the images that I created for the book. I'm also grateful to my younger daughter, Pavni, who patiently waited for my attention all these months when my focus was on the book. I thank my family for their unconditional support. The book would have been not been possible without their love and encouragement.

about this book

This book is written for developers with a working knowledge of Java who want to earn the OCA Java SE 7 Programmer certification. It uses powerful tools and features to make reaching your goal of certification a quick, smooth, and enjoyable experience. This section will explain the features used in the book and tell you how to use the book to get the most out of it as you prepare for the certification exam. More information on the exam and on how the book is organized is available in the Introduction.

Start your preparation with the chapter-based exam objective map

I strongly recommend a structured approach to preparing for this exam. To help you with this task, I've developed a chapter-based exam objective map, as shown in figure 1. The full version is in the Introduction (table I.3).

	Exam objectives	Covered in chapter/section	Your readiness score
1	**Java basics**	**Chapters 1 and 3**	
1.1	Define the scope of variables	Section 3.1	☆☆☆
1.2	Define the structure of a Java class	Section 1.1	☆☆☆
1.3	Create executable Java applications with a main method	Section 1.2	☆☆☆

Figure 1   The Introduction to this book provides a list of all exam objectives and the corresponding chapter and section numbers where they are covered. See the full table in the Introduction (table I.3).

As you go through your preparation, mark your readiness score for each section. Self-assessment is an important tool that will help you determine when you are ready to take the exam.

The map in the Introduction shows the complete exam objective list mapped to the relevant chapter and section numbers. You can jump to the relevant section number to work on a particular exam topic.

Chapter-based objectives

Each chapter starts with a list of the exam objectives covered in that chapter, as shown in figure 2. This list is followed by a quick comparison of the major concepts and topics covered in the chapter with real-world objects and scenarios.

Exam objectives covered in this chapter	What you need to know
[3.4] Create `if` and `if-else` constructs.	How to use `if`, `if-else`, `if-else-if-else`, and nested `if` constructs. 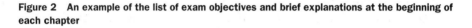 The differences between using these `if` constructs with and without curly braces { }.

Figure 2   An example of the list of exam objectives and brief explanations at the beginning of each chapter

Section-based objectives

Each main section in a chapter starts by identifying the exam objective(s) that it covers. Each listed exam topic starts with the exam objective and its subobjective number.

In figure 3, the number 4.4 refers to section 4.4 in chapter 4 (the complete list of chapters and sections can be found in the table of contents). The 4.3 preceding the exam objective refers to the objective's numbering in the list of exam objectives on Oracle's website (the complete numbered list of exam objectives is given in table I.3 in the Introduction).

4.4   ArrayList

   [4.3]   Declare and use an ArrayList

In this section, I'll cover how to use `ArrayList`, its commonly used methods, and the advantages it offers over an array.

Figure 3   An example of the beginning of a section, identifying the exam objective that it covers

Exam tips

Each chapter provides multiple *exam tips* to re-emphasize the points that are the most confusing, overlooked, or frequently answered incorrectly by candidates and that therefore require special attention for the exam. Figure 4 shows an example.

> **EXAM TIP** An `ArrayList` preserves the order of insertion of its elements. `Iterator`, `ListIterator`, and the enhanced `for` loop will return the elements in the order in which they were added to the `ArrayList`.

Figure 4   Example of an exam tip; they occur multiple times in a chapter

Notes

All chapters also include multiple notes, which draw your attention to points that should be noted while you're preparing for the exam. Figure 5 shows an example.

> **NOTE** Though the terms *method parameters* and *method arguments* are not the same, you may have noticed that they are used interchangeably by many programmers. *Method parameters* are the variables that appear in the definition of a method. *Method arguments* are the actual values that are passed to a method while executing it. In figure 3.13, variables `phNum` and `msg` are method parameters. If you execute this method as `sendMsg("123456", "Hello")`, then the `String` values `"123456"` and `"Hello"` are method arguments.

Figure 5   Example note

Sidebars

Sidebars contain information that may not be directly relevant to the exam but that is related to it. Figure 6 shows an example.

> ### Static classes and interfaces
> Certification aspirants frequently ask questions about `static` classes and interfaces, so I'll quickly cover these in this section to ward off any confusion related to them. But note that `static` classes and interfaces are types of nested classes and interfaces that aren't covered by the OCA Java 7 Programmer I exam.
>
> You can't prefix the definition of a top-level class or an interface with the keyword `static`. A top-level class or interface is one that isn't defined within another class or interface. The following code will fail to compile:
>
> ```
> static class Person {}
> ```

Figure 6   Example sidebar

Images

I've used a lot of images in the chapters for an immersive learning experience. I believe that a simple image can help you understand a concept quickly, and a little humor can help you to retain information longer.

Simple images are used to draw your attention to a particular line of code (as shown in figure 7).

```
public String replace(char oldChar, char newChar) {
    if (oldChar != newChar) {
        // code to create a new char array and
        // replace the desired char with the new char

        return new String(0, len, buf);
    }
    return this;
}
```

replace creates and
returns a new String
object. It doesn't modify
the existing array value.

Figure 7   An example image that draws your attention to a particular line of code

I've used pictorial representation of data in arrays (figure 8) and other data types to aid visualization and understanding.

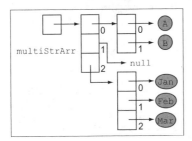

Figure 8   An example pictorial representation of data in an array

To reinforce important points and help you retain them longer, a little humor has been added using comic strips (as in figure 9).

Figure 9   An example of a little humor to help you remember that the `finally` block always executes

I've also used images to group and represent information for quick reference. Figure 10 shows an example of the protected members that can be accessed by derived or unrelated classes in the same or separate packages. I strongly recommend that you try to create a few of your own figures like these.

	Same package	Separate package
Derived classes	✓	✓
Unrelated classes	✓	✓

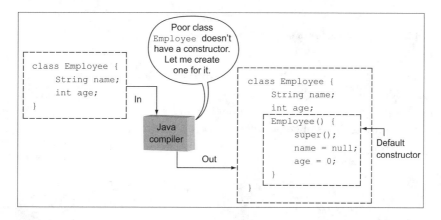

Figure 10 An example of grouping and representing information for quick reference

An image can also add more meaning to a sequence of steps also explained in the text. For example, figure 11 seems to bring the Java compiler to life by allowing it to talk with you and convey what it does when it gets to compile a class that doesn't define a constructor. Again, try a few of your own! It'll be fun!

Figure 11 An example pictorial representation of steps executed by the Java compiler when it compiles a class without a constructor

The exam requires that you know multiple methods from classes such as `String`, `StringBuilder`, `ArrayList`, and others. The number of these methods can be overwhelming, but grouping these methods according to their functionality can make this task a lot more manageable. Figure 12 shows an example of an image that groups methods of the `String` class according to their functionality.

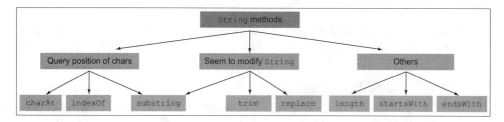

Figure 12 An example image used to group methods of the `String` class according to their functionality.

Expressions that involve multiple operands can be hard to comprehend. Figure 13 is an example of an image that can save you from the mayhem of unary increment and decrement operators used in prefix and postfix notation.

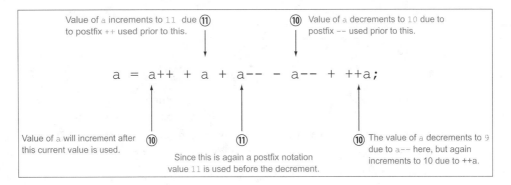

Figure 13   Example of values taken by the operands during execution of an expression

Code snippets that define multiple points and that may result in the nonlinear execution of code can be very difficult to comprehend. These may include selection statements, loops, or exception-handling code. Figure 14 is an example of an image that clearly outlines the lines of code that will execute.

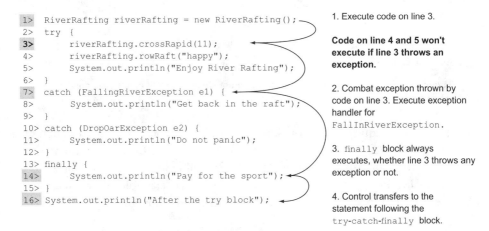

Figure 14   An example of flow of control in a code snippet that may define multiple points of nonlinear execution of code

Twist in the Tale exercises

Each chapter includes a few Twist in the Tale exercises. For these exercises, I've tried to use modified code from the examples already covered in a chapter, and the "Twist in the Tale" title refers to modified or tweaked code. These exercises highlight how even small code modifications can change the behavior of your code. They should encourage you to carefully examine all of the code in the exam.

My main reason for including these exercises is that on the real exam, you may get to answer more than one question that seems to define exactly the same question and answer options. But upon closer inspection, you'll realize that these questions differ slightly, and that these differences change the behavior of the code and the correct answer option.

The answers to all of the Twist in the Tale exercises are given in the appendix.

Code Indentation

Some of the examples in this book show incorrect indentation of code. This has been done on purpose because on the real exam you can't expect to see perfectly indented code. You should be able to comprehend incorrectly indented code to answer an exam question correctly.

Review notes

When you're ready to take your exam, don't forget to reread the review notes a day before or on the morning of the exam. These notes contain important points from each chapter as a quick refresher.

Exam questions

Each chapter concludes with a set of 10 to 11 exam questions. These follow the same pattern as the real exam questions. Attempt these exam questions after completing a chapter.

Answers to exam questions

The answers to all exam questions provide detailed explanations, including why options are correct or incorrect. Mark your incorrect answers and identify the sections that you need to reread. If possible, draw a few diagrams—you'll be amazed at how much they can help you retain the concepts. Give it a try—it'll be fun!

Author Online

The purchase of *OCA Java SE 7 Programmer I Certification Guide* includes free access to a private forum run by Manning Publications where you can make comments about the book, ask technical questions, and receive help from the author and other users. You can access and subscribe to the forum at www.manning.com/OCAJavaSE7ProgrammerICertification-Guide. This page provides information on how to get on the forum once you're registered, what kind of help is available, and the rules of conduct in the forum.

Manning's commitment to our readers is to provide a venue where a meaningful dialogue among individual readers and between readers and the author can take place. It's not a commitment to any specific amount of participation on the part of the authors, whose contribution to the book's forum remains voluntary (and unpaid). We suggest you try asking the author some challenging questions, lest her interest stray!

The Author Online forum and the archives of previous discussions will be accessible from the publisher's website as long as the book is in print.

about the author

Mala Gupta has a Master's degree in Computer Applications (MCA). She is an Oracle Certified Associate-Java SE 7 Programmer, Java Sun Certified Web Component Developer (SCWCD), and Sun Certified Java 2 Programmer (SCJP).

She has more than 12 years of experience in software design and development and training. Her work experience is in Java technologies, primarily as an analyst, programmer, and mentor.

Mala has worked with international training and software services organizations in Europe and development centers in India on various Java-based portals and web applications. She has experience in mentoring and ramping up teams' technical and process skills.

She is the founder and lead mentor of a portal (http://ejavaguru.com) that has offered an online Java course in Java Programmer certification since 2006.

about the cover illustration

The figure on the cover of the *OCA Java SE 7 Programmer I Certification Guide* is captioned a "Morlach." This illustration is taken from a recent reprint of Balthasar Hacquet's *Images and Descriptions of Southwestern and Eastern Wenda, Illyrians, and Slavs* published by the Ethnographic Museum in Split, Croatia, in 2008. Hacquet (1739–1815) was an Austrian physician and scientist who spent many years studying the botany, geology, and ethnography of many parts of the Austrian Empire, as well as the Veneto, the Julian Alps, and the western Balkans, inhabited in the past by peoples of many different tribes and nationalities. Hand-drawn illustrations accompany the many scientific papers and books that Hacquet published.

Morlachs were a rural population that lived in the Dinaric Alps in the western Balkans hundreds of years ago. Many of them were shepherds who migrated in search of better pastures for their flocks, alternating between the mountains in the summer and the seashore in the winter. They were also called "Vlachs" in Serbian and Croatian. The rich diversity of the drawings in Hacquet's publications speaks vividly of the uniqueness and individuality of Alpine and Balkan regions just 200 years ago. This was a time when the dress codes of two villages separated by a few miles identified people uniquely as belonging to one or the other, and when members of an ethnic tribe, social class, or trade could be easily distinguished by what they were wearing.

Dress codes have changed since then and the diversity by region, so rich at the time, has faded away. It is now often hard to tell the inhabitant of one continent from another and the residents of the picturesque towns and villages in the Balkans are not readily distinguishable from people who live in other parts of the world.

We at Manning celebrate the inventiveness, the initiative, and the fun of the computer business with book covers based on costumes from two centuries ago brought back to life by illustrations such as this one.

Introduction

This introduction covers

- Introduction to the Oracle Certified Associate (OCA) Java SE 7 Programmer certification (exam number 1Z0-803)
- Importance of OCA Java SE 7 Programmer certification
- Comparison of the OCA Java SE 7 Programmer I exam with OCA Java SE 5/6 exam
- Comparison of the OCA Java SE 7 Programmer I exam (1Z0-803) with OCP Java SE 7 Programmer II exam (1Z0-804)
- Detailed exam objectives, mapped to book chapters
- Readiness checklist to determine your readiness level for writing the exam
- FAQ on exam preparation and on taking the exam
- Introduction to the testing engine used for the exam

This book is intended specifically for individuals who wish to earn the Oracle Certified Associate (OCA) Java SE 7 Programmer certification (exam number 1Z0-803). It assumes that you are familiar with Java and have some experience working with it.

If you are completely new to Java or to object-oriented languages, I suggest that you start your journey with an entry-level book and then come back to this one.

1 Disclaimer

The information in this chapter is sourced from Oracle.com, public websites, and user forums. Input has been taken from real people who have earned Java certification, including the author. All efforts have been made to maintain the accuracy of the content, but the details of the exam—including the exam objectives, pricing, exam pass score, total number of questions, maximum exam duration, and others—are subject to change per Oracle's policies. The author and publisher of the book shall not be held responsible for any loss or damage accrued due to any information contained in this book or due to any direct or indirect use of this information.

2 Introduction to OCA Java SE 7 Programmer certification

The Oracle Certified Associate (OCA) Java SE 7 Programmer I exam (1Z0-803) covers the fundamentals of Java SE 7 programming, such as the importance of object-oriented programming, its implementation in code, and using flow control, arrays, and other constructs.

This exam is the first of the two steps in earning the title of Oracle Certified Professional (OCP) Java SE 7 Programmer. It certifies that an individual possesses a strong foundation in the Java programming language. Table 1 lists the details of this exam.

Table 1   Details for OCA Java SE 7 Programmer I exam (1Z0-803)

Exam number	1Z0-803
Java version	Based on Java version 7
Number of questions	90
Passing score	77%
Time duration	140 minutes
Pricing	US$300
Type of questions	Multiple-choice questions

2.1 The importance of OCA Java SE 7 Programmer certification

The OCA Java SE 7 Programmer I exam (1Z0-803) is an entry-level exam in your Java certification roadmap, as shown in figure 1. This exam is a prerequisite for the OCP Java SE 7 Programmer II exam (1Z0-804), which is itself a prerequisite for most of the other Oracle certifications in Java. The dashed lines and arrows in figure 1 depict the prerequisites for a certification.

As shown in figure 1, the Java certification tracks are offered under the categories Associate, Professional, Expert, and Master.

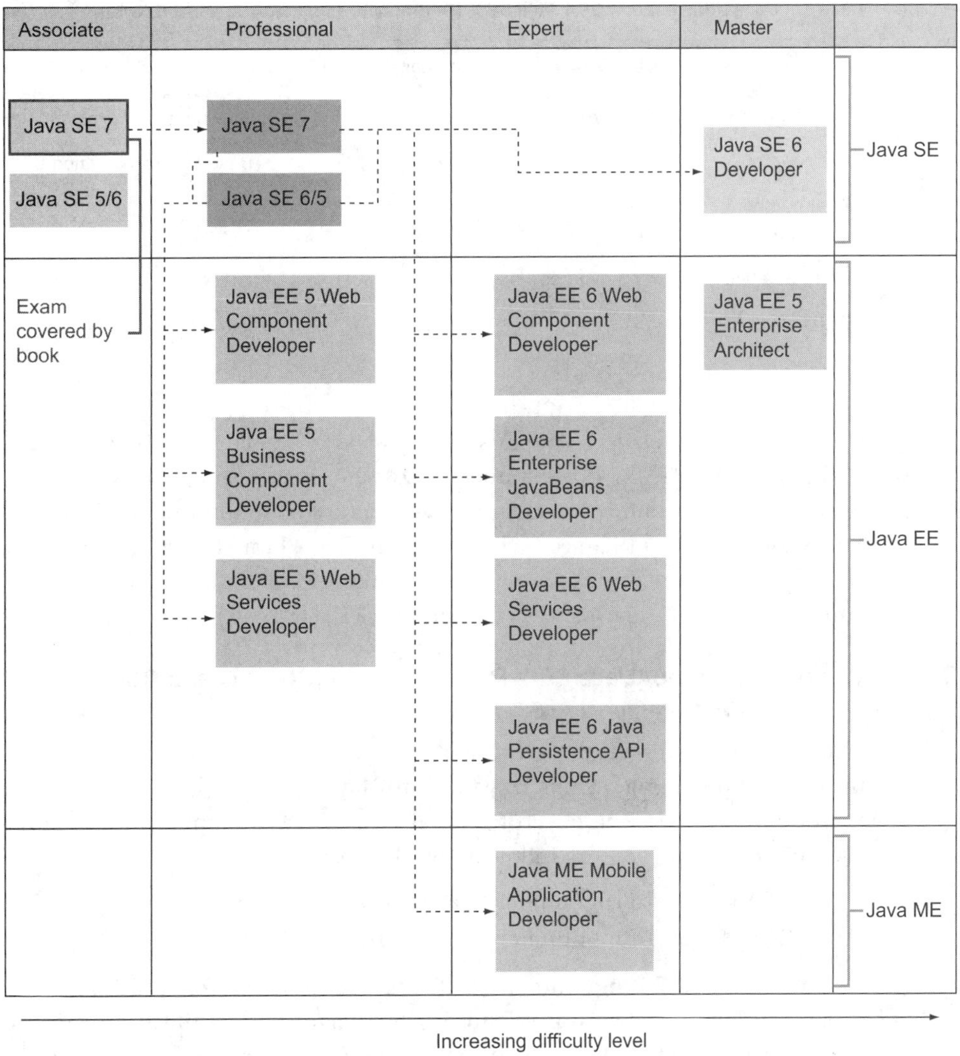

Associate	Professional	Expert	Master	
Java SE 7	Java SE 7		Java SE 6 Developer	Java SE
Java SE 5/6	Java SE 6/5			
Exam covered by book	Java EE 5 Web Component Developer	Java EE 6 Web Component Developer	Java EE 5 Enterprise Architect	
	Java EE 5 Business Component Developer	Java EE 6 Enterprise JavaBeans Developer		Java EE
	Java EE 5 Web Services Developer	Java EE 6 Web Services Developer		
		Java EE 6 Java Persistence API Developer		
		Java ME Mobile Application Developer		Java ME

Increasing difficulty level

Figure 1   OCA Java SE 7 Programmer certification is the entry-level certification in the Java certification roadmap. It's a prerequisite for the OCP Java SE 7 Programmer II exam (1Z0-804), which is a prerequisite for most of the other certifications in Java.

2.2   *Comparing OCA Java exam versions*

This section will clear up any confusion surrounding the different versions of the OCA Java exam. As of now, Oracle offers two versions of the OCA certification in Java:

- OCA Java SE 7 Programmer I (exam number: 1Z0-803)
- OCA Java SE 5/SE 6 (exam number: 1Z0-850)

These two exam versions are quite different as far target audience, total number of questions, passing score, and exam duration are concerned, as listed in table 2.

Table 2   Comparing exams: OCA Java SE 7 Programmer I and OCA Java SE 5/6

	OCA Java SE 7 Programmer I (1Z0-803)	OCA Java SE 5/SE 6 (1Z0-850)
Target audience	Java programmers	Java programmers and IT managers
Java version	Based on Java version 7	Based on Java version 5/6
Total number of questions	90	51
Exam duration	140 minutes	115 minutes
Passing score	77%	68%
Pricing	US$300	US$300

Figure 2 shows a detailed comparison of the exam objectives of OCA Java SE 5/6 (1Z0-850) and OCA Java SE 7 Programmer I (1Z0-803). It shows objectives that are exclusive to each of these exam versions and those that are common to both. The first column shows the objectives that are included only in OCA Java SE 5/6 (1Z0-850), the middle column shows common exam objectives, and the right column shows exam objectives covered only in OCA Java SE 7 Programmer I (1Z0-803).

2.3   Comparing the OCA Java SE 7 Programmer I (1Z0-803) and OCP Java SE 7 Programmer II (1Z0-804) exams

The confusion between these two exams is due to the similarity in their names, but these are two separate exams. Starting with Java 7, Oracle has raised the bar to earn the title of Oracle Certified Professional Java SE 7 Programmer, which now requires successfully completing the following two exams:

- OCA Java SE 7 Programmer I (exam number: 1Z0-803)
- OCP Java SE 7 Programmer II (exam number: 1Z0-804)

The OCP Java SE 7 Programmer certification is designed for individuals who possess advanced skills in the Java programming language. This certification covers comparatively advanced Java features, such as threads, concurrency, Java file I/O, inner classes, localization, and others.

2.4   Complete exam objectives, mapped to book chapters, and readiness checklist

Table 3 includes a complete list of exam objectives for the OCA Java SE 7 Programmer I exam, which was taken from Oracle's website. All the objectives are mapped to the book's chapters and the section numbers that cover them. You can also check your readiness to take the exam by selecting the appropriate stars. Here's the legend:

☆   Basic knowledge
☆☆   Intermediate (you can use it in code)
☆☆☆   Advanced (you can answer all questions about it)

OCA Java SE 5/6 1Z0-850	Common objectives	OCA Java SE 7 Programmer I 1Z0-803
Algorithm design and implementation	**Java basics**	
• Algorithm • Pseudocode	• Variable scope • Structure of Java class • `import` and `package` statements • `main` method	
	Working with Java data types	
• Enums	• Primitives, object references • Read/write to object fields • Call methods on objects • `String`s	• `StringBuilder`
Java development fundamentals	**Operators and decision constructs**	

• Use of `javac` command
 • Use of `java` command
 • Purpose and type of classes in packages
     `java.awt`
     `javax.swing`
     `java.io`
     `java.net`
     `java.util`
	• Java operators
	 • `if` and `if-else` constructs
	 • `switch` statement
		• Parentheses to override operator precedence
		 • Test equality between `String` and other objects using `==` and `equals()`

	Creating and using arrays	
	• One-dimensional arrays • Multidimensional arrays	• `ArrayList`
Java platforms and integration technologies	**Loop constructs**	
• Compare and contrast J2SE, J2ME, J2EE • RMI • JDBC, SQL, RDMS • JNDI, messaging, and JMS	• `for` and enhanced `for` loops • `while` and `do-while` loops • `break` and `continue` statements	
Client technologies	**Methods and encapsulation**	
• HTML, JavaScript • J2ME MIDlets • Applets • Swing	• Create methods with arguments and return types • Apply access modifiers • Effect on object references and primitives when they are passed to methods	• Apply `static` keyword to methods and fields • Overloaded constructors and methods • Default and user-defined constructors
Server technologies	**Inheritance**	
• EJB, servlets, JSP, JMS, SMTP, JAX-RBC, WebServices, JavaMail • Servlet and JSP for HTML • EJB session, entity, and message-driven beans • Web tier, business tier, EIS tier	• Implement inheritance • Polymorphism • Differentiate between type of a reference variable and object • Use abstract classes and interfaces	• Determine when casting is necessary • Use `super` and `this` to access objects and constructors
OOP concepts		**Handling exceptions**
• UML diagrams • Association • Composition • Association navigation		• Exceptions and errors • `try-catch` blocks • Use of exceptions • Methods that throw exceptions • Common exception classes and categories

Figure 2   Comparing objectives of exams OCA Java SE 5/6 and OCA Java SE 7 Programmer I

Table 3   Exam objectives and subobjectives mapped to chapter and section numbers, with readiness score

	Exam objectives	Covered in chapter/section	Your readiness score
1	**Java basics**	**Chapters 1 and 3**	
1.1	Define the scope of variables	Section 3.1	☆☆☆
1.2	Define the structure of a Java class	Section 1.1	☆☆☆
1.3	Create executable Java applications with a main method	Section 1.2	☆☆☆
1.4	Import other Java packages to make them accessible in your code	Section 1.3	☆☆☆
2	**Working with Java data types**	**Chapters 2, 3, and 4**	
2.1	Declare and initialize variables	Sections 2.1 and 2.3	☆☆☆
2.2	Differentiate between object reference variables and primitive variables	Sections 2.1 and 2.3	☆☆☆
2.3	Read or write to object fields	Section 3.6	☆☆☆
2.4	Explain an object's life cycle	Section 3.2	☆☆☆
2.5	Call methods on objects	Section 3.6	☆☆☆
2.6	Manipulate data using the `String-Builder` class and its methods	Section 4.2	☆☆☆
2.7	Create and manipulate strings	Section 4.1	☆☆☆
3	**Using operators and decision constructs**	**Chapters 2, 4, and 5**	
3.1	Use Java operators	Section 2.4	☆☆☆
3.2	Use parentheses to override operator precedence	Section 2.4	☆☆☆
3.3	Test equality between strings and other objects using `==` and `equals()`	Section 4.1	☆☆☆
3.4	Create `if` and `if-else` constructs	Section 5.1	☆☆☆
3.5	Use a `switch` statement	Section 5.2	☆☆☆
4	**Creating and using arrays**	**Chapter 4**	
4.1	Declare, instantiate, initialize, and use a one-dimensional array	Section 4.3	☆☆☆
4.2	Declare, instantiate, initialize, and use a multidimensional array	Section 4.3	☆☆☆
4.3	Declare and use an `ArrayList`	Section 4.4	☆☆☆

Table 3 Exam objectives and subobjectives mapped to chapter and section numbers, with readiness score *(continued)*

	Exam objectives	Covered in chapter/section	Your readiness score
5	**Using loop constructs**	**Chapter 5**	
5.1	Create and use `while` loops	Section 5.5	☆☆☆
5.2	Create and use `for` loops, including the enhanced `for` loop	Sections 5.3 and 5.4	☆☆☆
5.3	Create and use `do-while` loops	Section 5.5	☆☆☆
5.4	Compare loop constructs	Section 5.6	☆☆☆
5.5	Use `break` and `continue`	Section 5.7	☆☆☆
6	**Working with methods and encapsulation**	**Chapters 1 and 3**	
6.1	Create methods with arguments and return values	Section 3.3	☆☆☆
6.2	Apply the `static` keyword to methods and fields	Section 1.5	☆☆☆
6.3	Create an overloaded method	Section 3.4	☆☆☆
6.4	Differentiate between default and user-defined constructors	Section 3.5	☆☆☆
6.5	Create and overload constructors	Section 3.5	☆☆☆
6.6	Apply access modifiers	Section 1.4	☆☆☆
6.7	Apply encapsulation principles to a class	Section 3.7	☆☆☆
6.8	Determine the effect upon object references and primitive values when they are passed into methods that change the values	Section 3.8	☆☆☆
7	**Working with inheritance**	**Chapters 1 and 6**	
7.1	Implement inheritance	Section 6.1	☆☆☆
7.2	Develop code that demonstrates the use of polymorphism	Section 6.6	☆☆☆
7.3	Differentiate between the type of a reference and the type of an object	Section 6.3	☆☆☆
7.4	Determine when casting is necessary	Section 6.4	☆☆☆
7.5	Use `super` and `this` to access objects and constructors	Section 6.5	☆☆☆
7.6	Use abstract classes and interfaces	Sections 1.5, 6.2, and 6.6	☆☆☆

Table 3 Exam objectives and subobjectives mapped to chapter and section numbers, with readiness score *(continued)*

	Exam objectives	Covered in chapter/section	Your readiness score
8	**Handling exceptions**	**Chapter 7**	
8.1	Differentiate among checked exceptions, `RuntimeExceptions`, and `Errors`	Section 7.3	☆☆☆
8.2	Create a `try-catch` block and determine how exceptions alter normal program flow	Section 7.2	☆☆☆
8.3	Describe what exceptions are used for in Java	Section 7.1	☆☆☆
8.4	Invoke a method that throws an exception	Section 7.2	☆☆☆
8.5	Recognize common exception classes and categories	Section 7.4	☆☆☆

When you are ready to take the exam, you should ideally be able to select three stars for each item in the table. But let's define a better way to evaluate your exam readiness. Once you have marked all the stars in the previous chart, calculate your total points using the following values:

☆   1 point
☆☆   2 points
☆☆☆   4 points

As the maximum number of points is 172 (43 objectives × 4), a score in the range of 150–172 is considered a good score.

You can download a PDF version of the form from the book's web page at http://manning.com/gupta/ if you wish to mark yourself more than once.

3   *FAQs*

You might be anxious when you start your exam preparation or even think about getting certified. This section can help calm your nerves by answering frequently asked questions on exam preparation and on writing the exam.

3.1   *FAQs on exam preparation*

This sections answers frequently asked questions on how to prepare for the exam, including the best approach, study material, preparation duration, how to test self-readiness, and more.

WILL THE EXAM DETAILS EVER CHANGE FOR THE OCA JAVA SE 7 PROGRAMMER I EXAM?

Oracle can change the exam details for a certification even after the certification is made live. The changes can be to the exam objectives, pricing, exam duration, exam questions, and other parts. In the past, Oracle has made similar changes to certification exams. Such changes may not be major, but it is always advisable to check Oracle's website for the latest exam information when you start your exam preparation.

WHAT IS THE BEST WAY TO PREPARE FOR THIS EXAM?

At the time of writing this book, there weren't many resources available to prepare for this exam. Apart from this book, Oracle offers an online course on this exam.

Generally, candidates use a combination of resources, such as books, online study materials, articles on the exam, free and paid mock exams, and training to prepare for the exam. Different combinations work best for different people, and there is no one perfect formula to prepare. Depending on whether training or self-study works best for you, you can select the method that is most appropriate for you. Combine it with a lot of code practice and mock exams.

HOW DO I KNOW WHEN I AM READY FOR THE EXAM?

You can be sure about your exam readiness by *consistently* getting a good score in the mock exams. Generally, a score of 80% and above in approximately seven mock exams (the more the better) attempted consecutively will assure you of a similar score in the real exam. You can also test your exam readiness using table 3. This table contains exam objectives and subobjectives with multiple stars representing different levels of expertise.

HOW MANY MOCK TESTS SHOULD I ATTEMPT BEFORE THE REAL EXAM?

Ideally, you should attempt at least 10 mock exams before you attempt the real exam. The more the better!

I HAVE TWO YEARS' EXPERIENCE WORKING WITH JAVA. DO I STILL NEED TO PREPARE FOR THIS CERTIFICATION?

It is important to understand that there is a difference between the practical knowledge of having worked with Java and the knowledge required to pass this certification exam. The authors of the Java certification exams employ multiple tricks to test your knowledge. Hence, you need a structured preparation and approach to succeed in the certification exam.

WHAT IS THE IDEAL TIME REQUIRED TO PREPARE FOR THE EXAM?

The preparation time frame mainly depends on your experience with Java and the amount of time that you can spend to prepare yourself. On average, you will require approximately 150 hours of study over two or three months to prepare for this exam. Again, the number of study hours required depends on individual learning curves and backgrounds.

It's important to be consistent with your exam preparation. You cannot study for a month and then restart after, say, a gap of a month or more.

DOES THIS EXAM INCLUDE ANY UNSCORED QUESTIONS?

A few of the questions that you write in any Oracle exam may be marked unscored. Oracle's policy states that while writing an exam, you won't be informed whether a question will be scored. You may be surprised to learn that as many as 10 questions out of the 90 questions in the OCA Java SE 7 Programmer I exam may be unscored. Even if you answer a few questions incorrectly, you stand a chance of scoring 100%.

Oracle regularly updates its question bank for all its certification exams. These unscored questions may be used for research and to evaluate new questions that can be added to an exam.

CAN I START MY EXAM PREPARATION WITH THE MOCK EXAMS?

If you are quite comfortable with the Java language features, then yes, you can start your exam preparation with the mock exams. This will also help you to understand the types of questions to expect in the real certification exam. But if you have little or no experience working with Java, or if you are not quite comfortable with the language features of Java, I don't advise you to start with the mock exams. The exam authors often use a lot of tricks to evaluate a candidate in the real certification exam. Starting your exam preparation with mock exams will only leave you confused about the Java concepts.

SHOULD I REALLY BOTHER GETTING CERTIFIED?

Yes, you should, for the simple reason that employers bother about the certification of employees. Organizations prefer a certified Java developer over a noncertified Java developer with similar IT skills and experience. The certification can also get you a higher paycheck than uncertified peers with comparable skills.

3.2   *FAQs on taking the exam*

This section contains a list of frequently asked questions related to the exam registration, exam coupon, do's and don'ts while taking the exam, and exam retakes.

WHERE AND HOW DO I WRITE THIS EXAM?

You can write this exam at an Oracle Testing Center or Pearson VUE Authorized Testing Center. To sit for the exam, you must register for the exam and purchase an exam voucher. The following options are available:

- Register for the exam and pay Pearson VUE directly.
- Purchase an exam voucher from Oracle and register at Pearson VUE to take the exam.
- Register at an Oracle Testing Center.

Look for the nearest testing centers in your area, register yourself, and schedule an exam date and time. Most of the popular computer training institutes also have a testing center on their premises. You can locate a Pearson VUE testing site at www.pearsonvue .com/oracle/, which contains detailed information on locating testing centers and scheduling or rescheduling an exam. At the time of registration, you'll need to provide the following details along with your name, address, and contact numbers:

- Exam title and number (OCA Java SE 7 Programmer I, 1Z0-803)
- Any discount code that should be applied during registration
- Oracle Testing ID/Candidate ID, if you have written any other Oracle/Sun certification exam
- Your OPN Company ID (if your employer is in the Oracle Partner Network, you can find out the company ID and use any available discounts on the exam fee)

HOW LONG IS THE EXAM COUPON VALID FOR?

Each exam coupon is printed with an expiry date. Beware of any discounted coupons that come with an assurance that they can be used past the expiration date.

CAN I REFER TO NOTES OR BOOKS WHILE WRITING THIS EXAM?

You can't refer to any books or notes while writing this exam. You are not allowed to carry any blank paper for rough work or even your mobile phone inside the testing cubicle.

WHAT IS THE PURPOSE OF MARKING A QUESTION WHILE WRITING THE EXAM?

By marking a question, you can manage your time efficiently. Don't spend a lot of time on a single question. You can mark a difficult question to defer answering it while writing your exam. The exam gives you an option to review answers to the marked questions at the end of the exam. Also, navigating from one question to another using the Back and Next buttons is usually time consuming. If you are unsure of an answer, mark it and review it at the end.

CAN I WRITE DOWN THE EXAM QUESTIONS AND BRING THEM BACK WITH ME?

No. The exam centers no longer provide sheets of paper for the rough work that you may need to do while taking the exam. The testing center will provide you with either erasable or nonerasable boards. If you're provided with a nonerasable board, you may request another one if you need it.

Oracle is quite particular about certification candidates distributing or circulating the memorized questions in any form. If Oracle finds out that this is happening, it may cancel a candidate's certificate, bar that candidate forever from writing any Oracle certification, inform the employer, or take legal action.

WHAT HAPPENS IF I COMPLETE THE EXAM BEFORE OR AFTER THE TOTAL TIME?

If you complete the exam before the total exam time has elapsed, revise your answers and click the Submit or Finish button. The screen will display your score within 10 seconds of clicking the Submit button!

If you have not clicked the Submit button and you use up all the exam time, the exam engine will no longer allow you to modify any of the exam answers and will present the screen with the Submit button.

WILL I RECEIVE MY SCORE IMMEDIATELY AFTER THE EXAM?

Yes, you will. When you click the Submit button, the screen will show your total score. It will also show what you scored on each objective. The testing center will also give you hard copies of your certification score. The certificate itself will arrive via post within six to eight weeks.

WHAT HAPPENS IF I FAIL? CAN I RETAKE THE EXAM?

It's not the end of the world. Don't worry if you fail. You can retake the exam after 14 days (and the world will not know it's a retake).

However, you cannot retake a passed exam to improve your score. Also, you cannot retake a beta exam.

4   *The testing engine used in the exam*

The user interface of the testing engine used for the certification exam is quite simple. (You could even call it primitive, compared to today's web, desktop, and smartphone applications.)

Before you can start the exam, you will be required to accept the terms and conditions of the Oracle Certification Candidate Agreement. Your computer screen will display all these conditions and give you an option to accept the conditions. You can proceed with writing the exam only if you accept these conditions.

Here are the features of the testing engine used by Oracle:

- *Engine UI is divided into three sections*—The UI of the testing engine is divided into the following three segments:
  - *Static upper section*—Displays question number, time remaining, and a checkbox to mark a question for review.
  - *Scrollable middle section*—Displays the question text and the answer options.
  - *Static bottom section*—Displays buttons to display the previous question, display the next question, end the exam, and review marked questions.
- *Each question is displayed on a separate screen*—The exam engine displays one question on the screen at a time. It does not display multiple questions on a single screen, like a scrollable web page. All effort is made to display the complete question and answer options without scrolling, or with little scrolling.
- *Code Exhibit button*—Many questions include code. Such questions, together with their answers, may require significant scrolling to be viewed. As this can be quite inconvenient, such questions include a Code Exhibit button that displays the code in a separate window.
- *Mark questions to be reviewed*—The question screen displays a checkbox with the text "Mark for review" at the top-left corner. A question can be marked using this option. The marked questions can be quickly reviewed at the end of the exam.
- *Buttons to display the previous and next questions*—The test includes buttons to display the previous and next questions within the bottom section of the testing engine.
- *Buttons to end the exam and review marked questions*—The engine displays buttons to end the exam and to review the marked questions in the bottom section of the testing engine.
- *Remaining time*—The engine displays the time remaining for the exam at the top right of the screen.
- *Question number*—Each question displays its serial number.
- *Correct number of answer options*—Each question displays the correct number of options that should be selected from multiple options.

On behalf of all at Manning Publications, I wish you good luck and hope that you score very well on your exam.

Java basics 1

Exam objectives covered in this chapter	What you need to know
[1.2] Define the structure of a Java class.	Structure of a Java class, with its components: package and import statements, class declarations, comments, variables, and methods. Difference between the components of a Java class and that of a Java source code file.
[1.3] Create executable Java applications with a `main` method.	The right method signature for the `main` method to create an executable Java application. The arguments that are passed to the `main` method.
[1.4] Import other Java packages to make them accessible in your code.	Understand packages and import statements. Get the right syntax and semantics to import classes from packages and interfaces in your own classes.
[6.6] Apply access modifiers.	Application of access modifiers (`public`, `protected`, default, and `private`) to a class and its members. Determine the accessibility of code with these modifiers.
[7.6] Use `abstract` classes and interfaces.	The implication of defining classes, interfaces, and methods as `abstract` entities.
[6.2] Apply the `static` keyword to methods and fields.	The implication of defining fields and methods as `static` members.

Imagine you've set up a new IT organization that works with multiple developers. To ensure a smooth and efficient workflow, you'll define a structure for your organization and a set of departments with separate assigned responsibilities. These departments will interact with each other whenever required. Also, depending on confidentiality requirements, your organization's data will be available to employees on an as-needed basis, or you may assign special privileges to only some employees of the organization. This is an example of how organizations work with a well-defined structure and a set of rules to deliver the best results.

Similarly, Java has organized its workflow. The organization's structure and components can be compared with Java's class structure and components, and the organization's departments can be compared with Java packages. Restricting access to all data in the organization can be compared to Java's access modifiers. An organization's special privileges can be compared to nonaccess modifiers in Java.

In the OCA Java SE 7 Programmer I exam, you'll be asked questions on the structure of a Java class, packages, importing classes, and applying access and nonaccess modifiers. Given that information, this chapter will cover the following:

- Understanding the structure and components of a Java class
- Understanding executable Java applications
- Understanding Java packages
- Importing Java packages into your code
- Applying access and nonaccess modifiers

1.1 *The structure of a Java class and source code file*

> [1.2] Define the structure of a Java class

> **NOTE** When you see a certification objective callout such as the preceding one, it means that in this section, we'll cover this objective. The same objective may be covered in more than one section in this chapter or in other chapters.

This section covers the structure and components of both a Java source code file (.java file) and a Java class (defined using the keyword `class`). It also covers the differences between a Java source code file and a Java class.

First things first. Start your exam preparation with a clear understanding of what is required from you in the certification exam. For example, try to answer the following query from a certification aspirant: "I come across the term 'class' with different meanings—class `Person`, the Java source code file—Person.java, and Java bytecode stored in Person.class. Which of these structures is on the exam?" To answer this question, take a look at figure 1.1, which includes the class `Person`, the files Person.java and Person.class, and the relationship between them.

As you can see in figure 1.1, a person can be defined as a class `Person`. This class should reside in a Java source code file (Person.java). Using this Java source code file, the Java compiler (javac.exe on Windows or javac on Mac OS X/Linux/UNIX) generates bytecode (compiled code for the Java Virtual Machine) and stores it in Person.class. The scope of this exam objective is limited to Java classes (class `Person`) and Java source code files (Person.java).

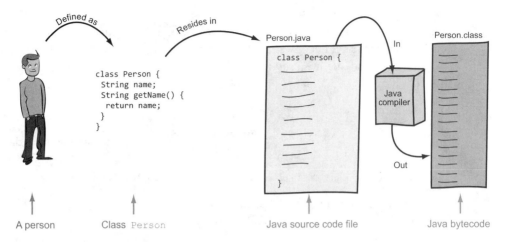

Figure 1.1 Relationship between the class `Person`, the files Person.java and Person.class, and how one transforms into another

1.1.1 Structure of a Java class

The OCA Java SE 7 Programmer I exam will question you on your understanding of the structure and components of a Java class defined using the keyword `class`. A class can define multiple components. All the Java components that you've heard of can be defined within a Java class. Figure 1.2 defines the components and structure of a Java class.

Here's a quick list of the components of a class (the ones that are on this exam), which we'll discuss in detail in this section:

- The `package` statement
- The `import` statement
- Comments
- Class declarations and definitions
- Variables
- Methods
- Constructors

Java class components

```
Package statement         —— 1
Import statements         —— 2
Comments                  —— 3a
Class declaration {       —— 4
         Variables        —— 5
         Comments         —— 3b
         Constructors     —— 6
         Methods          —— 7
         Nested classes   ⎤ Not included in OCA Java SE 7
         Nested interfaces ⎬ Programmer I exam
         Enum             ⎦
}
```

Figure 1.2 Components of a Java class

PACKAGE STATEMENT

All Java classes are part of a package. A Java class can be explicitly defined in a named package; otherwise it becomes part of a *default* package, which doesn't have a name.

A package statement is used to explicitly define which package a class is in. If a class includes a package statement, it must be the first statement in the class definition:

```
package certification;                                        The package statement
class Course {                                                should be the first
                            The rest of the code              statement in a class
                            for class Course
}
```

NOTE   Packages are covered in detail in section 1.3 of this chapter.

The package statement cannot appear within a class declaration or after the class declaration. The following code will fail to compile:

```
class Course {
                            The rest of the code for class Course
}
package certification;      If you place the package statement after
                            the class definition, the code won't compile
```

The following code will also fail to compile, because it places the package statement within the class definition:

```
class Course {              A package statement can't be placed within the curly
package com.cert;           braces that mark the start and end of a class definition
}
```

Also, if present, the package statement must appear exactly once in a class. The following code won't compile:

```
package com.cert;           A class can't define multiple
package com.exams;          package statements
class Course {
}
```

IMPORT STATEMENT

Classes and interfaces in the same package can use each other without prefixing their names with the package name. But to use a class or an interface from another package, you must use its fully qualified name. Because this can be tedious and can make your code difficult to read, you can use the import statement to use the simple name of a class or interface in your code.

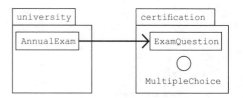

Figure 1.3   UML representation of the relationship between class `AnnualExam` and `ExamQuestion`

Let's look at this using an example class, `AnnualExam`, which is defined in the package `university`. Class `AnnualExam` is associated with the class `certification.ExamQuestion`, as shown using the Unified Modeling Language (UML) in figure 1.3.

Here's the code for class `AnnualExam`:

```
package university;
import certification.ExamQuestion;

class AnnualExam {
    ExamQuestion eq;
}
```

Define a variable of ExamQuestion

Note that the `import` statement follows the package statement but precedes the `class` declaration. What happens if the class `AnnualExam` isn't defined in a package? Will there be any change in the code if the class `AnnualExam` and `ExamQuestion` are related, as depicted in figure 1.4?

In this case, the class `AnnualExam` isn't part of an explicit package, but the class `ExamQuestion` is part of package `certification`. Here's the code for class `AnnualExam`:

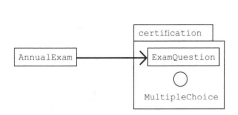

Figure 1.4   A UML representation of the relationship between the unpackaged class `AnnualExam` and `ExamQuestion`

```
import certification.ExamQuestion;
class AnnualExam {
    ExamQuestion eq;
}
```

Define a variable of ExamQuestion

As you can see in the previous example code, the class `AnnualExam` doesn't define the `package` statement, but it defines the `import` statement to import the class `certification.ExamQuestion`.

If a `package` statement is present in a class, the `import` statement must follow the package statement. It's important to maintain the order of the occurrence of the package and `import` statements. Reversing this order will result in your code failing to compile:

```
import certification.ExamQuestion;
package university;

class AnnualExam {
    ExamQuestion eq;
}
```

The code won't compile because an import statement can't be placed before a package statement

We'll discuss `import` statements in detail in section 1.3 of this chapter.

COMMENTS

You can also add comments to your Java code. Comments can appear at multiple places in a class. A comment can appear before and after a `package` statement, before and after the class definition, before and within and after a method definition. Comments come in two flavors: multiline comments and end-of-line comments.

Multiline comments span multiple lines of code. They start with `/*` and end with `*/`. Here's an example:

```
class MyClass {
    /*
       comments that span multiple          Multiline comments start
       lines of code                        with /* and end with */
    */
}
```

Multiline comments can contain any special characters (including Unicode characters). Here's an example:

```
class MyClass {
    /*
       Multi-line comments with
       special characters &%^*{}|\|:;"'      Multiline comment with
       ?/>.<,!@#$%^&*()                      special characters in it
    */
}
```

Most of the time, when you see a multiline comment in a Java source code file (.java file), you'll notice that it uses an asterisk (*) to start the comment in the next line. Please note that this isn't required—it's done more for aesthetic reasons. Here's an example:

```
class MyClass {
    /*                                     Multiline comments that start with * on a
     * comments that span multiple         new line—don't they look well organized?
     * lines of code                       The usage of * isn't mandatory; it's done
     */                                    for aesthetic reasons.
}
```

End-of-line comments start with // and, as evident by their name, they are placed at the end of a line of code. The text between // and the end of the line is treated as a comment, which you would normally use to briefly describe the line of code. Here's an example:

```
                                          Brief comment to describe variable fName
class Person {
    String fName;    // variable to store Person's first name    ←
    String id;       // a 6 letter id generated by the database   ←
}
                                          Brief comment to describe variable id
```

In the earlier section on the package statement, you read that a package statement, if present, should be the first line of code in a class. The only exception to this rule is the presence of comments. A comment can precede a package statement. The following code defines a package statement, with multiline and end-of-line comments:

```
/**
 * @author MGupta        // first name initial + last name   ←    End-of-line
 * @version 0.1                                                    comment within a
 *                                                            ①    multiline comment
 * Class to store the details of a monument
 */
package uni;              // package uni              ←─② End-of-line comment
class Monument {
    int startYear;
```

```
    String builtBy;    // individual/ architect    ◁─❸  End-of-line comment
}
// another comment                          ◁─❹  End-of-line comment at the beginning of a line
```

Line ❶ defines an end-of-line code comment within multiline code. This is acceptable. The end-of-line code comment is treated as part of the multiline comment, not as a separate end-of-line comment. Lines ❷ and ❸ define end-of-line code comments. Line ❹ defines an end-of-line code comment at the start of a line, after the class definition.

The multiline comment is placed before the `package` statement, which is acceptable because comments can appear anywhere in your code.

CLASS DECLARATION

The class declaration marks the start of a class. It can be as simple as the keyword `class` followed by the name of a class:

```
                                              Simplest class declaration: keyword
                                              class followed by the class name
class Person {                        ◁─┘
//..              A class can define a lot of things here, but we don't
//..              need these details to show the class declaration
}
```

Time to get more details. The declaration of a class is composed of the following parts:

- Access modifiers
- Nonaccess modifiers
- Class name
- Name of the base class, if the class is extending another class
- All implemented interfaces, if the class is implementing any interfaces
- Class body (class fields, methods, constructors), included within a pair of curly braces, {}

Don't worry if you don't understand this material at this point. I'll cover these details as we move through the exam preparation.

Let's look at the components of a class declaration using an example:

```
public final class Runner extends Person implements Athlete {}
```

The components of the preceding class can be pictorially depicted, as shown in figure 1.5. The following list summarizes the optional and compulsory components.

Compulsory	Optional
Keyword `class`	Access modifier, such as `public`
Name of the class	Nonaccess modifier, such as `final`
Class body, marked by the opening and closing curly braces, {}	Keyword `extends` together with the name of the base class
	Keyword `implements` together with the name of the interfaces being implemented

Class declaration components

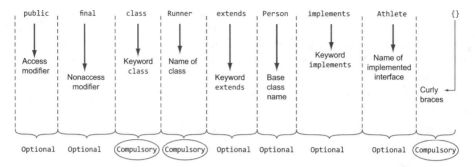

Figure 1.5   Components of a class declaration

We'll discuss the access and nonaccess modifiers in detail in sections 1.4 and 1.5 in this chapter.

CLASS DEFINITION

A class is a design used to specify the properties and behavior of an object. The properties of an object are implemented using *variables*, and the behavior is implemented using *methods*.

For example, consider a class as being like the design or specification of a mobile phone, and a mobile phone as being an object of that design. The same design can be used to create multiple mobile phones, just as the Java Virtual Machine (JVM) uses a class to create its objects. You can also consider a class as being like a mold that you can use to create meaningful and useful objects. A class is a design from which an object can be created.

Let's define a simple class to represent a mobile phone:

```java
class Phone {
    String model;
    String company;
    Phone(String model) {
        this.model = model;
    }
    double weight;
    void makeCall(String number) {
        // code
    }
    void receiveCall() {
        // code
    }
}
```

Points to remember:

- A class name starts with the keyword `class`. Watch out for the case of the keyword `class`. Java is case sEnSiTivE. `class` (lowercase *c*) isn't the same as `Class` (uppercase *C*). You can't use the word `Class` (capital *C*) to define a class.
- The state of a class is defined using attributes or instance variables.

- The behavior is defined using methods. The methods will include the argument list (if any). Don't worry if you don't understand these methods. The methods are covered in detail later in this chapter.
- A class definition may also include comments and constructors.

NOTE   A class is a design from which an object can be created.

VARIABLES

Revisit the previous example. Because the variables `model`, `company`, and `weight` are used to store the state of an object (also called an *instance*), they are called *instance variables* or *instance attributes*. Each object has its own copy of the instance variables. If you change the value of an instance variable for an object, the value for the same named instance variable won't change for another object. The instance variables are defined within a class but outside all methods in a class.

A single copy of a *class variable* or `static` variable is shared by all the objects of a class. The `static` variables are covered in section 1.5.3 with a detailed discussion of the nonaccess modifier `static`.

METHODS

Again, revisit the previous example. The methods `makeCall` and `receiveCall` are instance methods, which are generally used to manipulate the instance variables.

A *class method* or *static method* is used to work with the `static` variables, as discussed in detail in section 1.5.3.

CONSTRUCTORS

Class `Phone` in the previous example defines a single constructor. A class constructor is used to create and initialize the objects of a class. A class can define multiple constructors that accept different sets of method parameters.

1.1.2   Structure and components of a Java source code file

A Java source code file is used to define classes and interfaces. All your Java code should be defined in Java source code files (text files whose names end with .java). The exam covers the following aspects of the structure of a Java source code file:

- Definition of a class and an interface in a Java source code file
- Definition of single or multiple classes and interfaces within the same Java source code file
- Application of `import` and `package` statements to all the classes in a Java source code file

We've already covered the detailed structure and definition of classes in section 1.1.1. Let's get started with the definition of an interface.

DEFINITION OF INTERFACES IN A JAVA SOURCE CODE FILE

An interface is a grouping of related methods and constants, but the methods in an interface cannot define any implementation. An interface specifies a contract for the classes to implement.

Here's a quick example to help you to understand the essence of interfaces. No matter which brand of television each one of us has, every television provides the common functionality of changing the channel and adjusting the volume. You can compare the controls of a television set to an interface, and the design of a television set to a class that implements the interface controls.

Let's define this interface:

```java
interface Controls {
    void changeChannel(int channelNumber);
    void increaseVolume();
    void decreaseVolume();
}
```

The definition of an interface starts with the keyword `interface`. An interface can define constants and methods. Remember, Java is case-sensitive, so you can't use the word `Interface` (with a capital *I*) to define an interface.

DEFINITION OF SINGLE AND MULTIPLE CLASSES IN A SINGLE JAVA SOURCE CODE FILE

You can define either a single class or an interface in a single Java source code file, or many such files. Let's start with a simple example: a Java source code file called Single-Class.java that defines a single class `SingleClass`:

```java
class SingleClass {
    //.. we are not detailing this part
}
```
Contents of Java source code file SingleClass.java

Here's an example of a Java source code file, Multiple1.java, that defines multiple interfaces:

```java
interface Printable {
    //.. we are not detailing this part
}
interface Movable {
    //.. we are not detailing this part
}
```
Contents of Java source code file Multiple1.java

You can also define a combination of classes and interfaces in the same Java source code file. Here's an example:

```java
interface Printable {
    //.. we are not detailing this part
}
class MyClass {
    //.. we are not detailing this part
}
interface Movable {
    //.. we are not detailing this part
}
class Car {
    //.. we are not detailing this part
}
```
Contents of Java source code file Multiple2.java

There is no required order for the multiple classes or interfaces that can be defined in a single Java source code file.

EXAM TIP The classes and interfaces can be defined in any order of occurrence in a Java source code file.

If you define a `public` class or an interface in a class, its name should match the name of the Java source code file. Also, a source code file can't define more than one `public` class or interface. If you try to do so, your code won't compile, which leads to a small hands-on exercise for you that I call *Twist in the Tale*, as mentioned in the Preface. The answers to all these exercises are provided in the appendix.

> **About the Twist in the Tale exercises**
>
> For these exercises, I've tried to use modified code from the examples already covered in the chapter. The *Twist in the Tale* title refers to modified or tweaked code.
>
> These exercises will help you understand how even small code modifications can change the behavior of your code. They should also encourage you to carefully examine all of the code in the exam. The reason for these exercises is that in the exam, you may be asked more than one question that seems to require the same answer. But on closer inspection, you'll realize that the questions differ slightly, and this will change the behavior of the code and the correct answer option!

Twist in the Tale 1.1

Modify the contents of the Java source code file Multiple.java, and define a public interface in it. Execute the code and see how it affects your code.

Question: Examine the following content of Java source code file Multiple.java and select the correct answers:

```
// Contents of Multiple.java
public interface Printable {
    //.. we are not detailing this part
}
interface Movable {
    //.. we are not detailing this part
}
```

Options:

  a A Java source code file cannot define multiple interfaces.
  b A Java source code file can only define multiple classes.
  c A Java source code file can define multiple interfaces and classes.
  d The previous class will fail to compile.

If you need help getting your system set up to write Java, refer to Oracle's "Getting Started" tutorial, http://docs.oracle.com/javase/tutorial/getStarted/.

Twist in the Tale 1.2

Question: Examine the content of the following Java source code file, Multiple2.java, and select the correct option.

```
// contents of Multiple2.java
interface Printable {
    //.. we are not detailing this part
}
class MyClass {
    //.. we are not detailing this part
}
interface Movable {
    //.. we are not detailing this part
}
public class Car {
    //.. we are not detailing this part
}
public interface Multiple2 {}
```

Options:

a The code fails to compile.

b The code compiles successfully.

c Removing the definition of class `Car` will compile the code.

d Changing class `Car` to a non-public class will compile the code.

e Changing class Multiple2 to a non-public class will compile the code.

APPLICATION OF PACKAGE AND IMPORT STATEMENTS IN JAVA SOURCE CODE FILES

In the previous section, I mentioned that you can define multiple classes and interfaces in the same Java source code file. When you use a `package` or `import` statement within such Java files, both the `package` and `import` statements apply to all of the classes and interfaces defined in that source code file.

For example, if you include a `package` and an `import` statement in Java source code file Multiple.java (as in the following code), `Car`, `Movable`, and `Printable` will be become part of the same package `com.manning.code`:

```
// contents of Multiple.java
package com.manning.code;
import com.manning.*;

interface Printable {}
interface Movable {}
class Car {}
```

Printable, Movable, and Car are part of package com.manning.code

All classes and interfaces defined in package com.manning are accessible to Printable, Movable, and Car

EXAM TIP Classes and interfaces defined in the same Java source code file *can't* be defined in separate packages. Classes and interfaces imported using the `import` statement are available to all the classes and interfaces defined in the same Java source code file.

In the next section, you'll create executable Java applications—classes that are used to define an entry point of execution for a Java application.

1.2   Executable Java applications

The OCA Java SE 7 Programmer I exam requires that you understand the meaning of an executable Java application and its requirements, that is, what makes a regular Java class an executable Java class.

1.2.1   Executable Java classes versus nonexecutable Java classes

"Doesn't the Java Virtual Machine execute all the Java classes when they are used? If so, what is a nonexecutable Java class?"

An executable Java class is a class which, when handed over to the JVM, starts its execution at a particular point in the class—the main method, defined in the class. The JVM starts executing the code that is defined in the main method. You cannot hand over a nonexecutable Java class to the JVM and ask it to start executing the class. In this case, the JVM won't know how to execute it because no entry point is marked, for the JVM, in a nonexecutable class.

Typically, an application consists of a number of classes and interfaces that are defined in multiple Java source code files. Of all these files, a programmer designates one of the classes as an executable class. The programmer can define the steps that the JVM should execute as soon as it launches the application. For example, a programmer can define an executable Java class that includes code to display the appropriate GUI window to a user and to open a database connection.

In figure 1.6, the classes Window, UserData, ServerConnection, and UserPreferences don't define a main method. Class LaunchApplication defines a main method and is an executable class.

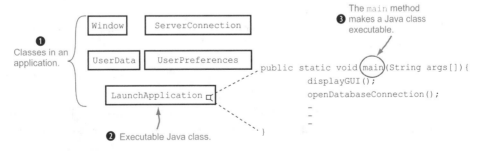

Figure 1.6   Class LaunchApplication is an executable Java class, but the rest of the classes—Window, UserData, ServerConnection, and UserPreferences—aren't.

1.2.2   *Main method*

The first requirement in creating an executable Java application is to create a class
with a method whose signature (name and method arguments) match the `main`
method, defined as follows:

```
public class HelloExam {
    public static void main(String args[]) {
        System.out.println("Hello exam");
    }
}
```

This `main` method should comply with the following rules:

- The method must be marked as a `public` method.
- The method must be marked as a `static` method.
- The name of the method must be `main`.
- The return type of this method must be `void`.
- The method must accept a method argument of a `String` array or a variable
  argument of type `String`.

Figure 1.7 illustrates the previous code and its related set of rules.

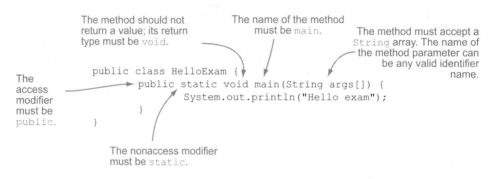

Figure 1.7   Ingredients of a correct `main` method

It's valid to define the method parameter passed to the `main` method as a variable
argument (*varargs*) of type `String`:

```
public static void main(String... args)
```
◁─┤ **It is valid to define args
as a variable argument**

To define a variable argument variable, the ellipsis (. . .) should follow the type of the
variable and not the variable itself (a mistake made by lot of new programmers):

```
public static void main(String args...)
```
◁─┤ **This won't compile. Ellipses should
follow the data type, String.**

As mentioned previously, the name of the `String` array passed to the `main` method need not be `args` to qualify it as the correct `main` method. Thus, the following examples are also correct definitions of the `main` method:

```
public static void main(String[] arguments)
public static void main(String[] HelloWorld)
```

The names of the method arguments are arguments and HelloWorld, which is acceptable

To define an array, the square brackets, `[]`, can follow either the variable name or its type. The following is a correct method declaration of the `main` method:

```
public static void main(String[] args)
public static void main(String minnieMouse[])
```

The square brackets, [], can follow either the variable name or its type

It's interesting to note that the placement of the keywords `public` and `static` can be interchanged, which means that the following are both correct method declarations of the `main` method:

```
public static void main(String[] args)
static public void main(String[] args)
```

The placement of the keywords public and static is interchangeable

On execution, the code shown in figure 1.7 outputs the following:

```
Hello exam
```

Almost all Java developers work with an Integrated Development Environment (IDE). The OCA Java SE 7 Programmer I exam, however, expects you to understand how to execute a Java application, or an executable Java class, using the command prompt. If you need help getting your system set up to compile or execute Java applications using the command prompt, refer to Oracle's detailed instructions at http://docs.oracle .com/javase/tutorial/getStarted/cupojava/index.html.

To execute the code shown in figure 1.7, issue the command `java HelloExam`, as shown in figure 1.8.

We discussed how the `main` method accepts an array of `String` as the method parameter. But how and where do you pass the array to the `main` method? Let's modify the previous code to access and output values from this array. Here's the relevant code:

```
public class HelloExamWithParameters {
    public static void main(String args[]) {
        System.out.println(args[0]);
        System.out.println(args[1]);
    }
}
```

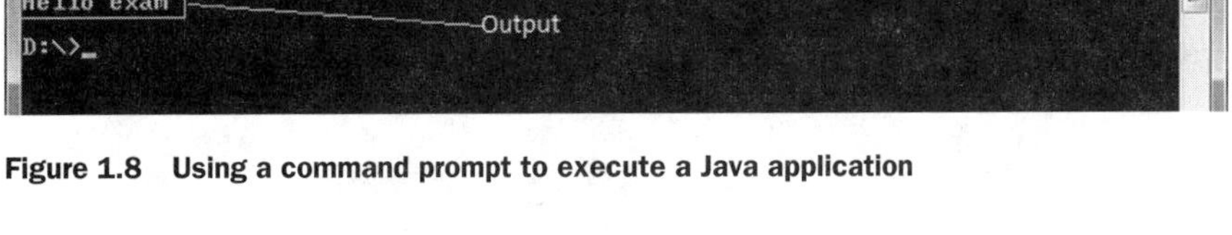

Figure 1.8   Using a command prompt to execute a Java application

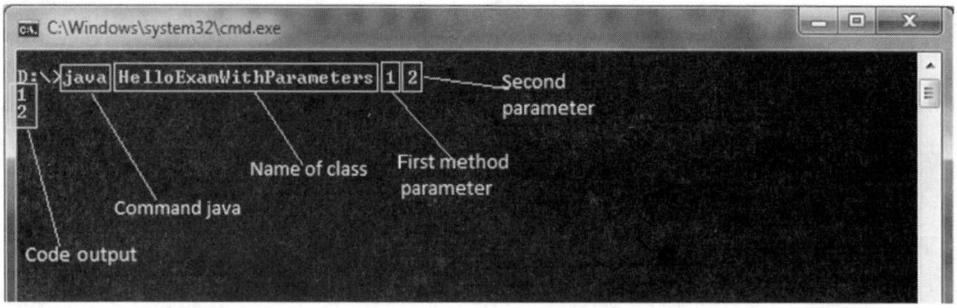

Figure 1.9   Passing command parameters to a `main` method

Execute the class in the preceding code at a command prompt, as shown in figure 1.9.

As you can see from the output shown in figure 1.9, the keyword `java` and the name of the class aren't passed on as command parameters to the `main` method. The OCA Java SE 7 Programmer I exam will test you on your knowledge of whether the keyword `java` and the class name are passed on to the `main` method.

> **EXAM TIP** The method parameters that are passed on to the `main` method are also called command-line parameters or command-line values. As the name implies, these values are passed on to a method from the command line.

If you weren't able to follow the code with respect to the arrays and class `String`, don't worry; we'll cover the class `String` and arrays in detail in chapter 4.

Here's the next Twist in the Tale exercise for you. In this exercise, and in the rest of the book, you'll see the names Shreya, Harry, Paul, and Selvan, who are hypothetical programmers also studying for this certification exam. The answer is provided in the appendix.

Twist in the Tale 1.3

One of the programmers, Harry, executed a program that gave the output "java one". Now he's trying to figure out which of the following classes outputs these results. Given that he executed the class using the command `java EJava java one one`, can you help him figure out the correct option(s)?

```
a  class EJava {
       public static void main(String sun[]) {
           System.out.println(sun[0] + " " + sun[2]);
       }
   }
b  class EJava {
       static public void main(String phone[]) {
           System.out.println(phone[0] + " " + phone[1]);
       }
   }
c  class EJava {
       static public void main(String[] arguments[]) {
```

```
            System.out.println(arguments[0] + " " + arguments[1]);
        }
    }
d   class EJava {
        static void public main(String args[]) {
            System.out.println(args[0] + " " + args[1]);
        }
    }
```

Confusion with command-line parameters

Programming languages like C pass on the name of a class as a command-line argument to the `main` method. Java doesn't do so. This is a simple but important point.

1.3 Java packages

[1.4] Import other Java packages to make them accessible in your code

In this section, you'll learn what Java packages are and how to create them. You'll use the `import` statement, which enables you to use simple names for classes and interfaces defined in separate packages.

1.3.1 The need for packages

Why do you think we need packages? First, answer this question: do you remember having known more than one Amit, Paul, Anu, or John to date? Harry knows more than one Paul (six, to be precise), whom he categorizes as managers, friends, and cousins. These are subcategorized by their location and relation, as shown in figure 1.10.

Similarly, you can use packages to group together a related set of classes and interfaces (I will not discuss enums here because they aren't covered on this exam). Packages also provide access protection and namespace management. You can create separate packages to define classes for separate projects, such as android games and online health-care systems. Further, you can create subpackages within these packages, such as separate subpackages for GUIs, database access, networking, and so on.

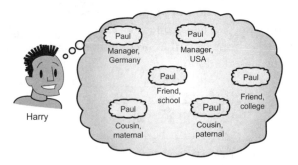

Figure 1.10   Harry knows six Pauls!

PRACTICAL TIP   In real-life projects, you will never work with an unpackaged class or interface. Almost all organizations that develop software have strict package-naming rules, which are often documented.

The OCA Java SE 7 Programmer I exam covers importing packaged classes into other classes. But after 12 years of experience, I've learned that before starting to *import* other classes into your own code, it's important to understand what the packaged classes are, how packaged and nonpackaged classes differ, and why you need to import the packaged classes.

Packaged classes are part of a named package—a namespace—and they're defined as being part of a package by including a `package` statement in a class. All classes and interfaces are packaged. If you don't include an explicit `package` statement in a class or an interface, it's part of a *default* package.

1.3.2   *Defining classes in a package using the package statement*

You can define which classes and interfaces are in a package by using the `package` statement as the first statement in your class or interface. Here's an example:

```
package certification;
class ExamQuestion {         Variables and
    //..code                 methods
}
```

The class in the previous code defines an `ExamQuestion` class in the `certification` package. You can define an interface, `MultipleChoice`, in a similar manner:

```
package certification;
interface MultipleChoice {
    void choice1();
    void choice2();
}
```

Figure 1.11 shows the UML representation of the package `certification`, with the class `ExamQuestion` and the interface `MultipleChoice`:

The name of the package in the previous examples is `certification`. You may use such names for small projects that contain only a few classes and interfaces, but it's common for organizations to use subpackages to define *all* their classes. For example, if folks at Oracle define a class to store exam questions for a Java Associate exam, they might use the package name `com.oracle.javacert.associate`. Figure 1.12 shows its UML representation, together with the corresponding class definition:

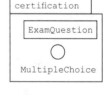

Figure 1.11
A UML representation of the package `certification`, **class Exam-Question, and interface** `MultipleChoice`

```
package com.oracle.javacert.associate;      com.oracle.javacert.associate
class ExamQuestion {
        // variables and methods                   ExamQuestion
}
```

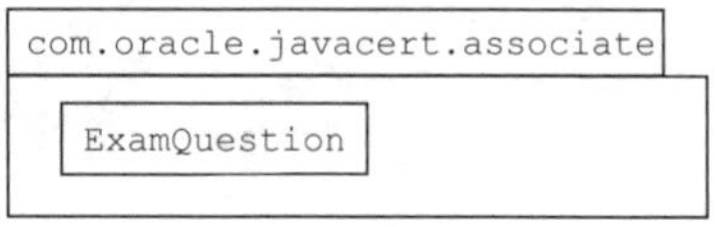

Figure 1.12   A subpackage and its corresponding class definition

The package name `com.oracle.javacert.associate` follows a package-naming convention recommended by Oracle and shown in table 1.1.

Table 1.1 Package-naming conventions used in the package name `com.oracle.javacert` `.associate`

Package or subpackage name	Its meaning
`com`	Commercial. A couple of the commonly used three-letter package abbreviations are gov—for government bodies edu—for educational institutions
`oracle`	Name of the organization
`javacert`	Further categorization of the project at Oracle
`associate`	Further subcategorization of Java certification

RULES TO REMEMBER
A few of important rules about packages:

- Per Java naming conventions, package names should all be in lowercase.
- The package and subpackage names are separated using a dot (.).
- Package names follow the rules defined for valid identifiers in Java.
- For packaged classes and interfaces, the `package` statement is the first statement in a Java source file (a .java file). The exception is that comments can appear before or after a `package` statement.
- There can be a maximum of one `package` statement per Java source code file (.java file).
- All the classes and interfaces defined in a Java source code file will be defined in the same package. There is no way to package classes and interfaces defined within the same Java source code file in different packages.

NOTE A fully qualified name for a class or interface is formed by prefixing its package name with its name (separated by a period). The fully qualified name of class `ExamQuestion` is `certification.ExamQuestion` in figure 1.11 and `com.oracle.javacert.associate.ExamQuestion` in figure 1.12.

DIRECTORY STRUCTURE AND PACKAGE HIERARCHY
The hierarchy of the packaged classes should match the hierarchy of the directories in which these classes and interfaces are defined in the code. For example, the class `ExamQuestion` in the `certification` package should be defined in a directory with the name "certification."

The name of the directory "certification" and its location are governed by the following rules:

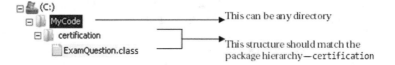

For the package example shown in figure 1.12, note that there isn't any constraint on the location of the base directory in which the directory structure is defined. Examine the following image:

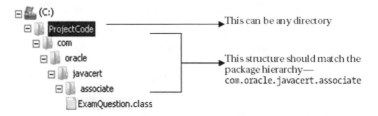

SETTING THE CLASSPATH FOR PACKAGED CLASSES

To enable the Java Runtime Environment (JRE) to find your classes, add the base directory that contains your packaged Java code to the classpath.

For example, to enable the JRE to locate the certification.ExamQuestion class from the previous examples, add the directory C:\MyCode to the classpath. To enable the JRE to locate the class com.oracle.javacert.associate.ExamQuestion, add the directory C:\ProjectCode to the classpath.

You don't need to bother setting the classpath if you're working with an IDE. But I strongly encourage you to learn how to work with a simple text editor and how to set a classpath. This can be particularly helpful with your projects at work. I have also witnessed many interviewers querying candidates on the need for classpaths.

1.3.3 Using simple names with import statements

The import statement enables you to use *simple names* instead of using *fully qualified names* for classes and interfaces defined in separate packages.

Let's work with a real-life example. Imagine your Home and your neighbor's Office. "LivingRoom" and "Kitchen" within your home can refer to each other without mentioning that they exist within the same home. Similarly, in an office, a Cubicle and a ConferenceHall can refer to each other without explicitly mentioning that they exist within the same office. But "Home" and "Office" can't access each other's rooms or cubicles without stating that they exist in a separate home or office. This situation is represented in figure 1.13.

To refer to the LivingRoom in Cubicle, you *must* specify its complete location, as shown in left part of the figure 1.14. As you can see in this figure, repeated references to the location of LivingRoom make the description of LivingRoom look tedious and redundant. To avoid this, you can display a notice in Cubicle that all occurrences of LivingRoom refer to LivingRoom in Home, and thereafter use its simple name. Home

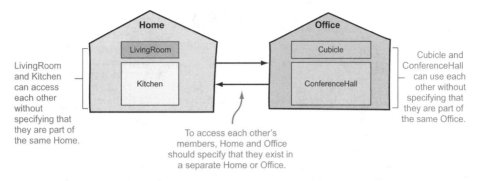

Figure 1.13 To refer to each other's members, Home and Office should specify that they exist in separate places.

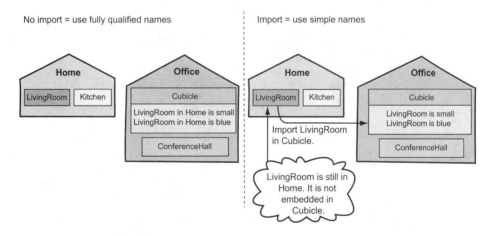

Figure 1.14 LivingRoom can be accessed in Cubicle by using its fully qualified name. It can also be accessed using its simple name if you also use the `import` statement.

and Office are like Java packages, and this notice is the equivalent of the `import` statement. Figure 1.14 shows the difference in using fully qualified names and simple names for Home in Cubicle.

Let's implement the previous example in code, where classes `LivingRoom` and `Kitchen` are defined in the package `home` and classes `Cubicle` and `ConferenceHall` are defined in the package `office`. The class `Cubicle` uses (is associated to) the class `LivingRoom` in the package `home`, as shown in figure 1.15.

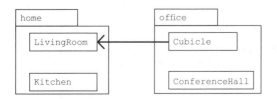

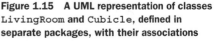

Figure 1.15 A UML representation of classes `LivingRoom` and `Cubicle`, defined in separate packages, with their associations

Class `Cubicle` can refer to class `LivingRoom` without using an `import` statement:

```
package office;
class Cubicle {
    home.LivingRoom livingRoom;
}
```

In the absence of an import statement, use the fully qualified name to access class **LivingRoom**

Class `Cubicle` can use the simple name for class `LivingRoom` by using the `import` statement:

```
package office;
import home.LivingRoom;
```

import statement

```
class Cubicle {
    LivingRoom livingRoom;
}
```

No need to use the fully qualified name of class **LivingRoom**

NOTE   The `import` statement doesn't embed the contents of the imported class in your class, which means that *importing* more classes doesn't increase the size of your own class. It lets you use the simple name for a class or interface defined in a separate package.

1.3.4   *Using packaged classes without using the import statement*

It is possible to use a packaged class or interface without using the `import` statement, by using its fully qualified name:

Missing import statement

```
class AnnualExam {
    certification.ExamQuestion eq;
}
```

Define a variable of ExamQuestion by using its fully qualified name

This approach can clutter your code if you create multiple variables of interfaces and classes defined in other packages. Use this approach sparingly in actual projects.

For the exam, it's important to note that you can't use the `import` statement to access multiple classes or interfaces with the same names from different packages. For example, the Java API defines the class `Date` in two commonly used packages: `java.util` and `java.sql`. To define variables of these classes in a class, use their fully qualified names with the variable declaration:

Missing import statement

```
class AnnualExam {
    java.util.Date date1;
    java.sql.Date date2;
}
```

◄── **Variable of type java.util.Date**

Variable of type java.sql.Date

An attempt to use an `import` statement to import both these classes in the same class will not compile:

```
import java.util.Date;
import java.sql.Date;
class AnnualExam { }
```

Code to import classes with the same name from different packages won't compile

1.3.5   *Importing a single member versus all members of a package*

You can import either a single member or all members (classes and interfaces) of a package using the import statement. First, revisit the UML notation of the certification package, as shown in figure 1.16.

Examine the following code for class AnnualExam:

```
import certification.ExamQuestion;    ⊲─┤ Imports only the
class AnnualExam {                          class ExamQuestion
    ExamQuestion eq;       ⊲── Compiles OK
    MultipleChoice mc;    ⊲─┐
}                              │ Will not compile
```

By using the wildcard character, an asterisk (*), you can import all of the public members, classes, and interfaces of a package. Compare the previous class definition with the following definition of the class AnnualExam:

```
import certification.*;               ⊲─┤ Imports all classes and
class AnnualExam {                          interfaces from certification
    ExamQuestion eq;       ⊲── Compiles OK
    MultipleChoice mc;    ⊲─┐
}                              │ This also compiles OK
```

Unlike in C or C++, *importing* a class doesn't add to the size of a Java .class file. An import statement enables Java to refer to the imported classes without embedding their source code in the target .class file.

When you work with an IDE, it may automatically add import statements for classes and interfaces that you reference in your code.

1.3.6   *Can you recursively import subpackages?*

You can't import classes from a subpackage by using an asterisk in the import statement.

For example, the following UML notation depicts the package com.oracle.javacert with the class Schedule, and two subpackages, associate and webdeveloper. Package associate contains class ExamQuestion, and package webdeveloper contains class MarkSheet, as shown in figure 1.17.

The following import statement will import only the class Schedule. It won't import the classes ExamQuestion and MarkSheet:

```
import com.oracle.javacert.*;         ⊲─┐ Imports the class
                                          Schedule only
```

certification

ExamQuestion

○
MultipleChoice

Figure 1.16
A UML representation of the certification package

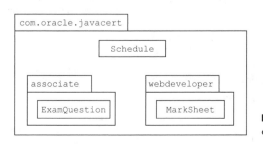

Figure 1.17   A UML representation of package com.oracle.javacert and its subpackages

Similarly, the following `import` statement will import all the classes from the packages associate and webdeveloper:

```
import com.oracle.javacert.associate.*;
import com.oracle.javacert.webdeveloper.*;
```

Imports class ExamQuestion only

Imports class MarkSheet only

1.3.7 Importing classes from the default package

What happens if you don't explicitly package your classes or interfaces? In that case, they're packaged in a *default, no-name* package. This default package is automatically imported in the Java classes and interfaces defined within the same directory on your system.

For example, the classes Person and Office, which are not defined in an explicit package, can use each other if they are defined in the same directory:

```
class Person {
    // code
}
class Office {
    Person p;
}
```

Not defined in an explicit package

Class Person accessible in class Office

A class from a default package can't be used in any named packaged class, regardless of whether they are defined within the same directory or not.

1.3.8 Static imports

You can import an individual `static` member of a class or all its `static` members by using the `import static` statement.

In the following code, the class ExamQuestion defines a `public static` variable named marks and a `public static` method named print:

```
package certification;
public class ExamQuestion {
    static public int marks;
    public static void print() {
        System.out.println(100);
    }
}
```

public static variable marks

public static method print

The variable marks can be accessed in the class AnnualExam using the `import static` statement. The order of the keywords `import` and `static` can't be reversed:

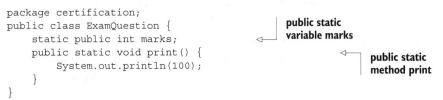

```
package university;
import static certification.ExamQuestion.marks;
class AnnualExam {
    AnnualExam() {
        marks = 20;
    }
}
```

Correct statement is import static, not static import

Access variable marks without prefixing it with its class name

To access all `public static` members of class ExamQuestion in class AnnualExam, you can use an asterisk with the `import static` statement:

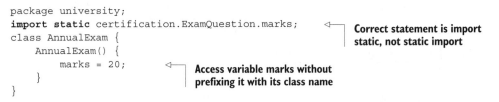

```
package university;
import static certification.ExamQuestion.*;
```

Imports all static members of class ExamQuestion

```
class AnnualExam {
    AnnualExam() {
        marks = 20;
        print();
    }
}
```

Accesses variable marks and method print without prefixing them with their class names

Because the variable `marks` and method `print` are defined as `public` members, they are accessible to the class `AnnualExam` using the `import static` statement. These wouldn't be accessible to the class `AnnualExam` if they were defined using any other access modifiers. The accessibility of a class, an interface, and their methods and variables are determined by their access modifiers, which are covered in the next section.

1.4 Java access modifiers

[6.6] Apply access modifiers

In this section, we'll cover all of the access modifiers—`public`, `protected`, and `private`—as well as default access, which is the result when you don't use an access modifier. We'll also look at how you can use access modifiers to restrict the visibility of a class and its members in the same and separate packages.

1.4.1 Access modifiers

Let's start with an example. Examine the definitions of the classes `House` and `Book` in the following code and the UML representation shown in figure 1.18.

```
package building;
class House {}

package library;
class Book {}
```

With the current class definitions, the class `House` cannot access the class `Book`. Can you make the necessary changes (in terms of the access modifiers) to make the class `Book` accessible to the class `House`?

This one shouldn't be difficult. From the discussion of class declarations in section 1.1, you know that a top-level class can be defined only using the `public` or default access modifiers. If you declare the class `Book` using the access modifier `public`, it'll be accessible outside the package in which it is defined.

> **NOTE** A top-level class is a class that isn't defined within any other class. A class that is defined within another class is called a *nested* or *inner class*. Nested and inner classes aren't on the OCA Java SE 7 Programmer I exam.

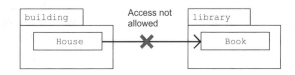

Figure 1.18 The nonpublic class `Book` cannot be accessed outside the package `library`.

WHAT DO THEY CONTROL?

Access modifiers control the accessibility of a class or an interface, including its members (methods and variables), by other classes and interfaces. For example, you can't access the `private` variables and methods of another class. By using the appropriate access modifiers, you can limit access to your class or interface, and their members, by other classes and interfaces.

CAN ACCESS MODIFIERS BE APPLIED TO ALL TYPES OF JAVA ENTITIES?

Access modifiers can be applied to classes, interfaces, and their members (instance and class variables and methods). Local variables and method parameters can't be defined using access modifiers. An attempt to do so will prevent the code from compiling.

HOW MANY ACCESS MODIFIERS ARE THERE: THREE OR FOUR?

Programmers are frequently confused about the number of access modifiers in Java because the *default access* isn't defined using an explicit keyword. If a Java entity (class, interface, method, or variable) isn't defined using an explicit access modifier, it is said to be defined using the *default access*, also called *package access*.

Java defines four access modifiers:

- `public` (least restrictive)
- `protected`
- *default*
- `private` (most restrictive)

To understand all of these access modifiers, we'll use the same set of classes: `Book`, `CourseBook`, `Librarian`, `StoryBook`, and `House`. Figure 1.19 depicts these classes using UML notation.

The classes `Book`, `CourseBook`, and `Librarian` are defined in the package `library`. The classes `StoryBook` and `House` are defined in the package `building`. Further, classes `StoryBook` and `CourseBook` (defined in separate packages) extend class `Book`. Using these classes, I'll show how the accessibility of a class and its members varies with different access modifiers, from unrelated to derived classes, across packages.

As we cover each of the access modifiers, we'll add a set of instance variables and a method to the class `Book` with the relevant access modifier. We'll then define code for the other classes that try to access class `Book` and its members.

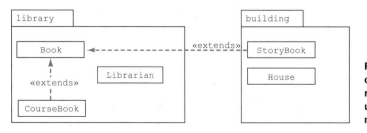

Figure 1.19   A set of classes and their relationships to help understand access modifiers

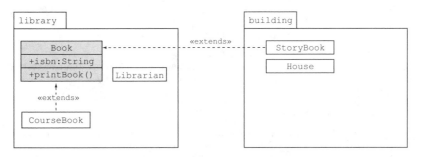

Figure 1.20 Understanding the `public` access modifier

1.4.2 Public access modifier

This is the least restrictive access modifier. Classes and interfaces defined using the public access modifier are accessible across all packages, from derived to unrelated classes.

To understand the public access modifier, let's define the class `Book` as a public class and add a public instance variable (`isbn`) and a public method (`printBook`) to it. Figure 1.20 shows the UML notation.

Definition of class `Book`:

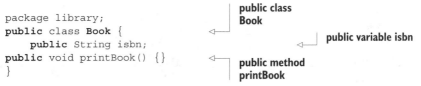

```
package library;
public class Book {
    public String isbn;
public void printBook() {}
}
```

> **public class Book**
> **public variable isbn**
> **public method printBook**

The public access modifier is said to be the least restrictive, so let's try to access the public class `Book` and its public members from class `House`. We'll use class `House` because `House` and `Book` are defined in separate packages and they're unrelated. Class `House` doesn't enjoy any advantages by being defined in the same package or being a derived class.

Here's the code for class `House`:

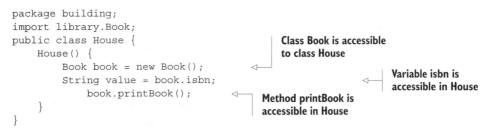

```
package building;
import library.Book;
public class House {
    House() {
        Book book = new Book();
        String value = book.isbn;
            book.printBook();
    }
}
```

> **Class Book is accessible to class House**
> **Variable isbn is accessible in House**
> **Method printBook is accessible in House**

As you may notice in the previous example, the class `Book` and its public members—instance variable `isbn` and method `printBook`—are accessible to the class `House`. They are also accessible to the other classes: `StoryBook`, `Librarian`, `House`, and `CourseBook`. Figure 1.21 shows the classes that can access a public class and its members.

Figure 1.21   **Classes that can access a public class and its members**

1.4.3   *Protected access modifier*

The members of a class defined using the `protected` access modifier are accessible to

- Classes and interfaces defined in the same package
- All derived classes, even if they're defined in separate packages

Let's add a `protected` instance variable `author` and method `modifyTemplate` to the class `Book`. Figure 1.22 shows the class representation.

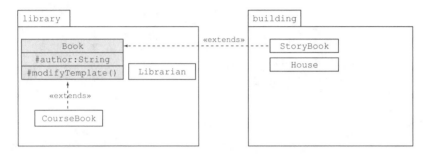

Figure 1.22   **Understanding the `protected` access modifier**

Here's the code for the class `Book` (I've deliberately left out its `public` members because they aren't required in this section):

```
package library;
public class Book {
    protected String author;
    protected void modifyTemplate() {}
}
```

Protected variable author

Protected method modifyTemplate

Figure 1.23 illustrates how classes from the same and separate packages, derived classes, and unrelated classes access the class `Book` and its `protected` members.

Class `House` throws a compilation error message for trying to access the method `modifyTemplate` and the variable `author`, as follows:

```
House.java:8: modifyTemplate() has protected access in library.Book
        book.modifyTemplate();
            ^
```

Notice that the derived classes `CourseBook` and `StoryBook` can access the class `Book`'s `protected` variable `author` and method `modifyTemplate` as if they were defined in their own classes. If class `StoryBook` tries to create an object of class `Book` and then tries to access its `protected` variable `author` and `modifyTemplate`, it will not compile:

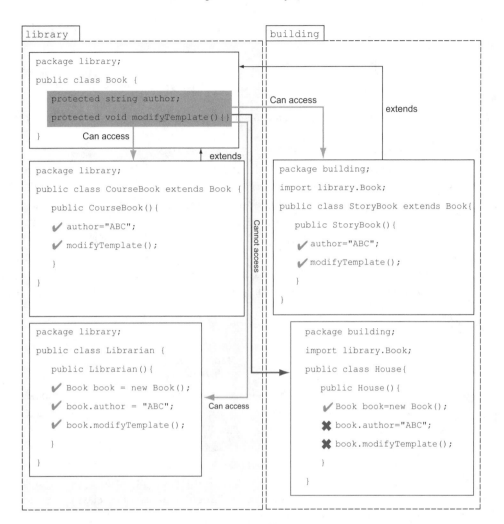

Figure 1.23   **Access of `protected` members of the class `Book` in unrelated and derived classes, from the same and separate packages**

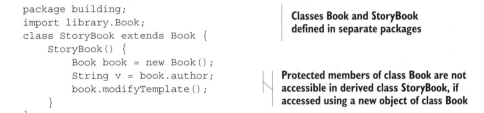

```
package building;
import library.Book;
class StoryBook extends Book {
    StoryBook() {
        Book book = new Book();
        String v = book.author;
        book.modifyTemplate();
    }
}
```

Classes Book and StoryBook defined in separate packages

Protected members of class Book are not accessible in derived class StoryBook, if accessed using a new object of class Book

EXAM TIP   A concise but not too simple way of stating the previous rule is this: a derived class can inherit and access `protected` members of its base class, regardless of the package in which it's defined. A derived class in a separate package can't access `protected` members of its base class using reference variables.

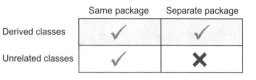

Figure 1.24 **Classes that can access protected members**

Figure 1.24 shows the classes that can access protected members of a class or interface.

1.4.4 *Default access (package access)*

The members of a class defined without using any explicit access modifier are defined with *package accessibility* (also called *default accessibility*). The members with package access are *only* accessible to classes and interfaces defined in the same package.

Let's define an instance variable issueCount and a method issueHistory with default access in class Book. Figure 1.25 shows the class representation with these new members.

Here's the code for the class Book (I've deliberately left out its public and protected members because they aren't required in this section):

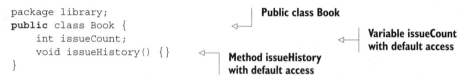

You can see how classes from the same package and separate packages, derived classes, and unrelated classes access the class Book and its members (the variable issueCount and the method issueHistory) in figure 1.26.

Because the classes CourseBook and Librarian are defined in the same package as the class Book, they can access the variables issueCount and issueHistory. Because the classes House and StoryBook don't reside in the same package as the class Book, they can't access the variables issueCount and issueHistory. The class StoryBook throws the following compilation error message:

```
StoryBook.java:6: issueHistory() is not public in library.Book; cannot be
    accessed from outside package
        book.issueHistory();
            ^
```

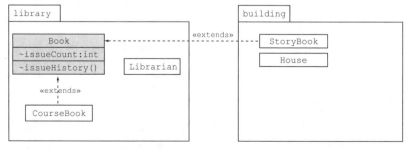

Figure 1.25 **Understanding class representation for default access**

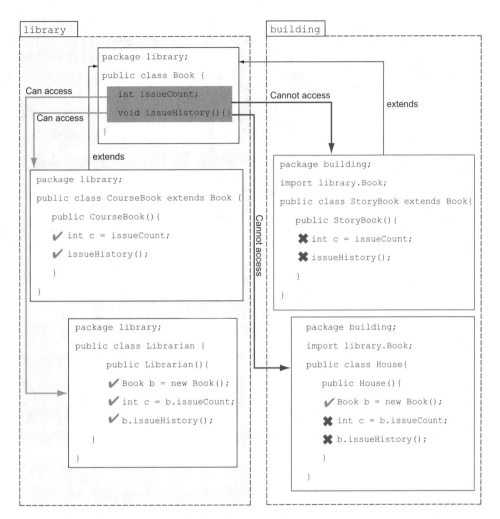

Figure 1.26   Access of members with default access to the class `Book` **in unrelated and derived classes from the same and separate packages**

The class `House` throws the following compilation error message (for trying to access `issueHistory`):

```
House.java:9: cannot find symbol
symbol  : method issueHistory()
location: class building.House
        issueHistory();
```

Defining a class Book with default access

What happens if we define a class with default access? What will happen to the accessibility of its members if the class itself has *default* (package) accessibility?

Let's consider this situation using an example: assume that Superfast Burgers opens a new outlet on a beautiful island and offers free meals to people from all over

---

How packages and class hierarchy affect default access to class members

From the compilation errors thrown by the Java compiler when trying to compile the classes `StoryBook` and `House`, you can see that the method `issueHistory` (defined in the class `Book`) is visible to its derived class `StoryBook` (defined in another package), but `StoryBook` cannot access it. The method `issueHistory` (defined in class `Book`) is not even visible to the unrelated class `House` defined in a separate package.

---

the world, which obviously includes inhabitants of the island. But the island is inaccessible by all means (air and water). Would the existence of this particular Superfast Burgers outlet make any sense to people who don't inhabit the island? An illustration of this example is shown in figure 1.27.

The island is like a package in Java, and the Superfast Burgers like a class defined with default access. In the same way that the Superfast Burgers cannot be accessed from outside the island in which it exists, a class defined with default (package) access is visible and accessible only from within the package in which it is defined. It can't be accessed from outside the package in which it resides.

Let's redefine the class `Book` with default (package) access, as follows:

```
package library;
class Book {
    //.. class members        ◁─┐  Class Book now
}                                └  has default access
```

The behavior of the class `Book` remains the same for the classes `CourseBook` and `Librarian`, which are defined in the same package. But the class `Book` can't be accessed by classes `House` and `StoryBook`, which reside in a separate package.

Let's start with the class `House`. Examine the following code:

```
package building;
import library.Book;        ◁─┐  Class Book isn't accessible
public class House {}         └  in class House
```

Can be accessed only by the inhabitants of the island

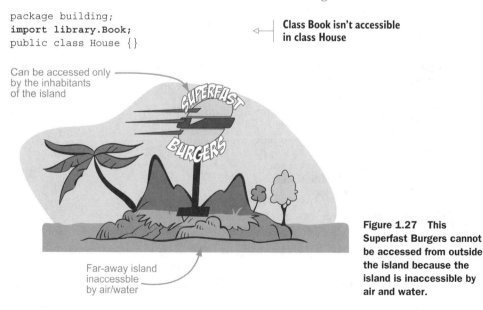

Far-away island inaccessble by air/water

Figure 1.27　This Superfast Burgers cannot be accessed from outside the island because the island is inaccessible by air and water.

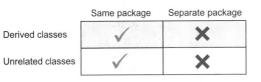

	Same package	Separate package
Derived classes	✓	✗
Unrelated classes	✓	✗

Figure 1.28 The classes that can access members with default (package) access

The class House generates the following compilation error message:

```
House.java:2: library.Book is not public in library; cannot be accessed from
    outside package
import library.Book;
```

Here's the code of the class StoryBook:

```
package building;
import library.Book;
class StoryBook extends Book {}
```

⟵┘ **Book isn't accessible in StoryBook**

⟵┘ **StoryBook cannot extend Book**

Figure 1.28 shows which classes can access members of a class or interface with default (package) access.

Because a lot of programmers are confused about which members are made accessible by using the protected and default access modifiers, the following exam tip offers a simple and interesting rule to help you remember their differences.

EXAM TIP Default access can be compared to package-private (accessible only within a package) and protected access can be compared to package-private + *kids* ("kids" refer to derived classes). Kids can access protected methods only by inheritance and not by reference (accessing members by using the dot operator on an object).

1.4.5 Private access modifier

The private access modifier is the most restrictive access modifier. The members of a class defined using the private access modifier are accessible only to themselves. It doesn't matter whether the class or interface in question is from another package or has extended the class—private members are *not* accessible outside the class in which they're defined. private members are accessible only to the classes and interfaces in which they are defined.

Let's see this in action by adding a private method countPages to the class Book. Figure 1.29 depicts the class representation using UML.

Examine the following definition of the class Book:

```
package library;
class Book {
    private void countPages() {}
    protected void modifyTemplate() {
        countPages();
    }
}
```

⟵┘ **private method**

⟵ **Only Book can access its own private method countPages**

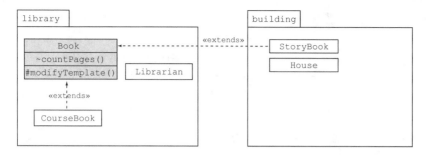

Figure 1.29   Understanding the `private` access modifier

None of the classes defined in any of the packages (whether derived or not) can access the `private` method `countPages`. But let's try to access it from the class `CourseBook`. I chose the class `CourseBook` because both of these classes are defined in the same package, and the class `CourseBook` extends the class `Book`. Here's the code of `CourseBook`:

```
package library;
class CourseBook extends Book {
    CourseBook() {
        countPages();
    }
}
```

CourseBook
extends Book

CourseBook cannot access
private method countPages

Because the class `CourseBook` tries to access private members of the class `Book`, it will not compile. Similarly, if any of the other classes (`StoryBook`, `Librarian`, `House`, or `CourseBook`) tries to access the `private` method `countPages()` of class `Book`, it will not compile. Figure 1.30 shows the classes that can access the `private` members of a class.

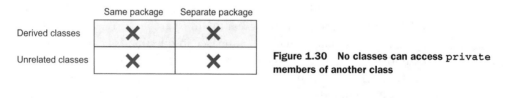

Figure 1.30   No classes can access `private` members of another class

Twist in the Tale 1.4

The following task was assigned to a group of programmers: "How can you declare a class `Curtain` in a package `building` so that it isn't visible outside the package `building`?"

These are the answers submitted by Paul, Shreya, Harry, and Selvan. Which of these do you think is correct, and why? (You can check your Twist in the Tale answers in the appendix.)

Programmer name	Submitted code
Paul	`package building;` `public class Curtain {}`
Shreya	`package building;` `protected class Curtain {}`
Harry	`package building;` `class Curtain {}`
Selvan	`package building;` `private class Curtain {}`

Your job title may assign special privileges or responsibilities to you. For example, if you work as a Java developer, you may be responsible for updating your programming skills or earning professional certifications in Java. Similarly, you can assign special privileges, responsibilities, and behaviors to your Java entities by using *nonaccess modifiers*, which are covered in the next section.

1.5 *Nonaccess modifiers*

> [7.6] Use abstract classes and interfaces

> [6.2] Apply the static keyword to methods and fields

This section discusses the nonaccess modifiers `abstract`, `final`, and `static`. Access modifiers control the accessibility of your class and its members outside the class and the package. Nonaccess modifiers change the default properties of a Java class and its members.

For example, if you add the keyword `abstract` to the definition of a class, it'll be considered an `abstract` class. None of the other classes will be able to create objects of this class. Such is the magic of the nonaccess modifiers.

You can characterize your classes, interfaces, methods, and variables with the following nonaccess modifiers (though not all are applicable to each Java entity):

- `abstract`
- `static`
- `final`
- `synchronized`
- `native`
- `strictfp`
- `transient`
- `volatile`

The OCA Java SE 7 Programmer I exam covers only three of these nonaccess modifiers: abstract, final, and static, which I'll cover in detail. To ward off any confusion about the rest of the modifiers, I'll describe them briefly here:

- synchronized—A synchronized method can't be accessed by multiple threads concurrently. This constraint is used to protect the integrity of data that might be accessed and changed by multiple threads concurrently. You can't mark classes, interfaces, or variables with this modifier.
- native—A native method calls and makes use of libraries and methods implemented in other programming languages such as C or C++. You can't mark classes, interfaces, or variables with this modifier.
- transient—A transient variable isn't serialized when the corresponding object is serialized. The transient modifier can't be applied to classes, interfaces, or methods.
- volatile—A volatile variable's value can be safely modified by different threads. Classes, interfaces, and methods cannot use this modifier.
- strictfp—Classes, interfaces, and methods defined using this keyword ensure that calculations using floating-point numbers are identical on all platforms. This modifier can't be used with variables.

Now let's look at the three nonaccess modifiers that are on the exam.

1.5.1   *Abstract modifier*

When added to the definition of a class, interface, or method, the abstract modifier changes its default behavior. Because it is a nonaccess modifier, abstract doesn't change the accessibility of a class, interface, or method.

Let's examine the behavior of each of these with the abstract modifier.

ABSTRACT CLASS

When the abstract keyword is prefixed to the definition of a concrete class, it changes it to an abstract class, even if the class doesn't define any abstract methods. The following code is a valid example of an abstract class:

```
abstract class Person {
    private String name;
    public void displayName() { }
}
```

An abstract class can't be instantiated, which means that the following code will fail to compile:

```
class University {
    Person p = new Person();          ⟵  This line of code
}                                          won't compile
```

Here's the compilation error thrown by the previous class:

```
University.java:4: Person is abstract; cannot be instantiated
    Person p = new Person();
                 ^
```

```
1 error
```

EXAM TIP   An abstract class may or may not define an abstract method; you can define an abstract class without any abstract methods. But a concrete class can't define an abstract method.

ABSTRACT INTERFACE

An interface is an abstract entity by default. The Java compiler automatically adds the keyword abstract to the definition of an interface. Thus, adding the keyword abstract to the definition of an interface is redundant. The following definitions of interfaces are the same:

```
interface Movable {}           ◁──┘  Interface defined without the
                                      explicit use of keyword abstract
abstract interface Movable {}  ◁──┐  Interface defined with the
                                      explicit use of keyword abstract
```

ABSTRACT METHOD

An abstract method doesn't have a body. Usually, an abstract method is implemented by a derived class. Here's an example:

```
abstract class Person {
    private String name;
    public void displayName() { }   ◁──┘  This isn't an abstract method.
                                            It has an empty body: {}.
    public abstract void perform();  ◁──┐  This is an abstract method.
}                                         It isn't followed by {}.
```

EXAM TIP   A method with an empty body isn't an abstract method.

ABSTRACT VARIABLES

None of the different types of variables (instance, static, local, and method parameters) can be defined as abstract.

EXAM TIP   Don't be tricked by code that tries to apply the nonaccess modifier abstract to a variable. Such code won't compile.

1.5.2   *Final modifier*

The keyword final changes the default behavior of a class, variable, or method.

FINAL CLASS

A class that is marked final cannot be extended by another class. The class Professor will not compile if the class Person is marked as final, as follows:

```
final class Person {}
class Professor extends Person {}   ◁──┘  Won't compile
```

FINAL INTERFACE

An interface cannot be marked as final. An interface is abstract by default and marking it with final will prevent your interface from compiling:

```
final interface MyInterface{}                    ◁─┐ Won't compile
```

FINAL VARIABLE

A final variable can't be reassigned a value. It can be assigned a value only once. See the following code:

```
class Person {
    final long MAX_AGE;
    Person() {                    ┌ Compiles successfully: value
        MAX_AGE = 99;      ◁─┘ assigned once to final variable
    }
}
```

Compare the previous example with the following code, which tries to reassign a value to a final variable:

```
class Person {
    final long MAX_AGE = 90;
    Person() {                    ┌ Won't compile;
        MAX_AGE = 99;      ◁─┘ reassignment not allowed
    }
}
```

It's easy to confuse reassigning a value to a final variable with *calling* a method on a final variable. If a reference variable is defined as a final variable, you can't reassign another object to it, but you can call methods on this variable:

```
class Person {
    final StringBuilder name = new StringBuilder("Sh");
    Person() {                                        ┌ Can call methods
        name.append("reya");              ◁─┘ on a final variable
        name = new StringBuilder();    ◁─┐
    }                                               │ Won't compile. You can't reassign
}                                                    └ another object to a final variable.
```

FINAL METHOD

A final method defined in a base class can't be overridden by a derived class. Examine the following code:

```
class Person {
    final void sing() {
        System.out.println("la..la..la..");
    }
}
class Professor extends Person {
    void sing() {                                        ◁─┐ Won't compile
        System.out.println("Alpha.. beta.. gamma");
    }
}
```

Figure 1.31   Comparing a shared bank vault with a static variable

If a method in a derived class has the same method signature as its base class's method, it is referred to as an *overridden method*. Overridden methods are discussed along with polymorphism in chapter 6.

1.5.3   *Static modifier*

The nonaccess modifier `static`, when applied to the definitions of variables, methods, classes, and interfaces, changes their default behavior. We'll examine each of them in following sections.

STATIC VARIABLES

`static` variables belong to a class. They are common to all instances of a class and aren't unique to any instance of a class. `static` attributes exist independently of any instances of a class and may be accessed even when no instances of the class have been created. You can compare a `static` variable with a shared variable. A `static` variable is shared by all of the objects of a class.

Think of a `static` variable as being like a common bank vault that's shared by the employees of an organization. Each of the employees accesses the same bank vault, so any change made by one employee is visible to all the other employees, as illustrated in figure 1.31.

Figure 1.32 defines a class `Emp` that defines a non-static variable `name` and a static variable `bankVault`.

It's time to test what we've been discussing up to this point. The following `TestEmp` class creates two objects of the class `Emp` (from figure 1.32) and modifies the value of the variable `bankVault` using these separate objects:

```
class Emp {                         We want this value to be
    String name;                    shared by all the objects of
    static int bankVault;           class Emp.
}
```

Figure 1.32   Definition of the class `Emp` with a static variable `bankVault` and non-static variable `name`

```
class TestEmp {
    public static void main(String[] args) {
    Emp emp1 = new Emp();
        Emp emp2 = new Emp();
        emp1.bankVault = 10;
        emp2.bankVault = 20;

        System.out.println(emp1.bankVault);
        System.out.println(emp2.bankVault);
        System.out.println(Emp.bankVault);
    }
}
```

Reference variables emp1 and emp2 refer to separate objects of class Emp

Variable bankVault of variable emp2 is assigned a value of 20

This will print 20

This will also print 20

Variable bankVault of variable emp1 is assigned a value of 10

This will print 20 as well

In the preceding code example, `emp1.bankVault`, `emp2.bankVault`, and `Emp.bankVault` all refer to the *same* static attribute: `bankVault`.

EXAM TIP   A `static` variable can be accessed using the name of the object reference variable or the name of a class.

The `static` and `final` nonaccess modifiers can be used to define *constants* (variables whose value can't change). In the following code, the class `Emp` defines the constants `MIN_AGE` and `MAX_AGE`:

```
class Emp {
    public static final int MIN_AGE = 20;
    static final int MAX_AGE = 70;
}
```

Constant MIN_AGE

Constant MAX_AGE

Though you can define a constant as a non-`static` member, it's common practice to define constants as `static` members, as doing so allows the constant values to be used across objects and classes.

STATIC METHODS

`static` methods aren't associated with objects and can't use any of the instance variables of a class. You can define `static` methods to access or manipulate `static` variables:

```
class Emp {
    String name;
    static int bankVault;

    static int getBankVaultValue() {
        return bankVault;
    }
}
```

static method getBankVaultValue returns the value of static variable bankVault

You can also use `static` methods to define *utility methods*, which are methods that usually manipulate the method parameters to compute and return an appropriate value:

```
static double interest(double num1, double num2, double num3) {
    return(num1+num2+num3)/3;
}
```

A `static` method may not always define method parameters. The method `average-OfFirst100Integers` computes and returns the average of numbers 1 to 100:

```
static double averageOfFirst100Integers() {
    int sum = 0;
    for (int i=1; i <= 100; ++i) {
        sum += i;
    }
    return (sum)/100;
}
```

Method averageOfFirst100Integers doesn't define method parameters

The non-private `static` variables and methods are inherited by derived classes. The `static` members aren't involved in runtime polymorphism. You can't override the `static` members in a derived class, but you can redefine them.

Any discussion of `static` methods and their behavior can be quite confusing if you aren't aware of inheritance and derived classes. But don't worry if you don't understand all of it. I'll cover derived classes and inheritance in chapter 6. For now, note that a `static` method can be accessed using the name of the object reference variables and the class in a manner similar to `static` variables.

> **NOTE** Even though you can use an object reference variable to access `static` members, it's not advisable to do so. Because `static` members belong to a class and not to individual objects, using object reference variables to access `static` members may make them appear to belong to an object. The proper way to access them is by using the class name.

WHAT CAN A STATIC METHOD ACCESS?

Neither `static` methods nor `static` variables can access the non-`static` variables and methods of a class. But the reverse is true: non-`static` variables and methods can access `static` variables and methods because the `static` members of a class exist even if no instances of the class exist. `static` members are forbidden from accessing instance methods and variables, which can exist only if an instance of the class is created.

Examine the following code:

```
class MyClass {
    static int x = count();
    int count() { return 10; }
}
```

Compilation error

This is the compilation error thrown by the previous class:

```
MyClass.java:3: nonstatic method count() cannot be referenced from a static
    context
    static int x = count();
                   ^

1 error
```

The following code is valid:

```
class MyClass {
    static int x = result();
    static int result() { return 20; }
```

static variable referencing a static method

```
    int nonStaticResult() { return result(); }
}
```
◁— **Non-static method using static method**

> ![owl] **EXAM TIP**   Static methods and variables can't access the instance members of a class.

Static classes and interfaces

Certification aspirants frequently ask questions about `static` classes and interfaces, so I'll quickly cover these in this section to ward off any confusion related to them. But note that `static` classes and interfaces are types of nested classes and interfaces that aren't covered by the OCA Java 7 Programmer I exam.

You can't prefix the definition of a top-level class or an interface with the keyword `static`. A top-level class or interface is one that isn't defined within another class or interface. The following code will fail to compile:

```
static class Person {}
static interface MyInterface {}
```

But you can define a class and an interface as a static member of another class. The following code is valid:

```
class Person {
    static class Address {}
    static interface MyInterface {}
}
```
◁— **Also known as a static nested class**

1.6   *Summary*

This chapter started with a look at the structure of a Java class. Although you should know how to work with Java classes, Java source code files (.java files), and Java bytecode files (.class files), the OCA Java SE 7 Programmer I exam will question you only on the structure and components of the first two—classes and source code—not on Java bytecode.

We discussed the components of a Java class and of Java source code files. A class can define multiple components, namely `import` and `package` statements, variables, constructors, methods, comments, nested classes, nested interfaces, annotations, and enums. A Java source code file (.java) can define multiple classes and interfaces.

We then covered the differences and similarities between executable and nonexecutable Java classes. An executable Java class defines the entry point (`main` method) for the JVM to start its execution. The `main` method should be defined with the required method signature; otherwise, the class will fail to be categorized as an executable Java class.

Packages are used to group together related classes and interfaces. They also provide access protection and namespace management. The `import` statement is used to import classes and interfaces from other packages. In the absence of an `import` statement, classes and interfaces should be referred to by their fully qualified names (complete package name plus class or interface name).

Access modifiers control the access of classes and their members within a package and across packages. Java defines four access modifiers: `public`, `protected`, default, and `private`. When default access is assigned to a class or its member, no access modifier is prefixed to it. The absence of an access modifier is equal to assigning the class or its members with default access. The least restrictive access modifier is `public`, and `private` is the most restrictive. `protected` access sits between `public` and default access, allowing access to derived classes outside of a package.

Finally, we covered the `abstract` and `static` nonaccess modifiers. A class or a method can be defined as an `abstract` member. `abstract` classes can't be instantiated. Methods and variables can be defined as `static` members. All the objects of a class share the same copy of `static` variables, which are also known as class-level variables.

1.7   Review notes

This section lists the main points covered in this chapter.

The structure of a Java class and source code file:

- The OCA Java SE 7 Programmer I exam covers the structure and components of a Java class and Java source code file (.java file). It doesn't cover the structure and components of Java bytecode files (.class files).
- A class can define multiple components. All the Java components you've heard of can be defined within a Java class: `import` and `package` statements, variables, constructors, methods, comments, nested classes, nested interfaces, annotations, and enums.
- The OCA Java SE 7 Programmer I exam doesn't cover the definitions of nested classes, nested interfaces, annotations, and enums.
- If a class defines a `package` statement, it should be the first statement in the class definition.
- The `package` statement can't appear within a class declaration or after the class declaration.
- If present, the `package` statement should appear exactly once in a class.
- The `import` statement uses simple names of classes and interfaces from within the class.
- The `import` statement can't be used to import multiple classes or interfaces with the same name.
- A class can include multiple `import` statements.
- If a class includes a `package` statement, all the `import` statements should follow the `package` statement.
- Comments are another component of a class. Comments are used to annotate Java code and can appear at multiple places within a class.
- A comment can appear before or after a `package` statement, before or after the class definition, and before, within, or after a method definition.
- Comments come in two flavors: multiline and end-of-line comments.

- Comments can contain any special characters (including characters from the Unicode charset).
- Multiline comments span multiple lines of code. They start with /* and end with */.
- End-of-line comments start with // and, as the name suggests, are placed at the end of a line of code. The text between // and the end of the line is treated as a comment.
- Class declarations and class definitions are components of a Java class.
- A Java class may define zero or more instance variables, methods, and constructors.
- The order of the definition of instance variables, constructors, and methods doesn't matter in a class.
- A class may define an instance variable before or after the definition of a method and still use it.
- A Java source code file (.java file) can define multiple classes and interfaces.
- A public class can be defined only in a source code file with the same name.
- package and import statements apply to all the classes and interfaces defined in the same source code file (.java file).

Executable Java applications:

- An executable Java class is a class that, when handed over to the Java Virtual Machine (JVM), starts its execution at a particular point in the class. This point of execution is the main method.
- For a class to be executable, the class should define a main method with the signature public static void main(String args[]) or public static void main(String... args). The positions of static and public can be interchanged, and the method parameter can use any valid name.
- A class can define multiple methods with the name main, provided that the signature of these methods doesn't match the signature of the main method defined in the previous point. These other methods with different signatures aren't considered *the* main method.
- The main method accepts an array of type String containing the method parameters passed to it by the JVM.
- The keyword java and the name of the class aren't passed on as command parameters to the main method.

Java packages:

- You can use packages to group together a related set of classes and interfaces.
- By default, all classes and interfaces in separate packages and subpackages aren't visible to each other.
- The package and subpackage names are separated using a period.
- All classes and interfaces in the same package are visible to each other.
- An import statement allows the use of simple names for packaged classes and interfaces defined in other packages.

- You can't use the `import` statement to access multiple classes or interfaces with the same names from different packages.
- You can import either a single member or all members (classes and interfaces) of a package using the `import` statement.
- You can't import classes from a subpackage by using the wildcard character, an asterisk (`*`), in the `import` statement.
- A class from a default package can't be used in any named packaged class, regardless of whether it's defined within the same directory or not.
- You can import an individual `static` member of a class or all its `static` members by using a `static import` statement.
- An `import` statement can't be placed before a `package` statement in a class. Any attempt to do so will cause the compilation of the class to fail.
- The members of default packages are accessible only to classes or interfaces defined in the same directory on your system.

Java access modifiers:

- The access modifiers control the accessibility of your class and its members outside the class and package.
- Java defines four access modifiers: `public`, `protected`, default, and `private`.
- The `public` access modifier is the least restrictive access modifier.
- Classes and interfaces defined using the `public` access modifier are accessible to related and unrelated classes outside the package in which they're defined.
- The members of a class defined using the `protected` access modifier are accessible to classes and interfaces defined in the same package and to all derived classes, even if they're defined in separate packages.
- The members of a class defined without using an explicit access modifier are defined with package accessibility (also called default accessibility).
- The members with package access are accessible only to classes and interfaces defined in the same package.
- A class defined using default access can't be accessed outside its package.
- The members of a class defined using a `private` access modifier are accessible only to the class in which they are defined. It doesn't matter whether the class or interface in question is from another package or has extended the class. Private members are not accessible outside the class in which they're defined.
- The `private` access modifier is the most restrictive access modifier.

Nonaccess modifiers:

- The nonaccess modifiers change the default properties of a Java class and its members.
- The OCA Java SE 7 Programmer I exam covers only two nonaccess modifiers: `abstract` and `static`.

- The abstract keyword, when prefixed to the definition of a concrete class, can change it to an abstract class, even if it doesn't define any abstract methods.
- An abstract class cannot be instantiated.
- An interface is an abstract entity by default. The Java compiler automatically adds the keyword abstract to the definition of an interface (which means that adding the keyword abstract to the definition of an interface is redundant).
- An abstract method doesn't have a body, which means it's implemented by the class that extends the class defining the abstract method.
- A variable can't be defined as an abstract variable.
- The static modifier can be applied to inner classes, inner interfaces, variables, and methods. Inner classes and interfaces aren't covered in this exam.
- A method can't be defined both as abstract and static.
- static attributes (fields and methods) are common to all instances of a class and aren't unique to any instance of a class.
- static attributes exist independent of any instances of a class and may be accessed even when no instances of the class have been created.
- static attributes are also known as *class fields* or *class methods* because they're said to belong to their class, not to any instance of that class.
- A static variable or method can be accessed using the name of a reference object variable or the name of a class.
- A static method or variable can't access non-static variables or methods of a class. But the reverse is true: non-static variables and methods can access static variables and methods.
- static classes and interfaces are a type of nested classes and interfaces but they aren't covered in the OCA Java SE 7 Programmer I exam.
- You can't prefix the definition of a top-level class or an interface with the keyword static. A top-level class or interface is one that isn't defined within another class or interface.

1.8   *Sample exam questions*

Q1-1. What are the valid components of a Java source file (choose all that apply):

  a package statement
  b import statements
  c methods
  d variables
  e Java compiler
  f Java Runtime Environment

Q1-2. The following numbered list of Java class components is not in any particular order. Select the correct order of their occurrence in a Java class (choose all that apply):

1 comments
2 import statement
3 package statement
4 methods
5 class declaration
6 variables

    a 1, 3, 2, 5, 6, 4
    b 3, 1, 2, 5, 4, 6
    c 3, 2, 1, 4, 5, 6
    d 3, 2, 1, 5, 6, 4

Q1-3. Which of the following examples define the correct Java class structure?

a
```
#connect java compiler;
#connect java virtual machine;
class EJavaGuru {}
```

b
```
package java compiler;
import java virtual machine;
class EJavaGuru {}
```

c
```
import javavirtualmachine.*;
package javacompiler;
class EJavaGuru {
    void method1() {}
    int count;
}
```

d
```
package javacompiler;
import javavirtualmachine.*;
class EJavaGuru {
    void method1() {}
    int count;
}
```

e
```
#package javacompiler;
$import javavirtualmachine;
class EJavaGuru {
    void method1() {}
    int count;
}
```

f
```
package javacompiler;
import javavirtualmachine;
Class EJavaGuru {
    void method1() {}
    int count;
}
```

Q1-4. Given the following contents of the Java source code file MyClass.java, select the correct options:

```
// contents of MyClass.java
package com.ejavaguru;
import java.util.Date;
class Student {}
class Course {}
```

   a The imported class, `java.util.Date`, can be accessed only in the class `Student`.

   b The imported class, `java.util.Date`, can be accessed by both the `Student` and `Course` classes.

   c Both of the classes `Student` and `Course` are defined in the package `com.ejavaguru`.

   d Only the class `Student` is defined in the package `com.ejavaguru`. The class `Course` is defined in the default Java package.

Q1-5. Given the following definition of the class `EJavaGuru`,

```
class EJavaGuru {
    public static void main(String[] args) {
        System.out.println(args[1]+":"+ args[2]+":"+ args[3]);
    }
}
```

what is the output of the previous class, if it is executed using the following command:

```
java EJavaGuru one two three four
```

   a `one:two:three`

   b `EJavaGuru:one:two`

   c `java:EJavaGuru:one`

   d `two:three:four`

Q1-6. Which of the following options, when inserted at `//INSERT CODE HERE`, will print out EJavaGuru?

```
public class EJavaGuru {
    // INSERT CODE HERE
    {
        System.out.println("EJavaGuru");
    }
}
```

   a `public void main (String[] args)`

   b `public void main(String    args[])`

   c `static public void main    (String[] array)`

   d `public static void main (String args)`

   e `static public main (String args[])`

Q1-7. Select the correct options:

    a You can start the execution of a Java application through the `main` method.

    b The Java compiler calls and executes the `main` method.

    c The Java Virtual Machine calls and executes the `main` method.

    d A class calls and executes the `main` method.

Q1-8. A class `Course` is defined in a package `com.ejavaguru`. Given that the physical location of the corresponding class file is /mycode/com/ejavaguru/Course.class and execution takes place within the mycode directory, which of the following lines of code, when inserted at // INSERT CODE HERE, will import the `Course` class into the class `MyCourse`?

```
// INSERT CODE HERE
class MyCourse {
    Course c;
}
```

    a `import mycode.com.ejavaguru.Course;`

    b `import com.ejavaguru.Course;`

    c `import mycode.com.ejavaguru;`

    d `import com.ejavaguru;`

    e `import mycode.com.ejavaguru*;`

    f `import com.ejavaguru*;`

Q1-9. Examine the following code:

```
class Course {
    String courseName;
}
class EJavaGuru {
    public static void main(String args[]) {
        Course c = new Course();
        c.courseName = "Java";
        System.out.println(c.courseName);
    }
}
```

Which of the following statements will be true if the variable `courseName` is defined as a `private` variable?

    a class `EJavaGuru` will print Java.

    b class `EJavaGuru` will print null.

    c class `EJavaGuru` won't compile.

    d class `EJavaGuru` will throw an exception at runtime.

Q1-10. Given the following definition of the class `Course`,

```
package com.ejavaguru.courses;
class Course {
    public String courseName;
}
```

what's the output of the following code?

```
package com.ejavaguru;
import com.ejavaguru.courses.Course;
class EJavaGuru {
    public static void main(String args[]) {
        Course c = new Course();
        c.courseName = "Java";
        System.out.println(c.courseName);
    }
}
```

a   The class EJavaGuru will print Java.

b   The class EJavaGuru will print null.

c   The class EJavaGuru won't compile.

d   The class EJavaGuru will throw an exception at runtime.

Q1-11. Given the following code, select the correct options:

```
package com.ejavaguru.courses;
class Course {
    public String courseName;
    public void setCourseName(private String name) {
        courseName = name;
    }
}
```

a   You can't define a method argument as a `private` variable.

b   A method argument should be defined with either `public` or default accessibility.

c   For overridden methods, method arguments should be defined with `protected` accessibility.

d   None of the above.

1.9   *Answers to sample exam questions*

Q1-1. What are the valid components of a Java source file (choose all that apply):

a   **package statement**

b   **import statements**

c   **methods**

d   **variables**

e   Java compiler

f   Java Runtime Environment

Answer: a, b, c, d

Explanation: The Java compiler and Java Runtime Environment aren't components of a Java source file.

Q1-2. The following numbered list of Java class components is not in any particular order. Select the correct order of their occurrence in a Java class (choose all that apply):

1 comments
2 import statement
3 package statement
4 methods
5 class declaration
6 variables

    a **1, 3, 2, 5, 6, 4**
    b **3, 1, 2, 5, 4, 6**
    c 3, 2, 1, 4, 5, 6
    d **3, 2, 1, 5, 6, 4**

Answer: a, b, d

Explanation: The comments can appear anywhere in a class. They can appear before and after `package` and `import` statements. They can appear before or after a class, method, or variable declaration.

The first statement (if present) in a class should be a `package` statement. It can't be placed after an `import` statement or a declaration of a class.

The `import` statement should follow a `package` statement and be followed by a class declaration.

The class declaration follows the `import` statements, if present. It's followed by the declaration of the methods and variables.

Answer (c) is incorrect. None of the variables or methods can be defined before the definition of a class or interface.

Q1-3. Which of the following examples define the correct Java class structure?

```
a  #connect java compiler;
   #connect java virtual machine;
   class EJavaGuru {}
```

```
b  package java compiler;
   import java virtual machine;
   class EJavaGuru {}
```

```
c  import javavirtualmachine.*;
   package javacompiler;
   class EJavaGuru {
       void method1() {}
       int count;
   }
```

```
d  package javacompiler;
   import javavirtualmachine.*;
   class EJavaGuru {
       void method1() {}
       int count;
   }
```

```
e  #package javacompiler;
   $import javavirtualmachine;
   class EJavaGuru {
       void method1() {}
       int count;
   }

f  package javacompiler;
   import javavirtualmachine;
   Class EJavaGuru {
       void method1() {}
       int count;
   }
```

Answer: d

Explanation: Answer (a) is incorrect because #connect isn't a statement in Java. # is used to add comments in UNIX.

Option (b) is incorrect because a package name (Java compiler) cannot contain spaces. Also, java virtual machine isn't a valid package name to be imported in a class. The package name to be imported cannot contain spaces.

Option (c) is incorrect because a package statement should be placed before an import statement.

Option (e) is incorrect. #package and $import aren't valid statements or directives in Java.

Option (f) is incorrect. Java is case-sensitive, so the word class is not the same as the word Class. The correct keyword to define a class is class.

Q1-4. Given the following contents of the Java source code file MyClass.java, select the correct options:

```
// contents of MyClass.java
package com.ejavaguru;
import java.util.Date;
class Student {}
class Course {}
```

    a The imported class, java.util.Date, can be accessed only in the class Student.

    b **The imported class, java.util.Date, can be accessed by both the Student and Course classes.**

    c **Both of the classes Student and Course are defined in the package com.ejavaguru.**

    d Only the class Student is defined in the package com.ejavaguru. The class Course is defined in the default Java package.

Answer: b, c

Explanation: You can define multiple classes, interfaces, and enums in a Java source code file.

Option (a) is incorrect. The import statement applies to all the classes, interfaces, and enums defined within the same Java source code file.

Option (d) is incorrect. If a package statement is defined in the source code file, all of the classes, interfaces, and enums defined within it will exist in the same Java package.

Q1-5. Given the following definition of the class EJavaGuru,

```
class EJavaGuru {
    public static void main(String[] args) {
        System.out.println(args[1]+":"+ args[2]+":"+ args[3]);
    }
}
```

what is the output of the previous class, if it is executed using the command:

```
java EJavaGuru one two three four
```

   a one:two:three
   b EJavaGuru:one:two
   c java:EJavaGuru:one
   d **two:three:four**

Answer: d

Explanation: The command-line arguments passed to the main method of a class do not contain the word Java and the name of the class.

Because the position of an array is zero-based, the method argument is assigned the following values:

args[0] -> one
args[1] -> two
args[2] -> three
args[3] -> four

The class prints two:three:four.

Q1-6. Which of the following options, when inserted at //INSERT CODE HERE, will print out EJavaGuru?

```
public class EJavaGuru {
    // INSERT CODE HERE
    {
        System.out.println("EJavaGuru");
    }
}
```

   a public void main (String[] args)
   b public void main(String   args[])
   c **static public void main   (String[] array)**
   d public static void main (String args)
   e static public main (String args[])

Answer: c

Explanation: Option (a) is incorrect. This option defines a valid method but not a valid main method. The main method should be defined as a static method, which is missing from the method declaration in option (a).

Option (b) is incorrect. This option is similar to the method defined in option (a), with one difference. In this option, the square brackets are placed after the name of the method argument. The main method accepts an array as a method argument, and to define an array, the square brackets can be placed after either the data type or the method argument name.

Option (c) is correct. Extra spaces in a class are ignored by the Java compiler.

Option (d) is incorrect. The main method accepts an array of String as a method argument. The method in this option accepts a single String object.

Option (e) is incorrect. It isn't a valid method definition and doesn't specify the return type of the method. This line of code will not compile.

Q1-7. Select the correct options:

   a **You can start the execution of a Java application through the main method.**
   b The Java compiler calls and executes the main method.
   c **The Java Virtual Machine calls and executes the main method.**
   d A class calls and executes the main method.

Answer: a, c

Explanation: The Java Virtual Machine calls and executes the main method.

Q1-8. A class Course is defined in a package com.ejavaguru. Given that the physical location of the corresponding class file is /mycode/com/ejavaguru/Course.class and execution takes place within the mycode directory, which of the following lines of code, when inserted at // INSERT CODE HERE, will import the Course class into the class MyCourse?

```
// INSERT CODE HERE
class MyCourse {
    Course c;
}
```

   a `import mycode.com.ejavaguru.Course;`
   b **`import com.ejavaguru.Course;`**
   c `import mycode.com.ejavaguru;`
   d `import com.ejavaguru;`
   e `import mycode.com.ejavaguru*;`
   f `import com.ejavaguru*;`

Answer: b

Explanation: Option (a) is incorrect. The path of the imported class used in an import statement isn't related to the class's physical location. It reflects the package and subpackage that a class is in.

Options (c) and (e) are incorrect. The class's physical location isn't specified in the import statement.

Options (d) and (f) are incorrect. `ejavaguru` is a package. To import a package and its members, the package name should be followed by `.*`, as follows:

```
import com.ejavaguru.*;
```

Q1-9. Examine the following code:

```
class Course {
    String courseName;
}
class EJavaGuru {
    public static void main(String args[]) {
        Course c = new Course();
        c.courseName = "Java";
        System.out.println(c.courseName);
    }
}
```

Which of the following statements will be true if the variable `courseName` is defined as a `private` variable?

    a   class `EJavaGuru` will print Java.

    b   class `EJavaGuru` will print null.

    c   **class `EJavaGuru` won't compile.**

    d   class `EJavaGuru` will throw an exception at runtime.

Answer: c

Explanation: If the variable `courseName` is defined as a `private` member, it won't be accessible from the class `EJavaGuru`. An attempt to do so will cause it to fail at compile time. Because the code won't compile, it can't execute.

Q1-10. Given the following definition of the class `Course`,

```
package com.ejavaguru.courses;
class Course {
    public String courseName;
}
```

what's the output of the following code?

```
package com.ejavaguru;
import com.ejavaguru.courses.Course;
class EJavaGuru {
    public static void main(String args[]) {
        Course c = new Course();
        c.courseName = "Java";
        System.out.println(c.courseName);
    }
}
```

    a   The class `EJavaGuru` will print Java.

    b   The class `EJavaGuru` will print null.

    c   **The class `EJavaGuru` will not compile.**

    d   The class `EJavaGuru` will throw an exception at runtime.

Answer: c

Explanation: The class will fail to compile because a non-public class cannot be accessed outside a package in which it is defined. The class Course therefore can't be accessed from within the class EJavaGuru, even if it is explicitly imported into it. If the class itself isn't accessible, there's no point in accessing a public member of a class.

Q1-11. Given the following code, select the correct options:

```
package com.ejavaguru.courses;
class Course {
    public String courseName;
    public void setCourseName(private String name) {
        courseName = name;
    }
}
```

    a **You can't define a method argument as a `private` variable.**

    b A method argument should be defined with either `public` or default accessibility.

    c For overridden methods, method arguments should be defined with `protected` accessibility.

    d None of the above.

Answer: a

Explanation: You can't add an explicit accessibility keyword to the method parameters. If you do, the code won't compile.

Working with
Java data types 2

Exam objectives covered in this chapter	What you need to know
[2.2] Differentiate between object reference variables and primitive variables.	The primitive data types in Java, including scenarios when a particular primitive data type should or can't be used. Similarities and differences between the primitive data types. Similarities and differences between primitive and object reference variables.
[2.1] Declare and initialize variables.	Declaration and initialization of primitives and object reference variables. Literal values for primitive and object reference variables.
[3.1] Use Java operators.	Use of assignment, arithmetic, relational, and logical operators with primitives and object reference variables. Valid operands for an operator. Output of an arithmetic expression. Determine the equality of two primitives.
[3.2] Use parentheses to override operator precedence.	How to override the default operator precedence by using parentheses.

Imagine that you've just purchased a new home! Unfortunately, it didn't come with all the kitchen stuff. You'll likely need to buy different-sized containers to store different types of food items, because one size can't fit all! Also, you might move around food items in your home—perhaps because of a change in the requirements over time (you wish to eat it or you wish to store it).

Your new kitchen is an analogy for how Java stores its data using different data types and manipulates the data using operators. The food items are like data types in Java, and the containers used to store the food are like variables in Java. The change in the requirements that triggers a change in the state of food items can be compared to the processing logic. The agents of change (fire, heat, or cooling) that change the state of the food items can be compared to Java operators. You need these agents of change so that you can process the raw food items to create delicacies.

In the OCA Java SE 7 Programmer I exam, you'll be asked questions on the various data types in Java, such as how to create and initialize them and what their similarities and differences are. The exam will also question you on using the Java operators. This chapter covers the following:

- Primitive data types in Java
- Literal values of primitive Java data types
- Object reference variables in Java
- Valid and invalid identifiers
- Usage of Java operators
- Modification of default operator precedence via parentheses

2.1   Primitive variables

> [2.1]   Declare and initialize variables

> [2.2]   Differentiate between object reference variables and primitive variables

In this section, you'll learn all the primitive data types in Java, their literal values, and the process of creating and initializing primitive variables. A variable defined as one of the primitive data types is a *primitive variable*.

Primitive data types, as the name suggests, are the simplest data types in a programming language. In the Java language, they're predefined. The names of the primitive types are quite descriptive of the values that they can store. Java defines the following eight primitive data types:

- `char`
- `byte`
- `short`
- `int`
- `long`
- `float`
- `double`
- `boolean`

Examine figure 2.1 and try to match the given value with the corresponding type.

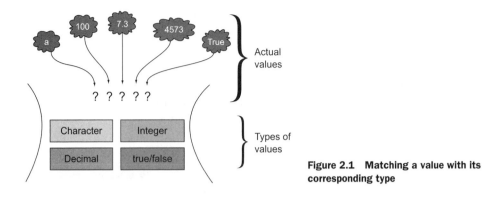

Figure 2.1   Matching a value with its corresponding type

This should be a simple exercise. Table 2.1 provides the answers.

Table 2.1   Matching a value with its corresponding data type

Character values	Integer values	Decimal values	true/false
a	100 4573	7.3	true

In the preceding exercise, I categorized the data that you need to store as follows: character, integer, decimal, and true/false values. This categorization will make your life simpler when confronted with selecting the most appropriate primitive data type to store a value. For example, to store an integer value, you need a primitive data type that is capable of storing integer values; to store decimal numbers, you need a primitive data type that can store decimal numbers. Simple, isn't it?

Let's map the types of data that the primitive data types can store, because it's always easy to group and remember information. The primitive data types can be categorized as follows: Boolean, character, and numeric (further categorized as integral and floating-point) types. Take a look at this categorization in figure 2.2.

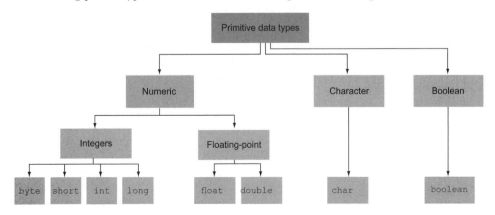

Figure 2.2   Categorization of primitive data types

This categorization in figure 2.2 will help you further associate each data type with the value that it can store. Let's start with the Boolean category.

2.1.1   *Category: Boolean*

The Boolean category has only one data type: `boolean`. A `boolean` variable can store one of two values: `true` or `false`. It is used in scenarios where only two states can exist. See table 2.2 for a list of questions and their probable answers.

Table 2.2   Suitable data that can be stored using a `boolean` data type

Question	Probable answers
Did you purchase the exam voucher?	Yes/No
Did you log in to your email account?	Yes/No
Did you tweet about your passion today?	Yes/No
Tax collected in financial year 2001–2002	Good question! But it can't be answered as yes/no.

 EXAM TIP   In this exam, the questions test your ability to select the best suitable data type for a condition that can only have two states: yes/no or true/false. The correct answer here is the `boolean` type.

Here's some code that defines `boolean` primitive variables:

```
boolean voucherPurchased = true;
boolean examPrepStarted = false;
boolean result = false;
boolean longDrive = true;
```

In some languages—such as JavaScript—you don't need to define the type of a variable before you use it. In JavaScript, the compiler defines the type of the variable according to the value that you assign to it. Java, in contrast, is a strongly typed language. You must declare a variable and define its type before you can assign a value to it. Figure 2.3 illustrates defining a `boolean` variable and assigning a value to it.

Another point to note here is the value that's assigned to a `boolean` variable. I used the literals `true` and `false` to initialize the `boolean` variables. A *literal* is a fixed value that doesn't need further calculations in order for it to be assigned to any variable. `true` and `false` are the only two `boolean` literals.

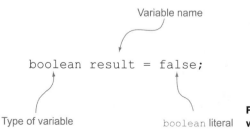

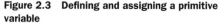

Figure 2.3   Defining and assigning a primitive variable

NOTE There are only two boolean literal values: true and false.

2.1.2 Category: Numeric

The numeric category defines two subcategories: integers and floating point (also called decimals). Let's start with the integers.

INTEGERS: BYTE, INT, SHORT, LONG

When you can count a value in whole numbers, the result is an integer. It includes both negative and positive numbers. Table 2.3 lists probable scenarios in which the data can be stored as integers.

Table 2.3 Data that can be categorized as numeric (nondecimal numbers) data type

Situation	Can be stored as integers?
Number of friends on Facebook	Yes
Number of tweets posted today	Yes
Number of photographs uploaded for printing	Yes
Your body temperature	Not always

You can use the byte, short, int, and long data types to store integer values. Wait a minute: why do you need so many types to store integers?

Each one of these can store a different range of values. The benefits of the smaller ones are obvious: they need less space in memory and are faster to work with. Table 2.4 lists all these data types, along with their sizes and the ranges of the values that they can store.

Table 2.4 Ranges of values stored by the numeric Java primitive data types

Data type	Size	Range of values
byte	8 bits	–128 to 127, inclusive
short	16 bits	–32,768 to 32,767, inclusive
int	32 bits	–2,147,483,648 to 2,147,483,647, inclusive
long	64 bits	–9,223,372,036,854,775,808 to 9,223,372,036,854,775,807, inclusive

The OCA Java SE 7 Programmer I exam may ask you questions about the range of integers that can be assigned to a byte data type, but it won't include questions on the ranges of integer values that can be stored by short, int, or long data types. Don't worry—you don't have to memorize the ranges for all these data types!

Here's some code that assigns literal values to primitive numeric variables within their acceptable ranges:

```
byte num = 100;
short sum = 1240;
int total = 48764;
long population = 214748368;
```

The default type of a nondecimal number is int. To designate an integer literal value as a long value, add the suffix L or l (L in lowercase), as follows:

```
long fishInSea = 764398609800L;
```

Integer literal values come in four flavors: binary, decimal, octal, and hexadecimal.

- *Binary number system*—A base-2 system, which uses only 2 digits, 0 and 1.
- *Octal number system*—A base-8 system, which uses digits 0 through 7 (a total of 8 digits). Here the decimal number 8 is represented as octal 10, decimal 9 as 11, and so on.
- *Decimal number system*—The base-10 number system that you use every day. It's based on 10 digits, from 0 through 9 (a total of 10 digits).
- *Hexadecimal number system*—A base-16 system, which uses digits 0 through 9 and the letters A through F (a total of 16 digits and letters). Here the number 10 is represented as A, 11 as B, 12 as C, 13 as D, 14 as E, and 15 as F.

Let's take quick look at how you can convert integers in the decimal number system to the other number systems. Figures 2.4, 2.5, and 2.6 show how to convert the decimal number 267 to the octal, hexadecimal, and binary number systems.

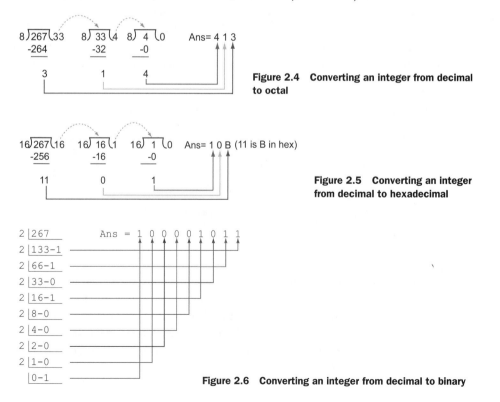

Figure 2.4   Converting an integer from decimal to octal

Figure 2.5   Converting an integer from decimal to hexadecimal

Figure 2.6   Converting an integer from decimal to binary

EXAM TIP In the OCA Java SE 7 Programmer I exam, you will not be asked to convert a number from the decimal number system to the octal and hexadecimal number systems and vice versa. But you can expect questions that ask you to select valid literals for integers. The previous figures will help you understand these number systems better and retain this information longer, which will in turn enable you to answer questions correctly during the exam.

You can assign integer literals in base decimal, binary, octal, and hexadecimal. For octal literals, use the prefix 0; for binary, use the prefix 0B or 0b; and for hexadecimal, use the prefix 0x or 0X. Here's an example of each of these:

267 in decimal number system

```
int baseDecimal = 267;
int octVal = 0413;
int hexVal = 0x10B;
int binVal = 0b100001011;
```

267 in decimal number system is equal to 413 in octal number system

267 in decimal number system is equal to 10B in hexadecimal number system

276 in decimal number system is equal to 100001011 in binary number system

With Java version 7, you can also use underscores as part of the literal values, which helps group the individual digits or letters of the literal values and is much more readable. The underscores have no effect on the values. The following is valid code:

```
long baseDecimal = 100_267_760;
long octVal = 04_13;
long hexVal = 0x10_BA_75;
long binVal = 0b1_0000_10_11;
```

More readable literal values in binary, decimal, octal, and hexadecimal that use underscores to group digits and letters

RULES TO REMEMBER

Pay attention to the use of underscores in the numeric literal values. Here are some of the rules:

- You can't start or end a literal value with an underscore.
- You can't place an underscore right after the prefixes 0b, 0B, 0x, and 0X, which are used to define binary and hexadecimal literal values.
- You can place an underscore right after the prefix 0, which is used to define an octal literal value.
- You can't place an underscore prior to an L suffix (the L suffix is used to mark a literal value as long).
- You can't use an underscore in positions where a string of digits is expected.

Because you are likely to be questioned on valid and invalid uses of underscores in literal values on the exam, let's look at some examples:

```
int intLiteral = _100;
int intLiteral2 = 100_999_;
long longLiteral = 100_L;
```

Can't start or end a literal value with an underscore

Can't place an underscore prior to suffix L

The following line of code will compile successfully but will fail at runtime:

```
int i = Integer.parseInt("45_98");
```

⟵ **Invalid use of underscore where a string of digits is expected**

Because a `String` value can accept underscores, the compiler will compile the previous code. But the runtime will throw an exception stating that an invalid format of value was passed to the method `parseInt`.

Here's the first Twist in the Tale exercise of this chapter for you to attempt. It uses multiple combinations of underscores in numeric literal values. See if you can get all of them right (answers in the appendix).

Twist in the Tale 2.1

Let's use the primitive variables `baseDecimal`, `octVal`, `hexVal`, and `binVal` defined earlier in this section and introduce additional code for printing the values of all these variables. Determine the output of the following code:

```
class TwistInTaleNumberSystems {
public static void main (String args[]) {
        int baseDecimal = 267;
        int octVal = 0413;
        int hexVal = 0x10B;
        int binVal = 0b100001011;
        System.out.println (baseDecimal + octVal);
        System.out.println (hexVal + binVal);
    }
}
```

Here's another quick exercise—let's define and initialize some `long` primitive variables that use underscores in the literal values assigned to them. Determine which of these does this job correctly:

```
long var1 = 0_100_267_760;
long var2 = 0_x_4_13;
long var3 = 0b_x10_BA_75;
long var4 = 0b_10000_10_11;
long var5 = 0xa10_AG_75;
long var6 = 0x1_0000_10;
long var7 = 100__12_12;
```

FLOATING-POINT NUMBERS: FLOAT AND DOUBLE

You need floating-point numbers where you expect decimal numbers. For example, can you define the probability of an event occurring as an integer? Table 2.5 lists probable scenarios in which the corresponding data is stored as a floating-point number.

In Java, you can use the `float` and `double` primitive data types to store decimal numbers. `float` requires less space than `double`, but it can store a smaller range of values than `double`. A `float` data type also has less precision, so even some of the numbers that are in the range of a `float` still can't be accurately represented when using `double`. Table 2.6 lists the sizes and ranges of values for `float` and `double`.

Table 2.5 Data that is stored as floating-point numbers

Situation	Is the answer a floating-point number?
Orbital mechanics of a spacecraft	Yes (very precise values are required)
Probability of your friend request being accepted	Yes; probability is between 0.0 (none) to 1.0 (sure)
Speed of Earth revolving around the Sun	Yes
Magnitude of an earthquake on the Richter scale	Yes

Table 2.6 Range of values for decimal numbers

Data type	Size	Range of values
float	32 bits	+/−1.4E−45 to +/−3.4028235E+38, +/−infinity, +/−0, NaN
double	64 bits	+/−4.9E−324 to +/−1.7976931348623157E+308, +/−infinity, +/−0, NaN

Here's some code in action:

```
float average = 20.129F;
float orbit = 1765.65f;
double inclination = 120.1762;
```

Did you notice the use of the suffixes F and f while initializing the variables average and orbit in the preceding code? The default type of a decimal literal is double, but by suffixing a decimal literal value with F or f, you tell the compiler that the literal value should be treated like a float and not a double.

You can also assign a literal decimal value in scientific notation as follows:

```
double inclination2 = 1.201762e2;
```
◁─┤ **120.1762 is same as 1.201762e2 (the latter is expressed in scientific notation)**

You can also add the suffix D or d to a decimal number value to specify that it is a double value. But because the default type of a decimal number is double, the use of the suffix D or d is redundant. Examine the following line of code:

```
double inclination = 120.1762D;
```
◁── **120.1762D is same as 120.1762**

Starting with Java version 7, you can also use underscores with the floating-point literal values. The rules are generally the same as previously mentioned for numeric literal values; the following rules are specific to floating-point literals:

- You can't place an underscore prior to a D, d, F, or f suffix (these suffixes are used to mark a floating-point literal as double or float).
- You can't place an underscore adjacent to a decimal point.

Let's look at some examples that demonstrate the invalid use of underscores in floating-point literal values:

```
float floatLiteral = 100._48F;
double doubleLiteral = 100_.87;
```
Can't use underscore adjacent to a decimal point

```
float floatLiteral2 = 100.48_F;
double doubleLiteral2 = 100.87_d;
```
Can't use underscore prior to suffix F, f, D, or d

2.1.3   *Category: Character*

The character category defines only one data type: char. A char can store a single 16-bit Unicode character; that is, it can store characters from virtually all the existing scripts and languages, including Japanese, Korean, Chinese, Devanagari, French, German, Spanish, and others. Because your keyboard may not have keys to represent all these characters, you can use a value from \u0000 (or 0) to a maximum value of \uffff (or 65,535) inclusive. The following code shows the assignment of a value to a char variable:

```
char c1 = 'D';
```
Use single quotes to assign a char, not double quotes

A very common mistake is using double quotes to assign a value to a char. The correct option is single quotes. Figure 2.7 shows a conversation between two (hypothetical) programmers, Paul and Harry.

What happens if you try to assign a char using double quotes? The code will fail to compile, with this message:

```
Type mismatch: cannot convert from String to char
```

> **EXAM TIP**   Never use double quotes to assign a letter to a char variable. Double quotes are used to assign a value to a variable of type String.

Internally, Java stores char data as an unsigned integer value (positive integer). It's therefore perfectly acceptable to assign a positive integer value to a char, as follows:

```
char c1 = 122;
```
◁—— **Assign z to c1**

The integer value 122 is equivalent to the letter z, but the integer value 122 is not equal to the Unicode value \u0122. The former is a number in base 10 (uses digits 0–9) and the latter is a number in base 16 (uses digits 0–9 and letters a–f). \u is used to mark

Figure 2.7   Never use double quotes to assign a letter as a char value.

the value as a Unicode value. You must use quotes to assign Unicode values to `char` variables. Here's an example:

```
char c2 = '\u0122';
System.out.println("c1 = " + c1);
System.out.println("c2 = " + c2);
```

Figure 2.8 shows the output of the preceding code on a system that supports Unicode characters.

c1 = z
c2 = Ģ   **Figure 2.8   The output of assigning a character using the integer value** `122` **versus the Unicode value** `\u0122`

As mentioned earlier, `char` values are unsigned integer values, so if you try to assign a negative number to one, the code will not compile. Here's an example:

```
char c3 = -122;            ◁—— Fails to compile
```

But you can forcefully assign a negative number to a char by casting it to `char`, as follows:

```
char c3 = (char)-122;                  ◁—┐ Compiles successfully
System.out.println("c3 = " + c3);
```

In the previous code, note how the literal value –122 is prefixed by (char). This practice is called *casting*. Casting is the forceful conversion of one data type to another data type.

You can cast only compatible data types. For example, you can cast a `char` to an `int` and vice versa. But you can't cast an `int` to a `boolean` value or vice versa. When you cast a bigger value to a data type that has a smaller range, you tell the compiler that you know what you're doing, so the compiler proceeds by chopping off any extra bits that may not fit into the smaller variable. Use casting with caution—it may not always give you the correct converted values.

Figure 2.9 shows the output of the preceding code that cast a value to c3 (the value looks weird!).

c3 = ⌐   **Figure 2.9   The output of assigning a negative value to a character variable**

The `char` data type in Java doesn't allocate space to store the sign of an integer. If you try to forcefully assign a negative integer to `char`, the sign bit is stored as the part of the integer value, which results in the storage of unexpected values.

EXAM TIP   The exam will test your understanding of the possible values that can be assigned to a variable of type `char`, including whether an assignment will result in a compilation error. Don't worry—it won't test you on the value that is actually displayed after assigning arbitrary integer values to a `char`!

2.1.4   *Confusion with the names of the primitive data types*

If you've previously worked in another programming language, there's a good chance that you might get confused with the names of the primitive data types in Java and other languages. For example, C defines a primitive `short int` data type. But short and int are two separate primitive data types in Java. The OCA Java SE 7 Programmer I exam will test you on your ability to recognize the names of the primitive data types, and the answers to these questions may not be immediately obvious. An example follows:

Question: What is the output of the following code?

```java
public class MyChar {
    public static void main(String[] args) {
        int myInt = 7;
        bool result = true;
        if (result == true)
            do
                System.out.println(myInt);
            while (myInt > 10);

    }
}
```

- a It prints 7 once.
- b It prints nothing.
- c Compilation error.
- d Runtime error.

The correct answer is (c). This question tries to trick you with complex code that doesn't use any if constructs or do-while loops! As you can see, it uses an incorrect data type name, bool, to declare and initialize the variable result. Therefore, the code will fail to compile.

> **EXAM TIP** Watch out for questions that use incorrect names for the primitive data types. For example, there isn't any bool primitive data type in Java. The correct data type is boolean. If you've worked with other programming languages, you might get confused trying to remember the exact names of all the primitive data types used in Java. Remember that just two of the primitive data types—int and char—are shortened; the rest of the primitive data types (byte, short, long, float, and double) are not.

2.2 *Identifiers*

Identifiers are names of packages, classes, interfaces, methods, and variables. Though identifying a valid identifier is not explicitly included in the OCA Java SE 7 Programmer I exam objectives, there's a good chance that you'll encounter a question similar to the following that will require you to identify valid and invalid identifiers:

Question: Which of the following lines of code will compile successfully?

- a byte exam_total = 7;
- b int exam-Total = 1090;

The correct answer is (a). Option (b) is incorrect because hyphens aren't allowed in the name of a Java identifier. Underscores are allowed. If you've worked with another programming language, this may be different from what you're used to.

2.2.1 Valid and invalid identifiers

Table 2.7 contains a list of rules that will enable you to correctly define valid (and invalid) identifiers, along with some examples.

Table 2.7 Ingredients of valid and invalid identifiers

Properties of valid Identifiers	Properties of invalid identifiers
Unlimited length	Same spelling as a Java reserved word or keyword (see table 2.8)
Starts with a letter (a–z, upper- or lowercase), a currency sign, or an underscore	Uses special characters: !, @, #, %, ^, &, *, (,), ', :, ;, [, /, \, }
Can use a digit (not at the starting position)	Starts with a Java digit (0–9)
Can use an underscore (in any position)	
Can use a currency sign (in any position): $, £, ¢, ¥ and others	

Examples of valid identifiers	Examples of invalid identifiers
`customerValueObject`	`7world` (identifier can't start with a digit)
`$rate, £Value, _sine`	`%value` (identifier can't use special char %)
`happy2Help, nullValue`	`Digital!`, `books@manning` (identifier can't use special char ! or @)
`Constant`	`null`, `true`, `false`, `goto` (identifier can't have the same name as a Java keyword or reserved word)

You can't define a variable with the same name as Java keywords or reserved words. As these names suggest, they're reserved for specific purposes. Table 2.8 lists Java keywords, reserved words, and literals that you can't use as an identifier name.

Table 2.8 Java keywords and reserved words that can't be used as names for Java variables

`abstract`	`default`	`goto`	`package`	`this`
`assert`	`do`	`if`	`private`	`throw`
`boolean`	`double`	`implements`	`protected`	`throws`
`break`	`else`	`import`	`public`	`transient`
`byte`	`enum`	`instanceof`	`return`	`true`
`case`	`extends`	`int`	`short`	`try`
`catch`	`false`	`interface`	`static`	`void`
`char`	`final`	`long`	`strictfp`	`volatile`
`class`	`finally`	`native`	`super`	`while`
`const`	`float`	`new`	`switch`	
`continue`	`for`	`null`	`synchronized`	

Let's combat some of the common mistakes when determining correct and incorrect variables using the following variable declarations:

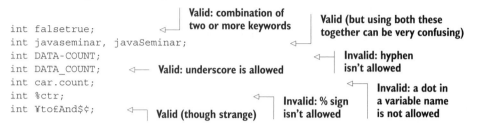

Next, let's look at the object reference variables and how they differ from the primitive variables.

2.3   *Object reference variables*

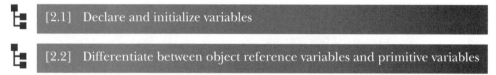

The variables in Java can be categorized into two types: *primitive variables* and *reference variables*. In this section, along with a quick introduction to reference variables, we'll cover the basic differences between reference variables and primitive variables.

Reference variables are also known as *object reference variables* or *object references*. I use all of these terms interchangeably in this text.

2.3.1   *What are object reference variables?*

Objects are instances of classes, including both predefined and user-defined classes. For a reference type in Java, the variable name evaluates to the address of the location in memory where the object referenced by the variable is stored. An object reference is, in fact, a memory address that points to a memory area where an object's data is located.

Let's quickly define a barebones class, `Person`, as follows:

```
class Person {}
```

When an object is instantiated with the `new` operator, a heap-memory address value to that object is returned. That address is usually assigned to the reference variable. Figure 2.10 shows a line of code that creates a reference variable `person` of type `Person` and assigns an object to it.

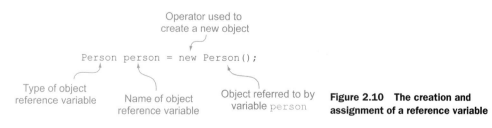

Figure 2.10   **The creation and assignment of a reference variable**

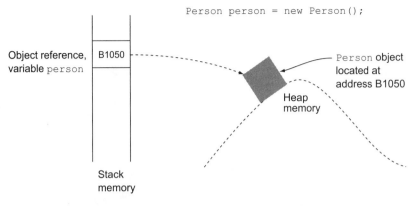

Figure 2.11 An object reference variable and the referenced object in memory

When the statement shown in figure 2.10 executes, three things happen:

- A new `Person` object is created.
- A variable named `person` is created in the stack with an empty (`null`) value.
- The variable `person` is assigned the memory address value where the object is located.

Figure 2.11 contains a pictorial representation of a reference variable and the object it refers to in memory.

You can think of an object reference variable as a *handle* to an object that allows you access to that object's attributes. The following analogy will help you understand object reference variables, the objects that they refer to, and their relationship. Think of objects as analogous to *dogs*, and think of object references as analogous to *leashes*. Although this analogy does not bear too much analysis, the following comparisons are valid:

- A leash not attached to a dog is a reference object variable with a `null` value.
- A dog without a leash is a Java object that's not referred to by any object reference variable.
- Just as an unleashed dog might be picked up by animal control, an object that is not referred to by a reference variable is liable to be garbage collected (removed from memory by the JVM).
- Several leashes may be tethered to a single dog. Similarly, several Java objects may be referenced by multiple object reference variables.

Figure 2.12 illustrates this analogy.

The literal value of all types of object reference variables is `null`. You can also assign a `null` value to a reference variable explicitly. Here's an example:

```
Person person = null;
```

In this case, the reference variable `person` can be compared to a leash without a dog.

NOTE The literal value for all types of object reference variables is `null`.

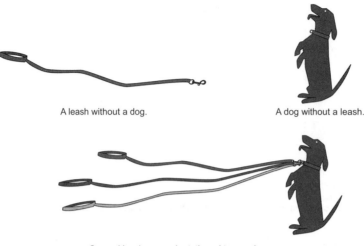

A leash without a dog.   A dog without a leash.

Several leashes may be tethered to one dog.

Figure 2.12   Dog leash analogy for understanding objects

2.3.2   *Differentiating between object reference variables and primitive variables*

Just as men and women are fundamentally different (according to John Gray, author of *Men Are from Mars, Women Are from Venus*), primitive variables and object reference variables differ from each other in multiple ways. The basic difference is that primitive variables store the actual values, whereas reference variables store the addresses of the objects they refer to.

Let's assume that a class Person is already defined. If you create an int variable a, and an object reference variable person, they will store their values in memory as shown in figure 2.13.

```
int a = 77;
Person person = new Person();
```

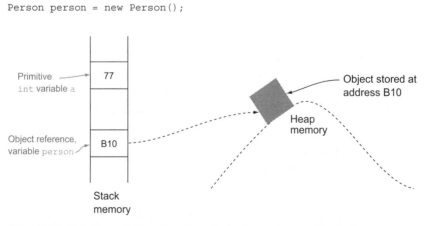

Figure 2.13   Primitive variables store the actual values, whereas object reference variables store the addresses of the objects they refer to.

Other important differences between primitive variables and object reference variables are shown in figure 2.14 as a conversation between a girl and a boy. The girl represents an object reference variable and the boy represents a primitive variable. (Don't worry if you don't understand all of these analogies. They'll make much more sense after you read related topics in later chapters.)

In the next section, you'll start manipulating these variables using operators.

2.4 Operators

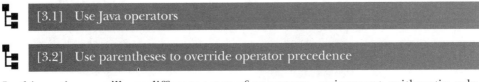

In this section, you'll use different types of operators—assignment, arithmetic, relational, and logical—to manipulate the values of variables. You'll also write code to

Figure 2.14 **Differences between object reference variables and primitive variables**

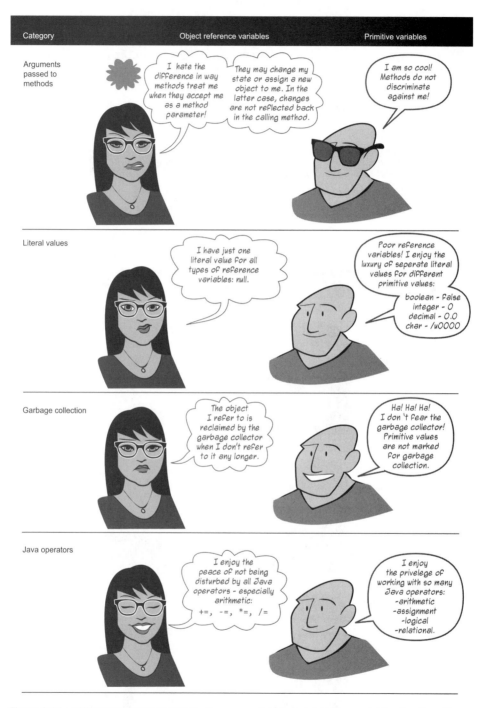

Figure 2.14   Differences between object reference variables and primitive variables *(continued)*

determine the equality of two primitive data types. You'll also learn how to modify the default precedence of an operator by using parentheses. For the OCA Java SE 7 Programmer I exam, you should be able to work with the operators listed in table 2.9.

Table 2.9 Operator types and the relevant operators

Operator type	Operators	Purpose
Assignment	=, +=, -=, *=, /=	Assign value to a variable
Arithmetic	+, -, *, /, %, ++, --	Add, subtract, multiply, divide, and modulus primitives
Relational	<, <=, >, >=, ==, !=	Compare primitives
Logical	!, &&, ||	Apply NOT, AND, and OR logic to primitives

> **NOTE** Not all operators can be used with all types of operands. For example, you can determine whether a number is greater than another number, but you can't determine whether `true` is greater than `false` or a number is greater than `true`. Take note of this as you learn the usage of all the operators on the OCA Java SE 7 Programmer I exam.

2.4.1 Assignment operators

The assignment operators that you need to know for the exam are =, +=, -=, *=, and /=.

The simple assignment operator, =, is the most frequently used operator. It's used to initialize variables with values and to reassign new values to them.

The +=, -=, *=, and /= operators are short forms of addition, subtraction, multiplication and division with assignment. The += operator can be read as "first add and then assign," and -= can be read as "first subtract and then assign." Similarly, *= can be read as "first multiply and then assign" and /= can be read as "first divide and then assign." If you apply these operators to two operands, a and b, they can be represented as follows:

```
a -= b is equal to a = a - b
a += b is equal to a = a + b
a *= b is equal to a = a * b
a /= b is equal to a = a / b
```

Let's have a look at some valid lines of code:

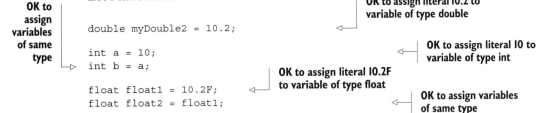

```
double myDouble2 = 10.2;

int a = 10;
int b = a;

float float1 = 10.2F;
float float2 = float1;
```

OK to assign variables of same type

OK to assign literal 10.2 to variable of type double

OK to assign literal 10 to variable of type int

OK to assign literal 10.2F to variable of type float

OK to assign variables of same type

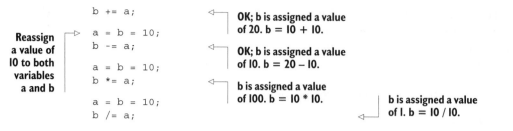

Reassign a value of 10 to both variables a and b

```
b += a;
a = b = 10;
b -= a;
a = b = 10;
b *= a;
a = b = 10;
b /= a;
```

OK; b is assigned a value of 20. b = 10 + 10.

OK; b is assigned a value of 10. b = 20 – 10.

b is assigned a value of 100. b = 10 * 10.

b is assigned a value of 1. b = 10 / 10.

Let's have a look at some invalid lines of code:

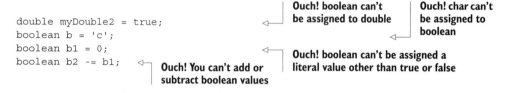

```
double myDouble2 = true;
boolean b = 'c';
boolean b1 = 0;
boolean b2 -= b1;
```

Ouch! boolean can't be assigned to double

Ouch! char can't be assigned to boolean

Ouch! boolean can't be assigned a literal value other than true or false

Ouch! You can't add or subtract boolean values

Now let's try to squeeze the variables that can store a larger range of values into variables with a shorter range. Try the following assignments:

```
long num = 100976543356L;
int val = num;
```

Compiler won't allow this

It's similar to what is shown in figure 2.15, where someone is forcefully trying to squeeze a bigger value (`long`) into a smaller container (`int`).

You can still assign a bigger value to a variable that can only store smaller ranges by explicitly casting the bigger value to a smaller value. By doing so, you tell the compiler that you know what you're doing. In that case, the compiler proceeds by chopping off any extra bits that may not fit into the smaller variable. Beware! This approach may not always give you the correct converted values.

Figure 2.15   Assigning a bigger value (`long`) to a variable (`int`) that is only capable of storing smaller value range

Compare the previous assignment example (assigning a `long` to an `int`) with the following example that assigns a smaller value (`int`) to a variable (`long`) that is capable of storing bigger value ranges:

```
int intVal = 1009;
long longVal = intVal;
```

Allowed

An `int` can easily fit into a `long` because there's enough room for it (as shown in figure 2.16).

EXAM TIP   You can't use the assignment operators to assign a `boolean` value to variables of type `char`, `byte`, `int`, `short`, `long`, `float`, or `double`, or vice versa.

You can also assign multiple values on the same line using the assignment operator. Examine the following lines of code:

Figure 2.16   Assigning a smaller value (`int`) to a variable (`long`) that is capable of storing a larger value range

<table>
<tr><td>

Define and initialize variables on the same line

</td><td>

```
int a = 7, b = 10, c = 8;
a = b = c;
System.out.println(a);    ◁─┐  Prints 8
```

</td></tr>
</table>

Assignment starts from right; the value of c is assigned to b and the value of b is assigned to a ❶

On line ❶, the assignment starts from right to left. The value of variable c is assigned to the variable b, and the value of variable b (which is already equal to c) is assigned to the variable a. This is proved by the fact that line 3 prints 8, and not 7!

The next Twist in the Tale throws in a few twists with variable assignment and initialization. Let's see if you can identify the incorrect ones (answers in the appendix).

Twist in the Tale 2.2

Let's modify the assignment and initialization of the boolean variables used in previous sections. Examine the following code initializations and select the incorrect answers:

```
public class Foo {
    public static void main (String args[]) {
        boolean b1, b2, b3, b4, b5, b6;    // line 1
        b1 = b2 = b3 = true;               // line 2
        b4 = 0;                            // line 3
        b5 = 'false';                      // line 4
        b6 = yes;                          // line 5
    }
}
```

a The code on line 1 will fail to compile.

b Can't initialize multiple variables like the code on line 2.

c The code on line 3 is correct.

d Can't assign 'false' to a boolean variable.

e The code on line 5 is correct.

2.4.2 Arithmetic operators

Let's take a quick look at each of these operators, together with a simple example, in table 2.10.

Table 2.10 Use of arithmetic operators with examples

Operator	Purpose	Usage	Answer
+	Addition	12 + 10	22
–	Subtraction	19 – 29	–10
*	Multiplication	101 * 45	4545
/	Division (quotient)	10 / 6 10.0 / 6.0	1 1.6666666666666667

Table 2.10   Use of arithmetic operators with examples *(continued)*

Operator	Purpose	Usage	Answer
%	Modulus (remainder in division)	`10 % 6` `10.0 % 6.0`	4 4.0
++	Unary increment operator; increments value by 1	`++10`	11
--	Unary decrement operator; decrements value by 1	`--10`	9

++ AND – (UNARY INCREMENT AND DECREMENT OPERATORS)

The operators ++ and -- are unary operators; they work with a single operand. They're used to increment or decrement the value of a variable by 1.

Unary operators can also be used in prefix and postfix notation. In *prefix notation*, the operator appears before its operand:

```
int a = 10;
++a;
```
Operator + + in prefix notation

In *postfix notation*, the operator appears after its operand:

```
int a = 10;
a++;
```
Operator + + in postfix notation

When these operators are not part of an expression, the postfix and prefix notations behave in exactly the same manner:

```
int a = 20;                        Assign 20 to a
int b = 10;                  Assign 10 to b
++a;
b++;
System.out.println(a);       Prints 21
System.out.println(b);             Prints 11
```

When a unary operator is used in an expression, its placement with respect to its operand decides whether its value will increment or decrement before the evaluation of the expression or after the evaluation of the expression. See the following code, where the operator ++ is used in prefix notation:

```
int a = 20;          Assign 20 to a
int b = 10;                   Assign 10 to b
int c = a - ++b;                      Assign 20 – (+ +10),
                                      that is, 20–11, or 9, to c
System.out.println(c);          Prints 9
System.out.println(b);      Prints 11
```

In the preceding example, the expression a - ++b uses the increment operator (++) in prefix notation. Therefore, the value of variable b increments to 11 before it is subtracted from 20, assigning the result 9 to variable c.

When ++ is used in postfix notation with an operand, its value increments after it has been used in the expression:

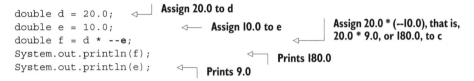

```
int a = 20;          ⊲⎤  Assign 20 to a
int b = 10;              ⊲—  Assign 10 to b           │ Assign 20 – (10++), that
int c = a - b++;                                ⊲⎤  │ is, 20–10, or 10, to c
System.out.println(c);              ⊲⎤  Prints 10
System.out.println(b);   ⊲⎤  Prints 11
```

The interesting part here is that the value of b is printed as 11 in both cases because the value of the variable increments (or decrements) as soon as the expression in which it's used is evaluated.

The same logic applies to the unary operator, --. Here's an example:

```
double d = 20.0;     ⊲⎤  Assign 20.0 to d
double e = 10.0;         ⊲—  Assign 10.0 to e           │ Assign 20.0 * (--10.0), that is,
double f = d * --e;                             ⊲⎤  │ 20.0 * 9.0, or 180.0, to c
System.out.println(f);              ⊲⎤  Prints 180.0
System.out.println(e);   ⊲⎤  Prints 9.0
```

Let's use the unary decrement operator (--) in postfix notation and see what happens:

```
double d = 20.0;     ⊲⎤  Assign 20.0 to d
double e = 10.0;         ⊲—  Assign 10.0 to e           │ Assign 20.0 * (10.0--), that is,
double f = d * e--;                             ⊲⎤  │ 20.0 * 10.0, or 200.0, to c
System.out.println(f);              ⊲⎤  Prints 200.0
System.out.println(e);   ⊲⎤  Prints 9.0
```

Let's check out some example code that uses unary increment and decrement operators in both prefix and postfix notation in the same line of code. What do you think the output of the following code will be?

```
int a = 10;
a = a++ + a + a-- - a-- + ++a;
System.out.println(a);
```

The output of this code is 32. The expression on the right-hand side evaluates from left to right, with the following values, which evaluate to 32:

```
a = 10 + 11 + 11 - 10 + 10;
```

The evaluation of an expression starts from left to right. For a prefix unary operator, the value of its operand increments or decrements just before its value is used in an expression. For a postfix unary operator, the value of its operand increments or decrements just after its value is used in an expression. Figure 2.17 illustrates what is happening in the preceding expression.

For the exam, it's important for you to have a good understanding of, and practice in, using postfix and prefix operators. In addition to the expressions shown in the previous examples, you can also find them in use as conditions in if statements, for loops, and do-while and while loops.

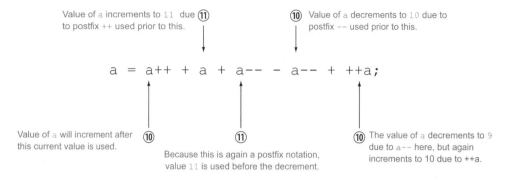

Figure 2.17   Evaluation of an expression that has multiple occurrences of unary operators in postfix and prefix notation

The next Twist in the Tale exercise will give you practice with unary operators used in prefix and postfix notation (answer in the appendix).

Twist in the Tale 2.3

Let's modify the expression used in figure 2.17 by replacing all occurrences of unary operators in prefix notation with postfix notations, and vice versa. So, ++a changes to a++, and vice versa. Similarly, --a changes to a--, and vice versa. Your task is to evaluate the modified expression and determine the output of the following code:

```
int a = 10;
a = ++a + a + --a - --a + a++;
System.out.println (a);
```

Try to form the expression by replacing the values of variable a in the expression and explain each of them, the way it was done for you in figure 2.17.

2.4.3   *Relational operators*

Relational operators are used to check one condition. You can use these operators to determine whether a primitive value is equal to another value or whether it is less than or greater than the other value.

These relational operators can be divided into two categories:

- Comparing greater (>, >=) and lesser values (<, <=)
- Comparing values for equality (==) and nonequality (!=)

The operators <, <=, >, and >= work with all types of numbers, both integers (including char) and floating point, that can be added and subtracted. Examine the following code:

```
int i1 = 10;
int i2 = 20;
System.out.println(i1 >= i2);          ⟵   Prints false
```

```
long long1 = 10;
long long2 = 20;
System.out.println(long1 <= long2);          ⟵┘ Prints true
```

The second category of operators is covered in the following section.

EXAM TIP   You cannot compare incomparable values. For example, you cannot compare a `boolean` with an `int`, a `char`, or a floating-point number. If
you try to do so, your code will not compile.

COMPARING PRIMITIVES FOR EQUALITY (USING == AND !=)

The operators `==` (equal to) and `!=` (not equal to) can be used to compare all types of
primitives: `char`, `byte`, `short`, `int`, `long`, `float`, `double`, and `boolean`. The operator
`==` returns the `boolean` value `true` if the primitive values that you're comparing are
equal, and `false` otherwise. The operator `!=` returns `true` if the primitive values that
you're comparing are *not* equal, and `false` otherwise. For the same set of values, if `==`
returns `true`, `!=` will return `false`. Sounds interesting!

Examine the following code:

```
int a = 10;
int b = 20;
System.out.println(a == b);          ⟵┘ Prints false
System.out.println(a != b);                ⟵── Prints true

boolean b1 = false;
System.out.println(b1 == true);      ⟵┘ Prints false
System.out.println(b1 != true);            ⟵── Prints true

System.out.println(b1 == false);     ⟵┘ Prints true
System.out.println(b1 != false);           ⟵── Prints false
```

Remember that you can't apply these operators to incomparable types. In the following code snippet, the code that compares an `int` variable to a `boolean` variable will fail
to compile:

```
int a = 10;
boolean b1 = false;                     Causes compilation
System.out.println(a == b1);      ⟵┘  error
```

Here's the compilation error:

```
incomparable types: int and boolean
System.out.println(a == b1);
                     ^
```

EXAM TIP   The result of the relational operation is always a `boolean` value.
You can't assign the result of a relational operation to a variable of type `char`,
`int`, `byte`, `short`, `long`, `float`, or `double`.

COMPARING PRIMITIVES USING THE ASSIGNMENT OPERATOR (=)

It's a very common mistake to use the assignment operator, `=`, in place of the equality
operator, `==`, to compare primitive values. Before reading any further, check out the
following code:

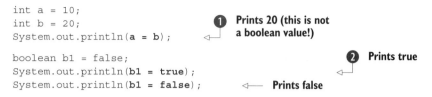

```
int a = 10;
int b = 20;                                  ❶ Prints 20 (this is not
System.out.println(a = b);          ◁┘         a boolean value!)

boolean b1 = false;                                    ❷ Prints true
System.out.println(b1 = true);          ◁┘
System.out.println(b1 = false);      ◁─── Prints false
```

❶ in the previous example isn't comparing the variables a and b. It's assigning the value of the variable b to a and then printing out the value of the variable a, which is 20. Similarly, ❷ isn't comparing the variable b1 with the boolean literal true. It's assigning the boolean literal true to variable b1 and printing out the value of the variable b1.

> **NOTE** You can't compare primitive values by using the assignment operator, =.

2.4.4   *Logical operators*

Logical operators are used to evaluate one or more expressions. These expressions should return a boolean value. You can use the logical operators AND, OR, and NOT to check multiple conditions and proceed accordingly. Here are a few real-life examples:

- *Case 1 (for managers)*—Request promotion if customer is extremely happy with the delivered project AND you think you deserve to be in your boss's seat!
- *Case 2 (for students)*—Accept job proposal if handsome pay and perks OR awesome work profile.
- *Case 3 (for entry-level Java programmers)*—If NOT happy with current job, change it.

In each of these example cases, you're making a decision (request promotion, accept job proposal, or change job) only if a set of conditions is satisfied. In case 1, a manager may request a promotion only if *both* the specified conditions are met. In case 2, a student may accept a new job if *either* of the conditions is true. In case 3, an entry-level Java programmer may change his or her current job if *not* happy with the current job; that is, if the specified condition (being happy with the current job) is false.

As illustrated in these examples, if you wish to proceed with a task when *both* the conditions are true, use the logical AND operator, &&. If you wish to proceed with a task when *either* of the conditions is true, use the logical OR operator, ||. If you wish to wish to reverse the outcome of a boolean value, use the negation operator, !.

Time to look at some code in action:

```
int a = 10;                                       ❶ Prints false
int b = 20;
System.out.println(a > 20 && b > 10);   ◁┘  ❷ Prints true
System.out.println(a > 20 || b > 10);   ◁─┘
System.out.println(! (b > 10));            ◁─❸ Prints false
System.out.println(! (a > 20));      ◁─❹ Prints true
```

❶ prints false because both the conditions, a > 20 and b > 10, are not true. The first one (a > 20) is false. ❷ prints true because one of these conditions (b > 10) is true.

❸ prints false because the specified condition, b > 10, is true. ❹ prints true because the specified condition, a > 20, is false.

Table 2.11 will help you understand the result of using all these logical operators.

Table 2.11 Outcome of using `boolean` literal values with the logical operators AND, OR, and NOT

Operators && (AND)	Operator || (OR)	Operator ! (NOT)
true && true → true true && false → false false && true → false false && false → false true && true && false → false	true || true → true true || false → true false || true → true false || false → false false || false || true → true	!true → false !false → true

Here's a summary of this table:

- *Logical* AND *(&&)*—Evaluates to true if *all* operands are true; false otherwise.
- *Logical* OR *(\|\|)*—Evaluates to true if *any* or all of the operands is true.
- *Logical negation (!)*—Negates the boolean value. Evaluates to true for false, and vice versa.

The operators | and & can also be used to manipulate individual bits of a number value, but I will not cover this usage here, because they are not on this exam.

&& AND \|\| ARE SHORT-CIRCUIT OPERATORS

Another interesting point to note with respect to the logical operators && and \|\| is that they're also called *short-circuit* operators because of the way they evaluate their operands to determine the result. Let's start with the operator &&.

The && operator returns true only if both the operands are true. If the first operand to this operator evaluates to false, the result can *never* be true. Therefore, && does not evaluate the second operand. Similarly, the \|\| operator does not evaluate the second operator if the first operand evaluates to true.

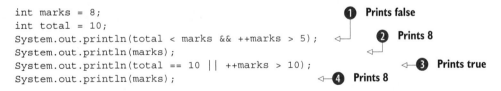

```
int marks = 8;
int total = 10;
System.out.println(total < marks && ++marks > 5);   ⤎┐   ❶ Prints false
System.out.println(marks);                                  ❷ Prints 8
System.out.println(total == 10 || ++marks > 10);        ⤎   ⤎❸ Prints true
System.out.println(marks);                          ⤎❹ Prints 8
```

In the first print statement at ❶, because the first condition, total < marks, evaluates to false, the next condition, ++marks > 5, is not even evaluated. As you can see ❷, the output value of marks is still 8 (the value to which it was initialized on line 1)! Similarly, in the next comparison ❸, because total == 10 evaluates to true, the second condition, ++marks > 10, isn't evaluated. Again, this can be verified when the value of marks is printed again ❹, and the output is 8.

NOTE All the relational and logical operators return a `boolean` value, which can be assigned to a primitive `boolean` variable.

The purpose of the next Twist in Tale is to encourage you to play with code that uses short-circuit operators. To determine whether a `boolean` expression passed as an operand to the short-circuit operators evaluates, you can apply a unary increment operator (in postfix notation) to the variable used in the expression. Compare the new variable value with the old value to verify whether the expression was evaluated (answers in the appendix).

Twist in the Tale 2.4

As you know, the short-circuit operators `&&` and `||` may not evaluate both their operands if they can determine the result of the expression by evaluating just the first operand. Examine the following code and circle the expressions that you think will evaluate. Draw a square around the expressions that you think may not execute. (For example, on line 1, both a++ > 10 and ++b < 30 will evaluate .)

```
class TwistInTaleLLogicalOperators {
    public static void main (String args[]) {
        int a = 10;
        int b = 20;
        int c = 40;
        System.out.println(a++ > 10 || ++b < 30);      // line1
        System.out.println(a > 90 && ++b < 30);
        System.out.println(!(c>20) && a==10 );
        System.out.println(a >= 99 || a <= 33 && b == 10);
        System.out.println(a >= 99 && a <= 33 || b == 10);
    }
}
```

Example use of the short-circuit operator `&&` in real projects

The logical operator `&&` is often used in code to check whether an object reference variable has been assigned a value before invoking a method on it:

```
String name = "hello";
if (name != null && name.length() > 0)
    System.out.println(name.toUpperCase());
```

2.4.5 *Operator precedence*

What happens if you use multiple operators within a single line of code with multiple operands? Which one should be treated like the king and given preference over the others?

Don't worry. Java already has a rule in place for just such a situation. Table 2.12 lists the precedence of operators: the operator on top has the highest precedence, and operators within the same group have the same precedence and are evaluated from left to right.

Table 2.12 Precedence of operators

Operator	Precedence
Postfix	`Expression++, expression--`
Unary	`++expression, --expression, +expression, -expression, !`
Multiplication	`* (multiply), / (divide), % (remainder)`
Addition	`+ (add), - (subtract)`
Relational	`<, >, <=, >=`
Equality	`==, !=`
Logical AND	`&&`
Logical OR	`||`
Assignment	`=, +=, -=, *=, /=, %=`

Let's execute an expression that uses multiple operators (with different precedence) in an expression:

```
int int1 = 10, int2 = 20, int3 = 30;
System.out.println(int1 % int2 * int3 + int1 / int2);
```
❶ **Prints 300**

Because this expression ❶ defines multiple operators with different precedence, it's evaluated as follows:

```
(((int1 % int2) * int3)) + (int1 / int2)
(((10  % 20)  * 30))  + (10 / 20)
( (10         * 30))  + (0)
( 300 )
```

What if you don't want to evaluate the expression in this way? The remedy is simple: use parentheses to override the default operator precedence. Here's an example that adds int3 and int1 before multiplying by int2:

```
int int1 = 10, int2 = 20, int3 = 30;
System.out.println(int1 % int2 * (int3 + int1) / int2);
```
Prints 20!

NOTE You can use parentheses to override the default operator precedence. If your expression defines multiple operators and you are unsure how your expression will be evaluated, use parentheses to evaluate in your preferred order. The inner parentheses are evaluated prior to the outer ones.

2.5   *Summary*

In this chapter, we started with the primitive data types in Java, including examples of where to use each of the kinds and their literal values. We also categorized the primitives into character type, integer type, and floating type. Then we covered the ingredients of valid and invalid Java identifiers.

We discussed the operators used to manipulate primitives (limited to the ones required for the OCA Java SE 7 Programmer I exam). We also covered the conditions in which a particular operator can be used. For example, if you wish to check whether a set of conditions is true, you can use the logical operators. It's also important to understand the operand types that can be used for each of these operators. For example, you can't use `boolean` operands with the operators >, >=, =<, and <.

2.6   *Review notes*

Primitive data types:

- Java defines eight primitive data types: `char`, `byte`, `short`, `int`, `long`, `float`, `double`, and `boolean`.
- Primitive data types are the simplest data types.
- Primitive data types are predefined by the programming language. A user can't define a primitive data type in Java.
- It's helpful to categorize the primitive data types as Boolean, numeric, and character data types.

The Boolean data type:

- The `boolean` data type is used to store data with only two possible values. These two possible values may be thought of as yes/no, 0/1, true/false, or any other combination. The actual values that a `boolean` can store are `true` and `false`.
- `true` and `false` are literal values.
- A literal is a fixed value that doesn't need further calculations to be assigned to any variable.

Numeric data types:

- Numeric values can be stored either as integers or decimal numbers.
- `byte`, `short`, `int`, and `long` can be used to store integers.
- The `byte`, `short`, `int`, and `long` data types use 8, 16, 32, and 64 bits, respectively, to store their values.
- `float` and `double` can be used to store decimal numbers.
- The float and double data types use 32 and 64 bits, respectively, to store their values.
- The default type of integers—that is, nondecimal numbers—is `int`.
- To designate an integer literal value as a `long` value, add the suffix L or l to the literal value.

- Numeric values can be stored in binary, octal, decimal, and hexadecimal number formats. The OCA Java SE 7 Programmer I exam will not ask you to convert a number from one number system to another.
- Literal values in the decimal number system use digits from 0 to 9 (a total of 10 digits).
- Literal values in the octal number system use digits from 0 to 7 (a total of 8 digits).
- Literal values in the hexadecimal number system use digits from 0 to 9 and letters from A to F (a total of 16 digits and letters).
- Literal values in the binary number system use digits 0 and 1 (a total of 2 digits).
- The literal values in the octal number system start with the prefix 0. For example, 0413 in the octal number system is 267 in the decimal number system.
- The literal values in the hexadecimal number system start with the prefix 0x. For example, 0x10B in the hexadecimal number system is 267 in the decimal number system.
- The literal values in the binary number system start with the prefix 0b or 0B. For example, the decimal value 267 is 0B100001011 in the binary system.
- Starting with Java 7, you can use underscores within the Java literal values to make them more readable. 0B1_0000_10_11, 0_413, and 0x10_B are valid binary, octal, and hexadecimal literal values.
- The default type of a decimal number is double.
- To designate a decimal literal value as a float value, add the suffix F or f to the literal value.
- The suffixes D and d can be used to mark a literal value as a double value. Though it's allowed, doing so is not required because the default value of decimal literals is double.

Character primitive data types:

- A char data type can store a single 16-bit Unicode character; that is, it can store characters from virtually all the world's existing scripts and languages.
- You can use values from \u0000 (or 0) to a maximum of \uffff (or 65,535 inclusive) to store a char. Unicode values are defined in the hexadecimal number system.
- Internally, the char data type is stored as an unsigned integer value (only positive integers).
- When you assign a letter to a char, Java stores its integer equivalent value. You may assign a positive integer value to a char instead of a letter, such as 122.
- The literal value 122 is not the same as the Unicode value \u0122. The former is a decimal number and the latter is a hexadecimal number.
- Single quotes, not double quotes, are used to assign a letter to a char variable.

Valid identifiers:

- A valid identifier starts with a letter (a–z, upper- or lowercase), a currency sign, or an underscore. There is no limit to its length.
- A valid identifier can contain digits, but not in the starting place.
- A valid identifier can use the underscore and currency sign at any position of the identifier.
- A valid identifier can't have the same spelling as a Java keyword, such as `switch`.
- A valid identifier can't use any special characters, including !, @, #, %, ^, &, *, (,), ', :, ;, [, /, \, or }

Operators:

- The OCA Java SE 7 Programmer I exam covers assignment, arithmetic, relational, and logical operators.

Assignment operators:

- Assignment operators can be used to assign or reassign values to all types of variables.
- A variable can't be assigned to an incompatible value. For example, character and numeric values cannot be assigned to a `boolean` variable, and vice versa.
- += and -= are short forms of addition/subtraction and assignment.
- += can be read as "first add and then assign" and -= can be read as "first subtract and then assign."

Arithmetic operators:

- Arithmetic operators can't be used with the `boolean` data type. Attempting to do so will make the code fail to compile.
- ++ and -- are unary increment and decrement operators. These operators work with single operands.
- Unary operators can be used in prefix or postfix notation.
- When the unary operators ++ and -- are used in prefix notation, the value of the variable increments/decrements just before the variable is used in an expression.
- When the unary operators ++ and -- are used in postfix notation, the value of the variable increments/decrements just after the variable is used in an expression.
- By default, unary operators have a higher precedence than multiplication operators and addition operators.

Relational operators:

- Relational operators are used to compare values for equality (==) and non-equality (!=). They are also used to determine whether two numeric values are greater than (>, >=) or less than (<, <=) each other.
- You can't compare incomparable values. For example, you can't compare a `boolean` with an `int`, a `char`, or a floating-point number. If you try to do so, your code will not compile.

- The operators equal to (==) and not equal to (!=) can be used to compare all types of primitives: char, byte, short, int, long, float, double, and boolean.
- The operator == returns true if the primitive values being compared are equal.
- The operator != returns true if the primitive values being compared are *not* equal.
- The result of the relational operator is always a boolean value.

Logical operators:

- You can use the logical operators to determine whether a set of conditions is true or false and proceed accordingly.
- Logical AND (&&) evaluates to true if all operands are true, and false otherwise.
- Logical OR (||) evaluates to true if any or all of the operands is true.
- Logical negation (!) negates the boolean value. It evaluates to true for false, and vice versa.
- The result of a logical operation is always a boolean value.
- The logical operators && and || are also called short-circuit operators. If these operators can determine the output of the expression with the evaluation of the first operand, they don't evaluate the second operand.
- The && operator returns true only if both of the operands are true. If the first operand to this operator evaluates to false, the result can never be true. Therefore, && does not evaluate the second operand.
- Similarly, the || operator returns true if any of the operands is true. If the first operand to this operator evaluates to true, the result can never be false. Therefore, || does not evaluate the second operator.

2.7 *Sample exam questions*

Q2-1. Select all incorrect statements:

    a A programmer can't define a new primitive data type.

    b A programmer can define a new primitive data type.

    c Once assigned, the value of a primitive can't be modified.

    d A value can't be assigned to a primitive variable.

Q2-2. Which of the options are correct for the following code?

```
public class Prim {                                  // line 1
    public static void main(String[] args) {         // line 2
        char a = 'a';                                // line 3
        char b = -10;                                // line 4
        char c = '1';                                // line 5
        integer d = 1000;                            // line 6
        System.out.println(++a + b++ * c - d);       // line 7
    }                                                // line 8
}                                                    // line 9
```

    a Code at line 4 fails to compile.

    b Code at line 5 fails to compile.

c Code at line 6 fails to compile.

d Code at line 7 fails to compile.

Q2-3. What is the output of the following code?

```java
public class Foo {
    public static void main(String[] args) {
        int a = 10;
        long b = 20;
        short c = 30;
        System.out.println(++a + b++ * c);
    }
}
```

a 611

b 641

c 930

d 960

Q2-4. Select the option(s) that is/are the best choice for the following:
_____ should be used to store a count of cars manufactured by a car manufacturing company. _____ should be used to store whether this car manufacturing company modifies the interiors on the customer's request. _____ should be used to store the maximum speed of a car.

a long, boolean, double

b long, int, float

c char, int, double

d long, boolean, float

Q2-5. Which of the following options contain correct code to declare and initialize variables to store whole numbers?

a bit a = 0;

b integer a2 = 7;

c long a3 = 0x10C;

d short a4 = 0512;

e double a5 = 10;

f byte a7 = -0;

g long a8 = 123456789;

Q2-6. Select the options that, when inserted at // INSERT CODE HERE, will make the following code output a value of 11:

```java
public class IncrementNum {
    public static void main(String[] args) {
        int ctr = 50;
        // INSERT CODE HERE
        System.out.println(ctr % 20);
    }
}
```

a   `ctr += 1;`

b   `ctr =+ 1;`

c   `++ctr;`

d   `ctr = 1;`

Q2-7. What is the output of the following code?

```
int a = 10;
int b = 20;
int c = (a * (b + 2)) - 10-4 * ((2*2) - 6;
System.out.println(c);
```

a   218

b   232

c   246

d   Compilation error

Q2-8. What is true about the following lines of code?

```
boolean b = false;
int i = 90;
System.out.println(i >= b);
```

a   Code prints `true`

b   Code prints `false`

c   Code prints `90 >= false`

d   Compilation error

Q2-9. Examine the following code and select the correct options:

```
public class Prim {                                    // line 1
    public static void main(String[] args) {           // line 2
        int num1 = 12;                                 // line 3
        float num2 = 17.8f;                            // line 4
        boolean eJavaResult = true;                    // line 5
        boolean returnVal = num1 >= 12 && num2 < 4.567 // line 6
                        || eJavaResult == true;
        System.out.println(returnVal);                 // line 7
    }                                                  // line 8
}                                                      // line 9
```

a   Code prints `false`

b   Code prints `true`

c   Code will print `true` if code on line 6 is modified to the following:

```
boolean returnVal = (num1 >= 12 && num2 < 4.567) || eJavaResult ==
true;
```

d   Code will print `true` if code on line 6 is modified to the following:

```
boolean returnVal = num1 >= 12 && (num2 < 4.567 || eJavaResult ==
false);
```

Q2-10. If the functionality of the operators = and > were to be swapped in Java (for the code on line numbers 4, 5, and 6), what would be the result of the following code?

```
boolean myBool = false;                                 // line 1
int yourInt = 10;                                       // line 2
float hisFloat = 19.54f;                                // line 3

System.out.println(hisFloat > yourInt);                 // line 4
System.out.println(yourInt = 10);                       // line 5
System.out.println(myBool > false);                     // line 6
```

   a true
      true
      false

   b 10.0
      false
      false

   c false
      false
      false

   d Compilation error

2.8   *Answers to sample exam questions*

Q2-1. Select all incorrect statements:

   a A programmer can't define a new primitive data type.
   b **A programmer can define a new primitive data type.**
   c **Once assigned, the value of a primitive can't be modified.**
   d **A value can't be assigned to a primitive variable.**

Answer: b, c, d

Explanation: Only option (a) is a correct statement. Java primitive data types are pre-defined by the programming language. They can't be defined by a programmer.

Q2-2. Which of the options are correct for the following code?

```
public class Prim {                                     // line 1
    public static void main(String[] args) {            // line 2
        char a = 'a';                                   // line 3
        char b = -10;                                   // line 4
        char c = '1';                                   // line 5
        integer d = 1000;                               // line 6
        System.out.println(++a + b++ * c - d);          // line 7
    }                                                   // line 8
}                                                       // line 9
```

   a **Code at line 4 fails to compile.**
   b Code at line 5 fails to compile.
   c **Code at line 6 fails to compile.**
   d **Code at line 7 fails to compile.**

Answer: a, c, d

Explanation:

Option (a) is correct. The code at line 4 fails to compile because you can't assign a negative value to a primitive `char` data type without casting.

Option (c) is correct. There is no primitive data type with the name "integer." The valid data types are `int` and `Integer` (a wrapper class with *I* in uppercase).

Option (d) is correct. The variable d remains undefined on line 7 because its declaration fails to compile on line 6. So the arithmetic expression (++a + b++ * c - d) that uses variable d fails to compile. There are no issues with using the variable c of the `char` data type in an arithmetic expression. The char data types are internally stored as unsigned integer values and can be used in arithmetic expressions.

Q2-3. What is the output of the following code?

```
public class Foo {
    public static void main(String[] args) {
        int a = 10;
        long b = 20;
        short c = 30;
        System.out.println(++a + b++ * c);
    }
}
```

    a **611**

    b 641

    c 930

    d 960

Answer: a

Explanation: The prefix increment operator (++) used with the variable a will increment its value before it is used in the expression ++a + b++ * c. The postfix increment operator (++) used with the variable b will increment its value *after* its initial value is used in the expression ++a + b++ * c.

Therefore, the expression ++a + b++ * c, evaluates with the following values:

```
11 + 20 * 30
```

Because the multiplication operator has a higher precedence than the addition operator, the values 20 and 30 are multiplied before the result is added to the value 11. The example expression evaluates as follows:

```
(++a + b++ * c)
= 11 + 20 * 30
= 11 + 600
= 611
```

 EXAM TIP   Although questions 2-2 and 2-3 seemed to test you on your understanding of operators, they actually tested you on different topics. Question 2-2 tested you on the name of the primitive data types. Beware! The real exam has a lot of such questions. A question that may seem to test you on threads may actually be testing you on the use of a do-while loop!

Q2-4. Select the option(s) that is/are the best choice for the following:
_____ should be used to store a count of cars manufactured by a car manufacturing company. _____ should be used to store whether this car manufacturing company modifies the interiors on the customer's request. _____ should be used to store the maximum speed of a car.

- a `long, boolean, double`
- b `long, int, float`
- c `char, int, double`
- d `long, boolean, float`

Answer: a, d

Explanation:

Options (a) and (d) are correct. Use a `long` data type to store big number values, a `boolean` data type to store yes/no values as `true/false`, and a `double` or `float` to store decimal numbers.

Option (b) is incorrect. You can't use an `int` to store yes/no or `true/false` values.

Option (c) is incorrect. You can't use a `char` data type to store very long values (such as the count of cars manufactured by the car manufacturer until a certain date). Also, it's conceptually incorrect to track counts using the `char` data type.

Q2-5. Which of the following options contain correct code to declare and initialize variables to store whole numbers?

- a `bit a = 0;`
- b `integer a2 = 7;`
- c `long a3 = 0x10C;`
- d `short a4 = 0512;`
- e `double a5 = 10;`
- f `byte a7 = -0;`
- g `long a8 = 123456789;`

Answer: c, d, f, g

Explanation:

Options (a) and (b) are incorrect. There are no primitive data types in Java with the names `bit` and `integer`. The correct names are `byte` and `int`.

Option (c) is correct. It assigns a hexadecimal literal value to the variable `a3`.

Option (d) is correct. It assigns an octal literal value to the variable `a4`.

Option (e) is incorrect. It defines a variable of type `double`, which is used to store decimal numbers, not integers.

Option (f) is correct. `-0` is a valid literal value.

Option (g) is correct. `123456789` is a valid integer literal value that can be assigned to a variable of type `long`.

Q2-6. Select the options that, when inserted at // INSERT CODE HERE, will make the following code output a value of 11:

```
public class IncrementNum {
    public static void main(String[] args) {
        int ctr = 50;
        // INSERT CODE HERE
        System.out.println(ctr % 20);
    }
}
```

 a **ctr += 1;**

 b ctr =+ 1;

 c **++ctr;**

 d ctr = 1;

Answer: a, c

Explanation: To output a value of 11, the value of the variable ctr should be 51 because 51%20 is 11. Operator % outputs the remainder from a division operation. The current value of the variable ctr is 50. It can be incremented by 1 using the correct assignment or increment operator.

 Option (b) is incorrect. Java does not define a =+ operator. The correct operator is +=.

 Option (d) is incorrect because it's assigning a value of 1 to the variable result, not incrementing it by 1.

Q2-7. What is the output of the following code?

```
int a = 10;
int b = 20;
int c = (a * (b + 2)) - 10-4 * ((2*2) - 6;
System.out.println(c);
```

 a 218

 b 232

 c 246

 d **Compilation error**

Answer: d

Explanation: First of all, whenever you answer any question that uses parentheses to override operator precedence, check whether the number of opening parentheses matches the number of closing parentheses. This code will not compile because the number of opening parentheses does not match the number of closing parentheses.

 Second, you may not have to answer complex expressions in the real exam. Whenever you see overly complex code, look for other possible issues in the code. Complex code may be used to distract your attention from the real issue.

Q2-8. What is true about the following lines of code?

```
boolean b = false;
int i = 90;
System.out.println(i >= b);
```

    a Code prints `true`

    b Code prints `false`

    c Code prints `90 >= false`

    d **Compilation error**

Answer: d

Explanation: The code will fail to compile; hence, it can't execute. You can't compare incomparable types, such as a `boolean` value with a number.

Q2-9. Examine the following code and select the correct options:

```java
public class Prim {                                     // line 1
    public static void main(String[] args) {            // line 2
        int num1 = 12;                                  // line 3
        float num2 = 17.8f;                             // line 4
        boolean eJavaResult = true;                     // line 5
        boolean returnVal = num1 >= 12 && num2 < 4.567  // line 6
                            || eJavaResult == true;
        System.out.println(returnVal);                  // line 7
    }                                                   // line 8
}                                                       // line 9
```

    a Code prints `false`

    b **Code prints `true`**

    c **Code will print `true` if code on line 6 is modified to the following:**

```java
boolean returnVal = (num1 >= 12 && num2 < 4.567) || eJavaResult ==
true;
```

    d Code will print `true` if code on line 6 is modified to the following:

```java
boolean returnVal = num1 >= 12 && (num2 < 4.567 || eJavaResult ==
false);
```

Answer: b, c

Explanation:

    Option (a) is incorrect because the code prints `true`.

    Option (d) is incorrect because the code prints `false`.

    Both the short-circuit operators `&&` and `||` have the same operator precedence. In the absence of any parentheses, they are evaluated from left to right. The first expression, `num1 >= 12`, evaluates to `true`. The `&&` operator evaluates the second operand only if the first evaluates to `true`. Because `&&` returns `true` for its first operand, it evaluates the second operand, which is `(num2 < 4.567 || eJavaResult == true)`. The second operand evaluates to `true`; hence the variable `returnVal` is assigned `true`.

Q2-10. If the functionality of the operators `=` and `>` were to be swapped in Java (for the code on line numbers 4, 5, and 6), what would be the result of the following code?

```java
boolean myBool = false;         // line 1
int yourInt = 10;               // line 2
float hisFloat = 19.54f;        // line 3
```

```
System.out.println(hisFloat > yourInt);          // line 4
System.out.println(yourInt = 10);                 // line 5
System.out.println(myBool > false);               // line 6
```

   a true
       true
       false

   b **10.0**
       false
       false

   c false
       false
       false

   d Compilation error

Answer: b

Explanation: Because the question mentioned swapping the functionality of the operator > with =, the code on lines 4, 5, and 6 will actually evaluate to the following:

```
System.out.println(hisFloat = yourInt);
System.out.println(yourInt > 10);
System.out.println(myBool = false);
```

The result is shown in b.

Note that the expression myBool = false uses the assignment operator (=) and not a comparison operator (==). This expression assigns boolean literal false to myBool; it doesn't compare false with myBool. Watch out for similar (trick) assignments in the exam, which may *seem* to be comparing values.

Methods and encapsulation 3

Exam objectives covered in this chapter	What you need to know
[1.1] Define the scope of variables.	Variables can have multiple scopes: class, instance, method, and local. Accessibility of a variable in a given scope.
[2.4] Explain an object's life cycle.	Difference between when an object is declared, initialized, accessible, and eligible to be collected by Java's garbage collection. Garbage collection in Java.
[6.1] Create methods with arguments and return values.	Creation of methods with correct return types and method argument lists.
[6.3] Create an overloaded method.	Creation of methods with the same names, but a different set of argument lists.
[6.4] Differentiate between default and user-defined constructors.	A default constructor isn't the same as a no-argument constructor. Java defines a no-argument constructor when no user-defined constructors are created. User-defined constructors can be overloaded.
[6.5] Create and overload constructors.	Like regular methods, constructors can be overloaded.
[2.3] Read or write to object fields.	Object fields can be read and written to by using both instance variables and methods. Access modifiers determine the variables and methods that can be accessed to read from or write to object fields.

Exam objectives covered in this chapter	What you need to know
[2.5] Call methods on objects.	The correct notation to call methods on an object. Access modifiers affect the methods that can be called using a reference variable. Methods may or may not change the value of instance variables. Nonstatic methods can't be called on uninitialized objects.
[6.7] Apply encapsulation principles to a class.	Need for and benefits of encapsulation. Definition of classes that correctly implement the encapsulation principle.
[6.8] Determine the effect upon object references and primitive values when they're passed into methods that change the values.	Object references and primitives are treated in a different manner when passed into methods. Unlike reference variables, the values of primitives are never changed in the calling method when they're passed to methods.

Take a look around, and you'll find multiple examples of *well-encapsulated objects*. For instance, most of us use the services of a bank, which applies a set of well-defined processes that enable us to secure our money and valuables (a bank vault). The bank may require input from us to execute some of its processes, such as depositing money into our accounts. But the bank may or may not inform us about the results of other processes; for example, it may inform us about an account balance after a transaction, but it likely won't inform us about its recruitment plans for new employees.

In Java, you can compare a bank to a well-encapsulated class and the bank processes to Java methods. In this analogy, your money and valuables are like object fields in Java. You can also compare inputs that a bank process requires to Java's method parameters, and the bank process result to a Java method's return value. Finally, you can compare the set of steps that a bank executes when it opens a bank account to constructors in Java.

In the exam, you must answer questions about methods and encapsulation. This chapter will help you get the correct answers by covering the following:

- Defining the scope of variables
- Explaining an object's life cycle
- Creating methods with primitive and object arguments and return values
- Creating overloaded methods and constructors
- Reading and writing to object fields
- Calling methods on objects
- Applying encapsulation principles to a class

We'll start the chapter by defining the scope of the variables; we'll then cover the class constructors, including the differences between user-defined and default constructors and the ways in which they're useful.

3.1   *Scope of variables*

> **[1.1]   Define the scope of variables**

The scope of a variable specifies its life span. In this section, we'll cover the scopes of the variables and the domains in which they're accessible. Here are the available scopes of variables:

- Local variables (also known as method-local variables)
- Method parameters (also known as method arguments)
- Instance variables (also known as attributes, fields, and nonstatic variables)
- Class variables (also known as static variables)

Let's get started by defining local variables.

3.1.1   *Local variables*

Local variables are defined within a method. They may or may not be defined within code constructs such as if-else constructs, looping constructs, or switch statements. Typically, you'd use local variables to store the intermediate results of a calculation. Compared to the other three previously listed variable scopes, they have the shortest scope (life span).

Look at the following code, in which a local variable avg is defined within the method getAverage():

```
class Student {
    private double marks1, marks2, marks3;      Instance variables
    private double maxMarks = 100;
    public double getAverage() {                        Local variable avg
        double avg = 0;
        avg = ((marks1 + marks2 + marks3) / (maxMarks*3)) * 100;
        return avg;
    }                                           This code won't compile
    public void setAverage(double val) {        because avg is inaccessible
        avg = val;                              outside the method getAverage
    }
}
```

As you can see, the variable avg, defined locally in the method getAverage, can't be accessed outside of it in the method setAverage. The scope of this local variable, avg, is depicted in figure 3.1. The unshaded area marks where avg is accessible and the shaded area is where it won't be available.

> **NOTE**   The life span of a variable is determined by its scope. If the scope of a variable is limited to a method, its life span is also limited to that method. You may notice that these terms are used interchangeably.

Let's define another variable, avg, local to the if block of an if statement (code that executes when the if condition evaluates to true):

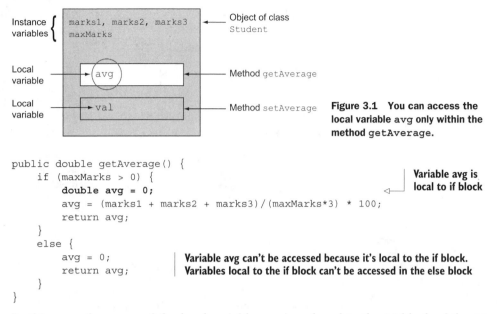

Figure 3.1 You can access the local variable `avg` only within the method `getAverage`.

```java
public double getAverage() {
    if (maxMarks > 0) {
        double avg = 0;
        avg = (marks1 + marks2 + marks3)/(maxMarks*3) * 100;
        return avg;
    }
    else {
        avg = 0;
        return avg;
    }
}
```

Variable avg is local to if block

Variable avg can't be accessed because it's local to the if block.
Variables local to the if block can't be accessed in the else block

In this case, the scope of the local variable `avg` is reduced to the `if` block of the `if`-`else` statement defined within the `getAverage` method. The scope of this local variable `avg` is depicted in figure 3.2, where the unshaded area marks where `avg` is accessible, and the shaded part marks the area where it won't be available.

Similarly, loop variables aren't accessible outside of the loop body:

```java
public void localVariableInLoop() {
    for (int ctr = 0; ctr < 5; ++ctr) {
        System.out.println(ctr);
    }
    System.out.println(ctr);
}
```

Variable ctr is defined within the for loop

Variable ctr isn't accessible outside the for loop. This line won't compile.

EXAM TIP The local variables topic is a favorite of OCA Java SE 7 Programmer I exam authors. You're likely to be asked a question that seems to be about a rather complex topic, such as inheritance or exception handling, but in fact it'll be testing your knowledge on the scope of a local variable.

The scope of a local variable depends on the location of its declaration within a method. The scope of local variables defined within a loop, `if`-`else`, or `switch` construct or within a code block (marked with {}) is limited to these constructs.

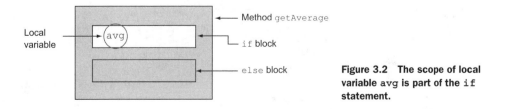

Figure 3.2 The scope of local variable `avg` is part of the `if` statement.

Local variables defined outside any of these constructs are accessible across the complete method.

The next section discusses the scope of method parameters.

3.1.2 *Method parameters*

The variables that accept values in a method are called *method parameters*. They're accessible only in the method that defines them. In the following example, a method parameter val is defined for the method setTested:

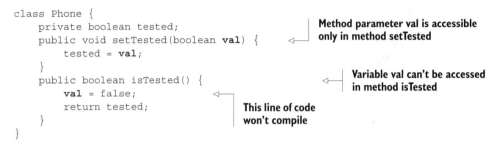

```
class Phone {
    private boolean tested;
    public void setTested(boolean val) {          Method parameter val is accessible
        tested = val;                             only in method setTested
    }
    public boolean isTested() {                   Variable val can't be accessed
        val = false;                              in method isTested
        return tested;
    }                         This line of code
}                             won't compile
```

In the previous code, you can access the method parameter val only within the method setTested. It can't be accessed in any other method.

The scope of the method parameter val is depicted in figure 3.3. The unshaded area marks where the variable is accessible, and the shaded part marks where it won't be available.

The scope of a method parameter may be as long as that of a local variable, or longer, but it can never be shorter. The following method, isPrime, defines a method parameter, num, and two local variables, result and ctr:

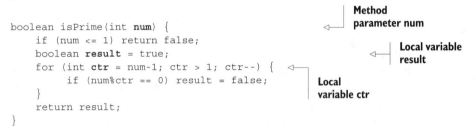

```
boolean isPrime(int num) {                     Method
    if (num <= 1) return false;                parameter num
    boolean result = true;
    for (int ctr = num-1; ctr > 1; ctr--) {    Local variable
        if (num%ctr == 0) result = false;      result
    }                        Local
    return result;           variable ctr
}
```

The scope of the method parameter num is as long as the scope of the local variable result. Because the scope of the local variable ctr is limited to the for block, it's

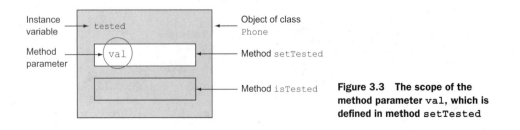

Figure 3.3   The scope of the method parameter val, which is defined in method setTested

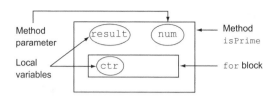
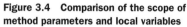

Figure 3.4   Comparison of the scope of method parameters and local variables

shorter than the method parameter num. The comparison of the scope of all of these three variables is shown in figure 3.4, where the scope of each variable (defined in an oval) is shown by the rectangle enclosing it.

Let's move on to instance variables, which have a larger scope than method parameters.

3.1.3   *Instance variables*

Instance is another name for an object. Hence, an *instance variable* is available for the life of an object. An instance variable is declared within a class, outside of all of the methods. It's accessible to all the nonstatic methods defined in a class.

In the following example, the variable tested is an instance variable—it's defined within the class Phone, outside of all of the methods. It can be accessed by all of the methods of class Phone:

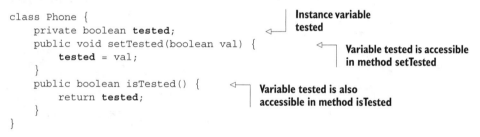

```
class Phone {
    private boolean tested;
    public void setTested(boolean val) {
        tested = val;
    }
    public boolean isTested() {
        return tested;
    }
}
```

Instance variable
tested

Variable tested is accessible
in method setTested

Variable tested is also
accessible in method isTested

The scope of the instance variable tested is depicted in figure 3.5. As you can see, the variable tested is accessible across the object of class Phone, represented by the unshaded area. It's accessible in the methods setTested and isTested.

> **EXAM TIP**   The scope of an instance variable is longer than that of a local variable or a method parameter.

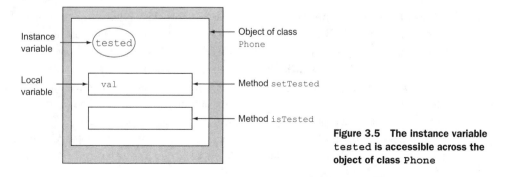

Figure 3.5   The instance variable tested is accessible across the object of class Phone

Class variables, covered in the next section, have the largest scope among all types of variables.

3.1.4   *Class variables*

A *class variable* is defined by using the keyword static. A class variable belongs to a class, not to individual objects of the class. A class variable is shared across all objects—objects don't have a separate copy of the class variables.

You don't even need an object to access a class variable. It can be accessed by using the name of the class in which it's defined:

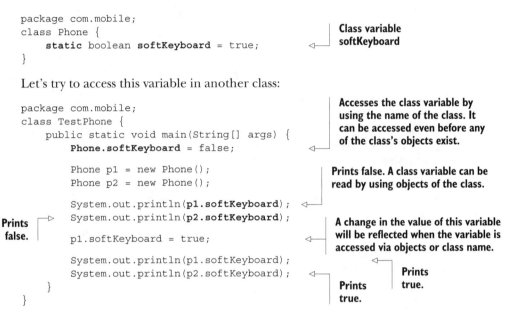

```
package com.mobile;
class Phone {
    static boolean softKeyboard = true;
}
```

**Class variable
softKeyboard**

Let's try to access this variable in another class:

```
package com.mobile;
class TestPhone {
    public static void main(String[] args) {
        Phone.softKeyboard = false;

        Phone p1 = new Phone();
        Phone p2 = new Phone();

        System.out.println(p1.softKeyboard);
        System.out.println(p2.softKeyboard);

        p1.softKeyboard = true;

        System.out.println(p1.softKeyboard);
        System.out.println(p2.softKeyboard);
    }
}
```

**Accesses the class variable by
using the name of the class. It
can be accessed even before any
of the class's objects exist.**

**Prints false. A class variable can be
read by using objects of the class.**

**A change in the value of this variable
will be reflected when the variable is
accessed via objects or class name.**

**Prints
false.**

**Prints
true.**

**Prints
true.**

As you can see in the previous code, the class variable softKeyboard is accessible using all of the following:

- Phone.softKeyboard
- p1.softKeyboard
- p2.softKeyboard

It doesn't matter whether you use the name of the class (Phone) or an object (p1) to access a class variable. You can change the value of a class variable using either of them because they all refer to a single shared copy.

The scope of the class variable softKeyboard is depicted in figure 3.6. As you can see, a single copy of this variable is accessible to all the objects of class Phone. The variable softKeyboard isn't defined within any object of class Phone, so it's accessible even without the existence of an object of class Phone. The class variable softKeyboard is made accessible by the JVM when it loads the Phone class into memory. The scope of the class variable softKeyboard depends on its access modifier and that of the Phone

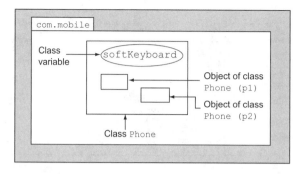

Figure 3.6 The scope of the class variable `softKeyboard` **is limited to the package** `com.mobile` **because it's defined in class** `Phone`**, which is defined with default access. The class variable** `softKeyboard` **is shared and accessible across all objects of class** `Phone`**.**

class. Because the class `Phone` and the class variable `softKeyboard` are defined using default access, they're accessible only within the package `com.mobile`.

COMPARING THE USE OF VARIABLES IN DIFFERENT SCOPES

Here is a quick comparison of the use of the local variables, method parameters, instance variables, and class variables:

- Local variables are defined within a method and are normally used to store the intermediate results of a calculation.
- Method parameters are used to pass values to a method. These values can be manipulated and may also be stored as the state of an object by assigning them to instance variables.
- Instance variables are used to store the state of an object. These are the values that need to be accessed by multiple methods.
- Class variables are used to store values that should be shared by all the objects of a class.

3.1.5 *Overlapping variable scopes*

In the previous sections on local variables, method parameters, instance variables, and class variables, did you notice that some of the variables are accessible in multiple places within an object? For example, all four variables will be accessible in a loop within a method.

This overlapping scope is shown in figure 3.7. The variables are defined in ovals and are accessible within all methods and blocks, as illustrated by their enclosing rectangles.

As shown in figure 3.7, an individual copy of `classVariable` can be accessed and shared by multiple objects (`object1` and `object2`) of a class. Both `object1` and `object2` have their own copy of the instance variable `instanceVariable1`, so `instance-Variable1` is accessible across all the methods of `object1`. The methods `method1` and `method2` have their own copies of `localVariable` and `methodParameter` when used with `object1` and `object2`.

The scope of `instanceVariable1` overlaps with the scope of `localVariable` and `methodParameter`, defined in `method1`. Hence, all three of these variables (`instance-Variable1`, `localVariable`, and `methodParameter`) can access each other in this

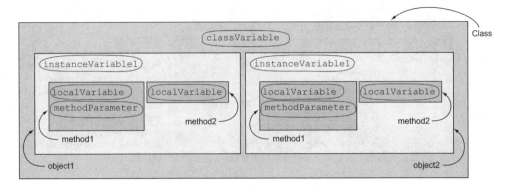

Figure 3.7   The scopes of variables can overlap

overlapped area. But `instanceVariable1` can't access `localVariable` and `method-Parameter` outside `method1`.

COMPARING THE SCOPE OF VARIABLES

Figure 3.8 compares the life spans of local variables, method parameters, instance variables, and class variables.

As you can see in figure 3.8, local variables have the shortest scope or life span, and class variables have the longest scope or life span.

> **EXAM TIP**   Different local variables can have different scopes. The scope of local variables may be shorter than or as long as the scope of method parameters. The scope of local variables is less than the duration of a method if they're declared in a sub-block (within braces { }) in a method. This sub-block can be an `if` statement, a `switch` construct, a loop, or a `try-catch` block (discussed in chapter 7).

VARIABLES WITH THE SAME NAME IN DIFFERENT SCOPES

The fact that the scopes of variables overlap results in interesting combinations of variables within different scopes but with the same names. Some rules are necessary to

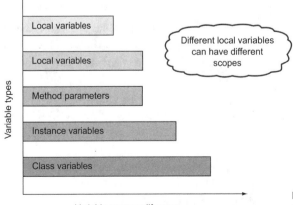

Figure 3.8   Comparing the scope, or life span, of all four variables

prevent conflicts. In particular, you can't define a static variable and an instance variable with the same name in a class:

```
class MyPhone {
    static boolean softKeyboard = true;
    boolean softKeyboard = true;
}
```
Won't compile. Class variable and instance variable can't be defined using the same name in a class

Similarly, local variables and method parameters can't be defined with the same name. The following code defines a method parameter and a local variable with the same name, so it won't compile:

```
void myMethod(int weight) {
    int weight = 10;
}
```
Won't compile. Method parameter and local variable can't be defined using the same name in a method

A class can define local variables with the same name as the instance or class variables. The following code defines a class variable and a local variable, softKeyboard, with the same name, and an instance variable and a local variable, phoneNumber, with the same name, which is acceptable:

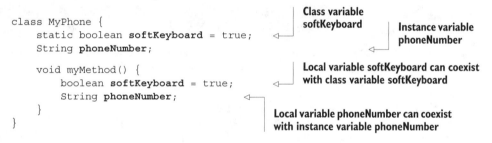

```
class MyPhone {
    static boolean softKeyboard = true;
    String phoneNumber;

    void myMethod() {
        boolean softKeyboard = true;
        String phoneNumber;
    }
}
```
Class variable softKeyboard

Instance variable phoneNumber

Local variable softKeyboard can coexist with class variable softKeyboard

Local variable phoneNumber can coexist with instance variable phoneNumber

What happens when you assign a value to a local variable that has the same name as an instance variable? Does the instance variable reflect this modified value? This question provides the food for thought in this chapter's first Twist in the Tale exercise. It should help you remember what happens when you assign a value to a local variable when an instance variable already exists with the same name in the class (answer in the appendix).

Twist in the Tale 3.1

The class Phone defines a local variable and an instance variable, phoneNumber, with the same name. Examine the definition of the method setNumber. Execute the class on your system and select the correct output of the class TestPhone from the given options:

```
class Phone {
    String phoneNumber = "123456789";
    void setNumber () {
        String phoneNumber;
        phoneNumber = "987654321";
    }
}
class TestPhone {
```

```
    public static void main(String[] args) {
        Phone p1 = new Phone();
        p1.setNumber();
        System.out.println (p1.phoneNumber);
    }
}
```

   a 123456789

   b 987654321

   c No output

   d The class Phone will not compile.

In this section, you worked with variables in different scopes. When variables go out of scope, they're no longer accessible by the remaining code. In the next section, you'll see how an object is created and made accessible and then inaccessible.

3.2 *Object's life cycle*

> [2.4] Explain an object's life cycle

The OCA Java SE 7 Programmer I exam will test your understanding of how to determine when an object is or isn't accessible. The exam also tests your ability to determine the total number of objects that are accessible at a particular line of code. Primitives aren't objects, so they're not relevant in this section.

Unlike some other programming languages, such as C, Java doesn't allow you to allocate or deallocate memory yourself when you create or destroy objects. Java manages memory for allocating objects and reclaiming the memory occupied by unused objects.

The task of reclaiming unused memory is taken care of by Java's garbage collector, which is a low-priority thread. It runs periodically and frees up space occupied by unused objects.

Java also provides a method called finalize, which is accessible to all of the classes. The method finalize is defined in the class java.lang.Object, which is the base class of all Java classes. All Java classes can override the method finalize, which executes just before an object is garbage collected. In theory, you can use this method to free up resources being used by an object, although doing so isn't recommended because its execution is not guaranteed to happen.

An object's life cycle starts when it's created and lasts until it goes out of its scope or is no longer referenced by a variable. When an object is accessible, it can be referenced by a variable and other classes can use it by calling its methods and accessing its variables. I'll discuss these stages in detail in the following subsections.

3.2.1 *An object is born*

An object comes into the picture when you use the keyword operator new. You can initialize a reference variable with this object. Note the difference between declaring a variable and initializing it. The following is an example of a class `Person` and another class `ObjectLifeCycle`:

```
class Person {}
class ObjectLifeCycle {
    Person person;
}
```

In the previous code, no objects of class `Person` are created in the class `ObjectLife-Cycle`; it declares only a variable of type `Person`. An object is created when a reference variable is initialized:

```
class ObjectLifeCycle2 {
    Person person = new Person();
}
```

> Declaring and initializing
> a variable of type Person

The difference in variable declaration and object creation is illustrated in figure 3.9, where you can compare a baby name to a reference variable and a real baby to an object. The left box in figure 3.9 represents variable declaration, because the baby hasn't been born yet. The right box in figure 3.9 represents object creation.

Syntactically, an object comes into being by using the `new` operator. Because `Strings` can also be initialized using the `=` operator, the following code is a valid example of `String` objects being created:

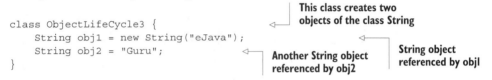

```
class ObjectLifeCycle3 {
    String obj1 = new String("eJava");
    String obj2 = "Guru";
}
```

> This class creates two
> objects of the class String

> Another String object
> referenced by obj2

> String object
> referenced by obj1

What happens when you create a new object without assigning it to any reference variable? Let's create a new object of class `Person` in class `ObjectLifeCycle2` without assigning it to any reference variable (modifications in **bold**):

```
class ObjectLifeCycle2 {
    Person person = new Person();
    ObjectLifeCycle2() {
        new Person();
    }
}
```

> An unreferenced
> object

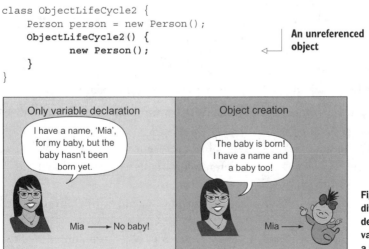

Figure 3.9 The difference between declaring a reference variable and initializing a reference variable

In the previous example, an object of class `Person` is created, but it can't be accessed using any reference variable. Creating an object in this manner will execute the relevant constructors of the class.

> **EXAM TIP**   Watch out for a count of the total objects created in any given code—the ones that can be accessed using a variable and the ones that can't be accessed using any variable. The exam may question you on the count of objects created.

In the next section, you'll learn what happens after an object is created.

3.2.2   *Object is accessible*

Once an object is created, it can be accessed using its reference variable. It remains accessible until it goes out of scope or its reference variable is explicitly set to `null`. Also, if you reassign another object to an initialized reference variable, the previous object becomes inaccessible. You can access and use an object within other classes and methods.

Take a look at the following definition of the class `Exam`:

```
class Exam {
    String name;
    public void setName(String newName) {
        name = newName;
    }
}
```

The class `ObjectLife1` declares a variable of type `Exam`, creates its object, calls its method, sets it to `null`, and then reinitializes it:

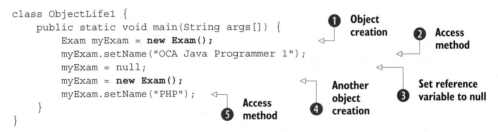

The previous example creates two objects of class `Exam` using the same reference variable `myExam`. Let's walk through what is happening in the example:

- ❶ creates a reference variable `myExam` and initializes it with an object of class `Exam`.
- ❷ calls method `setName` on the object referenced by the variable `myExam`.
- ❸ assigns a value `null` to the reference variable `myExam` such that the object referenced by this variable is no longer accessible.
- ❹ creates a new object of class `Exam` and assigns it to the reference variable `myExam`.
- ❺ calls method `setName`, on the second `Exam` object, created in method `main`.

When ❹ creates another object of class Exam and assigns it to the variable myExam, what happens to the first object created by ❶? Because the first object can no longer be accessed using any variable, it's considered garbage by Java and deemed eligible to be sent to the garbage bin by Java's garbage collector. As mentioned earlier, the garbage collector is a low-priority thread that reclaims the space used by unused or unreferenced objects in Java.

So what happens when an object become inaccessible? You'll find out in the next section.

3.2.3 *Object is inaccessible*

In the previous section, you learned that an object can become inaccessible if it can no longer be referenced by any variable. An object can also become inaccessible if it goes out of scope:

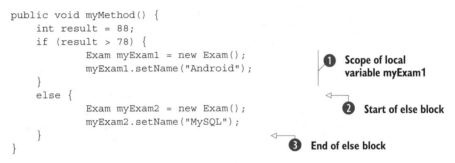

```java
public void myMethod() {
    int result = 88;
    if (result > 78) {
            Exam myExam1 = new Exam();
            myExam1.setName("Android");
    }
    else {
            Exam myExam2 = new Exam();
            myExam2.setName("MySQL");
    }
}
```

❶ Scope of local variable myExam1

❷ Start of else block

❸ End of else block

The variable myExam1 is a local variable defined within the if block. Its scope starts from the line where it is declared until the end of the if block, marked with a closing brace, at ❶. After this closing brace, the object referred by the variable myExam1 is no longer accessible. It goes out of scope and is marked as eligible for garbage collection by Java's garbage collector. Similarly, the object referred to by the variable myExam2 becomes inaccessible at the end of the else block, marked with a closing brace, at ❸.

> **EXAM TIP** An object is marked as eligible to be garbage collected when it can no longer be accessed, which can happen when the object goes out of scope. It can also happen when an object's reference variable is assigned an explicit null value or is reinitialized.

In the OCA Java SE 7 Programmer I exam, you're likely to answer questions on garbage collection for code that has multiple variable declarations and initializations. The exam may query you on the total number of objects that are eligible for garbage collection after a particular line of code.

As previously mentioned, the garbage collector is a low-priority thread that marks the objects eligible for garbage collection in the JVM and then clears the memory of these objects. You can determine only which objects are *eligible* to be garbage collected. You can *never* determine when a particular object *will* be garbage collected. A user can't control or determine the execution of a garbage collector. It's controlled by the JVM.

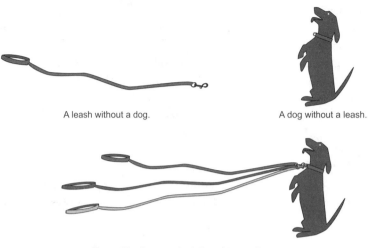

A leash without a dog.   A dog without a leash.

Several leashes may be tethered to one dog.

Figure 3.10   Comparing object reference variables and objects to dog leashes and leashed and unleashed dogs

 EXAM TIP   You can be sure only about which objects are marked for garbage collection. You can never be sure exactly when the object will be garbage collected. Watch for questions with wordings such as "which objects are sure to be collected during the next GC cycle," for which the real answer can never be known.

Let's revisit the dog leash and dog analogy I used in chapter 2 to define object reference variables. In figure 3.10, you can compare an object reference variable with a dog leash and a dog with an object. Review the following comparisons, which will help you to understand the life cycle of an object:

- An uninitialized reference variable can be compared to a dog leash without a dog.
- An initialized reference variable can be compared to a leashed dog.
- An unreferenced object can be compared to an unleashed dog.

You can compare Java's garbage collector to animal control. The way animal control picks up untethered dogs is like how Java's garbage collector reclaims the memory used by unreferenced objects.

Now that you're familiar with an object's life cycle, you can create methods that accept primitive data types and objects as method arguments; these methods return a value, which can be either a primitive data type or an object.

3.3   *Create methods with arguments and return values*

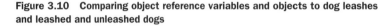 [6.1]   Create methods with arguments and return values

In this section, you'll work with the definitions of methods, which may or may not accept input parameters and may or may not return any values.

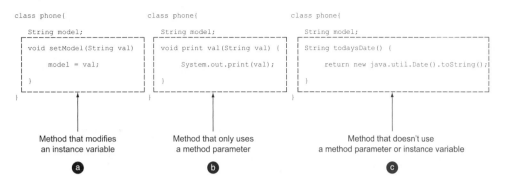

```
class phone{                    class phone{                    class phone{

    String model;                   String model;                   String model;

    void setModel(String val)       void print val(String val) {    String todaysDate() {

        model = val;                    System.out.print(val);          return new java.util.Date().toString();

    }                               }                               }

}                               }                               }
```

Method that modifies   Method that only uses   Method that doesn't use
an instance variable   a method parameter   a method parameter or instance variable

ⓐ   **ⓑ**   **ⓒ**

Figure 3.11   Different types of methods

A method is a group of statements identified with a name. Methods are used to define the behavior of an object. A method can perform different functions, as shown in figure 3.11:

a   The method `setModel` accesses and modifies the state of the object `Phone`.

b   The method `printVal` uses only the method parameter passed to it.

c   The method `todaysDate` accesses another class (`java.util.Date`) from the Java API and returns its `String` presentation.

In the following subsections, you'll learn about the components of a method:

- Return type
- Method parameters
- `return` statement
- Access modifiers (covered in chapter 1)
- Nonaccess modifiers (covered in chapter 1)

Figure 3.12 shows the code of a method accepting method parameters and defining a return type and a `return` statement.

Let's get started with a discussion of the return type of a method.

3.3.1   *Return type of a method*

In this section, you'll work with the return type of a method. The return type of a method states the type of value that a method will return.

A method may or may not return a value. One that doesn't return a value has a return type of `void`. A method can return a primitive value or an object of any class. The name of the return type can be any of the eight primitive types defined in Java, the name of any class, or an interface.

In the following code, the method `setWeight` doesn't return any value, and the method `getWeight` returns a value:

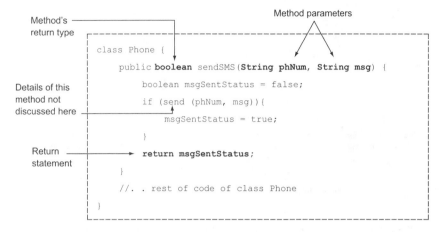

Figure 3.12 An example of a method that accepts method parameters and defines a return type and a `return` statement

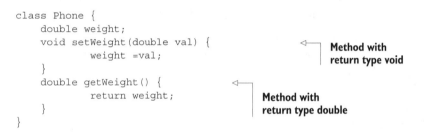

If a method doesn't return a value, you can't assign the result of that method to a variable. What do you think is the output of the following class `EJavaTestMethods`, which uses the previous class `Phone`?

```
class EJavaTestMethods {
    public static void main(String args[]) {
        Phone p = new Phone();
        double newWeight = p.setWeight(20.0);
    }
}
```

Because the method setWeight doesn't return any value, this line won't compile.

The previous code won't compile because the method `setWeight` doesn't return a value. Its return type is `void`. Because the method `setWeight` doesn't return a value, there's nothing to be assigned to the variable `newWeight`, so the code fails to compile.

If a method returns a value, the calling method may or may not bother to store the returned value from a method in a variable. Look at the following code:

```
class EJavaTestMethods2 {
    public static void main(String args[]) {
        Phone p = new Phone();
        p.getWeight();
    }
}
```

Method getWeight returns a double value, but this value isn't assigned to any variable

In the previous example, the value returned by the method `getWeight` isn't assigned to any variable, which isn't an issue for the Java compiler. The compiler will happily compile the code for you.

 EXAM TIP You can optionally assign the value returned by a method to a variable. If you don't assign the returned value from a method, it's neither a compilation error nor a runtime exception.

The variable you use to accept the returned value from a method must be compatible with the returned value. Consider this example:

```
class EJavaTestMethods2 {
    public static void main(String args[]) {
        Phone p = new Phone();
        double newWeight = p.getWeight();       ❶  Will compile
        int newWeight2 = p.getWeight();         ❷  Won't compile
    }
}
```

In the preceding code, ❶ will compile successfully because the return type of the method `getWeight` is `double` and the type of the variable `newWeight` is also `double`. But ❷ won't compile because the `double` value returned from method `getWeight` can't be assigned to variable `newWeight2`, which is of type `int`.

We've discussed how to transfer a value out from a method. To transfer value into a method, you can use method arguments.

3.3.2 *Method parameters*

Method parameters are the variables that appear in the definition of a method and specify the type and number of values that a method can accept. In figure 3.13, the variables `phNum` and `msg` are the method parameters.

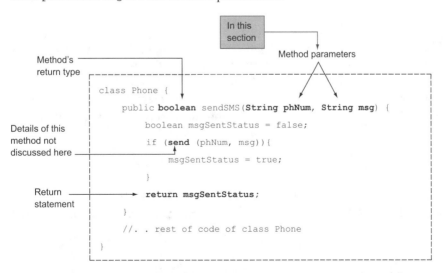

Figure 3.13 An example of a method that accepts method parameters and defines a return type and a `return` statement.

You can pass multiple values to a method as input. Theoretically, no limit exists on the number of method parameters that can be defined by a method, but practically it's not a good idea to define more than five or six method parameters. It's cumbersome to use a method with too many method parameters because you have to cross-check their types and purposes multiple times to ensure that you're passing the right values at the right positions.

> **NOTE** Though the terms *method parameters* and *method arguments* are not the same, you may have noticed that they're used interchangeably by many programmers. *Method parameters* are the variables that appear in the definition of a method. *Method arguments* are the actual values that are passed to a method while executing it. In figure 3.13, variables phNum and msg are method parameters. If you execute this method as sendMsg("123456", "Hello"), then the String values "123456" and "Hello" are method arguments. As you know, you can pass literal values or variables to a method. Thus, method arguments can be literal values or variables.

A method may accept zero or multiple method arguments. The following example accepts two int values and returns their average as a double value:

```
double calcAverage(int marks1, int marks2) {        ◁──┐  Multiple method parameters:
    double avg = 0;                                      marks1 and marks2
    avg = (marks1 + marks2)/2.0;
    return avg;
}
```

The following example shows a method that doesn't accept any method parameters:

```
void printHello() {
    System.out.println("Hello");
}
```

If a method doesn't accept any parameters, the parentheses that follow the name of the method are empty. Because the keyword void is used to specify that a method doesn't return a value, you may think it's correct to use the keyword void to specify that a method doesn't accept any method parameters, but this is incorrect. The following is an invalid definition of a method that accepts no parameters:

```
void printHello(void) {
    System.out.println("Hello");        ◁──┐  Won't compile
}
```

You can define a parameter that can accept variable arguments (varargs) in your methods. Following is an example of class Employee, which defines a method days-OffWork that accepts variable arguments:

```
class Employee {
    public int daysOffWork(int... days) {
        int daysOff = 0;
```

```
            for (int i = 0; i < days.length; i++)
                daysOff += days[i];
            return daysOff;
        }
    }
```

The ellipsis (. . .) that follows the data type indicates that the method parameter days may be passed an array or multiple comma-separated values. Re-examine the preceding code example and note the usage of the variable days in the method daysOff-Work—it works like an array. When you define a variable-length argument for a method, Java creates an array behind the scenes to implement it.

You can define only one variable argument in a parameter list, and it should be the last variable in the parameter list. If you don't comply with these two rules, your code won't compile:

```
class Employee {
    public int daysOffWork(String... months, int... days) {    ◁───  Won't compile.
        int daysOff = 0;                                              You can't define
        for (int i = 0; i < days.length; i++)                        multiple variables
            daysOff += days[i];                                      that can accept
        return daysOff;                                              variable
    }                                                                arguments.
}
```

If your method defines multiple method parameters, the variable that accepts variable arguments must be the last one in the parameter list:

```
class Employee {
    public int daysOffWork(int... days, String year) {    ◁───  Won't compile. If
        int daysOff = 0;                                         multiple parameters
        for (int i = 0; i < days.length; i++)                    are defined, the
            daysOff += days[i];                                  variable argument
        return daysOff;                                          must be the last in
    }                                                            the list.
}
```

 EXAM TIP   In the OCA exam, you may be questioned on the valid return types for a method that doesn't accept any method parameters. Note that there are no valid or invalid combinations of the number and type of method parameters that can be passed to a method and the value that it can return. They're independent of each other.

You can pass any type and number of parameters to a method, including primitives, objects of a class, or objects referenced by an interface.

RULES TO REMEMBER

Points to note with respect to defining method parameters:

- You can define multiple parameters for a method.
- The method parameter can be a primitive type or objects referenced by a class or referenced by an interface.

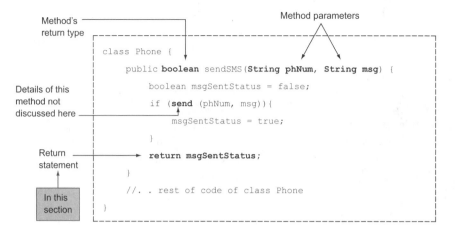

Figure 3.14   An example of a method that accepts method parameters and defines a return type and a `return` **statement**

- The method's parameters are separated by commas.
- Each method parameter is preceded by the name of its type. Each method parameter must have an explicit type declared with its name. You can't declare the type once and then list them separated by commas, as you can for variables.

3.3.3   *Return statement*

A `return` statement is used to exit from a method, with or without a value. For methods that define a return type, the `return` statement must be immediately followed by a return value. For methods that don't return a value, the `return` statement can be used without a return value to exit a method. Figure 3.14 illustrates the use of a `return` statement.

In this example, we'll revisit the previous example of method `calcAverage`, which returns a value of type `double`, using a `return` statement:

```
double calcAverage(int marks1, int marks2) {
    double avg = 0;
    avg = (marks1 + marks2)/2.0;                     return
    return avg;                                       statement
}
```

The methods that don't return a value (return type is `void`) are not required to define a return statement:

```
void setWeight(double val) {           return statement not required for
    weight = val;                      methods with return type void
}
```

But you can use the `return` statement in a method even if it doesn't return a value. Usually this statement is used to define an early exit from a method:

```
void setWeight(double val) {
    if (val < -1) return;
    weight = val;
}
```

This code compiles successfully. Control exits the method if this condition is true.

Method with return type void can use return statement.

Also, the return statement must be the last statement to *execute* in a method, if present. The return statement transfers control out of the method, which means that there's no point in defining any code after it. The compiler will fail to compile such code:

```
void setWeight(double val) {
    return;
    weight = val;
}
```

The return statement must be the last statement to execute in a method

This code can't execute due to the presence of the return statement before it

Note that there's a difference in the return statement being the last statement in a method and being the last statement to execute in a method. The return statement need not be the *last statement* in a method, but it must be the *last statement to execute* in a method:

```
void setWeight(double val) {
    if (val < 0)
        return;                    ← ❶
    else
        weight = val;
}
```

In the preceding example, the return statement ❶ isn't the last statement in this method. But it's the last statement to execute for method parameter values of less than zero.

RULES TO REMEMBER WHEN DEFINING A RETURN STATEMENT
Here are some items to note when defining a return statement:

- For a method that returns a value, the return statement must be followed immediately by a value.
- For a method that doesn't return a value (return type is void), the return statement must *not* be followed by a return value.
- If the compiler determines that a return statement isn't the last statement to *execute* in a method, the method will fail to compile.

RULES TO REMEMBER FOR DEFINING METHODS WITH ARGUMENTS AND RETURN TYPES
The previous list of rules will help you define a return statement in a method. Following is a set of rules to remember for the complete exam objective 6.1, "Create methods with arguments and return values":

- A method may or may not accept method arguments.
- A method may or may not return a value.

- A method returns a value by using the keyword `return`, followed by the name of a variable or an expression whose value is passed back to the calling method.
- The returned value from a method may or may not be assigned to a variable. If the value is assigned to a variable, the variable type must be compatible with the type of the return value.
- A `return` statement must be the last statement in a method. Statements placed after the `return` statements aren't reachable and fail to compile.
- A method can be an instance method (nonstatic) or a class method (static).
- A method can take zero or more parameters but can return only zero or one values.

Do you think we've covered all the rules for defining a method? Not yet! Do you think you can define multiple methods in a class with the same name? You can, but you need to be aware of some additional rules, which are discussed in the next section.

3.4   *Create an overloaded method*

[6.3]   Create an overloaded method

Overloaded methods are methods with the same name but different method parameter lists. In this section, you'll learn how to create and use overloaded methods.

Imagine that you're delivering a lecture and need to instruct the audience to take notes using paper, a smart phone, or a laptop—whichever is available to them for the day. One way to do this is give the audience a list of instructions as follows:

- Take notes using paper.
- Take notes using smartphones.
- Take notes using laptops.

Another method is to instruct them to "take notes" and then provide them with the paper, a smartphone, or a laptop they're supposed to use. Apart from the simplicity of the latter method, it also gives you the flexibility to add other media on which to take notes (such as one's hand, some cloth, or the wall) without needing to remember the list of all the instructions.

This second approach, providing one set of instructions (with the same name) but a different set of input values can be compared to overloaded methods in Java, as shown in figure 3.15.

Again, overloaded methods are methods that are defined in the same class with the same name but with different method argument lists. As shown in figure 3.15, overloaded methods make it easier to add methods with similar functionality that work with different sets of input values.

Let's work with an example from the Java API classes that we all use frequently: `System.out.println()`. The `println` method accepts multiple types of method parameters:

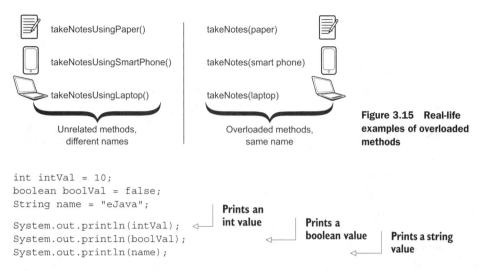

Figure 3.15 Real-life examples of overloaded methods

```
int intVal = 10;
boolean boolVal = false;
String name = "eJava";

System.out.println(intVal);     Prints an
                                int value
System.out.println(boolVal);                Prints a
                                            boolean value    Prints a string
System.out.println(name);                                    value
```

When you use the method `println`, you know that whatever you pass to it as a method argument will be printed to the console. Wouldn't it be crazy to use methods like `printlnInt`, `printlnBool`, and `printlnString` for the same functionality? I think so, too.

RULES TO REMEMBER FOR DEFINING OVERLOADED METHODS

Here are a few rules for defining overloaded methods:

- Overloaded methods must have different method parameters from one another.
- Overloaded methods may or may not define a different return type.
- Overloaded methods may or may not define different access modifiers.
- Overloaded methods can't be defined by only changing their return type or access modifiers.

Next, I'll describe in detail the method parameters that are passed to overloaded methods, their return types, and access modifiers.

3.4.1 Argument list

Overloaded methods accept different lists of arguments. The argument lists can differ in terms of any of the following:

- Change in the number of parameters that are accepted
- Change in the types of parameters that are accepted
- Change in the positions of the parameters that are accepted (based on parameter type, not variable names)

Following is an example of the overloaded method `calcAverage`, which accepts different numbers of method parameters:

```
double calcAverage(int marks1, double marks2) {      Two method
    return (marks1 + marks2)/2.0;                     arguments
}
```

```
double calcAverage(int marks1, int marks2, int marks3) {
    return (marks1 + marks2 + marks3)/3.0;
}
```
Three method arguments

The previous code is an example of the simplest flavor of overloaded methods. You can also define overloaded methods in which the difference in the argument list is in the types of the parameters that are accepted:

```
double calcAverage(int marks1, double marks2) {
    return (marks1 + marks2)/2.0;
}
double calcAverage(char marks1, char marks2) {
    return (marks1 + marks2)/2.0;
}
```
Arguments: int, double

Arguments: char, char

The methods are also correctly overloaded if they change only the positions of the parameters that are passed to them:

```
double calcAverage(double marks1, int marks2) {
    return (marks1 + marks2)/2.0;
}
double calcAverage(int marks1, double marks2) {
    return (marks1 + marks2)/2.0;
}
```
Arguments: double, int

Arguments: int, double

Although you might argue that the arguments being accepted are one and the same, with only their positions differing, the Java compiler treats them as different argument lists. Hence, the previous code is a valid example of overloaded methods.

But an issue arises when you try to execute this method using values that can be passed to both versions of the overloaded methods. In this case, the code will fail to compile:

```
class MyClass {
    double calcAverage(double marks1, int marks2) {
        return (marks1 + marks2)/2.0;
    }
    double calcAverage(int marks1, double marks2) {
        return (marks1 + marks2)/2.0;
    }
    public static void main(String args[]) {
        MyClass myClass = new MyClass();
        myClass.calcAverage(2, 3);
    }
}
```
❶ **Method parameters: double and int**

❷ **Method parameters: int and double**

❸ **Compiler can't determine which overloaded method calcAverage should be called**

In the previous code, ❶ defines the method calcAverage, which accepts two method parameters: a double and an int. ❷ defines the overloaded method calcAverage, which accepts two method parameters: an int and a double. Because an int literal value can be passed to a variable of type double, literal values 2 and 3 can be passed to both the overloaded methods declared at ❶ and ❷. Because this method call is dubious, ❸ fails to compile.

3.4.2 Return type

Methods can't be defined as overloaded methods if they differ only in their return types:

```
double calcAverage(int marks1, int marks2) {
    return (marks1 + marks2)/2.0;
}
int calcAverage(int marks1, int marks2) {
    return (marks1 + marks2)/2.0;
}
```

◁─┤ **Return type of method calcAverage is double**

◁─┐ **Return type is int**

The previous methods can't be termed overloaded methods. If they're defined within the same class, they won't compile. The code also won't compile if one of the methods is defined in a subclass or derived class.

3.4.3 Access modifier

Methods can't be defined as overloaded methods if they only differ in their access modifiers:

```
public double calcAverage(int marks1, int marks2) {
    return (marks1 + marks2)/2.0;
}
private double calcAverage(int marks1, int marks2) {
    return (marks1 + marks2)/2.0;
}
```

◁── **Access—public**

◁── **Access—private**

If you define overloaded calcAverage methods as shown in the preceding code, the code won't compile.

HOW TO REMEMBER THE RULES OF DEFINING OVERLOADED METHODS

An interesting way to remember the preceding rules for overloaded methods is illustrated in figure 3.16 with faces that have varying shapes. These faces also differ in the shapes of their noses and lips, and the number and shapes of their hairs. These faces are like methods and their parts are like the different parts of a method:

- Shape of face (triangle, oval, square) = method name
- Shape of nose = method's return type
- Shape of lips = method's access modifier
- Hair = method parameters

Your task is to encircle all the methods (faces) that you think overload the method (face) in the center. To get you started, I have circled one of the faces.

In the next section, you'll create special methods called constructors, which are used to create objects of a class.

Figure 3.16   An interesting exercise to remember method-overloading rules

3.5   *Constructors of a class*

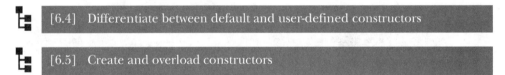

[6.4]   Differentiate between default and user-defined constructors

[6.5]   Create and overload constructors

In this section, you'll create constructors, learn the differences between default and user-defined constructors, and create overloaded constructors.

What happens when you open a new bank account? Depending on the services your bank provides, you may be assigned a new bank account number, provided with a checkbook, and given access to a new online account the bank has created for you. These details are created and returned to you as part of setting up your new bank account.

Compare these steps with what a constructor does in Java, as illustrated in figure 3.17.

Constructors are special methods that create and return an object of the class in which they're defined. Constructors have the same name as the name of the class in which they're defined, and they don't specify a return type—not even `void`.

A constructor can accomplish the following tasks:

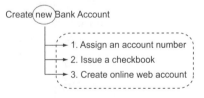

Figure 3.17   The series of steps that may be executed when you create a new bank account. These steps can be compared with what a constructor does in Java.

- Call the base class's constructor; this can be an implicit or explicit call.
- Initialize all of the instance variables of a class with their default values.

Constructors come in two flavors: user-defined constructors and default constructors, which we'll cover in detail in the next sections.

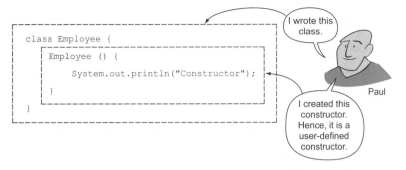

Figure 3.18 A class, `Employee`, with a constructor defined by the user Paul

3.5.1 *User-defined constructors*

The author of a class has full control over the definition of the class. An author may or may not define a constructor in a class. If the author does define a constructor in a class, it's known as a *user-defined constructor*. Here the word "user" doesn't refer to another person or class that uses this class, but instead refers to the person who created the class. It's called "user-defined" because it's not created by the Java compiler.

Figure 3.18 shows a class `Employee` that defines a constructor.

Here is a class, `Office`, which creates an object of class `Employee`:

```
class Office {
    public static void main(String args[]) {
        Employee emp = new Employee();
    }
}
```

❶ **Constructor is called on object creation**

In the previous example, ❶ creates an object of class `Employee` using the keyword `new`, which triggers the execution of the `Employee` class constructor. The output of the class `Office` is as follows:

```
Constructor
```

Because a constructor is called as soon as an object is created, you can use it to assign default values to the instance variable of your class, as follows (modified and additional code is highlighted in bold):

```
class Employee {
    String name;                              Instance variable
    int age;
    Employee() {
            age = 20;                         <--- Initialize age
            System.out.println("Constructor");
    }
}
```

Let's create an object of class `Employee` in class `Office` and see if there's any difference:

```
class Office {
    public static void main(String args[]) {
```

```
                    Employee emp = new Employee();
                    System.out.println(emp.age);              ◁─┤ Access and print the
        }                                                          value of variable age
}
```

The output of the previous code is as follows:

```
Constructor
20
```

Because a constructor is a method, you can also pass method parameters to it, as follows (changes are highlighted in bold):

```
class Employee {
    String name;
    int age;
    Employee(int newAge, String newName) {
            name = newName;
            age = newAge;
            System.out.println("Constructor");
    }
}
```

You can use this constructor in the class `Office` by passing to it the required method arguments, as follows:

```
class Office {
    public static void main(String args[]) {
            Employee emp = new Employee(30, "Pavni Gupta");
    }
}
```

Revisit the use and declaration of the previously mentioned constructors. Note that a constructor is called when you create an object of a class. A constructor does have an implicit return type, which is the class in which it's defined. It creates and returns an object of its class, which is why you can't define a return type for a constructor. Also note that you can define constructors using any of the four access modifiers.

 EXAM TIP You can define a constructor using all four access modifiers: `public`, `protected`, default, and `private`.

What happens if you define a return type for a constructor? Java will treat it as another method, not a constructor, which also implies that it won't be called implicitly when you create an object of its class:

```
class Employee {
    void Employee() {
            System.out.println("Constructor");
    }
}
class Office {                                          ❶ Doesn't call method
    public static void main(String args[]) {                Employee with
            Employee emp = new Employee();          ◁─┤    return type void
    }
}
```

In the previous example, ❶ won't call the method Employee with the return type void defined in the class Employee. Because the method Employee defines its return type as void, it's no longer treated as a constructor.

If the class Employee defines the return type of the method Employee as void, how can Java use it to create an object? The method (with the return type void) is reduced to the state of another method in the class Employee. This logic applies to all of the other data types: if you define the return type of a constructor to be any data type—such as char, int, String, long, double, or any other class—it'll no longer be treated as a constructor.

How do you execute such a method? By calling it explicitly, as in the following code (modified code is in bold):

```
class Employee {
    void Employee() {
            System.out.println("not a Constructor now");
    }
}
class Office {
    public static void main(String args[]) {
            Employee emp = new Employee();
            emp.Employee();
    }
}
```

Prints "not a Constructor now"

Note that the previous method is called like any other method defined in class Employee. It doesn't get called automatically when you create an object of class Employee. As you can see in the previous code, it's perfectly fine to define a method that's not a constructor in a class with the same name. Interesting.

But note that the authors of the OCA exam also found this interesting, and you're likely to get a few tricky questions regarding this concept. Don't worry: with the right information under your belt, you're sure to answer them correctly.

 EXAM TIP A constructor must not define any return type. Instead, it creates and returns an object of the class in which it's defined. If you define a return type for a constructor, it'll no longer be treated as a constructor. Instead, it'll be treated as a regular method, even though it shares the same name as its class.

INITIALIZER BLOCKS VERSUS CONSTRUCTORS

An *initializer block* is defined within a class, not as a part of a method. It executes for every object that's created for a class. In the following example, the class Employee defines an initializer block:

```
class Employee {
    {
        System.out.println("Employee:initializer");
    }
}
```

Initializer block

In the following code, the class `TestEmp` creates an object of class `Employee`:

```
class TestEmp {
    public static void main(String args[]) {
        Employee e = new Employee();
    }
}
```

**Prints
"Employee:initializer"**

If you define both an initializer and a constructor for a class, both of these will execute. The initializer block will execute prior to the constructor:

```
class Employee {
    Employee() {
        System.out.println("Employee:constructor");
    }
    {
        System.out.println("Employee:initializer");
    }
}
class TestEmp {
    public static void main(String args[]) {
        Employee e = new Employee();
    }
}
```

Constructor

Initializer block

**Creates an object of class
Employee; calls both the
initializer block and the
constructor**

The output of the class `TestEmp` is as follows:

```
Employee:initializer
Employee:constructor
```

Do the previous examples leave you wondering why we need both an initializer block and a constructor, if both of these execute upon the creation of an object? Initializer blocks are used to initialize the variables of anonymous classes. An *anonymous class* is a type of inner class. In the absence of a name, anonymous classes can't define a constructor and rely on an initializer block to initialize their variables upon the creation of an object of their class. Because inner classes are not on this exam, I won't discuss how to use an initializer block with an anonymous inner class.

A lot of action can happen within an initializer block: It can create local variables. It can access and assign values to instance and static variables. It can call methods and define loops, conditional statements, and `try-catch-finally` blocks. Unlike constructors, an initializer block can't accept method parameters.

> **NOTE**   Loops and conditional statements are covered in chapter 5, and `try-catch-finally` blocks are covered in chapter 7.

3.5.2   *Default constructor*

In the previous section on user-defined constructors, I discussed how a constructor is used to create an object. What happens if you don't define any constructor in a class?

The following code is an example of the class `Employee` that doesn't define a constructor:

```
class Employee {
    String name;
    int age;
}
```

**No constructor is defined
in class Employee**

You can create objects of this class in another class (`Office`), as follows:

```
class Office {
    public static void main(String args[]) {
        Employee emp = new Employee();
    }
}
```

**Class Employee doesn't
define a constructor,
but this code compiles
successfully**

In this case, which method creates the object of the class `Employee`? Figure 3.19 shows what happens when a class (`Employee`) is compiled that doesn't define any constructor. In the absence of a user-defined constructor, Java inserts a *default constructor*. This constructor doesn't accept any method arguments. It calls the constructor of the super (parent) class and assigns default values to all the instance variables.

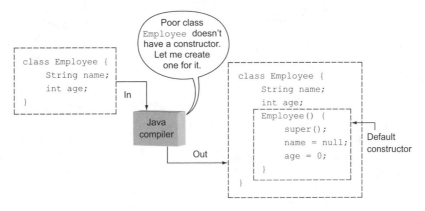

**Figure 3.19   When the Java compiler compiles a class that doesn't define a
constructor, the compiler creates one for it.**

What happens if you add another constructor to the class `Employee`, as in the following example?

```
class Employee {
    String name;
    int age;
    Employee(int newAge, String newName) {
        name = newName;
        age = newAge;
        System.out.println("User defined Constructor");
    }
}
```

**User-defined
constructor**

In this case, upon recompilation, the Java compiler will notice that you've defined a constructor in the class `Employee`. It won't add a default constructor to it, as shown in figure 3.20.

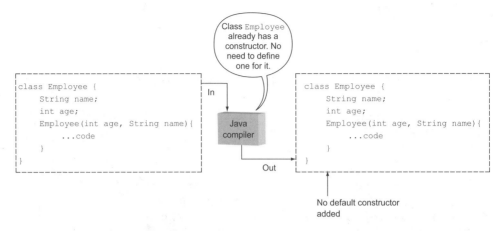

Figure 3.20   When a class with a constructor is compiled, the Java compiler doesn't add a default constructor to it.

In the absence of a no-argument constructor, the following code will fail to compile:

```
class Office {
    public static void main(String args[]) {
        Employee emp = new Employee();          ⟵——— Won't compile
    }
}
```

 EXAM TIP   Java defines a default constructor if and only if you don't define a constructor. If a class doesn't define a constructor, the compiler will add a default, no-argument constructor to the class. But if you modify the class later by adding a constructor to it, the Java compiler will remove the default, no-argument constructor that it initially added to the class.

3.5.3   *Overloaded constructors*

In the same way in which you can overload methods in a class, you can also overload the constructors in a class. *Overloaded constructors* follow the same rules as discussed in the previous section for overloaded methods. Here's a quick recap:

- Overloaded constructors must be defined using different argument lists.
- Overloaded constructors can't be defined by just a change in the access modifiers.

Because constructors don't define a return type, there's no point to defining invalid overloaded constructors with different return types.

The following is an example of an `Employee` class that defines four overloaded constructors:

```
class Employee {
    String name;
    int age;
    Employee() {
        name = "John";
```

① No-argument constructor

```
        age = 25;
    }
    Employee(String newName) {
        name = newName;
        age = 25;
    }
    Employee(int newAge, String newName) {
        name = newName;
        age = newAge;
    }
    Employee(String newName, int newAge) {
        name = newName;
        age = newAge;
    }
}
```

2 **Constructor with one String argument**

3 **Constructor with two arguments—int and String**

4 **Constructor with two arguments—String and int**

In the previous code, **1** defines a constructor that doesn't accept any method arguments. **2** defines another constructor that accepts a single method argument. Note the constructors defined at **3** and **4**. Both of these accept two method arguments, String and int. But the placement of these two method arguments is different in **3** and **4**, which is acceptable and valid for overloaded constructors and methods.

INVOKING AN OVERLOADED CONSTRUCTOR FROM ANOTHER CONSTRUCTOR

It's common to define multiple constructors in a class and reuse their functionality across constructors. Unlike overloaded methods, which can be invoked using the name of a method, overloaded constructors are invoked by using the keyword this— an implicit reference that's accessible to all objects that refer to an object itself:

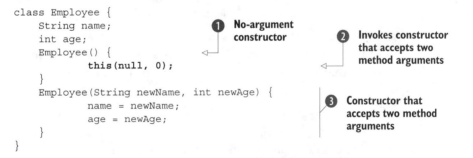

```
class Employee {
    String name;
    int age;
    Employee() {
        this(null, 0);
    }
    Employee(String newName, int newAge) {
        name = newName;
        age = newAge;
    }
}
```

1 **No-argument constructor**

2 **Invokes constructor that accepts two method arguments**

3 **Constructor that accepts two method arguments**

The code at **1** creates a no-argument constructor. At **2**, this constructor calls the overloaded constructor by passing to it values null and 0. **3** defines an overloaded constructor that accepts two method arguments.

Because a constructor is defined using the name of its class, it's a common mistake to try to invoke a constructor from another constructor using the class's name:

```
class Employee {
    String name;
    int age;
    Employee() {
        Employee(null, 0);
    }
}
```

Won't compile—you can't invoke a constructor within a class by using the class's name.

```
Employee(String newName, int newAge) {
        name = newName;
        age = newAge;
    }
}
```

Also, when you invoke an overloaded constructor using the keyword this, it must be the first statement in your constructor:

```
class Employee {
    String name;
    int age;
    Employee() {
            System.out.println("No-argument constructor");  ◁─┐
            this(null, 0);
    }
    Employee(String newName, int newAge) {
            name = newName;
            age = newAge;
    }
}
```

Won't compile— the call to the overloaded constructor must be the first statement in a constructor.

That's not all: you can't call a constructor from any other method in your class. None of the other methods of the class Employee can invoke its constructor.

RULES TO REMEMBER

Here's a quick list of rules to remember for the exam for defining and using overloaded constructors:

- Overloaded constructors must be defined using different argument lists.
- Overloaded constructors can't be defined by just a change in the access modifiers.
- Overloaded constructors may be defined using different access modifiers.
- A constructor can call another overloaded constructor by using the keyword this.
- A constructor can't invoke a constructor by using its class's name.
- If present, the call to another constructor must be the first statement in a constructor.

The next Twist in the Tale exercise hides an important concept within its code, which you can get to know only if you execute the modified code (answer in the appendix).

Twist in the Tale 3.2

Let's modify the definition of the class Employee that I used in the section on overloaded constructors, as follows:

```
class Employee {
    String name;
    int age;
    Employee() {
            this ();
    }
    Employee (String newName, int newAge) {
```

```
                    name = newName;
                    age = newAge;
        }
}
```

What is the output of this modified code, and why?

Now that you've seen how to create methods, constructors, and their overloaded variants, we'll turn to how all of these can be used to access and modify object fields in the next section.

3.6 Accessing object fields

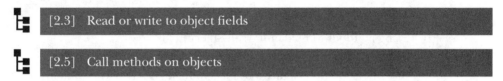

In this section, you'll read, initialize, and modify object fields. You'll also learn the correct notation used to call methods on objects. Access modifiers also determine whether you can call a method on an object.

3.6.1 What is an object field?

An *object field* is another name for an instance variable defined in a class. I've often seen certification aspirants who are confused over whether the object fields are the same as instance variables of a class.

Here's an example of the class `Star`:

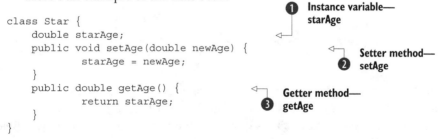

```
class Star {
    double starAge;
    public void setAge(double newAge) {
            starAge = newAge;
    }
    public double getAge() {
            return starAge;
    }
}
```

In the previous example, ❶ defines an instance variable, `starAge`. ❷ defines a *setter* method, `setAge`. A *setter* method is used to set the value of a variable. ❸ defines a *getter* method, `getAge`. A *getter* method is used to retrieve the value of a variable. In this example, the object field is `starAge`, not `age` or `newAge`. The name of an object field is not determined by the name of its *getter* or *setter* methods.

3.6.2 Read and write object fields

The OCA Java SE 7 Programmer I exam will test you on how to read values from and write them to fields of an object, which can be accomplished by any of following:

> **JavaBeans properties and object fields**
>
> The reason for the confusion over the name of the object field is that Java classes can also be used to define visual components called *JavaBeans*, which are used in visual environments. These classes are supposed to define getter and setter methods to retrieve and set the properties of the visual components. If a visual Java-Bean component defines a property such as age, then the name of its getter and setter methods would be getAge and setAge. For a JavaBean, you don't have to worry about the name of the variable that's used to store the value of this property. In a JavaBean, an object field thisIsMyAge can be used to store the value of its *property* age.
>
> Note that the JavaBeans I mentioned aren't Enterprise JavaBeans. Enterprise Java-Beans are used in enterprise applications written in Java, which run on servers.

- Using methods to read and write object fields
- Using constructors to write values to object fields
- Directly accessing instance variables to read and write object fields

This exam objective (2.3) will also test your understanding of how to assign different values to the same object fields for multiple objects. Let's start with an example:

```
class Employee {
    String name;                                    ❶ Object
    int age;                                          fields
    Employee() {
          age = 22;                                 ❷ Assign value
    }                                                  to age
    public void setName(String val) {
          name = val;                               ❸ Assign val
    }                                                  to name
    public void printEmp() {
          System.out.println("name = " + name + " age = " + age);
    }
}
```

In class Employee, ❶ defines two object fields: name and age. It defines a (no-argument) constructor. And ❷ assigns a value of 22 to its field age. This class also defines a method setName where ❸ assigns the value passed to it to the object field name. The method printEmp is used to print the values of object fields name and age.

The following is the definition of a class, Office, which creates two instances, e1 and e2, of the class Employee and assigns values to its fields. Let's look at the output of the class Office:

```
class Office {
    public static void main(String args[]) {
          Employee e1 = new Employee();
          Employee e2 = new Employee();
          e1.name = "Selvan";
          e2.setName("Harry");
```

```
        e1.printEmp();
        e2.printEmp();
    }
}
```

This is the output of the previous code:

```
name = Selvan age = 22
name = Harry age = 22
```

Figure 3.21 defines object diagrams (a diagram with the name and type of an object, the name of the object's fields, and their corresponding values), which will help you to better understand the previous output.

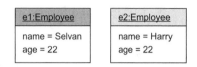

Figure 3.21   Two objects of class `Employee`

You can access the object field name of the object of class `Employee` either by using its variable name or by using the method setName. The following line of code assigns a value Selvan to the field name of object e1:

```
e1.name = "Selvan";
```

The following line of code uses the method setName to assign a value of Harry to the field name of object e2:

```
e2.setName("Harry");
```

Because the constructor of the class `Employee` assigns a value of 22 to the variable age, objects e1 and e2 both contain the same value, 22.

What happens if you don't assign any value to an object field and try to print out its value? All the instance variables (object fields) are assigned their default values if you try to access or read their values before writing any values to them:

```
class Employee {                                    Object field:
    String name;                              ⮜┘    name          Object field:
    int age;                                                      ⮜┘  age
    public void printEmp() {
            System.out.println("name = " + name + " age = " + age);
    }
}
class Office {
    public static void main(String args[]) {
            Employee e1 = new Employee();
            e1.printEmp();
    }
}
```

The output of the previous code is as follows (the default value of an object is null and int is 0):

```
name = null age = 0
```

What happens if you change the access modifier of the variable name to private, as shown here (modified code in bold)?

```
class Employee {
    private String name;              ◁─┤ Object field with
    int age;                             private access
    Employee() {
            age = 22;                 ◁─┤ Assign value
    }                                    to age
    public void setName(String val) {
            name = val;               ◁─┤ Assign val
    }                                    to name
    public void printEmp() {
            System.out.println("name = " + name + " age = " + age);
    }
}
```

Nonprivate object field ┌▷ (points to `int age;`)

You won't be able to set the value of the object field name as follows:

```
e1.name = "Selvan";
```

This line of code won't compile. Instead, it complains that the variable `name` has private access in the class `Employee` and can't be accessed from any other class:

```
Office.java:6:  name has private access in Employee
            e1.name = "Selvan";
```

When you answer questions on reading values from and writing them to an object field, watch out for the following points, which will help you escape traps laid by the authors of the OCA Java SE 7 Programmer I exam:

- Access modifier of the object field
- Access modifiers of methods used to read and write value of the object field
- Constructors that assign values to object fields

3.6.3   *Calling methods on objects*

You can call methods defined in a class using an object reference variable. In this exam objective, the OCA Java SE 7 Programmer I exam will specifically test you on the following:

- The correct notation used to call a method on an object reference variable
- The right number of method parameters that must be passed to a method
- The return value of a method that's assigned to a variable

Java uses the dot notation (`.`) to execute a method on a reference variable. Suppose the class `Employee` is defined as follows:

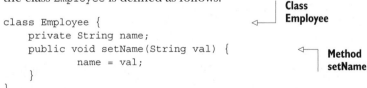

```
class Employee {                         ◁─┤ Class
    private String name;                    Employee
    public void setName(String val) {
            name = val;                  ◁─┐ Method
    }                                       setName
}
```

You can create an object of class `Employee` and call the method `setName` on it like this:

```
Employee e1 = new Employee();
e1.setName("Java");
```

The following method invocations aren't valid in Java:

```
e1->setName("Java");
e1->.setName("Java");          Invalid method
e1-setName("Java");            invocations
```

When you call a method, you must pass to it the exact number of method parameters that are defined by it. In the previous definition of the Employee class, the method set-Name defines a method parameter of type String. You can pass a literal value or a variable to a method, as a method parameter. The following code invocations are correct:

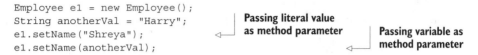

```
Employee e1 = new Employee();
String anotherVal = "Harry";                 Passing literal value
e1.setName("Shreya");                        as method parameter   Passing variable as
e1.setName(anotherVal);                                            method parameter
```

If the parameter list of the called method defines a variable argument at the rightmost position, you can call the method with a variable number of arguments. Let's add a method daysOffWork in the class Employee that accepts a variable list of arguments (modifications in bold):

```
class Employee {
    private String name;
    public void setName(String val) {
            name = val;
    }
    public int daysOffWork(int... days) {
        int daysOff = 0;
        for (int i = 0; i < days.length; i++)
            daysOff += days[i];
        return daysOff;
    }
}
```

You can call this method using a variable list of arguments:

```
Class Test {
    public static void main(String args[]) {          Call method
        Employee e = new Employee();                   daysOffWork with four
        System.out.println(e.daysOffWork(1, 2, 3, 4));  method arguments
        System.out.println(e.daysOffWork(1, 2, 3));
    }
}
```

Call method daysOffWork
with three method
arguments

The output of the previous code is as follows:

```
10
6
```

Let's add a method getName to the class Employee that returns a String value (changes in bold):

```
class Employee {
    private String name;
    public void setName(String val) {
            name = val;
    }
```

```
public String getName() {
        return name;
    }
}
```

You can assign the String value returned from the method getName to a String variable or pass it on to another method, as follows:

```
Employee e1 = new Employee();
Employee e2 = new Employee();
String name = e1.getName();          ◁──┘  Assign method's return
e2.setName(e1.getName());                  value to a variable
                                     ◁──┘  Pass the method's return
                                           value to another method
```

In the previous code, the return type of method setName is void; therefore, you can't use it to assign a value to a variable:

```
Employee e1 = new Employee();              Won't
String name = e1.setName();          ◁──┘  compile
```

Also, you can't assign a return value of a method to an incompatible variable, as follows:

```
Employee e1 = new Employee();              You can't assign the String returned from
int val = e1.getName();              ◁──┘  method getName to an int variable
```

You can read and write object fields either by using methods or by directly accessing the instance variables of a class. But it's not a good idea to enable access to the instance variables outside a class.

In the next section, you'll see the risks of exposing instance variables outside a class and the benefits of a well-encapsulated class.

3.7   *Apply encapsulation principles to a class*

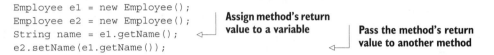

[6.7]   Apply encapsulation principles to a class

As the heading of this section suggests, we'll apply the encapsulation principle to a class. A well-encapsulated object doesn't expose its internal parts to the outside world. It defines a set of methods that enable the users of the class to interact with it.

As an example from the real world, you can compare a bank to a well-encapsulated class. A bank doesn't expose its internal parts—for example, its vaults and bank accounts—to the outside world, just as a well-encapsulated class in Java shouldn't expose the variables that it uses to store the state of an object outside of that object. The way a bank defines a set of procedures (such as key access to vaults and verification before money withdrawals) to protect its internal parts is much like the way a well-encapsulated class defines methods to access its variables.

3.7.1   *Need for encapsulation*

The private members of a class—its variables and methods—are used to hide information about a class. Why would you need to hide information in a class? Compare a class with yourself. Do you want anyone else to know about all of your weaknesses? Do you want anyone else to be able to control your mind? The same applies to a class that you define in Java. A class may need a number of variables and methods to store an object's state and define its behavior. But it wouldn't like all the other classes to know about it.

Let's work with an example to help you get the hang of this concept. Here's the definition of a class Phone:

```java
class Phone {
    String model;
    String company;
    double weight;
    void makeCall(String number) {

    }
    void receiveCall() {

    }
}
```

Instance variables that store the state of an object of Phone

Methods; details not relevant at this point

Because the variable weight isn't defined as a private member, any other class can access it and write any value to it, as follows:

```java
class Home {
    public static void main() {
        Phone ph = new Phone();
        ph.weight = -12.23;
    }
}
```

Assign a negative weight to Phone

3.7.2 *Apply encapsulation*

In the previous section, you might have noticed that the object fields of a class that isn't well encapsulated are exposed outside of the class. This approach enables the users of the class to assign arbitrary values to the object fields.

Should this be allowed? For example, going back to the example of the Phone class discussed in the previous section (3.7.1), how can the weight of a phone be a negative value?

Let's resolve this issue by defining the variable weight as a private variable in class Phone, as follows (irrelevant changes have been omitted):

```java
class Phone {
    private double weight;

}
```

But now this variable won't be accessible in class Home. Let's define methods using this variable, which can be accessible outside the class Phone (changes in bold):

```java
class Phone {
    private double weight;
    public void setWeight(double val) {
        if (val > 0 && val < 1000) {
            weight =val;
        }
    }
}
```

Negative and weight over 1,000 not allowed

```
    public double getWeight() {
            return weight;
    }
}
```

The method `setWeight` doesn't assign the value passed to it as a method parameter to the instance variable `weight` if it's a negative value or a value greater than 1,000. This behavior is known as exposing object functionality using public methods.

Let's see how this method is used to assign a value to the variable `weight` in the class `Home`:

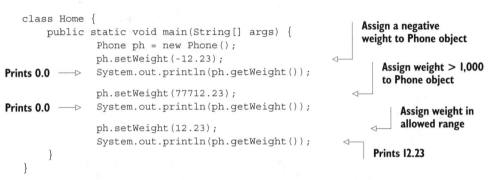

```
class Home {
    public static void main(String[] args) {
            Phone ph = new Phone();
            ph.setWeight(-12.23);
            System.out.println(ph.getWeight());

            ph.setWeight(77712.23);
            System.out.println(ph.getWeight());

            ph.setWeight(12.23);
            System.out.println(ph.getWeight());
    }
}
```

Assign a negative weight to Phone object

Assign weight > 1,000 to Phone object

Assign weight in allowed range

Prints 0.0

Prints 0.0

Prints 12.23

Note that when the class `Home` tries to set the value of the variable to `-12.23` or `77712.23` (out-of-range values), those values aren't assigned to the `Phone`'s private variable `weight`. It accepts the value `12.23`, which is within the defined range.

On the OCA Java SE 7 Programmer I exam, you may also find the term "information hiding." *Encapsulation* is the concept of defining variables and the methods together in a class. *Information hiding* originated from the application and purpose of the concept of encapsulation. These terms are also used interchangeably.

> **EXAM TIP** The terms *encapsulation* and *information hiding* are used interchangeably. By exposing object functionality only through methods, you can prevent your private variables from being assigned any values that don't fit your requirements. One of the best ways to create a well-encapsulated class is to define its instance variables as private variables and allow access to these variables using public methods.

The next Twist in the Tale exercise has a little hidden trick about determining a correctly encapsulated class. Let's see if you can find it (answer in the appendix).

Twist in the Tale 3.3

Let's modify the definition of the class `Phone` that I previously used to demonstrate the encapsulation principle in this section. Given the following definition of class `Phone`, which of the options, when replacing the code on lines 1–3, makes it a well-encapsulated class?

```
class Phone {
    public String model;
    double weight;                                    //LINE1
    public void setWeight(double w) {weight = w;}     //LINE2
    public double getWeight() {return weight;}        //LINE3
}
```

- **a** `public double weight;`
  `private void setWeight(double w) { weight = w; }`
  `private double getWeight() {    return weight; }`
- **b** `public double weight;`
  `void setWeight(double w) { weight = w; }`
  `double getWeight() {    return weight; }`
- **c** `public double weight;`
  `protected void setWeight(double w) { weight = w; }`
  `protected double getWeight() {    return weight; }`
- **d** `public double weight;`
  `public void setWeight(double w) { weight = w; }`
  `public double getWeight() {    return weight; }`
- **e** None of the above.

Well-encapsulated classes don't expose their instance variables outside their class. What happens when the methods of these classes modify the state of the method arguments that are passed to them? Is this acceptable behavior? I'll discuss what happens in the next section.

3.8 *Passing objects and primitives to methods*

> [6.8]   Determine the effect upon object references and primitive values
> when they are passed into methods that change the values

In this section, you'll learn the difference between passing object references and primitives to a method. You'll determine the effect upon object references and primitive values when they're passed into methods that change the values.

Object references and primitives behave in a different manner when they're passed to a method because of the differences in how these two data types are internally stored by Java. Let's start with passing primitives to methods.

3.8.1 *Passing primitives to methods*

The value of a primitive data type is copied and passed on to a method. Hence, the variable whose value was copied doesn't change:

```
class Employee {
    int age;
    void modifyVal(int a) {
        a = a + 1;
        System.out.println(a);
```

 Method modifyVal accepts method argument of type int

```
        }
    }
class Office {
    public static void main(String args[]) {
        Employee e = new Employee();
        System.out.println(e.age);
        e.modifyVal(e.age);
        System.out.println(e.age);
    }
}
```

Prints 0

Prints 0

Calls method
modifyVal on an object
❷ of class Employee

The output of the previous code is as follows:

```
0
1
0
```

The method modifyVal ❶ accepts a method argument a of type int. In this method, the variable a is a method parameter and holds a copy of the value that is passed to it. The method increments the value of the method parameter a and prints its value.

When the class Office calls the method modifyVal ❷, it passes a copy of the value of the object field age to it. The method modifyVal never accesses the object field age. Hence, after the execution of this method, the value of the method field age prints as 0 again.

What happens if the definition of the class Employee is modified as follows (modifications in bold):

```
class Employee {
    int age;
    void modifyVal(int age) {
        age = age + 1;
        System.out.println(age);
    }
}
```

The class Office will still print the same answer because the method modifyVal defines a method parameter with the name age. Note the following important points related to passing a method parameter to a method:

- It's okay to define a method parameter with the same name as an instance variable (or object field).
- Within a method, a method parameter takes precedence over an object field. When the method modifyVal refers to the variable age, it refers to the method parameter age, not the instance variable age. To access the instance variable age within the method modifyVal, the variable name age needs to be prefixed with the keyword this (this is a keyword that refers to the object itself).

The keyword this is discussed in detail in chapter 6.

EXAM TIP When you pass a primitive variable to a method, its value remains the same after the execution of the method. The value doesn't change, regardless of whether the method reassigns the primitive to another variable or modifies it.

3.8.2 Passing object references to methods

There are two main cases:

- When a method reassigns the object reference passed to it to another variable
- When a method modifies the state of the object reference passed to it

WHEN METHODS REASSIGN THE OBJECT REFERENCES PASSED TO THEM

When you pass an object reference to a method, the method can assign it to another variable. In this case, the state of the object, which was passed on to the method, remains intact.

The following code example explains this concept. Suppose you have the following definition of class Person:

```java
class Person {
    private String name;
    Person(String newName) {
        name = newName;
    }
    public String getName() {
        return name;
    }
    public void setName(String val) {
        name = val;
    }
}
```

What do you think is the output of the following code?

```java
class Test {
    public static void swap(Person p1, Person p2) {
        Person temp = p1;
        p1 = p2;
        p2 = temp;
    }
    public static void main(String args[]) {
        Person person1 = new Person("John");
        Person person2 = new Person("Paul");
        System.out.println(person1.getName()
                + ":" + person2.getName());

        swap(person1, person2);

        System.out.println(person1.getName()
                + ":" + person2.getName());
    }
}
```

Method to swap two object references

❶ Creates object

❷ Prints John:Paul before passing objects referred by variable person1 and person2 to method swap

Executes method swap

❸ Prints John:Paul after method swap completes execution

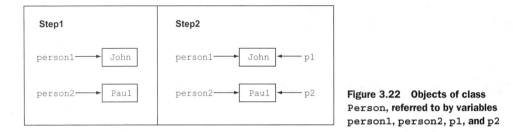

Figure 3.22   Objects of class Person, referred to by variables person1, person2, p1, and p2

In the previous code, ❶ creates two object references, person1 and person2, illustrated in step 1 of figure 3.22. The boxed values represent objects of class Person. ❷ prints John:Paul—the value of person1.name and person2.name.

The code then calls the method swap and passes to it the objects referred to by person1 and person2. When these objects are passed as arguments to the method swap, the method arguments p1 and p2 also refer to these objects. This behavior is illustrated in step 2 in figure 3.22.

The method swap defines three lines of code:

- Person temp = p1; makes temp refer to the object referred to by p1.
- p1 = p2; makes p1 refer to the object referred to by p2.
- p2 = temp; makes p2 refer to the object referred to by temp.

These three steps are represented in figure 3.23.

As you can see in figure 3.23, the reference variables person1 and person2 are still referring to the objects that they passed to the method swap. Because no change was made to the values of the objects referred to by variables person1 and person2, ❸ prints John:Paul again.

The output of the previous code is:

```
John:Paul
John:Paul
```

WHEN METHODS MODIFY THE STATE OF THE OBJECT REFERENCES PASSED TO THEM
Let's see how a method can change the state of an object so that the modified state is accessible in the calling method. Assume the same definition of the class Person, listed again for your convenience:

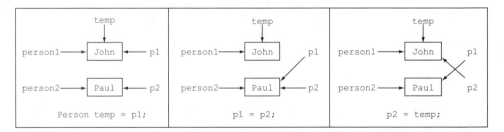

Figure 3.23   The change in the objects referred to by variables during the execution of the method swap

```
class Person {
    private String name;
    Person(String newName) {
            name = newName;
    }
    public String getName() {
            return name;
    }
    public void setName(String val) {
            name = val;
    }
}
```

What's the output of the following code?

```
class Test {
    public static void resetValueOfMemberVariable(Person p1) {
            p1.setName("Rodrigue");
    }
    public static void main(String args[]) {
            Person person1 = new Person("John");

            System.out.println(person1.getName());

            resetValueOfMemberVariable(person1);

            System.out.println(person1.getName());
    }
}
```

Create an object reference person1

Print person1.name before passing it to resetValueOfMemberVariable

Pass person1 to method resetValueOfMemberVariable

Print person1.name after passing it to resetValueOfMemberVariable

The output of the previous code is as follows:

```
John
Rodrigue
```

The method resetValueOfMemberVariable accepts the object referred to by person1 and assigns it to the method parameter p1. Now both the variables person1 and p1 refer to the same object. p1.setName("Rodrigue") modifies the value of the object referred to by variable p1. Because the variable person1 also refers to the same object, person1.getName() returns the new name, Rodrigue, in the method main. This sequence of actions is represented in figure 3.24.

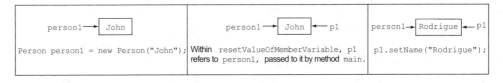

Person person1 = new Person("John"); Within resetValueOfMemberVariable, p1 refers to person1, passed to it by method main. p1.setName("Rodrigue");

Figure 3.24   Modification of the state of an object passed to the method resetValueOfMemberVariable

3.9   *Summary*

I started this chapter by discussing the scope of these variables: local, method parameter, instance, and class. Often these variables' scopes overlap with each other. I also covered the constructors of a class: the user-defined and default constructors. Java inserts a default constructor in a class that doesn't define any constructor. You can modify the source code of such a class, add a constructor, and recompile the class. Upon recompilation, the Java compiler removes the automatically generated constructor.

I then covered the subobjective of reading from and writing to object fields. The terms *object fields* and *instance variables* have the same meaning and are used interchangeably. You can read from and write to object fields by directly accessing them or by using accessor methods. I also showed you how to apply encapsulation principles to a class and explained why doing so is useful.

Finally, I explained the effect upon references and primitives when they're passed into methods that change their values. When you pass a primitive value to a method, its value never changes for the calling method. When you pass an object reference variable to a method, a change in its value may be reflected in the calling method—if the called method modifies an object field of the object passed to it. If the called method assigns a new object reference to the method argument before modifying the value of its fields, these changes aren't visible in the calling method.

3.10   *Review notes*

This section lists the main points covered in this chapter.

Scope of variables:

- Variables can have multiple scopes: class, instance, local, and method parameters.
- Local variables are defined within a method. Loop variables are local to the loop within which they're defined.
- The scope of local variables is less than the scope of a method if they're declared in a sub-block (within braces, {}) in a method. This sub-block can be an `if` statement, a `switch` construct, a loop, or a `try-catch` block (discussed in chapter 7).
- Local variables can't be accessed outside the method in which they're defined.
- Instance variables are defined and accessible within an object. They're accessible to all the instance methods of a class.
- Class variables are shared by all of the objects of a class—they can be accessed even if there are no objects of the class.
- Method parameters are used to accept arguments in a method. Their scope is limited to the method where they're defined.
- A method parameter and a local variable can't be defined using the same name.
- Class and instance variables can't be defined using the same name.

- Local and instance variables can be defined using the same name. In a method, if a local variable exists with the same name as an instance variable, the local variable takes precedence.

Object's lifecycle:

- An object's lifecycle starts when it's initialized and lasts until it goes out of scope or is no longer referenced by a variable.
- When an object is alive, it can be referenced by a variable and other classes can use it by calling its methods and accessing its variables.
- Declaring a reference object variable isn't the same as creating an object.
- An object is created using the operator new. Strings have special shorthand built into the compiler. Strings can be created by using double quotes, as in `"Hello"`.
- An object is marked as eligible for garbage collection when it can no longer be accessed.
- An object can become inaccessible if it can no longer be referenced by any variable, which happens when a reference variable is explicitly set to `null` or when it goes out of scope.
- You can be sure only about whether objects are marked for garbage collection. You can never be sure about whether an object has been garbage collected.

Create methods with arguments and return values:

- The return type of a method states the type of value that a method will return.
- You can define multiple method parameters for a method.
- The method parameter can be of a primitive type or objects of a class or interface.
- The method parameters are separated by commas.
- Each method parameter is preceded by the name of its type. You can't define the type of a method once, even when they're of the same type (the way you can when declaring multiple variables of same type).
- You can define only one variable argument in a parameter list, and it should be the final variable in the parameter list. If these two rules aren't followed, your code won't compile.
- For a method that returns a value, the `return` statement must be followed immediately by a value.
- For a method that doesn't return a value (return type is `void`), the `return` statement must not be followed by a return value.
- If there is code that can be executed only after a `return` statement, the class will fail to compile.
- A method can optionally accept method arguments.
- A method may optionally return a value.

- A method returns a value by using the keyword `return` followed by the name of a variable, whose value is passed back to the calling method.
- The returned value from a method may or may not be assigned to a variable. If the value is assigned to a variable, the variable type should be compatible with the type of the return value.
- A `return` statement should be the last statement in a method. Statements placed after the `return` statement aren't accessible and fail to compile.

Create an overloaded method:

- Overloaded methods accept different lists of arguments. The argument lists can differ by
  - Changes in the number of parameters that are accepted
  - Changes in the types of parameters that are accepted
  - Changes in the positions of parameters that are accepted
- Methods can't be defined as overloaded methods if they differ only in their return types or access modifiers.

Constructors of a class:

- Constructors are special methods defined in a class that create and return an object of the class in which they're defined.
- Constructors have the same name as the class, and they don't specify a return type—not even `void`.
- User-defined constructors are defined by the developer.
- Default constructors are defined by Java, but only if the developer doesn't define any constructor in a class.
- You can define a constructor using the four access modifiers: `public`, `protected`, default, and `private`.
- If you define a return type for a constructor, it'll no longer be treated like a constructor. It'll be treated like a regular method, even though it shares the same name as its class.
- An *initializer block* is defined within a class, not as a part of a method. It executes for every object that's created for a class.
- If you define both an initializer and a constructor for a class, both of these will execute. The initializer block will execute prior to the constructor.
- Unlike constructors, an initializer block can't accept method parameters.
- An initializer block can create local variables. It can access and assign values to instance and static variables. It can call methods and define loops, conditional statements, and `try-catch-finally` blocks.

Overloaded constructors:

- A class can also define overloaded constructors.
- Overloaded constructors should be defined using different argument lists.

- Overloaded constructors can't be defined by just a change in the access modifiers.
- Overloaded constructors may be defined using different access modifiers.
- A constructor can call another overloaded constructor by using the keyword this.
- A constructor can't invoke a constructor by using its class's name.
- If present, a call to another constructor should be the first statement in a constructor.

Accessing object fields:

- An object field is another name for an instance variable defined in a class.
- An object field can be read by either directly accessing the variable (if its access modifier permits) or by using a method that returns its value.
- An object field can be written by either directly accessing the variable (if its access modifier permits) or by using constructors and methods that accept a value and assign it to the instance variable.
- You can call methods defined in a class using an object reference variable.
- When calling a method, it must be passed the correct number and type of method arguments.

Applying encapsulation principles to a class:

- A well-encapsulated object doesn't expose the internal parts of an object outside it. It defines a set of well-defined interfaces (methods), which enables the users of the class to interact with it.
- A class that isn't well encapsulated is at risk of being assigned undesired values for its variables by the callers of the class, which can make the state of an object unstable.
- By exposing object functionality only through methods, you can prevent private variables from being assigned values that don't fit your requirements.
- The terms *encapsulation* and *information hiding* are also used interchangeably.
- One of the best ways to define a well-encapsulated class is to define its instance variables as private variables and allow access to these variables using methods.

Passing objects and primitives to methods:

- Objects and primitives behave in different manners when they're passed to a method, because of differences in the way these two data types are internally stored by Java.
- When you pass a primitive variable to a method, its value remains the same after the execution of the method. This doesn't change, regardless of whether the method reassigns the primitive to another variable or modifies it.
- When you pass an object to a method, the method can modify the object's state by executing its methods. In this case, the modified state of the object is reflected in the calling method.

3.11 *Sample exam questions*

Q3-1. How can you include encapsulation in your class design?

    a Define instance variables as private members.

    b Define public methods to access and modify the instance variables.

    c Define some of the instance variables as public members.

    d All of the above.

Q3-2. Examine the following code and select the correct option(s):

```
public class Person {
    public int height;
    public void setHeight(int newHeight) {
            if (newHeight <= 300)
                height = newHeight;
    }
}
```

    a The `height` of a `Person` can never be set to more than 300.

    b The previous code is an example of a well-encapsulated class.

    c The class would be better encapsulated if the height validation weren't set to 300.

    d Even though the class isn't well encapsulated, it can be inherited by other classes.

Q3-3. Which of the following methods correctly accepts three whole numbers as method arguments and returns their sum as a decimal number?

    a
```
public void addNumbers(byte arg1, int arg2, int arg3) {
    double sum = arg1 + arg2 + arg3;
}
```

    b
```
public double subtractNumbers(byte arg1, int arg2, int arg3) {
    double sum = arg1 + arg2 + arg3;
    return sum;
}
```

    c
```
public double numbers(long arg1, byte arg2, double arg3) {
    return arg1 + arg2 + arg3;
}
```

    d
```
public float wakaWakaAfrica(long a1, long a2, short a977) {
    double sum = a1 + a2 + a977;
    return (float)sum;
}
```

Q3-4. Which of the following statements are true?

    a If the return type of a method is `int`, the method can return a value of type `byte`.

    b A method may or may not return a value.

    c If the return type of a method is `void`, it can define a `return` statement without a value, as follows:

```
return;
```

   d A method may or may not accept any method arguments.

   e A method must accept at least one method argument or define its return type.

   f A method whose return type is `String` can't return `null`.

Q3-5. Given the following definition of class `Person`,

```
class Person {
    public String name;
    public int height;
}
```

what is the output of the following code?

```
class EJavaGuruPassObjects1 {
    public static void main(String args[]) {
            Person p = new Person();
            p.name = "EJava";

            anotherMethod(p);
            System.out.println(p.name);

            someMethod(p);
            System.out.println(p.name);
    }
    static void someMethod(Person p) {
            p.name = "someMethod";
            System.out.println(p.name);
    }
    static void anotherMethod(Person p) {
            p = new Person();
            p.name = "anotherMethod";
            System.out.println(p.name);
    }
}
```

   a anotherMethod
      anotherMethod
      someMethod
      someMethod

   b anotherMethod
      EJava
      someMethod
      someMethod

   c anotherMethod
      EJava
      someMethod
      EJava

   d Compilation error.

Q3-6. What is the output of the following code?

```
class EJavaGuruPassPrim {
    public static void main(String args[]) {
            int ejg = 10;
            anotherMethod(ejg);
            System.out.println(ejg);
```

```
            someMethod(ejg);
            System.out.println(ejg);
    }
    static void someMethod(int val) {
            ++val;
            System.out.println(val);
    }
    static void anotherMethod(int val) {
            val = 20;
            System.out.println(val);
    }
}
```

    a   20
         10
         11
         11

    b   20
         20
         11
         10

    c   20
         10
         11
         10

    d   Compilation error

Q3-7. Given the following signature of method eJava, choose the options that correctly overload this method:

```
public String eJava(int age, String name, double duration)
```

    a   `private String eJava(int val, String firstName, double dur)`
    b   `public void eJava(int val1, String val2, double val3)`
    c   `String eJava(String name, int age, double duration)`
    d   `float eJava(double name, String age, byte duration)`
    e   `ArrayList<String> eJava()`
    f   `char[] eJava(double numbers)`
    g   `String eJava()`

Q3-8. Given the following code,

```
class Course {
    void enroll(long duration) {
            System.out.println("long");
    }
    void enroll(int duration) {
            System.out.println("int");
    }
    void enroll(String s) {
            System.out.println("String");
    }
```

```
    void enroll(Object o) {
            System.out.println("Object");
    }
}
```

what is the output of the following code?

```
class EJavaGuru {
    public static void main(String args[]) {
            Course course = new Course();
            char c = 10;
            course.enroll(c);
            course.enroll("Object");
    }
}
```

- **a** Compilation error
- **b** Runtime exception
- **c** int
  String
- **d** long
  Object

Q3-9. Examine the following code and select the correct options:

```
class EJava {
    public EJava() {
            this(7);
            System.out.println("public");
    }
    private EJava(int val) {
            this("Sunday");
            System.out.println("private");
    }
    protected EJava(String val) {
            System.out.println("protected");
    }
}
class TestEJava {
    public static void main(String[] args) {
            EJava eJava = new EJava();
    }
}
```

- **a** The class EJava defines three overloaded constructors.
- **b** The class EJava defines two overloaded constructors. The private constructor isn't counted as an overloaded constructor.
- **c** Constructors with different access modifiers can't call each other.
- **d** The code prints the following:

  ```
  protected
  private
  public
  ```

e The code prints the following:

```
public
private
protected
```

Q3-10. Select the incorrect options:

a If a user defines a `private` constructor for a `public` class, Java creates a `public` default constructor for the class.

b A class that gets a default constructor doesn't have overloaded constructors.

c A user can overload the default constructor of a class.

d The following class is eligible for a default constructor:

```
class EJava {}
```

e The following class is also eligible for a default constructor:

```
class EJava {
        void EJava() {}
}
```

3.12   *Answers to sample exam questions*

Q3-1. How can you include encapsulation in your class design?

a **Define instance variables as private members.**

b **Define public methods to access and modify the instance variables.**

c Define some of the instance variables as public members.

d All of the previous.

Answer: a, b

Explanation: A well-encapsulated class should be like a capsule, hiding its instance variables from the outside world. The only way you should access and modify instance variables is through the public methods of a class to ensure that the outside world can access only the variables the class allows it to. By defining methods to assign values to its instance variables, a class can control the range of values that can be assigned to them.

Q3-2. Examine the following code and select the correct option(s):

```
public class Person {
    public int height;
    public void setHeight(int newHeight) {
            if (newHeight <= 300)
                height = newHeight;
    }
}
```

a The `height` of a `Person` can never be set to more than 300.

b The previous code is an example of a well-encapsulated class.

    c The class would be better encapsulated if the height validation weren't set to 300.

    d Even though the class isn't well encapsulated, it can be inherited by other classes.

Answer: d

Explanation: This class isn't well encapsulated because its instance variable `height` is defined as a `public` member. Because the instance variable can be directly accessed by other classes, the variable doesn't always use the method `setHeight` to set its height. The class `Person` can't control the values that can be assigned to its public variable `height`.

Q3-3. Which of the following methods correctly accepts three whole numbers as method arguments and returns their sum as a decimal number?

```
a  public void addNumbers(byte arg1, int arg2, int arg3) {
       double sum = arg1 + arg2 + arg3;
   }

b  public double subtractNumbers(byte arg1, int arg2, int arg3) {
       double sum = arg1 + arg2 + arg3;
       return sum;
   }

c  public double numbers(long arg1, byte arg2, double arg3) {
       return arg1 + arg2 + arg3;
   }

d  public float wakaWakaAfrica(long a1, long a2, short a977) {
       double sum = a1 + a2 + a977;
       return (float)sum;
   }
```

Answer: b, d

Explanation: Option (a) is incorrect. The question specifies the method should return a decimal number (type `double` or `float`), but this method doesn't return any value.

    Option (b) is correct. This method accepts three integer values: `byte`, `int`, and `int`. It computes the sum of these integer values and returns it as a decimal number (data type `double`). Note that the name of the method is `subtractNumbers`, which doesn't make it an invalid option. Practically, one wouldn't name a method `subtract-Numbers` if it's adding them. But syntactically and technically, this option meets the question's requirements and is a correct option.

    Option (c) is incorrect. This method doesn't accept integers as the method arguments. The type of the method argument `arg3` is `double`, which isn't an integer.

    Option (d) is correct. Even though the name of the method seems weird, it accepts the correct argument list (all integers) and returns the result in the correct data type (`float`).

Q3-4. Which of the following statements are true?

    a If the return type of a method is `int`, the method can return a value of type `byte`.

    b A method may or may not return a value.

   c **If the return type of a method is** void, **it can define a return statement without a value, as follows:**

```
return;
```

   d **A method may or may not accept any method arguments.**

   e A method should accept at least one method argument or define its return type.

   f A method whose return type is String can't return null.

Answer: a, b, c, d

Explanation: Option (e) is incorrect. There is no constraint on the number of arguments that can be passed on to a method, regardless of whether the method returns a value.

Option (f) is incorrect. You can't return the value null for methods that return primitive data types. You can return null for methods that return objects (String is a class and not a primitive data type).

Q3-5. Given the following definition of class Person,

```
class Person {
    public String name;
    public int height;
}
```

what is the output of the following code?

```
class EJavaGuruPassObjects1 {
    public static void main(String args[]) {
            Person p = new Person();
            p.name = "EJava";

            anotherMethod(p);
            System.out.println(p.name);

            someMethod(p);
            System.out.println(p.name);
    }
    static void someMethod(Person p) {
            p.name = "someMethod";
            System.out.println(p.name);
    }
    static void anotherMethod(Person p) {
            p = new Person();
            p.name = "anotherMethod";
            System.out.println(p.name);
    }
}
```

   a anotherMethod
      anotherMethod
      someMethod
      someMethod

b `anotherMethod`
  `EJava`
  `someMethod`
  `someMethod`

c `anotherMethod`
  `EJava`
  `someMethod`
  `EJava`

d Compilation error.

Answer: b

Explanation: The class `EJavaGuruPassObject1` defines two methods, `someMethod` and `anotherMethod`. The method `someMethod` modifies the value of the object parameter passed to it. Hence, the changes are visible within this method and in the calling method (method `main`). But the method `anotherMethod` reassigns the reference variable passed to it. Changes to any of the values of this object are limited to this method. They aren't reflected in the calling method (the `main` method).

Q3-6. What is the output of the following code?

```
class EJavaGuruPassPrim {
    public static void main(String args[]) {
            int ejg = 10;
            anotherMethod(ejg);
            System.out.println(ejg);
            someMethod(ejg);
            System.out.println(ejg);
    }
    static void someMethod(int val) {
            ++val;
            System.out.println(val);
    }
    static void anotherMethod(int val) {
            val = 20;
            System.out.println(val);
    }
}
```

  a 20
     10
     11
     11

  b 20
     20
     11
     10

  c **20**
     10
     11
     10

  d Compilation error

Answer: c

Explanation: When primitive data types are passed to a method, the values of the variables in the calling method remain the same. This behavior doesn't depend on whether the primitive values are reassigned other values or modified by addition, subtraction, or multiplication—or any other operation.

Q3-7. Given the following signature of method eJava, choose the options that correctly overload this method:

```
public String eJava(int age, String name, double duration)
```

    a `private String eJava(int val, String firstName, double dur)`
    b `public void eJava(int val1, String val2, double val3)`
    c `String eJava(String name, int age, double duration)`
    d `float eJava(double name, String age, byte duration)`
    e `ArrayList<String> eJava()`
    f `char[] eJava(double numbers)`
    g `String eJava()`

Answer: c, d, e, f, g

Explanation: Option (a) is incorrect. Overloaded methods can change the access modifiers, but changing the access modifier alone won't make it an overloaded method. This option also changes the names of the method parameters, but that doesn't make any difference to a method signature.

Option (b) is incorrect. Overloaded methods can change the return type of the method, but changing the return type won't make it an overloaded method.

Option (c) is correct. Changing the placement of the types of the method parameters overloads it.

Option (d) is correct. Changing the return type of a method and the placement of the types of the method parameters overloads it.

Option (e) is correct. Changing the return type of a method and making a change in the parameter list overload it.

Option (f) is correct. Changing the return type of a method and making a change in the parameter list overload it.

Option (g) is correct. Changing the parameter list also overloads a method.

Q3-8. Given the following code,

```
class Course {
    void enroll(long duration) {
            System.out.println("long");
    }
    void enroll(int duration) {
            System.out.println("int");
    }
    void enroll(String s) {
            System.out.println("String");
```

```
    }
    void enroll(Object o) {
            System.out.println("Object");
    }
}
```

what is the output of the following code?

```
class EJavaGuru {
    public static void main(String args[]) {
            Course course = new Course();
            char c = 10;
            course.enroll(c);
            course.enroll("Object");
    }
}
```

- a Compilation error
- b Runtime exception
- c `int`
  `String`
- d `long`
  `Object`

Answer: c

Explanation: No compilation issues exist with the code. You can overload methods by changing the type of the method arguments in the list. Using method arguments with data types having a base-derived class relationship (`Object` and `String` classes) is acceptable. Using method arguments with data types for which one can be automatically converted to the other (`int` and `long`) is also acceptable.

When the code executes `course.enroll(c)`, char can be passed to two overloaded enroll methods that accept `int` and `long`. The char gets expanded to its nearest type—`int`—so `course.enroll(c)` calls the overloaded method that accepts `int`, printing int. The code `course.enroll("Object")` is passed a `String` value. Although `String` is also an `Object`, this method calls the specific (not general) type of the argument passed to it. So `course.enroll("Object")` calls the overloaded method that accepts `String`, printing `String`.

Q3-9. Examine the following code and select the correct options:

```
class EJava {
    public EJava() {
            this(7);
            System.out.println("public");
    }
    private EJava(int val) {
            this("Sunday");
            System.out.println("private");
    }
```

```
    protected EJava(String val) {
            System.out.println("protected");
    }
}

class TestEJava {
    public static void main(String[] args) {
            EJava eJava = new EJava();
    }
}
```

a   **The class EJava defines three overloaded constructors.**

b   The class `EJava` defines two overloaded constructors. The private constructor isn't counted as an overloaded constructor.

c   Constructors with different access modifiers can't call each other.

d   **The code prints the following:**

```
protected
private
public
```

e   The code prints the following:

```
public
private
protected
```

Answer: a, d

Explanation: You can define overloaded constructors with different access modifiers in the same way that you define overloaded methods with different access modifiers. But a change in only the access modifier can't be used to define overloaded methods or constructors. `private` methods and constructors are also counted as overloaded methods.

The following line of code calls `EJava`'s constructor, which doesn't accept any method argument:

```
EJava eJava = new EJava();
```

The no-argument constructor of this class calls the constructor that accepts an `int` argument, which in turn calls the constructor with the `String` argument. Because the constructor with the `String` constructor doesn't call any other methods, it prints `protected` and returns control to the constructor that accepts an `int` argument. This constructor prints `private` and returns control back to the constructor that doesn't accept any method argument. This constructor prints `public` and returns control to the `main` method.

Q 3-10. Select the incorrect options:

a   **If a user defines a `private` constructor for a `public` class, Java creates a `public` default constructor for the class.**

b   A class that gets a default constructor doesn't have overloaded constructors.

c **A user can overload the default constructor of a class.**

d The following class is eligible for default constructor:

```
class EJava {}
```

e The following class is also eligible for a default constructor:

```
class EJava {
        void EJava() {}
}
```

Answer: a, c

Explanation: Option (a) is incorrect. If a user defines a constructor for a class with any access modifier, it's no longer an eligible candidate to be provided with a default constructor.

Option (b) is correct. A class gets a default constructor only when it doesn't have any constructor. A default or an automatic constructor can't exist with other constructors.

Option (c) is incorrect. A default constructor can't coexist with other constructors. A default constructor is automatically created by the Java compiler if the user doesn't define any constructor in a class. If the user reopens the source code file and adds a constructor to the class, upon recompilation no default constructor will be created for the class.

Option (d) is correct. Because this class doesn't have a constructor, Java will create a default constructor for it.

Option (e) is also correct. This class also doesn't have a constructor, so it's eligible for the creation of a default constructor. The following isn't a constructor because the return type of a constructor isn't void:

```
void EJava() {}
```

It's a regular and valid method, with the name same as its class.

String, StringBuilder, Arrays, and ArrayList

4

Exam objectives covered in this chapter	What you need to know
[2.7] Create and manipulate strings.	How to create `String` objects using the `assignment` and `new` operators. Use of the operators =, +=, !=, and == with `String` objects. Literal value for class `String`. Use of methods from class `String`. Immutable `String` values. All of the `String` methods manipulate and return a new `String` object.
[3.3] Test equality between strings and other objects using == and `equals()`.	How to determine the equality of two `String` objects. Differences between using operator == and method `equals()` to determine equality of `String` objects.
[2.6] Manipulate data using the `StringBuilder` class and its methods.	How to create `StringBuilder` classes and how to use their commonly used methods. Difference between `StringBuilder` and `String` classes. Difference between methods with similar names defined in both of these classes.
[4.1] Declare, instantiate, initialize, and use a one-dimensional array.	How to declare, instantiate, and initialize one-dimensional arrays using single and multiple steps. The do's and don'ts of each of these steps.
[4.2] Declare, instantiate, initialize, and use a multidimensional array.	How to declare, instantiate, and initialize multidimensional arrays using single and multiple steps, with do's and don'ts for each of these steps. Accessing elements in asymmetric multidimensional arrays.

Exam objectives covered in this chapter	What you need to know
[4.3] Declare and use an `ArrayList`.	How to declare, create, and use an `ArrayList`. Advantages of using an `ArrayList` over arrays. Use of methods that add, modify, and delete elements of an `ArrayList`.

In the OCA Java SE 7 Programmer I exam, you'll be asked many questions about how to create, modify, and delete `String` objects, `StringBuilder` objects, arrays, and `ArrayList` objects. To prepare you for such questions, in this chapter I'll provide insight into the variables you'll use to store these objects' values, along with definitions for some of their methods. This information should help you apply all of the methods correctly.

In this chapter, we'll cover the following:

- Creating and manipulating `String` and `StringBuilder` objects
- Using common methods from class `String` and `StringBuilder`
- Creating and using one-dimensional and multidimensional arrays in single and multiple steps
- Accessing elements in asymmetric multidimensional arrays
- Declaring, creating, and using an `ArrayList` and understanding the advantages of an `ArrayList` over arrays
- Using methods that add, modify, and delete elements of an `ArrayList`

4.1   *Welcome to the world of the String class*

 [2.7]   Create and manipulate strings

 [3.3]   Test equality between strings and other objects using == and equals()

In this section, we'll cover the class `String` defined in the Java API in the `java.lang` package. The `String` class represents character strings. We'll create objects of the class `String` and work with its commonly used methods, including `indexOf()`, `substring()`, `replace()`, `charAt()`, and others. You'll also learn how to determine the equality of two `String` objects.

The `String` class is perhaps the most used class in the Java API. You'll find instances of this class being used by every other class in the Java API. How many times do you think you've used the class `String`? Don't answer that question—it's like trying to count your hair.

Although many developers find the `String` class to be one of the simplest to work with, this perception can be deceptive. For example, in the `String` value `"Shreya"`, at which position do you think is r stored—second or third? The correct answer is second because the first letter of a `String` is stored at position 0 and not position 1. You'll learn many other facts about the `String` class in this section.

Let's start by creating new objects of this class.

4.1.1 Creating String objects

You can create objects of the class `String` by using the `new` operator, by using the assignment operator (=), or by enclosing a value within double quotes ("). But you may have noticed a *big* difference in how these objects are created, stored, and referred by Java.

Let's create two `String` objects with the value `"Paul"` using the operator new:

`String str1 = new String("Paul");`
`String str2 = new String("Paul");`
`System.out.println(str1 == str2);`
	Create two String objects by using the operator new	**When comparing the objects referred to by the variables str1 and str2, it prints false.**

Figure 4.1 illustrates the previous code.

```
str1 ─────────────────►  ┌──────┐  ⎫
                          │ Paul │  ⎬  Separate
str2 ─────────────────►  ├──────┤  ⎭  objects
                          │ Paul │
                          └──────┘
```

Figure 4.1 `String` objects created using the operator new always refer to separate objects, even if they store the same sequence of characters.

In the previous code, a comparison of the `String` reference variables `str1` and `str2` prints `false`. The operator `==` compares the addresses of the objects referred to by the variables `str1` and `str2`. Even though these `String` objects store the same sequence of characters, they refer to separate objects that are stored at separate locations.

Let's create two `String` objects with the value `"Harry"` using the assignment operator (=). Figure 4.2 illustrates the variables `str3` and `str4` and the objects referred to by these variables.

`String str3 = "Harry";`
`String str4 = "Harry";`
`System.out.println(str3 == str4);`
	Create two String objects by using assignment operator =	**Prints true because str3 and str4 refer to the same object**

In the previous example, the variables `str1` and `str2` referred to different `String` objects, even if they were created using the same sequence of characters. In the case of variables `str3` and `str4`, the objects are created and stored in a *pool* of `String` objects. Before creating a new object in the pool, Java first searches for an object with similar contents. When the following line of code executes, no `String` object with the value `"Harry"` is found in the pool of `String` objects:

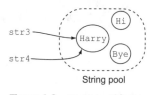

```
String str3 = "Harry";
```

Figure 4.2 `String` objects created using the assignment operator (=) may refer to the same object if they store the same sequence of characters.

As a result, Java creates a `String` object with the value `"Harry"` in the pool of `String` objects referred to by variable `str3`. This action is depicted in figure 4.3.

When the following line of code executes, Java is able to find a `String` object with the value `"Harry"` in the pool of `String` objects:

```
String str4 = "Harry";
```

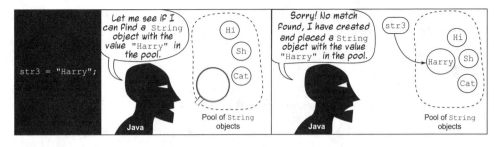

Figure 4.3 The sequence of steps that executes when Java is unable to locate a String in a pool of String objects

Java doesn't create a new String object in this case, and the variable str4 refers to the existing String object "Harry". As shown in figure 4.4, both variables str3 and str4 refer to the same String object in the pool of String objects.

You can also create a String object by enclosing a value within double quotes ("):

```
System.out.println("Morning");
```
⟵ **Creates a new String object with value Morning in the String constant pool**

These values are reused from the String constant pool if a matching value is found. If a matching value isn't found, the JVM creates a String object with the specified value and places it in the String constant pool:

```
String morning1 = "Morning";
System.out.println("Morning" == morning1);
```

Compare the preceding example with the following example, which creates a String object using the operator new and (only) double quotes and then compares their references:

```
String morning2 = new String("Morning");
System.out.println("Morning" == morning2);
```
⟵ **This String object is not placed in the String constant pool**

The preceding code shows that object references of String objects that exist in the String constant pool and object references of String objects that don't exist in

Figure 4.4 The sequence of actions that executes when Java locates a String in the pool of String objects

the String constant pool don't refer to the same String object, even if they define the same String value.

> **NOTE**   The terms "String constant pool" and "String pool" are used inter-changeably and refer to the same pool of String objects. Because String objects are immutable, the pool of String objects is also called the "String *constant* pool." You may see either of these terms on the exam.

You can also invoke other overloaded constructors of class String to create its objects by using the operator new:

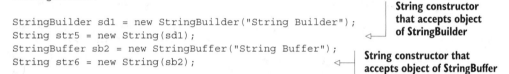

```
String girl = new String("Shreya");
char[] name = new char[]{'P','a','u','l'};
String boy = new String(name);
```

String constructor that accepts a String

String constructor that accepts a char array

You can also create objects of String using the classes StringBuilder and StringBuffer:

```
StringBuilder sd1 = new StringBuilder("String Builder");
String str5 = new String(sd1);
StringBuffer sb2 = new StringBuffer("String Buffer");
String str6 = new String(sb2);
```

String constructor that accepts object of StringBuilder

String constructor that accepts object of StringBuffer

Because String is a class, you can assign null to it, as shown in the next example:

```
String empName = null;
```

null is a literal value for objects

> **EXAM TIP**   The literal value for String is null.

COUNTING STRING OBJECTS

To test your understanding on the various ways in which a String object can be created, the exam may question you on the total number of String objects created in a given piece of code. Count the total number of String objects created in the following code, assuming that the String constant pool doesn't define any matching String values:

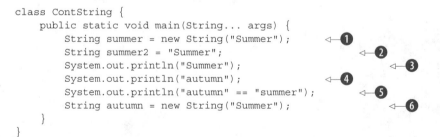

```
class ContString {
    public static void main(String... args) {
        String summer = new String("Summer");          ❶
        String summer2 = "Summer";                      ❷
        System.out.println("Summer");                   ❸
        System.out.println("autumn");                   ❹
        System.out.println("autumn" == "summer");       ❺
        String autumn = new String("Summer");           ❻
    }
}
```

I'll walk through the code with you step by step to calculate the total number of String objects created:

- The code at ❶ creates a new String object with the value "Summer". This object is not placed in the String constant pool.

- The code at ❷ creates a new String object with the value "Summer" and places it in the String constant pool.
- The code at ❸ doesn't need to create any new String object. It reuses the String object with the value "Summer" that already existed in the String constant pool.
- The code at ❹ creates a new String object with the value "autumn" and places it in the String constant pool.
- The code at ❺ reuses the String value "autumn" from the String constant pool. It creates a String object with the value "summer" in the String constant pool (note the difference in the case of letters—Java is case sEnSitIVe and "Summer" is not same as "summer").
- The code at ❻ creates a new String object with the value "Summer".
- The previous code creates a total of five String objects.

EXAM TIP   If a String object is created using the keyword new, it always results in the creation of a new String object. A new String object gets created using the assignment operator (=) or double quotes only if a matching String object with the same value isn't found in the String constant pool.

4.1.2   *The class String is immutable*

The concept that the class String is immutable is an important point to remember. Once created, the contents of an object of the class String can never be modified. The immutability of String objects helps the JVM reuse String objects, reducing memory overhead and increasing performance.

As shown previously in figure 4.4, the JVM creates a pool of String objects that can be referenced by multiple variables across the JVM. The JVM can make this optimization only because String is immutable. String objects can be shared across multiple reference variables without any fear of changes in their values. If the reference variables str1 and str2 refer to the same String object value "Java", str1 need not worry for its lifetime that the value "Java" might be changed by variable str2.

Let's take a quick look at how the immutability of class String is implemented by the authors of this class:

- The class String stores its values in a private variable of the type char array (char value[]). Arrays are fixed in size and don't grow once initialized.
- This value variable is marked as final in the class String. Note that final is a nonaccess modifier, and a final variable can be initialized only once.
- None of the methods defined in the class String manipulate the individual elements of the array value.

I'll discuss each of these points in detail in the following sections.

Code from Java API classes

To get a better understanding of how classes `String`, `StringBuilder`, and `Array-List` work, I'll explain the variables used to store these objects' values, along with definitions for some of their methods. My purpose is not to overwhelm you, but to prepare you. The exam won't question you on this subject, but these details will help you retain relevant information for the exam and implement similar requirements in code for practical projects.

The source code of the classes defined in the Java API is shipped with the Java Development Kit (JDK). You can access it by unzipping the folder src from your JDK's installation folder.

The rest of this section discusses how the authors of the Java API have implemented immutability in the class `String`.

STRING USES A CHAR ARRAY TO STORE ITS VALUE

Here's a partial definition of the class `String` from the Java source code file (String.java) that includes the array used to store the characters of a `String` value (the relevant code is in bold):

```
public final class String
    implements java.io.Serializable, Comparable<String>, CharSequence
{
    private final char value[];
```
        | The rest of the code   ◁─┐ The value array is used
        | of the class String   │ for character storage
```
}
```

The arrays are fixed in size—they can't grow once they're initialized.

Let's create a variable `name` of type `String` and see how it's stored internally:

```
String name = "Selvan";
```

Figure 4.5 shows a UML representation (class diagram on the left and object diagram on the right) of the class `String` and its object `name`, with only one relevant variable, `value`, which is an array of the type `char` and is used to store the sequence of characters assigned to a `String`.

As you can see in figure 4.5, the `String` value `Selvan` is stored in an array of type char. In this chapter, I'll cover arrays in detail, as well as how an array stores its first value at position 0.

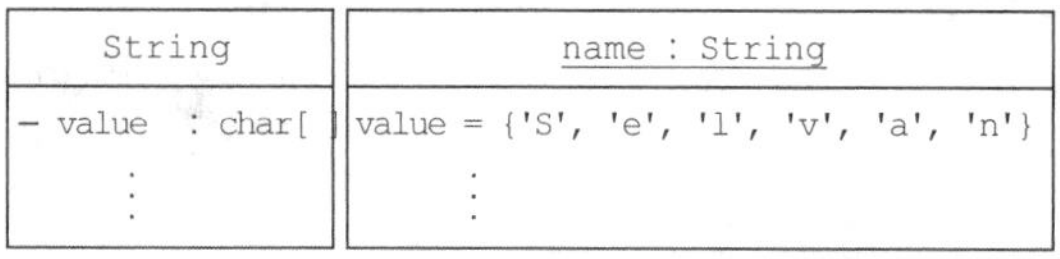

String	name : String
– value : char[	value = {'S', 'e', 'l', 'v', 'a', 'n'}
⋮	⋮

Figure 4.5 UML presentations of the class String and a String object with only one variable

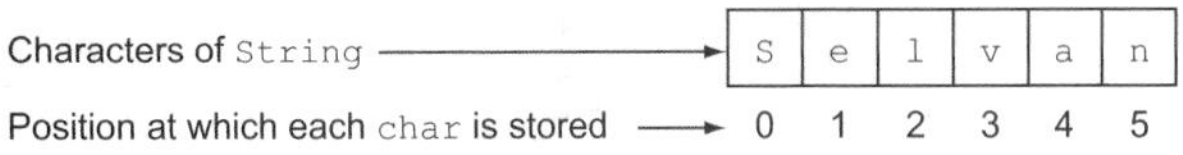

Characters of String ————————▶ | S | e | l | v | a | n |

Position at which each char is stored ——▶ 　0　1　2　3　4　5

Figure 4.6　Mapping characters stored by a String with the positions at which they're stored

Figure 4.6 shows how Selvan is stored as a char array.

What do you think you'll get when you request that this String return the character at position 4? If you said a and not v, you got the right answer (as in figure 4.6).

STRING USES FINAL VARIABLE TO STORE ITS VALUE

The variable value, which is used to store the value of a String object, is marked as final. Review the following code snippet from the class String.java:

```
private final char value[];
```
◁——| **value is used for character storage**

The basic characteristic of a final variable is that it can initialize a value only once. By marking the variable value as final, the class String makes sure that it can't be reassigned a value.

METHODS OF STRING DON'T MODIFY THE CHAR ARRAY

Although we can't reassign a value to a final char array (as mentioned in the previous section), we can reassign its individual characters. Wow—does this mean that the statement "Strings are immutable" isn't completely true?

No, that statement is still true. The char array used by the class String is marked private, which means that it isn't accessible outside the class for modification. The class String itself doesn't modify the value of this variable, either.

All the methods defined in the class String, such as substring, concat, toLowerCase, toUpperCase, trim, and so on, which *seem* to modify the contents of the String object on which they're called, create and return a new String object, rather than modifying the existing value. Figure 4.7 illustrates the partial definition of String's replace method.

I'll reiterate that the previous code from the class String will help you relate the theory to the code and understand how and why a particular concept works. If you understand a particular concept well in terms of how and why it works, you'll be able to retain that information longer.

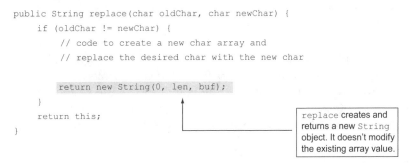

```
public String replace(char oldChar, char newChar) {
    if (oldChar != newChar) {
        // code to create a new char array and
        // replace the desired char with the new char

        return new String(0, len, buf);
    }
    return this;
}
```

replace creates and returns a new String object. It doesn't modify the existing array value.

Figure 4.7　The partial definition of the method replace from the class String shows that this method creates and returns a new String object rather than modifying the value of the String object on which it's called.

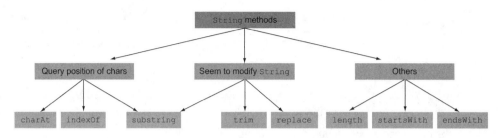

Figure 4.8 Categorization of the String methods

EXAM TIP Strings are immutable. Once initialized, a String value can't be modified. All the String methods that return a modified String value return a new String object with the modified value. The original String value always remains the same.

4.1.3 *Methods of the class String*

Figure 4.8 categorizes the methods that are on the exam into groups: ones that query positions of characters, ones that seem to modify String, and others.

Categorizing the methods in this way will help you better understand these methods. For example, the methods charAt(), indexOf(), and substring() query the position of individual characters in a String. The methods substring(), trim(), and replace() seem to be modifying the value of a String.

CHARAT()

You can use the method charAt(int index) to retrieve a character at a specified index of a String:

```
String name = new String("Paul");                  Prints P
System.out.println(name.charAt(0));        ⟵─┘
System.out.println(name.charAt(2));            ⟵── Prints u
```

Figure 4.9 illustrates the previous string, Paul.

Because the last character is placed at index 3, the following code will throw an exception at runtime:

```
System.out.println(name.charAt(4));
```

NOTE As a quick introduction, a *runtime exception* is a programming error determined by the Java Runtime Environment (JRE) during the execution of code. These errors occur because of the inappropriate use of another piece of code (exceptions are covered in detail in chapter 7). The previous code tries to access a nonexistent index position, so it causes an exception.

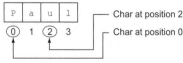

— Char at position 2

— Char at position 0

Figure 4.9 The sequence of characters of "Paul" stored by String and the corresponding array index positions

INDEXOF()

You can search a String for the occurrence of a char or a String. If the specified char or String is found in the target String, this method returns the first matching position; otherwise, it returns -1:

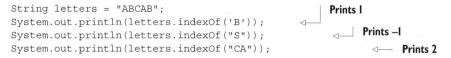

```
String letters = "ABCAB";
System.out.println(letters.indexOf('B'));
System.out.println(letters.indexOf("S"));
System.out.println(letters.indexOf("CA"));
```

Prints I
Prints –I
Prints 2

Figure 4.10 illustrates the previous string ABCAB.

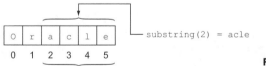

Start position of CA

Start position of B

Figure 4.10 The characters "ABCAB" stored by String

By default, the indexOf() method starts its search from the first char of the target String. If you wish, you can also set the starting position, as in the following example:

```
String letters = "ABCAB";
System.out.println(letters.indexOf('B', 2));
```

Prints 4

SUBSTRING()

The substring() method is shipped in two flavors. The first returns a substring of a String from the position you specify to the end of the String, as in the following example:

```
String exam = "Oracle";
String sub = exam.substring(2);
System.out.println(sub);
```

Prints acle

Figure 4.11 illustrates the previous example.

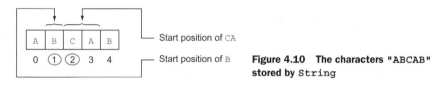

substring(2) = acle

Figure 4.11 The String "Oracle"

You can also specify the end position with this method:

```
String exam = "Oracle";
String result = exam.substring(2, 4);
System.out.println(result);
```

Prints ac

Figure 4.12 illustrates the String value "Oracle", including both a start and end point for the method substring.

An interesting point is that the substring method doesn't include the character at the end position. In the previous example, result is assigned the value ac (characters at positions 2 and 3), not the value acl (characters at positions 2, 3, and 4).

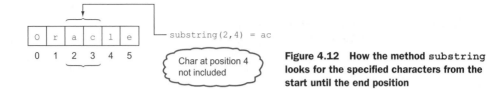

substring(2,4) = ac

0   1   2   3   4   5

Char at position 4
not included

**Figure 4.12   How the method `substring`
looks for the specified characters from the
start until the end position**

EXAM TIP   The `substring` method doesn't include the character at the end position in its return value.

TRIM()

The `trim()` method returns a new `String` by removing all the leading and trailing *white space* in a `String`. White spaces are blanks (new lines, spaces, or tabs).

Let's define and print a `String` with leading and trailing white space. (The colons printed before and after the `String` determine the start and end of the `String`.)

```
String varWithSpaces = " AB CB      ";
System.out.print(":");
System.out.print(varWithSpaces);
System.out.print(":");
```

**String with
white space**

Prints : AB CB   :

Here's another example that trims the leading and trailing white space:

```
System.out.print(":");
System.out.print(varWithSpaces.trim());
System.out.print(":");
```

Prints :AB CB:

Note that this method doesn't remove the space *within* a `String`.

REPLACE()

This method will return a new `String` by replacing all the occurrences of a `char` with another `char`. Instead of specifying a `char` to be replaced by another `char`, you can also specify a sequence of characters—a `String` to be replaced by another `String`:

```
String letters = "ABCAB";
System.out.println(letters.replace('B', 'b'));
System.out.println(letters.replace("CA", "12"));
```

Prints AbCAb

Prints AB12B

Notice the type of the method parameters passed on this method: either `char` or `String`. You can't mix these parameter types, as the following code shows:

```
String letters = "ABCAB";
System.out.println(letters.replace('B', "b"));
System.out.println(letters.replace("B", 'b'));
```

Won't compile

Again, notice that this method doesn't—or can't—change the value of the variable `letters`. Examine the following line of code and its output:

```
System.out.println(letters);
```

**Prints ABCAB because previous replace() method
calls don't affect the char[] array within letters**

LENGTH()

You can use the `length()` method to retrieve the length of a `String`. Here's an example showing its use:

```
System.out.println("Shreya".length());        ⟵── Prints 6
```

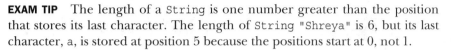 **EXAM TIP** The length of a `String` is one number greater than the position that stores its last character. The length of `String` "Shreya" is 6, but its last character, a, is stored at position 5 because the positions start at 0, not 1.

STARTSWITH() AND ENDSWITH()

The method `startsWith()` determines whether a `String` starts with a specified prefix, specified as a `String`. You can also specify whether you wish to search from the start of a `String` or from a particular position. This method returns `true` if a match is found and `false` otherwise:

```
String letters = "ABCAB";                              ┐  Prints true
System.out.println(letters.startsWith("AB"));    ⟵──┘
System.out.println(letters.startsWith("a"));     ⟵──┐  Prints false
System.out.println(letters.startsWith("A", 3));  ⟵── Prints true
```

The method `endsWith()` tests whether a `String` ends with a particular suffix. It returns `true` for a matching value and `false` otherwise:

```
                                                       ┐  Prints true
System.out.println(letters.endsWith("CAB"));     ⟵──┘
System.out.println(letters.endsWith("B"));       ⟵──┐  Prints true
System.out.println(letters.endsWith("b"));       ⟵── Prints false
```

METHOD CHAINING

It's common practice to use multiple `String` methods in a single line of code, as follows:

```
String result = "Sunday   ".replace(' ', 'Z').trim().concat("M n");
System.out.println(result);                      ⟵──┐ Prints SundayZZM n
```

The methods are evaluated from left to right. The first method to execute in this example is `replace`, not `concat`.

Method chaining is one of the favorite topics of the exam authors. You're sure to encounter a question on method chaining in the OCA Java SE 7 Programmer I exam.

 EXAM TIP When chained, the methods are evaluated from left to right.

Note that there's a difference between calling a chain of methods on a `String` object versus doing the same and then reassigning the return value to the same variable:

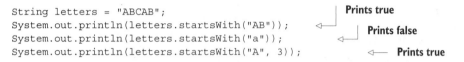

```
String day = "SunDday";                      ┐ Calls methods replace      │ String is immutable—
day.replace('D', 'Z').substring(3);    ⟵──┘ and substring on day.      │ no change in the value
System.out.println(day);                                                 │ variable day. Prints
                                                                         │ SunDday.
```

Prints ZDay. ⤵

```
day = day.replace('D', 'Z').substring(3);  ⟵──┐ Calls methods replace and
System.out.println(day);                       │ substring on day, and assigns
                                               │ the result back to variable day.
```

Because `String` objects are immutable, their values won't change if you execute methods on them. You can, of course, reassign a value to a reference variable of type `String`. Watch out for related questions in the exam.

Although the next Twist in the Tale exercise may seem simple, with only two lines of code, appearances can be deceptive (answers in the appendix).

Twist in the Tale 4.1

Let's modify some of the code used in the previous section. Execute this code on your system. Which answer correctly shows its output?

```
String letters = "ABCAB";
System.out.println(letters.substring(0, 2).startsWith('A'));
```

    a true

    b false

    c AB

    d ABC

    e Compilation error

4.1.4 *String objects and operators*

Of all the operators that are on this exam, you can use just a handful with the `String` objects:

- Concatenation: + and +=
- Equality: == and !=

In this section, we'll cover the concatenation operators. We'll cover the equality operators in the next section (4.1.5).

Concatenation operators (+ and +=) have a special meaning for `Strings`. The Java language has additional functionality defined for these operators for `String`. You can use the operators + and += to concatenate two `String` values. Behind the scenes, string concatenation is implemented by using the `StringBuilder` (covered in the next section) or `StringBuffer` (similar to `StringBuilder`) classes.

But remember that a `String` is immutable. You can't modify the value of any existing object of `String`. The + operator enables you to create a new object of class `String` with a value equal to the concatenated values of multiple `Strings`. Examine the following code:

```
String aString = "OCJA"+"Cert"+"Exam";
```
◁—| **aString contains OCJACertExam**

Here's another example:

```
int num = 10;
int val = 12;
String aStr = "OCJA";
```

```
String anotherStr = num + val + aStr;
System.out.println(anotherStr);
```
◁─┘ **Prints 22OCJA**

Why do you think the value of the variable `anotherStr` is 22OCJA and not 10120CJA? The + operator can be used with the primitive values, and the expression num + val + aStr is evaluated from left to right. Here's the sequence of steps executed by Java to evaluate the expression:

- Adds operands `num` and `val` to get 22.
- Concatenates 22 with OCJA to get 22OCJA.

If you wish to treat the numbers stored in variables `num` and `val` as `String` values, modify the expression as follows:

```
anotherStr = "" + num + val + aStr;
```
│ **Evaluates to**
◁─┘ **I0I2OCJA**

A practical tip on String concatenation

During my preparation for my Java Programmer certification, I learned how the output changes in String concatenation when the order of values being concatenated is changed. At work, it helped me to quickly debug a Java application that was logging incorrect values to a log file. It didn't take me long to discover that the offending line of code was `logToFile("Shipped:" + numReceived() + inTransit());`. The methods were returning correct values individually, but the return values of these methods were not being added. They were being *concatenated* as `String` values, resulting in the unexpected output.

One solution is to enclose the `int` addition within parentheses, as in `logToFile("Shipped:"+ (numReceived() + inTransit()));`. This code will log the text `"Shipped"` with the sum of the numeric values returned by the methods `numReceived()` and `inTransit()`.

When you use `+=` to concatenate `String` values, ensure that the variable you're using has been initialized (and doesn't contain `null`). Look at the following code:

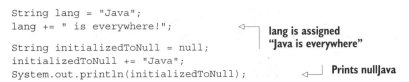

```
String lang = "Java";
lang += " is everywhere!";          ◁─┐  lang is assigned
                                       │  "Java is everywhere"
String initializedToNull = null;
initializedToNull += "Java";
System.out.println(initializedToNull);  ◁─┘ Prints nullJava
```

4.1.5   *Determining equality of Strings*

The correct way to compare two `String` values for equality is to use the `equals` method defined in the `String` class. This method returns a `true` value if the object being compared to it isn't `null`, is a `String` object, and represents the same sequence of characters as the object to which it's being compared.

The following listing shows the method definitions of the `equals` method defined in class `String` in the Java API.

Listing 4.1   Method definition of the `equals` method from the class `String`

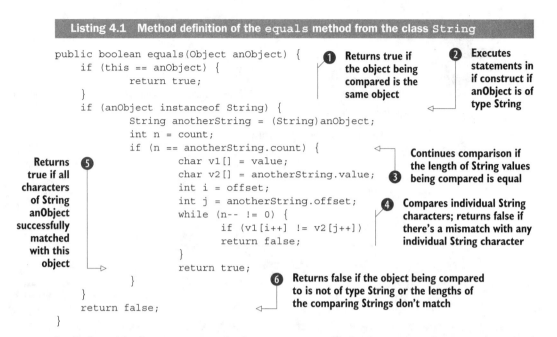

In listing 4.1, the `equals` method accepts a method parameter of type `Object` and returns a `boolean` value. Let's walk through the `equals` method defined by class `String`:

- **❶** compares the object reference variables. If the reference variables are the same, they refer to the same equal object.
- **❷** compares the type of the method parameter to this object. If the method parameter passed to this method is not of type `String`, **❻** returns `false`.
- **❸** checks whether the lengths of the `String` values being compared are equal.
- **❹** compares the individual characters of the `String` values. It returns `false` if a mismatch is found at any position. If no mismatch is found, **❺** returns `true`.

Examine the following code:

```
String var1 = new String("Java");
String var2 = new String("Java");
System.out.println(var1.equals(var2));      Prints true
System.out.println(var1 == var2);           ← Prints false
```

The operator `==` compares the reference variables, that is, whether the variables refer to the same object. Hence, `var1 == var2` in the previous code prints `false`. Now examine the following code:

```
String var3 = "code";
String var4 = "code";
System.out.println(var3.equals(var4));      Prints true
System.out.println(var3 == var4);           ← Prints true
```

Even though comparing `var3` and `var4` using the operator `==` prints `true`, you should *never* use this operator for comparing `String` values. The variables `var3` and `var4` refer to the same `String` object created and shared in the pool of `String` objects. (We discussed the pool of `String` objects in section 4.1.1 earlier in this chapter). This operator won't always return the value `true`, even if the two objects store the same `String` values.

 EXAM TIP The operator `==` compares whether the reference variables refer to the same objects, and the method `equals` compares the `String` values for equality. Always use the `equals` method to compare two `Strings` for equality. Never use the `==` operator for this purpose.

You can use the operator `!=` to compare the inequality of objects referred to by the `String` variables. It's the inverse of the operator `==`. Let's compare the usage of the operator `!=` with the operator `==` and the method `equals()`:

```
String var1 = new String("Java");
String var2 = new String("Java");
System.out.println(var1.equals(var2));
System.out.println(var1 == var2);
System.out.println(var1 != var2);
```

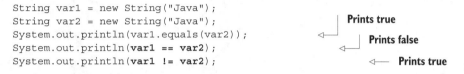

The following example uses the operators `!=` and `==` and the method `equals` to compare `String` variables that refer to the same object in the `String` constant pool:

```
String var3 = "code";
String var4 = "code";
System.out.println(var3.equals(var4));
System.out.println(var3 == var4);
System.out.println(var3 != var4);
```

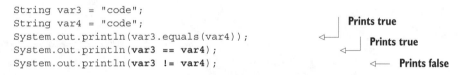

As you can see, in both of the previous examples the operator `!=` returns the inverse of the value returned by the operator `==`.

Because `Strings` are immutable, we also need a mutable sequence of characters that can be manipulated. Let's take a look at the other type of `String` on the OCA Java SE Programmer I exam: `StringBuilder`.

4.2 Mutable strings: StringBuilder

[2.6] Manipulate data using the StringBuilder class and its methods

The class `StringBuilder` is defined in the package `java.lang` and it has a mutable sequence of characters. You must use class `StringBuilder` when you're dealing with larger strings or modifying the contents of a string often. Doing so will improve the performance of your code. Unlike `StringBuilder`, the `String` class has an immutable sequence of characters. Every time you modify a string that's represented by the `String` class, your code actually creates new `String` objects instead of modifying the existing one.

 EXAM TIP You can expect questions on the need for the `StringBuilder` class and its comparison with the `String` class.

Let's work with the methods of the class `StringBuilder`. Because `StringBuilder` represents a mutable sequence of characters, the main operations on `StringBuilder` are related to the modification of its value by adding another value at the end or at a particular position, deletion of characters, or changing characters at a particular position.

4.2.1   *The StringBuilder class is mutable*

In contrast to the class `String`, the class `StringBuilder` uses a non–final `char` array to store its value. Following is a partial definition of the class `AbstractStringBuilder` (the base class of class `StringBuilder`). It includes the declaration of the variables `value` and `count`, which are used to store the value of `StringBuilder` and its `length` respectively (the relevant code is in bold):

```
abstract class AbstractStringBuilder implements Appendable, CharSequence {
    /**
     * The value is used for character storage.
     */
    char value[];

    /**
     * The count is the number of characters used.
     */
    int count;
//.. rest of the code
}
```

This information will come in handy when we discuss the methods of class `String-Builder` in the following sections.

4.2.2   *Creating StringBuilder objects*

You can create objects of class `StringBuilder` using multiple overloaded constructors, as follows:

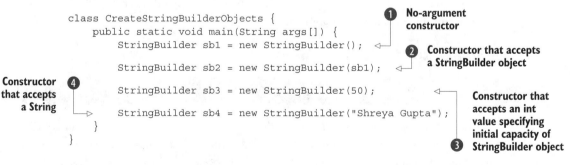

❶ constructs a `StringBuilder` object with no characters in it and an initial capacity of 16 characters. ❷ constructs a `StringBuilder` object that contains the same set of characters as contained by the `StringBuilder` object passed to it. ❸ constructs a `StringBuilder` object with no characters and an initial capacity of 50 characters. ❹ constructs a `StringBuilder` object with an initial value as contained by the `String` object. Figure 4.13 illustrates `StringBuilder` object sb4 with the value `Shreya Gupta`.

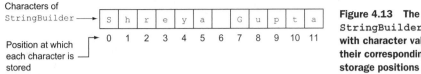

Characters of StringBuilder ⟶

Position at which each character is stored

Figure 4.13 The `StringBuilder` object with character values and their corresponding storage positions

When you create a `StringBuilder` object using its default constructor, the following code executes behind the scenes to initialize the array `value` defined in the class `StringBuilder` itself:

```
StringBuilder() {
    value = new char[16];
}
```
⟵| **Creates an array of length 16**

When you create a `StringBuilder` object by passing it a `String`, the following code executes behind the scenes to initialize the array `value`:

```
public StringBuilder(String str) {
    value = new char[str.length() + 16];
    append(str);
}
```
⟵| **Creates an array of length 16+ str.length**

The creation of objects for the class `StringBuilder` is the basis for the next Twist in the Tale exercise. Your task in this exercise is to look up the Java API documentation or the Java source code to answer the question. You can access the Java API documentation in a couple of ways:

- View it online at http://docs.oracle.com/javase/7/docs/api/.
- Download it to your system from www.oracle.com/technetwork/java/javase/documentation/java-se-7-doc-download-435117.html. Accept the license agreement and click on the link for jdk-7u6-apidocs.zip to download it. (These links may change eventually as Oracle updates its website.)

The answer to the following Twist in the Tale exercise is given in the appendix.

Twist in the Tale 4.2

Take a look at the Java API documentation or the Java source code files and answer the following question:

Which of the following options (there's just one correct answer) correctly creates an object of the class `StringBuilder` with a default capacity of 16 characters?

a `StringBuilder name = StringBuilder.getInstance();`

b `StringBuilder name = StringBuilder.createInstance();`

c `StringBuilder name = StringBuilder.buildInstance();`

d None of the above

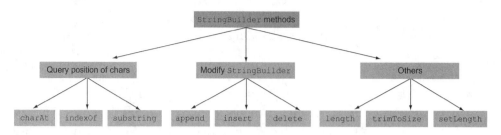

Figure 4.14   Categorization of `StringBuilder` **methods**

4.2.3   *Methods of class StringBuilder*

You'll be pleased to learn that a lot of the methods defined in the class `StringBuilder` work exactly like the versions in the class `String`—for example, methods such as `charAt`, `indexOf`, `substring`, and `length`. We won't discuss these again for the class `StringBuilder`. In this section, we'll discuss the other main methods of the class `String-Builder`: `append`, `insert`, and `delete`.

Figure 4.14 shows the categorization of this class's methods.

APPEND( )

The `append` method adds the specified value at the end of the existing value of a `StringBuilder` object. Because you may want to add data from multiple data types to a `StringBuilder` object, this method has been overloaded so that it can accept data of any type.

This method accepts all the primitives—`String`, char array, and `Object`—as method parameters, as shown in the following example:

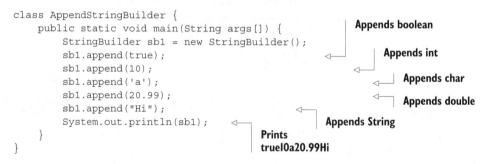

```
class AppendStringBuilder {
    public static void main(String args[]) {
        StringBuilder sb1 = new StringBuilder();
        sb1.append(true);          Appends boolean
        sb1.append(10);            Appends int
        sb1.append('a');           Appends char
        sb1.append(20.99);         Appends double
        sb1.append("Hi");          Appends String
        System.out.println(sb1);   Prints
    }                              true10a20.99Hi
}
```

You can append a complete char array, `StringBuffer`, or `String` or its subset as follows:

```
StringBuilder sb1 = new StringBuilder();
char[] name = {'J', 'a', 'v', 'a', '7'};
sb1.append(name, 1, 3);            Starting with position I
System.out.println(sb1);           append 3 characters,
                                   position I inclusive
                    Prints ava
```

Because the method `append` also accepts a method parameter of type `Object`, you can pass it any object from the Java API or your own user-defined object:

```
class AppendStringBuilder2 {
    public static void main(String args[]) {                    Append String
        StringBuilder sb1 = new StringBuilder();
        sb1.append("Java");
        sb1.append(new Person("Oracle"));                       Append object
                                                                of class Person
        System.out.println(sb1);                       Doesn't print
    }                                                   JavaOracle
}
class Person {
    String name;
    Person(String str) { name = str; }
}
```

The output of the previous code is:

```
JavaPerson@126b249
```

In this output, the hex value (126b249) that follows the @ sign may differ on your system.

When you append an object's value to a StringBuilder, the method append calls the target class's toString method to retrieve the object's String representation. If the toString method has been overridden by the class, then the method append adds the String value returned by it to the target StringBuilder object. In the absence of the overridden toString method, the toString method defined in the class Object executes. The default implementation of the method toString in the class Object returns the name of the class followed by the @ char and unsigned hexadecimal representation of the hash code of the object (the value returned by the object's hashcode method).

 EXAM TIP For classes that haven't overridden the toString method, the append method appends the output from the default implementation of method toString defined in class Object.

It's interesting to take a quick look at how the append method works for the class StringBuilder. Following is a partial code listing of the method append that accepts a boolean parameter (as explained in the comments):

```
public AbstractStringBuilder append(boolean b) {              ❶ Adds 4 (length of "true")
    if (b) {                                                    to count, which holds the
        int newCount = count + 4;                               number of characters in
        if (newCount > value.length)                            the StringBuilder
            expandCapacity(newCount);
        value[count++] = 't';                          ❷ Checks if value array is long
        value[count++] = 'r';                            enough and expands if required
        value[count++] = 'u';
        value[count++] = 'e';                          ❸ Adds the text "true",
    } else {                                             letter by letter
        ...
    }                                    Code to
    return this;                         append false
}
```

❶ and ❷ determine whether the array value can accommodate four additional characters corresponding to the boolean literal value true. It increases the capacity of the array value (used to store the characters of a StringBuilder object) if it isn't big enough. ❸ adds individual characters of the boolean value true to the array value.

INSERT()

The insert method is as powerful as the append method. It also exists in multiple flavors (read: overloaded methods) that accept any data type. The main difference between the append and insert methods is that the insert method enables you to insert the requested data at a particular position, but the append method only allows you to add the requested data at the end of the String-Builder object:

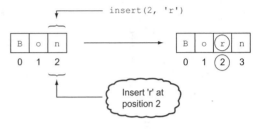

Figure 4.15   Inserting a char using the method insert in StringBuilder

```java
class InsertStringBuilder {
    public static void main(String args[]) {
        StringBuilder sb1 = new StringBuilder("Bon");
        sb1.insert(2, 'r');                          // Inserts r at
                                                     // position 2
        System.out.println(sb1);                     // Prints Born
    }
}
```

Figure 4.15 illustrates the previous code.

As with String objects, the first character of StringBuilder is stored at position 0. Hence, the previous code inserts the letter r at position 2, which is occupied by the letter n. You can also insert a complete char array, StringBuffer, or String or its subset, as follows:

```java
StringBuilder sb1 = new StringBuilder("123");
char[] name = {'J', 'a', 'v', 'a'};
sb1.insert(1, name, 1, 3);                  // Insert at sb1 position 1,
                                            // values ava from String name
System.out.println(sb1);                    // Prints 1ava23
```

Figure 4.16 illustrates the previous code.

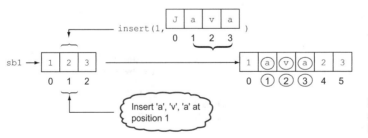

Figure 4.16   Inserting a substring of String in StringBuilder

EXAM TIP Take note of the start and end positions when inserting a value in a `StringBuilder`. Multiple flavors of the `insert` method defined in `String-Builder` may confuse you because they can be used to insert either single or multiple characters.

DELETE() AND DELETECHARAT()

The method `delete` removes the characters in a substring of the specified `String-Builder`. The method `deleteCharAt` removes the char at the specified position. Here's an example showing the method `delete`:

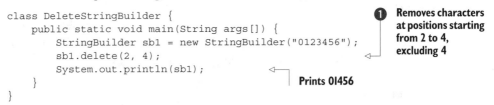

```
class DeleteStringBuilder {
    public static void main(String args[]) {
        StringBuilder sb1 = new StringBuilder("0123456");
        sb1.delete(2, 4);
        System.out.println(sb1);
    }
}
```

❶ Removes characters at positions starting from 2 to 4, excluding 4

Prints 01456

❶ removes characters at positions 2 and 3. The delete method doesn't remove the letter at position 4. Figure 4.17 illustrates the previous code.

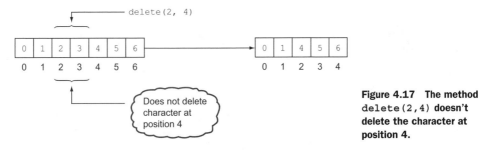

Figure 4.17 The method `delete(2,4)` doesn't delete the character at position 4.

The method `deleteCharAt` is simple. It removes a single character, as follows:

```
class DeleteStringBuilder {
    public static void main(String args[]) {
        StringBuilder sb1 = new StringBuilder("0123456");
        sb1.deleteCharAt(2);
        System.out.println(sb1);
    }
}
```

Deletes character at position 2

Prints 013456

 EXAM TIP Combinations of the `deleteCharAt` and `insert` methods can be quite confusing.

TRIM()

Unlike the class `String`, the class `StringBuilder` doesn't define the method `trim`. An attempt to use it with this class will prevent your code from compiling. The only reason I'm describing a nonexistent method here is to ward off any confusion.

REVERSE()

As the name suggests, the `reverse` method reverses the sequence of characters of a `StringBuilder`:

```
class ReverseStringBuilder {
    public static void main(String args[]) {
        StringBuilder sb1 = new StringBuilder("0123456");
        sb1.reverse();
        System.out.println(sb1);
    }
}
```

Prints
6543210

EXAM TIP   You can't use the method reverse to reverse a substring of StringBuilder.

REPLACE()

Unlike the replace method defined in the class String, the replace method in the class StringBuilder replaces a sequence of characters, identified by their positions, with another String, as in the following example:

```
class ReplaceStringBuilder {
    public static void main(String args[]) {
        StringBuilder sb1 = new StringBuilder("0123456");
        sb1.replace(2, 4, "ABCD");
        System.out.println(sb1);
    }
}
```

Prints
0IABCD456

Figure 4.18 shows a comparison of the replace methods defined in the classes String and StringBuilder.

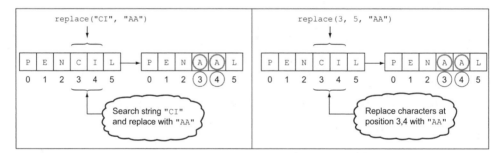

Figure 4.18   Comparing the replace methods in String (left) and StringBuilder (right). The method replace in String accepts the characters to be replaced. The method replace in StringBuilder accepts a position to be replaced.

SUBSEQUENCE()

Apart from using the method substring, you can also use the method subSequence to retrieve a subsequence of a StringBuilder object. This method returns objects of type CharSequence:

```
class SubSequenceStringBuilder {
    public static void main(String args[]) {
        StringBuilder sb1 = new StringBuilder("0123456");
        System.out.println(sb1.subSequence(2, 4));
        System.out.println(sb1);
    }
}
```

Prints 23

Prints 0123456

The method subsequence doesn't modify the existing value of a StringBuilder object.

4.2.4 *A quick note on the class StringBuffer*

Though the OCA Java SE 7 Programmer I exam objectives don't mention the class StringBuffer, you may see it in the list of (incorrect) answers in the OCA exam.

The classes StringBuffer and StringBuilder offer the same functionality, with one difference: the methods of the class StringBuffer are synchronized where necessary, whereas the methods of the class StringBuilder aren't. What does this mean? When you work with the class StringBuffer, only one thread out of multiple threads can execute your method. This arrangement prevents any inconsistencies in the values of the instance variables that are modified by these (synchronized) methods. But it introduces additional overhead, so working with synchronized methods and the StringBuffer class affects the performance of your code.

The class StringBuilder offers the same functionality as offered by StringBuffer, minus the additional feature of synchronized methods. Often your code won't be accessed by multiple threads, so it won't need the overhead of thread synchronization. If you need to access your code from multiple threads, use StringBuffer; otherwise use StringBuilder.

4.3 *Arrays*

> [4.1]   Declare, instantiate, initialize, and use a one-dimensional array

> [4.2]   Declare, instantiate, initialize, and use a multidimensional array

In this section, I'll cover declaration, allocation, and initialization of one-dimensional and multidimensional arrays. You'll learn about the differences between arrays of primitive data types and arrays of objects.

4.3.1 *What is an array?*

An array is an object that stores a collection of values. The fact that an array itself is an object is often overlooked. I'll reiterate: an array is an object itself, which implies that it stores references to the data it stores. Arrays can store two types of data:

- A collection of primitive data types
- A collection of objects

An array of primitives stores a collection of values that constitute the primitive values themselves. (With primitives, there are no objects to reference.) An array of objects stores a collection of values, which are in fact heap-memory addresses or pointers. The addresses point to (reference) the object instances that your array is said to store, which means that object arrays store references (to objects) and primitive arrays store primitive values.

The members of an array are defined in contiguous (continuous) memory locations and hence offer improved access speed. (You should be able to quickly access all the students of a class if they all can be found next to each other.)

The following code creates an array of primitive data and an array of objects:

```
class CreateArray {
    public static void main(String args[]) {

        int intArray[] = new int[] {4, 8, 107};
        String objArray[] = new String[] {"Harry", "Shreya",
                                          "Paul", "Selvan"};

    }
}
```

Array of primitive data

Array of objects

I'll discuss the details of creating arrays shortly. The previous example shows one of the ways to create arrays. Figure 4.19 illustrates the arrays `intArray` and `objArray`. Unlike `intArray`, `objArray` stores references to `String` objects.

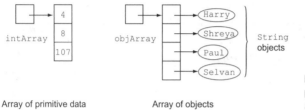

Array of primitive data   Array of objects

Figure 4.19   An array of `int` primitive data type and another of `String` objects

📝 **NOTE**   Arrays are objects and refer to a collection of primitive data types or other objects.

In Java, you can define one-dimensional and multidimensional arrays. A *one-dimensional array* is an object that refers to a collection of scalar values. A two-dimensional (or more) array is referred to as a *multidimensional array*. A two-dimensional array refers to a collection of objects in which each of the objects is a one-dimensional array. Similarly, a three-dimensional array refers to a collection of two-dimensional arrays, and so on. Figure 4.20 depicts a one-dimensional array and multidimensional arrays (two-dimensional and three-dimensional).

Note that multidimensional arrays may or may not contain the same number of elements in each row or column, as shown in the two-dimensional array in figure 4.20.

Creating an array involves three steps, as follows:

- Declaring the array
- Allocating the array
- Initializing the array elements

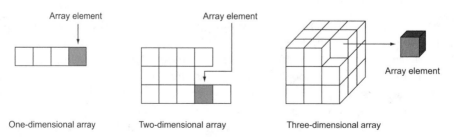

One-dimensional array   Two-dimensional array   Three-dimensional array

Figure 4.20   One-dimensional and multidimensional (two- and three-dimensional) arrays

You can create an array by executing the previous steps using separate lines of code or you can combine these steps on the same line of code. Let's start with the first approach: completing each step on a separate line of code.

4.3.2 *Array declaration*

An array declaration includes the array *type* and array *variable*, as shown in figure 4.21. The type of objects that an array can store depends on its type. An array type is followed by empty pairs of square brackets [].

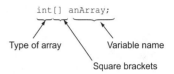

Figure 4.21 Array declaration includes the array type and array variable

To declare an array, specify its type, followed by the name of the array variable. Here's an example of declaring arrays of int and String values:

```
int intArray[];
String[] strArray;
int[] multiArray[];
```

One-dimensional array

Multidimensional array

The number of bracket pairs indicates the depth of array nesting. Java doesn't impose any theoretical limit on the level of array nesting. The square brackets can follow the array type or its name, as shown in figure 4.22.

Figure 4.22 Square brackets can follow either the variable name or its type. In the case of multidimensional arrays, it can follow both of them.

The array declaration only creates a variable that refers to null, as shown in figure 4.23.

Because no elements of an array are created when it's declared, it's invalid to define the size of an array with its declaration. The following code won't compile:

```
int intArray[2];
String[5] strArray;
int[2] multiArray[3];
```

Array size can't be defined with the array declaration. This code won't compile.

An array type can be any of the following:

- Primitive data type
- Interface
- Abstract class
- Concrete class

Figure 4.23 Array declaration creates a variable that refers to null.

We declared an array of an int primitive type and a concrete class String previously. I'll discuss some complex examples with abstract classes and interfaces in section 4.3.7.

 NOTE Arrays can be of any data type other than null.

4.3.3   *Array allocation*

As the name suggests, array allocation will allocate memory for the elements of an array. When you allocate memory for an array, you should specify its dimensions, such as the number of elements the array should store. Note that the size of an array can't expand or reduce once it is allocated. Here are a few examples:

```
int intArray[];
String[] strArray;
int[] multiArr[];
```
Array declaration

```
intArray = new int[2];
strArray = new String[4];
multiArr = new int[2][3];
```
Note use of keyword new to allocate an array

Because an array is an object, it's allocated using the keyword `new`, followed by the type of value that it stores, and then its size. The code won't compile if you don't specify the size of the array or if you place the array size on the left of the = sign, as follows:

```
intArray = new int[];
intArray[2] = new int;
```
Won't compile. Array size missing.

Won't compile. Array size placed incorrectly.

The size of the array should evaluate to an `int` value. You can't create an array with its size specified as a floating-point number. The following line of code won't compile:

```
intArray = new int[2.4];
```
Won't compile. Can't define size of an array as a floating-point number

Java accepts an expression to specify the size of an array, as long as it evaluates to an `int` value. The following are valid array allocations:

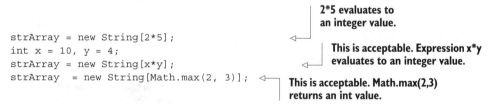

```
strArray = new String[2*5];
int x = 10, y = 4;
strArray = new String[x*y];
strArray  = new String[Math.max(2, 3)];
```
2*5 evaluates to an integer value.

This is acceptable. Expression x*y evaluates to an integer value.

This is acceptable. Math.max(2,3) returns an int value.

Let's allocate the multidimensional array `multiArr`, as follows:

```
int[] multiArr[];
multiArr = new int[2][3];
```
Array declaration

OK to define size in both the square brackets

You can also allocate the multidimensional array `multiArr` by defining size in only the first square bracket:

```
multiArr = new int[2][];
```
OK to define the size in only the first square brackets

It's interesting to note what happens when the multidimensional array `multiArr` is allocated by defining sizes for a single dimension and for both its dimensions. This difference is shown in figure 4.24.

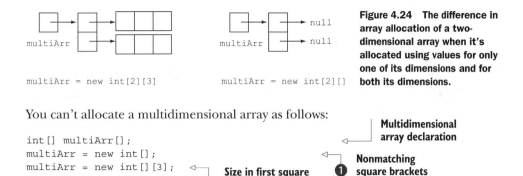

Figure 4.24 The difference in array allocation of a two-dimensional array when it's allocated using values for only one of its dimensions and for both its dimensions.

You can't allocate a multidimensional array as follows:

```
int[] multiArr[];
multiArr = new int[];
multiArr = new int[][3];
```

Multidimensional array declaration

❷ Nonmatching square brackets

❷ Size in first square bracket missing

❶ won't compile because there's a mismatch in the number of square brackets on both sides of the assignment operator (=). The compiler required [] [] on the right side of the assignment operator, but it finds only []. ❷ won't compile because you can't allocate a multidimensional array without including a size in the first square brackets and defining a size in the second square brackets.

Once allocated, the array elements store their default values. For arrays that store objects, all the allocated array's elements store null. For arrays that store primitive values, the default values depend on the exact data types stored by them.

> **EXAM TIP**   Once allocated, all the array elements store their default values. Elements in an array that store objects default to null. Elements of an array that store primitive data types store 0 for integer types (byte, short, int, long), 0.0 for decimal types (float and double), false for boolean, or /u0000 for char data.

4.3.4 *Array initialization*

You can initialize an array as follows:

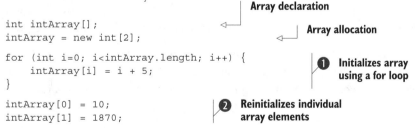

```
int intArray[];
intArray = new int[2];

for (int i=0; i<intArray.length; i++) {
    intArray[i] = i + 5;
}

intArray[0] = 10;
intArray[1] = 1870;
```

Array declaration

Array allocation

❶ Initializes array using a for loop

❷ Reinitializes individual array elements

❶ Uses a for loop to initialize the array intArray with the required values. ❷ initializes the individual array elements without using a for loop. Note that all array objects can access the instance variable length, which stores the array size.

Similarly, a String array can be declared, allocated, and initialized as follows:

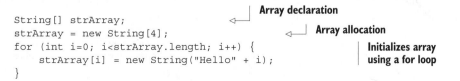

```
String[] strArray;
strArray = new String[4];
for (int i=0; i<strArray.length; i++) {
    strArray[i] = new String("Hello" + i);
}
```

Array declaration

Array allocation

Initializes array using a for loop

```
strArray[1] = "Summer";
strArray[3] = "Winter";                    Initializes array without
strArray[0] = "Autumn";                    using a for loop
strArray[2] = "Spring";
```

When you initialize a two-dimensional array, you can use nested for loops to initialize its array elements. Also notice that to access an element in a two-dimensional array, you should use two array position values, as follows:

```
int[] multiArr[];                                   Array declaration
multiArr = new int[2][3];                                Array allocation

for (int i=0; i<multiArr.length; i++) {
    for (int j=0; j<multiArr[i].length; j++) {
        multiArr[i][j] = i + j;                     Initializes array
    }                                               using a for loop
}

multiArr[0][0] = 10;
multiArr[1][2] = 1210;                              Initializes array without
multiArr[0][1] = 110;                               using a for loop
multiArr[0][2] = 1087;
```

What happens when you try to access a nonexistent array index position? The following code creates an array of size 2 but tries to access its array element at index 3:

```
                                           Length of
int intArray[] = new int[2];               intArray is 2     3 isn't a valid index
System.out.println(intArray[3]);                             position for intArray
```

The previous code will throw a runtime exception, `ArrayIndexOutOfBoundsException`. For an array of size 2, the only valid index positions are 0 and 1. All the rest of the array index positions will throw the exception `ArrayIndexOutOfBoundsException` at runtime.

> **NOTE** Don't worry if you can't immediately absorb all of the information related to exceptions here. Exceptions are covered in detail in chapter 7.

The Java compiler doesn't check the range of the index positions at which you try to access an array element. You may be surprised to learn that the following line of code will compile successfully even though it uses a negative array index value:

```
                                         Length of
int intArray[] = new int[2];             intArray is 2      Will compile successfully even
System.out.println(intArray[-10]);                          though it tries to access array
                                                            element at negative index
```

Though the previous code compiles successfully, it will throw the exception `Array-IndexOutOfBoundsException` at runtime. Code to access an array element will fail to compile if you don't pass it a `char`, `byte`, `short`, or `int` data type (wrapper classes are not on this exam, and I don't include them in this discussion):

```
int intArray[] = new int[2];             Won't compile—can't specify array
System.out.println(intArray[1.2]);       index using floating-point number
```

Also, you can't remove array positions. For an array of objects, you can set a position to value `null`, but it doesn't remove the array position:

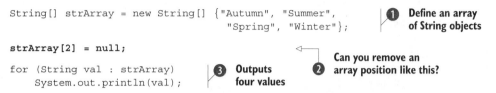

```
String[] strArray = new String[] {"Autumn", "Summer",
                                  "Spring", "Winter"};

strArray[2] = null;

for (String val : strArray)
    System.out.println(val);
```

❶ Define an array of String objects

❷ Can you remove an array position like this?

❸ Outputs four values

❶ creates an array of `String` and initializes it with four `String` values. ❷ sets the value at array index 2 to `null`. ❸ iterates over all the array elements. As shown in the following output, four (not three) values are printed:

```
Autumn
Summer
null
Winter
```

4.3.5 *Combining array declaration, allocation, and initialization*

You can combine all the previously mentioned steps of array declaration, allocation, and initialization into one step, as follows:

```
int intArray[] = {0, 1};
String[] strArray = {"Summer", "Winter"};
int multiArray[][] = { {0, 1}, {3, 4, 5} };
```

Notice that the previous code

- Doesn't use the keyword `new` to initialize an array
- Doesn't specify the size of the array
- Uses a single pair of braces to define values for a one-dimensional array and multiple pairs of braces to define a multidimensional array

All the previous steps of array declaration, allocation, and initialization can be combined in the following way, as well:

```
int intArray2[] = new int[]{0, 1};
String[] strArray2 = new String[]{"Summer", "Winter"};
int multiArray2[][] = new int[][]{ {0, 1}, {3, 4, 5}};
```

Unlike the first approach, the preceding code uses the keyword `new` to initialize an array.

If you try to specify the size of an array with the preceding approach, the code won't compile. Here are a few examples:

```
int intArray2[] = new int[2]{0, 1};
String[] strArray2 = new String[2]{"Summer", "Winter"};
int multiArray2[][] = new int[2][]{ {0, 1}, {3, 4, 5}};
```

EXAM TIP   When you combine an array declaration, allocation, and initialization in a single step, you can't specify the size of the array. The size of the array is calculated by the number of values that are assigned to the array.

Another important point to note is that if you declare and initialize an array using two separate lines of code, you'll use the keyword new to initialize the values. The following lines of code are correct:

```
int intArray[];
intArray = new int[]{0, 1};
```

But you can't miss the keyword new and initialize your array as follows:

```
int intArray[];
intArray = {0, 1};
```

4.3.6   *Asymmetrical multidimensional arrays*

At the beginning of this section, I mentioned that a multidimensional array can be asymmetrical. Arrays can define a different number of columns for each of its rows.

The following example is an asymmetrical two-dimensional array:

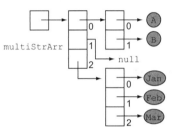

Figure 4.25   An asymmetrical array

```
String multiStrArr[][] = new String[][]{
                          {"A", "B"},
                          null,
                          {"Jan", "Feb", "Mar"},
                     };
```

Figure 4.25 shows this asymmetrical array.

As you might have noticed, multiStrArr[1] refers to a null value. An attempt to access any element of this array, such as multiStrArr[1][0], will throw an exception. This brings us to the next Twist in the Tale exercise (answers are in the appendix).

Twist in the Tale 4.3

Modify some of the code used in the previous example as follows:

```
Line1> String multiStrArr[][] = new String[][]{
Line2>                          {"A", "B"},
Line3>                          null,
Line4>                          {"Jan", "Feb", null},
Line5>                          };
```

Which of the following individual options are true for the previous code?

  a Code on line 4 is the same as {"Jan", "Feb", null, null},

  b No value is stored at multiStrArr[2][2]

  c No value is stored at multiStrArr[1][1]

  d Array multiStrArr is asymmetric.

4.3.7 *Arrays of type interface, abstract class, and class Object*

In the section on array declaration, I mentioned that the type of an array can also be an interface or an abstract class. What values do elements of these arrays store? Let's take a look at some examples.

INTERFACE TYPE

If the type of an array is an interface, its elements are either `null` or objects that implement the relevant interface type. For example, for the interface `MyInterface`, the array `interfaceArray` can store references to objects of either the class `MyClass1` or `MyClass2`:

```
interface MyInterface {}
class MyClass1 implements MyInterface {}
class MyClass2 implements MyInterface {}

class Test {
MyInterface[] interfaceArray = new MyInterface[]
                              {
                                        new MyClass1(),
                                        null,
                                        new MyClass2()
                              };
}
```

ABSTRACT CLASS TYPE

If the type of an array is an `abstract` class, its elements are either `null` or objects of concrete classes that extend the relevant `abstract` class:

```
abstract class Vehicle{}
class Car extends Vehicle {}
class Bus extends Vehicle {}

class Test {
        Vehicle[] vehicleArray = { new Car(),
                                   new Bus(),
                                   null};        ◁── │ null is a valid
                                                       element
}
```

Next, I'll discuss a special case in which the type of an array is `Object`.

OBJECT

Because all classes extend the class `java.lang.Object`, elements of an array whose type is `java.lang.Object` can refer to any object. Here's an example:

```
interface MyInterface {}
class MyClass1 implements MyInterface {}
abstract class Vehicle{}
class Car extends Vehicle {}
class Test {
Object[] objArray = new Object[] {
                        new MyClass1(),
                        null,                   ◁── │ null is a valid
                        new Car(),                    element
                        new java.util.Date(),
```

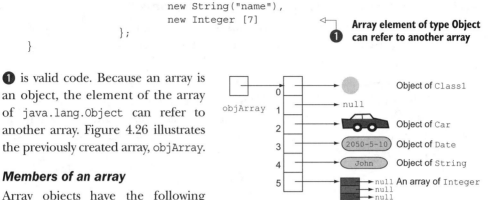

```
                new String("name"),
                new Integer [7]
        };
    }
```

Array element of type Object
❶ **can refer to another array**

❶ is valid code. Because an array is an object, the element of the array of `java.lang.Object` can refer to another array. Figure 4.26 illustrates the previously created array, `objArray`.

4.3.8   *Members of an array*

Array objects have the following public members:

- `length`—The variable `length` contains the number of components of the array.

Figure 4.26   An array of class `Object`

- `clone()`—This method overrides the method `clone` defined in class `Object` but doesn't throw checked exceptions. The return type of this method is the same as the array's type. For example, for an array of type `Type[]`, this method returns `Type[]`.
- *Inherited methods*—Methods inherited from the class `Object`, except the method `clone`.

As mentioned in the earlier section on the `String` class, a `String` uses method `length()` to retrieve its length. With an array, you can use the array's variable `length` to determine the number of the array's elements. In the exam, you may be tricked by code that tries to access the *length* of a `String` using variable `length`. Note the correct combination of class and member used to access its length:

- `String`—Retrieve length using the method `length()`
- *Array*—Determine element count using the variable `length`

I have an interesting way to remember this rule. As opposed to an array, you'll invoke a *lot* of methods on `String` objects. So you use *method* `length()` to retrieve the length of `String` and *variable* `length` to retrieve the length of an array.

4.4   *ArrayList*

[4.3]   Declare and use an ArrayList

In this section, I'll cover how to use `ArrayList`, its commonly used methods, and the advantages it offers over an array.

The OCA Java SE 7 Programmer I exam covers only one class from the Java Collection API: `ArrayList`. The rest of the classes from the Java Collection API are covered in the OCP Java SE 7 Programmer II exam (exam number 1Z0-804). One of the reasons to include this class in the Java Associate exam could be how frequently this class is used by all Java programmers.

ArrayList is one of the most widely used classes from the Collections framework. It offers the best combination of features offered by an *array* and the *List* data structure. The most commonly used operations with a list are: add items to a list, modify items in a list, delete items from a list, and iterate over the items.

One frequently asked question by Java developers is: "Why should I bother with an ArrayList when I can already store objects of the same type in an array?" The answer lies in the ease of use of an ArrayList. This is an important question, and the OCA Java SE 7 Programmer I exam contains explicit questions on the practical reasons for using an ArrayList.

You can compare an ArrayList with a resizable array. As you know, once it's created, you can't increase or decrease the size of an array. On the other hand, an Array-List automatically increases and decreases in size as elements are added to or removed from it. Also, unlike arrays, you don't need to specify an initial size to create an ArrayList.

Let's compare an ArrayList and an array with real-world objects. Just as a balloon can increase and decrease in size when it's inflated or deflated, an ArrayList can increase or decrease in size as values are added to it or removed from it. One comparison is a cricket ball, as it has a predefined size. Once created, like an array, it can't increase or decrease in size.

Here are a few more important properties of an ArrayList:

- It implements the interface List .
- It allows null values to be added to it.
- It implements all list operations (add, modify, and delete values).
- It allows duplicate values to be added to it.
- It maintains its insertion order.
- You can use either Iterator or ListIterator (an implementation of the Iterator interface) to iterate over the items of an ArrayList.
- It supports generics, making it type safe. (You have to declare the type of the elements that should be added to an ArrayList with its declaration.)

4.4.1 Creating an ArrayList

The following example shows you how to create an ArrayList:

```
import java.util.ArrayList;                                    ①  Import
public class CreateArrayList {                                    java.util.ArrayList
    public static void main(String args[]) {
            ArrayList<String> myArrList = new ArrayList<String>();  ←┐
    }
}                                                              Declare an
                                                            ArrayList object ②
```

Package `java.util` isn't implicitly imported into your class, which means that ❶ imports the class `ArrayList` in the class `CreateArrayList` defined previously. To create an `ArrayList`, you need to inform Java about the type of the objects that you want to store in this collection of objects. ❷ declares an `ArrayList` called `myArrList`, which can store `String` objects specified by the name of the class `String` between the angle brackets (`<>`). Note that the name `String` appears twice in the code at ❷, once on the left side of the equal sign and the other on the right. Do you think the second one seems redundant? Congratulations, Oracle agrees with you. Starting with Java version 7, you can omit the object type on the right side of the equal sign and create an `ArrayList` as follows:

```
ArrayList<String> myArrList = new ArrayList<>();
```
⟵ **Missing object type on right of = works in Java version 7 and above**

Many developers still work with Java SE versions prior to version 7, so you're likely to see some developers still using the older way of creating an `ArrayList`.

Take a look at what happens behind the scenes (in the Java source code) when you execute the previous statement to create an `ArrayList`. Because you didn't pass any arguments to the constructor of class `ArrayList`, its no-argument constructor will execute. Examine the definition of the following no-argument constructor defined in class `ArrayList.java`:

```
/**
 * Constructs an empty list with an initial capacity of ten.
 */
public ArrayList() {
    this(10);
}
```

Because you can use an `ArrayList` to store any type of `Object`, `ArrayList` defines an instance variable `elementData` of type `Object` to store all its individual elements. Following is a partial code listing from class `ArrayList`:

```
/**
 * The array buffer into which the elements of the ArrayList are stored.
 * The capacity of the ArrayList is the length of this array buffer.
 */
private transient Object[] elementData;
```

Figure 4.27 illustrates the variable `elementData` shown within an object of `ArrayList`.

Object of `ArrayList`

I am an array and I store data for `ArrayList`

Object [] elementData;

Figure 4.27   Variable `elementData` shown within an object of `ArrayList`

Here is the definition of the constructor from the class `ArrayList` (`ArrayList.java`), which initializes the previously defined instance variable, `elementData`:

```
/**
 * Constructs an empty list with the specified initial capacity.
 *
 * @param   initialCapacity  the initial capacity of the list
 * @exception IllegalArgumentException if the specified initial capacity
 *                 is negative
 */
public ArrayList(int initialCapacity) {
    super();
    if (initialCapacity < 0)
        throw new IllegalArgumentException("Illegal Capacity: "+
                                                    initialCapacity);
    this.elementData = new Object[initialCapacity];
}
```

Wait a minute. Did you notice that an `ArrayList` uses an array to store its individual elements? Does that make you wonder why on earth you would need another class if it uses a type (array, to be precise) that you already know how to work with? The simple answer is that you wouldn't want to reinvent the wheel.

For an example, answer this question: to decode an image, which of the following options would you prefer:

- Creating your own class using characters to decode the image
- Using an existing class that offers the same functionality

Obviously, it makes sense to go with the second option. If you use an existing class that offers the same functionality, you get more benefits with less work. The same logic applies to `ArrayList`. It offers you all of the benefits of using an array, with none of the disadvantages. It offers an expandable array that is modifiable.

> **NOTE** An `ArrayList` uses an array to store its elements. It provides you with the functionality of a dynamic array.

I'll cover how to add, modify, delete, and access the elements of an `ArrayList` in the following sections. Let's start with adding elements to an `ArrayList`.

4.4.2 Adding elements to an ArrayList

Let's start with adding elements to an `ArrayList`, as follows:

```
import java.util.ArrayList;
public class AddToArrayList {
    public static void main(String args[]) {
        ArrayList<String> list = new ArrayList<>();
        list.add("one");
        list.add("two");                                 ❶ Add element
        list.add("four");                                   at the end
        list.add(2, "three");          ❷ Add element at
    }                                     specified position
}
```

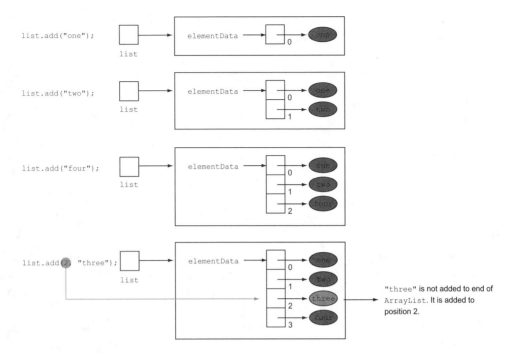

Figure 4.28   Code that adds elements to the end of an `ArrayList` and at a specified position

You can add a value to an `ArrayList` either at its end or at a specified position. ❶ adds elements at the end of `list`. ❷ adds an element to `list` at position 2. Please note that the first element of an `ArrayList` is stored at position 0. Hence, at ❷ the `String` literal value `"three"` will be inserted at position 2, which was occupied by the literal value `"four"`. When a value is added to a place that is already occupied by another element, the values shift by a place to accommodate the newly added value. In this case, the literal value `"four"` shifted to position 3 to make way for the literal value `"three"` (see figure 4.28).

Let's see what happens behind the scenes in an `ArrayList` when you add an element to it. Here's the definition of the method `add` from the class `ArrayList`:

```
/**
 * Appends the specified element to the end of this list.
 *
 * @param e element to be appended to this list
 * @return <tt>true</tt> (as specified by {@link Collection#add})
 */
public boolean add(E e) {
    ensureCapacity(size + 1);      // Create another array with
                                   // the increased capacity
                                   // and copy existing elements to it.
    elementData[size++] = e;       // Store the newly added variable
                                   // reference at the
                                   // end of the list.
```

```
        return true;
    }
```

When you add an element to the end of the list, the `ArrayList` first checks whether its instance variable `elementData` has an empty slot at the end. If there's an empty slot at its end, it stores the element at the first available empty slot. If no empty slots exist, the method `ensureCapacity` creates another array with a higher capacity and copies the existing values to this newly created array. It then copies the newly added value at the first available empty slot in the array.

When you add an element at a particular position, an `ArrayList` creates a new array and inserts all its elements at positions other than the position you specified. If there are any subsequent elements to the right of the position that you specified, it shifts them by one position. Then it adds the new element at the requested position.

PRACTICAL TIP Understanding how and why a class works in a particular manner will take you a long way, in regard to both the certification exam and your career. This understanding should help you retain the information for a longer time and help you answer questions in the certification exam that are looking to verify your practical knowledge of using this class. Last, but not least, the internal workings of a class will enable you to make informed decisions on using a particular class at your workplace and writing efficient code.

4.4.3 *Accessing elements of an ArrayList*

Before we modify or delete the elements of an `ArrayList`, let's see how to access them. To access the elements of an `ArrayList`, you can either use Java's enhanced `for` loop, `Iterator`, or `ListIterator`.

The following code accesses and prints all the elements of an `ArrayList` using the enhanced `for` loop (code to access elements is in bold):

```
import java.util.ArrayList;

public class AccessArrayList {
    public static void main(String args[]) {
        ArrayList<String> myArrList = new ArrayList<>();
        myArrList.add("One");
        myArrList.add("Two");
        myArrList.add("Four");
        myArrList.add(2, "Three");

        for (String element : myArrList) {          ❶ Code to access
            System.out.println(element);               ArrayList elements
        }
    }
}
```

The output of the previous code is as follows:

```
One
Two
Three
Four
```

❶ defines the enhanced for loop to access all the elements of the myArrList.

Let's take a look at how to use a ListIterator to loop through all the values of an ArrayList:

```
import java.util.ArrayList;
import java.util.ListIterator;

public class AccessArrayListUsingListIterator {
    public static void main(String args[]) {
        ArrayList<String> myArrList = new ArrayList<String>();
        myArrList.add("One");
        myArrList.add("Two");
        myArrList.add("Four");
        myArrList.add(2, "Three");
        ListIterator<String> iterator = myArrList.listIterator();
        while (iterator.hasNext()) {
            System.out.println(iterator.next());
        }
    }
}
```

❶ Get the iterator

❷ Use hasNext() to check whether more elements exist

❸ Call next() to get the next item from iterator

❶ gets the iterator associated with ArrayList myArrList. ❷ calls the method hasNext on iterator to check whether more elements of myArrList exist. The method hasNext returns a boolean true value if more of its elements exist, and false otherwise. ❸ calls the method next on iterator to get the next item from myArrList.

The previous code prints out the same results as the code that preceded it, the code that used an enhanced for loop to access ArrayList's elements. A ListIterator doesn't contain any reference to the *current* element of an ArrayList. ListIterator provides you with a method (hasNext) to check whether more elements exist for an ArrayList. If true, you can extract its *next* element using method next().

Note that an ArrayList preserves the insertion order of its elements. ListIterator and the enhanced for loop will return to you the elements in the order in which you added them.

> **EXAM TIP**   An ArrayList preserves the order of insertion of its elements. Iterator, ListIterator, and the enhanced for loop will return the elements in the order in which they were added to the ArrayList. An iterator (Iterator or ListIterator) lets you remove elements as you iterate an ArrayList. It's not possible to remove elements from an ArrayList while iterating it using a for loop.

4.4.4   *Modifying the elements of an ArrayList*

You can modify an ArrayList by either replacing an existing element in ArrayList or modifying all of its existing values. The following code uses the set method to replace an element in an ArrayList:

```
import java.util.ArrayList;

public class ReplaceElementInArrayList {
    public static void main(String args[]) {
        ArrayList<String> myArrList = new ArrayList<String>();
```

```
        myArrList.add("One");
        myArrList.add("Two");
        myArrList.add("Three");
        myArrList.set(1, "One and Half");    ◁──┤ Replace ArrayList element
                                                  at position 1 ("Two") with
        for (String element:myArrList)            "One and Half"
            System.out.println(element);
    }
}
```

The output of the previous code is as follows:

```
One
One and Half
Three
```

You can also modify the existing values of an `ArrayList` by accessing its individual elements. Because `Strings` are immutable, let's try this with `StringBuilder`. Here's the code:

```
import java.util.ArrayList;
public class ModifyArrayListWithStringBuilder {
    public static void main(String args[]) {
        ArrayList<StringBuilder> myArrList =
                                  new ArrayList<StringBuilder>();
        myArrList.add(new StringBuilder("One"));
        myArrList.add(new StringBuilder("Two"));
        myArrList.add(new StringBuilder("Three"));

        for (StringBuilder element : myArrList)      ❶ Access ArrayList elements
            element.append(element.length());           and modify them

        for (StringBuilder element : myArrList)
            System.out.println(element);
    }
}
```

The output of this code is as follows:

```
One3
Two3
Three5
```

❶ accesses all the elements of `myArrList` and modifies the element value by appending its length to it. The modified value is printed by accessing `myArrList` elements again.

4.4.5 *Deleting the elements of an ArrayList*

`ArrayList` defines two methods to remove its elements, as follows:

- `remove(int index)`—This method removes the element at the specified position in this list.
- `remove(Object o)`—This method removes the first occurrence of the specified element from this list, if it's present.

Let's take a look at some code that uses these removal methods:

```
import java.util.ArrayList;
public class DeleteElementsFromArrayList {
    public static void main(String args[]) {
        ArrayList<StringBuilder> myArrList = new ArrayList<>();

        StringBuilder sb1 = new StringBuilder("One");
        StringBuilder sb2 = new StringBuilder("Two");
        StringBuilder sb3 = new StringBuilder("Three");
        StringBuilder sb4 = new StringBuilder("Four");

        myArrList.add(sb1);
        myArrList.add(sb2);
        myArrList.add(sb3);
        myArrList.add(sb4);

        myArrList.remove(1);
        for (StringBuilder element:myArrList)
            System.out.println(element);

        myArrList.remove(sb3);
        myArrList.remove(new StringBuilder("Four"));

        System.out.println();
        for (StringBuilder element : myArrList)
            System.out.println(element);

    }
}
```

Remove element at position 1

Prints One, Three, and Four

Doesn't remove Four ❶

Removes Three from list

Prints One and Four

The output of the previous code is as follows:

```
One
Three
Four

One
Four
```

❶ tries to remove the StringBuilder with the value "Four" from myArrList. The removal of the specified element fails because of the manner in which the object references are compared for equality. Two objects are equal if their object references (the variables that store them) point to the same object.

You can always override the equals method in your own class to change this default behavior. The following is an example using the class MyPerson:

```
import java.util.ArrayList;
class MyPerson {
    String name;
    MyPerson(String name) { this.name = name; }

    @Override
    public boolean equals(Object obj) {
        if (obj instanceof MyPerson) {
            MyPerson p = (MyPerson)obj;
            boolean isEqual = p.name.equals(this.name);
            return isEqual;
        }
        else
```

❶ **Method equals**

null and objects of type other than MyPerson can't be equal to this object

Cast obj to MyPerson

Compare name of method parameter to that of this object's name

```
            return false;
        }
    }
public class DeleteElementsFromArrayList2 {
    public static void main(String args[]) {
        ArrayList<MyPerson> myArrList = new ArrayList<MyPerson>();

        MyPerson p1 = new MyPerson("Shreya");
        MyPerson p2 = new MyPerson("Paul");
        MyPerson p3 = new MyPerson("Harry");

        myArrList.add(p1);
        myArrList.add(p2);
        myArrList.add(p3);

        myArrList.remove(new MyPerson("Paul"));          ❷ Removes
                                                            Paul
        for (MyPerson element:myArrList)
            System.out.println(element.name);               Prints Shreya
                                                            and Harry
    }
}
```

At ❶, the method equals in class MyPerson overrides method equals in class Object. It returns false if a null value is passed to this method. It returns true if an object of MyPerson is passed to it with a matching value for its instance variable name.

At ❷, the method remove removes the element with the name Paul from myArr-List. As mentioned earlier, the method remove compares the objects for equality before removing it from ArrayList by calling method equals.

When elements of an ArrayList are removed, the remaining elements are rearranged at their correct positions. This change is required to retrieve all the remaining elements at their correct new positions.

4.4.6 *Other methods of ArrayList*

Let's briefly discuss the other important methods defined in ArrayList.

ADDING MULTIPLE ELEMENTS TO AN ARRAYLIST

You can add multiple elements to an ArrayList from another ArrayList or any other class that is a subclass of Collection by using the following overloaded versions of method addAll:

- addAll(Collection<? extends E> c)
- addAll(int index, Collection<? extends E> c)

Method addAll(Collection<? extends E> c) appends all of the elements in the specified collection to the end of this list in the order in which they're returned by the specified collection's Iterator. If you aren't familiar with generics, and the parameters of this method look scary to you, don't worry—other classes from the Collection API are not on this exam.

Method addAll(int index, Collection<? extends E> c) inserts all of the elements in the specified collection into this list, starting at the specified position.

In the following code example, all elements of ArrayList yourArrList are inserted into ArrayList myArrList, starting at position 1:

```
ArrayList<String> myArrList = new ArrayList<String>();
myArrList.add("One");
myArrList.add("Two");

ArrayList<String> yourArrList = new ArrayList<String>();
yourArrList.add("Three");
yourArrList.add("Four");

myArrList.addAll(1, yourArrList);              Add elements of yourArrList
for (String val : myArrList)                    to myArrList
    System.out.println(val);
```

The output of the previous code is as follows:

```
One
Three
Four
Two
```

The elements of yourArrList aren't removed from it. The objects that are stored in yourArrList can now be referred to from myArrList.

What happens if you modify the *common* object references in these lists, myArrList and yourArrList? We have two cases here: In the first one, you *reassign* the object reference using either of the lists. In this case, the value in the second list will remain unchanged. In the second case, you *modify* the internals of any of the common list elements—in this case, the change will be reflected in both of the lists.

> **EXAM TIP**   This is also one of the favorite topics of the exam authors. In the exam, you're likely to encounter a question that adds the same object reference to multiple lists and then tests you on your understanding of the state of the same object and reference variable in all the lists. If you have any questions on this issue, please refer to the section on reference variables (section 2.3).

Time for our next Twist in the Tale exercise. Let's modify some of the code that we've used in our previous examples and see how it affects the output (answers in the appendix).

Twist in the Tale 4.4

What is the output of the following code?

```
ArrayList<String> myArrList = new ArrayList<String>();
String one = "One";
String two = new String("Two");
myArrList.add(one);
myArrList.add(two);
ArrayList<String> yourArrList = myArrList;
one.replace("O", "B");
```

```
for (String val : myArrList)
    System.out.print(val + ":");

for (String val : yourArrList)
    System.out.print(val + ":");
```

   a One:Two:One:Two:

   b Bne:Two:Bne:Two:

   c One:Two:Bne:Two:

   d Bne:Two:One:Two:

CLEARING ARRAYLIST ELEMENTS

You can remove all the ArrayList elements by calling clear on it. Here's an example:

```
ArrayList<String> myArrList = new ArrayList<String>();
myArrList.add("One");
myArrList.add("Two");

myArrList.clear();

for (String val:myArrList)
    System.out.println(val);
```

The previous code won't print out anything because there are no more elements in myArrList.

ACCESSING INDIVIDUAL ARRAYLIST ELEMENTS

In this section, we'll cover the following methods for accessing elements of an ArrayList:

- get(int index)—This method returns the element at the specified position in this list.
- size()—This method returns the number of elements in this list.
- contains(Object o)—This method returns true if this list contains the specified element.
- indexOf(Object o)—This method returns the index of the first occurrence of the specified element in this list, or -1 if this list doesn't contain the element.
- lastIndexOf(Object o)—This method returns the index of the last occurrence of the specified element in this list, or -1 if this list doesn't contain the element.

You can retrieve an object at a particular position in ArrayList and determine its size as follows:

```
ArrayList<String> myArrList = new ArrayList<String>();
myArrList.add("One");
myArrList.add("Two");

String valFromList = myArrList.get(1);       Prints Two—element
System.out.println(valFromList);             at position 1

System.out.println(myArrList.size());            Prints 2
```

Behind the scenes, the method get will check whether the requested position exists in the ArrayList by comparing it with the array's size. If the requested element isn't within the range, the get method throws a java.lang.IndexOutOfBoundsException error at runtime.

All of the remaining three methods—contains, indexOf, and lastIndexOf—require you to have an unambiguous and strong understanding of how to determine the equality of objects. ArrayList stores objects, and these three methods will compare the values that you pass to these methods with all the elements of the ArrayList.

By default, objects are considered equal if they are referred to by the same variable (the String class is an exception with its pool of String objects). If you want to compare objects by their state (values of the instance variable), override the equals method in that class. I've already demonstrated the difference in how equality of objects of a class is determined, when the class overrides its equals method and when it doesn't, in section 4.4.5 with an overridden equals method in the class MyPerson.

Let's see the usage of all these methods:

```
public class MiscMethodsArrayList3 {
    public static void main(String args[]) {
        ArrayList<StringBuilder> myArrList =
                            new ArrayList<StringBuilder>();
        StringBuilder sb1 = new StringBuilder("Jan");
        StringBuilder sb2 = new StringBuilder("Feb");

        myArrList.add(sb1);
        myArrList.add(sb2);
        myArrList.add(sb2);

        System.out.println(myArrList.contains(new StringBuilder("Jan")));
        System.out.println(myArrList.contains(sb1));

        System.out.println(myArrList.indexOf(new StringBuilder("Feb")));
        System.out.println(myArrList.indexOf(sb2));

        System.out.println(myArrList.lastIndexOf(
                            new StringBuilder("Feb")));
        System.out.println(myArrList.lastIndexOf(sb2));
    }
}
```

Annotations (left): **Adds sb2 to the ArrayList again** → myArrList.add(sb2); · **Prints false** → contains(new StringBuilder("Jan")) · **Prints –1** → indexOf(new StringBuilder("Feb")) · **Prints –1** → lastIndexOf(new StringBuilder("Feb"))

Annotations (right): **Adds sb1 to the ArrayList** → myArrList.add(sb1); · **Adds sb2 to the ArrayList** → myArrList.add(sb2); · **Prints true** → contains(sb1) · **Prints 1** → indexOf(sb2) · **Prints 2** → lastIndexOf(sb2)

The output of the previous code is as follows:

```
false
true
-1
1
-1
2
```

Take a look at the output of the same code using a list of MyPerson objects that has overridden the equals method. First, here's the definition of the class MyPerson:

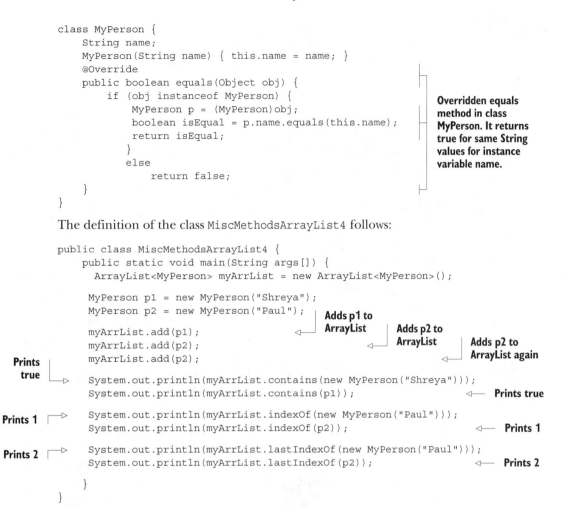

```
class MyPerson {
    String name;
    MyPerson(String name) { this.name = name; }
    @Override
    public boolean equals(Object obj) {
        if (obj instanceof MyPerson) {
            MyPerson p = (MyPerson)obj;
            boolean isEqual = p.name.equals(this.name);
            return isEqual;
        }
        else
            return false;
    }
}
```

Overridden equals method in class MyPerson. It returns true for same String values for instance variable name.

The definition of the class `MiscMethodsArrayList4` follows:

```
public class MiscMethodsArrayList4 {
    public static void main(String args[]) {
        ArrayList<MyPerson> myArrList = new ArrayList<MyPerson>();

        MyPerson p1 = new MyPerson("Shreya");
        MyPerson p2 = new MyPerson("Paul");

        myArrList.add(p1);
        myArrList.add(p2);
        myArrList.add(p2);

        System.out.println(myArrList.contains(new MyPerson("Shreya")));
        System.out.println(myArrList.contains(p1));

        System.out.println(myArrList.indexOf(new MyPerson("Paul")));
        System.out.println(myArrList.indexOf(p2));

        System.out.println(myArrList.lastIndexOf(new MyPerson("Paul")));
        System.out.println(myArrList.lastIndexOf(p2));
    }
}
```

Adds p1 to ArrayList

Adds p2 to ArrayList

Adds p2 to ArrayList again

Prints true

Prints true

Prints 1

Prints 1

Prints 2

Prints 2

As you can see from the output of the preceding code, equality of the objects of class `MyPerson` is determined by the rules defined in its `equals` method. Two objects of class `MyPerson` with the same value for its instance variable `name` are considered to be equal. `myArrList` stores objects of class `MyPerson`. To find a target object, `myArrList` will rely on the output given by the `equals` method of class `MyPerson`; it won't compare the object references of the stored and target objects.

EXAM TIP An `ArrayList` can accept duplicate object values.

CLONING AN ARRAYLIST
The method `clone` defined in the class `ArrayList` returns a *shallow copy* of this Array-List instance. "Shallow copy" means that this method creates a new instance of the `ArrayList` object to be cloned. Its element references are copied, but the objects themselves are not.

Here's an example:

```
public class MiscMethodsArrayList5 {
    public static void main(String args[]) {
        ArrayList<StringBuilder> myArrList = new ArrayList<StringBuilder>();
        StringBuilder sb1 = new StringBuilder("Jan");
        StringBuilder sb2 = new StringBuilder("Feb");

        myArrList.add(sb1);
        myArrList.add(sb2);
        myArrList.add(sb2);

        ArrayList<StringBuilder> assignedArrList = myArrList;

        ArrayList<StringBuilder> clonedArrList =
                  (ArrayList<StringBuilder>)myArrList.clone();

        System.out.println(myArrList == assignedArrList);

        System.out.println(myArrList == clonedArrList);

        StringBuilder myArrVal = myArrList.get(0);
        StringBuilder assignedArrVal = assignedArrList.get(0);
        StringBuilder clonedArrVal = clonedArrList.get(0);

        System.out.println(myArrVal == assignedArrVal);
        System.out.println(myArrVal == clonedArrVal);
    }
}
```

① Assigns object referred to by myArrList to assignedArrList

② Clones myArrList and assigns it to clonedArrList

③ Prints true

④ Prints false

⑤ All of these reference variables refer to the same object.

⑥ Prints true

⑦ Prints true

Let's go through the previous code:

- **①** assigns the object referred to by myArrList to assignedArrList. The variables myArrList and assignedArrList now refer to the same object.
- **②** assigns a *copy* of the object referred to by myArrList to clonedArrList. The variables myArrList and clonedArrList refer to different objects. Because method clone returns a value of the type Object, it is cast to ArrayList<String-Builder> to assign it to clonedArrList (don't worry if you can't follow this line—casting is covered in chapter 6).
- **③** prints true because myArrList and assignedArrList refer to the same object.
- **④** prints false because myArrList and clonedArrList refer to separate objects, because the method clone creates and returns a new object of Array-List (but with the same list members).
- **⑤** proves that the method clone didn't copy the elements of myArrList. All the variable references myArrVal, AssignedArrVal, and clonedArrVal refer to the same objects.
- Hence, both **⑥** and **⑦** print true.

CREATING AN ARRAY FROM AN ARRAYLIST

You can use the method toArray to return an array containing all of the elements in an ArrayList in sequence from the first to the last element. As mentioned earlier in this chapter (refer to figure 4.27 in section 4.4.1), an ArrayList uses a private variable, 'elementData' (an array), to store its own values. Method toArray doesn't return a reference to this array. It creates a new array, copies the elements of the ArrayList to it and then returns it.

Now comes the tricky part. No references to the returned array, which is itself an object, are maintained by the `ArrayList`. But the references to the individual `ArrayList` elements are copied to the returned array and are still referred to by the `ArrayList`.

This implies that if you modify the returned array by, say, swapping the position of its elements or by assigning new objects to its elements, the elements of `ArrayList` won't be affected. But, if you modify the state of (mutable) elements of the returned array, then the modified state of elements will be reflected in the `ArrayList`.

4.5　*Comparing objects for equality*

[3.3] Test equality between strings and other objects using == and equals()

In section 4.1, you saw how the class `String` defined a set of rules to determine whether two `String` values are equal, and how these rules were coded in the method `equals`. Similarly, any Java class can define a set of rules to determine whether its two objects should be considered equal. This comparison is accomplished using the method `equals`, which is described in the next section.

4.5.1　*The method equals in the class java.lang.Object*

The method `equals` is defined in class `java.lang.Object`. All of the Java classes directly or indirectly inherit from this class. Listing 4.2 contains the default implementation of the method `equals` from class `java.lang.Object`.

Listing 4.2　Implementation of `equals` method from the class `java.lang.Object`

```
public boolean equals(Object obj) {
    return (this == obj);
}
```

As you can see, the default implementation of the `equals` method only compares whether two object variables refer to the same object. Because instance variables are used to store the state of an object, it's common to compare the values of the instance variables to determine whether two objects should be considered equal.

4.5.2　*Comparing objects of a user-defined class*

Let's work with an example of class `BankAccount`, which defines two instance variables: `acctNumber`, of type `String`, and `acctType`, of type `int`. The `equals` method compares the values of these instance variables to determine the equality of two objects of class `BankAccount`.

Here's the relevant code:

```
class BankAccount {
    String acctNumber;
    int acctType;

    public boolean equals(Object anObject) {
        if (anObject instanceof BankAccount) {
```

Check whether we are comparing the same type of objects

```
        BankAccount b = (BankAccount)anObject;
        return (acctNumber.equals(b.acctNumber) &&
            acctType == b.acctType);
    }
    else
        return false;
    }
}
```

> Two bank objects are considered equal if they have the same values, for instance variables acctNumber and acctType

Let's verify the working of this `equals` method in the following code:

```
class Test {
    public static void main(String args[]) {
        BankAccount b1 = new BankAccount();
        b1.acctNumber = "0023490";
        b1.acctType = 4;

        BankAccount b2 = new BankAccount();
        b2.acctNumber = "11223344";
        b2.acctType = 3;

        BankAccount b3 = new BankAccount();
        b3.acctNumber = "11223344";
        b3.acctType = 3;

        System.out.println(b1.equals(b2));          ❶ Prints false

        System.out.println(b2.equals(b3));          ❷ Prints true

        System.out.println(b1.equals(new String("abc")));

                                                    ❸ Prints false
    }
}
```

❶ prints `false` because the value of the reference variables b1 and b2 do not match. ❷ prints `true` because the values of the reference variables b2 and b3 match each other. ❸ passes an object of type `String` to the method `equals` defined in the class `BankAccount`. This method returns `false` if the method parameter passed to it is not of type `BankAccount`. Hence ❸ prints `false`.

Even though the following implementation is unacceptable for classes used in the real world, it's still correct syntactically:

```
class BankAccount {
    String acctNumber;
    int acctType;

    public boolean equals(Object anObject) {
        return true;
    }
}
```

The previous definition of the `equals` method will return `true` for any object that's compared to an object of class `BankAccount` because it doesn't compare any values. Let's see what happens when you compare an object of class `String` with an object of class `BankAccount` and vice versa using `equals()`:

```
class TestBank {
    public static void main(String args[]) {
```

```
        BankAccount acct = new BankAccount();
        String str = "Bank";

        System.out.println(acct.equals(str));
        System.out.println(str.equals(acct));
    }
}
```

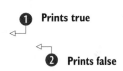

① **Prints true**

② **Prints false**

In the preceding code, **①** prints `true`, but **②** prints `false`. The `equals` method in the class `String` returns `true` only if the object that's being compared to is a `String` with the same sequence of characters.

> **EXAM TIP**   In the exam, watch out for questions about the correct implementation of the `equals` method to compare two objects versus questions about the equals methods that simply compile correctly. If you'd been asked whether `equals()` in the previous example code would compile correctly, the correct answer is yes.

4.5.3   *Incorrect method signature of the equals method*

It's a very common mistake to write an `equals` method that accepts a member of the class itself. In the following code, the only change is in the type of method parameter:

```
class BankAccount {
    String acctNumber;
    int acctType;

    public boolean equals(BankAccount anObject) {
        if (anObject instanceof BankAccount) {
            BankAccount b = (BankAccount)anObject;
            return (acctNumber.equals(b.acctNumber) &&
                acctType == b.acctType);
        }
        else
            return false;
    }
}
```

Type of method parameter is BankAccount, not Object

Though the previous definition of `equals()` may seem to be flawless, what happens when you try to add and retrieve an object of class `BankAccount` (as shown in the preceding code) from an `ArrayList`? The method `contains` defined in the class `ArrayList` compares two objects by calling the object's `equals` method. It does not compare object references.

In the following code, see what happens when you add an object of the class `BankAccount` to an `ArrayList` and then try to verify whether the list contains a `BankAccount` object with the same instance variables values for `acctNumber` and `acctType` as the object being searched for:

```
class TestMethodEquals {
    public static void main(String args[]) {
        BankAccount b1 = new BankAccount();
        b1.acctNumber = "0023490"; b1.acctType = 4;
```

① **Object b1**

```
                    ArrayList <BankAccount> list = new ArrayList<BankAccount>();
      Adds    ▷      list.add(b1);
    object
      b1 to          BankAccount b2 = new BankAccount();         ③  Creates b2 with
      list  ②        b2.acctNumber = "0023490"; b2.acctType = 4;    same state as b1

                     System.out.println(list.contains(b2));        ◁
             }                                                   ④  Prints false
      }
```

① and **③** define objects b1 and b2 of the class BankAccount with the same state. **②** adds b1 to the list. **④** compares the object b2 with the objects added to the list.

An ArrayList uses the method equals to compare two objects. Because the class BankAccount didn't follow the rules for correctly defining (overriding) the method equals, ArrayList uses the method equals from the base class Object, which compares object references. Because the code didn't add b2 to list, it prints false.

What do you think will be the output of the previous code if you change the definition of the method equals in the class BankAccount so that it accepts a method parameter of type Object? Try it for yourself!

EXAM TIP   The method equals defines a method parameter of type Object, and its return type is boolean. Don't change the name of the method, its return type, or the type of method parameter when you define (*override*) this method in your class to compare two objects.

4.5.4   *Contract of the equals method*

The Java API defines a *contract* for the equals method, which should be taken care of when you implement it in any of your classes. I've pulled the following contract explanation directly from the Java API documentation:[1]

> The equals method implements an equivalence relation on non-null object references:
>
> - It is reflexive: for any non-null reference value x, x.equals(x) should return true.
> - It is symmetric: for any non-null reference values x and y, x.equals(y) should return true if and only if y.equals(x) returns true.
> - It is transitive: for any non-null reference values x, y, and z, if x.equals(y) returns true and y.equals(z) returns true, then x.equals(z) should return true.
> - It is consistent: for any non-null reference values x and y, multiple invocations of x.equals(y) consistently return true or consistently return false, provided no information used in equals() comparisons on the objects is modified.
> - For any non-null reference value x, x.equals(null) should return false.

---

[1] The Java API documentation for equals can be found on the Oracle site: http://docs.oracle.com/javase/7/docs/api/java/lang/Object.html#equals(java.lang.Object).

As per the contract, the definition of the `equals` method that we defined for the class `BankAccount` in an earlier example violates the contract for the `equals` method. Take a look at the definition again:

```
public boolean equals(Object anObject) {
    return true;
}
```

This code returns `true`, even for `null` values passed to this method. According to the contract of the method `equals`, if a `null` value is passed to the `equals` method, the method should return `false`.

 EXAM TIP You may get to answer explicit questions on the contract of the `equals` method. An `equals` method that returns `true` for a `null` object passed to it will violate the contract. Also, if the `equals` method modifies the value of any of the instance variables of the method parameter passed to it, or of the object on which it is called, it will violate the `equals` contract.

The `hashCode()` method

A lot of programmers are confused about the role of the method `hashCode` in determining the equality of objects. The method `hashCode` is *not* called by the `equals` method to determine the equality of two objects. Because the `hashCode` method is not on the exam, I'll discuss it quickly here to ward off any confusion about this method.

The method `hashCode` is used by the collection classes (such as `TreeMap` and `HashMap`) that store *key-value* pairs, where a *key* is an object. These collection classes use the `hashCode` of a *key* to search efficiently for the corresponding *value*. The `hashCode` of the *key* (an object) is used to specify a *bucket* number, which should store its corresponding *value*. The `hashCode` values of two objects can be the same. When these collection classes find the right bucket, they call the `equals` method to select the correct *value* object (that shares the same *key* values). The `equals` method is called even if a *bucket* contains only one object. After all, it might be the same hash but a different `equals`, and there is no match to get!

According to the Java documentation, when you override the `equals` method in your class, you should also override the `hashCode` method. If you don't, objects of your classes won't behave as required if they're used as *keys* by collection classes that store *key-value* pairs. This method is not discussed in detail in this chapter because it isn't on the exam. But don't forget to override it with the method `equals` in your real-world projects.

4.6 Summary

In this chapter, you learned about the `String` class, its properties, and its methods. Because this is one of the most frequently used classes in Java, I'll reiterate that a good understanding of this class in terms of why its methods behave in a particular manner will go a long way to helping you successfully complete the OCA Java SE 7 Programmer I exam.

You also learned how to create objects of the class `String` using the operator `new` and the assignment operator (=). You also learned the differences between how `String` objects are stored using these two approaches. If you use the assignment operator to create your `String` objects, they're stored in a common pool of `String` objects (also known as the `String` constant pool) that can be used by others. This storage is possible because `String` objects are immutable—that is, their values can't be changed.

You also learned how a `char` array is used to store the value of a `String` object. This knowledge helps explain why the methods `charAt()`, `indexOf()`, and `substring()` search for the first character of a `String` at position 0, not position 1. We also reviewed the methods `replace()`, `trim()`, and `substring()`, which seem to modify the value of a `String` but will never be able to do it because `String` objects are immutable. You also learned the methods `length()`, `startsWith()`, and `endsWith()`.

Because all operators can't be used with `String`s, you learned about the ones that can be used with `String`: `+`, `+=`, `==`, and `!=`. You also learned that the equality of `String`s can be determined using the method `equals`. By using the operator `==`, you can only determine whether both the variables are referring to the same object; it doesn't compare the values stored by `String`s. As with all the other object types, the only literal value that can be assigned to a `String` is `null`.

We worked with the class `StringBuilder`, which is defined in the package `java.lang` and is used to store a mutable sequence of characters. The class `String-Builder` is usually used to store a sequence of characters that needs to be modified often—like when you're building a query for database applications. Like the `String` class, `StringBuilder` also uses a `char` array to store its characters. A lot of the methods defined in class `StringBuilder` work exactly as defined by the class `String`, such as the methods `charAt`, `indexOf`, `substring`, and `length`. The append method is used to add characters to the end of a `StringBuilder` object. The `insert` method is another important `StringBuilder` method that's used to insert either single or multiple characters at a specified position in a `StringBuilder` object. The class `StringBuilder` offers the same functionality offered by the class `StringBuffer`, minus the additional feature of methods that are synchronized where needed.

An array is an object that stores a collection of values. An array can store a collection of primitive data types or a collection of objects. You can define one-dimensional and multidimensional arrays. A one-dimensional array is an object that refers to a collection of scalar values. A two-dimensional (or more) array is referred to as a multidimensional array. A two-dimensional array refers to a collection of objects, where each of the objects is a one-dimensional array. Similarly, a three-dimensional array refers to a collection of two-dimension arrays, and so on. Arrays can be declared, allocated, and initialized in a single step or in multiple steps. A two-dimensional array does not need to be symmetrical, and each of its rows can define different numbers of members. You can define arrays of primitives, interfaces, abstract classes, and concrete classes. All arrays are objects and can access the variable `length` and methods inherited from the class `java.lang.Object`.

ArrayList is a resizable array that offers the best combination of features offered by an array and the List data structure. You can add objects to an ArrayList using the method add. You can access the objects of an ArrayList by using an enhanced for loop. An ArrayList preserves the order of insertion of its elements. ListIterator and the enhanced for loop will return the elements in the order in which they were added to the ArrayList. You can modify the elements of an ArrayList using the method set. You can remove the elements of an ArrayList by using the method remove, which accepts the element position or an object. You can also add multiple elements to an ArrayList by using the method addAll. The method clone defined in the class ArrayList returns a *shallow copy* of this ArrayList instance. "Shallow copy" means that the method creates a new instance of the ArrayList to be cloned, but the ArrayList elements aren't copied.

You can compare the objects of your class by overriding the equals method. The equals method is defined in the class java.lang.Object, which is the base class of all classes in Java. The default implementation of the method equals only compares the object references for equality. Because instance variables are used to store the state of an object, it's common to compare the values of these variables to determine whether two objects should be considered equal in the equals method. The Java API documentation defines a contract for the equals method. In the exam, for a given definition of the method equals, it is important to note the differences between an equals method that compiles successfully, one that fails compilation, and one that doesn't follow the contract.

4.7 Review notes

This section lists the main points covered in this chapter.

The class String:

- The class String represents an immutable sequence of characters.
- A String object can be created by using the operator new, by using the assignment operator (=), or by using double quotes (as in System.out.println ("Four")).
- String objects created using the assignment operator are placed in a *pool* of String objects. Whenever the JRE receives a new request to create a String object using the assignment operator, it checks whether a String object with the same value already exists in the pool. If found, it returns the object reference for the existing String object from the pool.
- String objects created using the operator new are never placed in the pool of String objects.
- The comparison operator (==) compares String references, whereas the equals method compares the String values.
- None of the methods defined in the class String can modify its value.
- The method charAt(int index) retrieves a character at a specified index of a String.

- The method `indexOf` can be used to search a `String` for the occurrence of a `char` or a `String`, starting from the first position or a specified position.
- The method `substring` can be used to retrieve a portion of a `String` object. The `substring` method doesn't include the character at the end position.
- The `trim` method will return a new `String` by removing all the leading and trailing white spaces in a `String`. This method doesn't remove any white space *within* a `String`.
- You can use the method `length` to retrieve the length of a `String`.
- The method `startsWith` determines whether a `String` starts with a specified `String`.
- The method `endsWith` determines whether a `String` ends with a specified `String`.
- It's a common practice to use multiple `String` methods in a single line of code. When chained, the methods are evaluated from left to right.
- You can use the concatenation operators + and += and comparison operators != and == with `String` objects.
- The Java language provides special support for concatenating `String` objects by using the operators + and +=.
- The right technique for comparing two `String` values for equality is to use the method `equals` defined in the `String` class. This method returns a `true` value if the object being compared isn't `null` and is a `String` object that represents the same sequence of characters as the object to which it's being compared.
- The comparison operator == determines whether both the reference variables are referring to the same `String` objects. Hence, it's not the right operator for comparing `String` values.

The class `StringBuilder`:

- The class `StringBuilder` is defined in the package `java.lang` and represents a mutable sequence of characters.
- The `StringBuilder` class is very efficient when a user needs to modify a sequence of characters often. Because it's mutable, the value of a `String-Builder` object can be modified without the need to create a new `String-Builder` object.
- A `StringBuilder` object can be created using its constructors, which can accept either a `String` object, another `StringBuilder` object, an int value to specify the capacity of `StringBuilder`, or nothing.
- The methods `charAt`, `indexOf`, `substring`, and `length` defined in the class `StringBuilder` work in the same way as methods with the same names defined in the class `String`.
- The `append` method adds the specified value at the end of the existing value of a `StringBuilder` object.
- The `insert` method enables you to insert characters at a specified position in a `StringBuilder` object. The main difference between the `append` and `insert`

methods is that the `insert` method enables you to insert the requested data at a particular position, whereas the `append` method only allows you to add the requested data at the end of the `StringBuilder` object.

- The method `delete` removes the characters in a substring of the specified `StringBuilder`. The method `deleteCharAt` removes the `char` at the specified position.
- Unlike the class `String`, the class `StringBuilder` doesn't define the method `trim`.
- The method `reverse` reverses the sequence of characters of a `StringBuilder`.
- The `replace` method in the class `StringBuilder` replaces a sequence of characters, identified by their position, with another `String`.
- In addition to using the method `substring`, you can also use the method `subSequence` to retrieve a subsequence of a `StringBuilder` object.

Arrays:

- An array is an object that stores a collection of values.
- An array itself is an object.
- An array can store two types of data—a collection of primitive data types and a collection of objects.
- You can define one-dimensional and multidimensional arrays.
- A one-dimensional array is an object that refers to a collection of scalar values.
- A two-dimensional (or more) array is referred to as a multidimensional array.
- A two-dimensional array refers to a collection of objects, in which each of the objects is a one-dimensional array.
- Similarly, a three-dimensional array refers to a collection of two-dimensional arrays, and so on.
- Multidimensional arrays may or may not contain the same number of elements in each row or column.
- The creation of an array involves three steps: declaration of an array, allocation of an array, and initialization of array elements.
- An array declaration is composed of an array type, a variable name, and one or more occurrences of `[]`.
- Square brackets can follow either the variable name or its type. In the case of multidimensional arrays, it can follow both of them.
- An array declaration creates a variable that refers to `null`.
- Because no elements of an array are created when it's declared, it's invalid to define the size of an array with its declaration.
- *Array allocation* allocates memory for the elements of an array. When you allocate memory for an array, you must specify its dimensions, such as the number of elements the array should store.
- Because an array is an object, it's allocated using the keyword `new`, followed by the type of value that it stores, and then its size.

- Once allocated, all the array elements store their default values. Elements of an array that store objects refer to `null`. Elements of an array that store primitive data types store `0` for integer types (`byte`, `short`, `int`, `long`), `0.0` for decimal types (`float` and `double`), `false` for `boolean`, or `/u0000` for `char` data.

- To access an element in a two-dimensional array, use two array position values.

- You can combine all the steps of array declaration, allocation, and initialization into one single step.

- When you combine array declaration, allocation, and initialization in a single step, you can't specify the size of the array. The size of the array is calculated by the number of values that are assigned to the array.

- You can declare and allocate an array but choose not to initialize it (for example, `int[] a = new int[5];`).

- The Java compiler doesn't check the range of the index positions at which you try to access an array element. The code throws an `ArrayIndexOutOfBoundsException` exception if the requested index position doesn't fall in the valid range at runtime.

- A multidimensional array can be asymmetrical; it may not define the same number of columns for each of its rows.

- The type of an array can also be an `interface` or `abstract` class. Such an array can be used to store objects of classes that inherit from the `interface` type or the `abstract` class type.

- The type of an array can also be `java.lang.Object`. Because all classes extend the class `java.lang.Object` class, elements of this array can refer to any object.

- All the arrays are objects and can access the variable `length`, which specifies the number or components stored by the array.

- Because all arrays are objects, they inherit and can access all methods from the class `Object`.

`ArrayList:`

- `ArrayList` is one of the most widely used classes from the Collections framework. It offers the best combination of features offered by an array and the List data structure.

- An `ArrayList` is like a resizable array.

- Unlike arrays, you may not specify an initial size to create an `ArrayList`.

- `ArrayList` implements the interface `List` and allows `null` values to be added to it.

- `ArrayList` implements all list operations (`add`, `modify`, and `delete` values).

- `ArrayList` allows duplicate values to be added to it and maintains its insertion order.

- You can use either `Iterator` or `ListIterator` to iterate over the items of an `ArrayList`.

- ArrayList supports generics, making it type safe.
- Internally, an array of type java.lang.Object is used to store the data in an ArrayList.
- You can add a value to an ArrayList either at its end or at a specified position by using the method add.
- To access the elements of an ArrayList, you can use either the enhanced for loop, Iterator, or ListIterator.
- An iterator (Iterator or ListIterator) lets you remove elements as you iterate through an ArrayList. It's not possible to remove elements from an ArrayList while iterating through it using a for loop.
- An ArrayList preserves the order of insertion of its elements. ListIterator and the enhanced for loop will return the elements in the order in which they were added to the ArrayList.
- You can use the method set to modify an ArrayList by either replacing an existing element in ArrayList or modifying its existing values.
- remove(int) removes the element at the specified position in the list.
- remove(Object o) removes the first occurrence of the specified element from the list, if it's present.
- You can add multiple elements to an ArrayList from another ArrayList or any other class that's a subclass of Collection by using the method addAll.
- You can remove all the ArrayList elements by calling the method clear on it.
- get(int index) returns the element at the specified position in the list.
- size() returns the number of elements in the list.
- contains(Object o) returns true if the list contains the specified element.
- indexOf(Object o) returns the index of the first occurrence of the specified element in the list, or -1 if the list doesn't contain the element.
- lastIndexOf(Object o) returns the index of the last occurrence of the specified element in the list, or -1 if the list doesn't contain the element.
- The method clone defined in the class ArrayList returns a *shallow copy* of this ArrayList instance. "Shallow copy" means that the method creates a new instance of the ArrayList to be cloned, but the ArrayList elements aren't copied.
- You can use the method toArray to return an array containing all of the elements in ArrayList in sequence from the first to the last element.

Comparing objects for equality:

- Any Java class can define a set of rules to determine whether two objects should be considered equal.
- The method equals is defined in the class java.lang.Object. All the Java classes directly or indirectly inherit this class.
- The default implementation of the equals method only compares whether two object variables refer to the same object.

- Because instance variables are used to store the state of an object, it's common to compare the values of the instance variables to determine whether two objects should be considered equal.
- When you override the equals method in your class, make sure that you use the correct method signature for the equals method.
- The Java API defines a contract for the equals method, which should be taken care of when you implement the method in any of your classes.
- According to the contract of the method equals, if a null value is passed to it, the method equals should return false.
- If the equals method modifies the value of any of the instance variables of the method parameter passed to it, or of the object on which it is called, it will violate the contract.

4.8   *Sample exam questions*

Q4-1. What is the output of the following code?

```
class EJavaGuruArray {
    public static void main(String args[]) {
            int[] arr = new int[5];
            byte b = 4; char c = 'c'; long longVar = 10;
            arr[0] = b;
            arr[1] = c;
            arr[3] = longVar;
            System.out.println(arr[0] + arr[1] + arr[2] + arr[3]);
    }
}
```

    a 4c010

    b 4c10

    c 113

    d 103

    e Compilation error

Q4-2. What is the output of the following code?

```
class EJavaGuruArray2 {
    public static void main(String args[]) {
        int[] arr1;
        int[] arr2 = new int[3];
        char[] arr3 = {'a', 'b'};
        arr1 = arr2;
        arr1 = arr3;
        System.out.println(arr1[0] + ":" + arr1[1]);
    }
}
```

    a 0:0

    b a:b

    c 0:b

d a:0

e Compilation error

Q4-3. Which of the following are valid lines of code to define a multidimensional int array?

a `int[][] array1 = {{1, 2, 3}, {}, {1, 2,3, 4, 5}};`

b `int[][] array2 = new array() {{1, 2, 3}, {}, {1, 2,3, 4, 5}};`

c `int[][] array3 = {1, 2, 3}, {0}, {1, 2,3, 4, 5};`

d `int[][] array5 = new int[2][];`

Q4-4. Which of the following statements are correct?

a By default, an `ArrayList` creates an array with an initial size of 16 to store its elements.

b Because `ArrayList` stores only objects, you can't pass an element of an `Array-List` to a `switch` construct.

c Calling `clear()` and `remove()` on an `ArrayList` will remove all its elements.

d If you frequently add elements to an `ArrayList`, specifying a larger capacity will improve the code efficiency.

e Calling the method `clone()` on an `ArrayList` creates its shallow copy; that is, it doesn't clone the individual list elements.

Q4-5. Which of the following statements are correct?

a An `ArrayList` offers a resizable array, which is easily managed using the methods it provides. You can add and remove elements from an `ArrayList`.

b Values stored by an `ArrayList` can be modified.

c You can iterate through elements of an `ArrayList` using a for loop, `Iterator`, or `ListIterator`.

d An `ArrayList` requires you to specify the total number of elements before you can store any elements in it.

e An `ArrayList` can store any type of object.

Q4-6. What is the output of the following code?

```
import java.util.*;                                          // line 1
class EJavaGuruArrayList {                                   // line 2
    public static void main(String args[]) {                // line 3
        ArrayList<String> ejg = new ArrayList<>();          // line 4
        ejg.add("One");                                     // line 5
        ejg.add("Two");                                     // line 6

        System.out.println(ejg.contains(new String("One"))); // line 7
        System.out.println(ejg.indexOf("Two"));            // line 8
        ejg.clear();                                        // line 9
        System.out.println(ejg);                            // line 10
        System.out.println(ejg.get(1));                     // line 11

    }                                                        // line 12
}                                                            // line 13
```

a Line 7 prints `true`

b Line 7 prints `false`

c Line 8 prints `-1`

d Line 8 prints `1`

e Line 9 removes all elements of the list `ejg`

f Line 9 sets the list `ejg` to `null`

g Line 10 prints `null`

h Line 10 prints `[]`

i Line 10 prints a value similar to `ArrayList@16356`

k Line 11 throws an exception

l Line 11 prints `null`

Q4-7. What is the output of the following code?

```
class EJavaGuruString {
    public static void main(String args[]) {
            String ejg1 = new String("E Java");
            String ejg2 = new String("E Java");
            String ejg3 = "E Java";
            String ejg4 = "E Java";
            do
                    System.out.println(ejg1.equals(ejg2));
            while (ejg3 == ejg4);
    }
}
```

a true printed once

b false printed once

c true printed in an infinite loop

d false printed in an infinite loop

Q4-8. What is the output of the following code?

```
class EJavaGuruString2 {
    public static void main(String args[]) {
            String ejg = "game".replace('a', 'Z').trim().concat("Aa");
            ejg.substring(0, 2);
            System.out.println(ejg);
    }
}
```

a gZmeAZ

b gZmeAa

c gZm

d gZ

e game

Q4-9. What is the output of the following code?

```
class EJavaGuruString2 {
    public static void main(String args[]) {
        String ejg = "game";
        ejg.replace('a', 'Z').trim().concat("Aa");
        ejg.substring(0, 2);
        System.out.println(ejg);
    }
}
```

a gZmeAZ

b gZmeAa

c gZm

d gZ

e game

Q4-10. What is the output of the following code?

```
class EJavaGuruStringBuilder {
    public static void main(String args[]) {
        StringBuilder ejg = new StringBuilder(10 + 2 + "SUN" + 4 + 5);
        ejg.append(ejg.delete(3, 6));
        System.out.println(ejg);
    }
}
```

a 12S512S5

b 12S12S

c 1025102S

d Runtime exception

Q4-11. What is the output of the following code?

```
class EJavaGuruStringBuilder2 {
    public static void main(String args[]) {
        StringBuilder sb1 = new StringBuilder("123456");
        sb1.subSequence(2, 4);
        sb1.deleteCharAt(3);
        sb1.reverse();
        System.out.println(sb1);
    }
}
```

a 521

b Runtime exception

c 65321

d 65431

4.9   *Answers to sample exam questions*

Q4-1. What is the output of the following code?

```
class EJavaGuruArray {
    public static void main(String args[]) {
            int[] arr = new int[5];
            byte b = 4; char c = 'c'; long longVar = 10;
            arr[0] = b;
            arr[1] = c;
            arr[3] = longVar;
            System.out.println(arr[0] + arr[1] + arr[2] + arr[3]);
    }
}
```

   a 4c010

   b 4c10

   c 113

   d 103

   e **Compilation error**

Answer: e

Explanation: The previous code won't compile due to the following line of code:

```
arr[3] = longVar;
```

This line of code tries to assign a value of type long to a variable of type int. Because Java does support implicit widening conversions for variables, the previous code fails to compile. Also, the previous code tries to trick you regarding your understanding of the following:

- Assigning a char value to an int array element (arr[1] = c)
- Adding a byte value to an int array element (arr[0] = b)
- Whether an unassigned int array element is assigned a default value (arr[2])
- Whether arr[0] + arr[1] + arr[2] + arr[3] prints the sum of all these values, or a concatenated value

When answering questions in the OCA Java SE 7 Java Programmer I exam, be careful about such tactics. If any of the answers list a compilation error or a runtime exception as an option, look for obvious lines of code that could result in it. In this example, arr[3] = longVar will result in compilation error.

Q4-2. What is the output of the following code?

```
class EJavaGuruArray2 {
    public static void main(String args[]) {
            int[] arr1;
            int[] arr2 = new int[3];
            char[] arr3 = {'a', 'b'};
            arr1 = arr2;
            arr1 = arr3;
```

```
            System.out.println(arr1[0] + ":" + arr1[1]);
    }
}
```

   a   0:0

   b   a:b

   c   0:b

   d   a:0

   e   **Compilation error**

Answer: e

Explanation: Because a char value can be assigned to an int value, you might assume that a char array can be assigned to an int array. But we're talking about arrays of int and char primitives, which aren't the same as a primitive int or char. Arrays themselves are reference variables, which refer to a collection of objects of similar type.

Q4-3. Which of the following are valid lines of code to define a multidimensional int array?

   a   `int[][] array1 = {{1, 2, 3}, {}, {1, 2,3, 4, 5}};`

   b   `int[][] array2 = new array() {{1, 2, 3}, {}, {1, 2,3, 4, 5}};`

   c   `int[][] array3 = {1, 2, 3}, {0}, {1, 2,3, 4, 5};`

   d   `int[][] array5 = new int[2][];`

Answer: a, d

Explanation: Option (b) is incorrect. This line of code won't compile because new array() isn't valid code. Unlike objects of other classes, an array isn't initialized using the keyword new followed by the word array. When the keyword new is used to initialize an array, it's followed by the type of the array, not the word array.

    Option (c) is incorrect. To initialize a two-dimensional array, all of these values must be enclosed within another pair of curly braces, as shown in option (a).

Q4-4. Which of the following statements are correct?

   a   By default, an ArrayList creates an array with an initial size of 16 to store its elements.

   b   Because ArrayList stores only objects, you can't pass element of an ArrayList to a switch construct.

   c   Calling clear() or remove() on an ArrayList, will remove all its elements.

   d   **If you frequently add elements to an ArrayList, specifying a larger capacity will improve the code efficiency.**

   e   **Calling the method clone() on an ArrayList creates its shallow copy; that is, it doesn't clone the individual list elements.**

Answer: d, e

Explanation: Option (a) is incorrect. By default, an ArrayList creates an array with an initial size of 10 to store its elements.

Option (b) is incorrect. Starting with Java 7, `switch` also accepts variables of type `String`. Because a `String` can be stored in an `ArrayList`, you can use elements of an `ArrayList` in a `switch` construct.

Option (c) is incorrect. Only `remove()` will remove all elements of an `ArrayList`.

Option (d) is correct. An `ArrayList` internally uses an array to store all its elements. Whenever you add an element to an `ArrayList`, it checks whether the array can accommodate the new value. If it can't, `ArrayList` creates a larger array, copies all the existing values to the new array, and then adds the new value at the end of the array. If you frequently add elements to an `ArrayList`, it makes sense to create an `ArrayList` with a bigger capacity because the previous process isn't repeated for each `ArrayList` insertion.

Option (e) is correct. Calling `clone()` on an `ArrayList` will create a separate reference variable that stores the same number of elements as the `ArrayList` to be cloned. But each individual `ArrayList` element will refer to the same object; that is, the individual `ArrayList` elements aren't cloned.

Q4-5. Which of the following statements are correct?

   a **An `ArrayList` offers a resizable array, which is easily managed using the methods it provides. You can add and remove elements from an `ArrayList`.**

   b **Values stored by an `ArrayList` can be modified.**

   c **You can iterate through elements of an `ArrayList` using a for loop, `Iterator`, or `ListIterator`.**

   d An ArrayList requires you to specify the total elements before you can store any elements in it.

   e **An `ArrayList` can store any type of object.**

Answer: a, b, c, e

Explanation: Option (a) is correct. A developer may prefer using an `ArrayList` over an array because it offers all the benefits of an array and a list. For example, you can easily add or remove elements from an `ArrayList`.

Option (b) is correct.

Option (c) is correct. An `ArrayList` can be easily searched, sorted, and have its values compared using the methods provided by the Collection framework classes.

Option (d) is incorrect. An array requires you to specify the total number of elements before you can add any element to it. But you don't need to specify the total number of elements that you may add to an `ArrayList` at any time in your code.

Option (e) is correct.

Q4-6. What is the output of the following code?

```
import java.util.*;                                        // line 1
class EJavaGuruArrayList {                                  // line 2
    public static void main(String args[]) {               // line 3
        ArrayList<String> ejg = new ArrayList<>();         // line 4
```

```
    ejg.add("One");                                        // line 5
    ejg.add("Two");                                        // line 6

    System.out.println(ejg.contains(new String("One")));   // line 7
    System.out.println(ejg.indexOf("Two"));                // line 8
    ejg.clear();                                           // line 9
    System.out.println(ejg);                               // line 10
    System.out.println(ejg.get(1));                        // line 11

  }                                                        // line 12
}                                                          // line 13
```

a **Line 7 prints `true`**

b Line 7 prints `false`

c Line 8 prints `-1`

d **Line 8 prints `1`**

e **Line 9 removes all elements of the list `ejg`**

f Line 9 sets `ejg` to `null`

g Line 10 prints `null`

h **Line 10 prints `[]`**

i Line 10 prints a value similar to `ArrayList@16356`

k **Line 11 throws an exception**

l Line 11 prints `null`

Answer: a, d, e, h, k

Explanation: Line 7: The method `contains` accepts an object and compares it with the values stored in the list. It returns `true` if the method finds a match and `false` otherwise. This method uses the `equals` method defined by the object stored in the list. In the example, the `ArrayList` stores objects of class `String`, which has overridden the `equals` method. The `equals` method of the `String` class compares the values stored by it. This is why line 7 returns the value `true`.

Line 8: `indexOf` returns the index position of an element if a match is found; otherwise, it returns `-1`. This method also uses the `equals` method behind the scenes to compare the values in an `ArrayList`. Because the `equals` method in class `String` compares its values and not the reference variables, the `indexOf` method finds a match in position 1.

Line 9: The `clear` method removes all the individual elements of an `ArrayList` such that an attempt to access any of the earlier `ArrayList` elements will throw a runtime exception. It doesn't set the `ArrayList` reference variable to `null`.

Line 10: `ArrayList` has overridden the `toString` method such that it returns a list of all its elements enclosed within square brackets. To print each element, the `toString` method is called to retrieve its `String` representation.

Line 11: The `clear` method removes all the elements of an `ArrayList`. An attempt to access the (nonexistent) `ArrayList` element throws a runtime `IndexOutOfBounds-Exception` exception.

This question tests your understanding of `ArrayList` and determining the equality of `String` objects.

Q4-7. What is the output of the following code?

```
class EJavaGuruString {
    public static void main(String args[]) {
            String ejg1 = new String("E Java");
            String ejg2 = new String("E Java");
            String ejg3 = "E Java";
            String ejg4 = "E Java";
            do
                System.out.println(ejg1.equals(ejg2));
            while (ejg3 == ejg4);
    }
}
```

 a true printed once

 b false printed once

 c **true printed in an infinite loop**

 d false printed in an infinite loop

Answer: c

Explanation: `String` objects that are created without using the `new` operator are placed in a pool of `String`s. Hence, the `String` object referred to by the variable `ejg3` is placed in a pool of `String`s. The variable `ejg4` is also defined without using the `new` operator. Before Java creates another `String` object in the `String` pool for the variable `ejg4`, it looks for a `String` object with the same value in the pool. Because this value already exists in the pool, it makes the variable `ejg4` refer to the same `String` object. This, in turn, makes the variables `ejg3` and `ejg4` refer to the same `String` objects. Hence, both of the following comparisons will return `true`:

- `ejg3 == ejg4` (compare the object references)
- `ejg3.equals(ejg4)` (compare the object values)

Even though the variables `ejg1` and `ejg2` refer to different `String` objects, they define the same values. So `ejg1.equals(ejg2)` also returns `true`. Because the loop condition (`ejg3==ejg4`) always returns `true`, the code prints `true` in an infinite loop.

Q4-8. What is the output of the following code?

```
class EJavaGuruString2 {
    public static void main(String args[]) {
            String ejg = "game".replace('a', 'Z').trim().concat("Aa");
            ejg.substring(0, 2);
            System.out.println(ejg);
    }
}
```

 a gZmeAZ

 b **gZmeAa**

 c gZm

 d gZ

 e game

Answer: b

Explanation: When chained, methods are evaluated from left to right. The first method to execute is replace, not concat. Strings are immutable. Calling the method substring on the reference variable ejg doesn't change the contents of the variable ejg. It returns a String object that isn't referred to by any other variable in the code. In fact, none of the methods defined in the String class modifies the object's own value. They all create and return new String objects.

Q4-9. What is the output of the following code?

```
class EJavaGuruString2 {
    public static void main(String args[]) {
        String ejg = "game";
        ejg.replace('a', 'Z').trim().concat("Aa");
        ejg.substring(0, 2);
        System.out.println(ejg);
    }
}
```

 a gZmeAZ

 b gZmeAa

 c gZm

 d gZ

 e **game**

Answer: e

Explanation: String objects are immutable. It doesn't matter how many methods you execute on a String object; its value won't change. Variable ejg is initialized with the String value "game". This value won't change, and the code prints game.

Q4-10. What is the output of the following code?

```
class EJavaGuruStringBuilder {
    public static void main(String args[]) {
        StringBuilder ejg = new StringBuilder(10 + 2 + "SUN" + 4 + 5);
        ejg.append(ejg.delete(3, 6));
        System.out.println(ejg);
    }
}
```

 a **12S512S5**

 b 12S12S

 c 1025102S

 d dRuntime exception

Answer: a

Explanation: This question tests you on your understanding of operators, `String`, and `StringBuilder`. The following line of code returns `12SUN45`:

```
10 + 2 + "SUN" + 4 + 5
```

The + operator adds two numbers but concatenates the last two numbers. When the + operator encounters a `String` object, it treats all the remaining operands as `String` objects.

Unlike the `String` objects, `StringBuilder` objects are mutable. The append and delete methods defined in this class change its value. `ejg.delete(3, 6)` modifies the existing value of the `StringBuilder` to `12S5`. It then appends the same value to itself when calling `ejg.append()`, resulting in the value `12S512S5`.

Q4-11. What is the output of the following code?

```
class EJavaGuruStringBuilder2 {
    public static void main(String args[]) {
            StringBuilder sb1 = new StringBuilder("123456");
            sb1.subSequence(2, 4);
            sb1.deleteCharAt(3);
            sb1.reverse();
            System.out.println(sb1);
    }
}
```

   a 521

   b Runtime exception

   c **65321**

   d 65431

Answer: c

Explanation: Like the method `substring`, the method `subSequence` doesn't modify the contents of a `StringBuilder`. Hence, the value of the variable `sb1` remains `123456`, even after the execution of the following line of code:

```
sb1.subSequence(2, 4);
```

The method `deleteCharAt` deletes a char value at position 3. Because the positions are zero-based, the digit 4 is deleted from the value `123456`, resulting in `12356`. The method `reverse` modifies the value of a `StringBuilder` by assigning to it the reverse representation of its value. The reverse of `12356` is `65321`.

Flow control

5

Exam objectives covered in this chapter	What you need to know
[3.4] Create `if` and `if-else` constructs.	How to use `if`, `if-else`, `if-else-if-else`, and nested `if` constructs. The differences between using these `if` constructs with and without curly braces { }.
[3.5] Use a `switch` statement.	How to use a `switch` statement by passing the correct type of arguments to the `switch` statement and `case` and `default` labels. The change in the code flow when `break` and `return` statements are used in the `switch` statement.
[5.1] Create and use `while` loops.	How to use the `while` loop, including determining when to apply the `while` loop.
[5.2] Create and use `for` loops, including the enhanced `for` loop.	How to use `for` and enhanced `for` loops. The advantages and disadvantages of the `for` loop and enhanced `for` loop. Scenarios when you may not be able to use the enhanced `for` loop.
[5.3] Create and use `do-while` loops.	Creation and use of `do-while` loops. Every `do-while` loop executes at least once, even if its condition evaluates to `false` for the first iteration.
[5.4] Compare loop constructs.	The differences and similarities between `for`, enhanced `for`, `do-while`, and `while` loops. Given a scenario or a code snippet, knowing which is the most appropriate loop.

Exam objectives covered in this chapter	What you need to know
[5.5] Use break and continue statements.	The use of break and continue statements. A break statement can be used within loops and switch statement. A continue statement can be used only within loops. The difference in the code flow when a break or continue statement is used. Identify the right scenarios for using break and continue statements.

We all make multiple decisions on a daily basis, and we often have to choose from a number of available options to make each decision. These decisions range from the complex, such as selecting what subjects to study in school or which profession to choose, to the simple, such as what food to eat or what clothes to wear. The option you choose that leads to a decision can potentially change the course of your life, in a small or big way. For example, if you choose to study medicine at a university, you have the option to become a research scientist; if you choose fine arts, you have the option to become a painter. But deciding whether to eat pasta or pizza for dinner isn't likely to have a huge impact on your life.

You may also repeat particular sets of actions. These actions can range from eating an ice cream cone every day to phoning a friend until you connect, or passing exams at school or university in order to achieve a desired degree. These repetitions can also change the course of your life: you might relish having ice cream everyday, or enjoy the benefits that come from earning a higher degree.

In Java, the selection statements (if and switch) and looping statements (for, enhanced for, while, and do-while) are used to define and choose among different courses of action, as well as to repeat lines of code. You use these types of statements to define the flow of control in code.

In the OCA Java SE 7 Programmer I exam, you'll be asked how to define and control the flow in your code. To prepare you, I'll cover the following topics in this chapter:

- Creating and using if, if-else, and switch constructs to execute statements selectively
- Creating and using loops—while, do-while, for, and enhanced for
- Creating nested constructs for selection and iteration statements
- Comparing the do-while, while, for, and enhanced for loop constructs
- Using break and continue statements

In Java, you can execute your code conditionally by using either the if or switch constructs. Let's start with the if construct.

5.1 The if and if-else constructs

 [3.4]   Create if and if-else constructs

In this section, we'll cover if and if-else constructs. We'll examine what happens when these constructs are used with and without curly braces {}. We'll also cover nested if and if-else constructs.

5.1.1 The if construct and its flavors

An if construct enables you to execute a set of statements in your code based on the result of a condition. This condition must always evaluate to a boolean or a Boolean value. (The Boolean wrapper class isn't covered in the OCA Java SE 7 Programmer I exam, so you won't see it being used in the coding examples in this book.) You can specify a set of statements to execute when this condition evaluates to true or false. (In many Java books, the terms *constructs* and *statements* are used interchangeably.)

Multiple flavors of the if statement are illustrated in figure 5.1:

- if
- if-else
- if-else-if-else

In figure 5.1, *condition1* and *condition2* refer to a variable or an expression that must evaluate to a boolean or Boolean value. In the figure, *statement1, statement2, and statement3* refer to either a single line of code or a code block.

Because the Boolean wrapper class isn't covered in the OCA Java SE 7 Programmer I exam, I won't cover it in the coding examples in this book. We'll work with only the boolean data type.

EXAM TIP   In Java, *then* isn't a keyword, so it shouldn't be used with the if statement.

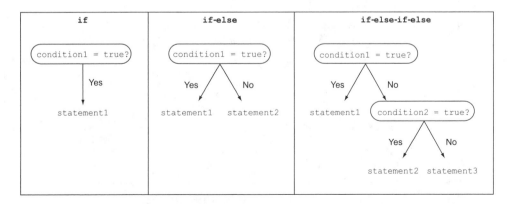

Figure 5.1   Multiple flavors of the if statement: if, if-else, and if-else-if-else

Let's look at the use of the previously mentioned if statement flavors by first defining a set of variables: score, result, name, and file, as follows:

```
int score = 100;
String result = "";
String name = "Lion";
java.io.File file = new java.io.File("F");
```

Figure 5.2 shows the use of if, if-else, and if-else-if-else constructs and compares them by showing the code side by side.

Let's quickly go through the code used in figure 5.2's if, if-else, and if-else-if-else statements. In the following example code, if the condition name.equals("Lion") evaluates to true, a value of 200 is assigned to the variable score:

```
if (name.equals("Lion"))
    score = 200;
```
**Example of
if construct**

In the following example, if the condition name.equals("Lion") evaluates to true, a value of 200 is assigned to the variable score. If this condition were to evaluate to false, a value of 300 would be assigned to the variable score:

```
if (name.equals("Lion"))
    score = 200;
else
    score = 300;
```
**Example of if-else
construct**

In the following example, if score is equal to 100, the variable result is assigned a value of A. If score is equal to 50, the variable result is assigned a value of B. If score is equal to 10, the variable result is assigned a value of C. If score doesn't match any of 100, 50, or 10, a value of F is assigned to the variable result. An if-else-if-else construct can use different conditions for all its if constructs:

if	if-else	if-else-if-else

`if (name.equals("Lion"))`
 	
`    score = 200;`
	`if (name.equals("Lion"))`
	
	`    score = 200;`
	
	`else`
	
	`    score = 300;`
		`if (score == 100)`
		
		`    result = "A";`
		
		`else if (score == 50)`
		
		`    result = "B";`
		
		`else if (score == 10)`
		
		`    result = "C";`
		
		`else`
		
		`    result = "F";`

Figure 5.2   Multiple flavors of if statements implemented in code

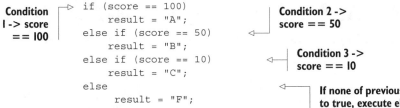

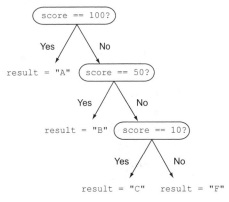

Figure 5.3 illustrates the previous code and makes several points clear:

- The last `else` statement is part of the last `if` construct, not any of the `if` constructs before it.
- The `if-else-if-else` is an if-else construct in which the `else` part defines another `if` construct. A few other programming languages, such as VB and C#, use `if-elsif` and `if-elseif` (without a space) constructs to define `if-else-if` constructs. If you've programmed with any of these languages, note the difference in Java. The following code is equal to the previous code:

Figure 5.3 Execution of the `if-else-if-else` code

```
if (score == 100)
    result = "A";
else
    if (score == 50)
        result = "B";
    else
        if (score == 10)
            result = "C";
        else
            result="F";
```

Again, note that none of the previous `if` constructs use *then* to define the code to execute if a condition evaluates to `true`. Unlike other programming languages, *then* isn't a keyword in Java and isn't used with the `if` construct.

 EXAM TIP The `if-else-if-else` is an if-else construct in which the `else` part defines another `if` construct.

The `boolean` expression used as a condition for the `if` construct can also include assignment operation. The following Twist in the Tale exercise throws in a twist by modifying the value of a variable that the `if` statement is comparing. Let's see if you can answer it correctly (answer in the appendix).

Twist in the Tale 5.1

Let's modify the code used in the previous example as follows. What is the output of this code?

```
String result = "1";
int score = 10;
if ((score = score+10) == 100)
    result = "A";
else if ((score = score+29) == 50)
    result = "B";
else if ((score = score+200) == 10)
    result = "C";
else
    result = "F";

System.out.println(result + ":" + score);
```

    a A:10

    b C:10

    c A:20

    d B:29

    e C:249

    f F:249

5.1.2   *Missing else blocks*

What happens if you don't define the `else` statement for an `if` construct? It's acceptable to define one course of action for an `if` construct as follows (omitting the `else` part):

```
boolean testValue = false;
if (testValue == true)
    System.out.println("value is true");
```

But you can't define the `else` part for an `if` construct, skipping the `if` code block. The following code won't compile:

```
boolean testValue = false;
if (testValue == true)                    Won't
else                                      compile
    System.out.println("value is false");
```

Here is another interesting and bizarre piece of code:

```
int score = 100;                          ① Missing then
if((score=score+10) > 110);                  or else part
```

① is a valid line of code, even if it doesn't define either the *then* or `else` part of the `if` statement. In this case, the `if` condition evaluates and that's it. The `if` construct doesn't define any code that should execute based on the result of this condition.

NOTE Using if(testValue==true) is the same as using if(testValue). Similarly, if(testValue==false) is the same as using if(!testValue). This book includes examples of both these approaches. A lot of beginners in Java programming find the latter approach (without the explicit ==) confusing.

5.1.3 Implications of the presence and absence of {} in if-else constructs

You can execute a single statement or a block of statements when an if condition evaluates to true or false. An if block is marked by enclosing one or more statements within a pair of curly braces, {}. An if block will execute a single line of code if there are no braces, but will execute an unlimited number of lines if they're contained within a block (defined using braces). The braces are optional if there's only one line in the if statement.

The following code executes only one statement of assigning value 200 to variable score if the expression used in the if statement evaluates to true:

```
String name = "Lion";
int score = 100;
if (name.equals("Lion"))
    score = 200;
```

What happens if you want to execute another line of code if the value of the variable name is equal to Lion? Is the following code correct?

```
String name = "Lion";
int score = 100;
if (name.equals("Lion"))
    score = 200;            Set name
    name = "Larry";         to Larry
```

The statement score = 200; executes if the if condition is true. Although it looks like the statement name = "Larry"; is part of the if statement, it isn't. It will execute regardless of the result of the if condition because of the lack of braces, {}.

EXAM TIP In the exam, watch out for code like this that uses misleading indentation in if constructs. In the absence of a defined code block (marked with a pair of {}), only the statement following the if construct will be considered to be part of it.

What happens to the same code if you define an else part for your if construct, as follows:

```
String name = "Lion";
int score = 100;
if (name.equals("Lion"))
    score = 200;            This statement isn't
    name = "Larry";         part of the if construct
else
    score = 129;
```

In this case, the code won't compile. The compiler will report that the `else` part is defined without an `if` statement. If this leaves you confused, examine the following code, which is indented in order to emphasize the fact that the `name = "Larry"` line isn't part of the `else` construct:

```
String name = "Lion";
int score = 100;
if (name.equals ("Lion"))
    score = 200;

name = "Larry";

else
    score = 129;
```

This statement isn't part of the if construct

The else statement seems to be defined without a preceding if construct

If you want to execute multiple statements for an `if` construct, define them within a block of code. You can do so by defining all this code within curly braces: {}. Here's an example:

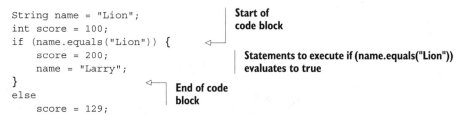

```
String name = "Lion";
int score = 100;
if (name.equals("Lion")) {
    score = 200;
    name = "Larry";
}
else
    score = 129;
```

Start of code block

Statements to execute if (name.equals("Lion")) evaluates to true

End of code block

Similarly, you can define multiple lines of code for the `else` part. The following example does so incorrectly:

```
String name = "Lion";
if (name.equals("Lion"))
    System.out.println("Lion");
else
    System.out.println("Not a Lion");
    System.out.println("Again, not a Lion");
```

1 Not part of the else construct. Will execute regardless of value of variable name.

The output of the previous code is as follows:

```
Lion
Again, not a Lion
```

Though the code at **1** *looks* like it will execute only if the value of the variable `name` matches the value `Lion`, this is not the case. It is indented incorrectly to trick you into believing that it is a part of the `else` block. The previous code is the same as the following code (with correct indentation):

```
String name = "Lion";
if (name.equals("Lion"))
    System.out.println("Lion");
else
    System.out.println("Not a Lion");
System.out.println("Again, not a Lion");
```

Not part of the else construct. Will execute regardless of value of variable name.

If you wish to execute the last two statements in the previous code only if the `if` condition evaluates to `false`, you can do so by using `{}`:

```
String name = "Lion";
if (name.equals("Lion"))
    System.out.println("Lion");
else {
    System.out.println("Not a Lion");
    System.out.println("Again, not a Lion");
}
```

> **Now part of the else construct. Will execute only when if condition evaluates to false.**

You can define another statement, construct, or loop to execute for an `if` condition, without using `{}`, as follows:

```
String name = "Lion";
if (name.equals("Lion"))
    for (int i = 0; i < 3; ++i)
        System.out.println(i);
```

> **An if condition**
>
> **A for loop is a single construct that will execute if name.equals("Lion") evaluates to true**
>
> **This code is part of the for loop defined on previous line**

`System.out.println(i)` is part of the `for` loop, not an unrelated statement that follows the `for` loop. So this code is correct and gives the following output:

```
0
1
2
```

5.1.4 *Appropriate versus inappropriate expressions passed as arguments to an if statement*

The result of a variable or an expression used in an `if` construct must evaluate to `true` or `false`. Assume the following definitions of variables:

```
int score = 100;
boolean allow = false;
String name = "Lion";
```

Let's look at a few examples of some of the valid variables and expressions that can be passed to an `if` statement.

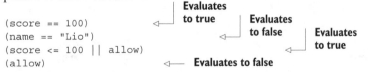

```
(score == 100)
(name == "Lio")
(score <= 100 || allow)
(allow)
```

> **Evaluates to true**
>
> **Evaluates to false**
>
> **Evaluates to true**
>
> **Evaluates to false**

Note that using `==` is not good practice for comparing two `String` objects for equality. As mentioned in chapter 4, the correct approach for comparing two `String` objects is to use the `equals` method from the `String` class. But comparing two `String` values using `==` is a valid expression that returns a `boolean` value, and it may be used in the exam.

Now comes the tricky part of passing an assignment operation to an `if` construct. What do you think is the output of the following code?

```
boolean allow = false;
if (allow = true)
    System.out.println("value is true");
```

> **This is assignment, not comparison**

```
else
    System.out.println("value is false");
```

You may think that because the value of the boolean variable allow is set to false, the previous code output's value is false. Revisit the code and notice that the assignment operation allow = true assigns the value true to the boolean variable allow. Also, its result is also a boolean value, which makes it eligible to be passed on as an argument to the if construct.

Although the previous code has no syntactical errors, there is a *logical error*—an error in the program logic. The correct code to compare a boolean variable with a boolean literal value is as follows:

```
boolean allow = false;
if (allow == true)                                   ⟵⌐  This is
    System.out.println("value is true");                 comparison
else
    System.out.println("value is false");
```

> **EXAM TIP** Watch out for code in the exam that uses the assignment operator (=) to compare a boolean value in the if condition. It won't compare the boolean value; it'll assign a value to it. The correct operator for comparing a boolean value is the equality operator (==).

5.1.5 *Nested if constructs*

A nested if construct is an if construct defined within another if construct. Theoretically, there is no limit on the levels of nested if and if-else constructs.

Whenever you come across nested if and if-else constructs, you need to be careful about determining the else part of an if statement. If this statement doesn't make a lot of sense, take a look at the following code and determine its output:

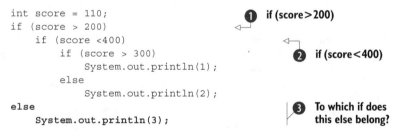

```
int score = 110;                        ❶ if (score>200)
if (score > 200)                      ⟵⌐
    if (score <400)
        if (score > 300)                ❷ if (score<400)
            System.out.println(1);
        else
            System.out.println(2);
else                                    ❸ To which if does
    System.out.println(3);                   this else belong?
```

Based on the way the code is indented, you may believe that the else at ❸ belongs to the if defined at ❶. But it belongs to the if defined at ❷. Here's the code with the correct indentation:

```
int score = 110;
if (score > 200)
    if (score <400)
        if (score > 300)
            System.out.println(1);
        else
            System.out.println(2);
```

```
else
        System.out.println(3);
```

> This else belongs to the if
> with condition (score<400)

Next, you need to understand how to do the following:

- How to define an else for an outer if other than the one that it'll be assigned to by default
- How to determine to which if an else belongs in nested if constructs

Both of these tasks are simple. Let's start with the first one.

HOW TO DEFINE AN ELSE FOR AN OUTER IF OTHER THAN THE ONE THAT IT'LL BE ASSIGNED TO BY DEFAULT

The key point is to use curly braces, as follows:

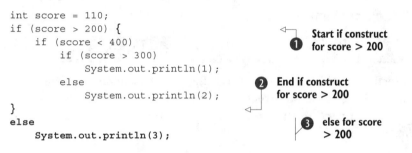

```
int score = 110;
if (score > 200) {
    if (score < 400)
        if (score > 300)
            System.out.println(1);
        else
            System.out.println(2);
}
else
    System.out.println(3);
```

① Start if construct for score > 200

② End if construct for score > 200

③ else for score > 200

Curly braces at **①** and **②** mark the start and end of the if condition (score > 200) defined at **①**. Hence, the else at **③** that follows **②** belongs to the if defined at **①**.

HOW TO DETERMINE TO WHICH IF AN ELSE BELONGS IN NESTED IF CONSTRUCTS

If code uses curly braces to mark the start and end of the territory of an if or else construct, it can be simple to determine which else goes with which if, as mentioned in the previous section. When the if constructs don't use curly braces, don't get confused by the code indentation, which may or may not be correct.

Try to match the ifs with their corresponding elses in the following poorly indented code:

```
if (score > 200)
if (score < 400)
if (score > 300)
    System.out.println(1);
else
    System.out.println(2);
else
    System.out.println(3);
```

Start working from the inside out, with the innermost if-else statement, matching each else with its nearest unmatched if statement. Figure 5.4 shows how to match the if-else pairs for the previous code, marked with *1, 2,* and *3*.

You can alternatively use the switch statement to execute code conditionally. Even though both if-else constructs and switch statements are used to execute statements selectively, they differ in their usage, which you'll notice as you work with the switch statement in the next section.

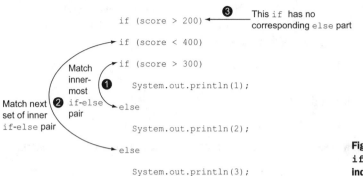

Figure 5.4 How to match if-else pairs for poorly indented code

5.2   *The switch statement*

[3.5] Use a switch statement

In this section, you'll learn how to use the switch statement and see how it compares to nested if-else constructs. You'll learn the right ingredients for defining values that are passed to the switch labels and the correct use of the break statement in these labels.

5.2.1   *Create and use a switch statement*

You can use a switch statement to compare the value of a variable with multiple values. For each of these values, you can define a set of statements to execute.

The following example uses a switch statement to compare the value of the variable marks with the literal values 10, 20, and 30, defined using the case keyword:

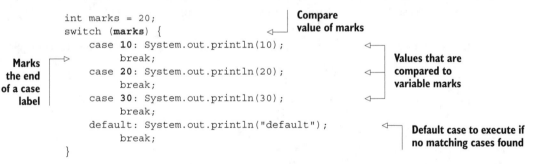

A switch statement can define multiple case labels within its switch block, but only a single default label. The default label executes when no matching value is found in the case labels. A break statement is used to exit a switch statement, after the code completes its execution for a matching case.

5.2.2   *Comparing a switch statement with multiple if-else constructs*

A switch statement can improve the readability of your code by replacing a set of (rather complicated-looking) related if-else-if-else statements with a switch and multiple case statements.

Examine the following code, which uses if-else-if-else statements to check the value of a String variable day and display an appropriate message:

```
String day = "SUN";
if (day.equals("MON") || day.equals("TUE")||
    day.equals("WED") || day.equals("THU"))
    System.out.println("Time to work");
else if (day.equals("FRI"))
    System.out.println("Nearing weekend");
else if (day.equals("SAT") || day.equals("SUN"))
    System.out.println("Weekend!");
else
    System.out.println("Invalid day?");
```

Multiple comparisons

Now examine this implementation of the previous logic using the switch statement:

```
String day = "SUN";
switch (day) {
    case "MON":
    case "TUE":
    case "WED":
    case "THU": System.out.println("Time to work");
                break;
    case "FRI": System.out.println("Nearing weekend");
                break;
    case "SAT":
    case "SUN": System.out.println("Weekend!");
                break;
    default: System.out.println("Invalid day?");
}
```

The two previous snippets of code perform the same function of comparing the value of the variable day and printing an appropriate value. But the latter code, which uses the switch statement, is simpler and easier to read and follow.

Note that the previous switch statement doesn't define code for all the case values. What happens if the value of the variable day matches TUE? When the code control enters the label matching TUE in the switch construct, it'll execute all of the code until it encounters a break statement or it reaches the end of the switch statement.

Figure 5.5 depicts the execution of the multiple if-else-if-else statements used in the example code in this section. You can compare it to a series of questions and answers that continue until a match is found or all the conditions are evaluated.

Figure 5.5 The if-else-if-else construct is like a series of questions and answers.

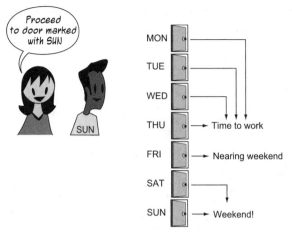

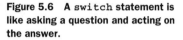

Figure 5.6 A `switch` statement is like asking a question and acting on the answer.

As opposed to an `if-else-if-else` construct, you can compare a `switch` statement to asking a single question and evaluating its answer to determine which code to execute. Figure 5.6 illustrates the `switch` statement and its `case` labels.

EXAM TIP The `if-else-if-else` construct evaluates all of the conditions until it finds a match. A `switch` construct compares the argument passed to it with its labels.

Let's see if you can find the twist in the next exercise. Hint: it defines code to compare `String` values (answers can be found in the appendix).

Twist in the Tale 5.2

Let's modify the code used in the previous example as follows. What is the output of this code?

```
String day = new String("SUN");
switch (day) {
    case "MON":
    case "TUE":
    case "WED":
    case "THU": System.out.println("Time to work");
                break;
    case "FRI": System.out.println("Nearing weekend");
                break;
    case "SAT":
    case "SUN": System.out.println("Weekend!");
                break;
    default: System.out.println("Invalid day?");
}
```

- **a** Time to work
- **b** Nearing weekend
- **c** Weekend!
- **d** Invalid day?

5.2.3   *Arguments passed to a switch statement*

You can't use the switch statement to compare all types of values, such as all types of objects and primitives. There are limitations on the types of arguments that a switch statement can accept.

Figure 5.7 shows the types of arguments that can be passed to a switch statement and to an if construct.

A switch statement accepts arguments of type char, byte, short, int, and String (starting in Java version 7). It also accepts arguments and expressions of types enum, Character, Byte, Integer, and Short, but because these aren't on the OCA Java SE 7 Programmer I exam objectives, I won't cover them any further. The switch statement doesn't accept arguments of type long, float, or double, or any object besides String.

Apart from passing a variable to a switch statement, you can also pass an expression to the switch statement as long as it returns one of the allowed types. The following code is valid:

```
int score =10, num = 20;
switch (score+num) {             Type of score+num is int and
    // ..code                    can thus be passed as an
}                                argument to switch statement
```

The following code won't compile because the type of history is double, which is a type that isn't accepted by the switch statement:

```
double history = 20;
switch (history) {               Double variable can't be
    // ..code                    passed as an argument to
}                                switch statement
```

EXAM TIP   Watch out for questions in the exam that try to pass a primitive decimal type such as float or double to a switch statement. Code that tries to do so will not compile.

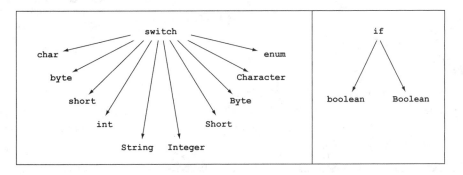

Figure 5.7   Types of arguments that can be passed to a switch **statement and an** if **construct**

5.2.4   *Values passed to the label case of a switch statement*

You're constrained in a couple of ways when it comes to the value that can be passed to the case label in a switch statement, as the following subsections explain.

CASE VALUES SHOULD BE COMPILE-TIME CONSTANTS

The value of a case label must be a compile-time constant value; that is, the value should be known at the time of code compilation:

```
int a=10, b=20, c=30;
switch (a) {                                              ❶ Not allowed
    case b+c: System.out.println(b+c); break;     ◁┘
    case 10*7: System.out.println(10*7512+10); break;   ◁─❷ Allowed
}
```

Note that b+c in the previous code defined at ❶ can't be determined at the time of compilation and isn't allowed. But 10*7 defined at ❷ is a valid case label value.

You can use variables in an expression if they're marked final because the value of final variables can't change once they're initialized:

```
final int a = 10;
final int b = 20;
final int c = 30;

switch (a) {                                    ❶ Expression b+c is
    case b+c: System.out.println(b+c); break;   ◁┘ compile-time constant
}
```

Because the variables b and c are final variables here, at ❶ the value of b+c can be known at compile time. This makes it a compile-time constant value, which can be used in a case label.

You may be surprised to learn that if you don't assign a value to a final variable with its declaration, it isn't considered a compile-time constant:

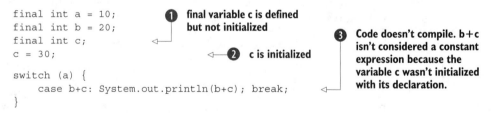

```
final int a = 10;        ❶ final variable c is defined
final int b = 20;          but not initialized
final int c;          ◁┘                                 ❸ Code doesn't compile. b+c
c = 30;                           ◁─❷ c is initialized      isn't considered a constant
                                                            expression because the
switch (a) {                                                variable c wasn't initialized
    case b+c: System.out.println(b+c); break;   ◁┘          with its declaration.
}
```

This code defines a final variable c at line ❶ but doesn't initialize it. The final variable c is initialized at line ❷. Because the final variable c isn't initialized with its declaration, at ❸ the expression b+c isn't considered a compile-time constant, so it can't be used as a case label.

CASE VALUES SHOULD BE ASSIGNABLE TO THE ARGUMENT PASSED TO THE SWITCH STATEMENT

Examine the following code, in which the type of argument passed to the switch statement is byte and the case label value is of the type float. Such code won't compile:

```
byte myByte = 10;
switch (myByte) {
    case 1.2: System.out.println(1); break;        ◁──┐ Floating-point number can't
}                                                        be assigned to byte variable
```

NULL ISN'T ALLOWED AS A CASE LABEL

Code that tries to compare the variable passed to the switch statement with null won't compile, as demonstrated in the following code:

```
String name = "Paul";
switch (name) {
    case "Paul": System.out.println(1);
            break;
    case null: System.out.println("null");        ◁──┐ null isn't allowed
}                                                        as a case label
```

ONE CODE BLOCK CAN BE DEFINED FOR MULTIPLE CASES

It's acceptable to define a single code block for multiple case labels in a switch statement, as shown by the following code:

```
int score =10;
switch (score) {
    case 100:                                          You can define
    case 50 :                                          multiple cases, which
    case 10 : System.out.println("Average score");     should execute the
        break;                                         same code block
    case 200: System.out.println("Good score");
}
```

This example code will output Average score if the value of the variable score matches any of the values 100, 50, and 10.

5.2.5 *Use of break statements within a switch statement*

In the previous examples, note the use of break to exit the switch construct once a matching case is found. In the absence of the break statement, control will *fall through* the remaining code and execute the code corresponding to all the *remaining* cases that *follow* that matching case.

Consider the examples shown in figure 5.8—one with a break statement and the other without a break statement. Examine the flow of code (depicted using arrows) in this figure when the value of the variable score is equal to 50.

Our (hypothetical) enthusiastic programmers, Harry and Selvan, who are also preparing for this exam, sent in some of their code. Can you choose the correct code for them in the following Twist in the Tale exercise? (Answers are in the appendix).

> #### Twist in the Tale 5.3

Which of the following code submissions by our two hypothetical programmers, Harry and Selvan, examines the value of the long variable dayCount and prints out the name of any one month that matches the day count?

a   Submission by Harry:

```
long dayCount = 31;
if (dayCount == 28 || dayCount == 29)
    System.out.println("Feb");
else if (dayCount == 30)
    System.out.println("Apr");
else if (dayCount == 31)
    System.out.println("Jan");
```

b   Submission by Selvan:

```
long dayCount = 31;
switch (dayCount) {
    case 28:
    case 29: System.out.println("Feb"); break;
    case 30: System.out.println("Apr"); break;
    case 31: System.out.println("Jan"); break;
}
```

In the next section, I'll cover the iteration statements known as loop statements. Just as you'd like to repeat the action of "eating an ice cream" every day, loops are used to execute the same lines of code multiple times. You can use a for loop, an enhanced for (for-each) loop, or the do-while and while loops to repeat a block of code. Let's start with the for loop.

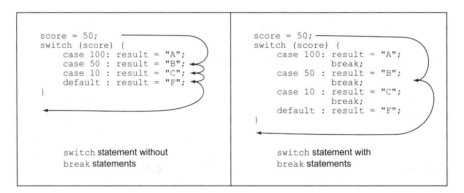

Figure 5.8   Differences in code flow for a switch statement with and without break statements

5.3   *The for loop*

[5.2]   Create and use for loops including the enhanced for loop

In this section, I'll cover the regular for loop. The enhanced for loop is covered in the next section.

A `for` loop is *usually* used to execute a set of statements a fixed number of times. It takes the following form:

```
for (initialization; condition; update) {
    statements;
}
```

Here's a simple example:

```
int tableOf = 25;
for (int ctr = 1; ctr <= 5; ctr++) {
    System.out.println(tableOf * ctr);
}
```

1 **Executes multiple times**

The output of the previous code is as follows:

```
25
50
75
100
125
```

In the previous example, the code at **1** will execute five times. It'll start with an initial value of 1 for the variable `ctr` and execute while the value of the variable `ctr` is less than or equal to 5. The value of variable `ctr` will increment by 1 (ctr++) after the execution of the code at **1**.

The code at **1** executes for `ctr` values 1, 2, 3, 4, and 5. Because 6 <= 5 evaluates to `false`, the `for` loop completes its execution without executing the code at **1** any further.

In the previous example, notice that the `for` loop defines three types of statements separated with semicolons (;), as follows:

- Initialization statements
- Termination condition
- Update clause (executable statement)

This loop is depicted as a flowchart in figure 5.9. The statements defined within the loop body execute until the termination condition is `false`.

One important point to note with respect to the `for` loop is that the update clause executes after all the statements defined within the `for` loop body. In other words, you can consider the update clause to be a last statement in the `for` loop. The initialization section, which executes only once, may define multiple initialization statements. Similarly, the update clause may define multiple statements. But there can be only one termination condition for a `for` loop.

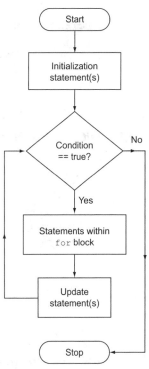

Figure 5.9   The flow of control in a `for` loop

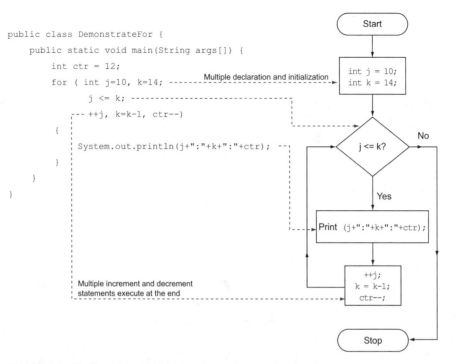

Figure 5.10   The flow of control in a `for` loop using a code example

In figure 5.10, I've provided a code snippet and a flowchart that depicts the corresponding flow of execution of statements to explain the previous concept.

Let's explore the initialization block, termination condition, and update clause of a `for` loop in detail.

5.3.1   *Initialization block*

An initialization block executes only once. A `for` loop can declare and initialize multiple variables in its initialization block, but the variables it declares should be of the same type. The following code is valid:

```
int tableOf = 25;
for (int ctr = 1, num = 100000; ctr <= 5; ++ctr) {      ◁──┐ Define and assign
    System.out.println(tableOf * ctr);                        multiple variables
    System.out.println(num * ctr);
}
```

But you can't declare variables of different types in an initialization block. The following code will fail to compile:

```
                                                        Can't define variables of different
                                                        types in an initialization block
for (int j=10, long longVar = 10; j <= 1; ++j) { }  ◁──┘
```

It's a common programming mistake to try to use the variables defined in a `for`'s initialization block outside the `for` block. Please note that the scope of the variables declared in the initialization block is limited to the `for` block. An example follows:

```
int tableOf = 25;
for (int ctr = 1; ctr <= 5; ++ctr) {           Variable ctr is accessible
    System.out.println(tableOf * ctr);          only within for loop body
}
ctr = 20;                                      Variable ctr isn't accessible
                                               outside for loop
```

5.3.2 Termination condition

The termination condition is evaluated once for each iteration before executing the statements defined within the body of the loop. The `for` loop terminates when the termination condition evaluates to `false`:

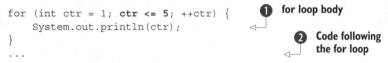

```
for (int ctr = 1; ctr <= 5; ++ctr) {           ❶ for loop body
    System.out.println(ctr);
}                                              ❷ Code following
...                                              the for loop
```

The termination condition—`ctr <= 5` in this example—is checked before ❶ executes. If the condition evaluates to `false`, control is transferred to ❷. A `for` loop can define exactly one termination condition—no more, no less.

5.3.3 The update clause

Usually, you'd use this block to manipulate the value of the variable that you used to specify the termination condition. In the previous example, I defined the following code in this section:

```
++ctr;
```

Code defined in this block executes *after* all the code defined in the body of the `for` loop. The previous code increments the value of the variable `ctr` by 1 after the following code executes:

```
System.out.println(ctr);
```

The termination condition is evaluated next. This execution continues until the termination condition evaluates to `false`.

You can define multiple statements in the update clause, including calls to other methods. The only limit is that these statements will execute in the order in which they appear, at the end of all the statements defined in the `for` block. Examine the following code, which calls a method in the update block:

```
public class ForIncrementStatements {
    public static void main(String args[]) {          The increment
        String line = "ab";                           block can also
        for (int i=0; i < line.length(); ++i, printMethod())   call methods
            System.out.println(line.charAt(i));
    }
    private static void printMethod() {               printMethod is called
        System.out.println("Happy");                  by the for loop's
    }                                                 increment block
}
```

The output of this code is as follows:

```
a
Happy
b
Happy
```

5.3.4   *Nested for loop*

If a loop encloses another loop, they are called *nested loops*. The loop that encloses another loop is called the *outer loop*, and the enclosed loop is called the *inner loop*. Theoretically, there are no limits on the levels of nesting for loops.

Let's get started with a single-level nested loop. For an example, you can compare the hour hand of a clock to an outer loop and its minute hand to an inner loop. Each hour can be compared with an iteration of the outer loop, and each minute can be compared with an iteration of the inner loop. Because an hour has 60 minutes, the inner loop should iterate 60 times *for each iteration* of the outer loop. This comparison between a clock and a nested loop is shown in figure 5.11.

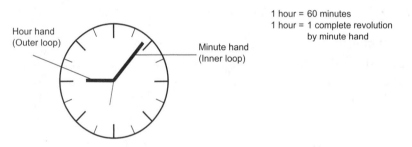

Figure 5.11   Comparison of the hands of a clock to a nested loop

You can use the following nested for loops to print out each minute (1 to 60) for hours from 1 to 6:

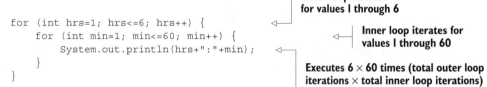

```java
for (int hrs=1; hrs<=6; hrs++) {
    for (int min=1; min<=60; min++) {
        System.out.println(hrs+":"+min);
    }
}
```

- Outer loop iterates for values I through 6
- Inner loop iterates for values I through 60
- Executes 6 × 60 times (total outer loop iterations × total inner loop iterations)

Nested loops are often used to initialize or iterate multidimensional arrays. The following code initializes a multidimensional array using nested for loops:

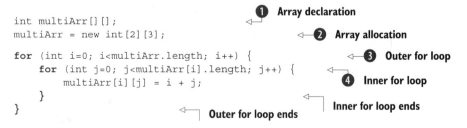

```java
int multiArr[][];
multiArr = new int[2][3];

for (int i=0; i<multiArr.length; i++) {
    for (int j=0; j<multiArr[i].length; j++) {
        multiArr[i][j] = i + j;
    }
}
```

- ❶ Array declaration
- ❷ Array allocation
- ❸ Outer for loop
- ❹ Inner for loop
- Inner for loop ends
- Outer for loop ends

❶ defines a two-dimensional array `multiArr`. ❷ allocates this array, creating two rows and three columns, and assigns all array members the default `int` value of 0.

❸ defines an outer `for` loop. Because the value of `multiArr.length` is 2 (the value of the first subscript at ❷), the outer `for` loop executes twice, with variable i having values 0 and 1. The inner `for` loop is defined at ❹. Because the length of each of the rows of the `multiArr` array is 3 (the value of the second subscript at ❷), the inner loop executes three times for each iteration of the outer `for` loop, with variable j having values 0, 1, and 2.

Figure 5.12 illustrates the array `multiArr` after it's initialized using the previous code.

In the next section, I discuss another flavor of the `for` loop: the *enhanced* `for` loop or `for`-each loop.

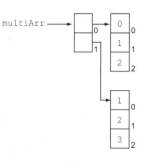

Figure 5.12   The array `multiArr` after it's initialized using the previous code

5.4   *The enhanced for loop*

[5.2]   Create and use for loops including the enhanced for loop

The enhanced `for` loop is also called the *for-each* loop, and it offers some advantages over the regular `for` loop. It also has some limitations.

To start with, the regular `for` loop is cumbersome to use when it comes to iterating through a collection or an array. You need to create a looping variable and specify the start and end positions of the collection or the array, even if you want to iterate through the complete collection or list. The enhanced `for` loop makes the previously mentioned routine task quite a breeze, as the following example demonstrates for an `ArrayList myList`:

```
ArrayList<String> myList= new ArrayList<String>();
myList.add("Java");
myList.add("Loop");
```

The following code uses the regular `for` loop to iterate through this list:

```
for(Iterator<String> i = myList.iterator(); i.hasNext();)
    System.out.println(i.next());
```

The following code uses the enhanced `for` loop to iterate through the list `myList`:

```
for (String val : myList)
    System.out.println(val);
```

You can read the colon (`:`) in a `for`-each loop as "in".

The `for`-each loop is a breeze to implement: there's no code clutter, and the code is easy to write and comprehend. In the previous example, the `for`-each loop is read as "for each element `val` in collection `myList`, print the value of `val`."

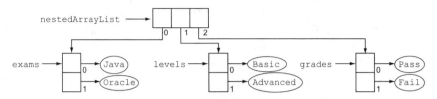

Figure 5.13   Pictorial representation of `nestedArrayList`

You can also easily iterate through *nested collections* using the enhanced `for` loop. In this example, assume that an `ArrayList` of `exams`, `levels`, and `grades` are defined as follows:

```
ArrayList<String> exams= new ArrayList<String>();
exams.add("Java"); exams.add("Oracle");

ArrayList<String> levels= new ArrayList<String>();
levels.add("Basic"); levels.add("Advanced");

ArrayList<String> grades= new ArrayList<String>();
grades.add("Pass"); grades.add("Fail");
```

The following code creates a nested `ArrayList`, `nestedArrayList`, every element of which is itself an `ArrayList` of `String` objects:

```
ArrayList<ArrayList<String>> nestedArrayList =
                      new ArrayList< ArrayList<String>>();
nestedArrayList.add(exams);
nestedArrayList.add(levels);
nestedArrayList.add(grades);
```

ArrayList of ArrayList

Add object of ArrayList to nestedArrayList

The `nestedArrayList` can be compared to a multidimensional array, as shown in figure 5.13.

A nested enhanced `for` loop can be used to iterate through the nested `ArrayList` `nestedArrayList`. Here's the relevant code:

```
for (ArrayList<String> nestedListElement : nestedArrayList)
    for (String element : nestedListElement)
        System.out.println(element);
```

The output of this code is as follows:

```
Java
Oracle
Basic
Advanced
Pass
Fail
```

The enhanced `for` loop is again a breeze to use to iterate through *nested or non-nested* arrays. For example, you can use the following code to iterate through an array of elements and calculate its total:

```
int total = 0;
int primeNums[] = {2, 3, 7, 11};
for (int num : primeNums)
    total += num;
```

What happens when you try to modify the value of the loop variable in an enhanced for loop? The result depends on whether you're iterating through a collection of primitive values or objects. If you're iterating through an array of primitive values, manipulation of the loop variable will never change the value of the array being iterated because the primitive values are passed by value to the loop variable in an enhanced for loop.

When you iterate through a collection of objects, the value of the collection is passed by reference to the loop variable. Therefore, if the value of the loop variable is manipulated by executing methods on it, the modified value will be reflected in the collection of objects being iterated:

```
StringBuilder myArr[] = {
                new StringBuilder("Java"),
                new StringBuilder("Loop")
                };

for (StringBuilder val : myArr)          Iterates through array myArr
    System.out.println(val);             and prints Java and Loop

for (StringBuilder val : myArr)                 Appends Oracle to value
    val.append("Oracle");                       referred by loop variable val

for (StringBuilder val : myArr)          Iterates through array myArr and
    System.out.println(val);             prints JavaOracle and LoopOracle
```

The output of the previous code is:

```
Java
Loop
JavaOracle
LoopOracle
```

Let's modify the previous code. Instead of calling the method append on the loop variable val, let's assign to it another StringBuilder object. In this case, the original elements of the array being iterated will not be affected and will remain the same:

```
StringBuilder myArr[] = {
                new StringBuilder("Java"),
                new StringBuilder("Loop")
                };

or (StringBuilder val : myArr)          Iterates through array myArr
    System.out.println (val);           and prints Java and Loop

for (StringBuilder val : myArr)                 Assigns new StringBuilder object to
    val = new StringBuilder("Oracle");          reference variable val with value Oracle

for (StringBuilder val : myArr)          Iterates through array myArray
    System.out.println (val);            and still prints Java and Loop
```

The output of previous code is:

```
Java
Loop
Java
Loop
```

EXAM TIP   Watch out for code that uses an enhanced `for` loop and its loop variable to change the values of elements in the collection that it iterates. This behavior often serves as food for thought for the exam authors.

5.4.1   *Limitations of the enhanced for loop*

Though a `for`-each loop is a good choice for iterating through collections and arrays, it can't be used in some places.

CAN'T BE USED TO INITIALIZE AN ARRAY AND MODIFY ITS ELEMENTS

Can you use an enhanced `for` loop in place of the regular `for` loop in the following code?

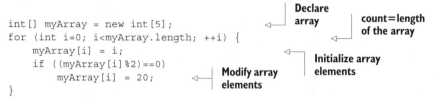

The simple answer is "no." Although you can define a "counter" outside of the enhanced `for` loop and use it to initialize and modify the array elements, this approach defeats the purpose of the `for`-each loop. The existing `for` loop is easier to use in this case.

CAN'T BE USED TO DELETE OR REMOVE THE ELEMENTS OF A COLLECTION

Because the `for` loop hides the *iterator* used to iterate through the elements of a collection, you can't use it to remove or delete the existing collection values because you can't call the `remove` method.

If you assign a `null` value to the loop variable, it won't remove the element from a collection:

```
ArrayList<StringBuilder> myList= new ArrayList<>();
myList.add(new StringBuilder("One"));
myList.add(new StringBuilder("Two"));

for (StringBuilder val : myList)
    System.out.println (val);

for (StringBuilder val : myList)
    val = null;

for (StringBuilder val : myList)
    System.out.println(val);
```

> Doesn't remove an object from list; sets value of loop variable to null

The output of the previous code is:

```
One
Two
One
Two
```

CAN'T BE USED TO ITERATE OVER MULTIPLE COLLECTIONS OR ARRAYS IN THE SAME LOOP
Though it's perfectly fine for you to iterate through nested collections or arrays using a for loop, you can't iterate over multiple collections or arrays in the same for-each loop because the for-each loop allows for the creation of only one looping variable. Unlike the regular for loop, you can't define multiple looping variables in a for-each loop.

 EXAM TIP Use the for-each loop to iterate arrays and collections. Don't use it to initialize, modify, or filter them.

5.4.2 *Nested enhanced for loop*

First of all, working with a nested collection is not the same as working with a nested loop. A nested loop can also work with unrelated collections.

As discussed in section 5.3.4, loops defined within another loop are called *nested loops*. The loop that defines another loop within itself is called the *outer loop*, and the loop that's defined within another loop is called the *inner loop*. Theoretically, the level of nesting for any of the loops has no limits, including the enhanced for loop.

In this section, we'll work with three nested enhanced for loops. You can compare a three-level nested loop with a clock that has hour, minute, and second hands. The second hand of the clock completes a full circle each minute. Similarly, the minute hand completes a full circle each hour. This comparison is shown in figure 5.14.

The following is a coding example of the nested, enhanced for loop, which I discussed in a previous section:

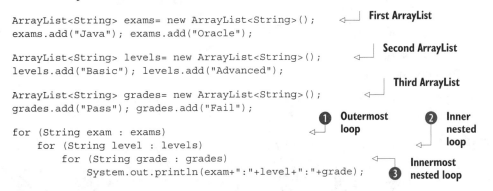

```
ArrayList<String> exams= new ArrayList<String>();          ⟵⌐ First ArrayList
exams.add("Java"); exams.add("Oracle");

ArrayList<String> levels= new ArrayList<String>();         ⟵⌐ Second ArrayList
levels.add("Basic"); levels.add("Advanced");

ArrayList<String> grades= new ArrayList<String>();         ⟵⌐ Third ArrayList
grades.add("Pass"); grades.add("Fail");
                                                    ❶ Outermost     ❷ Inner
for (String exam : exams)                        ⟵⌐    loop              nested
    for (String level : levels)                                     ⟵⌐   loop
        for (String grade : grades)                          ⟵⌐
            System.out.println(exam+":"+level+":"+grade);    ❸ Innermost
                                                                nested loop
```

An inner loop in a nested loop executes for each iteration of its outer loop. The previous example defines three enhanced for loops: the outermost loop at ❶, the inner nested loop at ❷, and the innermost loop at ❸. The complete innermost loop at ❸ executes for each iteration of its immediate outer loop defined at ❷. Similarly, the complete inner loop defined at ❷ executes for each iteration of its

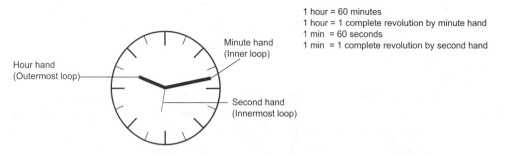

1 hour = 60 minutes
1 hour = 1 complete revolution by minute hand
1 min = 60 seconds
1 min = 1 complete revolution by second hand

Figure 5.14   Comparison between a clock with three hands and the levels of a nested `for` **loop**

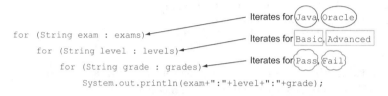

Figure 5.15   Nested `for` **loop with the loop values for which each of these nested loop iterates**

immediate outer loop defined at ❶. Figure 5.15 shows the loop values for which all of these loops iterate.

The output of the previous code is as follows:

```
Java:Basic:Pass
Java:Basic:Fail
Java:Advanced:Pass
Java:Advanced:Fail
Oracle:Basic:Pass
Oracle:Basic:Fail
Oracle:Advanced:Pass
Oracle:Advanced:Fail
```

EXAM TIP   A nested loop executes all its iterations for each single iteration of its immediate outer loop.

Apart from the `for` loops, the other looping statements on the exam are `while` and `do-while`, which are discussed in the next section.

5.5   *The while and do-while loops*

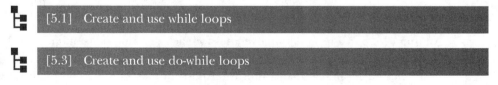

[5.1]   Create and use while loops

[5.3]   Create and use do-while loops

You'll learn about `while` and `do-while` loops in this section. Both of these loops execute a set of statements as long as their condition evaluates to `true`. Both of these loops work in exactly the same manner, except for one difference: the while loops checks its condition before evaluating its loop body, and the do-while loop checks its condition after executing the statements defined in its loop body.

Does this difference in behavior make a difference in their execution? Yes, it does, and in this section, you'll see how.

5.5.1 *The while loop*

A while loop is used to repeatedly execute a set of statements as long as its condition evaluates to true. This loop checks the condition *before* it starts the execution of the statement.

For example, at famous fast-food chain Superfast Burgers, an employee may be instructed to prepare burgers as long as buns are available. In this example, the availability of buns is the while condition and the preparation of burgers is the while's loop body. We can represent this in code as follows:

```
boolean bunsAvailable = true;
while (bunsAvailable) {
    ... prepare burger ...
    if (noMoreBuns)
        bunsAvailable = false;
}
```

The previous example is for demonstration purposes only, because the loop body isn't completely defined. The condition used in the while loop to check whether or not to execute the loop body again should evaluate to false at some point in time; otherwise, the loop will execute indefinitely. The value of this loop variable may be changed by the while loop or by another method if it's an instance or a static variable.

The while loop accepts arguments of type boolean or Boolean. Because the Boolean wrapper class isn't covered in the OCA Java SE 7 Programmer I exam, I won't cover it any further. In the previous code, the loop body checks whether more buns are available. If none are available, it sets the value of the variable bunsAvailable to false. The loop body doesn't execute for the next iteration because bunsAvailable evaluates to false.

The execution of the previous while loop is shown in figure 5.16 as a simple flow-chart to help you understand the concept better.

Now, let's examine another simple example that uses the while loop:

```
int num = 9;
boolean divisibleBy7 = false;
while (!divisibleBy7) {
    System.out.println(num);
    if (num % 7 == 0) divisibleBy7 = true;
    --num;
}
```

The output of this code is as follows:

```
9
8
7
```

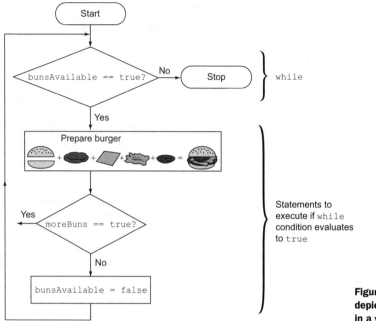

Figure 5.16   **A flowchart depicting the flow of code in a while loop**

What happens if you change the code as follows (changes in bold):

```
int num = 9;
boolean divisibleBy7 = true;
while (divisibleBy7 == false) {
    System.out.println(num);
    if (num % 7 == 0) divisibleBy7 = true;
    --num;
}
```

The code won't enter the loop because the condition `divisibleBy7==false` isn't `true`.

5.5.2   *The do-while loop*

A do-while loop is used to repeatedly execute a set of statements until the condition that it uses evaluates to `false`. This loop checks the condition *after* it completes the execution of all the statements in its loop body.

You could compare this structure to a software application that displays a menu at startup. Each menu option will execute a set of steps and redisplay the menu. The last menu option is "exit," which exits the application and does not redisplay the menu:

```
boolean exitSelected = false;
do {
    String selectedOption = displayMenuToUser();
    if (selectedOption.equals("exit"))
        exitSelected = true;
    else
        executeCommand(selectedOption);
} while (exitSelected == false);
```

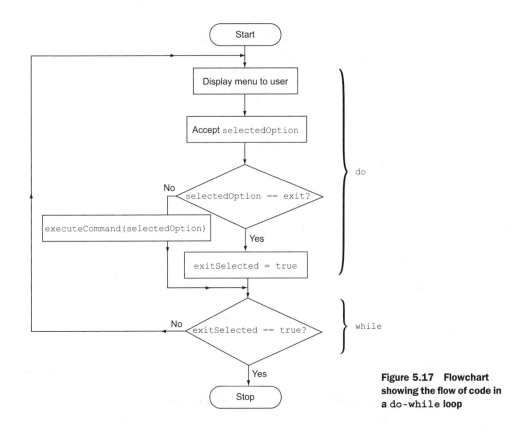

Figure 5.17 Flowchart showing the flow of code in a do-while loop

The previous code is represented by a simple flowchart in figure 5.17 that will help you to better understand the code.

The previous example is for demonstration purposes only because the methods used in the do-while loop aren't defined. As discussed in the previous section on while loops, the condition that's used in the do-while loop to check whether or not to execute the loop body again should evaluate to false at some point in time, or the loop will execute indefinitely. The value of this loop variable may be changed by the while loop or by another method, if it's an instance or static variable.

> **NOTE** Don't forget to use a semicolon (;) to end the do-while loop after specifying its condition. Even some experienced programmers overlook this step!

The do-while loop accepts arguments of type boolean or Boolean. Because the Boolean wrapper class isn't covered in the OCA Java SE 7 Programmer I exam, I won't cover it any further.

Let's modify the example used in section 5.5.1 to use the do-while loop instead of a while loop, as follows:

```
int num = 9;
boolean divisibleBy7 = false;
do {
```

```
        System.out.println(num);
        if (num % 7 == 0) divisibleBy7 = true;
        num--;
} while (divisibleBy7 == false);
```

The output of this code is as follows:

```
9
8
7
```

What happens if you change the code as follows (changes in bold):

```
int num = 9;
boolean divisibleBy7 = true;
do {
        System.out.println(num);
        if (num % 7 == 0) divisibleBy7 = true;
        num--;
} while (divisibleBy7 == false);
```

The output of the previous code is as follows:

```
9
```

The do-while loop executes once, even though the condition specified in the do-while loop evaluates to false because the condition is evaluated at the end of execution of the loop body.

5.5.3   *While and do-while block, expression, and nesting rules*

You can use the curly braces {} with while and do-while loops to define multiple lines of code to execute for every iteration. Without the use of curly braces, only the first line of code will be considered a part of the while or do-while loop, as specified in the if-else construct in section 5.1.3.

Similarly, the rules that define an appropriate expression to be passed to while and do-while loops are as for the if-else construct in section 5.1.4. Also, the rules for defining nested while and do-while loops are the same as for an if-else construct in section 5.1.5.

5.6   *Comparing loop constructs*

[5.4]   Compare loop constructs

In this section, I'll discuss the differences and similarities between the following looping constructs: do-while, while, for, and enhanced for.

5.6.1   *Comparing do-while and while loops*

Both do-while and while loops execute a set of statements until their termination condition evaluates to false. The only difference between these two statements is that the do-while loop executes the code at least once, even if the condition evaluates to

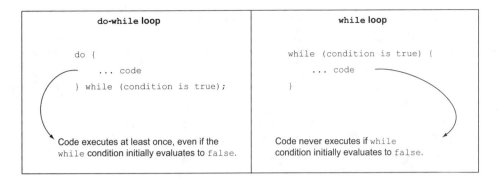

Figure 5.18 Comparing do-while **and** while **loops**

false. The do-while loop evaluates the termination condition *after* executing the statements, whereas the while loop evaluates the termination condition *before* executing its statements.

The forms taken by these statements are depicted in figure 5.18.

What do you think the output of the following code is?

The output of the previous code is as follows:

```
12
```

What do you think the output of the following code is?

```
int num=10;
while (++num > 20) {
    num++;
}
System.out.println(num);
```
Because 11 isn't > 20,
num++ doesn't execute.

The output of the previous code is as follows

```
11
```

5.6.2 *Comparing for and enhanced for loops*

The regular for loop, although cumbersome to use, is much more powerful than the enhanced for loop (as mentioned in section 5.4.1):

- The enhanced for loop can't be used to initialize an array and modify its elements.
- The enhanced for loop can't be used to delete the elements of a collection.
- The enhanced for loop can't be used to iterate over multiple collections or arrays in the same loop.

5.6.3   *Comparing for and while loops*

You should *try* to use a `for` loop when you know the number of iterations—for example, when you're iterating through a collection or an array, or when you're executing a loop for a fixed number of times, say to "ping" a server five times.

You should *try* to use a `do-while` or a `while` loop when you don't know the number of iterations beforehand, and when the number of iterations depends on a condition being `true`—for example, when accepting passport renewal applications from applicants until there are no more applicants. In this case, you'd be unaware of the number of applicants who have submitted their applications on a given day.

5.7   *Loop statements: break and continue*

[5.5]   Use break and continue

Imagine that you've defined a loop to iterate through a list of managers, and you're looking for at least one manager whose name starts with the letter *D*. You'd like to exit the loop after you find the first match, but how? You can do this by using the `break` statement in your loop.

Now imagine that you want to iterate through all of the folders on your laptop and scan any files larger than 10 MB for viruses. If all those files are found to be okay, you want to upload them to a server. But what if you'd like to skip the steps of *virus checking* and *file uploading* for file sizes less than 10 MB, yet still proceed with the remaining files on your laptop? You can! You'd use the `continue` statement in your loop.

In this section, I'll discuss the `break` and `continue` statements, which you can use to exit a loop completely or to skip the remaining statements in a loop iteration. At the end of this section, I'll discuss labeled statements.

5.7.1   *The break statement*

The `break` statement is used to *exit*—or *break out of*—the `for`, for-each, `do`, and `do-while` loops, as well as `switch` constructs. Alternatively, the `continue` statement can be used to skip the remaining steps in the current iteration and start with the next loop iteration.

The difference between these statements can be best demonstrated with an example. You could use the following code to browse and print all of the values of a `String` array:

```
String[] programmers = {"Paul", "Shreya", "Selvan", "Harry"};
for (String name : programmers) {
    System.out.println(name);
}
```

The output of the previous code is as follows:

```
Paul
Shreya
Selvan
Harry
```

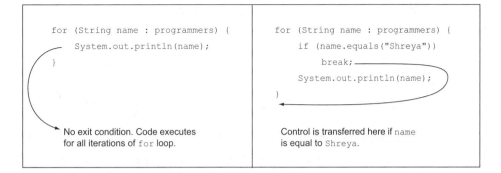

Figure 5.19 **The flow of control when the** `break` **statement executes within a loop**

Let's modify the previous code to exit the loop when the array value is equal to Shreya. Here's the required code:

```
String[] programmers = {"Paul", "Shreya", "Selvan", "Harry"};
for (String name : programmers) {
    if (name.equals("Shreya"))
        break;                              Break out
    System.out.println(name);               of the loop
}
```

The output of the previous code is as follows:

```
Paul
```

As soon as a loop encounters a `break`, it exits the loop. Hence, only the first value of this array—that is, `Paul`—is printed. As mentioned in the section on the `switch` construct, the `break` statement can be defined after every case in order for the control to exit the `switch` construct once it finds a matching case.

The previous code snippets are depicted in figure 5.19, which shows the transfer of control upon execution of the `break` statement.

When you use the `break` statement with nested loops, it exits the inner loop. The next Twist in the Tale exercise looks at a small code snippet to see how the control transfers when you use a `break` statement in nested `for` loops (answers in the appendix).

> **Twist in the Tale 5.4**

Let's modify the code used in the previous example as follows. What is the output of this code?

```
String[] programmers = {"Outer", "Inner"};
for (String outer : programmers) {
    for (String inner : programmers) {
        if (inner.equals("Inner"))
            break;
        System.out.print(inner + ":");
    }
}
```

a `Outer:Outer:`

b `Outer:Inner:Outer:Inner:`

c `Outer:`

d `Outer:Inner:`

, **e** `Inner:Inner:`

5.7.2 *The continue statement*

The `continue` statement is used to skip the remaining steps in the current iteration and start with the next loop iteration. Let's replace the `break` statement in the previous example with `continue` and examine its output:

```
String[] programmers = {"Paul", "Shreya", "Selvan", "Harry"};
for (String name : programmers) {
    if (name.equals("Shreya"))
        continue;                         ◁—|  Skip the remaining
    System.out.println(name);                |  loop statements
}
```

The output of the previous code is as follows:

```
Paul
Selvan
Harry
```

As soon as a loop encounters `continue`, it exits the current iteration of the loop. In this example, it skips the printing step for the array value `Shreya`. Unlike the `break` statement, `continue` doesn't exit the loop—it restarts with the next loop iteration, printing the remaining array values (that is, `Selvan` and `Harry`).

When you use the `continue` statement with nested loops, it exits the current iteration of the inner loop.

Figure 5.20 compares how the control transfers out of the loop and to the next iteration when `break` and `continue` statements are used.

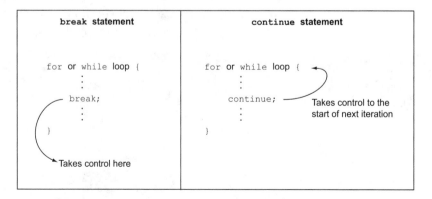

Figure 5.20 Comparing the flow of control when using `break` and `continue` statements in a loop

5.7.3 *Labeled statements*

In Java, you can add labels to the following types of statements:

- A code block defined using {}
- All looping statements (for, enhanced for, while, do-while)
- Conditional constructs (if and switch statements)
- Expressions
- Assignments
- return statements
- try blocks
- throws statements

An example of a labeled loop is given here:

```
String[] programmers = {"Outer", "Inner"};
outer:
for (int i = 0; i < programmers.length; i++) {
}
```

You can't add labels to declarations. The following labeled declaration won't compile:

```
outer :
    int[] myArray = {1,2,3};
```
⟵┘ **Variable declaration**
that fails compilation

It's interesting to note that the previous declaration can be defined within a block statement, as follows:

```
outer : {
    int[] myArray = {1,2,3};
}
```
⟵┘ **Start definition**
of block

⟵┤ **Variable declaration,**
compiles

⟵┐ **End block**

LABELED BREAK STATEMENTS

You can use a labeled break statement to exit an outer loop. Here's an example:

```
String[] programmers = {"Outer", "Inner"};
outer:
for (String outer : programmers) {
    for (String inner : programmers) {
        if (inner.equals("Inner"))
            break outer;
        System.out.print(inner + ":");
    }
}
```
⟵┘ **Exits the outer loop,**
marked with label outer

The output of the previous code is:

```
Outer:
```

When this code executes break outer:, control transfers to the line of text that marks the end of this block. It doesn't transfer control to the label outer.

LABELED CONTINUE STATEMENTS

You can use a labeled continue statement to skip an iteration of the outer loop. Here's an example:

```
String[] programmers = {"Paul", "Shreya", "Selvan", "Harry"};
outer:
for (String name1 : programmers) {
    for (String name : programmers) {
        if (name.equals("Shreya"))
            continue outer;
        System.out.println(name);
    }
}
```

> **Skips remaining code for current iteration of outer loop and starts with its next iteration**

The output of the previous code is:

```
Paul
Paul
Paul
Paul
```

5.8   *Summary*

We started this chapter with the selection statements if and switch. We covered the different flavors of the if construct. Then we looked at the switch construct, which accepts a limited set of argument types including byte, char, short, int, and String. The humble if-else construct can define virtually any set of simple or complicated conditions.

We also saw how you can execute your code using all types of loops: for, for-each, do, and do-while. The for, do, and do-while loops have been around since the Java language was first introduced, whereas the enhanced for loop (the for-each loop) was added to the language as of Java version 5.0. I recommend that you use the for-each loop to iterate through arrays and collections.

At the end of this chapter, we looked at the break and continue statements. You use the break statement to *exit*—or *break out of*—a for, for-each, do, do-while, or switch construct. You use the continue statement to skip the remaining steps in the current iteration and start with the next loop iteration.

5.9   *Review notes*

if and if-else constructs:

- The if statement enables you to execute a set of statements in your code based on the result of a condition, which should evaluate to a boolean or Boolean value.
- The multiple flavors of an if statement are if, if-else, and if-else-if-else.
- The if construct doesn't use the keyword *then* to define code to execute when an if condition evaluates to true. The *then* part of the if construct follows the if condition.
- An if construct may or may not define its else part.
- The else part of an if construct can't exist without the definition of its *then* part.
- It's easy to get confused with the common *if-else* syntax used in other programming languages. The if-elsif and if-elseif statements aren't used in Java to define if-else-if-else constructs. The correct keywords are if and else.

- You can execute a single statement or a block of statements for corresponding `true` and `false` conditions. A pair of braces marks a block of statements: { }.
- If an `if` construct doesn't use { } to define a block of code to execute for its *then* or `else` part, only the first line of code is part of the `if` construct.
- An assignment of a `boolean` variable can also be passed as an argument to the `if` construct. It's valid because the resultant value is `boolean`, which is accepted by `if` constructs.
- Theoretically, nested `if` and `if-else` constructs have no limits on their levels. When using nested `if-else` constructs, be careful about matching the `else` part with the right `if` part.

`switch` statements:

- A `switch` statement is used to compare the value of a variable with multiple pre-defined values.
- A `switch` statement accepts arguments of type `char`, `byte`, `short`, `int`, and `String`. It also accepts arguments of wrapper classes: `Character`, `Byte`, `Short`, `Integer`, and `Enum`. These wrapper classes aren't on the OCA Java SE 7 Programmer I exam.
- A `switch` statement can be compared with multiple related `if-else-if-else` constructs.
- You can pass an expression as an argument to a `switch` statement, as long as the type of the expression is one of the acceptable data types.
- The `case` value should be a compile-time constant, assignable to the argument passed to the `switch` statement.
- The `case` value can't be the literal value `null`.
- The `case` value can define expressions that use literal values; that is, they can be evaluated at compile time, as in `7+2`.
- One code block can be defined to execute for multiple `case` values in a `switch` statement.
- A `break` statement is used to exit a `switch` construct once a matching case is found and the required code statements have executed.
- In absence of the `break` statement, control will *fall through* all the remaining case values in a `switch` statement until the first `break` statement is found, evaluating the code for the `case` statements in order.

`for` loops:

- A `for` loop is usually used to execute a set of statements a fixed number of times.
- A `for` loop defines three types of statements separated by semicolons (;): initialization statements, termination condition, and update clause.
- The definition of any of the three `for` statements—initialization statements, termination condition, and update clause—is optional. For example, `for (;;);`

and for (;;) {} are valid code for defining a for loop. Also, defining any one of these statements is also valid code.

- An initialization block executes only once. A for loop can declare and initialize multiple variables in its initialization block, but the variables that it declares should be of the same type.
- The termination condition is evaluated once, for all the iterations, before the statements defined within the body of the loop are executed.
- The for loop terminates when the termination condition evaluates to false.
- The update block is usually used to increment or decrement the value of the variables that are defined in the initialization block. It can also execute multiple other statements, including method calls.
- Nested for loops have no limits on levels.
- Nested for loops are frequently used to work with multidimensional arrays.

Enhanced for loops:

- The enhanced for loop is also called the for-each loop.
- The enhanced for loop offers some benefits over the regular for loop, but it's not as flexible as the regular for loop.
- The enhanced for loop offers simple syntax to iterate through a collection of values—an array, ArrayList, or other classes from Java's Collection framework that store a collection of values.
- The enhanced for loop can't be used to initialize an array and modify its elements.
- The enhanced for loop can't be used to delete the elements of a collection.
- The enhanced for loop can't be used to iterate over multiple collections or arrays in the same loop.
- Nested enhanced for loops have no limits on levels.

while and do-while loops:

- A while loop is used to keep executing a set of statements until the condition that it uses evaluates to false. This loop checks the condition *before* it starts the execution of the statement.
- A do-while loop is used to keep executing a set of statements until the condition that it uses evaluates to false. This loop checks the condition *after* it completes the execution of all the statements in its loop body.
- The levels of nested do-while or while loops have no limitations.
- Both do-while and while loops can define either a single line of code or a code block to execute. The latter is defined by using curly braces, {}.

Comparing loop constructs:

- Both the do-while and while loops execute a set of statements until the termination condition evaluates to false. The only difference between these two statements is that the do-while loop executes the code at least once, even if the condition evaluates to false.

- The regular for loop, though cumbersome to use, is much more powerful than the enhanced for loop.
- The enhanced for loop can't be used to initialize an array and modify its elements. The enhanced for loop can't be used to delete or remove the elements of a collection.
- The enhanced for loop can't be used to iterate over multiple collections or arrays in the same loop.
- You should try to use a for loop when you know the number of iterations—for example, iterating through a collection or an array, or executing a loop for a fixed number of times, say to "ping" a server five times.
- You should try to use a do-while or a while loop when you don't know the number of iterations beforehand and the number of iterations depends on a condition being true—for example, accepting passport renewal applications until all applicants have been attended to.

Loop statements (break and continue):

- The break statement is used to *exit*—or *break out of*—the for, for-each, do, and do-while loops and the switch construct.
- The continue statement is used to skip the remaining steps in the current iteration and start with the next loop iteration. The continue statement works with the for, for-each, do, and do-while loops and the switch construct.
- When you use the break statement with nested loops, it exits the inner loop.
- When you use the continue statement with nested loops, it exits the current iteration of the inner loop.

Labeled statements:

- You can add labels to a code block defined using braces, {}, all looping statements (for, enhanced for loop, while, do-while), conditional constructs (if and switch statements), expressions and assignments, return statements, try blocks, and throws statements.
- You can't add labels to declarations of variables.
- You can use a labeled break statement to exit an outer loop.
- You can use a labeled continue statement to skip the iteration of the outer loop.

5.10 Sample exam questions

Q5-1. What's the output of the following code?

```
class Loop2 {
    public static void main(String[] args) {
        int i = 10;
        do
```

```
            while (i < 15)
                i = i + 20;
        while (i < 2);
        System.out.println(i);
    }
}
```

     a   10

     b   30

     c   31

     d   32

Q5-2. What's the output of the following code?

```
class Loop2 {
    public static void main(String[] args) {
        int i = 10;
        do
            while (i++ < 15)
                i = i + 20;
        while (i < 2);
        System.out.println(i);
    }
}
```

     a   10

     b   30

     c   31

     d   32

Q5-3. Which of the following statements is true?

     a   The enhanced for loop can't be used within a regular for loop.

     b   The enhanced for loop can't be used within a while loop.

     c   The enhanced for loop can be used within a do-while loop.

     d   The enhanced for loop can't be used within a switch construct.

     e   All of the above statements are false.

Q5-4. What's the output of the following code?

```
int a =  10;
if (a++ > 10) {
    System.out.println("true");
}
{
    System.out.println("false");
}
System.out.println("ABC");
```

     a   true
         false
         ABC

b false
   ABC

c true
   ABC

d Compilation error

Q5-5. Given the following code, which of the following lines of code can individually replace the //INSERT CODE HERE line so that the code compiles successfully?

```
class EJavaGuru {
    public static int getVal() {
        return 100;
    }
    public static void main(String args[]) {
        int num = 10;
        final int num2 = 20;
        switch (num) {
            // INSERT CODE HERE
            break;
            default: System.out.println("default");
        }
    }
}
```

a case 10*3: System.out.println(2);

b case num: System.out.println(3);

c case 10/3: System.out.println(4);

d case num2: System.out.println(5);

Q5-6. What's the output of the following code?

```
class EJavaGuru {
    public static void main(String args[]) {
        int num = 20;
        final int num2;
        num2 = 20;

        switch (num) {
            default: System.out.println("default");
            case num2: System.out.println(4);
            break;
        }
    }
}
```

a default

b default
   4

c 4

d Compilation error

Q5-7. What's the output of the following code?

```
class EJavaGuru {
    public static void main(String args[]) {
        int num = 120;

        switch (num) {
            default: System.out.println("default");
            case 0: System.out.println("case1");
            case 10*2-20: System.out.println("case2");
            break;
        }
    }
}
```

   a default
       case1
       case2

   b case1
       case2

   c case2

   d Compilation error

   e Runtime exception

Q5-8. What's the output of the following code?

```
class EJavaGuru3 {
    public static void main(String args[]) {
        byte foo = 120;
        switch (foo) {
            default: System.out.println("ejavaguru"); break;
            case 2: System.out.println("e"); break;
            case 120: System.out.println("ejava");
            case 121: System.out.println("enum");
            case 127: System.out.println("guru"); break;
        }
    }
}
```

   a ejava
       enum
       guru

   b ejava

   c ejavaguru
       e

   d ejava
       enum
       guru
       ejavaguru

Q5-9. What's the output of the following code?

```
class EJavaGuru4 {
    public static void main(String args[]) {
```

```
        boolean myVal = false;
        if (myVal=true)
        for (int i = 0; i < 2; i++) System.out.println(i);
        else System.out.println("else");
    }
}
```

a else

b 0
   1
   2

c 0
   1

d Compilation error

Q5-10. What's the output of the following code?

```
class EJavaGuru5 {
    public static void main(String args[]) {
        int i = 0;
        for (; i < 2; i=i+5) {
            if (i < 5) continue;
            System.out.println(i);
        }
        System.out.println(i);
    }
}
```

a Compilation error

b 0
   5

c 0
   5
   10

d 10

e 0
   1
   5

f 5

5.11 Answers to sample exam questions

Q5-1. What's the output of the following code?

```
class Loop2 {
    public static void main(String[] args) {
        int i = 10;
        do
            while (i < 15)
                i = i + 20;
        while (i < 2);
        System.out.println(i);
    }
}
```

    a 10

    b **30**

    c 31

    d 32

Answer: b

Explanation: The condition specified in the do-while loop evaluates to false (because 10<2 evaluates to false). But the control enters the do-while loop because the do-while loop executes at least once—its condition is checked at the end of the loop. The while evaluates to true for the first iteration and adds 20 to i, making it 30. The while loop doesn't execute for the second time. Hence, the value of the variable i at the end of the execution of the previous code is 30.

Q5-2. What's the output of the following code?

```
class Loop2 {
    public static void main(String[] args) {
        int i = 10;
        do
            while (i++ < 15)
                i = i + 20;
        while (i < 2);
        System.out.println(i);
    }
}
```

    a 10

    b 30

    c 31

    d **32**

Answer: d

Explanation: If you've attempted to answer question 5-1, it's likely that you would select the same answer for this question, too. I've deliberately used the same question text and variable names (with a small difference) because you may encounter a similar pattern in the OCA Java SE 7 Programmer I exam. This question includes one difference: unlike question 5-1, it uses a postfix unary operator in the while condition.

    The condition specified in the do-while loop evaluates to false (because 10<2 evaluates to false). But the control enters the do-while loop because the do-while loop executes at least once—its condition is checked at the end of the loop. This question prints outs 32, not 30, because the condition specified in the while loop (which has an increment operator) executes twice.

    In this question, the while loop condition executes twice. For the first evaluation, i++ < 15 (that is, 10<15) returns true and increments the value of variable i by 1 (due to the postfix increment operator). The loop body modifies the value of i to 31. The second condition evaluates i++<15 (that is, 31<15) to false. But due to the postfix increment operator value of i, it increments to 32. The final value is printed as 32.

Q5-3. Which of the following statements is true?

   a The enhanced for loop can't be used within a regular for loop.

   b The enhanced for loop can't be used within a while loop.

   c **The enhanced for loop can be used within a do-while loop.**

   d The enhanced for loop can't be used within a switch construct.

   e All of the above statements are false.

Answer: c

Explanation: The enhanced for loop can be used within all types of looping and conditional constructs. Notice the use of "can" and "can't" in the answer options. It's important to take note of these subtle differences.

Q5-4. What's the output of the following code?

```
int a =  10;
if (a++ > 10) {
    System.out.println("true");
}
{
    System.out.println("false");
}
System.out.println("ABC");
```

   a true
      false
      ABC

   b **false**
      ABC

   c true
      ABC

   d Compilation error

Answer: b

Explanation: First of all, the code has no compilation errors. This question has a trick—the following code snippet isn't part of the if construct:

```
{
    System.out.println("false");
}
```

Hence, the value false will print no matter what, regardless of whether the condition in the if construct evaluates to true or false.

Because the opening and closing braces for this code snippet are placed right after the if construct, it leads us to believe that this code snippet is the else part of the if construct. Also, note that an if construct uses the keyword else to define the else part. This keyword is missing in this question.

The `if` condition (that is, a++ > 10) evaluates to `false` because the postfix increment operator (a++) increments the value of the variable a immediately after its earlier value is used. `10` isn't greater than `10` so this condition evaluates to `false`.

Q5-5. Given the following code, which of the following lines of code can individually replace the `//INSERT CODE HERE` line so that the code compiles successfully?

```
class EJavaGuru {
    public static int getVal() {
        return 100;
    }
    public static void main(String args[]) {
        int num = 10;
        final int num2 = 20;
        switch (num) {
            // INSERT CODE HERE
            break;
            default: System.out.println("default");
        }
    }
}
```

a `case 10*3: System.out.println(2);`

b case num: System.out.println(3);

c `case 10/3: System.out.println(4);`

d `case num2: System.out.println(5);`

Answer: a, c, d

Explanation: Option (a) is correct. Compile-time constants, including expressions, are permissible in the `case` labels.

Option (b) is incorrect. The `case` labels should be compile-time constants. A non-final variable isn't a compile-time constant because it can be reassigned a value during the course of a class's execution. Although the previous class doesn't assign a value to it, the compiler still treats it as a changeable variable.

Option (c) is correct. The value specified in the `case` labels should be assignable to the variable used in the `switch` construct. You may think that `10/3` will return a decimal number, which can't be assigned to the variable num, but this operation discards the decimal part and compares `3` with the variable num.

Option (d) is correct. The variable num2 is defined as a `final` variable and assigned a value on the same line of code, with its declaration. Hence, it's considered to be a compile-time constant.

Q5-6. What's the output of the following code?

```
class EJavaGuru {
    public static void main(String args[]) {
        int num = 20;
        final int num2;
        num2 = 20;
```

```
        switch (num) {
            default: System.out.println("default");
            case num2: System.out.println(4);
            break;
        }
    }
}
```

a `default`

b `default`
`4`

c `4`

d Compilation error

Answer: d

Explanation: The code will fail to compile. The `case` labels require compile-time constant values, and the variable `num2` doesn't qualify as such. Although the variable `num2` is defined as a `final` variable, it isn't assigned a value with its declaration. The code assigns a literal value `20` to this variable after its declaration, but it isn't considered to be a compile-time constant by the Java compiler.

Q5-7. What's the output of the following code?

```
class EJavaGuru {
    public static void main(String args[]) {
        int num = 120;

        switch (num) {
            default: System.out.println("default");
            case 0: System.out.println("case1");
            case 10*2-20: System.out.println("case2");
            break;
        }
    }
}
```

a `default`
`case1`
`case2`

b `case1`
`case2`

c `case2`

d Compilation error

e Runtime exception

Answer: d

Explanation: The expressions used for both case labels—that is, `0` and `10*2-20`—evaluate to the constant value `0`. Because you can't define duplicate case labels for the switch statement, the code will fail to compile with an error message that states that the code defines a duplicate case label.

Q5-8. What's the output of the following code?

```
class EJavaGuru3 {
    public static void main(String args[]) {
        byte foo = 120;
        switch (foo) {
            default: System.out.println("ejavaguru"); break;
            case 2: System.out.println("e"); break;
            case 120: System.out.println("ejava");
            case 121: System.out.println("enum");
            case 127: System.out.println("guru"); break;
        }
    }
}
```

   a **ejava**
      enum
      guru

   b ejava

   c ejavaguru
      e

   d ejava
      enum
      guru
      ejavaguru

Answer: a

Explanation: For a switch case construct, control enters the case labels when a matching case is found. The control then falls through the remaining case labels until it's terminated by a break statement. The control exits the switch construct when it encounters a break statement or it reaches the end of the switch construct.

In this example, a matching label is found for case label 120. The control executes the statement for this case label and prints ejava to the console. Because a break statement doesn't terminate the case label, the control falls through to case label 121. The control executes the statement for this case label and prints enum to the console. Because a break statement also doesn't terminate this case label, the control falls through to case label 127. The control executes the statement for this case label and prints guru to the console. This case label is terminated by a break statement, so the control exits the switch construct.

Q5-9. What's the output of the following code?

```
class EJavaGuru4 {
    public static void main(String args[]) {
        boolean myVal = false;
        if (myVal=true)
            for (int i = 0; i < 2; i++) System.out.println(i);
```

```
        else System.out.println("else");
    }
}
```

a else

b 0
1
2

c 0
1

d Compilation error

Answer: c

Explanation: First of all, the expression used in the `if` construct isn't comparing the value of the variable `myVal` with the literal value `true`—it's assigning the literal value `true` to it. The assignment operator (`=`) assigns the literal value. The comparison operator (`==`) is used to compare values. Because the resulting value is a `boolean` value, the compiler doesn't complain about the assignment in the `if` construct.

The code is deliberately poorly indented because you may encounter similarly poor indentation in the OCA Java SE 7 Programmer I exam. The `for` loop is part of the `if` construct, which prints 0 and 1. The `else` part doesn't execute because the `if` condition evaluates to `true`. The code has no compilation errors.

Q5-10. What's the output of the following code?

```
class EJavaGuru5 {
    public static void main(String args[]) {
        int i = 0;
        for (; i < 2; i=i+5) {
            if (i < 5) continue;
            System.out.println(i);
        }
        System.out.println(i);
    }
}
```

a Compilation error

b 0
5

c 0
5
10

d 10

e 0
1
5

f 5

Answer: f

Explanation: First of all, the following line of code has no compilation errors:

```
for (; i < 2; i=i+5) {
```

Using the initialization block is optional in a `for` loop. In this case, using a semicolon (`;`) terminates it.

For the first `for` iteration, the variable `i` has a value of `0`. Because this value is less than `2`, the following `if` construct evaluates to `true` and the `continue` statement executes:

```
if (i < 5) continue;
```

Because the `continue` statement ignores all of the remaining statements in a `for` loop iteration, the control doesn't print the value of the variable `i`, which leads the control to move on to the next `for` iteration. In the next `for` iteration, the value of the variable `i` is `5`. The `for` loop condition evaluates to `false` and the control moves out of the `for` loop. After the `for` loop, the code prints out the value of the variable `i`, which increments once using the code `i=i+5`.

Working with inheritance

6

Exam objectives covered in this chapter	What you need to know
[7.1] Implement inheritance.	The need for inheriting classes. How to implement inheritance using classes.
[7.2] Develop code that demonstrates the use of polymorphism.	How to implement polymorphism with classes and interfaces. How to define polymorphic or overridden methods.
[7.3] Differentiate between the type of a reference and the type of an object.	How to determine the valid types of the variables that can be used to refer to an object. How to determine the differences in the members of an object, which ones are accessible, and when an object is referred to using a variable of an inherited base class or an implemented interface.
[7.4] Determine when casting is necessary.	The need for casting. How to cast an object to another class or an interface.
[7.5] Use `super` and `this` to access objects and constructors.	How to access variables, methods, and constructors using `super` and `this`. What happens if a derived class tries to access variables of a base class when they're not accessible to the derived class.
[7.6] Use abstract classes and interfaces.	The role of abstract classes and interfaces in implementing polymorphism.

All living beings inherit the characteristics and behaviors of their parents. The off-spring of a fly looks and behaves like a fly, and that of a lion looks and behaves like a lion. But despite being similar to their parents, all offspring are also different and unique in their own ways. Additionally, a single action may have different meanings for different beings. For example, the action "eat" has different meanings for a fly and a lion. A fly eats nectar, whereas a lion eats antelope.

Something similar happens in Java. The concept of inheriting characteristics and behaviors from parents can be compared to classes inheriting variables and methods from a parent class. Being different and unique in one's own way is similar to how a class can both inherit from a parent and also define additional variables and methods. Single actions having different meanings can be compared to polymorphism in Java.

In the OCA Java SE 7 Programmer I exam, you'll be asked questions on how to implement inheritance and polymorphism and how to use classes and interfaces. Hence, this chapter covers the following:

- Understanding and implementing inheritance
- Developing code that demonstrates the use of polymorphism
- Differentiating between the type of a reference and an object
- Determining when casting is required
- Using `super` and `this` to access objects and constructors
- Using abstract classes and interfaces

6.1   *Inheritance with classes*

[7.1]   Implement inheritance

When we discuss inheritance in the context of an object-oriented programming language such as Java, we talk about how a class can inherit the properties and behavior of another class. The class that inherits from another class can also define additional properties and behaviors. The exam will ask you explicit questions about the need to inherit classes and how to implement inheritance using classes.

Let's get started with the need to inherit classes.

6.1.1   *Need to inherit classes*

Imagine the positions *Programmer* and *Manager* within an organization. Both of these positions have a common set of properties, including name, address, and phone number. These positions also have different properties. A *Programmer* may be concerned about a project's programming languages, whereas a *Manager* may be concerned with project status reports.

Let's assume you're supposed to store details of all Programmers and Managers in your office. Figure 6.1 shows the properties and behavior that you may have identified for a Programmer and a Manager, together with their representations as classes.

Did you notice that the classes `Programmer` and `Manager` have common properties, namely, `name`, `address`, `phoneNumber`, and `experience`? The next step is to pull out these common properties into a new position and name it something like *Employee*. This step is shown in figure 6.2.

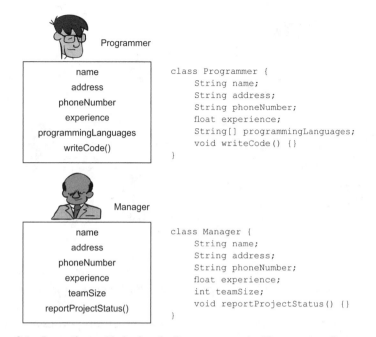

```
class Programmer {
    String name;
    String address;
    String phoneNumber;
    float experience;
    String[] programmingLanguages;
    void writeCode() {}
}
```

```
class Manager {
    String name;
    String address;
    String phoneNumber;
    float experience;
    int teamSize;
    void reportProjectStatus() {}
}
```

Figure 6.1 Properties and behavior of a Programmer and a Manager, together with their representations as classes

This new position, Employee, can be defined as a new class, `Employee`, which is inherited by the classes `Programmer` and `Manager`. A class uses the keyword `extends` to *inherit* a class, as shown in figure 6.3.

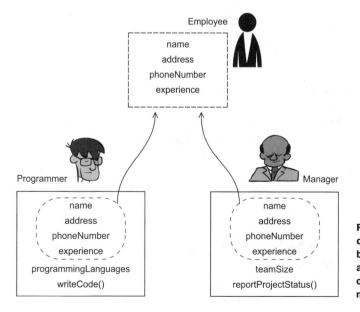

Figure 6.2 Identify common properties and behaviors of a Programmer and a Manager, pull them out into a new position, and name it Employee

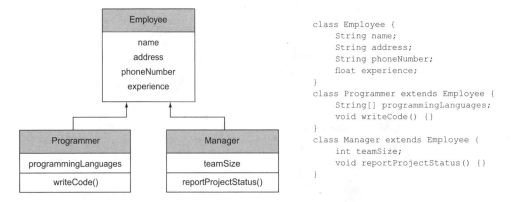

Figure 6.3   The classes `Programmer` and `Manager` extend the class `Employee`

Inheriting a class is also referred to as *subclassing*. In figure 6.3, the inherited class `Employee` is also referred to as the *superclass, base class,* or *parent class.* The classes `Programmer` and `Manager` that inherit the class `Employee` are called *subclasses, derived classes, extended classes,* or *child classes.*

Why do you think you need to pull out the common properties and behaviors into a separate class `Employee` and make the `Programmer` and `Manager` classes inherit it?

SMALLER DERIVED CLASS DEFINITIONS

What if you were supposed to write more specialized classes, such as `Astronaut` and `Doctor`, which have the same common characteristics and behaviors as those of the class `Employee`? With the class `Employee` in place, you only need to define the variables and methods that are specific to the classes `Astronaut` and `Doctor`, and have the classes inherit `Employee`.

Figure 6.4 is a UML representation of the classes `Astronaut`, `Doctor`, `Programmer`, and `Manager`, both with and without inheritance from class `Employee`. As you can see in this figure, the definitions of these classes is smaller when they inherit the class `Employee`.

EASE OF MODIFICATION TO COMMON PROPERTIES AND BEHAVIOR

What happens if your boss steps in and tells you that all of these specialized classes—`Astronaut`, `Doctor`, `Programmer`, and `Manager`—should now have a property `facebookId`? Figure 6.5 shows that with the base class `Employee` in place, you just need to add this variable to that base class. If you haven't inherited from the class `Employee`, you need to add the variable `facebookId` to *each* of these four classes.

Note that common code can be modified and deleted from the base class `Employee` fairly easily.

EXTENSIBILITY

Code that works with the base class in a hierarchy tree can work with all classes that are added using inheritance later.

Assume that an organization needs to send out invitations to all its employees and that it uses the following method to do so:

```
class HR {
    void sendInvitation(Employee emp) {
        System.out.println("Send invitation to" +
                                    emp.name + " at " + emp.address);
    }
}
```

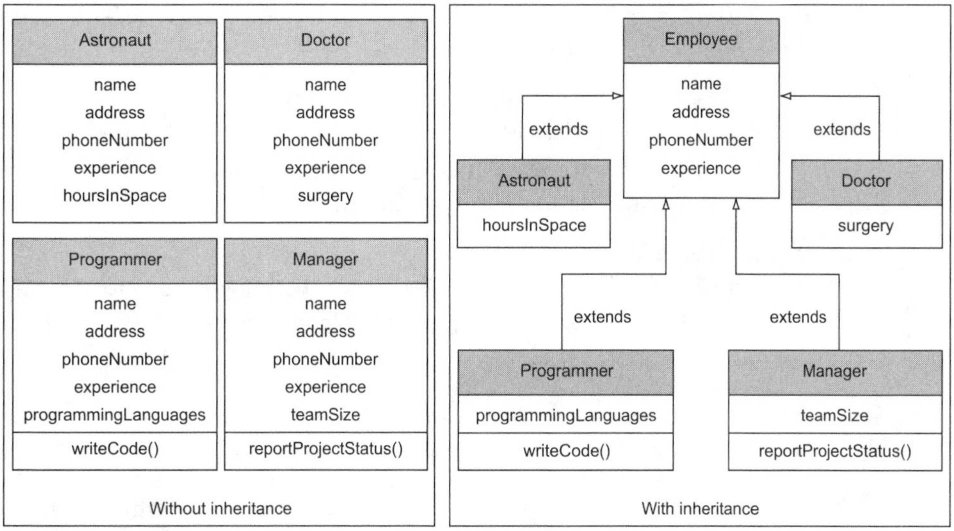

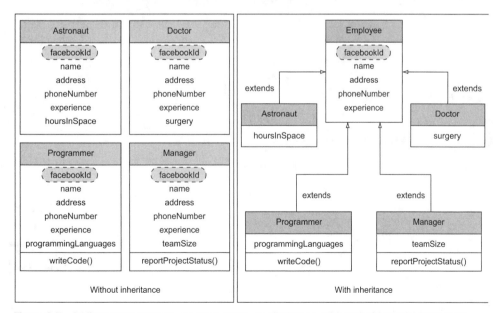

Figure 6.4   Differences in the size of the classes `Astronaut`, `Doctor`, `Programmer`, **and** `Manager`,
both with and without inheriting from the class `Employee`

Figure 6.5   Adding a new property, `facebookId`, **to all classes, with and without the base class**
`Employee`

Because method `sendInvitation` accepts an argument of type `Employee`, you can also pass to it a subclass of `Employee`. Essentially, this design means that you can use the previous method with a class defined later that has `Employee` as its base class. Inheritance makes code extensible.

USE TRIED-AND-TESTED CODE FROM A BASE CLASS

You don't need to reinvent the wheel. With inheritance in place, subclasses can use tried-and-tested code from a base class.

CONCENTRATE ON THE SPECIALIZED BEHAVIOR OF YOUR CLASSES

Inheriting a class enables you to concentrate on the variables and methods that define the special behavior of your class. Inheritance lets you make use of existing code from a base class without having to define it yourself.

LOGICAL STRUCTURES AND GROUPING

When multiple classes inherit a base class, it creates a logical group. For an example, see figure 6.5. The classes `Astronaut`, `Doctor`, `Programmer`, and `Manager` are all grouped as types of the class `Employee`.

> **EXAM TIP** Inheritance enables you to reuse code that has already been defined by a class. Inheritance can be implemented by extending a class.

The next section solves the mystery of how you can access the inherited members of a base class directly in a derived class.

6.1.2 A derived class contains within it an object of its base class

The classes `Programmer` and `Manager` inherit the variables and methods defined in the class `Employee` and use them directly, as if they were defined in their own classes. Examine the following code:

```
class Employee {
    String name;
    String address;
    String phoneNumber;
    float experience;
}
class Manager extends Employee {
    int teamSize;
    void reportProjectStatus() {}
}
class Programmer extends Employee {
    String[] programmingLanguages;
    void writeCode() {}
    void accessBaseClassMembers() {
        name = "Programmer";
    }
}
```

Derived class Programmer can directly access members of its base class.

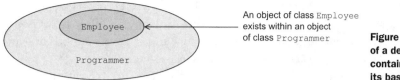

An object of class `Employee` exists within an object of class `Programmer`

Figure 6.6   An object of a derived class contains an object of its base class.

How can the class `Programmer` assign a value to a variable that's defined in the class `Employee`? You can think of this arrangement as follows: when a class inherits another class, it encloses within it an object of the inherited class. Hence, all the members (variables and methods) of the inherited class are available to the class, as shown in figure 6.6.

But a derived class can't inherit all the members of its base class. The next two sections discuss which base class members are and aren't inherited by a derived class.

6.1.3   Which base class members are inherited by a derived class?

The access modifiers play an important role in determining the inheritance of base class members in derived classes. A derived class inherits all the non-private members of its base class. A derived class inherits base class members with the following accessibility modifiers:

- *Default*—Members with default access can be accessed in a derived class only if base and derived classes reside in the same package.
- `protected`—Members with `protected` access are accessible to all the derived classes, regardless of the packages in which the base and derived classes are defined.
- `public`—Members with `public` access are visible to all the other classes.

6.1.4   Which base class members aren't inherited by a derived class?

A derived class doesn't inherit the following members:

- `private` members of the base class.
- Base class members with default access, if the base class and derived classes exist in separate packages.
- Constructors of the base class. A derived class can call a base class's constructors, but it doesn't inherit them (section 6.5 discusses how a derived class can call a base class's constructors using the implicit reference `super`).

Apart from inheriting the properties and behavior of its base class, a derived class can also define additional properties and behaviors, as discussed in the next section.

6.1.5   Derived classes can define additional properties and behaviors

Though derived classes are similar to their base classes, they generally also have differences. Derived classes can define additional properties and behaviors. You may see explicit questions on the exam about how a derived class can differ from its base class.

Take a quick look back at figure 6.5. All the derived classes—Manager, Programmer, Doctor, and Astronaut—define additional variables, methods, or both. Derived classes can also define their own constructors and static methods and variables. A derived class can also *hide* or *override* its base class's members.

When a derived class defines an instance or class variable with the same name as one defined from its base class, only these new variables and methods are visible to code using the derived class. When a derived class defines different code for a method inherited from a base class by defining the method again, this method is treated as a special method—an *overridden* method.

You can implement inheritance by using either a concrete class or an abstract class as a base class, but there are some important differences that you should be aware of. These are discussed in the next section.

6.1.6   *Abstract base class versus concrete base class*

Figures 6.2 and 6.3 showed how you can pull out the common properties and behavior of a Programmer and Manager and represent these as a new class, Employee. You can define class Employee as an abstract class, if you think that it's only a categorization and no real employee exists in real life—that is, if all employees are really either *Programmers* or *Managers*. That's the essence of an abstract class: it groups the common properties and behavior of its derived classes, but it prevents itself from being instantiated. Also, an abstract class can force all its derived classes to define their own implementations for a behavior by defining it as an abstract method (a method without a body).

It isn't mandatory for an abstract class to define an abstract method. It may or may not define any abstract methods. But if an abstract base class defines one or more abstract methods, the class must be marked as abstract and the abstract methods must be implemented in all its derived classes. If a derived class doesn't implement all the abstract methods defined by its base class, then it also needs to be an abstract class.

For the exam, you need to remember the following important points about implementing inheritance using an abstract base class:

- You can never create objects of an abstract class.
- A base class can be defined as an abstract class, even if it doesn't define any abstract methods.
- A derived class should implement all the abstract methods of its base class. If it doesn't, it must be defined as an abstract derived class.
- You can use variables of an abstract base class to refer to objects of its derived class (discussed in detail in section 6.3).

The first Twist in the Tale exercise for this chapter queries you on the relationship between base and derived classes (answer in the appendix).

Let's modify the code used in the previous example as follows. Which of the options is correct for this modified code?

```
class Employee {
    private String name;
    String address;
    protected String phoneNumber;
    public float experience;
}
class Programmer extends Employee {
    Programmer (String val) {
        name = val;
    }
    String getName() {
        return name;
    }
}
class Office {
    public static void main(String args[]) {
        new Programmer ("Harry").getName();
    }
}
```

   a The class Office prints Harry.

   b The derived class Programmer can't define a getter method for a variable defined in its base class Employee.

   c The derived class Programmer can't access variables of its base class in its constructors.

   d new Programmer ("Harry").getName(); isn't the right way to create an object of class Programmer.

   e Compilation error.

TERMS AND DEFINITIONS TO REMEMBER

Following is a list of terms and their corresponding definitions that you should remember; they're used throughout the chapter, and you'll come across them while answering questions on inheritance in the OCA Java SE 7 Programmer I exam.

   ■ *Base class*—A class inherited by another class. The class Employee is a *base class* for the classes Programmer and Manager in the previous examples.

   ■ *Superclass*—A base class is also known as a *superclass*.

   ■ *Parent class*—A base class is also known as a *parent class*.

   ■ *Derived class*—A class that inherits from another class. The classes Programmer and Manager are *derived classes* in the previous example.

   ■ *Subclass*—A derived class is also known as a *subclass*.

   ■ *Extended class*—A derived class is also known as an *extended class*.

- *Child class*—A derived class is also known as a *child class*.
- *IS-A relationship*—A relationship shared by base and derived classes. In the previous examples, a Programmer IS-A Person. A Manager IS-A Person. Because a derived class represents a specialized type of a base class, a derived IS-A class is a kind of base class.
- extends—The keyword used by a class to inherit another class and by an interface to inherit another interface.
- implements—The keyword used by a class to implement an interface (interfaces are covered in the next section).

NOTE   The terms *base class*, *superclass*, and *parent class* are used interchangeably. Similarly, the terms *derived class* and *subclass* are also used interchangeably.

In this section, you learned that an abstract class may define abstract methods. Let's take it a step further to interfaces, which can define only abstract methods and constants. In the next section, we'll discuss why you need interfaces and how to use them.

6.2   *Use interfaces*

[7.6]   Use abstract classes and interfaces

Interfaces are abstract classes taken to extremes. An interface can define only abstract methods and constants. All the members of an interface are implicitly public.

Let's go back to the example used in section 6.1 with classes Employee, Programmer, and Manager, where Programmer and Manager inherit the class Employee. Imagine that your boss steps in and commands that Programmer and Manager *must* support additional behaviors, as listed in table 6.1.

Table 6.1   Additional behaviors that need to be supported by the classes Programmer and Manager

Entity	New expected behavior
Programmer	Attend training
Manager	Attend training, conduct interviews

How will you accomplish this task? One approach you can take is to define all the relevant methods in class Employee. Because both Programmer and Manager extend the class Employee, they'd be able to access these methods. But wait: Programmer doesn't need the behavior of the conducting interview task; only Manager should support the functionality of conducting interviews.

Another obvious approach would be to define the relevant methods in the desired classes. You could define methods to conduct interviews in Manager and methods to attend training in both Programmer and Manager. Again, this is not an ideal solution. What will happen if your boss later informs you that all the Employees who attend

training should accept a *training schedule*, that is, there is a change in the signature of
the method that defines the behavior "attends training"? Can you define separate
classes for this behavior and make the classes `Programmer` and `Manager` implement
them? No, you can't. Java doesn't allow a class to inherit multiple classes.

Let's try interfaces. Create two interfaces to define the specified behavior:

```
interface Trainable {
    public void attendTraining();
}
interface Interviewer {
    public void conductInterview();
}
```

Though Java does not allow a class to inherit from more than one class, it allows a class
to implement multiple interfaces. A class uses the keyword `implements` to implement
an interface. In the following code, the classes `Programmer` and `Manager` implement the
relevant interfaces (modified code in bold):

```
class Employee {                                              Manager
    String name;                                              implements
    String address;                                           Interviewer
    String phoneNumber;                                       and Trainable
    float experience;
}
class Manager extends Employee implements Interviewer, Trainable {  ◁——
    int teamSize;
    void reportProjectStatus() {}
    public void conductInterview() {
        System.out.println("Mgr - conductInterview");
    }
    public void attendTraining() {
        System.out.println("Mgr - attendTraining");
    }                                                         Programmer
}                                                             implements
class Programmer extends Employee implements Trainable{       only Trainable
    String[] programmingLanguages;                              ◁——
    void writeCode() {}
    public void attendTraining() {
        System.out.println("Prog - attendTraining");
    }
}
```

Figure 6.7 displays the relationships between these classes in a UML diagram.

An `interface` can be represented using either a rectangle with the text <<inter-
face>> or a circle. Both these notations are popular; you may see them in various websites or books. The same relationships can also be represented as depicted in figure 6.8,
where the interfaces are defined as circles.

Each class can implement these methods in its own particular manner. As mentioned previously, let's change the method `attendTraining` in the interface `Trainable`
so it accepts a `trainingSchedule`, as follows:

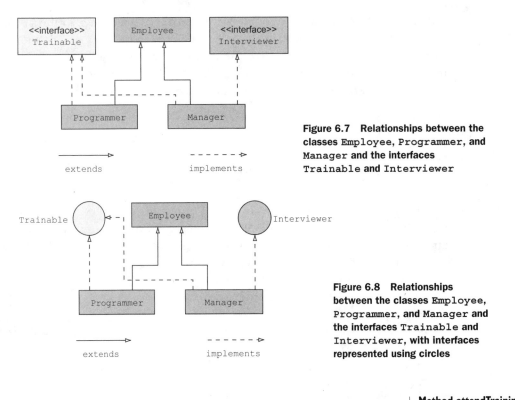

Figure 6.7 Relationships between the classes `Employee`, `Programmer`, **and** `Manager` **and the interfaces** `Trainable` **and** `Interviewer`

Figure 6.8 Relationships between the classes `Employee`, `Programmer`, **and** `Manager` **and the interfaces** `Trainable` **and** `Interviewer`**, with interfaces represented using circles**

```
interface Trainable {
    public void attendTraining(String[] trainingSchedule);
}
```

◁— **Method attendTraining now accepts a trainingSchedule as an array of String**

Does a change in the signature of a method in an interface have any impact on the definition of this method in the classes that implement it? Yes, it does. If the signature of a method is changed in an interface, all classes that implement the interface will fail to compile. Now that the method signature has been modified, the classes `Programmer` and `Manager` must be modified so that the signature of the method `attendTraining` matches in all three: the interface `Trainable` and the classes `Programmer` and `Manager`.

The changes are as follows (in bold):

```
interface Trainable {
    public void attendTraining(String[] trainingSchedule);
}
interface Interviewer {
    public void conductInterview();
}
class Employee {
    String name;
    String address;
    String phoneNumber;
    float experience;
}
```

◁— **Signature of method attendTraining should match in interface Trainable, class Manager, and class Programmer**

```
class Manager extends Employee implements Interviewer, Trainable {
    int teamSize;
    void reportProjectStatus() {}
    public void conductInterview() {
        System.out.println("Mgr - conductInterview");
    }
    public void attendTraining(String[] trainingSchedule) {
        System.out.println("Mgr - attendTraining");
    }
}
class Programmer extends Employee implements Trainable{
    String[] programmingLanguages;
    void writeCode() {}
    public void attendTraining(String[] trainingSchedule) {
        System.out.println("Prog - attendTraining");
    }
}
```

Signature of method attendTraining should match in interface Trainable, class Manager, and class Programmer

 EXAM TIP The method signatures of a method defined in an interface and the classes that implement the interface must match, or the classes won't compile.

6.2.1 Properties of members of an interface

An interface can only define constants. Once it's assigned, you can't change the value of a constant. The variables of an interface are implicitly public, final, and static.

For example, the following definition of the interface MyInterface,

```
interface MyInterface {
    int age = 10;
}
```

is equivalent to the following definition:

```
interface MyInterface {
    public static final int AGE = 10;
}
```

public, static, and final modifiers are implicitly added to variables defined in an interface.

You should initialize all variables in an interface, or your code won't compile:

```
interface MyInterface {
    int AGE;
}
```

Won't compile. Should assign a value to a final variable.

The methods of an interface are implicitly public. When you implement an interface, you must implement all its methods by using the access modifier public. A class that implements an interface can't make the interface's methods more restrictive. Although the following class and interface definitions look acceptable, they're not:

```
interface Relocatable {
    void move();
}
class CEO implements Relocatable {
    void move() {}
}
```

Implicitly public

Won't compile. Can't assign weaker access (default access) to public method move in class CEO.

The following code is correct and compiles happily:

```
interface Relocatable {
    void move();
}
class CEO implements Relocatable {
    public void move() {}
}
```

Implicitly
public

Will
compile

Unlike a class, an interface can't define constructors.

6.2.2 *Why a class can't extend multiple classes*

In Java, a class can't extend multiple classes. Why do you think this is so? Let's examine this issue using an example, in which the class Programmer *is* allowed to inherit two classes: Employee and Philanthropist. Figure 6.9 shows the relationship between these classes and the corresponding code.

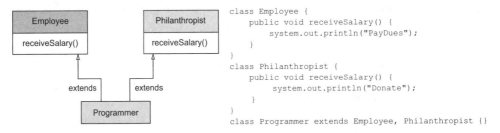

Figure 6.9 **What happens if a class is allowed to extend multiple classes?**

If class Programmer inherited the method receiveSalary, defined in both Employee and Philanthropist, what do you think a Programmer would do with his or her salary: pay dues (like an Employee) or donate it (like a Philanthropist)? What do you think would be the output of the following code?

```
class Test {
    public static void main(String args[]) {
        Programmer p = new Programmer();
        p.receiveSalary();
    }
}
```

Would this print
"PayDues" or "Donate"?

In this case, class Programmer can access two receiveSalary methods with identical method signatures but different implementations, so it is impossible to resolve this method call. This is why classes aren't allowed to inherit multiple classes in Java.

EXAM TIP   Because a derived class may inherit different implementations for the same method signature from multiple base *classes*, multiple inheritance is not allowed in Java.

6.2.3 *Implementing multiple interfaces*

In the previous section, you learned that a class can't inherit multiple classes, but a class can implement multiple interfaces. Also, an interface can extend multiple interfaces.

Why is this allowed, when Java doesn't allow a class to extend multiple classes? What's the catch?

An interface defines barebones methods—methods without any body—and when an interface extends another interface, it inherits the methods defined in the base interface. What happens if the base interface and subinterface define methods with the same signatures? Or when an interface extends more than one interface that defines the same method?

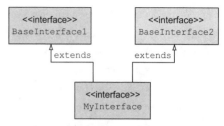

Figure 6.10 **The interface** `MyInterface` **extends the interfaces** `BaseInterface1` **and** `BaseInterface2`.

Consider the following code, whose UML representation is shown in figure 6.10. Which of the `getName` methods will be inherited by the interface `MyInterface`? Will `MyInterface` inherit the `getName` method defined in `BaseInterface1` or the one defined in `BaseInterface2`?

```
interface BaseInterface1 {
    String getName();
}
interface BaseInterface2 {
    String getName();
}
interface MyInterface extends BaseInterface1, BaseInterface2 {}
```

Because neither of the `getName` methods defined in `BaseInterface1` and `Base-Interface2` define a method body (as shown in figure 6.11), the question of which of the methods `MyInterface` inherits is irrelevant. Interface `MyInterface` has access to a single `getName` method, which should be implemented by all the classes that implement `MyInterface`.

Let's make the `Employee` class implement the interface `MyInterface`, as follows:

```
class Employee implements MyInterface {
    String name;
    public String getName() {
        return name;
    }
}
```

Employee defines a body for method getName, inherited from interface MyInterface

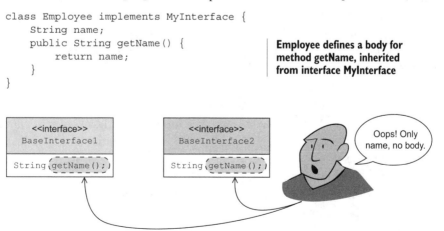

Figure 6.11 Methods defined in an interface don't have a method body.

POINTS TO NOTE ABOUT CLASS AND INTERFACE INHERITANCE:

- A class can inherit zero or one class.
- A class uses the keyword `extends` to inherit a class.
- A class can implement multiple interfaces.
- A class uses the keyword `implements` to implement an interface.
- An interface can't implement any class.
- An interface can inherit zero or more interfaces.
- An interface uses the keyword `extends` to inherit interfaces.
- An abstract class can extend a concrete class and vice versa.
- An abstract class can implement interfaces.
- An abstract class can extend another abstract class.
- The first concrete class in the hierarchy must supply actual method implementations for all `abstract` methods.

You can use a reference variable of a base class to refer to an object of its derived class. Similarly, you can use a reference variable of an interface to refer to an object of a class that implements it. It's interesting to note that these variables can't access all the variables and methods defined in the derived class or the class that implements the interface.

Let's dig into some more details about this in the next section.

6.3   *Reference variable and object types*

> [7.3]   Differentiate between the type of a reference and the type of an object

For this exam objective, you need to understand that when you refer to an object, the type of the *object reference variable* and the type of the *object* being referred to may be different. But there are rules on *how different* these can be. This concept may take a while to sink in, so don't worry if you don't get it on your first attempt.

In the same way in which you can refer to a person using their first name, last name, or both names, objects of derived classes can be referred to using a reference variable of either of the following types:

- *Its own type*—An object of a class `HRExecutive` can be referred to using an object reference variable of type `HRExecutive`.
- *Its base class*—If the class `HRExecutive` inherits the class `Employee`, an object of the class `HRExecutive` can be referred to using a variable of type `Employee`. If the class `Employee` inherits the class `Person`, an object of the class `HRExecutive` can also be referred to using a variable of type `Person`.
- *Implemented interfaces*—If the class `HRExecutive` implements the interface `Interviewer`, an object of the class `HRExecutive` can be referred using a variable of type `Interviewer`.

There are differences, however, when you try to access an object using a reference variable of its own type, its base class, or an implemented interface. Let's start with accessing an object with a variable of its own type.

6.3.1 *Using a variable of the derived class to access its own object*

Let's start with the code of the class HRExecutive, which inherits the class Employee and implements the interface Interviewer, as follows:

```
class Employee {
    String name;
    String address;
    String phoneNumber;
    float experience;
}
interface Interviewer {
    public void conductInterview();
}
class HRExecutive extends Employee implements Interviewer {    ◁─┐
    String[] specialization;
    public void conductInterview() {
        System.out.println("HRExecutive - conducting interview");
    }
}
```

Class HRExecutive inherits class Employee and implements interface Interview

Here's some code that demonstrates that an object of class HRExecutive can be referred to using a variable of type HRExecutive:

```
class Office {
    public static void main(String args[]) {
        HRExecutive hr = new HRExecutive();    ◁─┐
    }
}
```

A variable of type HRExecutive can be used to refer to its object.

You can access variables and methods defined in the class Employee, the class HRExecutive, and the interface Interviewer using the variable hr (with the type HRExecutive), as follows:

```
class Office {
    public static void main(String args[]) {
        HRExecutive hr = new HRExecutive();

        hr.specialization = new String[] {"Staffing"};
        System.out.println(hr.specialization[0]);

        hr.name = "Pavni Gupta";
        System.out.println(hr.name);

        hr.conductInterview();    ◁─┐
    }
}
```

Access variable defined in class HRExecutive

Access variable defined in class Employee

Access method defined in interface Interviewer

When you access an object of the class HRExecutive using its own type, you can access all the variables and methods that are defined in its base class and interface—the class

Employee and the interface Interviewer. Can you do the same if the type of the reference variable is changed to the class Employee, as defined in the next section?

6.3.2   *Using a variable of the base class to access an object of a derived class*

Let's access an object of type HRExecutive using a reference variable of type Employee, as follows:

```
class Office {
    public static void main(String args[]) {
        Employee emp = new HRExecutive();
    }
}
```

Variable of type Employee can also be used to refer to an object of class HRExecutive because class HRExecutive extends Employee.

Now let's see whether changing the type of the reference variable makes any difference when accessing the members of the class Employee, the class HRExecutive, or the interface Interviewer. Will the following code compile successfully?

Type of variable emp is Employee.

```
class Office {
    public static void main(String args[]) {
        Employee emp = new HRExecutive();

        emp.specialization = new String[] {"Staffing"};
        System.out.println(emp.specialization[0]);

        emp.name = "Pavni Gupta";
        System.out.println(emp.name);

        emp.conductInterview();
    }
}
```

①   Variable emp can't access member specialization defined in class HRExecutive.

Variable emp can access member name defined in class Employee.

Variable emp can't access method conductInterview defined in interface Interviewer.

The code at ① fails to compile because the type of the variable emp is defined as Employee. Picture it like this: the variable emp can see only the Employee object. Hence, it can access only the variables and methods defined in the class Employee, as illustrated in figure 6.12.

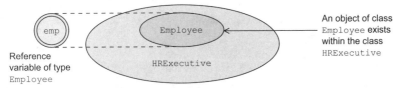

Reference variable of type Employee

An object of class Employee exists within the class HRExecutive

Figure 6.12   A variable of type Employee can see only the members defined in the class Employee.

6.3.3   *Using a variable of an implemented interface to access a derived class object*

Here's another interesting equation: what happens when you change the type of the reference variable to the interface Interviewer? A variable of type Interviewer can also be used to refer to an object of the class `HRExecutive` because the class `HRExecutive` implements `Interviewer`. See the following code:

```
class Office {
    public static void main(String args[]) {
        Interviewer interviewer = new HRExecutive();
    }
}
```

Now try to access the same set of variables and methods using the variable `inter-viewer`, which refers to an object of the class `HRExecutive`:

```
class Office {
    public static void main(String args[]) {
        Interviewer interviewer = new HRExecutive();    ⟵   Type of variable
                                                             interviewer is
                                                             Interviewer.

①      interviewer.specialization = new String[] {"Staffing"};
        System.out.println(interviewer.specialization[0]);

        interviewer.name = "Pavni Gupta";
        System.out.println(interviewer.name);

        interviewer.conductInterview();    ⟵   Variable interviewer can access
    }                                            the method conductInterview
}                                                defined in interface Interviewer.
```

Variable interviewer can't access members of class Employee or HRExecutive. ①

The code at ① doesn't compile because the type of the variable `interviewer` is defined as `Interviewer`. Picture it like this: the variable `interviewer` can only *access* the methods defined in the interface `Interviewer`, as illustrated in figure 6.13.

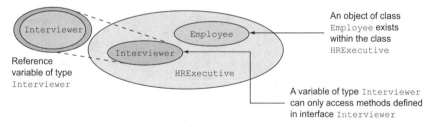

An object of class `Employee` exists within the class `HRExecutive`

Reference variable of type `Interviewer`

A variable of type `Interviewer` can only access methods defined in interface `Interviewer`

Figure 6.13   A variable of type `Interviewer` can see only the members defined in the interface `Interviewer`.

6.3.4   *The need for accessing an object using the variables of its base class or implemented interfaces*

You may be wondering why you need a reference variable of a base class or an implemented interface to access an object of a derived class if a variable can't access all the members that are available to an object of a derived class? The simple answer is that you might not be interested in *all* the members of a derived class.

Confused? Compare it with the following situation. When you enroll in flying classes, do you care whether the instructor can cook Italian cuisine or knows how to swim? No! You don't care about characteristics and behavior that are unrelated to flying. Here is

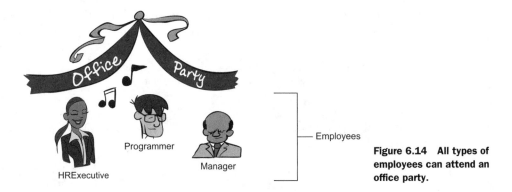

Figure 6.14   All types of employees can attend an office party.

another example. At an office party, all the employees are welcome, whether they are Programmers, HRExecutives, or Managers, as shown in figure 6.14.

The same logic applies when you access an object of the class HRExecutive using a reference variable of type Interviewer. When you do so, you're only concerned about the behavior of HRExecutive that relates to its capability as an Interviewer.

This arrangement also makes it possible to create an array (or a list) of the objects that refers to different types of objects grouped by a common base class or an interface. The following code segment defines an array of type Interviewer and stores in it objects of the classes HRExecutive and Manager:

```
class OfficeInheritanceList {
    public static void main(String args[]) {
        Interviewer[] interviewers = new Interviewer[2];

        interviewers[0] = new Manager();

        interviewers[1] = new HRExecutive();

        for (Interviewer interviewer : interviewers) {
            interviewer.conductInterview();
        }
    }
}
```

Array of type Interviewer— an interface

Because Manager implements interface Interviewer, it can be stored here.

Because HRExecutive implements interface Interviewer, it can be stored here.

Loop through the array and call method conductInterview

The class HRExecutive extends the class Employee and implements the interface Interviewer. Hence, you can assign an object of HRExecutive to any of the following types of variables:

- HRExecutive
- Employee
- Interviewer

Please note that the reverse of these assignments will fail compilation. To start with, you can't refer to an object of a base class by using a reference variable of its derived class. Because *all* members of a derived class can't be accessed using an object of the base class, it isn't allowed. The following statement will not compile:

```
HRExecutive hr = new Employee();
```
            ◁——— **Not allowed—won't compile**

Because you can't create an object of an interface, the following line of code will also fail to compile:

```
HRExecutive hr = new Interviewer();        ◁──── Not allowed—won't compile
```

It's now time for you to try to add objects of the previously defined related classes—Employee, Manager, and HRExecutive—to an array in your next Twist in the Tale exercise (answers in the appendix).

Twist in the Tale 6.2

Given the following definition of the classes and interface Employee, Manager, HRExecutive, and Interviewer, select the correct options for the class TwistInTale2:

```
class Employee {}
interface Interviewer {}
class Manager extends Employee implements Interviewer {}
class HRExecutive extends Employee implements Interviewer {}

class TwistInTale2 {
    public static void main (String args[]) {
        Interviewer[] interviewer = new Interviewer[] {
                new Manager(),           // Line 1
                new Employee(),          // Line 2
                new HRExecutive(),       // Line 3
                new Interviewer()        // Line 4
            };
    }
}
```

  a An object of the class Manager can be added to an array of the interface Interviewer. Code on line 1 will compile successfully.

  b An object of the class Employee can be added to an array of the interface Interviewer. Code on line 2 will compile successfully.

  c An object of the class HRExecutive can be added to an array of the interface Interviewer. Code on line 3 will compile successfully.

  d An object of the interface Interviewer can be added to an array of the interface Interviewer. Code on line 4 will compile successfully.

EXAM TIP You may see multiple questions in the exam that try to assign an object of a base class to a reference variable of a derived class. Note that a derived class can be referred to using a reference variable of its base class. The reverse is not allowed and won't compile.

In this section, you learned that the variables of a base class or interface are not able to access all the members of the object to which they refer. Don't worry; this can be resolved by *casting* a reference variable of a base class or an interface to the exact type of the object they refer to, as discussed in the next section.

6.4   *Casting*

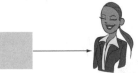

[7.4]   Determine when casting is necessary

Casting is the process of forcefully making a variable behave as a variable of another type. If a class shares an IS-A or inheritance relationship with another class or interface, their variables can be cast to each other's type.

In section 6.3, you learned that you can't access all the members of the class HRExecutive (derived class) if you refer to it via a variable of type Interviewer (implemented interface) or Employee (base class). In this section, you'll learn how to cast a variable of type Interviewer to access variables defined in the class HRExecutive, and why you'd want to.

6.4.1   *How to cast a variable to another type*

We'll start with the definitions of interface Interviewer and classes HRExecutive and Manager:

```
class Employee {}
interface Interviewer {
    public void conductInterview();
}
class HRExecutive extends Employee implements Interviewer {
    String[] specialization;
    public void conductInterview() {
        System.out.println("HRExecutive - conducting interview");
    }
}
class Manager implements Interviewer{
    int teamSize;
    public void conductInterview() {
        System.out.println("Manager - conducting interview");
    }
}
```

Create a variable of type Interviewer and assign to it an object of type HRExecutive (as depicted in figure 6.15).

```
Interviewer interviewer = new HRExecutive();
```

Try to access the variable specialization defined in the class HRExecutive using the previous variable:

```
interviewer.specialization = new String[] {"Staffing"};          ⟵── Won't compile
```

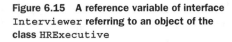

Variable of type   Object of
Interviewer   HRExecutive

**Figure 6.15   A reference variable of interface
Interviewer referring to an object of the
class HRExecutive**

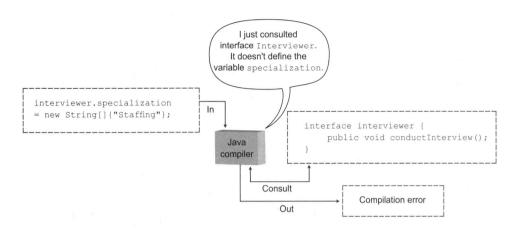

Figure 6.16 The Java compiler doesn't compile code if you try to access the variable specialization, defined in the class HRExecutive, by using a variable of the interface Interviewer.

The previous line of code won't compile. The compiler knows that the type of the variable interviewer is Interviewer and that the interface Interviewer doesn't define any variable with the name specialization (as shown in figure 6.16).

On the other hand, the JRE knows that the object referred to by the variable interviewer is of type HRExecutive, so you can use casting to get past the Java compiler and access the members of the object being referred to, as follows (see also figure 6.17):

```
((HRExecutive)interviewer).specialization = new String[] {"Staffing"};
```

In the previous example code, (HRExecutive) is placed just before the name of the variable, interviewer, to cast it to HRExecutive. A pair of parentheses surrounds

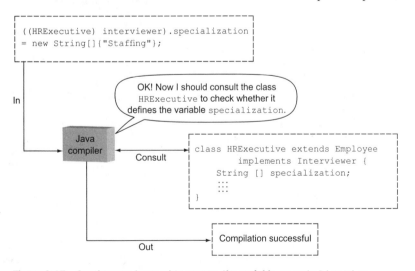

Figure 6.17 Casting can be used to access the variable specialization, defined in the class HRExecutive, by using a variable of interface Interviewer.

(HRExecutive)interviewer, which lets Java know you're sure that the object being referred to is an object of the class HRExecutive. Casting is another method of telling Java: "Look, I know that the actual object being referred to is HRExecutive, even though I'm using a reference variable of type Interviewer."

6.4.2   *Need for casting*

In section 6.3.4, I discussed the need to use a reference variable of an inherited class or an implemented interface to refer to an object of a derived class. I also used an example of enrolling in flying classes, where you don't care about whether the instructor can cook Italian cuisine or knows how to swim. You don't care about characteristics and behavior that are unrelated to flying.

But think about a situation in which you do care about the swimming skills of your instructor. Imagine that when you're attending flying classes, you friend enquires about whether your flying instructor also conducts swimming classes, and if so, whether your friend could enroll. In this case, a *need* arises to enquire about the swimming skills of your flying instructor.

Let's apply this situation to Java. You can't access all the members of an object if you access it using a reference variable of any of its implemented interfaces or of a base class. But if a need arises, you *might* choose to access some of the members of a derived class, which are not explicitly available, by using the reference variable of the base type or the implemented interface. This is where casting comes in!

Time to see this in code. Here's an example that exhibits the need for casting. An application maintains a list of interviewers, and depending on the type of interviewer (HRExecutive or Manager), it performs a different set of actions. If the interviewer is a Manager, the code calls conductInterview only if the value for the Manager's team-Size is greater than 10. Here's the code that implements this logic:

```
class OfficeWhyCasting {                              Array to store objects of
    public static void main(String args[]) {          classes that implement
        Interviewer[] interviewers = new Interviewer[2];    interface Interviewer

        interviewers[0] = new Manager();                    Store object of Manager
Store object of                                             at array position 0
HRExecutive at
array position 1    interviewers[1] = new HRExecutive();

        for (Interviewer interviewer : interviewers) {      Loop through
                                                            values of array
If object                if (interviewer instanceof Manager) {   interviewers
referred to by               int teamSize =((Manager)interviewer).teamSize;
interviewer is of
class Manager,               if (teamSize > 10) {                If interviewer's
use casting to                   interviewer.conductInterview();  teamSize > 10, call
retrieve value               }                                   conductInterview
for its teamSize             else {
                                 System.out.println("Mgr can't " +   If interviewer's
                                     "interview with team size less than 10");  teamSize <= 10,
                             }                                      print message
            }
    }
```

```
        else if (interviewer instanceof HRExecutive) {
            interviewer.conductInterview();
        }
    }
  }
}
```

> **Otherwise, if object stored is of class HRExecutive, call conductInterview method on the object; no casting is required in this case**

6.5   *Use this and super to access objects and constructors*

> **[7.5]   Use super and this to access objects and constructors**

In this section, you'll use the this and super keywords to access objects and constructors. this and super are *implicit* object references. These variables are defined and initialized by the JVM for every object in its memory.

Let's examine the capabilities and use of each of these reference variables.

6.5.1   *Object reference: this*

The this reference always points to an object's *own instance.* Any object can use the this reference to refer to its own instance. Think of the words *me, myself,* and *I:* anyone using those words is always referring to themselves, as shown in figure 6.18.

this = I, me, myself

USING THIS TO ACCESS VARIABLES AND METHODS
You can use the keyword this to refer to all methods and variables that are accessible to a class. For example, here's a modified definition of the class Employee:

Figure 6.18   The keyword this can be compared to the words *me, myself,* and *I.*

```
class Employee {
    String name;
}
```

The variable name can be accessed in the class Programmer (which extends the class Employee) as follows:

```
class Programmer extends Employee {
    void accessEmployeeVariables() {
        name = "Programmer";
    }
}
```

Because there exists an object of class Employee within the class Programmer, the variable name is accessible to an object of Programmer. The variable name can also be accessed in the class Programmer as follows:

```
class Programmer extends Employee {
    void accessEmployeeVariables() {
        this.name = "Programmer";
    }
}
```

The this reference may be used only when code executing within a method block needs to differentiate between an instance variable and its local variable or method parameters. But some developers use the keyword this all over their code, even when it's not required. Some use this as a means to differentiate instance variables from local variables or method parameters.

Figure 6.19 shows the constructor of the class Employee, which uses the reference variable this to differentiate between local and instance variables name, which are declared with the same name.

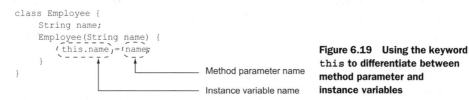

Figure 6.19   Using the keyword this to differentiate between method parameter and instance variables

In the previous example, the class Employee defines an instance variable with the name name. The Employee class constructor also defines a method parameter name, which is effectively a local variable defined within the scope of the method block. Hence, within the scope of the previously defined Employee constructor, there's a clash of names, and the local variable will take precedence. Using name within the scope of the Employee class constructor block will implicitly refer to that method's parameter, not the instance variable. In order to refer to the instance variable name from within the scope of the Employee class constructor, you are obliged to use a this reference.

USING THIS TO ACCESS CONSTRUCTORS
You can also differentiate one constructor from another by using the keyword this. Here's an example in which the class Employee defines two constructors, with the second constructor calling the first one:

```
class Employee {
    String name;                                    Instance variables are
    String address;                                 name and address

    Employee(String name) {                         Constructor that
        this.name = name;                           accepts only name
    }

    Employee(String name, String address) {         Calls constructor that
        this(name);                                 accepts only name

        this.address = address;                     Assigns value of method parameter
    }                                               address to instance variable
}
```

Constructor that accepts name and address

To call the default constructor (one that doesn't accept any method parameters), call
`this()`. Here's an example:

Calls constructor that doesn't accept any arguments. Must be the first statement in this method.

```
class Employee {
    String name;
    String address;

    Employee() {
        name = "NoName";
        address = "NoAddress";
    }

    Employee(String name, String address) {
        this();

        if (name != null) this.name = name;
        if (address != null) this.address = address;
    }
}
```

Instance variables are name and address

Constructor that doesn't accept any arguments

Constructor that accepts name and address

Assigns value of not null method parameters

If present, a call to a constructor from another constructor must be done on the first
line of code of the calling constructor.

> **EXAM TIP**   `this` refers to the instance of the class in which it's used. `this` can
> be used to access the inherited members of a base class in the derived class.

6.5.2   *Object reference: super*

In the previous section, I discussed how `this` refers to the
object instance itself. Similarly, `super` is also an object reference, but `super` refers to the parent or base class of a class.
Think of the words *my parent, my base*: anyone using those
terms is always referring to their parent or the base class, as
shown in figure 6.20.

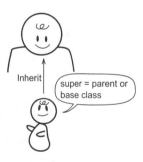

USING SUPER TO ACCESS VARIABLES AND METHODS OF
THE BASE CLASS

The variable reference `super` can be used to access a variable or method from the base class if there's a clash
between these names. This situation normally occurs when
a derived class defines variables and methods with the same
name as the base class.

Figure 6.20   When a class mentions `super`, it refers to its parent or the base class.

Here's an example:

Assign value to instance variable— name, defined in Programmer

```
class Employee {
    String name;
}
class Programmer extends Employee {
    String name;

    void setNames() {
        this.name = "Programmer";

        super.name = "Employee";
    }
}
```

Instance variable— name, in Employee

Instance variable— name, in Programmer

Assign value to instance variable—name, defined in Employee

```
    void printNames() {
        System.out.println(super.name);     ◁──┤  Print value of instance variable—
                                                   name, defined in Employee
        System.out.println(this.name);      ◁──
    }                                              Print value of instance
}                                                  variable—name, defined
class UsingThisAndSuper {                          in Programmer
    public static void main(String[] args) {
        Programmer programmer = new Programmer();  ◁──┐  Create an object of
        programmer.setNames();                          class Programmer
        programmer.printNames();
    }
}
```

The output of the preceding code is as follows:

```
Employee
Programmer
```

Similarly, you can use the reference variable super to access a method defined with the same name in the base or the parent class.

USING SUPER TO ACCESS CONSTRUCTORS OF BASE CLASS

The reference variable super can also be used to refer to the constructors of the base class in a derived class.

Here's an example in which the base class, Employee, defines a constructor that assigns default values to its variables. Its derived class calls the base class constructor in its own constructor.

```
class Employee {
    String name;                            │ Instance variables—
    String address;                           name and address

    Employee(String name, String address) {     ◁──┐  Constructor that accepts
        this.name = name;                               name and address
        this.address = address;
    }
}
class Programmer extends Employee {          │ Instance variable—
    String progLanguage;                     ◁──┘ progLanguage

    Programmer(String name, String address, String progLang) {
        super(name, address);                          ◁──┐  Calls
        this.progLanguage = progLang;                        Employee
    }                                                    ❶  constructor
}
```
Constructor that accepts values for superclass variables also ──▷

The code at ❶ calls the superclass constructor by passing it the reference variables, name and address, which it accepts itself.

EXAM TIP If present, a call to a superclass's constructor must be the first statement in a derived class's constructor. Otherwise, a call to super(); (the no-arg constructor) is inserted automatically by the compiler.

USING SUPER AND THIS IN STATIC METHODS

The keywords `super` and `this` are implicit object references. Because `static` methods belong to a class, not to objects of a class, you can't use `this` and `super` in `static` methods. Code that tries to do so won't compile:

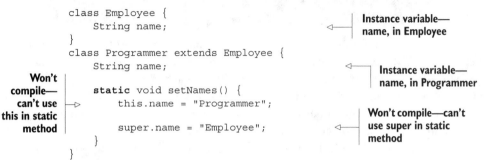

It's time to attempt the next Twist in the Tale exercise, using `this` and `super` keywords (answer in the appendix).

Twist in the Tale 6.3

Let's modify the definition of the `Employee` and `Programmer` classes as follows. What is the output of class `TwistInTale3`?

```
class Employee {
    String name = "Emp";
    String address = "EmpAddress";
}
class Programmer extends Employee{
    String name = "Prog";
    void printValues() {
        System.out.print(this.name + ":");
        System.out.print(this.address + ":");
        System.out.print(super.name + ":");
        System.out.print(super.address);
    }
}
class TwistInTale3 {
    public static void main(String args[]) {
        new Programmer().printValues();
    }
}
```

    a `Prog:null:Emp:EmpAddress`

    b `Prog:EmpAddress:Emp:EmpAddress`

    c `Prog::Emp:EmpAddress`

    d Compilation error

6.6   *Polymorphism*

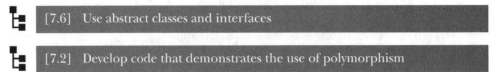

[7.6]   Use abstract classes and interfaces

[7.2]   Develop code that demonstrates the use of polymorphism

The literal meaning of the word "polymorphism" is "many forms." At the beginning of this chapter, I used a practical example to explain the meaning of polymorphism; the same action may have different meanings for different living beings. The action *eat* has a different meaning for a *fly* and a *lion*. A *fly* may eat *nectar*, whereas a *lion* may eat an antelope. Reacting to the same action in one's own unique manner in living beings can be compared to polymorphism in Java.

For the exam, you need to know what polymorphism in Java is, why you need it, and how to implement it in code.

6.6.1   *Polymorphism with classes*

Polymorphism comes into the picture when a class inherits another class and both the base and the derived classes define methods with the same method signature (the same method name and method parameters). As discussed in the previous section, an object can also be referred to using a reference variable of its base class. In this case, depending upon the type of the object used to execute a method, the Java runtime executes the method defined in the base or derived class.

Let's consider polymorphism using the classes `Employee`, `Programmer`, and `Manager`, where the classes `Programmer` and `Manager` inherit the class `Employee`. Figure 6.21 shows a UML diagram depicting the relationships among these classes.

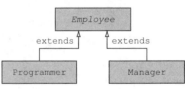

Figure 6.21   Relationships among the classes `Employee`, `Programmer`, and `Manager`

Let's start with the `Employee` class, which is not quite sure about what must be done to start work on a project (execute method `startProjectWork`). Hence, the method `startProjectWork` is defined as an `abstract` method, and the class `Employee` is defined as an `abstract` class, as follows:

```
abstract class Employee {
    public void reachOffice() {
        System.out.println("reached office - Gurgaon, India");
    }
    public abstract void startProjectWork();           Doesn't know how to
}                                                      work on a project
```

The class `Programmer` extends the class `Employee`, which essentially means that it has access to the method `reachOffice` defined in `Employee`. `Programmer` must also implement the abstract method `startProjectWork`, inherited from `Employee`. How do you think a programmer will typically start work on a programming project? Most probably, he will define classes and unit test them. This behavior is contained in the definition of the class `Programmer`, which implements the method `startProjectWork`, as follows:

```java
class Programmer extends Employee {
    public void startProjectWork() {
        defineClasses();
        unitTestCode();
    }
    private void defineClasses() { System.out.println("define classes"); }
    private void unitTestCode() { System.out.println("unit test code"); }
}
```

We are fortunate to have another special type of employee, a manager, who knows how to start work on a project. How do you think a manager will typically start work on a programming project? Most probably, she will meet with the customers, define a project schedule, and assign work to the team members. Here's the definition of class `Manager` that extends class `Employee` and implements the method `startProjectWork`:

```java
class Manager extends Employee {
    public void startProjectWork() {
        meetingWithCustomer();
        defineProjectSchedule();
        assignRespToTeam();
    }
    private void meetingWithCustomer() {
        System.out.println("meet Customer");
    }
    private void defineProjectSchedule() {
        System.out.println("Project Schedule");
    }
    private void assignRespToTeam() {
        System.out.println("team work starts");
    }
}
```

Let's see how this method behaves with different types of employees. Here's the relevant code:

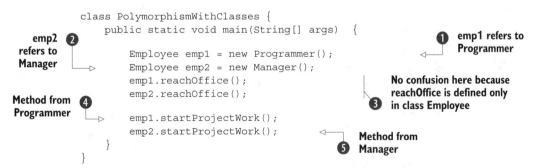

Here's the output of the code (blank lines added for clarity):

```
reached office - Gurgaon, India
reached office - Gurgaon, India
```

```
define classes
unit test code
```

```
meet Customer
Project Schedule
team work starts
```

The code at ❶ creates an object of the class `Programmer` and assigns it to a variable of type `Employee`. ❷ creates an object of the class `Manager` and assigns it to a variable of type `Employee`. So far, so good!

Now comes the complicated part. ❸ executes the method `reachOffice`. Because this method is defined only in the class `Employee`, there isn't any confusion and the same method executes, printing the following:

```
reached office - Gurgaon, India
reached office - Gurgaon, India
```

The code at ❹ executes the code `emp1.startProjectWork()` and calls the method `startProjectWork` defined in the class `Programmer`, because `emp1` refers to an object of the class `Programmer`. Here's the output of this method call:

```
define classes
unit test code
```

The code at ❺ executes `emp2.startProjectWork()` and calls the method `start-ProjectWork` defined in the class `Manager`, because `emp2` refers to an object of the class `Manager`. Here's the output of this method call:

```
meet Customer
Project Schedule
team work starts
```

Figure 6.22 illustrates this code.

As discussed in the beginning of this section, the usefulness of polymorphism lies in the ability of an object to behave in its own specific manner when the same action is passed to it. In the previous example, reference variables (`emp1` and `emp2`) of type `Employee` are used to store objects of class `Programmer` and `Manager`. When the same action—that is, method call `startProjectWork`—is invoked on these reference variables (`emp1` and `emp2`), each method call results in the method defined in the respective classes being executed.

POLYMORPHIC METHODS ARE ALSO CALLED OVERRIDDEN METHODS

Take a quick look at the method `startProjectWork`, as defined in the following classes `Employee`, `Programmer`, and `Manager` (only the relevant code is shown):

```
abstract class Employee {                              Method
    public abstract void startProjectWork();      ◁─┤ startProjectWork in
}                                                      class Employee
class Programmer extends Employee {
    public void startProjectWork() {              ◁─  Method
        ...                                           startProjectWork in
    }                                                 class Programmer
}
class Manager extends Employee {
```

```
public void startProjectWork() {
    ...
}
```
}

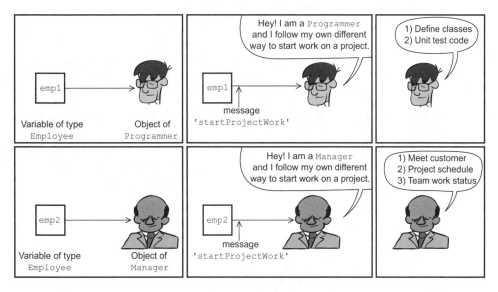 **Method startProjectWork in class Manager**

Note that the name of method `startProjectWork` is same in all these classes. Also, it accepts the same number of method arguments and defines the same return type in all the three classes: `Employee`, `Programmer`, and `Manager`. This is a contract specified to define overridden methods. Failing to use the same method name, same argument list, or same return type won't mark a method as an overridden method.

RULES TO REMEMBER WHEN DEFINING OVERRIDDEN METHODS

- Overridden methods are defined by classes and interfaces that share inheritance relationships.
- The name of the overridden method must be the same in both the base class and the derived class.
- The argument list passed to the overridden method must be the same in both the base class and derived class.
- The return type of an overriding method in the derived class can be the same, or a subclass of the return type of the overridden method in the base class. When the overriding method returns a subclass of the return type of the overridden method, it is known as a *covariant return type.*
- An overridden method defined in the base class can be an `abstract` method or a non-`abstract` method.
- Access modifiers for an overriding method can be the same or less restrictive than the method being overridden, but they can't be more restrictive.

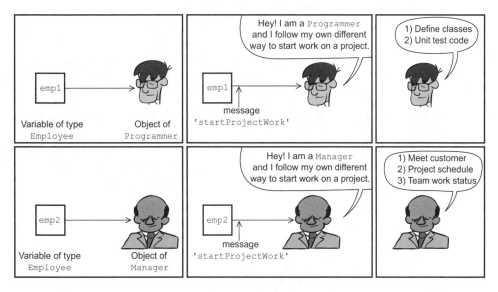

Figure 6.22 The objects are aware of their own type and execute the overridden method defined in their own class, even if a base class variable is used to refer to them.

DO POLYMORPHIC METHODS ALWAYS HAVE TO BE ABSTRACT?

No, polymorphic methods don't always have to be `abstract`. You can define the class `Employee` as a concrete class and the method `startProjectWork` as a non-abstract method and still get the same results (changes in bold):

```
class Employee {
    public void reachOffice() {
        System.out.println("reached office - Gurgaon, India");
    }
    public void startProjectWork() {
        System.out.println("procure hardware");
        System.out.println("install software");
    }
}
```

Because there's no change in the definition of the rest of the classes—`Programmer`, `Manager`, and `PolymorphismWithClasses`—I haven't listed them here. If you create an object of the class `Employee` (not of any of its derived classes), you can execute the method `startProjectWork` as follows:

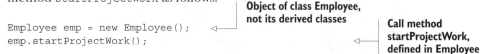

Object of class Employee, not its derived classes

```
Employee emp = new Employee();
emp.startProjectWork();
```

Call method startProjectWork, defined in Employee

EXAM TIP   To implement polymorphism with classes, you can define `abstract` or non-abstract methods in the base class and override them in the derived classes.

CAN POLYMORPHISM WORK WITH OVERLOADED METHODS?

No, polymorphism works only with overridden methods. Overridden methods have the same number and type of method arguments, whereas overloaded methods define a method argument list with either a different number or type of method parameters.

Overloaded methods only share the same name; the JRE treats them like different methods. In the case of overridden methods, the JRE decides at runtime which method should be called based on the exact type of the object on which it's called.

It's time for the next Twist in the Tale exercise. As usual, you can find the answers in the appendix.

Twist in the Tale 6.4

Given the following definition of classes `Employee` and `Programmer`, which of the options when inserted at `//INSERT CODE HERE//` will define the method run as a polymorphic method?

```
class Employee {
    //INSERT CODE HERE// {
        System.out.println("Emp-run");
        return null;
    }
}
class Programmer extends Employee{
    String run() {
        System.out.println("Programmer-run");
```

```
            return null;
        }
    }
    class TwistInTale4 {
        public static void main(String args[]) {
            new Programmer().run();
        }
    }
```

   a `String run()`

   b `void run(int meters)`

   c `void run()`

   d `int run(String race)`

6.6.2 *Binding of variables and methods at compile time and runtime*

You can use reference variables of a base class to refer to an object of a derived class. But there's a major difference in how Java accesses the variables and methods for these objects. With inheritance, the instance variables bind at compile time and the methods bind at runtime.

Examine the following code:

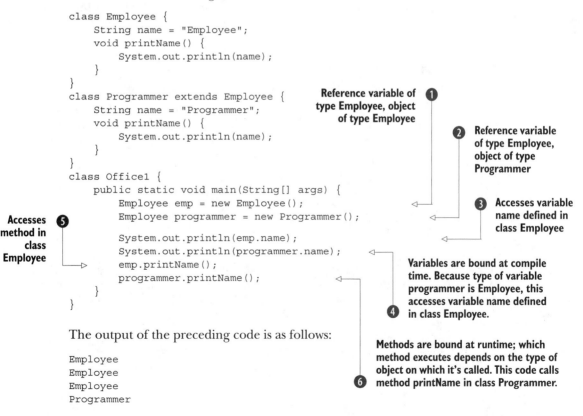

```
class Employee {
    String name = "Employee";
    void printName() {
        System.out.println(name);
    }
}
class Programmer extends Employee {
    String name = "Programmer";
    void printName() {
        System.out.println(name);
    }
}
class Office1 {
    public static void main(String[] args) {
        Employee emp = new Employee();
        Employee programmer = new Programmer();

        System.out.println(emp.name);
        System.out.println(programmer.name);
        emp.printName();
        programmer.printName();
    }
}
```

① Reference variable of type Employee, object of type Employee

② Reference variable of type Employee, object of type Programmer

③ Accesses variable name defined in class Employee

④ Variables are bound at compile time. Because type of variable programmer is Employee, this accesses variable name defined in class Employee.

⑤ Accesses method in class Employee

⑥ Methods are bound at runtime; which method executes depends on the type of object on which it's called. This code calls method printName in class Programmer.

The output of the preceding code is as follows:

```
Employee
Employee
Employee
Programmer
```

Let's see what's happening in the code, step by step:

- ❶ creates an object of class `Employee`, referenced by a variable of its own type—`Employee`.
- ❷ creates an object of class `Programmer`, referenced by a variable of its base type—`Employee`.
- ❸ accesses variable `name` defined in class `Employee` and prints `Employee`.
- ❹ also prints `Employee`. The type of the variable `programmer` is `Employee`. Because the variables are bound at compile time, the type of the object that's referenced by the variable `emp` doesn't make a difference. `programmer.name` will access the variable `name` defined in the class `Employee`.
- ❺ prints `Employee`. Because the type of the reference variable `emp` and the type of object referenced by it are the same (`Employee`), there's no confusion with the method call.
- ❻ prints `Programmer`. Even though the method `printName` is called using a reference of type `Employee`, the JRE is aware that the method is invoked on a `Programmer` object and hence executes the overridden `printName` method in the class `Programmer`.

 EXAM TIP Watch out for code in the exam that uses variables of the base class to refer to objects of the derived class and then accesses variables and methods of the referenced object. Remember that variables bind at compile time, whereas methods bind at runtime.

6.6.3 *Polymorphism with interfaces*

Polymorphism can also be implemented using interfaces. Whereas polymorphism with classes has a class as the base class, polymorphism with interfaces requires a class to implement an interface. Polymorphism with interfaces *always* involves `abstract` methods from the implemented interface because interfaces can define only `abstract` methods.

Let's start with an example. Here's an interface, `MobileAppExpert`, which defines a method, `deliverMobileApp`:

```
interface MobileAppExpert {
    void deliverMobileApp();
}
```

As you know, all the methods defined in an interface are implicitly `abstract` and `public`. Here are the classes `Programmer` and `Manager` that implement this interface and the method `deliverMobileApp`:

```
class Employee {}
class Programmer extends Employee implements MobileAppExpert {
    public void deliverMobileApp() {
        System.out.println("testing complete on real device");
    }
}
```

```
class Manager extends Employee implements MobileAppExpert {
    public void deliverMobileApp() {
        System.out.println("QA complete");
        System.out.println("code delivered with release notes");
    }
}
```

NOTE I've deliberately removed the methods previously defined in `Employee`, `Programmer`, and `Manager` because they are not relevant in this section.

The relationships among the two classes and the interface are shown in figure 6.23.

In the real world, the delivery of a mobile application would have different meaning for a programmer and a manager. For a *programmer*, the delivery of a mobile application may require the completion of testing on the real mobile device. However, for a *manager*, the delivery of a mobile application may mean completing the QA process and handing over code to the client along with any release notes. The bottom line is that the same message, `deliverMobileApp`, results in the execution of different sets of steps for a programmer and a manager.

Here's a class `PolymorphismWithInterfaces` that creates objects of the classes `Programmer` and `Manager` and calls the method `deliverMobileApp`:

```
class PolymorphismWithInterfaces {
    public static void main(String[] args)  {
        MobileAppExpert expert1 = new Programmer();
        MobileAppExpert expert2 = new Manager();

        expert1.deliverMobileApp();
        expert2.deliverMobileApp();
    }
}
```

① **Reference type of variables expert1 and expert2 is MobileAppExpert**

The output of the preceding code is as follows:

```
testing complete on real device
QA complete
code delivered with release notes
```

At **①**, the type of the variable is `MobileAppExpert`. Because the classes `Manager` and `Programmer` implement the interface `MobileAppExpert`, a reference variable of type

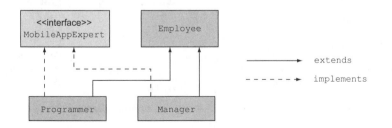

Figure 6.23 Relationships among classes `Employee`, `Programmer`, and `Manager` and the interface `MobileAppExpert`

MobileAppExpert can also be used to store objects of the classes Programmer and Manager.

Because both these classes also extend the class Employee, you can use a variable of type Employee to store objects of the classes Programmer and Manager. But in this case you won't be able to call method deliverMobileApp because it isn't visible to the class Employee. Examine the following code:

```
class PolymorphismWithInterfaces {
    public static void main(String[] args)  {          Employee can't see
        Employee expert1 = new Programmer();           deliverMobileApp
        Employee expert2 = new Manager();         ◁┘

        expert1.deliverMobileApp();                    Won't compile
        expert2.deliverMobileApp();
    }
}
```

Let's see what happens if we modify the class Employee to implement the interface MobileAppExpert, as follows:

```
class Employee implements MobileAppExpert {
    // code
}
interface MobileAppExpert {
    // code
}
```

Now the classes Programmer and Manager can just extend the class Employee. They no longer need to implement the interface MobileAppExpert because their base class, Employee, implements it:

```
class Programmer extends Employee {
    // code
}
class Manager extends Employee {
    // code
}
```

With the modified code, the new relationships among the classes Employee, Manager, and Programmer and the interface MobileAppExpert are shown in figure 6.24.

Let's try to access the method deliverMobileApp using a reference variable of type Employee class, as follows:

```
class PolymorphismWithInterfaces {
    public static void main(String[] args)  {          Employee can see
        Employee expert1 = new Programmer();           deliverMobileApp
        Employee expert2 = new Manager();         ◁┘

        expert1.deliverMobileApp();                    Will work!
        expert2.deliverMobileApp();
    }           .
}
```

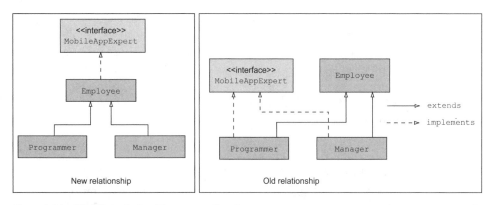

Figure 6.24 **Modified relationships among the classes** `Employee`, `Manager`, **and** `Programmer` **and the interface** `MobileAppExpert`

Figure 6.25 shows what's accessible to the variable `expert1`.

> **EXAM TIP** Watch out for overloaded methods that seem to participate in polymorphism—overloaded methods don't participate in polymorphism. Only overridden methods—methods with the same method signatures—participate in polymorphism.

6.7 Summary

We started the chapter with a discussion of inheritance and polymorphism, using an example from everyday life: all creatures inherit properties and behavior of their parents, and the same action (such as *reproduce*) may have different meanings for different species. Inheritance enables the reuse of existing code, and it can be implemented using classes and interfaces. A class can't extend more than one class, but it can implement more than one interface. Inheriting a class is also called *subclassing*, and the inherited class is referred to as the *base* or *parent class*. A class that inherits another class or implements an interface is called a *derived class* or *subclass*.

Just as it's common to address someone using a last name or family name, an object of a derived class can be referred to with a variable of a base class or an interface that it implements. But when you refer to an object using a variable of the base class, the variable can access only the members defined in the base class. Similarly, a variable of type interface can access only the members defined in that interface. Even

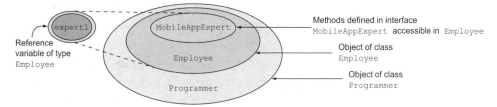

Figure 6.25 **What's accessible to the variable** `expert1`

with this limitation, you may wish to refer to objects using variables of their base class to work with multiple objects that have common base classes.

Objects of related classes—the ones that share an inheritance relationship—can be cast to another object. You may wish to cast an object when you wish to access its members that are not available by default using the variable that's used to refer to the object.

The keywords `this` and `super` are object references and are used to access an object and its base class respectively. You can use the keyword `this` to access a class's variables, methods, and constructors. Similarly, the keyword `super` is used to access a base class's variables, methods, and constructors.

Polymorphism is the ability of objects to execute methods defined in a superclass or base class, depending upon their type. Classes that share an inheritance relationship exhibit polymorphism. The polymorphic method should be defined in both the base class and the inherited class.

You can implement polymorphism by using either classes or interfaces. In the case of polymorphism with classes, the base class can be either an abstract class or a concrete class. The method in question here also need not be an abstract method. When you implement polymorphism using interfaces, you must use an `abstract` method from the interface.

6.8   *Review notes*

Inheritance with interfaces and classes:

- A class can inherit the properties and behavior of another class.
- A class can implement multiple interfaces.
- An interface can inherit zero or more interfaces. An interface cannot inherit a class.
- Inheritance enables you to use existing code.
- Inheriting a class is also known as subclassing.
- A class that inherits another class is called a derived class or subclass.
- A class that is inherited is called a parent or base class.
- Private members of a base class cannot be inherited in the derived class.
- A derived class can only inherit members with the default access modifier if both the base class and the derived class are in the same package.
- A class uses the keyword `extends` to inherit a class.
- An interface uses the keyword `extends` to inherit another interface.
- A class uses the keyword `implements` to implement an interface.
- A class can implement multiple interfaces but can inherit only one class.
- An interface can extend multiple interfaces.
- The method signatures of a method defined in an interface and in the class that implements the interface must match; otherwise, the class won't compile.
- An `abstract` class can inherit a concrete class, and a concrete class can inherit an `abstract` class.

Reference variable and object types:

- With inheritance, you can also refer to an object of a derived class using a variable of a base class or interface.
- An object of a base class can't be referred to using a reference variable of its derived class.
- When an object is referred to by a reference variable of a base class, the reference variable can only access the variables and members that are defined in the base class.
- When an object is referred to by a reference variable of an interface implemented by a class, the reference variable can access only the variables and methods defined in the interface.
- You may need to access an object of a derived class using a reference variable of the base class to group and use all the classes with common parent classes or interfaces.

The need for casting:

- Casting is the process of forcefully making a variable behave as a variable of another type.
- If the class `Manager` extends the class `Employee`, and a reference variable `emp` of type `Employee` is used to refer to an object of the class `Manager`, `((Manager)emp)` will cast the variable `emp` to `Manager`.

Using `super` and `this` to access objects and constructors:

- Keywords `super` and `this` are object references. These variables are defined and initialized by the JVM for every object in its memory.
- The `this` reference always points to an object's *own instance.*
- You can use the keyword `this` to refer to all methods and variables that are accessible to a class.
- If a method defines a local variable or method parameter with the same name as an instance variable, the keyword `this` must be used to access the instance variable in the method.
- You can call one constructor from another constructor by using the keyword `this`.
- `super`, an object reference, refers to the parent class or the base class of a class.
- The reference variable `super` can be used to access a variable or method from the base class if there is a clash of these names. This situation normally occurs when a derived class defines variables and methods with the same names as in the base class.
- The reference variable `super` can also be used to refer to the constructors of the base class in a derived class.

Polymorphism with classes:

- The literal meaning of the word "polymorphism" is "many forms."
- In Java, polymorphism comes into the picture when there's an inheritance relationship between classes, and both the base and derived classes define methods with the same name.
- The polymorphic methods are also called *overridden methods*.
- Overridden methods should define methods with the same name, same argument list, same list of method parameters. The return type of the overriding method can be the same, or a subclass of the return type of the overridden method in the base class, which is also known as covariant return type.
- Access modifiers for an overriding method can be the same or less restrictive but can't be more restrictive than the method being overridden.
- A derived class is said to override a method in the base class if it defines a method with the same name, same parameter list, and same return type as in the derived class.
- If a method defined in a base class is overloaded in the derived classes, then these two methods (in the base class and the derived class) are not called polymorphic methods.
- When implementing polymorphism with classes, a method defined in the base class may or may not be `abstract`.
- When implementing polymorphism with interfaces, a method defined in the base interface is always `abstract`.

6.9   *Sample exam questions*

Q6-1. What is the output of the following code?

```
class Animal {
    void jump() { System.out.println("Animal"); }
}
class Cat extends Animal {
    void jump(int a) { System.out.println("Cat"); }
}
class Rabbit extends Animal {
    void jump() { System.out.println("Rabbit"); }
}
class Circus {
    public static void main(String args[]) {
        Animal cat = new Cat();
        Rabbit rabbit = new Rabbit();
        cat.jump();
        rabbit.jump();
    }
}
```

   a Animal
      Rabbit

b `Cat`
   `Rabbit`

c `Animal`
   `Animal`

d None of the above

Q6-2. Given the following code, select the correct statements:

```
class Flower {
    public void fragrance() {System.out.println("Flower"); }
}
class Rose {
    public void fragrance() {System.out.println("Rose"); }
}
class Lily {
    public void fragrance() {System.out.println("Lily"); }
}
class Bouquet {
    public void arrangeFlowers() {
        Flower f1 = new Rose();
        Flower f2 = new Lily();
        f1.fragrance();
    }
}
```

a The output of the code is:

   `Flower`

b The output of the code is:

   `Rose`

c The output of the code is:

   `Lily`

d The code fails to compile.

Q6-3. Examine the following code and select the correct method declaration to be inserted at `//INSERT CODE HERE`:

```
interface Movable {
    void move();
}
class Person implements Movable {
    public void move() { System.out.println("Person move"); }
}
class Vehicle implements Movable {
    public void move() { System.out.println("Vehicle move"); }
}
class Test {
    // INSERT CODE HERE
        movable.move();
    }
}
```

   a   `void walk(Movable movable) {`

   b   `void walk(Person movable) {`

   c   `void walk(Vehicle movable) {`

   d   `void walk() {`

Q6-4. Select the correct statements:

   a   Only an `abstract` class can be used as a base class to implement polymorphism with classes.

   b   Polymorphic methods are also called overridden methods.

   c   In polymorphism, depending on the exact type of object, the JVM executes the appropriate method at compile time.

   d   None of the above.

Q6-5. Given the following code, select the correct statements:

```
class Person {}
class Employee extends Person {}
class Doctor extends Person {}
```

   a   The code exhibits polymorphism with classes.

   b   The code exhibits polymorphism with interfaces.

   c   The code exhibits polymorphism with classes and interfaces.

   d   None of the above.

Q6-6. Which of the following statements are true?

   a   Inheritance enables you to reuse existing code.

   b   Inheritance saves you from having to modify common code in multiple classes.

   c   Polymorphism passes special instructions to the compiler so that the code can run on multiple platforms.

   d   Polymorphic methods cannot throw exceptions.

Q6-7. Given the following code, which of the options are true?

```
class Satellite {
    void orbit() {}
}
class Moon extends Satellite {
    void orbit() {}
}
class ArtificialSatellite extends Satellite {
    void orbit() {}
}
```

   a   The method `orbit` defined in the classes `Satellite`, `Moon`, and `Artificial-Satellite` is polymorphic.

   b   Only the method `orbit` defined in the classes `Satellite` and `Artificial-Satellite` is polymorphic.

    c Only the method `orbit` defined in the class `ArtificialSatellite` is polymorphic.

    d None of the above.

Q6-8. Examine the following code:

```
class Programmer {
    void print() {
        System.out.println("Programmer - Mala Gupta");
    }
}
class Author extends Programmer {
    void print() {
        System.out.println("Author - Mala Gupta");
    }
}
class TestEJava {
    Programmer a = new Programmer();
    // INSERT CODE HERE
    a.print();
    b.print();
}
```

Which of the following lines of code can be individually inserted at `//INSERT CODE HERE` so that the output of the code is as follows:

```
Programmer - Mala Gupta
Author - Mala Gupta
```

    a `Programmer b = new Programmer();`

    b `Programmer b = new Author();`

    c `Author b = new Author();`

    d `Author b = new Programmer();`

    e `Programmer b = ((Author)new Programmer());`

    f `Author b = ((Author)new Programmer());`

Q6-9. Given the following code, which of the options, when applied individually, will make it compile successfully?

```
Line1>    interface Employee {}

Line2>    interface Printable extends Employee {
Line3>        String print();
Line4>    }

Line5>    class Programmer {
Line6>        String print() { return("Programmer - Mala Gupta"); }
Line7>    }

Line8>    class Author extends Programmer implements Printable, Employee {
Line9>        String print() { return("Author - Mala Gupta"); }
Line10>   }
```

    a Modify code on line 2 to: `interface Printable{`

    b Modify code on line 3 to: `publicStringprint();`

    c Define the accessibility of the print methods to public on lines 6 and 9.

    d Modify code on line 8 so that it implements only the interface Printable.

Q6-10. What is the output of the following code?

```
class Base {
    String var = "EJava";
    void printVar() {
        System.out.println(var);
    }
}
class Derived extends Base {
    String var = "Guru";
    void printVar() {
        System.out.println(var);
    }
}
class QReference {
    public static void main(String[] args) {
        Base base = new Base();
        Base derived = new Derived();

        System.out.println(base.var);
        System.out.println(derived.var);
        base.printVar();
        derived.printVar();
    }
}
```

    a EJava
       EJava
       EJava
       Guru

    b EJava
       Guru
       EJava
       Guru

    c EJava
       EJava
       EJava
       EJava

    d EJava
       Guru
       Guru
       Guru

6.10 *Answers to sample exam questions*

Q6-1. What is the output of the following code?

```
class Animal {
    void jump() { System.out.println("Animal"); }
}
class Cat extends Animal {
    void jump(int a) { System.out.println("Cat"); }
```

```
}
class Rabbit extends Animal {
    void jump() { System.out.println("Rabbit"); }
}
class Circus {
    public static void main(String args[]) {
        Animal cat = new Cat();
        Rabbit rabbit = new Rabbit();
        cat.jump();
        rabbit.jump();
    }
}
```

   a **Animal**
     Rabbit

   b Cat
     Rabbit

   c Animal
     Animal

   d None of the above

Answer: a

Explanation: Although the classes Cat and Rabbit seem to override the method jump, the class Cat doesn't override the method jump() defined in the class Animal. The class Cat defines a method parameter with the method jump, which makes it an overloaded method, not an overridden method. Because the class Cat extends the class Animal, it has access to the following two overloaded jump methods:

```
void jump() { System.out.println("Animal"); }
void jump(int a) { System.out.println("Cat"); }
```

The following line of code creates an object of class Cat and assigns it to a variable of type Animal:

```
Animal cat = new Cat();
```

When you call the method jump on the previous object, it executes the method jump, which doesn't accept any method parameters, printing the following value:

```
Animal
```

The following code will also print Animal and not Cat:

```
Cat cat = new Cat();
cat.jump();
```

Q6-2. Given the following code, select the correct statements:

```
class Flower {
    public void fragrance() {System.out.println("Flower"); }
}
class Rose {
    public void fragrance() {System.out.println("Rose"); }
}
```

```
class Lily {
    public void fragrance() {System.out.println("Lily"); }
}
class Bouquet {
    public void arrangeFlowers() {
        Flower f1 = new Rose();
        Flower f2 = new Lily();
        f1.fragrance();
    }
}
```

a The output of the code is:

```
Flower
```

b The output of the code is:

```
Rose
```

c The output of the code is:

```
Lily
```

d **The code fails to compile.**

Answer: d

Explanation: Although the code seems to implement polymorphism using classes, note that neither of the classes Rose or Lily *extends* the class Flower. Hence, a variable of type Flower can't be used to store objects of the classes Rose or Lily. The following lines of code will fail to compile:

```
Flower f1 = new Rose();
Flower f2 = new Lily();
```

Q6-3. Examine the following code and select the correct method declaration to be inserted at //INSERT CODE HERE:

```
interface Movable {
    void move();
}
class Person implements Movable {
    public void move() { System.out.println("Person move"); }
}
class Vehicle implements Movable {
    public void move() { System.out.println("Vehicle move"); }
}
class Test {
    // INSERT CODE HERE
        movable.move();
    }
}
```

a **void walk(Movable movable) {**
b **void walk(Person movable) {**
c **void walk(Vehicle movable) {**
d void walk() {

Answer: a, b, c

Explanation: You need to insert code in the class Test that makes the following line of code work:

```
movable.move();
```

Hence, option (d) is incorrect. Because class Test doesn't define any instance methods, the only way that the question's line of code can execute is when a method parameter movable is passed to the method walk.

Option (a) is correct. Because the interface Movable defines the method move, you can pass a variable of its type to the method move.

Option (b) is correct. Because the class Person implements the interface Movable and defines the method move, you can pass a variable of its type to the method walk. With this version of the method walk, you can pass it an object of the class Person or any of its subclasses.

Option (c) is correct. Because the class Vehicle implements the interface Movable and defines the method move, you can pass a variable of its type to the method walk. With this version of method walk, you can pass it an object of the class Vehicle or any of its subclasses.

Q6-4. Select the correct statements:

   a Only an abstract class can be used as a base class to implement polymorphism with classes.

   b **Polymorphic methods are also called overridden methods.**

   c In polymorphism, depending on the exact type of object, the JVM executes the appropriate method at compile time.

   d None of the above.

Answer: b

Option (a) is incorrect. To implement polymorphism with classes, either an abstract class or a concrete class can be used as a base class.

Option (c) is incorrect. First of all, no code execution takes place at compile time. Code can only execute at runtime. In polymorphism, the determination of the exact method to execute is deferred until runtime and is determined by the exact type of the object on which a method needs to be called.

Q6-5. Given the following code, select the correct statements:

```
class Person {}
class Employee extends Person {}
class Doctor extends Person {}
```

   a The code exhibits polymorphism with classes.

   b The code exhibits polymorphism with interfaces.

   c The code exhibits polymorphism with classes and interfaces.

   d **None of the above.**

Answer: d

Explanation: The given code does not define any method in the class `Person` that is redefined or implemented in the classes `Employee` and `Doctor`. Though the classes `Employee` and `Doctor` extend the class `Person`, all these three polymorphism concepts or design principles are based on a method, which is missing in these classes.

Q6-6. Which of the following statements are true?

    a   **Inheritance enables you to reuse existing code.**

    b   **Inheritance saves you from having to modify common code in multiple classes.**

    c   Polymorphism passes special instructions to the compiler so that the code can run on multiple platforms.

    d   Polymorphic methods cannot throw exceptions.

Answer: a, b

Explanation: Option (a) is correct. Inheritance can allow you to reuse existing code by extending a class. In this way, the functionality that is already defined in the base class need not be defined in the derived class. The functionality offered by the base class can be accessed in the derived class as if it were defined in the derived class.

Option (b) is correct. Common code can be placed in the base class, which can be extended by all the derived classes. If any changes need to be made to this common code, it can be modified in the base class. The modified code will be accessible to all the derived classes.

Option (c) is incorrect. Polymorphism doesn't pass any special instructions to the compiler to make the Java code execute on multiple platforms. Java code can execute on multiple platforms because the Java compiler compiles to virtual machine code, which is platform-neutral. Different platforms implement this virtual machine.

Option (d) is incorrect. Polymorphic methods can throw exceptions.

Q6-7. Given the following code, which of the options are true?

```
class Satellite {
    void orbit() {}
}
class Moon extends Satellite {
    void orbit() {}
}
class ArtificialSatellite extends Satellite {
    void orbit() {}
}
```

    a   **The method `orbit` defined in the classes `Satellite`, `Moon`, and `Artificial-Satellite` is polymorphic.**

    b   Only the method `orbit` defined in the classes `Satellite` and `Artificial-Satellite` is polymorphic.

    c   Only the method `orbit` defined in the class `ArtificialSatellite` is polymorphic.

    d   None of the above.

Answer: a

Explanation: All of these options define classes. When methods with the same method signature are defined in classes that share an inheritance relationship, the methods are considered polymorphic.

Q6-8. Examine the following code:

```
class Programmer {
    void print() {
        System.out.println("Programmer - Mala Gupta");
    }
}
class Author extends Programmer {
    void print() {
        System.out.println("Author - Mala Gupta");
    }
}
class TestEJava {
    Programmer a = new Programmer();
    // INSERT CODE HERE
    a.print();
    b.print();
}
```

Which of the following lines of code can be individually inserted at //INSERT CODE HERE so that the output of the code is as follows:

```
Programmer - Mala Gupta
Author - Mala Gupta
```

   a `Programmer b = new Programmer();`
   b **`Programmer b = new Author();`**
   c **`Author b = new Author();`**
   d `Author b = new Programmer();`
   e `Programmer b = ((Author)new Programmer());`
   f `Author b = ((Author)new Programmer());`

Answer: b, c

Explanation: Option (a) is incorrect. This code will compile, but because both the reference variable and object are of type `Programmer`, calling `print` on this object will print `Programmer - Mala Gupta`, not `Author - Mala Gupta`.

Option (d) is incorrect. This code will not compile. You can't assign an object of a base class to a reference variable of a derived class.

Option (e) is incorrect. This line of code will compile successfully, but it will fail at runtime with a `ClassCastException`. An object of a base class can't be cast to an object of its derived class.

Option (f) is incorrect. The expression `((Author)new Programmer())` is evaluated before it can be assigned to a reference variable of type `Author`. This line of code also tries to cast an object of the base class—`Programmer`—to an object of its derived class—Author. This code will also compile successfully but will fail at runtime with a ClassCastException. Using a reference variable of type Author won't make a difference here.

Q6-9. Given the following code, which of the options, when applied individually, will make it compile successfully?

```
Line1>    interface Employee {}

Line2>    interface Printable extends Employee {
Line3>        String print();
Line4>    }

Line5>    class Programmer {
Line6>        String print() { return("Programmer - Mala Gupta"); }
Line7>    }

Line8>     class Author extends Programmer implements Printable, Employee {
Line9>        String print() { return("Author - Mala Gupta"); }
Line10>    }
```

  a Modify code on line 2 to: interface Printable {
  b Modify code on line 3 to: public String print();
  c **Define the accessibility of the print methods to public on lines 6 and 9.**
  d Modify code on line 8 so that it implements only the interface Printable.

Answer: c

Explanation: The methods in an interface are implicitly public. A non-abstract class that implements an interface must implement all the methods defined in the interface. While overriding or implementing the methods, the accessibility of the implemented method must be public. An overriding method can't be assigned a weaker access privilege than public.

  Option (a) is incorrect. There are no issues with the interface Printable extending the interface Employee and the class Author implementing both of these interfaces.

  Option (b) is incorrect. Adding the access modifier to the method print on line 3 will not make any difference to the existing code. The methods defined in an interface are implicitly public.

  Option (d) is incorrect. There are no issues with a class implementing two interfaces when one of the interfaces extends the other interface.

Q6-10. What is the output of the following code?

```
class Base {
    String var = "EJava";
    void printVar() {
        System.out.println(var);
    }
}
class Derived extends Base {
    String var = "Guru";
    void printVar() {
```

```
            System.out.println(var);
        }
    }
class QReference {
    public static void main(String[] args) {
        Base base = new Base();
        Base derived = new Derived();

        System.out.println(base.var);
        System.out.println(derived.var);
        base.printVar();
        derived.printVar();
    }
}
```

a **EJava**
    EJava
    EJava
    Guru

b EJava
    Guru
    EJava
    Guru

c EJava
    EJava
    EJava
    EJava

d EJava
    Guru
    Guru
    Guru

Answer: a

Explanation: With inheritance, the instance variables bind at compile time and the methods bind at runtime. The following line of code refers to an object of the class Base, using a reference variable of type Base. Hence, both of the following lines of code print EJava:

```
System.out.println(base.var);
base.printVar();
```

But the following line of code refers to an object of the class Derived using a reference variable of type Base:

```
Base derived = new Derived();
```

Because the instance variables bind at compile time, the following line of code accesses and prints the value of the instance variable defined in the class Base:

```
System.out.println(derived.var);    // prints EJava
```

In derived.printVar(), even though the method printVar is called using a reference of type Base, the JVM is aware that the method is invoked on a Derived object and so executes the overridden printVar method in the class Derived.

Exception handling 7

Exam objectives covered in this chapter	What you need to know
[8.3] Describe what exceptions are used for in Java.	Need for the exception handlers; their advantages and disadvantages.
[8.1] Differentiate among checked exceptions, `RuntimeExceptions`, and `Errors`.	Differences and similarities between checked exceptions, `RuntimeExceptions`, and `Errors`. Differences and similarities in the way these exceptions and errors are handled in code.
[8.2] Create a `try-catch` block and determine how exceptions alter normal program flow.	How to create a `try-catch-finally` block. Understand the flow of code when the enclosed code throws an exception or error. How to create nested `try-catch-finally` blocks.
[8.4] Invoke a method that throws an exception.	How to determine the flow of control when an invoked method throws an exception. How to apply this to cases when it's thrown without a `try` block, and from a `try` block (with appropriate and insufficient exception handlers). The difference in calling methods that throw or don't throw exceptions.
[8.5] Recognize common exception classes and categories.	Common exception classes and categories, and how to recognize the code that can throw these exceptions and handle them appropriately.

Imagine you're about to board an airplane to Geneva to attend an important conference. At the last minute, you learn that the flight has been cancelled because the pilot isn't feeling well. Fortunately, the airline quickly arranges for an alternative pilot, allowing the flight to take off at its originally scheduled time. What a relief.

This example illustrates how exceptional conditions can modify the initial flow of an action and demonstrates the need to handle those conditions appropriately. In Java, an exceptional condition (like the illness of a pilot) can affect the normal code flow (airline flight operation). In this context, the arrangement for an alternative pilot can be compared to an exception handler.

Depending on the nature of the exceptional condition, you may or may not be able to recover completely. For example, would airline management have been able to get your flight off the ground if instead an earthquake had damaged much of the airport?

In the exam, you'll be asked similar questions with respect to Java code and exceptions. With that in mind, this chapter covers the following:

- Understanding and identifying exceptions arising in code
- Determining how exceptions alter the normal program flow
- Understanding the need to handle exceptions separately in your code
- Using `try-catch-finally` blocks to handle exceptions
- Differentiating among checked exceptions, unchecked exceptions, and errors
- Invoking methods that may throw exceptions
- Recognizing common exception categories and classes

You might feel like we're covering a lot in this chapter, but remember that we aren't going to delve into too much background information because we assume you already know the definitions and uses of classes and methods, class inheritance, arrays, and ArrayLists. Our focus in this chapter will be on the exam objectives and what you need to know about exceptions.

In this chapter, I won't discuss a `try` statement with multiple `catch` clauses, automatic closing of resources with a `try-with-resources` statement, or the creation of custom exceptions. These topics are covered in the next level of Java certification (in the OCP Java SE 7 Programmer II exam).

7.1 Exceptions in Java

> [8.3] Describe what exceptions are used for in Java

In this section, you'll learn what exceptions are in Java, why you need to handle exceptions separately from the main code, and all about their advantages and disadvantages.

7.1.1 A taste of exceptions

In figure 7.1, do you think the code in bold in the classes `ArrayAccess`, `OpenFile`, and `MethodAccess` have anything in common?

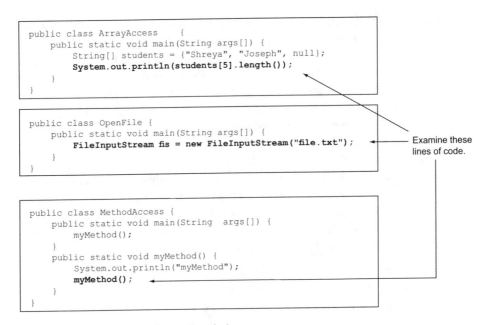

Figure 7.1   Getting a taste of exceptions in Java

I'm sure, given this chapter's title, that this question was easy to answer. Each of these three statements is associated with throwing an exception or an error. Let's look at them individually:

- *Class* `ArrayAccess`—Because the length of the array `students` is 3, trying to access the element at array position 5 is an exceptional condition, as shown in figure 7.2.
- *Class* `OpenFile`—The constructor of the class `FileInputStream` throws a checked exception `FileNotFoundException` (as shown in figure 7.3). If you try to compile this code without enclosing it within a `try` block or *catching* this exception, your code will fail to compile. (I'll discuss checked exceptions in detail in section 7.3.2.)
- *Class* `MethodAccess`—As you can see in figure 7.4, the method `myMethod` calls itself recursively, without specifying an exit condition. These recursive calls result in a `StackOverflowError` at runtime.

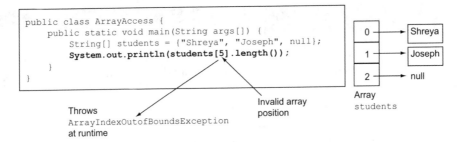

Figure 7.2   An example of `ArrayIndexOutOfBoundsException`

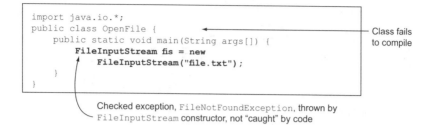

```
import java.io.*;
public class OpenFile {
    public static void main(String args[]) {
        FileInputStream fis = new
            FileInputStream("file.txt");
    }
}
```

— Class fails to compile

Checked exception, `FileNotFoundException`, thrown by `FileInputStream` constructor, not "caught" by code

Figure 7.3   An example of `FileNotFoundException`

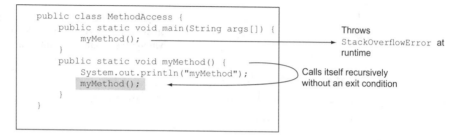

```
public class MethodAccess {
    public static void main(String args[]) {
        myMethod();
    }
    public static void myMethod() {
        System.out.println("myMethod");
        myMethod();
    }
}
```

Throws `StackOverflowError` at runtime

Calls itself recursively without an exit condition

Figure 7.4   An example of `StackOverflowError`

These examples of exceptions are typical of what you'll find on the OCA Java SE 7 Programmer I exam. Let's move on and explore exceptions and their handling in Java so that you can spot code that throws exceptions and handles them accordingly.

File I/O in Java

File I/O isn't covered in the OCA Java SE 7 Programmer I exam, but you may notice it mentioned in questions related to exception handling. I'll cover it quickly here just to the extent that it's required for this exam.

File I/O involves multiple classes that enable you to read data from and write it to a source. This data source can be persistent storage, memory, or even network connections. Data can be read and written as streams of binary or character data. Some file I/O classes only read data from a source, some write data to a source, and some do both.

In this chapter, you'll work with three classes from the file I/O API: `java.io.File`, `java.io.FileInputStream`, and `java.io.FileOutputStream`. `File` is an abstract representation of file and directory pathnames. You can *open* a `File` and then read from and write to it. A `FileInputStream` obtains input bytes using an object of class `File`. It defines the methods `read` to read bytes and `close` to close this stream. A `FileOutputStream` is an output stream for writing data to a `File`. It defines the methods `write` to write bytes and `close` to close this stream.

Creating an object of class `File` can throw the checked exception `java.io.FileNotFoundException`. The methods `read`, `write`, and `close` defined in classes `FileInputStream` and `FileOutputStream` can throw the checked exception `java.io.IOException`. Note that `FileNotFoundException` subclasses `IOException`.

```
Access the blogging website
if (website available) {
        Login to your account
        if (login successful) {
                Select the blog to be commented on
                if (database error in accessing data) {
                        Try again later
                }
                else {
                        Post your comments
                }
        }
        else {
                    Request for new password
        }
}
else {
            Try to access website again later
}
```

**Expected code flow
lost in combating
exceptional
conditions**

**Figure 7.5   Expected code flow lost
in combating exception conditions,
without separate exception handlers**

7.1.2   Why handle exceptions separately?

Imagine you want to post some comments on a blogging website. To make a comment, you must complete the following steps:

   a   Access the blogging website.
   b   Log into your account.
   c   Select the blog you want to comment on.
   d   Post your comments.

The preceding list might seem like an ideal set of steps. In actual conditions, you may have to verify whether you've completed a previous step before you can progress with the next step. Figure 7.5 modifies the previous steps.

The modified logic (figure 7.5) requires the code to check conditions before a user can continue with the next step. This checking of conditions at multiple places introduces new steps for users and also new paths of execution of the original steps. The difficult part of these modified paths is that they may leave users confused about the steps involved in the tasks they're trying to accomplish. Figure 7.6 shows how exception handling can help.

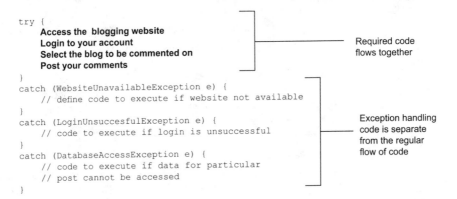

```
try {
        Access the blogging website
        Login to your account
        Select the blog to be commented on
        Post your comments
}
catch (WebsiteUnavailableException e) {
        // define code to execute if website not available
}
catch (LoginUnsuccesfulException e) {
        // code to execute if login is unsuccessful
}
catch (DatabaseAccessException e) {
        // code to execute if data for particular
        // post cannot be accessed
}
```

**Required code
flows together**

**Exception handling
code is separate
from the regular
flow of code**

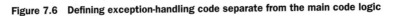

Figure 7.6   Defining exception-handling code separate from the main code logic

The code in figure 7.6 defines the original steps required to post comments to a blog, along with some exception-handling code. Because the exception handlers are defined separately, any confusion with what steps you need to accomplish to post comments on the website has been clarified. Additionally, this code doesn't compromise on checking the completion of a step before moving on to the next step, courtesy of appropriate exception handlers.

7.1.3 Do exceptions offer any other benefits?

Apart from separating concerns between defining the regular program logic and the exception handling code, exceptions also can help pinpoint the offending code (code that throws an exception), together with the method in which it is defined, by providing a stack trace of the exception or error. An example:

```
public class Trace {                                    // line 1
    public static void main(String args[]) {            // line 2
        method1();                                      // line 3
    }                                                   // line 4
    public static void method1() {                      // line 5
        method2();                                      // line 6
    }                                                   // line 7
    public static void method2() {                      // line 8
        String[] students = {"Shreya", "Joseph"};       // line 9
        System.out.println(students[5]);                // line 10
    }                                                   // line 11
}                                                       // line 12
```

method2() tries to access the array element of students at index 5, which is an invalid index for array students, so the code throws the exception ArrayIndexOutOfBounds-Exception at runtime. Figure 7.7 shows the stack trace when this exception is thrown. It includes the runtime exception message and the list of methods that were involved in calling the code that threw the exception, starting from the entry point of this application, the main method. You can match the line numbers specified in the stack trace in figure 7.7 to the line numbers in the code.

> **NOTE** The stack trace gives you a trace of the methods that were called when the JVM encountered an unhandled exception. Stack traces are read from the bottom. In figure 7.7, the trace starts with the main method (last line of the stack trace) and continues up to the method containing the code that threw the exception. Depending on the complexity of your code, a stack trace can

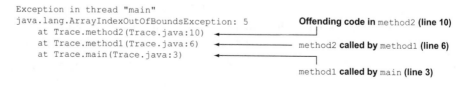

```
Exception in thread "main"
java.lang.ArrayIndexOutOfBoundsException: 5          Offending code in method2 (line 10)
        at Trace.method2(Trace.java:10)
        at Trace.method1(Trace.java:6)               method2 called by method1 (line 6)
        at Trace.main(Trace.java:3)

                                                     method1 called by main (line 3)
```

Figure 7.7 Tracing the line of code that threw an exception at runtime

range from a few lines to hundreds of lines of code. A stack trace works with handled and unhandled exceptions.

Let's move on and look at more details of exception propagation and at the creation of try-catch-finally blocks to take care of exceptions in code.

7.2   *What happens when an exception is thrown?*

> [8.2]   Create a try-catch block and determine how exceptions alter normal program flow

> [8.4]   Invoke a method that throws an exception

In this section, we'll uncover what happens when an exception is thrown in Java. We'll work through a lot of examples to learn how the normal flow of code is disrupted when an exception is thrown. You'll also define an alternative program flow for code that may throw exceptions.

As with all other Java objects, an exception is an object. All types of exceptions subclass java.lang.Throwable. When a piece of code hits an obstacle in the form of an exceptional condition, it creates an object of class java.lang.Throwable (at runtime an object of the most appropriate subtype is created), initializes it with the necessary information (such as its type, an optional textual description, and the offending program's state), and hands it over to the JVM. The JVM blows a siren in the form of this exception and looks for an appropriate code block that can "handle" this exception. The JVM keeps an account of all the methods that were called when it hit the offending code, so to find an appropriate exception handler it looks through all of the tracked method calls.

Re-examine the class Trace and the ArrayIndexOutOfBoundsException thrown by it, as mentioned in the previous section (7.1.3). Figure 7.8 illustrates the propagation of the exception ArrayIndexOutOfBoundsException thrown by method2 through all the methods.

To understand how an exception propagates through method calls, it's important to understand how method calls work. An application starts its execution with the method main, and main may call other methods. When main calls another method, the called method should complete its execution before main can complete its own execution.

An operating system (OS) keeps track of the code that it needs to execute using a *stack*. A stack is a type of list in which the items that are added last to it are the first ones to be taken off it—Last In First Out. This stack uses a *stack pointer* to point to the instructions that the OS should execute.

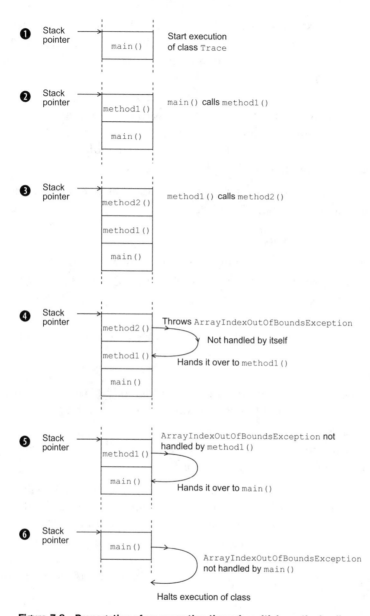

Figure 7.8 Propagation of an exception through multiple method calls

Now that you have this basic information under your belt, here's a step-by-step discussion of exception propagation, as shown in figure 7.8:

1 When the method main starts its execution, its instructions are pushed onto the stack.

2 The method main calls the method method1, and instructions for method1 are pushed onto the stack.

3 `method1` calls `method2`; instructions for `method2` are pushed onto the stack.

4 `method2` throws an exception: `ArrayIndexOutOfBoundsException`. Because `method2` doesn't handle this exception itself, it's passed on to the method that called it—`method1`.

5 `method1` doesn't define any exception handler for `ArrayIndexOutOfBounds-Exception`, so it hands this exception over to its calling method—`main`.

6 There are no exception handlers for `ArrayIndexOutOfBoundsException` in `main`. Because there are no further methods that handle `ArrayIndexOutOf-BoundsException`, execution of the class `Trace` stops.

You can use `try-catch-finally` blocks to define code that doesn't halt execution when it encounters an exceptional condition.

7.2.1   *Creating try-catch-finally blocks*

When you work with exception handlers, you often hear the terms `try`, `catch`, and `finally`. Before you start to work with these concepts, I'll answer three simple questions:

- *Try what?*
  First you *try* to execute your code. If it doesn't execute as planned, you handle the exceptional conditions using a *catch* block.

- *Catch what?*
  You *catch* the exceptional event arising from the code enclosed within the *try* block and handle the event by defining appropriate exception handlers.

- *What does finally do?*
  Finally, you execute a set of code, in all conditions, regardless of whether the code in the *try* block throws any exceptions.

Let's compare a `try-catch-finally` block with a real-life example. Imagine you're going river rafting on your vacation. Your instructor informs you that while rafting, you *might* fall off the raft into the river while crossing the rapids. In such a condition, you should try to use your oar or the rope thrown toward you to get back into the raft. You *might* also drop your oar into the river while rowing your raft. In such a condition, you should not panic and should stay seated. Whatever happens, you're paying for this adventure sport.

Compare this to Java code:

- You can compare river rafting to a class whose methods *might* throw exceptions.
- Crossing the rapids and rowing a raft are methods that *might* throw exceptions.
- Falling off the raft and dropping your oar are the exceptions.
- The steps for getting back into the raft and not panicking are the exception handlers—code that executes when an exception arises.
- The fact that you pay for the sport, whether you stay in the boat or not, can be compared to the `finally` block.

Let's implement the previous real-life examples by defining appropriate classes and methods. To start with, here are two barebones exception classes—FallInRiver-Exception and DropOarException—that can be thrown by methods in the class RiverRafting:

```
class FallInRiverException extends Exception {}
class DropOarException extends Exception {}
```

> **NOTE** You can create an exception of your own—a custom exception—by extending the class Exception (or any of its subclasses). Although the creation of custom classes is *not* on this exam, you may see questions in the exam that create and use custom exceptions. Perhaps these are included because hardly any checked exceptions from the Java API are on this exam. Coding questions on the exam may create and use custom exceptions.

Following is a definition of class RiverRafting. Its methods crossRapid and rowRaft may throw exceptions of type FallInRiverException and DropOarException:

```
class RiverRafting {
    void crossRapid(int degree) throws FallInRiverException {      ◁┐   Method crossRapid
        System.out.println("Cross Rapid");                            │   may throw
        if (degree > 10) throw new FallInRiverException();         ❶   FallInRiverException
    }

    void rowRaft(String state) throws DropOarException {          ◁┐   Method rowRaft
        System.out.println("Row Raft");                              │   may throw
        if (state.equals("nervous")) throw new DropOarException(); ❷   DropOarException
    }
}
```

Method crossRapid at ❶ throws the exception FallInRiverException. When you call this method, you should define an exception handler for this exception. Similarly, the method rowRaft at ❷ throws the exception DropOarException. When you call this method, you should define an exception handler for this exception.

When you execute methods that may throw *checked exceptions* (exceptions that don't extend the class RuntimeException), enclose the code within a try block. catch blocks that follow a try block should handle all the checked exceptions thrown by the code enclosed in the try block (checked exceptions are covered in detail in section 7.3).

The code shown in figure 7.9 uses the class RiverRafting as defined previously and depicts the flow of control when the code on line 3 (riverRafting.cross-Rapid(11);) throws an exception of type FallInRiverException.

The example in figure 7.9 shows how exceptions alter the normal program flow. If the code on line 3 throws an exception (FallInRiverException), the code on lines 4 and 5 won't execute. In this case, control is transferred to the code block that handles FallInRiverException. Then control is transferred to the finally block. After the execution of the finally block, the code that follows the try-catch-finally block is executed. The output of the previous code is:

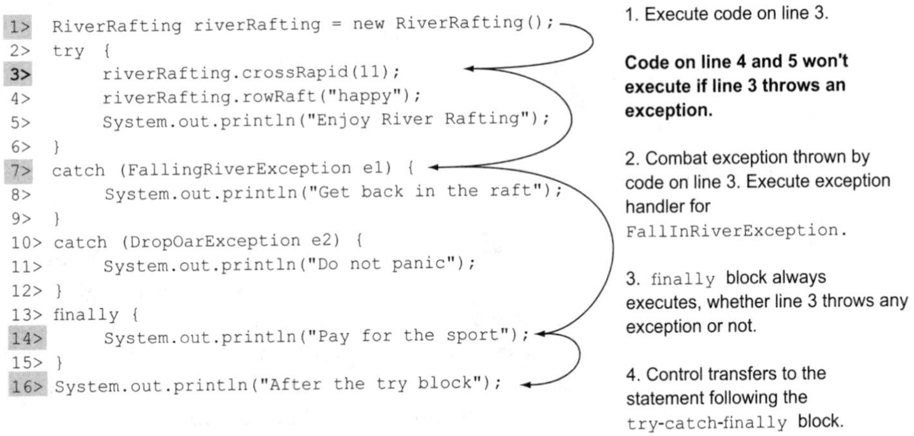

```
1>   RiverRafting riverRafting = new RiverRafting();
2>   try {
3>        riverRafting.crossRapid(11);
4>        riverRafting.rowRaft("happy");
5>        System.out.println("Enjoy River Rafting");
6>   }
7>   catch (FallingRiverException e1) {
8>        System.out.println("Get back in the raft");
9>   }
10>  catch (DropOarException e2) {
11>       System.out.println("Do not panic");
12>  }
13>  finally {
14>       System.out.println("Pay for the sport");
15>  }
16>  System.out.println("After the try block");
```

1. Execute code on line 3.

Code on line 4 and 5 won't execute if line 3 throws an exception.

2. Combat exception thrown by code on line 3. Execute exception handler for `FallInRiverException`.

3. `finally` block always executes, whether line 3 throws any exception or not.

4. Control transfers to the statement following the `try-catch-finally` block.

Figure 7.9   Modified flow of control when an exception is thrown

```
Cross Rapid
Get back in the raft
Pay for the sport
After the try block
```

If you modify the previous example code as follows, no exceptions are thrown by the code on line 3 (modifications in bold):

```
class TestRiverRafting {
    public static void main(String args[]) {
        RiverRafting riverRafting = new RiverRafting();
        try {
            riverRafting.crossRapid(7);                      ←─┐ No exceptions
            riverRafting.rowRaft("happy");                     │ thrown by this
            System.out.println("Enjoy River Rafting");         │ line of code
        }
        catch (FallInRiverException e1) {
            System.out.println("Get back in the raft");
        }
        catch (DropOarException e2) {
            System.out.println("Do not panic");
        }
        finally {
            System.out.println("Pay for the sport");
        }
        System.out.println("After the try block");
    }
}
```

The output of the previous code is as follows:

```
Cross Rapid
Row Raft
Enjoy River Rafting
Pay for the sport
After the try block
```

What do you think the output of the code would be if the method rowRaft threw an exception? Try it for yourself!

EXAM TIP   The finally block executes regardless of whether the try block throws an exception.

SINGLE TRY BLOCK, MULTIPLE CATCH BLOCKS, AND A FINALLY BLOCK

For a try block, you can define multiple catch blocks, but only a single finally block. Multiple catch blocks are used to handle different types of exceptions. A finally block is used to define *cleanup* code—code that closes and releases resources, such as file handlers and database or network connections.

When it comes to code, it makes sense to verify a concept by watching it in action. Let's work through a simple example so that you can better understand how to use the try-catch-finally block.

In listing 7.1, the constructor of the class FileInputStream may throw a FileNot-FoundException, and calling the method read on an object of FileInputStream, such as fis, may throw an IOException.

Listing 7.1   Code flow with multiple `catch` statements and a `finally` block

```java
import java.io.*;
public class MultipleExceptions {
    public static void main(String args[]) {
        FileInputStream fis = null;
        try {
            fis = new FileInputStream("file.txt");       // May throw FileNotFoundException
            System.out.println("File Opened");
            fis.read();                                   // May throw IOException
            System.out.println("Read File ");
        }
        catch (FileNotFoundException fnfe) {
            System.out.println("File not found");
        }
        catch (IOException ioe) {
            System.out.println("File Closing Exception");
        }
        finally {                                         // Positioning of catch and finally blocks can't be interchanged
            System.out.println("finally");
        }
        System.out.println("Next task..");
    }
}
```

Table 7.1 compares the code output that occurs depending on whether the system is able or unable to open (and read) file.txt.

In either of the cases described in table 7.1, the finally block executes, and after its execution, control is transferred to the statement following the try-catch block. Here's the output of the class MultipleExceptions if none of its code throws an exception:

Table 7.1 Output of code in listing 7.1 when the system is unable to open file.txt and when the system is able to open file.txt but unable to read it

Output if the system is unable to open file.txt	Output if the system is able to open file.txt, but unable to read it
File not found finally Next task..	File Opened File Closing Exception finally Next task..

```
File Opened
Read File
finally
Next task..
```

It's time now to attempt this chapter's first Twist in the Tale exercise. When you execute the code in this exercise, you'll understand what happens when you change the placement of the exception handlers (answers are in the appendix).

Twist in the Tale 7.1

Let's modify the placement of the finally block in listing 7.1 and see what happens.

Given that file.txt doesn't exist on your system, what is the output of the following code?

```java
import java.io.*;
public class MultipleExceptions {
    public static void main(String args[]) {
        FileInputStream fis = null;
        try {
            fis = new FileInputStream("file.txt");
            System.out.println("File Opened");
            fis.read();
            System.out.println("Read File");
        }
        finally {
            System.out.println("finally");
        }
        catch (FileNotFoundException fnfe) {
            System.out.println("File not found");
        }
        catch (IOException ioe) {
            System.out.println("File Closing Exception");
        }
        System.out.println("Next task..");
    }
}
```

a   The code prints

```
File not found
finally
Next task..
```

b The code prints

```
File Opened
File Closing Exception
finally
Next task..
```

c The code prints `File not found`

d The code fails to compile

In the remainder of this section, we'll look at some frequently asked questions on `try-catch-finally` blocks that often overwhelm certification aspirants.

7.2.2 Will a finally block execute even if the catch block defines a return statement?

Image the following scenario: a guy promises to buy diamonds for his girlfriend and treat her to coffee. The girl inquires about what will happen if he meets with an exceptional condition during the diamond purchase, such as inadequate funds. To the girl's disappointment, the boy replies that he'll still treat her to coffee.

You can compare the `try` block to the purchase of diamonds and the `finally` block to the coffee treat. The girl gets the coffee treat regardless of whether the boy successfully purchases the diamonds. Figure 7.10 shows this conversation.

It is interesting to note that a `finally` block will execute even if the code in the `try` block or any of the `catch` blocks defines a `return` statement. Examine the code in figure 7.11 and its output, and note when the class `ReturnFromCatchBlock` is unable to open file.txt:

As you can see from figure 7.11's code output, the flow of control doesn't return to the method `main` when the `return` statement executes in the `catch` handler of `File-NotFoundException`. It continues with the execution of the `finally` block before the control is transferred back to the `main` method. Note that the control isn't transferred

Figure 7.10 A little humor to help you remember that a `finally` block executes regardless of whether an exception is thrown.

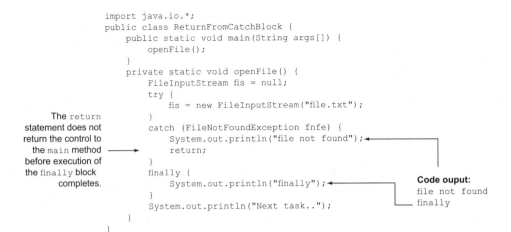

Figure 7.11   The `finally` block executes even if an exception handler defines a `return` statement.

to the `println` statement "Nexttask..." that follows the `try` block because the `return` statement is encountered in the `catch` block, as mentioned previously.

Going back to the example of the guy and his girlfriend, a few tragic conditions, such as an earthquake or tornado, can cancel the coffee treat. Similarly, there are a few scenarios in Java in which a `finally` block does not execute:

- *Application termination*—The `try` or the `catch` block executes `System.exit`, which terminates the application
- *Fatal errors*—A crash of the JVM or the OS

In the exam, you may be questioned on the correct order of two or more exception handlers. Does order matter? See for yourself in the next section.

7.2.3   *What happens if both a catch and a finally block define return statements?*

In the previous section, you saw that the `finally` block executes even if a `catch` block defines a `return` statement. For a method that defines a `try-catch-finally` block, what is returned to the calling method if both `catch` and `finally` return a value?

Here's an example:

```
class MultipleReturn {
    int getInt() {
        try {
            String[] students = {"Harry", "Paul"};
            System.out.println(students[5]);            Throws
        }                                               ArrayIndexOutOfBoundsException
        catch (Exception e) {
            return 10;                                  Returns value 10
        }                                               from catch block
        finally {
            return 20;            Returns value 20
        }                         from finally block
```

```
        }
    }
    public static void main(String args[]) {
        MultipleReturn var = new MultipleReturn();
        System.out.println(var.getInt());
    }
}
```

The output of the preceding code is

```
20
```

If both `catch` and `finally` blocks define `return` statements, the calling method will receive a value from the `finally` block.

7.2.4 What happens if a finally block modifies the value returned from a catch block?

If a `catch` block returns a primitive data type, the `finally` block can't modify the value being returned by it. An example:

```
class MultipleReturn {
    int getInt() {
        int returnVal = 10;
        try {
            String[] students = {"Harry", "Paul"};          Throws
            System.out.println(students[5]);          ◁——  ArrayIndexOutOfBoundsException
        }
        catch (Exception e) {
            System.out.println("About to return :" + returnVal);
            return returnVal;                            ◁——  Returns value 10
        }                                                      from catch block
        finally {
            returnVal += 10;                                              ◁——
            System.out.println("Return value is now :" + returnVal);
        }                                                      Modifies value
        return returnVal;                                      of variable to
    }                                                          be returned in
    public static void main(String args[]) {                   finally block
        MultipleReturn var = new MultipleReturn();
        System.out.println("In Main:" + var.getInt());
    }
}
```

The output of the preceding code is as follows:

```
About to return :10
Return value is now :20
In Main:10
```

Even though the `finally` block adds 10 to variable `returnVal`, this modified value is not returned to the method `main`. Control in the `catch` block *copies* the value of `returnVal` to be returned before it executes the `finally` block, so the returned value is not modified when `finally` executes.

Will the preceding code behave in a similar manner if the method returns an object? See for yourself:

```java
class MultipleReturn {
    StringBuilder getStringBuilder() {
        StringBuilder returnVal = new StringBuilder("10");
        try {
            String[] students = {"Harry", "Paul"};
            System.out.println(students[5]);
        }
        catch (Exception e) {
            System.out.println("About to return :" + returnVal);
            return returnVal;
        }
        finally {
            returnVal.append("10");
            System.out.println("Return value is now :" + returnVal);
        }
        return returnVal;
    }
    public static void main(String args[]) {
        MultipleReturn var = new MultipleReturn();
        System.out.println("In Main:" + var.getStringBuilder());
    }
}
```

Throws ArrayIndexOutOfBoundsException

Returns StringBuilder object value from catch block

Modifies value of variable to be returned in finally block

This is the output of the preceding code:

```
About to return :10
Return value is now :1010
In Main:1010
```

In this case, the `catch` block returns an object of the class `StringBuilder`. When the `finally` block executes, it can access the value of the object referred to by the variable `returnVal` and can modify it. The modified value is returned to the method `main`. Remember that primitives are passed by value and objects are passed by reference.

EXAM TIP   Watch out for code that returns a value from the `catch` block and modifies it in the `finally` block. If a `catch` block returns a primitive data type, the `finally` block can't modify the value being returned by it. If a `catch` block returns an object, the `finally` block can modify the value being returned by it.

7.2.5   *Does the order of the exceptions caught in the catch blocks matter?*

Order doesn't matter for unrelated classes. But it does matter for related classes sharing an IS-A relationship.

In the latter case, if you try to catch an exception of the base class before an exception of the derived class, your code will fail to compile. This behavior may seem bizarre, but there's a valid reason for it. As you know, an object of a derived class can

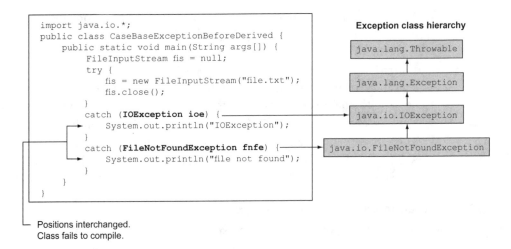

```
import java.io.*;
public class CaseBaseExceptionBeforeDerived {
    public static void main(String args[]) {
        FileInputStream fis = null;
        try {
            fis = new FileInputStream("file.txt");
            fis.close();
        }
        catch (IOException ioe) {
            System.out.println("IOException");
        }
        catch (FileNotFoundException fnfe) {
            System.out.println("file not found");
        }
    }
}
```

Exception class hierarchy

java.lang.Throwable

java.lang.Exception

java.io.IOException

java.io.FileNotFoundException

Positions interchanged.
Class fails to compile.

Figure 7.12   The order of placement of exception handlers is important.

be assigned to a variable of a base class. Similarly, if you try to catch an exception of a base class before its derived class, the exception handler for the derived class can never be reached, so the code will fail to compile.

Examine the code in figure 7.12, which has been modified by defining the catch block for IOException before the catch block for FileNotFoundException.

Figure 7.13 depicts an interesting way to remember that the order matters. As you know, a thrown exception looks for an appropriate exception handler, starting with the first handler and working toward the last. Let's compare a thrown exception to a tiger and the exception handlers to doors that allow certain types of creatures to enter. Like a thrown exception, the tiger should start with the first door and move on to the rest of the doors until a match is found.

The tiger starts with the first door, which allows all animals to enter. Voilà.

❶   ❷

Door 1   Door 2
Animals only   Tiger only

Figure 7.13   A visual way to remember that the order matters for exceptions caught in the catch blocks

The tiger enters the first door and never reaches the second door, which is meant specifically for tigers. In Java, when such a condition arises, the Java compiler refuses to compile the code because the later exception handler code will never execute. Java doesn't compile code if it contains unreachable statements.

RULES TO REMEMBER

Here are a few more rules you'll need to answer the questions in the OCA Java SE 7 Programmer I exam:

- A try block may be followed by multiple catch blocks, and the catch blocks may be followed by a single finally block.
- A try block may be followed by either a catch or a finally block or both. But a finally block alone wouldn't suffice if code in the try block throws a checked exception. In this case, you need to catch the checked exception or declare it to be thrown by your method. Otherwise your code won't compile.
- The try, catch, and finally blocks can't exist independently.
- The finally block can't appear before a catch block.
- A finally block always executes, regardless of whether the code throws an exception.

7.2.6 *Can I rethrow an exception or the error I catch?*

You can do whatever you want with an exception. Rethrow it, pass it on to a method, assign it to another variable, upload it to a server, send it in an SMS, and so on. Examine the following code:

```
import java.io.*;
public class ReThrowException {
    FileInputStream soccer;
    public void myMethod() {
        try {
            soccer = new FileInputStream("soccer.txt");
        }
        catch (FileNotFoundException fnfe) {
            throw fnfe;                          ◁──┐  Use throw keyword to
        }                                           │  throw exception caught
    }                                               │  in exception handler
}
```

Oops. The previous code fails to compile, and you get the following compilation error message:

```
ReThrowException.java:9: unreported exception java.io.FileNotFoundException;
    must be caught or declared to be thrown
            throw fnfe;
         ^
```

When you rethrow a checked exception, it's treated like a regular thrown checked exception, meaning that all the rules of handling a checked exception apply to it. In the previous example, the code neither "caught" the rethrown FileNotFoundException exception nor declared that the method myMethod would throw it using the throw clause. Hence, the code failed to compile.

The following (modified) code declares that the method myMethod throws a File-NotFoundException, and it compiles successfully:

```
import java.io.*;                                            Throws
public class ReThrowException {                    FileNotFoundException
    FileInputStream soccer;
    public void myMethod() throws FileNotFoundException {   ◁──┘
```

```
        try {
            soccer = new FileInputStream("soccer.txt");
        }
        catch (FileNotFoundException fnfe) {
            throw fnfe;                                    Exception
        }                                                 rethrown
    }
}
```

Another interesting point to note is that the previous code doesn't apply to a RuntimeException. You can rethrow a runtime exception, but you're not required to catch it, nor must you modify your method signature to include the throws clause. The simple reason for this rule is that RuntimeExceptions aren't checked exceptions, and they may not be caught or declared to be thrown by your code (exception categories are discussed in detail in section 7.3).

7.2.7 Can I declare my methods to throw a checked exception, instead of handling it?

If a method doesn't wish to handle the checked exceptions thrown by a method it calls, it can *throw* these exceptions using the throws clause in its own method signature. Examine the following example, in which the method myMethod doesn't include an exception handler; instead, it rethrows the IOException thrown by a constructor of the class FileInputStream using the throws clause in its method signature:

```
import java.io.*;                                        myMethod throws
public class ReThrowException2 {                         checked exception
    public void myMethod() throws IOException {
        FileInputStream soccer = new FileInputStream("soccer.txt");
        soccer.close();
    }
}
```

Any method that calls myMethod must now either catch the exception IOException or declare that it will be rethrown in its method signature.

7.2.8 I can create nested loops, so can I create nested try-catch blocks too?

The simple answer is yes, you can define a try-catch-finally block within another try-catch-finally block. Theoretically, the levels of nesting for the try-catch-finally blocks have no limits.

In the following example, another set of try-catch blocks is defined in the try and finally blocks of the outer try block:

```
import java.io.*;
public class NestedTryCatch {
    FileInputStream players, coach;
    public void myMethod() {                             Outer try
        try {                                            block
            players = new FileInputStream("players.txt");
```

```
        try {
            coach = new FileInputStream("coach.txt");           ←──┐  Inner try
            //.. rest of the code                                   │  block
        }
        catch (FileNotFoundException e) {
            System.out.println("coach.txt not found");
        }
        //.. rest of the code                                           Outer
    }                                                                    catch
    catch (FileNotFoundException fnfe) {                         ←──┘   block
        System.out.println("players.txt not found");
    }                                                               Outer finally
    finally {                                                    ←── block
        try {
            players.close();                           ←──┐  Another Inner
            coach.close();                                │  try block
        }
        catch (IOException ioe) {
            System.out.println(ioe);
        }
    }
  }
}
```

Now comes another Twist in the Tale exercise that'll test your understanding of the exceptions thrown and caught by nested try-catch blocks. In this one, an inner try block defines code that throws a NullPointerException. But the inner try block doesn't define an exception handler for this exception. Will the outer try block catch this exception? See for yourself (answer in the appendix).

Twist in the Tale 7.2

Given that players.txt exists on your system and that the assignment of players, shown in bold, doesn't throw any exceptions, what is the output of the following code?

```
import java.io.*;
public class TwistInTaleNestedTryCatch {
    static FileInputStream players, coach;
    public static void main(String args[]) {
        try {
            players = new FileInputStream("players.txt");
            System.out.println("players.txt found");
            try {
                coach.close();
            }
            catch (IOException e) {
                System.out.println("coach.txt not found");
            }
        }
        catch (FileNotFoundException fnfe) {
            System.out.println("players.txt not found");
        }
```

```
    catch (NullPointerException ne) {
        System.out.println("NullPointerException");
    }
  }
}
```

a The code prints

```
players.txt found
NullPointerException
```

b The code prints

```
players.txt found
coach.txt not found
```

c The code throws a runtime exception.

d The code fails to compile.

7.3   *Categories of exceptions*

[8.1] Differentiate among checked exceptions, RuntimeExceptions, and Errors

In this section, you'll learn about the categories of exceptions in Java, including checked exceptions, unchecked exceptions, and errors. I'll use code examples to explain the differences between these categories.

7.3.1   *Identifying exception categories*

As depicted in figure 7.14, exceptions can be divided into three main categories:

- Checked exceptions
- Runtime exceptions (unchecked exceptions)
- Errors

Of these three types, checked exceptions require most of your attention when it comes to coding and using methods. Normally, you shouldn't try to catch runtime exceptions, and there are few options you can use for the errors, because they're thrown by the JVM.

For the OCA Java SE 7 Programmer I exam, it's important to have a crystal-clear understanding of these three categories of exceptions, including their similarities and differences.

These categories are related to each other, and subclasses of the class `java.lang.Exception`

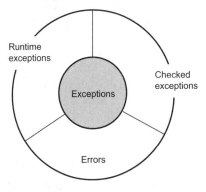

Figure 7.14 Categories of exceptions: checked exceptions, runtime exceptions, and errors

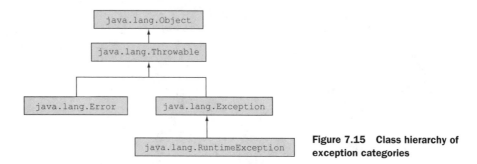

Figure 7.15   Class hierarchy of exception categories

are categorized as checked exceptions if they aren't subclasses of the class `java.lang` `.RuntimeException`. Subclasses of the class `java.lang.RuntimeException` are categorized as runtime exceptions. Subclasses of the class `java.lang.Error` are categorized as errors. Figure 7.15 illustrates the class hierarchy of these exception categories.

As you can see in figure 7.15, all of the errors and exceptions extend the class `java.lang.Throwable`. Let's examine each of these categories in detail.

7.3.2   *Checked exceptions*

When we talk about handling exceptions, it's *checked* exceptions that take up most of our attention. What is a checked exception?

- A checked exception is an unacceptable condition *foreseen* by the author of a method but outside the immediate control of the code. For example, `FileNot-FoundException` is a checked exception. This exception is thrown if the file that the code is trying to access can't be found. When it's thrown, this condition is outside the immediate control of the author of the code but it was *foreseen* by the author.

- A checked exception is a subclass of class `java.lang.Exception`, but it's not a subclass of `java.lang.RuntimeException`. It's interesting to note, however, that the class `java.lang.RuntimeException` itself is a subclass of the class `java.lang.Exception`.

EXAM TIP   In the OCA Java SE 7 Programmer I exam, you may have to select which type of reference variable to use to store the object of the thrown checked exception in a handler. To answer such questions correctly, remember that a checked exception is a subclass of the `java.lang.Exception` class, but not a subclass of `java.lang.RuntimeException`.

If a method uses another method that may throw a checked exception, one of the two following things should be true:

- The method should be enclosed within a `try-catch` block

or

- The method should specify this exception to be thrown in its method signature

Let's quickly review the class OpenFile, which we discussed in an earlier section:

```
import java.io.*;                                    Throws checked exception
public class OpenFile {                                  FileNotFoundException
    public static void main(String args[]) {
        FileInputStream fis = new FileInputStream("file.txt");
    }
}
```

As mentioned earlier, this will fail to compile because the code in bold throws the checked exception FileNotFoundException, and the previous class neither enclosed this line of code within a try block nor specified that it would be thrown in its method signature.

If a method chooses not to handle the checked exception thrown by its code, it may choose to throw it, and its method signature must specify that. Examine the following definition of the FileInputStream constructor (from the source code of the Java API), which is used in the previously mentioned class OpenFile:

```
public FileInputStream(String name) throws FileNotFoundException {
        this(name != null ? new File(name) : null);
}
```

Now examine the corresponding description of this constructor in the Java API documentation:

```
public FileInputStream(File file)
                throws FileNotFoundException
```

A checked exception is part of the API and is well documented. Checked exceptions are unacceptable conditions that a programmer *foresees* at the time of writing a method. By declaring these exceptions as checked exceptions, the author of the method makes its users aware of the exceptional conditions that can arise from its use. The user of a method with a checked exception must handle the exceptional condition accordingly.

7.3.3 *Runtime exceptions (also known as unchecked exceptions)*

Although you'll spend most of your time and energy combating checked exceptions, it's the runtime exceptions that'll give you the most headaches. This is particularly true when you're preparing to work on real-life projects. Some examples of runtime exceptions are NullPointerException (the most common one), ArrayIndexOutOfBoundsException, and ClassCastException.

What is a runtime exception?

- A runtime exception is a representation of a programming error. These occur from inappropriate use of another piece of code. For example, NullPointerException is a runtime exception that occurs when a piece of code tries to execute some code on a variable that hasn't been assigned an object and points to null. Another example is ArrayIndexOutOfBoundsException, which is thrown when a piece of code tries to access an array list element at a nonexistent position.
- A runtime exception is a subclass of java.lang.RuntimeException.

- A runtime exception may not be a part of the method signature, even if a method may throw it.

How about an example, now that you've read the previous definitions of runtime exceptions? Examine the following code, which throws a runtime exception (Array-IndexOutOfBoundsException):

```java
public class InvalidArrayAccess {
    public static void main(String args[]) {
        String[] students = {"Shreya", "Joseph"};
        System.out.println(students[5]);
        System.out.println("All seems to be well");
    }
}
```

students[5] tries to access nonexistent array position; Exception thrown: ArrayIndexOutOfBoundsException

The preceding code doesn't print output from System.out.println().

It's possible to create an exception handler for the exception ArrayIndexOutOf-BoundsException thrown by the previous example code, as follows:

```java
public class InvalidArrayAccess {
    public static void main(String args[]) {
        String[] students = {"Shreya", "Joseph"};
        try {
            System.out.println(students[5]);
        }
        catch (ArrayIndexOutOfBoundsException e){
            System.out.println("Exception");
        }
        System.out.println("All seems to be well");
    }
}
```

The output of the previous code is as follows:

```
Exception
All seems to be well
```

In the same way you can *catch* a checked exception, you can also catch a Runtime-Exception. In the previous code, you can prevent ArrayIndexOutOfBoundsException from being thrown by using appropriate checks:

```java
public class InvalidArrayAccess {
    public static void main(String args[]) {
        String[] students = {"Shreya", "Joseph"};
        int pos = 1;
        if (pos > 0 && pos < students.length)
            System.out.println(students[pos]);
    }
}
```

This line won't execute because pos is greater than length of array students.

7.3.4   Errors

Whether you're preparing for the OCA Java SE 7 Programmer I exam or your real-life projects, you need to know when the JVM throws errors. These errors are considered to be *serious* exceptional conditions and they can't be directly controlled by your code.

What's an error?

- An error is a serious exception thrown by the JVM as a result of an error in the environment state that processes your code. For example, NoClassDefFound-Error is an error thrown by the JVM when it's unable to locate the .class file that it's supposed to run. StackOverflowError is another error thrown by the JVM when the size of the memory required by the stack of a Java program is greater than what the JRE has offered for the Java application. This error usually occurs as a result of infinite or highly nested loops.
- An error is a subclass of class java.lang.Error.
- An error need not be a part of a method signature.
- An error can be caught by an exception handler, but it shouldn't be.

The following example shows how it's possible to "catch" an error:

```
public class CatchError {
    public static void main(String args[]) {
        try {
            myMethod();
        }
        catch (StackOverflowError s) {
            System.out.println(s);
        }
    }
    public static void myMethod() {
        System.out.println("myMethod");
        myMethod();
    }
}
```

> A class can catch and handle an error, but it shouldn't—it should instead let the JVM handle the error itself.

I agree that you shouldn't handle errors in your code. But if you do, will the exception handler that handles the code be executed? See for yourself by answering the question in the following Twist in the Tale exercise (answer in the appendix).

Twist in the Tale 7.3

Will the code in the error-handling block execute? What do you think is the output of the following code?

```
public class TwistInTaleCatchError {
    public static void main(String args[]) {
        try {
            myMethod();
        }
        catch (StackOverflowError s) {
            for (int i=0; i<2; ++i)
                System.out.println(i);
        }
    }
    public static void myMethod() {
        myMethod();
    }
}
```

```
a   0
    java.lang.StackOverFlowError
b   0
    1
c   0
    1
    2
    java.lang.StackOverFlowError
```

7.4   *Common exception classes and categories*

[8.5] Recognize common exception classes and categories

In this section, we'll take a look at common exception classes and categories of exceptions. You'll also learn about the scenarios in which these exceptions are thrown and how to handle them.

For the OCA Java SE 7 Programmer I exam, you should be familiar with the scenarios that lead to these commonly thrown exception classes and categories, and how to handle them. Table 7.2 lists common errors and exceptions.

Table 7.2   Common errors and exceptions

Runtime exceptions	Errors
ArrayIndexOutOfBoundsException	ExceptionInInitializerError
IndexOutOfBoundsException	StackOverflowError
ClassCastException	NoClassDefFoundError
IllegalArgumentException	OutOfMemoryError
IllegalStateException	
NullPointerException	
NumberFormatException	

The OCA Java SE 7 Programmer I exam objectives require that you understand which of the previously mentioned errors and exceptions are thrown by the JVM and which should be thrown programmatically. From the discussion of errors earlier in this chapter, you know that the errors represent issues associated with the JRE, such as OutOfMemoryError. As a programmer, you *shouldn't* throw or catch these errors—leave them for the JVM. The definition of the runtime exception notes that these are the kind of exceptions that are thrown by the JVM, which shouldn't be thrown by you programmatically.

Let's review each of these in detail.

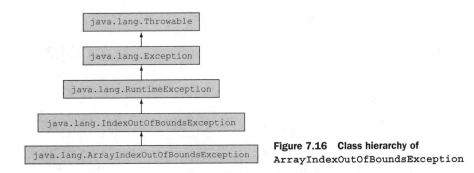

Figure 7.16 Class hierarchy of `ArrayIndexOutOfBoundsException`

7.4.1   *ArrayIndexOutOfBoundsException and IndexOutOfBoundsException*

As shown in figure 7.16, `ArrayIndexOutOfBoundsException` and `IndexOutOfBounds-Exception` are runtime exceptions, which share an IS-A relationship. `IndexOutOf-BoundsException` is subclassed by `ArrayIndexOutOfBoundsException`.

`ArrayIndexOutOfBoundsException` is thrown when a piece of code tries to access an array out of its bounds (either an array is accessed at a position less than 0 or at a position greater than or equal to its length). `IndexOutOfBoundsException` is thrown when a piece of code tries to access a list, like an `ArrayList`, using an illegal index.

Assuming that an array and list have been defined as follows,

```
String[] season = {"Spring", "Summer"};
ArrayList<String> exams = new ArrayList<>();
exams.add("SCJP");
exams.add("SCWCD");
```

The following lines of code will throw `ArrayIndexOutOfBoundsException`:

```
System.out.println(season[5]);      ⟵ Can't access position >= array length
System.out.println(season[-9]);     ⟵ Can't access array at negative position
```

The following lines of code will throw `IndexOutOfBoundsException`:

```
System.out.println(exams.get(-1));  ⟵ Can't access list at negative position
System.out.println(exams.get(4));   ⟵ Can't access list at position >= its size
```

Why do you think the JVM has taken the responsibility to throw this exception itself? One of the main reasons is that this exception isn't known until runtime and depends on the array or list position that's being accessed by a piece of code. Most often, a variable is used to specify this array or list position, and its value may not be known until runtime.

> **NOTE** When you try to access an invalid array position, `ArrayIndexOutOf-BoundsException` is thrown. When you try to access an invalid `ArrayList` position, `IndexOutOfBoundsException` is thrown.

You can avoid these exceptions from being thrown if you check whether the index position you are trying to access is greater than or equal to 0 and less than the size of your array or ArrayList.

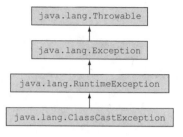

Figure 7.17   Class hierarchy of
ClassCastException

7.4.2   *ClassCastException*

Before I start discussing the example I'll use for this exception, take a quick look at figure 7.17 to review the class hierarchy of this exception.

Examine the code in listing 7.2, where the line of code that throws the ClassCastException is shown in bold.

Listing 7.2   An example of code that throws ClassCastException

```
import java.util.ArrayList;
public class ListAccess {
    public static void main(String args[]) {
        ArrayList<Ink> inks = new ArrayList<Ink>();
        inks.add(new ColorInk());
        inks.add(new BlackInk());
        Ink ink = (BlackInk)inks.get(0);            Throws
    }                                               ClassCastException
}
class Ink{}
class ColorInk extends Ink{}
class BlackInk extends Ink{}
```

ClassCastException is thrown when an object fails an IS-A test with the class type to which it's being cast. In the preceding example, class Ink is the base class for classes ColorInk and BlackInk. The JVM throws a ClassCastException in the previous case because the line of code in bold tries to explicitly cast an object of ColorInk to BlackInk.

Note that this line of code avoided the compilation error because the variable inks defines an ArrayList of type Ink, which is capable of storing objects of type Ink and all its subclasses. The code then correctly adds the allowed objects: one each of BlackInk and ColorInk. If the code had defined an ArrayList of type BlackInk or ColorInk, the code would have failed the compilation, as follows:

```
import java.util.ArrayList;
public class Invalid {
    public static void main(String args[]) {
        ArrayList<ColorInk> inks = new ArrayList<ColorInk>();
        inks.add(new ColorInk());
        Ink ink = (BlackInk)inks.get(0);            Compilation
    }                                               issues
}
class Ink{}
class ColorInk extends Ink{}
class BlackInk extends Ink{}
```

Here's the compilation error thrown by the previously modified piece of code:

```
Invalid.java:6: inconvertible types
found   : ColorInk
required: BlackInk
        Ink ink = (BlackInk)inks.get(0);
                            ^
```

You can use the `instanceof` operator to verify whether an object can be cast to another class before casting it. Assuming that the definition of classes `Ink`, `ColorInk`, and `BlackInk` are the same as defined in the previous example, the following lines of code will avoid the `ClassCastException`:

```
import java.util.ArrayList;
public class AvoidClassCastException {
    public static void main(String args[]) {
        ArrayList<Ink> inks = new ArrayList<Ink>();
        inks.add(new ColorInk());
        inks.add(new BlackInk());
        if (inks.get(0) instanceof BlackInk) {
            BlackInk ink = (BlackInk)inks.get(0);      ⟵⎤  No
        }                                                 ⎦  ClassCastException
    }
}
```

In the previous example, the condition (`inks.get(0) instanceof BlackInk`) evaluates to `false`, so the then part of the `if` statement doesn't execute.

In the following Twist in the Tale exercise, we'll introduce an interface used in the casting example in listing 7.2 (answer in the appendix).

Twist in the Tale 7.4

Let's introduce an interface used in listing 7.2 and see how it behaves. Following is the modified code. Examine the code and select the correct options:

```
class Ink{}
interface Printable {}
class ColorInk extends Ink implements Printable {}
class BlackInk extends Ink{}

class TwistInTaleCasting {
    public static void main(String args[]) {
        Printable printable = null;
        BlackInk blackInk = new BlackInk();
        printable = (Printable)blackInk;
    }
}
```

  a `printable = (Printable)blackInk` will throw compilation error.

  b `printable = (Printable)blackInk` will throw runtime exception.

  c `printable = (Printable)blackInk` will throw checked exception.

  d The following line of code will fail to compile:

     `printable = blackInk;`

7.4.3   *IllegalArgumentException*

As the name of this exception suggests, `Illegal-ArgumentException` is thrown to specify that a method has passed illegal or inappropriate arguments. Its class hierarchy is shown in figure 7.18.

Even though it's a runtime exception, programmers usually use this exception to validate the arguments that are passed to a method. The exception constructor is passed a descriptive message, specifying the exception details. Examine the following code:

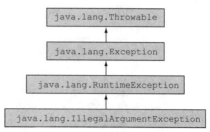

Figure 7.18   Class hierarchy of
`IllegalArgumentException`

```java
public void login(String username, String pwd, int maxLoginAttempt) {

    if (username == null || username.length() < 6)
        throw new IllegalArgumentException
                    ("Login:username can't be shorter than 6 chars");

    if (pwd == null || pwd.length() < 8)
        throw new IllegalArgumentException
                    ("Login: pwd cannot be shorter than 8 chars");

    if (maxLoginAttempt < 0)
        throw new IllegalArgumentException
                    ("Login: Invalid loginattempt val");

    //.. rest of the method code
}
```

The previous method validates the various method parameters passed to it and throws an appropriate `IllegalArgumentException` if they don't meet the requirements of the method. Each object of the `IllegalArgumentException` is passed a different `String` message that briefly describes it.

7.4.4   *IllegalStateException*

According to the Java API documentation, an `IllegalStateException` "signals that a method has been invoked at an illegal or inappropriate time. In other words, the Java environment or Java application is not in an appropriate state for the requested operation."[1]

The class hierarchy for `IllegalStateException` is shown in figure 7.19.

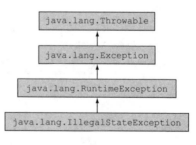

Figure 7.19   Class hierarchy of
`IllegalStateException`

---

[1]   The `IllegalStateException` documentation can be found in the Javadoc: http://docs.oracle.com/javase/7/docs/api/java/lang/IllegalStateException.html.

As an author of code, you can throw IllegalStateException to signal to the calling method that the method being requested for execution can't be called for the current state of an object.

For example, what happens if an application tries to modify an SMS that is already in transmission? Examine the following code:

```java
class SMS {
    private String msg;
    private boolean inTransit = false;

    public void create() {
        msg = "A new Message";
    }

    public void transmit() {
        ........                                    Code to transmit
        inTransit = true;                           message
    }

    public void modify() {
        if (!inTransit)
            msg = "new modified message";
        else
            throw new IllegalStateException
                            ("Msg in transit. Can't modify it");
    }
}
public class ThrowIllegalStateException {
    public static void main(String[] args) {
        SMS sms = new SMS();
        sms.create();
        sms.transmit();
        sms.modify();
    }
}
```

On execution, the class ThrowIllegalStateException throws the following exception:

```
Exception in thread "main" java.lang.IllegalStateException: Msg in transit.
    Can't modify it
    at SMS.modify(ThrowIllegalStateException.java:18)
    at ThrowIllegalStateException.main(ThrowIllegalStateException.java:27)
```

In the example code, the method modify in the class SMS throws an IllegalStateException if another piece of code tries to call it after the method send has been executed.

7.4.5 *NullPointerException*

NullPointerException, shown in figure 7.20, is the quintessential exception. I imagine that almost all Java programmers have had a taste of this exception, but let's look at an explanation for it.

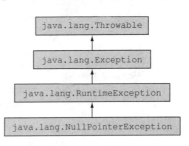

Figure 7.20 Class hierarchy of
NullPointerException

This exception is thrown by the JVM if you try to access a method or a variable with a `null` value. The exam can have interesting code combinations to test you on whether a particular piece of code will throw a `NullPointerException`. The key is to ensure that the reference variable has been assigned a non-`null` value. In particular, I'll address the following cases:

- Accessing members of a reference variable that is explicitly assigned a `null` value.
- Accessing members of an uninitialized instance or `static` reference variable. These are implicitly assigned a `null` value.
- Using an uninitialized local variable, which may *seem* to throw a `NullPointer-Exception`.
- Attempting to access nonexistent array positions.
- Using members of an array element that are assigned a `null` value.

Let's get started with the first case, in which a variable is explicitly assigned a `null` value:

```
import java.util.ArrayList;
class ThrowNullPointerException {                          list is null
    static ArrayList<String> list = null;
    public static void main(String[] args) {
        list.add("1");                        Attempt to call method
    }                                         add on list throws
}                                             NullPointerException
```

The preceding code tries to access the method `add` on variable `list`, which has been assigned a `null` value. It throws an exception, as follows:

```
Exception in thread "main" java.lang.NullPointerException
    at ThrowNullPointerException.main(ThrowNullPointerException.java:5)
```

By default, the `static` and instance variables of a class are assigned a `null` value. In the previous example, the static variable `list` is assigned an explicit `null` value. When the method `main` tries to execute the method `add` on variable `list`, it calls a method on a `null` value. This call causes the JVM to throw a `NullPointerException` (which is a `RuntimeException`). If you define the variable `list` as an instance variable and don't assign an explicit value to it, you'll get the same result (`NullPointerException` being thrown at runtime). Because the `static` method `main` can't access the instance variable `list`, you'll need to create an object of class `ThrowNullPointerException` to access it:

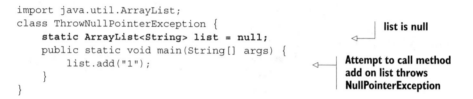

```
import java.util.ArrayList;                         list is implicitly
class ThrowNullPointerException {                   assigned a null
    ArrayList<String> list;                         value
    public static void main(String[] args) {
        ThrowNullPointerException obj = new ThrowNullPointerException();
        obj.list.add("1");
    }                                  Attempt to call method add on list
}                                      throws NullPointerException
```

You can prevent a `NullPointerException` from being thrown by checking whether an object is `null` before trying to access its member:

```
import java.util.ArrayList;
class ThrowNullPointerException {
    static ArrayList<String> list;
    public static void main(String[] args) {
        if (list!=null)
            list.add("1");
    }
}
```

Ascertain that list is not null ◁───

What happens if you modify the previous code as follows? Will it still throw a `Null-PointerException`?

```
import java.util.ArrayList;
class ThrowNullPointerException {
    public static void main(String[] args) {
        ArrayList<String> list;
        if (list!=null)
            list.add("1");
    }
}
```

Fails to compile ◁───

Interestingly, the previous code fails to compile. `list` is defined as a local variable inside the method `main`, and by default, local variables aren't assigned a value—not even a `null` value. If you attempt to use an uninitialized local variable, your code will fail to compile. Watch out for similar questions in the exam.

Another set of conditions when code may throw the `NullPointerException` involves use of arrays:

```
class ThrowAnotherNullPointerException {
    static String[] oldLaptops;
    public static void main(String[] args) {
        System.out.println(oldLaptops[1]);

        String[] newLaptops = new String[2];
        System.out.println(newLaptops[1].toString());
    }
}
```

◁─── **Throws NullPointerException**

◁─┐ **Throws NullPointerException**

The variable `oldLaptops` is assigned a `null` value by default because it's a `static` variable. Its array elements are neither initialized nor assigned a value. The code that tries to access the array's second element throws a `NullPointerException`.

In the second case, two array elements of the variable `newLaptops` are initialized and assigned a default value of `null`. If you call method `toString` on the second element of variable `newLaptops`, it results in a `NullPointerException` being thrown.

If you modify that line as shown in the following code, it won't throw an exception—it'll print the value `null`:

```
System.out.println(newLaptops[1]);
```

◁─── **No RuntimeException. Prints "null".**

EXAM TIP   In the exam, watch out for code that tries to use an uninitialized local variable. Because such variables aren't initialized with even a null value, you can't print their value using the System.out.println method. Such code *won't* compile.

Let's modify the previous code that uses the variable oldLaptops and check your understanding of NullPointerExceptions. Here's another Twist in the Tale hands-on exercise for you (answers in the appendix).

Twist in the Tale 7.5

Let's check your understanding of the NullPointerException. Here's a code snippet. Examine the code and select the correct answers.

```
class TwistInTaleNullPointerException {
    public static void main(String[] args) {
        String[][] oldLaptops =
            { {"Dell", "Toshiba", "Vaio"}, null,
{"IBM"}, new String[10] };
        System.out.println(oldLaptops[0][0]);          // line 1
        System.out.println(oldLaptops[1]);             // line 2
        System.out.println(oldLaptops[3][6]);          // line 3
        System.out.println(oldLaptops[3][0].length()); // line 4
        System.out.println(oldLaptops);                // line 5
    }
}
```

   a   Code on line 1 will throw NullPointerException
   b   Code on lines 1 and 3 will throw NullPointerException
   c   Only code on line 4 will throw NullPointerException
   d   Code on lines 3 and 5 will throw NullPointerException

7.4.6 *NumberFormatException*

What happens if you try to convert "87" and "9m#" to numeric values? The former value is okay, but you can't convert the latter value to a numeric value unless it's an encoded value, straight from a James Bond movie, that can be converted to anything.

As shown in figure 7.21, NumberFormat-Exception is a runtime exception. It's thrown to indicate that the application has tried to convert a string (with an inappropriate format) to one of the numeric types.

Multiple classes in the Java API define parsing methods. One of the most frequently used

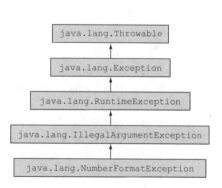

Figure 7.21   Class hierarchy of NumberFormatException

methods is parseInt from the class Integer. It's used to parse a String argument as a signed (negative or positive) decimal integer. Here are some examples:

Valid String values that can be converted to numeric values

```
System.out.println(Integer.parseInt("-123"));
System.out.println(Integer.parseInt("123"));
System.out.println(Integer.parseInt("+123"));
System.out.println(Integer.parseInt("123_45"));     ◁─
System.out.println(Integer.parseInt("12ABCD"));     ◁─
```

Will throw NumberFormatException. Use of underscores in string values isn't allowed.

Will throw NumberFormatException. Characters ABCD can't be converted to integers in base 10.

Starting in Java 7, you can use underscores (_) in numeric literal values. But you can't use them in String values passed to the method parseInt. The letters ABCD are not used in the decimal number system, but they can be used in the hexadecimal number system, so you can convert the hexadecimal literal value "12ABCD" to the decimal number system by specifying the base of the number system as 16:

```
System.out.println(Integer.parseInt("123ABCD", 16));     ◁───── Prints 1223629
```

Note that the argument 16 is passed to the method parseInt, not to the method println. The following will not compile:

```
System.out.println(Integer.parseInt("123ABCD"), 16);     ◁───── Won't compile
```

You may throw NumberFormatException from your own method to indicate that there's an issue with the conversion of a String value to a specified numeric format (decimal, octal, hexadecimal, binary), and you can add a customized exception message. One of the most common candidates for this exception is methods that are used to convert a command-line argument (accepted as a String value) to a numeric value. Please note that all command-line arguments are accepted in a String array as String values.

The following is an example of code that rethrows NumberFormatException programmatically:

```
public class ThrowNumberFormatException {
    public static int convertToNum(String val) {
        int num = 0;
        try {
            num = Integer.parseInt(val, 16);
        }
        catch (NumberFormatException e) {
            throw new NumberFormatException(val+
                " cannot be converted to hexadecimal number");
        }
        return num;
    }
    public static void main(String args[]) {
        System.out.println(convertToNum("16b"));
        System.out.println(convertToNum("65v"));
    }
}
```

Rethrows NumberFormatException thrown by method parseInt with modified exception message

The conversion of the hexadecimal literal 16b to the decimal number system is successful. But the conversion of the hexadecimal literal 65v to the decimal number system fails, and the previous code will give the following output:

```
363
Exception in thread "main" java.lang.NumberFormatException: 65v cannot be
    converted to hexadecimal number
    at
    ThrowNumberFormatException.convertToNum(ThrowNumberFormatException.java:
    8)
    at ThrowNumberFormatException.main(ThrowNumberFormatException.java:14)
```

Now let's take a look at some of the common errors that are covered on this exam.

7.4.7   *ExceptionInInitializerError*

The ExceptionInInitializerError error is typically thrown by the JVM when a static initializer in your code throws any type of RuntimeException. Figure 7.22 shows the class hierarchy of ExceptionIn-InitializerError.

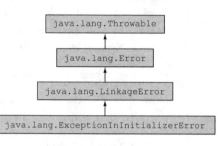

Figure 7.22   Class hierarchy of ExceptionInInitializerError

A static initializer block is defined using the keyword static, followed by curly braces, in a class. This block is defined within a class, but not within a method. It's usually used to execute code when a class loads for the first time. Runtime exceptions arising from any of the following will throw this error:

- Execution of an anonymous static block
- Initialization of a static variable
- Execution of a static method (called from either of the previous two items)

The static initializer block of the class defined in the following example will throw a NumberFormatException, and when the JVM tries to load this class, it'll throw an ExceptionInInitializerError:

```
public class DemoExceptionInInitializerError {
    static {
        int num = Integer.parseInt("sd", 16);
    }
}
```

Following is the error message when JVM tries to load the class DemoExceptionIn-InitializerError:

```
java.lang.ExceptionInInitializerError
Caused by: java.lang.NumberFormatException: For input string: "sd"
    at
    java.lang.NumberFormatException.forInputString(NumberFormatException.jav
    a:48)
```

```
      at java.lang.Integer.parseInt(Integer.java:447)
      at
       DemoExceptionInInitializerError.<clinit>(DemoExceptionInInitializerError
       .java:3)
```

EXAM TIP Beware of code that seems to be simple in the OCA Java SE 7 Programmer I exam. The class DemoExceptionInInitializerError (mentioned previously) seems deceptively simple, but it's a good candidate for an exam question. As you know, this class throws the error ExceptionInInitializer-Error when the JVM tries to load it.

In the following example, initialization of a static variable results in a NullPointer-Exception being thrown. When this class is loaded by the JVM, it throws an Exception-InInitializerError:

```
public class DemoExceptionInInitializerError1 {
    static String name = null;
    static int nameLength = name.length();
}
```

The error message when the JVM tries to load the DemoExceptionInInitializer-Error1 class is as follows:

```
java.lang.ExceptionInInitializerError
Caused by: java.lang.NullPointerException
      at
       DemoExceptionInInitializerError1.<clinit>(DemoExceptionInInitializerErro
       r1.java:3)
Exception in thread "main"
```

Now let's move on to the exception thrown by a static method, which may be called by the static initializer block or to initialize a static variable. Examine the following code, in which MyException is a user-defined RuntimeException:

```
public class DemoExceptionInInitializerError2 {
    static String name = getName();
    static String getName() {
        throw new MyException();           ◁─┐  MyException is a
    }                                           runtime exception
}
class MyException extends RuntimeException{}
```

This is the error thrown by the class DemoExceptionInInitializerError2:

```
java.lang.ExceptionInInitializerError
Caused by: MyException
      at
       DemoExceptionInInitializerError2.getName(DemoExceptionInInitializerError
       2.java:4)
      at
       DemoExceptionInInitializerError2.<clinit>(DemoExceptionInInitializerErro
       r2.java:2)
```

Did you notice that the error ExceptionInInitializerError can be caused only by a runtime exception? This happens for valid reasons, of course.

If a static initializer block throws an error, it doesn't recover from it to come back to the code to throw an `ExceptionInInitializerError`. This error can't be thrown if a `static` initializer block throws an object of a checked exception because the Java compiler is intelligent enough to determine this condition and doesn't allow you to throw an unhandled checked exception from a static initialization block.

EXAM TIP `ExceptionInInitializerError` can be caused by an object of `RuntimeException` only. It can't occur as the result of an error or checked exception thrown by the `static` initialization block.

7.4.8   *StackOverflowError*

The `StackOverflowError` error extends `Virtual-MachineError` (as shown in figure 7.23). As its name suggests, it should be left to be managed by the JVM.

This error is thrown by the JVM when a Java program calls itself so many times that the memory stack allocated to execute the Java program "overflows." Examine the following code, in which a method calls itself recursively without an exit condition:

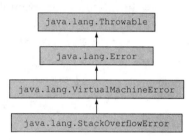

Figure 7.23   Class hierarchy of StackOverflowError

```
public class DemoStackOverflowError{
    static void recursion() {
        recursion();
    }
    public static void main(String args[]) {
        recursion();
    }
}
```

Calls itself recursively, without exit condition

The following error is thrown by the previous code:

```
Exception in thread "main" java.lang.StackOverflowError
    at DemoStackOverflowError.recursion(DemoStackOverflowError.java:3)
```

7.4.9   *NoClassDefFoundError*

What would happen if you failed to set your classpath and, as a result, the JVM was unable to load the class that you wanted to access or execute? Or what happens if you try to run your application before compiling it? In both these conditions, the JVM would throw `NoClassDefFoundError` (class hierarchy shown in figure 7.24).

This is what the Java API documentation says about this error:

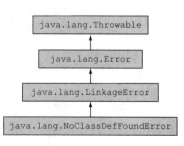

Figure 7.24   Class hierarchy of NoClassDefFoundError

Thrown if the Java Virtual Machine or a ClassLoader *instance tries to load in the definition of a class (as part of a normal method call or as part of creating a new instance using the* new *expression) and no definition of the class could be found.*[2]

Because this particular error is not a coding issue, I don't have a coding example for you. As you can see from the error hierarchy diagram in figure 7.24, this is a linkage error arising from a missing class file definition at runtime. This error should not be handled by the code and should be left to be handled exclusively by the JVM.

NOTE Don't confuse the exception thrown by Class.forName(), used to load the class, and NoClassDefFoundError thrown by the JVM. Class.for-Name() throws ClassNotFoundException.

7.4.10 *OutOfMemoryError*

What happens if you create and use a *lot* of objects in your application—for example, if you load a large chunk of persistent data to be processed by your application. In such a case, the JVM may run out of memory *on the heap*, and the garbage collector may not be able to free more memory for the JVM. In this case, the JVM is unable to create any more objects on the heap. An OutOfMemoryError will be thrown (class hierarchy shown in figure 7.25).

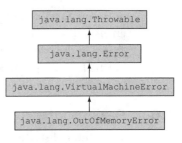

Figure 7.25 Class hierarchy of OutOfMemoryError

You'll always work with a finite heap size, no matter what platform you work on, so you can't create and use an unlimited number of objects in your application. To get around this error, you need to either limit the number of resources or objects that your application creates or increase the heap size on the platform you're working with.

A number of tools are available (which are beyond the scope of this book) that can help you monitor the number of objects created in your application.

7.5 *Summary*

In this chapter, we discussed the need for exception handling, as well as the advantages of defining the exception-handling code separate from the program logic. You saw how this approach helps separate concerns about defining the regular program logic and exception-handling code. We also looked at the code syntax, specifically the try-catch-finally blocks, for implementing the exception-handling code. Code that throws an exception should be enclosed within a try block that is immediately followed by a catch and/or a finally block. A try block can be followed by multiple catch blocks, but only a single finally block. A finally block can't be placed before

---

[2] The NoClassDefFoundError documentation can be found in the Javadoc: http://docs.oracle.com/javase/7/docs/api/java/lang/NoClassDefFoundError.html.

a try block. A try block must be followed by at least one catch or finally block. The try, catch, and finally blocks can't exist independently.

Next, we delved into the different categories of exceptions: checked exceptions, runtime or unchecked exceptions, and errors. Checked exceptions are subclasses of the class java.lang.Exception. Unchecked exceptions are subclasses of the class java .lang.RuntimeException, which itself is a subclass of the class java.lang.Exception. Errors are subclasses of java.lang.Error. All of these exceptions are subclasses of java.lang.Throwable.

A checked exception is an unacceptable condition foreseen by the author of a method but outside the immediate control of the code. A runtime exception represents a programming error—these occur because of inappropriate use of another piece of code. Errors are serious exceptions, thrown by the JVM, as a result of an error in the environment state that processes your code.

In the final sections of this chapter, we covered commonly occurring exceptions and errors, such as NullPointerException, IllegalArgumentException, StackOverflow-Error, and more. For each of these errors and exceptions, I explained the conditions in which they may be thrown in code and whether they should be explicitly handled in exception handlers.

7.6   *Review notes*

This section lists the main points of all the sections covered in this chapter.

A taste of exceptions:

- Trying to access an array element at a position that is greater than or equal to the array's length is considered an exceptional condition.
- Trying to execute a method that throws a checked exception without handling the thrown exception causes a compilation error.
- Trying to call a method recursively without defining an exit condition is considered an exceptional condition.
- Proper handling of exceptions is important in Java. It enables a programmer to define alternative code to execute in case an exceptional condition is met.

Why handle exceptions separately:

- Exception handlers refer to the blocks of code that execute when an exceptional condition arises during code execution.
- Handling exceptions separately enables you to define the main logic of your code together.
- Without the use of separate exception handlers, the main logic of your code would be lost in combating the exceptional conditions. (See figure 7.5 for an example.)
- Separate exception handlers enable you to define alternative code to execute separately from your main code flow when an exceptional condition is met.
- Exception handlers separate the concerns of defining the regular program logic from exception-handling code.

- Exceptions also help pinpoint the offending code, together with the method in which it is defined, by providing a stack trace of the exception or error.
- The stack trace of an exception enables you to get a list of all the exceptions that executed before the exception was reported.
- The stack trace of an exception is available within an exception handler.
- The JVM may send the stack trace of an unhandled exception to the Java console.

An exception is thrown:

- An exception is an object of the class `java.lang.Throwable`.
- When a piece of code hits an obstacle in the form of an exceptional condition, it creates an object of subclass `java.lang.Throwable`, initializes it with the necessary information (such as its type and optionally a textual description and the offending program's state), and hands it over to the JVM.
- The JVM keeps an account of all the methods that were called when it hits the code that throws an exception. To find an appropriate exception handler, it looks through all these method calls.
- Enclose the code that may throw an exception within a `try` block.
- Define `catch` blocks to include alternative code to execute when an exceptional condition arises.
- A `try` block can be followed by one or more `catch` blocks.
- The `catch` blocks must be followed by zero or one `finally` block.
- The `finally` block executes regardless of whether the code in the `try` block throws an exception.
- A `try` block can't define multiple `finally` blocks.
- The order in which the `catch` blocks are placed matters. If the caught exceptions have an inheritance relationship, the base class exceptions can't be caught before the derived class exceptions. An attempt to do this will result in compilation failure.
- A `finally` block will execute even if a `try` or `catch` block defines a `return` statement.
- A `try` block may be followed by either a `catch` or a `finally` block or both.
- If both `catch` and `finally` blocks define `return` statements, the calling method will receive the value from the `finally` block.
- If a `catch` block returns a primitive data type, a `finally` block can't modify the value being returned by it.
- If a `catch` block returns an object, a `finally` block can modify the value being returned by it.
- A `finally` block alone wouldn't suffice with a `try` block if code in the `try` block throws a checked exception. In this case, you need to catch the checked exception or define in the method signature that the exception is thrown, or your code won't compile.

- None of the try, catch, and finally blocks can exist independently.
- The finally block can't appear before a catch block.
- You can rethrow an error that you *catch* in an exception handler.
- You can either handle an exception or declare it to be thrown by your method. In the latter case, you need not handle the exception in your code. This applies to checked exceptions.
- You can create nested exception handlers.
- A try, catch, or finally block can define another try-catch-finally block. Theoretically, there is no limit on the allowed level of nesting of try-catch-finally blocks.

Categories of exceptions:

- Exceptions are divided into three categories: checked exceptions, runtime (or unchecked exceptions), and errors. These three categories share IS-A relationships (inheritance).
- Subclasses of the class java.lang.RuntimeException are categorized as runtime exceptions.
- Subclasses of the class java.lang.Error are categorized as errors.
- Subclasses of the class java.lang.Exception are categorized as checked exceptions if they are not subclasses of class java.lang.Runtime.
- The class java.lang.RuntimeException is a subclass of the class java.lang.Exception.
- The class java.lang.Exception is a subclass of the class java.lang.Throwable.
- The class java.lang.Error is also a subclass of the class java.lang.Throwable.
- The class java.lang.Throwable inherits the class java.lang.Object.

Checked exceptions:

- A checked exception is an unacceptable condition foreseen by the author of a method, but outside the immediate control of the code.
- FileNotFoundException is a checked exception. This exception is thrown if the file that the code is trying to access can't be found.
- All checked exceptions are a subclass of the java.lang.Exception class, not a subclass of java.lang.RuntimeException. It's interesting to note, however, that the class java.lang.RuntimeException itself is a subclass of the class java.lang.Exception.
- If a method calls another method that may throw a checked exception, either it must be enclosed within a try-catch block or the method should declare this exception to be thrown in its method signature.

Runtime exceptions:

- Runtime exceptions represent programming errors. These occur from inappropriate use of another piece of code. For example, NullPointerException is a runtime exception that occurs when a piece of code tries to execute some code on a variable that hasn't been assigned an object and points to `null`. Another example is `ArrayIndexOutOfBoundsException`, which is thrown when a piece of code tries to access an array of list elements at a nonexistent position.

- A runtime exception is a subclass of `java.lang.RuntimeException`.
- A runtime exception isn't a part of the method signature, even if a method may throw it.
- A runtime exception may not necessarily be caught by a `try-catch` block.

Errors:

- An error is a serious exception, thrown by the JVM as a result of an error in the environment state, which processes your code. For example, `NoClassDefFound-Error` is an error thrown by the JVM when it is unable to locate the .class file it is supposed to run.
- `StackOverflowError` is another error, thrown by the JVM when the size of the memory required by the stack of the Java program is greater than what the JRE has offered for the Java application. This error usually occurs as a result of infinite or highly nested loops.
- An error is a subclass of the class `java.lang.Error`.
- An error need not be a part of a method signature.
- Though you can handle the errors syntactically, there is little that you can do when these errors occur. For example, when the JVM throws `OutOfMemory-Error`, your code execution will halt, even if you define an exception handler for it.

Commonly occurring exceptions, categories, and classes:

- For the OCA Java SE 7 Programmer I exam, you need to be aware of commonly occurring exception categories and classes, when are they thrown, whether you should handle them, and how to handle them.
- `ArrayIndexOutOfBoundsException` is a runtime exception that's thrown when a piece of code tries to access an array position out of its bounds—when an array is accessed either at a position less than 0 or at a position greater than or equal to its length.
- `IndexOutOfBoundsException` is a runtime exception that's thrown when a piece of code tries to access a list position that's out of its bounds—when the position is either less than 0 or greater than or equal to the list's size.
- The class `ArrayIndexOutOfBoundsException` extends the class `java.lang.Index-OutOfBoundsException`, which extends the class `java.lang.RuntimeException`.
- In typical programming conditions, the `ArrayIndexOutOfBoundsException` shouldn't be thrown programmatically.
- One of the main reasons for the JVM taking the responsibility for throwing this exception itself is that this exception isn't known until runtime and depends on

the array or list position that's being accessed by a piece of code. Most often, a variable is used to specify this array or list position, and its value may not be known until runtime.

- `ClassCastException` is a runtime exception. `java.lang.ClassCastException` extends `java.lang.RuntimeException`.

- `ClassCastException` is thrown when an object fails an IS-A test with the class type it is being cast to.

- You can use the operator `instanceof` to verify whether an object can be cast to another class before casting it.

- `IllegalArgumentException` is a runtime exception. `java.lang.Illegal-ArgumentException` extends `java.lang.RuntimeException`.

- `IllegalArgumentException` is thrown to specify that a method has been passed illegal or inappropriate arguments.

- Even though `IllegalArgumentException` is a runtime exception, programmers usually use this exception to validate the arguments that are passed to a method, and the exception constructor is passed a descriptive message specifying the exception details.

- `IllegalStateException` is a runtime exception. `java.lang.IllegalState-Exception` extends `java.lang.RuntimeException`.

- `IllegalStateException` may be thrown programmatically.

- As a programmer, you can throw `IllegalStateException` to signal to the calling method that the method that's being requested for execution isn't ready to start its execution or is in a state in which it can't execute.

- For example, you can throw `IllegalStateException` from your code if an application tries to modify an SMS that has already been sent.

- `NullPointerException` is a runtime exception. The class `java.lang.Null-PointerException` extends `java.lang.RuntimeException`.

- `NullPointerException` is thrown by the JVM if you try to access a method or variable of an uninitialized reference variable.

- `NumberFormatException` is a runtime exception. `java.lang.NumberFormat-Exception` extends `java.lang.IllegalArgumentException`. `java.lang.Illegal-ArgumentException` extends `java.lang.RuntimeException`.

- You can throw `NumberFormatException` from your own method to indicate that there's an issue with the conversion of a `String` value to a specified numeric format (decimal, octal, hexadecimal, or binary).

- Runtime exceptions arising from any of the following may throw `ExceptionIn-InitializerError`:
  - Execution of an anonymous `static` block
  - Initialization of a `static` variable
  - Execution of a `static` method (called from either of the previous two items)

- The error `ExceptionInInitializerError` can be thrown only by an object of a runtime exception.
- `ExceptionInInitializerError` can't be thrown if a `static` initializer block throws an object of a checked exception, because the Java compiler is intelligent enough to determine this condition and it doesn't allow you to throw an unhandled checked exception from a `static` initialization block.
- `StackOverflowError` is an error. `java.lang.StackOverflowError` extends `java.lang.VirtualMachineError`.
- Because `StackOverflowError` extends `VirtualMachineError`, it should be left to be managed by the JVM.
- The `StackOverflowError` error is thrown by the JVM when a Java program calls itself so many times that the memory stack allocated to execute the Java program "overflows."
- `NoClassDefFoundError` is an Error. `java.lang.NoClassDefFoundError` extends `java.lang.LinkageError`. `java.lang.LinkageError` extends `java.lang.Error`.
- `NoClassDefFoundError` is thrown by the JVM or a `ClassLoader` when it is unable to load the definition of a class required to create an object of the class.
- Don't confuse the exception thrown by `Class.forName()`, used to load the class, and `NoClassDefFoundError` thrown by the JVM. `Class.forName()` throws `ClassNotFoundException`.
- `OutOfMemoryError` is thrown by the JVM when it's unable to create objects on the heap and the garbage collector may not be able to free more memory for the JVM.

7.7 Sample exam questions

Q7-1. What is the output of the following code:

```
class Course {
    String courseName;
    Course() {
        Course c = new Course();
        c.courseName = "Oracle";
    }
}
class EJavaGuruPrivate2 {
    public static void main(String args[]) {
        Course c = new Course();
        c.courseName = "Java";
        System.out.println(c.courseName);
    }
}
```

- **a** The code will print `Java`.
- **b** The code will print `Oracle`.
- **c** The code will not compile.
- **d** The code will throw an exception or an error at runtime.

Q7-2. Select the correct option(s):

   a You cannot handle runtime exceptions.

   b You should not handle errors.

   c If a method throws a checked exception, it must be either handled by the method or specified in its `throws` clause.

   d If a method throws a runtime exception, it may include the exception in its `throws` clause.

   e Runtime exceptions are checked exceptions.

Q7-3. Examine the following code and select the correct option(s):

```
class EJavaGuruExcep2 {
    public static void main(String args[]) {
        EJavaGuruExcep2 var = new EJavaGuruExcep2();
        var.printArrValues(args);
    }
    void printArrValues(String[] arr) {
        try {
            System.out.println(arr[0] + ":" + arr[1]);
        }
        catch (NullPointerException e) {
            System.out.println("NullPointerException");
        }
        catch (IndexOutOfBoundsException e) {
            System.out.println("IndexOutOfBoundsException");
        }
        catch (ArrayIndexOutOfBoundsException e) {
            System.out.println("ArrayIndexOutOfBoundsException");
        }
    }
}
```

   a If the class `EJavaGuruExcep2` is executed using the following command, it prints `NullPointerException`:

     `javaEJavaGuruExcep2`

   b If the class `EJavaGuruExcep2` is executed using the following command, it prints `IndexOutOfBoundsException`:

     `javaEJavaGuruExcep2`

   c If the class `EJavaGuruExcep2` is executed using the following command, it prints `ArrayIndexOutOfBoundsException`:

     `javaEJavaGuruExcep2one`

   d The code will fail to compile.

Q7-4. What is the output of the following code?

```
class EJava {
    void method() {
        try {
```

```
            guru();
            return;
        }
        finally {
            System.out.println("finally 1");
        }
    }
    void guru() {
        System.out.println("guru");
        throw new StackOverflowError();
    }
    public static void main(String args[]) {
        EJava var = new EJava();
        var.method();
    }
}
```

    a guru
       finally 1

    b guru
       finally 1
       Exception in thread "main" java.lang.StackOverflowError

    c guru
       Exception in thread "main" java.lang.StackOverflowError

    d guru

    e The code fails to compile.

Q7-5. Select the incorrect statement(s):

    a Exceptions enable a developer to define the programming logic separate from the exception-handling code.

    b Exception handling speeds up execution of the code.

    c Exception handing is used to define code that should execute when a piece of code throws an exception.

    d Code that handles all the checked exceptions can still throw unchecked exceptions.

Q7-6. Select the incorrect statement(s):

    a `java.lang.Throwable` is the base class of all types of exceptions.

    b If a class is a subclass of `java.lang.Exception`, it may or may not be a checked exception.

    c `Error` is an unchecked exception.

    d `Error` and checked exceptions need not be part of a method signature.

Q7-7. What is the output of the following code?

```
class TryFinally {
    int tryAgain() {
        int a = 10;
```

```
        try {
            ++a;
        }
        finally {
            a++;
        }
        return a;
    }
    public static void main(String args[]) {
        System.out.println(new TryFinally().tryAgain());
    }
}
```

   a 10

   b 11

   c 12

   d Compilation error

   e Runtime exception

Q7-8. What is the output of the following code?

```
class EJavaBase {
    void myMethod() throws ExceptionInInitializerError {
        System.out.println("Base");
    }
}
class EJavaDerived extends EJavaBase {
    void myMethod() throws RuntimeException {
        System.out.println("Derived");
    }
}
class EJava3 {
    public static void main(String args[]) {
        EJavaBase obj = new EJavaDerived();
        obj.myMethod();
    }
}
```

   a Base

   b Derived

   c Derived
      Base

   d Base
      Derived

   e Compilation error

Q7-9. Which of the following statements are true?

   a A user-defined class may not throw an `IllegalStateException`. It must be thrown only by Java API classes.

   b `System.out.println` will throw `NullPointerException` if an uninitialized instance variable of type `String` is passed to it to print its value.

   c `NumberFormatException` is thrown by multiple methods from the Java API when invalid numbers are passed on as `Strings` to be converted to the specified number format.

   d `ExceptionInInitializerError` may be thrown by the JVM when a `static` initializer in your code throws a `NullPointerException`.

Q7-10. What is the output of the following code?

```
class EJava4 {
    void foo() {
        try {
            String s = null;
            System.out.println("1");
            try {
                System.out.println(s.length());
            }
            catch (NullPointerException e) {
                System.out.println("inner");
            }
            System.out.println("2");
        }
        catch (NullPointerException e) {
            System.out.println("outer");
        }
    }
    public static void main(String args[]) {
        EJava4 obj = new EJava4();
        obj.foo();
    }
}
```

  a 1
     inner
     2
     outer

  b 1
     outer

  c 1
     inner

  d 1
     inner
     2

7.8   Answers to sample exam questions

Q7-1. What is the output of the following code:

```
class Course {
    String courseName;
    Course() {
        Course c = new Course();
        c.courseName = "Oracle";
    }
```

```
}
class EJavaGuruPrivate2 {
    public static void main(String args[]) {
        Course c = new Course();
        c.courseName = "Java";
        System.out.println(c.courseName);
    }
}
```

    a The code will print Java.

    b The code will print Oracle.

    c The code will not compile.

    d **The code will throw an exception or an error at runtime.**

Answer: d

Explanation: This class will throw StackOverflowError at runtime. The easiest way to look for a StackOverflowError is to locate recursive method calls. In the question's code, the constructor of the class Course creates an object of the class Course, which will call the constructor again. Hence, this becomes a recursive call and ends up throwing StackOverflowError at runtime. (As you know, an exception or an error can be thrown only at runtime, not compile time.)

Q7-2. Select the correct option(s):

    a You cannot handle runtime exceptions.

    b **You should not handle errors.**

    c **If a method throws a checked exception, it must be either handled by the method or specified in its throws clause.**

    d **If a method throws a runtime exception, it may include the exception in its throws clause.**

    e Runtime exceptions are checked exceptions.

Answer: b, c, d

Explanation: Option (a) is incorrect. You can handle runtime exceptions the way you can handle a checked exception in your code: using a try-catch block.

    Option (b) is correct. You shouldn't try to handle errors in your code. Or, to put it another way, you can't do much when an error is thrown by your code. Instead of trying to handle errors in your code, you should resolve the code that results in these errors. For example, StackOverflowError is an error that will be thrown by your code if your code executes a method recursively without any exit condition. This repetition will consume all the space on the stack and result in a StackOverflowError.

    Option (c) is correct. If you fail to implement either of these options, your code won't compile.

    Option (d) is correct. It isn't mandatory for runtime exceptions to be included in a method's throws clause. Usually this inclusion is unnecessary, but if you do include it, your code will execute without any issues.

Option (e) is incorrect. Runtime exception and all its subclasses are *not* checked exceptions.

Q7-3. Examine the following code and select the correct option(s):

```
class EJavaGuruExcep2 {
    public static void main(String args[]) {
        EJavaGuruExcep2 var = new EJavaGuruExcep2();
        var.printArrValues(args);
    }
    void printArrValues(String[] arr) {
        try {
            System.out.println(arr[0] + ":" + arr[1]);
        }
        catch (NullPointerException e) {
            System.out.println("NullPointerException");
        }
        catch (IndexOutOfBoundsException e) {
            System.out.println("IndexOutOfBoundsException");
        }
        catch (ArrayIndexOutOfBoundsException e) {
            System.out.println("ArrayIndexOutOfBoundsException");
        }
    }
}
```

a If the class EJavaGuruExcep2 is executed using the following command, it prints NullPointerException:

   javaEJavaGuruExcep2

b If the class EJavaGuruExcep2 is executed using the following command, it prints IndexOutOfBoundsException:

   javaEJavaGuruExcep2

c If the class EJavaGuruExcep2 is executed using the following command, it prints ArrayIndexOutOfBoundsException:

   javaEJavaGuruExcep2one

d **The code will fail to compile.**

Answer: d

Explanation: The key to answering this question is to be aware of the following two facts:

- Exceptions are classes. If an exception's base class is used in a catch block, it can catch all the exceptions of its derived class. If you try to catch an exception from its derived class afterward, the code won't compile.

- ArrayIndexOutOfBoundsException is a derived class of IndexOutOfBounds-Exception.

The rest of the points try to trick you into believing that the question is based on the arguments passed to a main method.

Q7-4. What is the output of the following code?

```
class EJava {
    void method() {
        try {
            guru();
            return;
        }
        finally {
            System.out.println("finally 1");
        }
    }
    void guru() {
        System.out.println("guru");
        throw new StackOverflowError();
    }
    public static void main(String args[]) {
        EJava var = new EJava();
        var.method();
    }
}
```

   a guru
      finally 1

   b **guru**
      finally 1
      Exception in thread "main" java.lang.StackOverflowError

   c guru
      Exception in thread "main" java.lang.StackOverflowError

   d guru

   e The code fails to compile.

Answer: b

Explanation: No compilation errors exist with the code.

The method guru throws StackOverflowError, which is not a checked exception. Even though your code should not throw an error, it is possible syntactically. Your code will compile successfully.

The call to the method guru is immediately followed by the keyword return, which is supposed to end the execution of the method method. But the call to guru is placed within a try-catch block, with a finally block. Because guru doesn't handle the error StackOverflowError itself, the control looks for the exception handler in the method method. This calling method doesn't handle this error, but defines a finally block. The control then executes the finally block. Because the code can't find an appropriate handler to handle this error, it propagates to the JVM, which abruptly halts the code.

Q7-5. Select the incorrect statement(s):

   a Exceptions enable a developer to define the programming logic separate from the exception-handling code.

   b **Exception handling speeds up execution of the code.**

   c Exception handing is used to define code that should execute when a piece of code throws an exception.

   d Code that handles all the checked exceptions can still throw unchecked exceptions.

Answer: b

Explanation: No direct relationship exists between exception handling and improved execution of code. Code that handles all the checked exceptions can throw unchecked exceptions and vice versa.

Q7-6. Select the incorrect statement(s):

   a `java.lang.Throwable` is the base class of all type of exceptions.

   b If a class is a subclass of `java.lang.Exception`, it may or may not be a checked exception.

   c **`Error` is an unchecked exception.**

   d **`Error` and checked exceptions need not be part of a method signature.**

Answer: c, d

Explanation:

   Option (a) is a true statement. A checked exception is a subclass of `java.lang.Exception`, and a runtime exception is a subclass of `java.lang.RuntimeException`. `java.lang.RuntimeException` is a subclass of `java.lang.Exception`, and `java.lang.Exception` is a subclass of `java.lang.Throwable`. Hence, all the exceptions are subclasses of `java.lang.Throwable`.

   Option (b) is also a true statement. Unchecked exceptions are subclasses of class `java.lang.RuntimeException`, which itself is a subclass of `java.lang.Exception`. Hence, a class can be a subclass of class `java.lang.Exception` and either a checked or an unchecked exception.

   Option (c) is a false statement. `Error` is *not* an exception. It does not subclass `java.lang.Exception`.

   Option (d) is also a false statement. `Error` need not be part of a method signature, but checked exceptions must be a part of the method signatures.

Q7-7. What is the output of the following code?

```java
class TryFinally {
    int tryAgain() {
        int a = 10;
        try {
            ++a;
        }
        finally {
            a++;
        }
        return a;
    }
```

```
        public static void main(String args[]) {
            System.out.println(new TryFinally().tryAgain());
        }
    }
```

   a   10

   b   11

   c   **12**

   d   Compilation error

   e   Runtime exception

Answer: c

Explanation: The `try` block executes, incrementing the value of variable a to 11. This step is followed by execution of the `finally` block, which also increments the value of variable a by 1, to 12. The method `tryAgain` returns the value 12, which is printed by the method `main`.

There are no compilation issues with the code. A `try` block can be followed by a `finally` block, without any `catch` blocks. Even though the `try` block doesn't throw any exceptions, it compiles successfully. The following is an example of a try-catch block that won't compile because it tries to *catch* a checked exception that's never thrown by the `try` block:

```
try {
    ++a;
}
catch (java.io.FileNotFoundException e) {
}
```

Q7-8. What is the output of the following code?

```
class EJavaBase {
    void myMethod() throws ExceptionInInitializerError {
        System.out.println("Base");
    }
}
class EJavaDerived extends EJavaBase {
    void myMethod() throws RuntimeException {
        System.out.println("Derived");
    }
}
class EJava3 {
    public static void main(String args[]) {
        EJavaBase obj = new EJavaDerived();
        obj.myMethod();
    }
}
```

   a   Base

   b   Derived

   c   Derived
       Base

   d `Base`
     `Derived`

   e Compilation error

Answer: b

Explanation: The rule that if a base class method doesn't throw an exception, an overriding method in the derived class can't throw a exception applies only to checked exceptions. It doesn't apply to runtime (unchecked) exceptions or errors. A base or overridden method is free to throw any `Error` or runtime exception.

Q7-9. Which of the following statements are true?

   a A user-defined class may not throw an `IllegalStateException`. It must be thrown only by Java API classes.

   b `System.out.println` will throw `NullPointerException` if an uninitialized instance variable of type `String` is passed to it to print its value.

   c **`NumberFormatException` is thrown by multiple methods from the Java API when invalid numbers are passed on as `Strings` to be converted to the specified number format.**

   d **`ExceptionInInitializerError` may be thrown by the JVM when a `static` initializer in your code throws a `NullPointerException`.**

Answer: c, d

Option (a) is incorrect. A user-defined class can throw any exception from the Java API.

   Option (b) is incorrect. An uninitialized instance variable of type `String` will be assigned a default value of `null`. When you pass this variable to `System.out.println` to print it, it will print `null`. If you try to access any member (variable or method) of this `null` object, then `NullPointerException` will be thrown.

Q7-10. What is the output of the following code?

```
class EJava4 {
    void foo() {
        try {
            String s = null;
            System.out.println("1");
            try {
                System.out.println(s.length());
            }
            catch (NullPointerException e) {
                System.out.println("inner");
            }
            System.out.println("2");
        }
        catch (NullPointerException e) {
            System.out.println("outer");
        }
    }
    public static void main(String args[]) {
```

```
        EJava4 obj = new EJava4();
        obj.foo();
    }
}
```

a 1
   inner
   2
   outer

b 1
   outer

c 1
   inner

d 1
   inner
   2

Answer: d

Explanation: First of all, nested `try-catch` statements don't throw compilation errors.

Because the variable s hasn't been initialized, an attempt to access its method `length()` will throw a `NullPointerException`. The inner `try-catch` block handles this exception and prints `inner`. The control then moves on to complete the remaining code in the outer `try-catch` block, printing 2. Because the `NullPointerException` was already handled in the inner `try-catch` block, it's not handled in the outer `try-catch` block.

Full mock exam

This chapter covers

- Complete mock exam with 90 questions
- Answers to all mock exam questions with extensive explanations and the subobjective on which each exam question is based

On the real exam, each question displays the count of correct options that you should select. The exam engine won't allow you to select more answer options than are specified by this number. If you try to do so, a warning will be displayed. The questions in this mock exam also specify the correct number of answer options to align it more closely to the real exam.

8.1 Mock exam

ME-Q1. Given the following definition of the classes Animal, Lion, and Jumpable, select the correct combinations of assignments of a variable (select 2 options):

```
interface Jumpable {}
class Animal {}
class Lion extends Animal implements Jumpable {}
```

☐ **a** Jumpable var1 = new Jumpable();
☐ **b** Animal var2 = new Animal();

   ☐ **c** `Lion var3 = new Animal();`

   ☐ **d** `Jumpable var4 = new Animal();`

   ☐ **e** `Jumpable var5 = new Lion();`

ME-Q2. Which of the following statements are true? (Select 3 options.)

   ☐ **a** A Java class can define multiple methods.

   ☐ **b** A Java class can define multiple variables.

   ☐ **c** A Java class can be defined in multiple packages.

   ☐ **d** A Java class can import multiple packages.

   ☐ **e** A Java class can't define more than 108 constructors.

   ☐ **f** End-of-line comments can't follow `import` or `package` statements.

   ☐ **g** Multiline comments can only be defined within a method definition.

ME-Q3. Given the following code, which option, if used to replace `/* INSERT CODE HERE */`, will make the code print 1? (Select 1 option.)

```
try {
    String[][] names = {{"Andre", "Mike"}, null, {"Pedro"}};
    System.out.println(names[2][1].substring(0, 2));
}
catch (/* INSERT CODE HERE */) {
    System.out.println(1);
}
```

   ◎ **a** `IndexPositionException e`

   ◎ **b** `NullPointerException e`

   ◎ **c** `ArrayIndexOutOfBoundsException e`

   ◎ **d** `ArrayOutOfBoundsException e`

ME-Q4. What is the output of the following code? (Select 1 option.)

```
int a = 10; String name = null;
try {
    a = name.length();
    a++;
}
catch (RuntimeException e){
    ++a;
}
System.out.println(a);
```

   ◎ **a** 5

   ◎ **b** 6

   ◎ **c** 10

   ◎ **d** 11

   ◎ **e** 12

   ◎ **f** Runtime exception

ME-Q5. Given the following class definition,

```
class Student { int marks = 10; }
```

what is the output of the following code? (Select 1 option.)

```
class Result {
    public static void main(String... args) {
        Student s = new Student();
        switch (s.marks) {
            default: System.out.println("100");
            case 10: System.out.println("10");
            case 98: System.out.println("98");
        }
    }
}
```

- a 100
  10
  98

- b 10
  98

- c 100

- d 10

ME-Q6. Given the following code, which code can be used to create and initialize an object of class `ColorPencil`? (Select 2 options.)

```
class Pencil {}
class ColorPencil extends Pencil {
    String color;
    ColorPencil(String color) {this.color = color;}
}
```

- a ColorPencil var1 = new ColorPencil();
- b ColorPencil var2 = new ColorPencil(RED);
- c ColorPencil var3 = new ColorPencil("RED");
- d Pencil var4 = new ColorPencil("BLUE");

ME-Q7. What is the output of the following code? (Select 1 option.)

```
class Doctor {
    protected int age;
    protected void setAge(int val) { age = val; }
    protected int getAge() { return age; }
}
class Surgeon extends Doctor {
    Surgeon(String val) {
        specialization = val;
    }
    String specialization;
    String getSpecialization() { return specialization; }
}
```

```
class Hospital {
    public static void main(String args[]) {
        Surgeon s1 = new Surgeon("Liver");
        Surgeon s2 = new Surgeon("Heart");
        s1.age = 45;
        System.out.println(s1.age + s2.getSpecialization());
        System.out.println(s2.age + s1.getSpecialization());
    }
}
```

- **a** 45Heart
  0Liver

- **b** 45Liver
  0Heart

- **c** 45Liver
  45Heart

- **d** 45Heart
  45Heart

- **e** Class fails to compile.

ME-Q8. What is the output of the following code? (Select 1 option.)

```
class RocketScience {
    public static void main(String args[]) {
        int a = 0;
        while (a == a++) {
            a++;
            System.out.println(a);
        }
    }
}
```

- **a** The while loop won't execute; nothing will be printed.
- **b** The while loop will execute indefinitely, printing all numbers, starting from 1.
- **c** The while loop will execute indefinitely, printing all even numbers, starting from 0.
- **d** The while loop will execute indefinitely, printing all even numbers, starting from 2.
- **e** The while loop will execute indefinitely, printing all odd numbers, starting from 1.
- **f** The while loop will execute indefinitely, printing all odd numbers, starting from 3.

ME-Q9. Given the following statements,

- com.ejava is a package
- class Person is defined in package com.ejava
- class Course is defined in package com.ejava

which of the following options correctly imports the classes `Person` and `Course` in the class `MyEJava`? (Select 3 options.)

- ☐ **a**
  ```
  import com.ejava.*;
  class MyEJava {}
  ```

- ☐ **b**
  ```
  import com.ejava;
  class MyEJava {}
  ```

- ☐ **c**
  ```
  import com.ejava.Person;
  import com.ejava.Course;
  class MyEJava {}
  ```

- ☐ **d**
  ```
  import com.ejava.Person;
  import com.ejava.*;
  class MyEJava {}
  ```

ME-Q10. Given that the following classes `Animal` and `Forest` are defined in the same package, examine the code and select the correct statements (select 2 options):

```
line1>     class Animal {
line2>         public void printKing() {
line3>             System.out.println("Lion");
line4>         }
line5>     }

line6>     class Forest {
line7>         public static void main(String... args) {
line8>             Animal anAnimal = new Animal();
line9>             anAnimal.printKing();
line10>        }
line11>    }
```

- ☐ **a** The class `Forest` prints `Lion`.
- ☐ **b** If the code on line 2 is changed as follows, the class `Forest` will print `Lion`:
  ```
  private void printKing() {
  ```
- ☐ **c** If the code on line 2 is changed as follows, the class `Forest` will print `Lion`:
  ```
  void printKing() {
  ```
- ☐ **d** If the code on line 2 is changed as follows, the class `Forest` will print `Lion`:
  ```
  default void printKing() {
  ```

ME-Q11. Which of the following statements are true? (Select 2 options.)

- ☐ **a** Given that you changed the access of a `public` method B, in class A, to a private method, class C that uses method B will fail to compile.
- ☐ **b** Given that you changed the access of a `private` method B, in class A, to a public method, none of the classes that use class A will fail to compile.
- ☐ **c** Given that you changed the access of a `protected` method B, in class A, to a method with default access, class C from the same package as class A won't be able to access method B.
- ☐ **d** A change in the accessibility of the methods in your class never affects any other class that uses your class.

ME-Q12. Which of the following statements are correct? (Select 3 options.)

☐ **a** You may not be able to handle all the checked exceptions in your code.

☐ **b** If required, you can handle all the runtime exceptions in your code.

☐ **c** You can handle an exception in your code even if you don't know its exact name.

☐ **d** A single exception handler can be used to handle all types of runtime and checked exceptions.

☐ **e** You must handle all errors that can be thrown by your code.

☐ **f** Runtime exceptions are also known as checked exceptions.

ME-Q13. Given the following code,

```
class MainMethod {
    public static void main(String... args) {
        System.out.println(args[0]+":"+ args[2]);
    }
}
```

what's its output if it's executed using the following command? (Select 1 option.)

```
java MainMethod 1+2 2*3 4-3 5+1
```

◯ **a** java:1+2

◯ **b** java:3

◯ **c** MainMethod:2*3

◯ **d** MainMethod:6

◯ **e** 1+2:2*3

◯ **f** 3:3

◯ **g** 6

◯ **h** 1+2:4-3

◯ **i** 31

◯ **j** 4

ME-Q14. What is the output of the following code? (Select 1 option.)

```
class Person {
    int age;
    float height;
    boolean result;
    String name;
}
public class EJava {
    public static void main(String arguments[]) {
        Person person = new Person();
        System.out.println(person.name + person.height + person.result
                            + person.age);
    }
}
```

◯ **a** null0.0false0

◯ **b** null0false0

○ **c** null0.0ffalse0

○ **d** 0.0false0

○ **e** 0false0

○ **f** 0.0ffalse0

○ **g** null0.0true0

○ **h** 0true0

○ **i** 0.0ftrue0

ME-Q15. Given the following code, which option, if used to replace /* INSERT CODE HERE */, will make the code print the value of the variable pagesPerMin? (Select 1 option.)

```
class Printer {
    int inkLevel;
}
class LaserPrinter extends Printer {
    int pagesPerMin;
    public static void main(String args[]) {
        Printer myPrinter = new LaserPrinter();
        System.out.println(/* INSERT CODE HERE */);
    }
}
```

○ **a** (LaserPrinter)myPrinter.pagesPerMin

○ **b** myPrinter.pagesPerMin

○ **c** LaserPrinter.myPrinter.pagesPerMin

○ **d** ((LaserPrinter)myPrinter).pagesPerMin

ME-Q16. Which statements describe the use of exception handling in Java? (Select 2 options.)

☐ **a** Exception handling can prevent an application from crashing or producing incorrect outputs or incorrect input values.

☐ **b** Exception handlers can't define an alternative flow of action in the event of an exception.

☐ **c** Exception handlers enable a programmer to define separate code blocks for handling different types of exceptions.

☐ **d** Exception handlers help to define well-encapsulated classes.

☐ **e** Exception handlers help with efficient inheritance.

ME-Q17. Which statements are true for reference and primitive variables? (Select 3 options.)

☐ **a** The names of the reference variables are limited to a length of 256 characters.

☐ **b** There is no limit on the length of the names of primitive variables.

☐ **c** Multiple reference variables may refer to exactly the same object in memory.

☐ **d** Values stored by primitive and reference variables can be compared for equality by using the equals operator (==) or by using the method equals.

☐ **e** A primitive variable can't refer to an object and vice versa.

ME-Q18. What is the output of the following code? (Select 1 option.)

```java
public class Handset {
    public static void main(String... args) {
        double price;
        String model;
        System.out.println(model + price);
    }
}
```

   ◉ **a** null0

   ◉ **b** null0.0

   ◉ **c** 0

   ◉ **d** 0.0

   ◉ **e** Compilation error

ME-Q19. What is the output of the following code? (Select 1 option.)

```java
public class Sales {
    public static void main(String args[]) {
        int salesPhone = 1;
        System.out.println(salesPhone++ + ++salesPhone +
                                                ++salesPhone);
    }
}
```

   ◉ **a** 5

   ◉ **b** 6

   ◉ **c** 8

   ◉ **d** 9

ME-Q20. Which of the following options defines the correct structure of a Java class?
(Select 1 option.)

   ◉ **a** `package com.ejava.guru;`
        `package com.ejava.oracle;`
        `class MyClass { }`

   ◉ **b** `import com.ejava.guru.*;`
        `import com.ejava.oracle.*;`
        `package com.ejava;`
        `class MyClass { }`

   ◉ **c** `class MyClass {`
             `import com.ejava.guru.*;`
        `}`

   ◉ **d** `class MyClass {`
             `int abc;`
        `}`

ME-Q21. What is the output of the following code? (Select 1 option.)

```java
class OpPre {
    public static void main(String... args) {
        int x = 10;
```

```
        int y = 20;
        int z = 30;
        if (x+y%z > (x+(-y)*(-z))) {
            System.out.println(x + y + z);
        }
    }
}
```

○ **a** 60

○ **b** 59

○ **c** 61

○ **d** No output.

○ **e** The code fails to compile.

ME-Q22. Select the most appropriate definition of the variable name and the line number on which it should be declared so that the following code compiles successfully (choose 1 option):

```
class EJava {
    // LINE 1
    public EJava() {
        System.out.println(name);
    }
    void calc() {
        // LINE 2
        if (8 > 2) {
            System.out.println(name);
        }
    }
    public static void main(String... args) {
        // LINE 3
        System.out.println(name);
    }
}
```

○ **a** Define static String name; on line 1.

○ **b** Define String name; on line 1.

○ **c** Define String name; on line 2.

○ **d** Define String name; on line 3.

ME-Q23. Examine the following code and select the correct statement (choose 1 option):

```
line1>    class Emp {
line2>        Emp mgr = new Emp();
line3>    }
line4>    class Office {
line5>        public static void main(String args[]) {
line6>            Emp e = null;
line7>            e = new Emp();
line8>            e = null;
line9>        }
line10>   }
```

○ **a** The object referred to by object e is eligible for garbage collection on line 8.

○ **b** The object referred to by object e is eligible for garbage collection on line 9.

○ **c** The object referred to by object e isn't eligible for garbage collection because its member variable mgr isn't set to null.

○ **d** The code throws a runtime exception and the code execution never reaches line 8 or 9.

ME-Q24. Which of the following is the correct declaration of a method that accepts two String arguments and an int argument and doesn't return any value? (Select 2 options.)

☐ **a** `void myMethod(String str1, int str2, String str3)`

☐ **b** `myMethod(String val1, int val2, String val3)`

☐ **c** `void myMethod(String str1, str2, int a)`

☐ **d** `void myMethod(String val1, val2, int val3)`

☐ **e** `void myMethod(int str2, String str3, String str1)`

ME-Q25. Which of the following will compile successfully? (Select 3 options.)

☐ **a** `int eArr1[] = {10, 23, 10, 2};`

☐ **b** `int[] eArr2 = new int[10];`

☐ **c** `int[] eArr3 = new int[] {};`

☐ **d** `int[] eArr4 = new int[10] {};`

☐ **e** `int eArr5[] = new int[2] {10, 20};`

ME-Q26. Assume that Oracle has asked you to create a method that returns the concatenated value of two String objects. Which of the following methods do you think can accomplish this job? (Select 2 options.)

☐ **a**
```
public String add(String 1, String 2) {
    return str1 + str2;
}
```

☐ **b**
```
private String add(String s1, String s2) {
    return s1.concat(s2);
}
```

☐ **c**
```
protected String add(String value1, String value2) {
    return value2.append(value2);
}
```

☐ **d**
```
String subtract(String first, String second) {
    return first.concat(second.substring(0));
}
```

ME-Q27. In Java, the class String is defined in the package java.lang, and this package is automatically imported in all the Java classes. Given this statement, which of the following options represents the correct definition of class EJava, which can define a variable of class String? (Choose 2 options.)

```
a import java.lang;
  class EJava {
      String guru;
  }
```

```
b import java.lang.String.*;
  class EJava {
      String guru;
  }
```

```
c class EJava {
      String guru;
  }
```

```
d import java.lang.String;
  import java.lang.String;
  class EJava {
      String guru;
  }
```

ME-Q28. Given the following definitions of the class `ChemistryBook`, select the statements that are correct individually (choose 2 options):

```
import java.util.ArrayList;
class ChemistryBook extends Book {
    public void read() {}                       //METHOD1
    public String read() { return null; }       //METHOD2
    ArrayList read(int a) { return null; }       //METHOD3
}
```

- **a** Methods marked with `//METHOD1` and `//METHOD2` are correctly overloaded methods.
- **b** Methods marked with `//METHOD2` and `//METHOD3` are correctly overloaded methods.
- **c** Methods marked with `//METHOD1` and `//METHOD3` are correctly overloaded methods.
- **d** All the methods—methods marked with `//METHOD1`, `//METHOD2`, and `//METHOD3`— are correctly overloaded methods.

ME-Q29) Given the following definition of the class `Home`, select the correct statements (choose 4 options):

```
class Home {
    String name;
    int rooms;
    Home() {}
}
```

- **a** The class `Home` will be provided a default constructor.
- **b** The class `Home` won't be provided a default constructor.
- **c** A default constructor can't coexist with overloaded constructors.
- **d** A default constructor doesn't accept any method parameters.
- **e** After compilation, the class `Home` has only a no-argument constructor.

☐ **f** After compilation, the class Home has two constructors: a no-argument constructor and a default constructor.

☐ **g** When an object of class Home is created, its variables name and rooms are not assigned any default values.

ME-Q30. Given the following code, which option, if used to replace /* INSERT CODE HERE */, will make the code print numbers that are completely divisible by 14? (Select 1 option.)

```
for (int ctr = 2; ctr <= 30; ++ctr) {
    if (ctr % 7 != 0)
        //INSERT CODE HERE
    if (ctr % 14 == 0)
        System.out.println(ctr);
}
```

◉ **a** continue;

◉ **b** exit;

◉ **c** break;

◉ **d** end;

ME-Q31. Ideally, which of the following should never be handled by an exception handler? (Select 2 options.)

☐ **a** StackOverflowError

☐ **b** OutOfMemoryError

☐ **c** ArrayIndexOutOfBoundError

☐ **d** ClassLoadingException

☐ **e** CompilationError

☐ **f** OutOfStorageError

ME-Q32. What is the output of the following code? (Select 1 option.)

```
public class MyCalendar {
    public static void main(String arguments[]) {
        Season season1 = new Season();
        season1.name = "Spring";

        Season season2 = new Season();
        season2.name = "Autumn";

        season1 = season2;
        System.out.println(season1.name);
        System.out.println(season2.name);
    }
}
class Season {
    String name;
}
```

        ○ **a** `String`
          `Autumn`

        ● **b** `Spring`
          `String`

        ○ **c** `Autumn`
          `Autumn`

        ○ **d** `Autumn`
          `String`

ME-Q33. What is true about the following code? (Select 1 option.)

```
class Shoe {}
class Boot extends Shoe {}
class ShoeFactory {
    ShoeFactory(Boot val) {
        System.out.println("boot");
    }
    ShoeFactory(Shoe val) {
        System.out.println("shoe");
    }
}
```

   ● **a** The class `ShoeFactory` has a total of two overloaded constructors.
   ○ **b** The class `ShoeFactory` has three overloaded constructors, two user-defined
     constructors, and one default constructor.
   ○ **c** The class `ShoeFactory` will fail to compile.
   ○ **d** The addition of the following constructor will increment the number of con-
     structors of the class `ShoeFactory` to 3:

     `private ShoeFactory (Shoe arg) {}`

ME-Q34. Given the following definitions of the classes `ColorPencil` and `TestColor`,
which option, if used to replace `/* INSERT CODE HERE */`, will initialize the instance
variable `color` of reference variable `myPencil` with the `String` literal value `"RED"`?
(Select 1 option.)

```
class ColorPencil {
    String color;
    ColorPencil(String color) {
        //INSERT CODE HERE
    }
}
class TestColor {
    ColorPencil myPencil = new ColorPencil("RED");
}
```

   ○ **a** `this.color = color;`
   ○ **b** `color = color;`
   ○ **c** `color = RED;`
   ○ **d** `this.color = RED;`

ME-Q35. What is the output of the following code? (Select 1 option.)

```
class EJavaCourse {
    String courseName = "Java";
}
class University {
    public static void main(String args[]) {
        EJavaCourse courses[] = { new EJavaCourse(), new EJavaCourse() };
        courses[0].courseName = "OCA";
        for (EJavaCourse c : courses) c = new EJavaCourse();
        for (EJavaCourse c : courses) System.out.println(c.courseName);
    }
}
```

- ⊙ **a** Java
     Java

- ⊙ **b** OCA
     Java

- ⊙ **c** OCA
     OCA

- ⊙ **d** None of the above.

ME-Q36. Given the following code, which option, if used to replace /* INSERT CODE HERE */, will make the code print the value of the variable screenSize? (Select 1 option.)

```
class Tablet {
    float screenSize = 7.0f;
    float getScreenSize() {
        return screenSize;
    }
    void setScreenSize(float val) {
        screenSize = val;
    }
}

class DemoTabs {
    public static void main(String args[]) {
        Tablet tab = new Tablet();
        System.out.println(/* INSERT CODE HERE */);

    }
}
```

- ⊙ **a** tab.screenSize
- ⊙ **b** tab->getScreensize()
- ⊙ **c** tab::getScreen()
- ⊙ **d** tab:screenSize

ME-Q37. Given the following definitions of the class Person and the interface Movable, the task is to declare a class Emp that inherits from the class Person and implements the interface Movable. Select the correct option to accomplish this task (choose 1 option):

```
class Person {}
interface Movable {}
```

⊙ **a** `class Emp implements Person extends Movable{}`

⊙ **b** `class Emp implements Person, Movable{}`

⊙ **c** `class Emp extends Person implements Movable{}`

⊙ **d** `class Emp extends Person, Movable{}`

ME-Q38. What is the output of the following code? (Select 1 option.)

```
class Phone {
    static void call() {
        System.out.println("Call-Phone");
    }
}
class SmartPhone extends Phone{
    static void call() {
        System.out.println("Call-SmartPhone");
    }
}
class TestPhones {
    public static void main(String... args) {
        Phone phone = new Phone();
        Phone smartPhone = new SmartPhone();
        phone.call();
        smartPhone.call();
    }
}
```

⊙ **a** Call-Phone
   Call-Phone

⊙ **b** Call-Phone
   Call-SmartPhone

⊙ **c** Call-Phone
   null

⊙ **d** null
   Call-SmartPhone

ME-Q39. Given the following code, which of the following statements are true? (Select 3 options.)

```
class MyExam {
    void question() {
        try {
            question();
        }
        catch (StackOverflowError e) {
            System.out.println("caught");
        }
    }
    public static void main(String args[]) {
        new MyExam().question();
    }
}
```

- ☐ **a** The code will print caught.
- ☐ **b** The code won't print caught.
- ☐ **c** The code would print caught if StackOverflowError were a runtime exception.
- ☐ **d** The code would print caught if StackOverflowError were a checked exception.
- ☐ **e** The code will print caught if question() throws exception NullPointer-Exception.

ME-Q40. A class Student is defined as follows:

```
public class Student {
    private String fName;
    private String lName;
    public Student(String first, String last) {
        fName = first; lName = last;
    }
    public String getName() { return fName + lName; }
}
```

The creator of the class later changes the method getName as follows:

```
public String getName() {
    return fName + " " + lName;
}
```

What are the implications of this change? (Select 2 options.)

- ☐ **a** The classes that were using the class Student will fail to compile.
- ☐ **b** The classes that were using the class Student will work without any compilation issues.
- ☐ **c** The class Student is an example of a well-encapsulated class.
- ☐ **d** The class Student exposes its instance variable outside the class.

ME-Q41. What is the output of the following code? (Select 1 option.)

```
class ColorPack {
    int shadeCount = 12;
    static int getShadeCount() {
        return shadeCount;
    }
}
class Artist {
    public static void main(String args[]) {
        ColorPack pack1 = new ColorPack();
        System.out.println(pack1.getShadeCount());
    }
}
```

- ○ **a** 10
- ○ **b** 12
- ○ **c** No output
- ○ **d** Compilation error

ME-Q42. Paul defined his `Laptop` and `Workshop` classes to upgrade his laptop's memory. Do you think he succeeded? What is the output of this code? (Select 1 option.)

```
class Laptop {
    String memory = "1GB";
}
class Workshop {
    public static void main(String args[]) {
        Laptop life = new Laptop();
        repair(life);
        System.out.println(life.memory);
    }
    public static void repair(Laptop laptop) {
        laptop.memory = "2GB";
    }
}
```

    ◯ **a** 1 GB

    ◯ **b** 2 GB

    ◯ **c** Compilation error

    ◯ **d** Runtime exception

ME-Q43. What is the output of the following code? (Select 1 option.)

```
public class Application {
    public static void main(String... args) {
        double price = 10;
        String model;
        if (price > 10)
            model = "Smartphone";
        else if (price <= 10)
            model = "landline";
        System.out.println(model);
    }
}
```

    ◯ **a** landline

    ◯ **b** Smartphone

    ◯ **c** No output

    ◯ **d** Compilation error

ME-Q44. What is the output of the following code? (Select 1 option.)

```
class EString {
    public static void main(String args[]) {
        String eVal = "123456789";
System.out.println(eVal.substring(eVal.indexOf("2"),eVal.indexOf("0")).concat
    ("0"));
    }
}
```

- ◉ **a** 234567890
- ◉ **b** 34567890
- ◉ **c** 234456789
- ◉ **d** 3456789
- ◉ **e** Compilation error
- ◉ **f** Runtime exception

ME-Q45. Examine the following code and select the correct statements (choose 2 options):

```java
class Artist {
    Artist assistant;
}
class Studio {
    public static void main(String... args) {
        Artist a1 = new Artist();
        Artist a2 = new Artist();
        a2.assistant = a1;
        a2 = null;                          // Line 1
    }
                                            // Line 2
}
```

- ☐ **a** At least two objects are garbage collected on line 1.
- ☐ **b** At least one object is garbage collected on line 1.
- ☐ **c** No objects are garbage collected on line 1.
- ☐ **d** The number of objects that are garbage collected on line 1 is unknown.
- ☐ **e** At least two objects are eligible for garbage collection on line 2.

ME-Q46. What is the output of the following code? (Select 1 option.)

```java
class Book {
    String ISBN;
    Book(String val) {
        ISBN = val;
    }
}
class TestEquals {
    public static void main(String... args) {
        Book b1 = new Book("1234-4657");
        Book b2 = new Book("1234-4657");
        System.out.print(b1.equals(b2) +":");
        System.out.print(b1 == b2);
    }
}
```

- ◉ **a** true:false
- ◉ **b** true:true
- ◉ **c** false:true
- ◉ **d** false:false
- ◉ **e** Compilation error—there is no equals method in the class Book.

ME-Q47. Which of the following statements are correct? (Select 2 options.)

☐ **a** `StringBuilder sb1 = new StringBuilder()` will create a `StringBuilder` object with no characters, but with an initial capacity to store 16 chars.

☐ **b** `StringBuilder sb1 = new StringBuilder(5*10)` will create a `StringBuilder` object with a value 50.

☐ **c** Unlike the class `String`, the concat method in `StringBuilder` modifies the value of a `StringBuilder` object.

☐ **d** The `insert` method can be used to insert a character, number, or `String` at the start or end or at a specified position of a `StringBuilder` object.

ME-Q48. Given the following definition of the class `Animal` and the interface `Jump`, select the correct array declarations and initialization (choose 3 options):

```
interface Jump {}
class Animal implements Jump {}
```

☐ **a** `Jump eJump1[] = {null, new Animal()};`

☐ **b** `Jump[] eJump2 = new Animal()[22];`

☐ **c** `Jump[] eJump3 = new Jump[10];`

☐ **d** `Jump[] eJump4 = new Animal[87];`

☐ **e** `Jump[] eJump5 = new Jump()[12];`

ME-Q49. What is the output of the following code? (Select 1 option.)

```
import java.util.*;
class EJGArrayL {
    public static void main(String args[]) {
        ArrayList<String> seasons = new ArrayList<String>();
        seasons.add(1, "Spring"); seasons.add(2, "Summer");
        seasons.add(3, "Autumn"); seasons.add(4, "Winter");
        seasons.remove(2);

        for (String s : seasons)
            System.out.print(s + ", ");
    }
}
```

◉ **a** `Spring, Summer, Winter,`

◉ **b** `Spring, Autumn, Winter,`

◉ **c** `Autumn, Winter,`

◉ **d** Compilation error

◉ **e** Runtime exception

ME-Q50. What is the output of the following code? (Select 1 option.)

```
class EIf {
    public static void main(String args[]) {
        bool boolean = false;
        if (boolean = true)
            System.out.println("true");
```

```
        else
            System.out.println("false");
    }
}
```

   ○ **a** The class will print `true`.

   ○ **b** The class will print `false`.

   ○ **c** The class will print `true` if the `if` condition is changed to `boolean == true`.

   ○ **d** The class will print `false` if the `if` condition is changed to `boolean != true`.

   ○ **e** The class won't compile.

ME-Q51. How many `Fish` did the `Whale` (defined as follows) manage to eat? Examine the following code and select the correct statements (choose 2 options):

```
class Whale {
    public static void main(String args[]) {
        boolean hungry = false;
        while (hungry=true) {
            ++Fish.count;
        }
        System.out.println(Fish.count);
    }
}
class Fish {
    static byte count;
}
```

   ☐ **a** The code doesn't compile.

   ☐ **b** The code doesn't print a value.

   ☐ **c** The code prints `0`.

   ☐ **d** Changing `++Fish.count` to `Fish.count++` will give the same results.

ME-Q52. Given the following code, which option, if used to replace `/* INSERT CODE HERE */`, will make the code print the name of the phone with the position at which it's stored in the array phone? (Select 1 option.)

```
class Phones {
    public static void main(String args[]) {
        String phones[]= {"BlackBerry", "Android", "iPhone"};
        for (String phone : phones)
            /* REPLACE CODE HERE */
    }
}
```

   ○ **a** `System.out.println(phones.count + ":" + phone);`

   ○ **b** `System.out.println(phones.counter + ":" + phone);`

   ○ **c** `System.out.println(phones.getPosition() + ":" + phone);`

   ○ **d** `System.out.println(phones.getCtr() + ":" + phone);`

   ○ **e** `System.out.println(phones.getCount() + ":" + phone);`

   ○ **f** `System.out.println(phones.pos + ":" + phone);`

   ○ **g** None of the above

ME-Q53. Which of the following classes represent runtime exceptions in Java (select 4 options):

- ☐ **a** RuntimeException
- ☐ **b** CheckedException
- ☐ **c** NullPointerException
- ☐ **d** ArrayIndexOutOfBoundsException
- ☐ **e** CompilationException
- ☐ **f** Throwable
- ☐ **g** StackOverflowException
- ☐ **h** MemoryOutOfBoundsException
- ☐ **i** IllegalArgumentException
- ☐ **j** NumberException

ME-Q54. What is the output of the following code? (Select 1 option.)

```java
class Book {
    String ISBN;
    Book(String val) {
        ISBN = val;
    }
    public boolean equals(Object b) {
        if (b instanceof Book) {
            return ((Book)b).ISBN.equals(ISBN);
        }
        else
            return false;
    }
}

class TestEquals {
    public static void main(String args[]) {
        Book b1 = new Book("1234-4657");
        Book b2 = new Book("1234-4657");
        System.out.print(b1.equals(b2) +":");
        System.out.print(b1 == b2);
    }
}
```

- ⦿ **a** true:false
- ⦿ **b** true:true
- ⦿ **c** false:true
- ⦿ **d** false:false

ME-Q55. What is the output of the following code? (Select 1 option.)

```java
int a = 10;
for (; a <= 20; ++a) {
    if (a%3 == 0) a++; else if (a%2 == 0) a=a*2;
    System.out.println(a);
}
```

- **a** 11
  13
  15
  17
  19

- **b** 20

- **c** 11
  14
  17
  20

- **d** 40

- **e** Compilation error

ME-Q56. Given the following code, which option, if used to replace /* INSERT CODE HERE */, will define an overloaded `rideWave` method (select 1 option):

```
class Raft {
    public String rideWave() { return null; }
    //INSERT CODE HERE
}
```

- **a** `public String[] rideWave() { return null; }`
- **b** `protected void riceWave(int a) {}`
- **c** `private void rideWave(int value, String value2) {}`
- **d** `default StringBuilder rideWave(StringBuffer a) { return null; }`

ME-Q57. Given the following code, which option, if used to replace /* INSERT CODE HERE */, will correctly calculate the sum of all the even numbers in the array num and store it in variable sum? (Select 1 option.)

```
int num[] = {10, 15, 2, 17};
int sum = 0;
for (int number : num) {
    //INSERT CODE HERE
    sum += number;
}
```

- **a** `if (number % 2 == 0)`
       `continue;`

- **b** `if (number % 2 == 0)`
       `break;`

- **c** `if (number % 2 != 0)`
       `continue;`

- **d** `if (number % 2 != 0)`
       `break;`

ME-Q58. What is the output of the following code? (Select 1 option.)

```
class Op {
    public static void main(String... args) {
        int a = 0;
```

```
        int b = 100;
        if (!b++ > 100 && a++ == 10) {
            System.out.println(a+b);
        }
    }
}
```

-   a 100
-   b 101
-   c 102
-   d Code fails to compile.
-   e No output is produced.

ME-Q59. Given the following definitions of the interfaces `Movable` and `Jumpable`, the task is to declare a class `Person` that inherits both of these interfaces. Which of the following code snippets will accomplish this task? (Select 2 options.)

```
interface Movable {}
interface Jumpable {}
```

-   a
```
interface Movable {}
interface Jumpable {}
class Person implements Movable, Jumpable {}
```
-   b
```
interface Movable {}
interface Jumpable {}
class Person extends Movable, Jumpable {}
```
-   c
```
interface Movable {}
interface Jumpable {}
class Person implements Movable extends Jumpable {}
```
-   d
```
interface Movable {}
interface Jumpable implements Movable {}
class Person implements Jumpable {}
```
-   e
```
interface Movable {}
interface Jumpable extends Movable {}
class Person implements Jumpable {}
```

ME-Q60. Choose the option that meets the following specification: Create a well-encapsulated class `Pencil` with one instance variable `model`. The value of `model` should be accessible and modifiable outside `Pencil`. (Select 1 option.)

-   a
```
class Pencil {
    public String model;
}
```
-   b
```
class Pencil {
    public String model;
    public String getModel() { return model; }
    public void setModel(String val) { model = val; }
}
```

```
  ● c class Pencil {
         private String model;
         public String getModel() { return model; }
         public void setModel(String val) { model = val; }
     }

  ● d class Pencil {
         public String model;
         private String getModel() { return model; }
         private void setModel(String val) { model = val; }
     }
```

ME-Q61. What is the output of the following code? (Select 1 option.)

```java
class Phone {
    void call() {
        System.out.println("Call-Phone");
    }
}
class SmartPhone extends Phone{
    void call() {
        System.out.println("Call-SmartPhone");
    }
}
class TestPhones {
    public static void main(String[] args) {
        Phone phone = new Phone();
        Phone smartPhone = new SmartPhone();
        phone.call();
        smartPhone.call();
    }
}
```

   ● a Call-Phone
      Call-Phone

   ● b Call-Phone
      Call-SmartPhone

   ● c Call-Phone
      null

   ● d null
      Call-SmartPhone

ME-Q62. Given the following requirements, choose the best looping construct to implement them (choose 1 option):

Step 1:   Meet the director of Oracle.

Step 2:   Schedule another meeting with the director.

Step 3:   Repeat steps 1 and 2, as long as more meetings are required.

   ● a for loop
   ● b enhanced for loop
   ● c do-while loop
   ● d while loop

ME-Q63. What is the output of the following code? (Select 1 option.)

```
class Phone {
    String keyboard = "in-built";
}
class Tablet extends Phone {
    boolean playMovie = false;
}
class College2 {
    public static void main(String args[]) {
        Phone phone = new Tablet();
        System.out.println(phone.keyboard + ":" + phone.playMovie);
    }
}
```

    ◉ **a** in-built:false

    ◉ **b** in-built:true

    ◉ **c** null:false

    ◉ **d** null:true

    ◉ **e** Compilation error

ME-Q64. What is the output of the following code? (Select 1 option.)

```
public class Wall {
    public static void main(String args[]) {
        double area = 10.98;
        String color;
        if (area < 5)
            color = "red";
        else
            color = "blue";
        System.out.println(color);
    }
}
```

    ◉ **a** red

    ◉ **b** blue

    ◉ **c** No output

    ◉ **d** Compilation error

ME-Q65. What is the output of the following code? (Select 1 option.)

```
class Diary {
    int pageCount = 100;
    int getPageCount() {
        return pageCount;
    }
    void setPageCount(int val) {
        pageCount = val;
    }
}
class ClassRoom {
    public static void main(String args[]) {
```

```
            System.out.println(new Diary().getPageCount());
            new Diary().setPageCount(200);
            System.out.println(new Diary().getPageCount());
        }
    }
```

    ○ **a** 100
        200

    ○ **b** 100
        100

    ○ **c** 200
        200

    ○ **d** Code fails to compile.

ME-Q66. How many times do you think you can shop with the following code (that is, what's the output of the following code)? (Select 1 option.)

```
class Shopping {
    public static void main(String args[]) {
        boolean bankrupt = true;
        do System.out.println("enjoying shopping"); bankrupt = false;
        while (!bankrupt);
    }
}
```

    ○ **a** The code prints enjoying shopping once.
    ○ **b** The code prints enjoying shopping twice.
    ○ **c** The code prints enjoying shopping in an infinite loop.
    ○ **d** The code fails to compile.

ME-Q67. Which of the following options are valid for defining multidimensional arrays? (Choose 4 options.)

    ☐ **a** `String ejg1[][] = new String[1][2];`
    ☐ **b** `String ejg2[][] = new String[][] { {}, {} };`
    ☐ **c** `String ejg3[][] = new String[2][2];`
    ☐ **d** `String ejg4[][] = new String[][]{{null},new String[]{"a","b","c"},`
        `{new String()}};`
    ☐ **e** `String ejg5[][] = new String[][2];`
    ☐ **f** `String ejg6[][] = new String[][]{"A", "B"};`
    ☐ **g** `String ejg7[][] = new String[]{{"A"}, {"B"}};`

ME-Q68. What is the output of the following code? (Select 1 option.)

```
class Laptop {
    String memory = "1GB";
}
class Workshop {
    public static void main(String args[]) {
        Laptop life = new Laptop();
```

```
        repair(life);
        System.out.println(life.memory);
    }
    public static void repair(Laptop laptop) {
        laptop = new Laptop();
        laptop.memory = "2GB";
    }
}
```

- ⊙ **a** 1 GB
- ⊙ **b** 2 GB
- ⊙ **c** Compilation error
- ⊙ **d** Runtime exception

ME-Q69. Given the following code, which option, if used to replace /* INSERT CODE HERE */, will enable a reference variable of type Roamable to refer to an object of the Phone class? (Select 1 option.)

```
interface Roamable{}
class Phone {}
class Tablet extends Phone implements Roamable {
    //INSERT CODE HERE
}
```

- ⊙ **a** Roamable var = new Phone();
- ⊙ **b** Roamable var = (Roamable)Phone();
- ⊙ **c** Roamable var = (Roamable)new Phone();
- ⊙ **d** Because the interface Roamable and the class Phone are unrelated, a reference variable of type Roamable can't refer to an object of class Phone.

ME-Q70. Which of the following statements are incorrect about *the* main method used to start a Java application? (Select 2 options.)

- ☐ **a** A class can't define multiple main methods.
- ☐ **b** More than one class in an application can define the main method.
- ☐ **c** The main method may accept a String, a String array, or varargs (String... arg) as a method argument.
- ☐ **d** The main method shouldn't define an object of the class in which the main method itself is defined.

ME-Q71. What is the output of the following code? (Select 1 option.)

```
class Paper {
    Paper() {
        this(10);
        System.out.println("Paper:0");
    }
    Paper(int a) { System.out.println("Paper:1"); }
}
```

```
class PostIt extends Paper {}
class TestPostIt {
    public static void main(String[] args) {
        Paper paper = new PostIt();
    }
}
```

    ○   **a**   Paper:1

    ○   **b**   Paper:0

    ○   **c**   Paper:0
              Paper:1

    ○   **d**   Paper:1
              Paper:0

ME-Q72. Examine the following code and select the correct statement (choose 1 option):

```
line1> class StringBuilders {
line2>     public static void main(String... args) {
line3>         StringBuilder sb1 = new StringBuilder("eLion");
line4>         String ejg = null;
line5>         ejg = sb1.append("X").substring(sb1.indexOf("L"),
     sb1.indexOf("X"));
line6>         System.out.println(ejg);
line7>     }
line8> }
```

    ○   **a**   The code will print LionX.

    ○   **b**   The code will print Lion.

    ○   **c**   The code will print Lion if line 5 is changed to the following:

```
ejg = sb1.append("X").substring(sb1.indexOf('L'), sb1.indexOf('X'));
```

    ○   **d**   The code will compile correctly if line 4 is changed to the following:

```
StringBuilder ejg = null;
```

ME-Q73. When considered individually, which of the options is correct for the following code? (Select 1 option.)

```
interface Jumpable { void jump(); }
class Chair implements Jumpable {
    public void jump() {
        System.out.println("Chair cannot jump");
    }
}
```

    ○   **a**   The class Chair can't implement the interface Jumpable because a Chair can't define a method jump.

    ○   **b**   If the name of the interface is changed to Movable and the definition of class Chair is updated to class Chair implements Movable, class Chair will compile successfully.

   ◉ **c** If the definition of the method `jump` is removed from the definition of the class `Chair`, it will compile successfully.

   ◎ **d** If the name of the method `jump` is changed to `run` in the interface `Jumpable`, the class `Chair` will compile successfully.

ME-Q74. Given the following code, which option, if used to replace `/* INSERT CODE HERE */`, will enable the class `Jungle` to determine whether the reference variable `animal` refers to an object of the class `Lion` and print 1? (Select 1 option.)

```
class Animal{ float age; }
class Lion extends Animal { int claws;}
class Jungle {
    public static void main(String args[]) {
        Animal animal = new Lion();
        /* INSERT CODE HERE */
        System.out.println(1);
    }
}
```

   ◎ **a** `if (animal instanceof Lion)`

   ◎ **b** `if (animal instanceOf Lion)`

   ◎ **c** `if (animal == Lion)`

   ◎ **d** `if (animal = Lion)`

ME-Q75. Given that the file Test.java, which defines the following code, fails to compile, select the reasons for the compilation failure (choose 2 options):

```
class Person {
    Person(String value) {}
}
class Employee extends Person {}
class Test {
    public static void main(String args[]) {
        Employee e = new Employee();
    }
}
```

   ☐ **a** The class `Person` fails to compile.

   ☐ **b** The class `Employee` fails to compile.

   ☐ **c** The default constructor can call only a no-argument constructor of a base class.

   ☐ **d** Code that creates an object of class `Employee` in class `Test` didn't pass a `String` value to the constructor of class `Employee`.

ME-Q76. Select the correct statements. (Choose 4 options.)

   ☐ **a** Checked exceptions are subclasses of `java.lang.Throwable`.

   ☐ **b** Runtime exceptions are subclasses of `java.lang.Exception`.

   ☐ **c** Errors are subclasses of `java.lang.Throwable`.

   ☐ **d** `java.lang.Throwable` is a subclass of `java.lang.Exception`.

   ☐ **e** `java.lang.Exception` is a subclass of `java.lang.Error`.

☐ **f** Errors aren't subclasses of java.lang.Exception.

☐ **g** java.lang.Throwable is a subclass of java.lang.Error.

☐ **h** Checked exceptions are subclasses of java.lang.CheckedException.

ME-Q77. Examine the following code and select the correct statements (choose 2 options):

```
class Bottle {
    void Bottle() {}
    void Bottle(WaterBottle w) {}
}
class WaterBottle extends Bottle {}
```

☐ **a** A base class can't pass reference variables of its defined class as method parameters in constructors.

☐ **b** The class compiles successfully—a base class can use reference variables of its derived class as method parameters.

☐ **c** The class Bottle defines two overloaded constructors.

☐ **d** The class Bottle can access only one constructor.

ME-Q78. Given the following code, which option, if used to replace /* INSERT CODE HERE */, will cause the code to print 110? (Select 1 option.)

```
class Book {
    private int pages = 100;
}
class Magazine extends Book {
    private int interviews = 2;
    private int totalPages() { /* INSERT CODE HERE */ }

    public static void main(String[] args) {
        System.out.println(new Magazine().totalPages());
    }

}
```

⊙ **a** return super.pages + this.interviews*5;

⊙ **b** return this.pages + this.interviews*5;

⊙ **c** return super.pages + interviews*5;

⊙ **d** return pages + this.interviews*5;

⊙ **e** None of the above

ME-Q79. Given that the method write has been defined as follows,

```
class NoInkException extends Exception {}
class Pen{
    void write(String val) throws NoInkException {
        //.. some code
    }
    void article() {
        //INSERT CODE HERE
    }
}
```

which of the following options, when inserted at //INSERT CODE HERE, will define valid use of the method `write` in the method `article`? (Select 2 options.)

☐ **a**
```
try {
    new Pen().write("story");
}
catch (NoInkException e) {}
```

☐ **b**
```
try {
    new Pen().write("story");
}
finally {}
```

☐ **c**
```
try {
    write("story");
}
catch (Exception e) {}
```

☐ **d**
```
try {
    new Pen().write("story");
}
catch (RuntimeException e) {}
```

ME-Q80. What is the output of the following code? (Select 1 option.)

```java
class EMyMethods {
    static String name = "m1";
    void riverRafting() {
        String name = "m2";
        if (8 > 2) {
            String name = "m3";
            System.out.println(name);
        }
    }
    public static void main(String[] args) {
        EMyMethods m1 = new EMyMethods();
        m1.riverRafting();
    }
}
```

   ◎ **a** m1

   ◎ **b** m2

   ◎ **c** m3

   ◎ **d** Code fails to compile.

ME-Q81. What is the output of the following code? (Select 1 option.)

```java
class EBowl {
    public static void main(String args[]) {
        String eFood = "Corn";
        System.out.println(eFood);
        mix(eFood);
        System.out.println(eFood);
    }
```

```
    static void mix(String foodIn) {
        foodIn.concat("A");
        foodIn.replace('C', 'B');
    }
}
```

○ **a** Corn
   BornA

○ **b** Corn
   CornA

○ **c** Corn
   Born

○ **d** Corn
   Corn

ME-Q82. Which statement is true for the following code? (Select 1 option.)

```
class SwJava {
    public static void main(String args[]) {
        String[] shapes = {"Circle", "Square", "Triangle"};
        switch (shapes) {
            case "Square": System.out.println("Circle"); break;
            case "Triangle": System.out.println("Square"); break;
            case "Circle": System.out.println("Triangle"); break;
        }
    }
}
```

○ **a** The code prints `Circle`.
○ **b** The code prints `Square`.
○ **c** The code prints `Triangle`.
○ **d** The code prints

   Circle
   Square
   Triangle

○ **e** The code prints

   Triangle
   Circle
   Square

○ **f** The code fails to compile.

ME-Q83. Which of the following options include the ideal conditions for choosing to use a do-while loop over a while loop? (Select 2 options.)

☐ **a** Repeatedly display a menu to a user and accept input until the user chooses to exit the application.

☐ **b** Repeatedly allow a student to sit in the exam only if she carries her identity card.

☐ **c** Repeatedly serve food to a person until he wants no more.

☐ **d** Repeatedly allow each passenger to board an airplane if the passengers have their boarding passes.

ME-Q84. Given the following definition of the classes Person, Father, and Home, which options, if used to replace /* INSERT CODE HERE */, will cause the code to compile successfully (select 3 options):

```
class Person {}
class Father extends Person {
    public void dance() throws ClassCastException {}
}
class Home {
    public static void main(String args[]) {
        Person p = new Person();
        try {
            ((Father)p).dance();
        }
        //INSERT CODE HERE
    }
}
```

   ☐ **a** catch (NullPointerException e) {}
       catch (ClassCastException e) {}
       catch (Exception e) {}
       catch (Throwable t) {}

   ☐ **b** catch (ClassCastException e) {}
       catch (NullPointerException e) {}
       catch (Exception e) {}
       catch (Throwable t) {}

   ☐ **c** catch (ClassCastException e) {}
       catch (Exception e) {}
       catch (NullPointerException e) {}
       catch (Throwable t) {}

   ☐ **d** catch (Throwable t) {}
       catch (Exception e) {}
       catch (ClassCastException e) {}
       catch (NullPointerException e) {}

   ☐ **e** finally {}

ME-Q85. What is the output of the following code? (Select 1 option.)

```
class Camera {
    public static void main(String args[]) {
        String settings;
        while (false) {
            settings = "Adjust settings manually";
        }
        System.out.println("Camera:" + settings);
    }
}
```

   ◉ **a** The code prints Camera:null.
   ◉ **b** The code prints Camera:Adjust settings manually.
   ◉ **c** The code will print Camera:.
   ◉ **d** The code will fail to compile.

ME-Q86. The output of the class TestEJavaCourse, defined as follows, is 300:

```
class Course {
    int enrollments;
}
class TestEJavaCourse {
    public static void main(String args[]) {
        Course c1 = new Course();
        Course c2 = new Course();
        c1.enrollments = 100;
        c2.enrollments = 200;
        System.out.println(c1.enrollments + c2.enrollments);
    }
}
```

What will happen if the variable enrollments is defined as a static variable? (Select 1 option.)

   ◎ **a** No change in output. TestEJavaCourse prints 300.

   ◎ **b** Change in output. TestEJavaCourse prints 200.

   ◎ **c** Change in output. TestEJavaCourse prints 400.

   ◎ **d** The class TestEJavaCourse fails to compile.

ME-Q87. What is the output of the following code? (Select 1 option.)

```
String ejgStr[] = new String[][]{{null},new String[]{"a","b","c"},{new
    String()}}[0] ;
String ejgStr1[] = null;
String ejgStr2[] = {null};

System.out.println(ejgStr[0]);
System.out.println(ejgStr2[0]);
System.out.println(ejgStr1[0]);
```

   ◎ **a** null
       NullPointerException

   ◎ **b** null
       null
       NullPointerException

   ◎ **c** NullPointerException

   ◎ **d** null
       null
       null

ME-Q88. Examine the following code and select the correct statement (choose 1 option):

```
import java.util.*;
class Person {}
class Emp extends Person {}

class TestArrayList {
    public static void main(String[] args) {
        ArrayList<Object> list = new ArrayList<Object>();
```

```
        list.add(new String("1234"));        //LINE1
        list.add(new Person());               //LINE2
        list.add(new Emp());                  //LINE3
        list.add(new String[]{"abcd", "xyz"});//LINE4
    }
}
```

   ◎ **a** The code on line 1 won't compile.

   ◎ **b** The code on line 2 won't compile.

   ◎ **c** The code on line 3 won't compile.

   ◎ **d** The code on line 4 won't compile.

   ◎ **e** None of the above.

ME-Q89. What is the output of the following code? (Select 1 option.)

```
public class If2 {
    public static void main(String args[]) {
        int a = 10; int b = 20; boolean c = false;
        if (b > a) if (++a == 10) if (c!=true) System.out.println(1);
        else System.out.println(2); else System.out.println(3);
    }
}
```

   ◎ **a** 1

   ◎ **b** 2

   ◎ **c** 3

   ◎ **d** No output

ME-Q90. Select the incorrect statement (choose 1 option):

   ◎ **a** An enhanced `for` loop can be used to iterate through the elements of an array and `ArrayList`.

   ◎ **b** The loop counter of an enhanced `for` loop can be used to modify the current element of the array being iterated over.

   ◎ **c** do-while and `while` loops can be used to iterate through the elements of an array and `ArrayList`.

   ◎ **d** The loop counter of a regular `for` loop can be used to modify the current element of an `ArrayList` being iterated over.

8.2   *Answers to mock exam questions*

This section contains answers to all the mock exam questions in section 8.1. Also, each question is preceded by the exam objective that the question is based on.

[7.3]   Differentiate between the type of a reference and the type of an object

ME-Q1. Given the following definition of the classes `Animal`, `Lion`, and `Jumpable`, select the correct combinations of assignments of a variable (select 2 options):

```
interface Jumpable {}
class Animal {}
class Lion extends Animal implements Jumpable {}
```

    ☐ **a** `Jumpable var1 = new Jumpable();`

    ☑ **b** `Animal var2 = new Animal();`

    ☐ **c** `Lion var3 = new Animal();`

    ☐ **d** `Jumpable var4 = new Animal();`

    ☑ **e** `Jumpable var5 = new Lion();`

Answer: b, e

Explanation: Option (a) is incorrect. An `interface` can't be instantiated.

    Option (c) is incorrect. A reference variable of a derived class can't be used to refer to an object of its base class.

    Option (d) is incorrect. A reference variable of type `Jumpable` can't be used to refer to an object of the class `Animal` because `Animal` doesn't implement the interface `Jumpable`.

[1.2]   Define the structure of a Java class

ME-Q2. Which of the following statements are true? (Select 3 options.)

    ☑ **a** **A Java class can define multiple methods.**

    ☑ **b** **A Java class can define multiple variables.**

    ☐ **c** A Java class can be defined in multiple packages.

    ☑ **d** **A Java class can import multiple packages.**

    ☐ **e** A Java class can't define more than 108 constructors.

    ☐ **f** End-of-line comments can't follow `import` or `package` statements.

    ☐ **g** Multiline comments can only be defined within a method definition.

Answer: a, b, d

Explanation: Option (c) is incorrect. The same class can't be defined in multiple packages. If you try to define the same class—say, the class `Person`—in the packages `com.ejava` and `com.eoracle`, you're defining two classes with the same name but in separate packages. In this case, `com.ejava.Person` and `com.eoracle.Person` will refer to two different classes.

    Option (e) is incorrect because there is no theoretical limit on the number of constructors that can be defined by a class.

    Option (f) is incorrect because end-of-line comments can follow any line of code.

    Option (g) is incorrect because multiline comments can also be placed outside a method definition.

> [8.2] Create a try-catch block and determine how exceptions alter normal program flow

ME-Q3. Given the following code, which option, if used to replace /* INSERT CODE HERE */, will make the code print 1? (Select 1 option.)

```
try {
    String[][] names = {{"Andre", "Mike"}, null, {"Pedro"}};
    System.out.println (names[2][1].substring(0, 2));
}
catch (/*INSERT CODE HERE*/) {
    System.out.println(1);
}
```

- a IndexPositionException e
- b NullPointerException e
- **c ArrayIndexOutOfBoundsException e**
- d ArrayOutOfBoundsException e

Answer: c

Explanation: Options (a) and (d) are incorrect because the Java API doesn't define any exception classes with these names.

Here's a list of the array values that are initialized by the code in this question:

```
names[0][0] = "Andre"
names[0][1] = "Mike"
names[1] = null
names[2][0] = "Pedro"
```

Because the array position [2][1] isn't defined, any attempt to access it will throw ArrayIndexOutOfBoundsException.

An attempt to access any position of the second array—that is, names[1][0]—will throw NullPointerException because names[1] is set to null.

> [8.2] Create a try-catch block and determine how exceptions alter normal program flow

ME-Q4. What is the output of the following code? (Select 1 option.)

```
int a = 10; String name = null;
try {
    a = name.length();
    a++;
}
catch (RuntimeException e){
    ++a;
}
System.out.println(a);
```

- **a** 5
- **b** 6
- **c** 10
- ● **d** 11
- **e** 12
- **f** Runtime exception

Answer: d

Explanation: Because the variable name isn't assigned a value, the following line of code will throw NullPointerException:

```
name.length();
```

Hence, the original value of the variable a isn't modified and the control is transferred to the exception handler, which increments the value of the variable a to 11.

> **[3.5]   Use a switch statement**

ME-Q5. Given the following class definition,

```
class Student { int marks = 10; }
```

what is the output of the following code? (Select 1 option.)

```
class Result {
    public static void main(String... args) {
        Student s = new Student();
        switch (s.marks) {
            default: System.out.println("100");
            case 10: System.out.println("10");
            case 98: System.out.println("98");
        }
    }
}
```

- **a** 100
     10
     98
- ● **b** 10
     98
- **c** 100
- **d** 10

Answer: b

Explanation: The default case executes only if no matching values are found. In this case, a matching value of 10 is found and the case label prints 10. Because a break statement doesn't terminate this case label, the code execution continues and executes the remaining statements within the switch block, until a break statement terminates it or it ends.

 [7.5]   Use super and this to access objects and constructors

ME-Q6. Given the following code, which code can be used to create and initialize an object of class ColorPencil? (Select 2 options.)

```
class Pencil {}
class ColorPencil extends Pencil {
    String color;
    ColorPencil(String color) {this.color = color;}
}
```

☐ **a** ColorPencil var1 = new ColorPencil();

☐ **b** ColorPencil var2 = new ColorPencil(RED);

☑ **c** ColorPencil var3 = new ColorPencil("RED");

☑ **d** Pencil var4 = new ColorPencil("BLUE");

Answer: c, d

Explanation: Option (a) is incorrect because new ColorPencil() tries to invoke the no-argument constructor of class ColorPencil, which isn't defined in class ColorPencil.

Option (b) is incorrect because new ColorPencil(RED) tries to pass a variable RED, which isn't defined in the code.

[2.3]   Read or write to object fields

ME-Q7. What is the output of the following code? (Select 1 option.)

```
class Doctor {
    protected int age;
    protected void setAge(int val) { age = val; }
    protected int getAge() { return age; }
}
class Surgeon extends Doctor {
    Surgeon(String val) {
        specialization = val;
    }
    String specialization;
    String getSpecialization() { return specialization; }
}
class Hospital {
    public static void main(String args[]) {
        Surgeon s1 = new Surgeon("Liver");
        Surgeon s2 = new Surgeon("Heart");
        s1.age = 45;
        System.out.println(s1.age + s2.getSpecialization());
```

```
        System.out.println(s2.age + s1.getSpecialization());
    }
}
```

- ◉ **a** `45Heart`
     `0Liver`

- ○ **b** `45Liver`
     `0Heart`

- ○ **c** `45Liver`
     `45Heart`

- ○ **d** `45Heart`
     `45Heart`

- ○ **e** Class fails to compile.

Answer: a

Explanation: The constructor of the class `Surgeon` assigns the values `"Liver"` and `"Heart"` to the variable `specialization` of objects `s1` and `s2`. The variable `age` is protected in the class `Doctor`. Also, the class `Surgeon` extends the class `Doctor`. Hence, the variable `age` is accessible to reference variables `s1` and `s2`. The code assigns a value of `45` to the member variable `age` of reference variable `s1`. The variable `age` of reference variable `s2` is initialized to the default value of an `int`, which is `0`. Hence, the code prints the values mentioned in option (a).

[3.1]   Use Java operators

ME-Q8. What is the output of the following code? (Select 1 option.)

```
class RocketScience {
    public static void main(String args[]) {
        int a = 0;
        while (a == a++) {
            a++;
            System.out.println(a);
        }
    }
}
```

- ○ **a** The `while` loop won't execute; nothing will be printed.
- ○ **b** The `while` loop will execute indefinitely, printing all numbers, starting from 1.
- ○ **c** The `while` loop will execute indefinitely, printing all even numbers, starting from 0.
- ◉ **d** **The `while` loop will execute indefinitely, printing all even numbers, starting from 2.**
- ○ **e** The `while` loop will execute indefinitely, printing all odd numbers, starting from 1.
- ○ **f** The `while` loop will execute indefinitely, printing all odd numbers, starting from 3.

Answer: d

Explanation: The while loop will execute indefinitely because the condition a == a++ will always evaluate to true. The postfix unary operator will increment the value of the variable a after it's used in the comparison expression. a++ within the loop body will increment the value of a by 1. Hence, the value of a increments by 2 in a single loop.

[1.4] Import other Java packages to make them accessible in your code

ME-Q9. Given the following statements,

- com.ejava is a package
- class Person is defined in package com.ejava
- class Course is defined in package com.ejava

which of the following options correctly import the classes Person and Course in the class MyEJava? (Select 3 options.)

☑ **a** `import com.ejava.*;`
`class MyEJava {}`

☐ **b** `import com.ejava;`
`class MyEJava {}`

☑ **c** `import com.ejava.Person;`
`import com.ejava.Course;`
`class MyEJava {}`

☑ **d** `import com.ejava.Person;`
`import com.ejava.*;`
`class MyEJava {}`

Answer: a, c, d

Explanation: Option (a) is correct. The statement `import com.ejava.*;` imports all the public members of the package com.ejava in class MyEJava.

Option (b) is incorrect. Because com.ejava is a package, to import all the classes defined in this package, the package name should be followed by .*:

```
import com.ejava.*;
```

Option (c) is correct. It uses two separate import statements to import each of the classes Person and Course individually, which is correct.

Option (d) is also correct. The first import statement imports only the class Person in MyClass. But the second import statement imports both the Person and Course classes from the package com.ejava. You can import the same class more than once in a Java class with no issues. This code is correct.

In Java, the import statement makes the imported class *visible* to the Java compiler, allowing it to be referred to by the class that's importing it. In Java, the import statement doesn't embed the imported class in the target class.

[6.6] Apply access modifiers

ME-Q10. Given that the following classes `Animal` and `Forest` are defined in the same package, examine the code and select the correct statements (select 2 options):

```
line1>    class Animal {
line2>        public void printKing() {
line3>            System.out.println("Lion");
line4>        }
line5>    }

line6>    class Forest {
line7>        public static void main(String... args) {
line8>            Animal anAnimal = new Animal();
line9>            anAnimal.printKing();
line10>       }
line11>    }
```

☑ **a The class `Forest` prints `Lion`.**

☐ b If the code on line 2 is changed as follows, the class `Forest` will print `Lion`:

```
private void printKing() {
```

☑ **c If the code on line 2 is changed as follows, the class `Forest` will print `Lion`:**

```
void printKing() {
```

☐ d If the code on line 2 is changed as follows, the class `Forest` will print `Lion`:

```
default void printKing() {
```

Answer: a, c

Explanation: Option (a) is correct. The code will compile successfully and print `Lion`.

Option (b) is incorrect. The code won't compile if the access modifier of the method `printKing` is changed to `private`. `private` members of a class can't be accessed outside the class.

Option (c) is correct. The classes `Animal` and `Forest` are defined in the same package, so changing the access modifier of the method `printKing` to default access will still make it accessible in the class `Forest`. The class will compile successfully and print `Lion`.

Option (d) is incorrect. "default" isn't a valid access modifier or keyword in Java. In Java, the default accessibility is marked by the absence of any explicit access modifier. This code will fail to compile.

[6.6] Apply access modifiers

ME-Q11. Which of the following statements are true? (Select 2 options.)

☑ **a Given that you changed the access of a `public` method B, in class A, to a private method, class C that uses method B will fail to compile.**

☑ **b Given that you changed the access of a `private` method B, in class A, to a public method, none of the classes that use class A will fail to compile.**

☐ c Given that you changed the access of a `protected` method B, in class A, to a method with default access, class C from the same package as class A won't be able to access method B.

☐ d A change in the accessibility of the methods in your class never affects any other class that uses your class.

Answer: a, b

Explanation: Option (a) is correct. A `public` method is accessible to other classes. If you change the accessibility of a `public` method to a `private` method, it will no longer be accessible outside its class. Any class that uses such a method will fail to compile after this modification.

Option (b) is correct. A `private` method isn't accessible outside the class in which it's defined. In other words, a `private` method isn't known to the other classes, so it can't be accessed by other classes. If classes can't even access the private methods of other classes, it won't make a difference to them if their accessibility is changed.

Option (c) is incorrect. A method with default access can be accessed by classes defined in the same package.

Option (d) is incorrect. A change in the accessibility of the methods in your class affects other classes that use your class. If you assign a weaker accessibility to any of your methods, it may no longer be accessible to the other classes. If this happens, the other class will fail to compile.

[8.1]   Differentiate among checked exceptions, RuntimeExceptions, and Errors

ME-Q12. Which of the following statements are correct? (Select 3 options)

☐ a You may not be able to handle all the checked exceptions in your code.

☑ **b If required, you can handle all the runtime exceptions in your code.**

☑ **c You can handle an exception in your code even if you don't know its exact name.**

☑ **d A single exception handler can be used to handle all types of runtime and checked exceptions.**

☐ e You must handle all errors that can be thrown by your code.

☐ f Runtime exceptions are also known as checked exceptions.

Answer: b, c, d

Explanation: Option (a) is incorrect. If, for example, `callingMethod()` calls `calledMethod()`, which throws checked exceptions, `callingMethod()` can't ignore checked exceptions thrown by `calledMethod()`. `callingMethod()` should handle these exceptions itself or declare them to be thrown. `callingMethod()` can't ignore *any* checked exceptions thrown by `calledMethod()`. If it tries to do so, the code won't compile.

Option (b) is correct. It is indeed possible to handle all the runtime exceptions in your code.

Options (c) and (d) are correct. The superclass of all types of exceptions (checked and runtime) is class java.lang.Exception, so if you define a handler for java.lang.Exception in your code, you are able to handle all runtime and checked exceptions, and this will include any exceptions whose names you don't know.

Option (e) is incorrect. Even though errors can be caught by an exception handler, you shouldn't handle them because they're serious exceptions thrown by the JVM as a result of an error in the environment state that processes your code.

Option (f) is incorrect because runtime exceptions are also known as unchecked exceptions.

[1.3] Create executable Java applications with a main method

ME-Q13. Given the following code,

```
class MainMethod {
    public static void main(String... args) {
        System.out.println(args[0]+":"+ args[2]);
    }
}
```

what's its output if it's executed using the following command? (Select 1 option.)

```
java MainMethod 1+2 2*3 4-3 5+1
```

- ⊙ **a** java:1+2
- ⊙ **b** java:3
- ⊙ **c** MainMethod:2*3
- ⊙ **d** MainMethod:6
- ⊙ **e** 1+2:2*3
- ⊙ **f** 3:3
- ⊙ **g** 6
- ⦿ **h** 1+2:4-3
- ⊙ **i** 31
- ⊙ **j** 4

Answer: h

Explanation: This question tests you on multiple points:

- *The arguments that are passed on to the main method*—The keyword java and the name of the class (MainMethod) aren't passed as arguments to the main method. The arguments following the class name are passed to the main method. In this case, four method arguments are passed to the main method, as follows:

```
args[0]: 1+2
args[1]: 2*3
```

```
args[2]: 4-3
args[3]: 5+1
```

- *The type of the arguments that are passed to the main method*—The `main` method accepts arguments of type `String`. All the numeric expressions—1+2, 2*3, 5+1 and 4-3—are passed as literal `String` values. These won't be evaluated when you try to print their values. Hence, `args[0]` won't be printed as 3. It will be printed as 1+2.

- *+ operations with `String` array elements*—Because the array passed to the `main` method contains all the `String` values, using the + operand with its individual values will concatenate its values. It won't add the values, if they are numeric expressions. Hence, `"1+2"+"4-3"` won't evaluate to 31 or 4.

[2.2] Differentiate between object reference variables and primitive variables

ME-Q14. What is the output of the following code? (Select 1 option.)

```java
class Person {
    int age;
    float height;
    boolean result;
    String name;
}
public class EJava {
    public static void main(String arguments[]) {
        Person person = new Person();
        System.out.println(person.name + person.height + person.result
                                    + person.age);
    }
}
```

- ● **a null0.0false0**
- ○ b null0false0
- ○ c null0.0ffalse0
- ○ d 0.0false0
- ○ e 0false0
- ○ f 0.0ffalse0
- ○ g null0.0true0
- ○ h 0true0
- ○ i 0.0ftrue0

Answer: a

Explanation: The instance variables of a class are all assigned default values if no explicit value is assigned to them. Here are the default values of the primitive data types and the objects:

```
char -> \u0000
byte, short, int -> 0
```

```
long -> 0L
float-> 0.0f
double -> 0.0d
boolean -> false
objects -> null
```

▟▟ **[7.4]** Determine when casting is necessary

ME-Q15. Given the following code, which option, if used to replace /* INSERT CODE HERE */, will make the code print the value of the variable pagesPerMin? (Select 1 option.)

```
class Printer {
    int inkLevel;
}
class LaserPrinter extends Printer {
    int pagesPerMin;
    public static void main(String args[]) {
        Printer myPrinter = new LaserPrinter();
        System.out.println(/* INSERT CODE HERE */);
    }
}
```

○ a (LaserPrinter)myPrinter.pagesPerMin

○ b myPrinter.pagesPerMin

○ c LaserPrinter.myPrinter.pagesPerMin

◉ **d ((LaserPrinter)myPrinter).pagesPerMin**

Answer: d

Explanation: Option (a) is incorrect because (LaserPrinter) tries to cast myPrinter.pagesPerMin to LaserPrinter, which is incorrect. This code won't compile.

Option (b) is incorrect. The type of reference variable myPrinter is Printer. myPrinter refers to an object of the class LaserPrinter, which extends the class Printer. A reference variable of the base class can't access the variables and methods defined in its subclass without an explicit cast.

Option (c) is incorrect. LaserPrinter.myPrinter treats LaserPrinter as a variable, although no variable with this name exists in the question's code. This code fails to compile.

▟▟ **[8.3]** Describe what exceptions are used for in Java

ME-Q16. Which statements describe the use of exception handling in Java? (Select 2 options.)

☑ **a Exception handling can prevent an application from crashing or producing incorrect outputs or incorrect input values.**

☐ b Exception handlers can't define an alternative flow of action in the event of an exception.

☑ **c Exception handlers enable a programmer to define separate code blocks for handling different types of exceptions.**

☐ d Exception handlers help to define well-encapsulated classes.

☐ e Exception handlers help with efficient inheritance.

Answer: a, c

Explanation: Option (b) is incorrect. One of the main purposes of an exception handler is to define an alternative flow of action.

Options (d) and (e) are incorrect. Definitions of exception handlers, well-encapsulated classes, and efficient inheritance aren't related in behavior as stated by these options.

[2.2] Differentiate between object reference variables and primitive variables

ME-Q17. Which statements are true for reference and primitive variables? (Select 3 options.)

☐ a The names of the reference variables are limited to a length of 256 characters.

☑ **b There is no limit on the length of the names of primitive variables.**

☑ **c Multiple reference variables may refer to exactly the same object in memory.**

☐ d Values stored by primitive and reference variables can be compared for equality by using the equals operator (==) or by using the method `equals`.

☑ **e A primitive variable can't refer to an object and vice versa.**

Answer: b, c, e

Explanation: Option (a) is incorrect. Theoretically, there is no limit on the number of characters that can be used to define the name of a primitive variable or object reference.

Option (d) is incorrect. Unlike object references, primitive variables can be compared for equality by using the equals operator (==) only.

Option (e) is correct. A primitive variable can never refer to an object and vice versa.

[2.1] Declare and initialize variables

ME-Q18. What is the output of the following code? (Select 1 option.)

```
public class Handset {
    public static void main(String... args) {
        double price;
        String model;
        System.out.println(model + price);
    }
}
```

○ **a** null0

○ **b** null0.0

○ **c** 0

⊚ **d** 0.0

◉ **e** **Compilation error**

Answer: e

Explanation: The local variables (variables that are declared within a method) aren't initialized with their default values. If you try to print the value of a local variable before initializing it, the code won't compile.

[3.1]   Use Java operators

ME-Q19. What is the output of the following code? (Select 1 option.)

```java
public class Sales {
    public static void main(String args[]) {
        int salesPhone = 1;
        System.out.println(salesPhone++ + ++salesPhone +
                                                ++salesPhone);
    }
}
```

⊚ **a** 5

⊚ **b** 6

◉ **c** 8

⊚ **d** 9

Answer: c

Explanation: Understanding the following rules will enable you to answer this question correctly:

- An arithmetic expression is evaluated from left to right.
- When an expression uses the unary increment operator (++) in postfix notation, its value increments just *after* its original value is used in an expression.
- When an expression uses the unary increment operator (++) in prefix notation, its value increments just *before* its value is used in an expression.

The initial value of the variable salesPhone is 1. Let's evaluate the result of the arithmetic expression salesPhone++ + ++salesPhone + ++salesPhone step by step:

1 The first occurrence of salesPhone uses ++ in postfix notation, so its value is used in the expression *before* it is incremented by 1. This means that the expression evaluates to

```
1 + ++salesPhone + ++salesPhone
```

2 Note that the previous usage of ++ in postfix increments has already incremented the value of salesPhone to 2. The second occurrence of salesPhone uses ++ in prefix notation, so its value is used in the expression *after* it is incremented by 1, to 3. This means that the expression evaluates to

```
1 + 3 + ++salesPhone
```

3 The third occurrence of salesPhone again uses ++ in prefix notation, so its value is used in the expression *after* it is incremented by 1, to 4. This means that the expression evaluates to

```
1 + 3 + 4
```

The previous expression evaluates to 8.

[1.2] Define the structure of a Java class

ME-Q20. Which of the following options defines the correct structure of a Java class? (Select 1 option.)

- **a** `package com.ejava.guru;`
  `package com.ejava.oracle;`
  `class MyClass { }`

- **b** `import com.ejava.guru.*;`
  `import com.ejava.oracle.*;`
  `package com.ejava;`
  `class MyClass { }`

- **c** `class MyClass {`
  `        import com.ejava.guru.*;`
  `}`

- **d** `class MyClass {`
  `        int abc;`
  `}`

Answer: d

Explanation: Option (a) is incorrect. A class can't define more than one package statement.

Option (b) is incorrect. Though a class can import multiple packages in a class, the package statement must be placed before the import statement.

Option (c) is incorrect. A class can't define an import statement within its class body. The import statement appears before the class body.

Option (d) is correct. In the absence of any package information, this class becomes part of the default package.

[3.2] Use parentheses to override operator precedence

ME-Q21. What is the output of the following code? (Select 1 option.)

```
class OpPre {
    public static void main(String... args) {
        int x = 10;
        int y = 20;
        int z = 30;
```

```
        if (x+y%z > (x+(-y)*(-z))) {
            System.out.println(x + y + z);
        }
    }
}
```

- ⊙ **a** 60
- ⊙ **b** 59
- ⊙ **c** 61
- ⦿ **d No output.**
- ⊙ **e** The code fails to compile.

Answer: d

Explanation: x+y%z evaluates to 30; (x+(y%z)) and (x+(-y)*(-z)) evaluate to 610. The if condition returns false and the line of code that prints the sum of x, y, and z doesn't execute. Hence, the code doesn't provide any output.

  [1.1]   Define the scope of variables

ME-Q22. Select the most appropriate definition of the variable name and the line number on which it should be declared so that the following code compiles successfully (choose 1 option):

```
class EJava {
    // LINE 1
    public EJava() {
        System.out.println(name);
    }
    void calc() {
        // LINE 2
        if (8 > 2) {
            System.out.println(name);
        }
    }
    public static void main(String... args) {
        // LINE 3
        System.out.println(name);
    }
}
```

- ⦿ **a Define static String name; on line 1.**
- ⊙ **b** Define String name; on line 1.
- ⊙ **c** Define String name; on line 2.
- ⊙ **d** Define String name; on line 3.

Answer: a

Explanation: The variable name must be accessible in the instance method calc, the class constructor, and the static method main. A non-static variable can't be accessed by a static method. Hence, the only appropriate option is to define a static variable name that can be accessed by all—the constructor of class EJava, and methods calc and main.

[2.4]   Explain an object's life cycle

ME-Q23. Examine the following code and select the correct statement (choose 1 option):

```
line1>    class Emp {
line2>        Emp mgr = new Emp();
line3>    }
line4>    class Office {
line5>        public static void main(String args[]) {
line6>            Emp e = null;
line7>            e = new Emp();
line8>            e = null;
line9>        }
line10>   }
```

    ◎ **a** The object referred to by object e is eligible for garbage collection on line 8.

    ◎ **b** The object referred to by object e is eligible for garbage collection on line 9.

    ◎ **c** The object referred to by object e isn't eligible for garbage collection because its member variable mgr isn't set to null.

    ◉ **d The code throws a runtime exception and the code execution never reaches line 8 or 9.**

Answer: d

Explanation: The code throws java.lang.StackOverflowError at runtime. Line 7 creates an instance of class Emp. Creation of an object of the class Emp requires the creation of an instance variable mgr and its initialization with an object of the same class. As you see, the Emp object creation calls itself recursively, resulting in java.lang .StackOverflowError.

[6.1]   Create methods with arguments and return values

ME-Q24. Which of the following is the correct declaration of a method that accepts two String arguments and an int argument and doesn't return any value? (Select 2 options.)

    ☑ **a void myMethod(String str1, int str2, String str3)**

    ☐ **b** myMethod(String val1, int val2, String val3)

    ☐ **c** void myMethod(String str1, str2, int a)

    ☐ **d** void myMethod(String val1, val2, int val3)

    ☑ **e void myMethod(int str2, String str3, String str1)**

Answer: a, e

Explanation: The placement of the type of method parameters and the name of the method parameters doesn't matter. You can accept two `String` variables and then an `int` variable or a `String` variable followed by `int` and again a `String`. The name of an `int` variable can be `str2`. As long as the names are valid identifiers, any name is acceptable. The return type of the method should be `void` to specify that the method doesn't return any value.

Option (b) is incorrect. It won't compile because the method signature doesn't include a return type.

Options (c) and (d) are incorrect. The method signatures of these methods don't define data types for all their method parameters.

[4.1]　Declare, instantiate, initialize, and use a one-dimensional array

ME-Q25. Which of the following will compile successfully? (Select 3 options.)

☑ **a** `int eArr1[] = {10, 23, 10, 2};`
☑ **b** `int[] eArr2 = new int[10];`
☑ **c** `int[] eArr3 = new int[] {};`
☐ **d** `int[] eArr4 = new int[10] {};`
☐ **e** `int eArr5[] = new int[2] {10, 20};`

Answer: a, b, c

Explanation: Option (d) is incorrect because it defines the size of the array while using {}, which isn't allowed. Both of the following lines of code are correct:

```
int[] eArr4 = new int[10];
int[] eArr4 = new int[]{};
```

Option (e) is incorrect because it's invalid to specify the size of the array within the square brackets when you're declaring, instantiating, and initializing an array in a single line of code.

[6.1]　Create methods with arguments and return values

ME-Q26. Assume that Oracle has asked you to create a method that returns the concatenated value of two `String` objects. Which of the following methods do you think can accomplish this job? (Select 2 options.)

☐ **a**
```
public String add(String 1, String 2) {
    return str1 + str2;
}
```

☑ **b**
```
private String add(String s1, String s2) {
    return s1.concat(s2);
}
```

```
☐ c protected String add(String value1, String value2) {
       return value2.append(value2);
   }
☑ d String subtract(String first, String second) {
       return first.concat(second.substring(0));
   }
```

Answer: b, d

Explanation: Option (a) is incorrect. This method defines method parameters with invalid identifier names. Identifiers can't start with a digit.

Option (b) is correct. The method requirements don't talk about the access modifier of the required method. It can have any accessibility.

Option (c) is incorrect because the class `String` doesn't define any append method.

Option (d) is correct. Even though the name of the method—`subtract`—isn't an appropriate name for a method that tries to concatenate two values, it does accomplish the required job.

[1.4] Import other Java packages to make them accessible in your code

---

ME-Q27. In Java, the class `String` is defined in the package `java.lang`, and this package is automatically imported in all the Java classes. Given this statement, which of the following options represents the correct definition of class `EJava`, which can define a variable of class `String`? (Choose 2 options.)

```
☐ a import java.lang;
     class EJava {
         String guru;
     }
☐ b import java.lang.String.*;
     class EJava {
         String guru;
     }
☑ c class EJava {
         String guru;
     }
☑ d import java.lang.String;
     import java.lang.String;
     class EJava {
         String guru;
     }
```

Answer: c, d

Explanation: Options (a) and (b) are incorrect. The code in both these options won't compile because they use incorrect `import` statement. The following line of code will import all the classes from package `java.lang` (including class `String`):

```
import java.lang.*;
```

You can use the following `import` statement to import just the class `String`:

```
import java.lang.String;
```

Option (c) is correct. The class `EJava` can create variables of the class `String` because the class `java.lang.String` is automatically imported in all the Java classes. Hence, it's available to `EJava`, even if this class doesn't import it explicitly.

Option (d) is correct. It doesn't make a difference if you import the same class more than once in your code.

[6.3]   Create an overloaded method

ME-Q28. Given the following definitions of the class `ChemistryBook`, select the statements that are correct individually (choose 2 options):

```
import java.util.ArrayList;
class ChemistryBook {
    public void read() {}                       //METHOD1
    public String read() { return null; }       //METHOD2
    ArrayList read(int a) { return null; }       //METHOD3
}
```

☐ **a** Methods marked with `//METHOD1` and `//METHOD2` are correctly overloaded methods.

☑ **b** **Methods marked with `//METHOD2` and `//METHOD3` are correctly overloaded methods.**

☑ **c** **Methods marked with `//METHOD1` and `//METHOD3` are correctly overloaded methods.**

☐ **d** All the methods—methods marked with `//METHOD1`, `//METHOD2`, and `//METHOD3`— are correctly overloaded methods.

Answer: b, c

Explanation: Options (a) and (d) are incorrect because the methods `read` marked with `//METHOD1` and `//METHOD2` only differ in their return types, `void` and `String`. Overloaded methods can't be defined with only a change in their return types; hence, these methods don't qualify as correctly overloaded methods.

Note that the presence of methods marked with `//METHOD1` and `//METHOD2` together will cause a compilation error.

[6.4]   Differentiate between default and user-defined constructors

ME-Q29. Given the following definition of the class `Home`, select the correct statements (choose 4 options):

```
class Home {
    String name;
```

```
        int rooms;
        Home() {}
}
```

☐ **a** The class `Home` will be provided a default constructor.

☑ **b** **The class `Home` won't be provided a default constructor.**

☑ **c** **A default constructor can't coexist with overloaded constructors.**

☑ **d** **A default constructor doesn't accept any method parameters.**

☑ **e** **After compilation, the class `Home` has only a no-argument constructor.**

☐ **f** After compilation, the class `Home` has two constructors: a no-argument constructor and a default constructor.

☐ **g** When an object of class `Home` is created, its variables `name` and `rooms` are not assigned any default values.

Answer: b, c, d, e

Explanation: Option (b) is correct. The class `Home` doesn't contain a default constructor. A default constructor is generated by Java when the user doesn't define any constructor. In this case, the class `Home` does define a constructor.

Option (c) is correct. A default constructor is generated only in the absence of a constructor. Hence, it can't coexist with other constructors.

Option (d) is correct. The default constructor doesn't accept any method parameters. It initializes the instance variables of a class to their default values.

Option (e) is correct and (f) is incorrect. No default constructor will be generated for class `Home` because `Home` already defines a no-argument constructor. A no-argument constructor is a constructor that defines no method parameters. After compilation, class `Home` has only one constructor that doesn't accept any method parameters.

Option (g) is incorrect. If you don't assign explicit values to instance variables of a class, they are initialized to their default values.

[5.5] Use break and continue

ME-Q30. Given the following code, which option, if used to replace /* INSERT CODE HERE */, will make the code print numbers that are completely divisible by 14? (Select 1 option.)

```
for (int ctr = 2; ctr <= 30; ++ctr) {
    if (ctr % 7 != 0)
        //INSERT CODE HERE
    if (ctr % 14 == 0)
        System.out.println(ctr);
}
```

◉ **a** `continue;`

◯ **b** `exit;`

◯ **c** `break;`

◯ **d** `end;`

Answer: a

Explanation: Options (b) and (d) are incorrect because exit and end aren't valid statements in Java.

Option (c) is incorrect. Using break will terminate the for loop during the first iteration of the for loop so that no output is printed.

[8.5]   Recognize common exception classes and categories

ME-Q31. Ideally, which of the following should never be handled by an exception handler? (Select 2 options.)

- ☑ a `StackOverflowError`
- ☑ b `OutOfMemoryError`
- ☐ c `ArrayIndexOutOfBoundError`
- ☐ d `ClassLoadingException`
- ☐ e `CompilationError`
- ☐ f `OutOfStorageError`

Answer: a, b

Explanation: Options (c), (d), (e), and (f) are incorrect because the Java API doesn't define these exception or error classes.

Options (a) and (b) are correct. You should never try to handle these errors in your code because `StackOverflowError` and `OutOfMemoryError` are serious errors.

[2.1]   Declare and initialize variables

ME-Q32. What is the output of the following code? (Select 1 option.)

```
public class MyCalendar {
    public static void main(String arguments[]) {
        Season season1 = new Season();
        season1.name = "Spring";

        Season season2 = new Season();
        season2.name = "Autumn";

        season1 = season2;
        System.out.println(season1.name);
        System.out.println(season2.name);
    }
}
class Season {
    String name;
}
```

- ◎ a `String`
     `Autumn`

○ **b** Spring
   String

◉ **c** **Autumn**
   Autumn

○ **d** Autumn
   String

Answer: c

Explanation: Multiple variable references can point to the same object. The following lines of code define a reference variable `season1`, which refers to an object that has the value of its instance variable (`name`) set to `Spring`:

```
Season season1 = new Season();
season1.name = "Spring";
```

The following lines of code define a reference variable `season2`, which refers to an object that has the value of its instance variable (`name`) set to `Autumn`:

```
Season season2 = new Season();
season2.name = "Autumn";
```

The following line of code reinitializes the reference variable `season1` and assigns it to the object referred to by the variable `season2`:

```
season1 = season2;
```

Now the variable `season1` refers to the object that is also referred to by the variable `season2`. Both of these variables refer to the same object—the one that has the value of the instance variable set to `Autumn`. Hence, the output of the previous code is as follows:

```
Autumn
Autumn
```

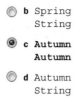 [6.5]   Create and overload constructors

ME-Q33. What is true about the following code? (Select 1 option.)

```
class Shoe {}
class Boot extends Shoe {}
class ShoeFactory {
    ShoeFactory(Boot val) {
        System.out.println("boot");
    }
    ShoeFactory(Shoe val) {
        System.out.println("shoe");
    }
}
```

◉ **a** **The class `ShoeFactory` has a total of two overloaded constructors.**

○ **b** The class `ShoeFactory` has three overloaded constructors, two user-defined constructors, and one default constructor.

  ◉ **c** The class `ShoeFactory` will fail to compile.

  ◉ **d** The addition of the following constructor will increment the number of constructors of the class `ShoeFactory` to 3:

```
private ShoeFactory (Shoe arg) {}
```

Answer: a

Explanation: Java accepts changes in the objects of base-derived classes as the sole criterion to define overloaded constructors and methods.

Option (b) is incorrect because Java doesn't generate a default constructor for a class that has already defined a constructor.

Option (c) is incorrect. All classes defined for this example compile successfully.

Option (d) is incorrect. The class `ShoeFactory` already defines a constructor that accepts a method argument of type `Shoe`. You can't overload a constructor with a mere change in its access modifier.

[7.5]   Use super and this to access objects and constructors

ME-Q34. Given the following definitions of the classes `ColorPencil` and `TestColor`, which option, if used to replace /* INSERT CODE HERE */, will initialize the instance variable `color` of reference variable `myPencil` with the `String` literal value `"RED"`? (Select 1 option.)

```
class ColorPencil {
    String color;
    ColorPencil(String color) {
        //INSERT CODE HERE
    }
}
class TestColor {
    ColorPencil myPencil = new ColorPencil("RED");
}
```

  ◉ **a** `this.color = color;`

  ◉ **b** `color = color;`

  ◉ **c** `color = RED;`

  ◉ **d** `this.color = RED;`

Answer: a

Explanation: Option (b) is incorrect. This line of code will assign the value of the method parameter to itself. The constructor of the class `ColorPencil` defines a method parameter with the same name as its instance variable, `color`. To access an instance variable in the constructor, it must be prefixed with the keyword `this`, or it will refer to the method parameter `color`.

Options (c) and (d) are incorrect. They try to access the value of variable `RED`, which isn't defined in the code.

[2.3] Read or write to object fields

ME-Q35. What is the output of the following code? (Select 1 option.)

```
class EJavaCourse {
    String courseName = "Java";
}
class University {
    public static void main(String args[]) {
        EJavaCourse courses[] = { new EJavaCourse(), new EJavaCourse() };
        courses[0].courseName = "OCA";
        for (EJavaCourse c : courses) c = new EJavaCourse();
        for (EJavaCourse c : courses) System.out.println(c.courseName);
    }
}
```

- **a** Java
     Java

- **b** **OCA**
     Java

- **c** OCA
     OCA

- **d** None of the above.

Answer: b

Explanation: This question tests you on multiple concepts: how to read from and write to object fields, how to use arrays, the enhanced `for` loop, and assigning a value to a loop variable.

The code defines an array of the class `EJavaCourse` with two elements. The default value of the variable `courseName`—Java—is assigned to each of these two elements. `courses[0].courseName = "OCA"` changes the value `courseName`, for the object stored at array position 0. `c = new EJavaCourse()` assigns a new object to the loop variable c. This assignment doesn't reassign new objects to the array reference variables. `System.out.println(c.courseName)` prints the name of the `courseName` of the objects initially stored by the array, using the loop variable c.

The loop variable in the enhanced `for` loop refers to a copy of the array or list element. If you modify the state of the loop variable, the modified object state will be reflected in the array. But if you assign a new object to the loop variable, it won't be reflected in the list or the array that's being iterated. You can compare this behavior of the enhanced `for` loop variable with the behavior of object references passed as arguments to a method.

[2.5] Call methods on objects

ME-Q36. Given the following code, which option, if used to replace /* INSERT CODE HERE */, will make the code print the value of the variable `screenSize`? (Select 1 option.)

```
class Tablet {
    float screenSize = 7.0f;
    float getScreenSize() {
        return screenSize;
    }
    void setScreenSize(float val) {
        screenSize = val;
    }
}

class DemoTabs {
    public static void main(String args[]) {
        Tablet tab = new Tablet();
        System.out.println(/* INSERT CODE HERE */);

    }
}
```

- ◉ **a tab.screenSize**
- ◎ b tab->getScreensize()
- ◎ c tab::getScreen()
- ◎ d tab:screenSize

Answer: a

Explanation: Only the dot operator (.) can be used to access an instance variable or a method of an object in Java. The rest of the operators (->, ::, and :) used in options (b), (c), and (d), respectively, aren't valid operators in Java.

[7.1]   Implement inheritance

ME-Q37. Given the following definitions of the class Person and the interface Movable, the task is to declare a class Emp that inherits from the class Person and implements the interface Movable. Select the correct option to accomplish this task (choose 1 option):

```
class Person {}
interface Movable {}
```

- ◎ a class Emp implements Person extends Movable{}
- ◎ b class Emp implements Person, Movable{}
- ◉ **c class Emp extends Person implements Movable{}**
- ◎ d class Emp extends Person, Movable{}

Answer: c

Explanation: Options (a) and (b) are incorrect because a class can't use the keyword implements to inherit a class.

Option (d) is incorrect because a class can't use the keyword extends to inherit an interface.

[7.2] Develop code that demonstrates the use of polymorphism

ME-Q38. What is the output of the following code? (Select 1 option.)

```
class Phone {
    static void call() {
        System.out.println("Call-Phone");
    }
}
class SmartPhone extends Phone{
    static void call() {
        System.out.println("Call-SmartPhone");
    }
}
class TestPhones {
    public static void main(String... args) {
        Phone phone = new Phone();
        Phone smartPhone = new SmartPhone();
        phone.call();
        smartPhone.call();
    }
}
```

- ⊙ **a** `Call-Phone`
       `Call-Phone`
- ○ **b** `Call-Phone`
       `Call-SmartPhone`
- ○ **c** `Call-Phone`
       `null`
- ○ **d** `null`
       `Call-SmartPhone`

Answer: a

Explanation: Invocation of a `static` method is tied to the type of the reference variable and doesn't depend on the type of the object that's assigned to the reference variable. The `static` method belongs to a class, not to its objects. Re-examine the following code:

```
Phone smartPhone = new SmartPhone();
smartPhone.call();
```

In the preceding code, the type of the reference variable `smartPhone` is `Phone`. Because `call` is a `static` method, `smartPhone.call()` calls the method `call` defined in the class `Phone`.

 [8.1] Differentiate among checked exceptions, RuntimeExceptions, and Errors

ME-Q39. Given the following code, which of the following statements are true? (Select 3 options.)

```
class MyExam {
    void question() {
        try {
            question();
        }
        catch (StackOverflowError e) {
            System.out.println("caught");
        }
    }
    public static void main(String args[]) {
        new MyExam().question();
    }
}
```

☑ **a** **The code will print `caught`.**

☐ **b** The code won't print `caught`.

☑ **c** **The code would print `caught` if `StackOverflowError` were a runtime exception.**

☑ **d** **The code would print `caught` if `StackOverflowError` were a checked exception.**

☐ **e** The code will print `caught` if `question()` throws exception `NullPointer-Exception`.

Answer: a, c, d

Explanation: Option (a) is correct. The control will be transferred to the exception handler for `StackOverflowError` when it's encountered. Hence it will print `caught`.

Options (c) and (d) are correct. Exception handlers execute when the corresponding checked or runtime exceptions are thrown.

Option (e) is incorrect. An exception handler for class `StackOverflow` can't handle exceptions of class `NullPointerException` because `NullPointerException` is not a superclass of `StackOverflowError`.

[6.7]   Apply encapsulation principles to a class

ME-Q40. A class `Student` is defined as follows:

```
public class Student {
    private String fName;
    private String lName;
    public Student(String first, String last) {
        fName = first; lName = last;
    }
    public String getName() { return fName + lName; }
}
```

The creator of the class later changes the method `getName` as follows:

```
public String getName() {
    return fName + " " + lName;
}
```

What are the implications of this change? (Select 2 options.)

☐ **a** The classes that were using the class Student will fail to compile.

☑ **b** **The classes that were using the class Student will work without any compilation issues.**

☑ **c** **The class Student is an example of a well-encapsulated class.**

☐ **d** The class Student exposes its instance variable outside the class.

Answer: b, c

Explanation: This is an example of a well-encapsulated class. There is no change in the method signature of method getName after it's modified. Hence, none of the code that uses this class and method will face any compilation issues. Its instance variables (fName and lName) aren't exposed outside the class. They are available only via a public method: getName.

 [6.2] Apply the static keyword to methods and fields

ME-Q41. What is the output of the following code? (Select 1 option.)

```
class ColorPack {
    int shadeCount = 12;
    static int getShadeCount() {
        return shadeCount;
    }
}
class Artist {
    public static void main(String args[]) {
        ColorPack pack1 = new ColorPack();
        System.out.println(pack1.getShadeCount());
    }
}
```

⚪ **a** 10

⚪ **b** 12

⚪ **c** No output

⚫ **d** **Compilation error**

Answer: d

Explanation: A static method can't access non-static instance variables of a class. Hence, the class ColorPack fails to compile.

[6.8] Determine the effect upon object references and primitive values when they are passed into methods that change the values

ME-Q42. Paul defined his Laptop and Workshop classes to upgrade his laptop's memory. Do you think he succeeded? What is the output of this code? (Select 1 option.)

```
class Laptop {
    String memory = "1GB";
}
class Workshop {
    public static void main(String args[]) {
        Laptop life = new Laptop();
        repair(life);
        System.out.println(life.memory);
    }
    public static void repair(Laptop laptop) {
        laptop.memory = "2GB";
    }
}
```

- ○ **a** 1 GB
- ◉ **b** 2 GB
- ○ **c** Compilation error
- ○ **d** Runtime exception

Answer: b

Explanation: The method `repair` defined in this example modifies the state of the method parameter `laptop` that is passed to it. It does so by modifying the value of the instance variable `memory`.

When a method modifies the state of an object reference variable that is passed to it, the changes made are visible in the calling method. The method `repair` makes changes to the state of the method parameter `laptop`; these changes are visible in the method `main`. Hence, the method `main` prints the value of `life.memory` as 2 GB.

 [2.1]   Declare and initialize variables

ME-Q43. What is the output of the following code? (Select 1 option.)

```
public class Application {
    public static void main(String... args) {
        double price = 10;
        String model;
        if (price > 10)
            model = "Smartphone";
        else if (price <= 10)
            model = "landline";
        System.out.println(model);
    }
}
```

- ○ **a** landline
- ○ **b** Smartphone
- ○ **c** No output
- ◉ **d** **Compilation error**

Answer: d

Explanation: The local variables aren't initialized with default values. Code that tries to print the value of an uninitialized local variable fails to compile.

In this code, the local variable `model` is only declared, not initialized. The initialization of the variable `model` is placed within the `if` and `else-if` constructs. If you initialize a variable within an `if` or `else-if` construct, the compiler can't be sure whether these conditions will evaluate to `true`, resulting in no initialization of the local variable. Because there is no `else` at the bottom and the compiler can't tell whether the `if` and `else-if` are mutually exclusive, the code won't compile.

If you remove the condition `if (price <= 10)` from the preceding code, the code will compile successfully:

```
public class Application {
    public static void main(String... args) {
        double price = 10;
        String model;
        if (price > 10)
            model = "Smartphone";
        else
            model = "landline";
        System.out.println(model);
    }
}
```

In this code, the compiler can be sure about the initialization of the local variable `model`.

[2.7] Create and manipulate strings

ME-Q44. What is the output of the following code? (Select 1 option.)

```
class EString {
    public static void main(String args[]) {
        String eVal = "123456789";

        System.out.println(eVal.substring(eVal.indexOf("2"),eVal.indexOf("0")).c
        oncat("0"));
    }
}
```

- ○ **a** 234567890
- ○ **b** 34567890
- ○ **c** 234456789
- ○ **d** 3456789
- ○ **e** Compilation error
- ◉ **f Runtime exception**

Answer: f

Explanation: When multiple methods are chained on a single code statement, the methods execute from left to right, not from right to left. `eVal.indexOf("0")` returns a negative value because, as you can see, the String eVal doesn't contain the digit 0. Hence, eVal.substring is passed a negative end value, which results in a RuntimeException.

[2.4] Explain an object's life cycle

ME-Q45. Examine the following code and select the correct statements (choose 2 options):

```
class Artist {
    Artist assistant;
}
class Studio {
    public static void main(String... args) {
        Artist a1 = new Artist();
        Artist a2 = new Artist();
        a2.assistant = a1;
        a2 = null;          // Line 1
    }
      // Line 2
}
```

- ☐ **a** At least two objects are garbage collected on line 1.
- ☐ **b** At least one object is garbage collected on line 1.
- ☐ **c** No objects are garbage collected on line 1
- ☑ **d** **The number of objects that are garbage collected on line 1 is unknown.**
- ☑ **e** **At least two objects are eligible for garbage collection on line 2.**

Answer: d, e

Explanation: Options (a), (b), and (c) are incorrect.

When an object reference is marked as null, the object is marked for garbage collection. But you can't be sure exactly when a garbage collector will kick in to garbage collect the objects. A garbage collector is a low-priority thread, and its exact execution time will depend on the OS. The OS will start this thread to claim unused space if it needs to claim unused space. You can be sure only about the number of objects that are eligible for garbage collection. You can never be sure about which objects have been garbage collected, so any statement that asserts that a particular number of objects *have* been garbage collected is incorrect.

Option (d) is correct. As mentioned previously, the exact number of objects garbage collected at any point in time can't be determined.

Option (e) is correct. If you marked this option incorrect, think again. The question wants you to select the correct statements, and this is a correct statement. You may argue that at least two objects were already made eligible for garbage collection at line 1, and you are correct. But because nothing changes on line 2, at least two objects are still eligible for garbage collection.

[3.3] Test equality between strings and other objects using == and equals()

ME-Q46. What is the output of the following code? (Select 1 option.)

```
class Book {
    String ISBN;
    Book(String val) {
        ISBN = val;
    }
}
class TestEquals {
    public static void main(String... args) {
        Book b1 = new Book("1234-4657");
        Book b2 = new Book("1234-4657");
        System.out.print(b1.equals(b2) +":");
        System.out.print(b1 == b2);
    }
}
```

- a true:false
- b true:true
- c false:true
- **d false:false**
- e Compilation error—there is no equals method in the class Book.

Answer: d

Explanation: The comparison operator determines whether the reference variables refer to the same object. Because the reference variables b1 and b2 refer to different objects, b1==b2 prints false.

The method equals is a public method defined in the class java.lang.Object. Because the class Object is the superclass for all the classes in Java, the method equals is inherited by all classes. Hence, the code compiles successfully. The default implementation of method equals in the base class compares the object references and returns true if both the reference variables refer to the same object and false otherwise.

Because the class Book doesn't override this method, the method equals in the base class Object is called for b1.equals(b2), which returns false. Hence, the code prints:

```
false:false
```

[2.6] Manipulate data using the StringBuilder class and its methods

ME-Q47. Which of the following statements are correct? (Select 2 options.)

- ☑ a **StringBuilder sb1 = new StringBuilder()** will create a **StringBuilder** object with no characters, but with an initial capacity to store 16 chars.

- ☐ **b** `StringBuilder sb1 = new StringBuilder(5*10)` will create a `StringBuilder` object with a value `50`.
- ☐ **c** Unlike the class `String`, the `concat` method in `StringBuilder` modifies the value of a `StringBuilder` object.
- ☑ **d** **The insert method can be used to insert a character, number, or String at the start or end or a specified position of a StringBuilder.**

Answer: a, d

Explanation: There is no `concat` method in the `StringBuilder` class. It defines a whole army of `append` methods (overloaded methods) to add data at the end to a `String-Builder` object.

new `StringBuilder(50)` creates a `StringBuilder` object with no characters, but with an initial capacity to store 50 chars.

[4.1]   Declare, instantiate, initialize, and use a one-dimensional array

ME-Q48. Given the following definition of the class `Animal` and the interface `Jump`, select the correct array declarations and initialization (choose 3 options):

```
interface Jump {}
class Animal implements Jump {}
```

- ☑ **a** `Jump eJump1[] = {null, new Animal()};`
- ☐ **b** `Jump[] eJump2 = new Animal()[22];`
- ☑ **c** `Jump[] eJump3 = new Jump[10];`
- ☑ **d** `Jump[] eJump4 = new Animal[87];`
- ☐ **e** `Jump[] eJump5 = new Jump()[12];`

Answer: a, c, d

Explanation: Option (b) is incorrect because the right side of the expression is trying to create a single object of the class `Animal` by using round brackets, `()`. At the same time, it's also using the square brackets, `[]`, to define an array. This combination is invalid.

Option (e) is incorrect. Apart from using an invalid syntax to initialize an array (as mentioned previously), it also tries to create objects of the interface `Jump`. Objects of interfaces can't be created.

[4.3]   Declare and use an ArrayList

ME-Q49. What is the output of the following code? (Select 1 option.)

```
import java.util.*;
class EJGArrayL {
    public static void main(String args[]) {
```

```
        ArrayList<String> seasons = new ArrayList<>();
        seasons.add(1, "Spring"); seasons.add(2, "Summer");
        seasons.add(3, "Autumn"); seasons.add(4, "Winter");
        seasons.remove(2);

        for (String s : seasons)
            System.out.print(s + ", ");
    }
}
```

- ○ **a** Spring, Summer, Winter,
- ○ **b** Spring, Autumn, Winter,
- ○ **c** Autumn, Winter,
- ○ **d** Compilation error
- ◉ **e Runtime exception**

Answer: e

Explanation: The code throws a runtime exception, IndexOutOfBoundsException, because the ArrayList is trying to insert its first element at position 0. Before the first call to the method add, the size of the ArrayList seasons is 0. Because season's first element is stored at position 0, a call to store its first element at position 1 will throw a RuntimeException. The elements of an ArrayList can't be added to a higher position if lower positions are available.

[3.4]   Create if and if-else constructs

ME-Q50. What is the output of the following code? (Select 1 option.)

```
class EIf {
    public static void main(String args[]) {
        bool boolean = false;
        if (boolean = true)
            System.out.println("true");
        else
            System.out.println("false");
    }
}
```

- ○ **a** The class will print true.
- ○ **b** The class will print false.
- ○ **c** The class will print true if the if condition is changed to boolean == true.
- ○ **d** The class will print false if the if condition is changed to boolean != true.
- ◉ **e The class won't compile.**

Answer: e

Explanation: This question tries to trick you on two points. First, there is no data type bool in Java. Second, the name of an identifier can't be the same as a reserved word. The code tries to define an identifier of type bool with the name boolean.

[5.1]   Create and use while loops

ME-Q51. How many `Fish` did the `Whale` (defined as follows) manage to eat? Examine the following code and select the correct statements (choose 2 options):

```
class Whale {
    public static void main(String args[]) {
        boolean hungry = false;
        while (hungry=true) {
            ++Fish.count;
        }
        System.out.println(Fish.count);
    }
}
class Fish {
    static byte count;
}
```

- ☐ **a** The code doesn't compile.
- ☑ **b The code doesn't print a value.**
- ☐ **c** The code prints 0.
- ☑ **d Changing `++Fish.count` to `Fish.count++` will give the same results.**

Answer: b, d

Explanation: Option (a) is incorrect because the code compiles successfully.

Option (c) is incorrect. This question tries to trick you by comparing a `boolean` value when it's assigning a `boolean` value in the `while` construct. Because the `while` loop assigns a value `true` to the variable `hungry`, it will always return `true`, incrementing the value of the variable `count`, and thus getting stuck in an infinite loop.

Option (d) is correct because when the unary increment operator (`++`) is not part of an expression, postfix and prefix notation behave in exactly the same manner.

[5.2]   Create and use for loops including the enhanced for loop

ME-Q52. Given the following code, which option, if used to replace `/* INSERT CODE HERE */`, will make the code print the name of the phone with the position at which it's stored in the array phone? (Select 1 option.)

```
class Phones {
    public static void main(String args[]) {
        String phones[]= {"BlackBerry", "Android", "iPhone"};
        for (String phone : phones)
            /* REPLACE CODE HERE */
    }
}
```

- ○ **a** `System.out.println(phones.count + ":" + phone);`
- ○ **b** `System.out.println(phones.counter + ":" + phone);`

    ◎ **c** `System.out.println(phones.getPosition() + ":" + phone);`

    ◎ **d** `System.out.println(phones.getCtr() + ":" + phone);`

    ◎ **e** `System.out.println(phones.getCount() + ":" + phone);`

    ◎ **f** `System.out.println(phones.pos + ":" + phone);`

    ◉ **g None of the above**

Answer: g

Explanation: The enhanced `for` loop doesn't provide you with a variable to access the position of the array that it's being used to iterate over. This facility comes with the regular `for` loop.

 [8.5] Recognize common exception classes and categories

ME-Q53. Which of the following classes represent runtime exceptions in Java (select 4 options):

    ☑ **a `RuntimeException`**

    ☐ **b** `CheckedException`

    ☑ **c `NullPointerException`**

    ☑ **d `ArrayIndexOutOfBoundsException`**

    ☐ **e** `CompilationException`

    ☐ **f** `Throwable`

    ☐ **g** `StackOverflowException`

    ☐ **h** `MemoryOutOfBoundsException`

    ☑ **i `IllegalArgumentException`**

    ☐ **j** `NumberException`

Answer: a, c, d, i

Explanation: Options (b), (e), (g), (h), and (j) are incorrect because there are no exception classes by these names in the Java API.

    Option (f) is incorrect because `Throwable` is the base class of all the exceptions—checked and runtime—and errors in Java. `RuntimeExceptions` is a subset of this class.

 [3.3] Test equality between strings and other objects using `==` and `equals()`

ME-Q54. What is the output of the following code? (Select 1 option.)

```
class Book {
    String ISBN;
    Book(String val) {
        ISBN = val;
    }
```

```
    public boolean equals(Object b) {
        if (b instanceof Book) {
            return ((Book)b).ISBN.equals(ISBN);
        }
        else
            return false;
    }
}

class TestEquals {
    public static void main(String args[]) {
        Book b1 = new Book("1234-4657");
        Book b2 = new Book("1234-4657");
        System.out.print(b1.equals(b2) +":");
        System.out.print(b1 == b2);
    }
}
```

◉ **a** **true:false**

◉ **b** true:true

◉ **c** false:true

◉ **d** false:false

Answer: a

Explanation: The comparison operator determines whether the reference variables refer to the same object. Because the reference variables b1 and b2 refer to different objects, b1==b2 prints false.

The method equals is a public method defined in the class java.lang.Object. Because the class Object is the superclass for all the classes in Java, equals is inherited by all classes. The default implementation of equals in the base class compares the object references and returns true if both the reference variables refer to the same object, and false otherwise. If a class has overridden this method, it returns a boolean value depending on the logic defined in this class. The class Book overrides the equals method and returns true if the Book object defines the same ISBN value as the Book object being compared to. Because the ISBN object value of both the variables b1 and b2 is the same, b1.equals(b2) returns true.

⌶   [5.2] Create and use for loops including the enhanced for loop

ME-Q55. What is the output of the following code? (Select 1 option.)

```
int a = 10;
for (; a <= 20; ++a) {
    if (a%3 == 0) a++; else if (a%2 == 0) a=a*2;
    System.out.println(a);
}
```

○ **a** 11
     13
     15
     17
     19

◉ **b** 20

○ **c** 11
     14
     17
     20

○ **d** 40

○ **e** Compilation error

Answer: b

Explanation: This question requires multiple skills: understanding the declaration of a for loop, use of operators, and use of the if-else construct.

The for loop is correctly defined in the code. The for loop in this code doesn't use its variable initialization block; it starts with ; to mark the absence of its variable initialization block. The code for the if construct is deliberately incorrect, because you may encounter similar code in the exam.

For the first iteration of the for loop, the value of the variable a is 10. Because a <= 20 evaluates to true, control moves on to the execution of the if construct. This if construct can be indented properly as follows:

```
if (a%3 == 0)
    a++;
else if (a%2 == 0)
    a=a*2;
```

(a%3 == 0) evaluates to false and (a%2 == 0) evaluates to true, so a value of 20 (a*2) is assigned to a. The subsequent line prints the value of a as 20.

The increment part of the loop statement, (++a), increments the value of variable a to 21. For the next loop iteration, its condition evaluates to false (a <= 20), and the loop terminates.

[6.3]   Create an overloaded method

ME-Q56. Given the following code, which option, if used to replace /* INSERT CODE HERE */, will define an overloaded rideWave method (select 1 option):

```
class Raft {
    public String rideWave() { return null; }
    //INSERT CODE HERE
}
```

○ **a** public String[] rideWave() { return null; }

○ **b** protected void riceWave(int a) {}

    ◉ **c** `private void rideWave(int value, String value2) {}`

    ◎ **d** `default StringBuilder rideWave (StringBuffer a) { return null; }`

Answer: c

Explanation: Option (a) is incorrect. Making a change in the return value of a method doesn't define a valid overloaded method.

    Option (b) is incorrect. The name of the method in this option is `riceWave` and not `rideWave`. Overloaded methods should have the same method name.

    Option (d) is incorrect. `default` isn't a valid access modifier. The default modifier is marked by the absence of an access modifier.

[5.5]   Use break and continue

ME-Q57. Given the following code, which option, if used to replace `/* INSERT CODE HERE */`, will correctly calculate the sum of all the even numbers in the array `num` and store it in variable `sum`? (Select 1 option.)

```
int num[] = {10, 15, 2, 17};
int sum = 0;
for (int number : num) {
    //INSERT CODE HERE
    sum += number;
}
```

    ◎ **a** `if (number % 2 == 0)`
              `continue;`

    ◎ **b** `if (number % 2 == 0)`
              `break;`

    ◉ **c** `if (number % 2 != 0)`
              `continue;`

    ◎ **d** `if (number % 2 != 0)`
              `break;`

Answer: c

Explanation: To find the sum of the even numbers, you first need to determine whether a number is an even number. Then you need to add the even numbers to the variable `sum`.

    Option (c) determines whether the array element is completely divisible by 2. If it isn't, it skips the remaining statements in the `for` loop by using the `continue` statement, which starts execution of the `for` loop with the next array element. If the array element is completely divisible by 2, `continue` doesn't execute, and the array number is added to the variable `sum`.

[3.1] Use Java operators

ME-Q58. What is the output of the following code? (Select 1 option.)

```
class Op {
    public static void main(String... args) {
        int a = 0;
        int b = 100;
        if (!b++ > 100 && a++ == 10) {
            System.out.println(a+b);
        }
    }
}
```

   ◉ **a** 100
   ◉ **b** 101
   ◉ **c** 102
   ⦿ **d Code fails to compile.**
   ◉ **e** No output is produced.

Answer: d

Explanation: Although it may seem that the negation unary operator (!) is being applied to the expression b++ > 100, it's actually being applied to the variable b of type int. Because a unary negation operator (!) can't be applied to a variable of type int, the code fails to compile. The correct if condition would be as follows:

```
if (!(b++ > 100) && a++ == 10) {
```

[7.1] Implement inheritance

ME-Q59. Given the following definitions of the interfaces Movable and Jumpable, the task is to declare a class Person that inherits both of these interfaces. Which of the following code snippets will accomplish this task? (Select 2 options.)

```
interface Movable {}
interface Jumpable {}
```

   ☑ **a interface Movable {}**
       interface Jumpable {}
       class Person implements Movable, Jumpable {}

   ☐ **b** interface Movable {}
       interface Jumpable {}
       class Person extends Movable, Jumpable {}

   ☐ **c** interface Movable {}
       interface Jumpable {}
       class Person implements Movable extends Jumpable {}

☐ **d** `interface Movable {}`
   `interface Jumpable implements Movable {}`
   `class Person implements Jumpable {}`

☑ **e** `interface Movable {}`
   `interface Jumpable extends Movable {}`
   `class Person implements Jumpable {}`

Answer: a, e

Explanation: Option (b) is incorrect because the right keyword for a `class` to inherit interfaces is `implements` and not `extends`.

Option (c) is incorrect because a class can't use the keyword `extends` to inherit interfaces.

Option (d) is incorrect because an interface should use the keyword `extends` to inherit another interface.

[6.7]   Apply encapsulation principles to a class

ME-Q60. Choose the options that meets the following specification: Create a well-encapsulated class `Pencil` with one instance variable `model`. The value of `model` should be accessible and modifiable outside `Pencil`. (Select 1 option.)

○ **a** `class Pencil {`
     `public String model;`
   `}`

○ **b** `class Pencil {`
     `public String model;`
     `public String getModel() { return model; }`
     `public void setModel(String val) { model = val; }`
   `}`

◉ **c** `class Pencil {`
     `private String model;`
     `public String getModel() { return model; }`
     `public void setModel(String val) { model = val; }`
   `}`

○ **d** `class Pencil {`
     `public String model;`
     `private String getModel() { return model; }`
     `private void setModel(String val) { model = val; }`
   `}`

Answer: c

Explanation: A well-encapsulated class's instance variables shouldn't be directly accessible outside the class. It should be accessible via non-`private` getter and setter methods.

[7.2] Develop code that demonstrates the use of polymorphism

ME-Q61. What is the output of the following code? (Select 1 option.)

```
class Phone {
    void call() {
        System.out.println("Call-Phone");
    }
}
class SmartPhone extends Phone{
    void call() {
        System.out.println("Call-SmartPhone");
    }
}
class TestPhones {
    public static void main(String[] args) {
        Phone phone = new Phone();
        Phone smartPhone = new SmartPhone();
        phone.call();
        smartPhone.call();
    }
}
```

○ **a** Call-Phone
    Call-Phone

◉ **b** **Call-Phone**
    Call-SmartPhone

○ **c** Call-Phone
    null

○ **d** null
    Call-SmartPhone

Answer: b

Explanation: The method call is defined in the base class Phone. This method call is inherited and overridden by the derived class SmartPhone. The type of both reference variables, phone and smartphone, is Phone. But the reference variable phone refers to an object of the class Phone, and the variable smartPhone refers to an object of the class SmartPhone. When the method call is called on the reference variable smart-Phone, it calls the method call defined in the class SmartPhone, because a call to an overridden method is resolved at runtime and is based on the type of the object on which a method is called.

[5.4] Compare loop constructs

ME-Q62. Given the following requirements, choose the best looping construct to implement them (choose 1 option):

Step 1:   Meet the director of Oracle.

Step 2:   Schedule another meeting with the director.

Step 3:   Repeat 1 and 2, as long as more meetings are required.

    ○ **a** `for` loop

    ○ **b** enhanced `for` loop

    ◉ **c** `do-while` **loop**

    ○ **d** `while` loop

Answer: c

Explanation: The question asks you to choose the best looping construct. The condition requires meeting the director at least once, without checking any other condition. This requirement is best implemented using a `do-while` loop.

    A regular `for` loop and `while` loop will check the condition of whether a meeting is required before the first meeting. This condition doesn't match with the requirements. An enhanced `for` loop is normally used to iterate through elements of a collection. We don't have any collection to iterate through here.

[7.3]   Differentiate between the type of a reference and the type of an object

ME-Q63. What is the output of the following code? (Select 1 option.)

```
class Phone {
    String keyboard = "in-built";
}
class Tablet extends Phone {
    boolean playMovie = false;
}
class College2 {
    public static void main(String args[]) {
        Phone phone = new Tablet();
        System.out.println(phone.keyboard + ":" + phone.playMovie);
    }
}
```

    ○ **a** `in-built:false`

    ○ **b** `in-built:true`

    ○ **c** `null:false`

    ○ **d** `null:true`

    ◉ **e** **Compilation error**

Answer: e

Explanation: This code won't compile. The object reference variable, `phone`, of type `Phone`, can be used to refer to an object of its derived type—`Tablet`. But variables of a base class can't access variables and methods of its derived classes without an explicit cast to the object of the derived class. So `phone` can access `keyboard`, but not `playMovie`.

[2.1] Declare and initialize variables

ME-Q64. What is the output of the following code? (Select 1 option.)

```
public class Wall {
    public static void main(String args[]) {
        double area = 10.98;
        String color;
        if (area < 5)
            color = "red";
        else
            color = "blue";
        System.out.println(color);
    }
}
```

- ⊙ **a** red
- ◉ **b** **blue**
- ⊙ **c** No output
- ⊙ **d** Compilation error

Answer: b

Explanation: In this piece of code, the local variable will always be initialized. It's initialized using the if-else construct. One of these constructs (if or else) is sure to execute, initializing the local variable color with a value. Hence, there are no issues with the initialization of the variable color. The code will execute successfully, printing blue.

[2.5] Call methods on objects

ME-Q65. What is the output of the following code? (Select 1 option.)

```
class Diary {
    int pageCount = 100;
    int getPageCount() {
        return pageCount;
    }
    void setPageCount(int val) {
        pageCount = val;
    }
}
class ClassRoom {
    public static void main(String args[]) {
        System.out.println(new Diary().getPageCount());
        new Diary().setPageCount(200);
        System.out.println(new Diary().getPageCount());
    }
}
```

○ **a** 100
    200

◉ **b** 100
    100

○ **c** 200
    200

○ **d** Code fails to compile.

Answer: b

Explanation: The constructor of a class creates an object of the class in which it's defined and returns the created object. This returned object can be assigned to a reference variable. In case the returned object isn't assigned to any reference variable, none of the variables or methods of this object can be accessed again. This is what happens in class `ClassRoom`. All calls to the methods `getPageCount` and `setPageCount` in the example operate on unrelated objects.

[5.3] Create and use do-while loops

ME-Q66. How many times do you think you can shop with the following code (that is, what's the output of the following code)? (Select 1 option.)

```
class Shopping {
    public static void main(String args[]) {
        boolean bankrupt = true;
        do System.out.println("enjoying shopping"); bankrupt = false;
        while (!bankrupt);
    }
}
```

○ **a** The code prints `enjoying shopping` once.

○ **b** The code prints `enjoying shopping` twice.

○ **c** The code prints `enjoying shopping` in an infinite loop.

◉ **d** **The code fails to compile.**

Answer: d

Explanation: The code fails to compile because it's trying to stuff two lines of code between the `do` and `while` statements without using curly braces.

[4.2] Declare, instantiate, initialize, and use a multidimensional array

ME-Q67. Which of the following options are valid for defining multidimensional arrays? (Choose 4 options.)

☑ **a** `String ejg1[][] = new String[1][2];`

☑ **b** `String ejg2[][] = new String[][] { {}, {} };`

☑ **c** `String ejg3[][] = new String[2][2];`

☑ **d** `String ejg4 [] [] = new String[] []{{null},new String[]{"a","b","c"},`
   `{new String()}};`

☐ **e** `String ejg5 [] [] = new String[] [2];`

☐ **f** `String ejg6 [] [] = new String[] []{"A", "B"};`

☐ **g** `String ejg7 [] [] = new String[]{{"A"}, {"B"}};`

Answer: a, b, c, d

Explanation: Options (a), (b), (c), and (d) define multidimensional arrays correctly.

Option (e) is incorrect because the size in the first pair of square brackets is missing.

Option (f) is incorrect. The correct code must use an additional pair of {} on the right side, as follows:

```
String ejg6[] [] = new String[] []{{"A"}, {"B"}};
```

Option (g) is incorrect. The correct code must use an additional pair of [] on the right side as follows:

```
String ejg7[] [] = new String[] []{{"A"}, {"B"}};
```

 [6.8] Determine the effect upon object references and primitive values when they are passed into methods that change the values

ME-Q68. What is the output of the following code? (Select 1 option.)

```
class Laptop {
    String memory = "1GB";
}
class Workshop {
    public static void main(String args[]) {
        Laptop life = new Laptop();
        repair(life);
        System.out.println(life.memory);
    }
    public static void repair(Laptop laptop) {
        laptop = new Laptop();
        laptop.memory = "2GB";
    }
}
```

◉ **a** 1 GB

◎ **b** 2 GB

◎ **c** Compilation error

◎ **d** Runtime exception

Answer: a

Explanation: The method `repair` defined in this example assigns a new object to the method parameter `laptop` that is passed to it. Then it modifies the state of this new assigned object by assigning 1 GB to its instance variable, `memory`.

When a method reassigns an object reference variable that is passed to it, the changes made to its state aren't visible in the calling method. This is because the changes are made to a new object and not to the one that was initially passed to this method. The method `repair` assigns a new object to the reference variable `laptop` that is passed to it and then modifies its state. Hence, the changes made to the state of the method parameter `laptop` aren't visible in method `main`, and it prints the value of `life.memory` as 1 GB.

[7.4]   Determine when casting is necessary

ME-Q69. Given the following code, which option, if used to replace `/* INSERT CODE HERE */`, will enable a reference variable of type `Roamable` to refer to an object of the Phone class? (Select 1 option.)

```
interface Roamable{}
class Phone {}
class Tablet extends Phone implements Roamable {
    //INSERT CODE HERE
}
```

- ○ **a** `Roamable var = new Phone();`
- ○ **b** `Roamable var = (Roamable)Phone();`
- ◉ **c** `Roamable var = (Roamable)new Phone();`
- ○ **d** Because interface `Roamable` and class `Phone` are unrelated, a reference variable of type `Roamable` can't refer to an object of class `Phone`.

Answer: c

Explanation: Option (a) is incorrect. Without explicit casting, a reference variable of type `Roamable` can't refer to an object of the class `Phone`.

Option (b) is incorrect because this is an invalid line of code that will fail to compile.

Option (d) is incorrect because a reference variable of type `Roamable` can refer to an object of the class `Phone` with an explicit cast.

Note that although option (c) will compile, it will throw a `ClassCastException` if it is executed.

[1.3]   Create executable Java applications with a main method

ME-Q70. Which of the following statements is incorrect about *the* main method used to start a Java application? (Select 2 options.)

- ☐ **a** A class can't define multiple `main` methods.
- ☐ **b** More than one class in an application can define the `main` method.
- ☑ **c** **The main method may accept a `String`, a `String` array, or varargs (`String...` arg) as a method argument.**
- ☑ **d** **The main method shouldn't define an object of the class in which the main method itself is defined.**

Answer: c, d

Explanation: Option (a) is a true statement. Even though you can define multiple methods with the name main in a class, you can define only one main method to start a Java application. This question specifically asks you about the main method used to start a Java application.

Option (b) is a true statement. Multiple classes in an application may define the main method.

Option (c) is a false statement. The main method must accept either a String array or varargs (String... arg) as a method argument. It can't accept a String object.

Option (d) is a false statement. There are no limitations on the types of the objects that this method can create. This includes the object of the class in which the main method is defined.

[7.5]   Use super and this to access objects and constructors

ME Q71. What is the output of the following code? (Select 1 option.)

```
class Paper {
    Paper() {
        this(10);
        System.out.println("Paper:0");
    }
    Paper(int a) { System.out.println("Paper:1"); }
}
class PostIt extends Paper {}
class TestPostIt {
    public static void main(String[] args) {
        Paper paper = new PostIt();
    }
}
```

   ⦿ **a** Paper:1

   ⦿ **b** Paper:0

   ⦿ **c** Paper:0
       Paper:1

   ◉ **d Paper:1**
       Paper:0

Answer: d

Explanation: new PostIt() creates an object of the class PostIt by calling its compiler-provided no-argument constructor. The no-argument constructor of class PostIt calls its base class no-argument constructor, which calls the other constructor that accepts one int method argument. The constructor that accepts an int argument prints Paper:1 and then returns the control to the no-argument constructor. The no-argument constructor then prints Paper:0.

[2.6] Manipulate data using the StringBuilder class and its methods

ME-Q72. Examine the following code and select the correct statement (choose 1 option):

```
line1> class StringBuilders {
line2>    public static void main(String... args) {
line3>        StringBuilder sb1 = new StringBuilder("eLion");
line4>        String ejg = null;
line5>        ejg = sb1.append("X").substring(sb1.indexOf("L"),
    sb1.indexOf("X"));
line6>        System.out.println(ejg);
line7>    }
line8> }
```

- ⊙ **a** The code will print `LionX`.
- ⦿ **b** **The code will print `Lion`.**
- ⊙ **c** The code will print `Lion` if line 5 is changed to the following:

    ```
    ejg = sb1.append("X").substring(sb1.indexOf('L'), sb1.indexOf('X'));
    ```

- ⊙ **d** The code will compile correctly if line 4 is changed to the following:

    ```
    StringBuilder ejg = null;
    ```

Answer: b

Explanation: Option (a) is incorrect and option (b) is correct. The `substring` method doesn't include the character at the end position in the result that it returns. Hence, the code prints `Lion`.

Option (c) is incorrect. If line 5 is changed as suggested in this option, the code won't compile. You can't pass a `char` to `StringBuilder`'s method `indexOf`; it accepts `String`.

Option (d) is incorrect because there are no compilation issues with the code.

[7.6] Use abstract classes and interfaces

ME-Q73. When considered individually, which of the options is correct for the following code? (Select 1 option.)

```
interface Jumpable { void jump(); }
class Chair implements Jumpable {
    public void jump() {
        System.out.println("Chair cannot jump");
    }
}
```

- ⊙ **a** The class `Chair` can't implement the interface `Jumpable` because a `Chair` can't define a method `jump`.
- ⦿ **b** **If the name of the interface is changed to `Movable` and definition of class `Chair` is updated to `class Chair implements Movable`, class `Chair` will compile successfully.**

    ◉ **c** If the definition of the method `jump` is removed from the definition of the class `Chair`, it will compile successfully.

    ◉ **d** If the name of the method `jump` is changed to `run` in the interface `Jumpable`, the class `Chair` will compile successfully.

Answer: b

Explanation: Option (a) is incorrect. The name of the interface or class doesn't matter when it comes to whether a class can implement an interface. If a class implements an interface, it should implement all of the methods defined by the interface.

    Option (c) is incorrect. If the definition of the method `jump` is removed from the class `Chair`, it will no longer compile. Because `Chair` implements the interface `Jumpable`, it should implement all of the methods defined in the interface `Jumpable`.

    Option (d) is incorrect. If the name of the method `jump` is changed to `run` in the interface `Jumpable`, the class `Chair` should implement this method to compile successfully.

[7.4]   Determine when casting is necessary

ME-Q74. Given the following code, which option, if used to replace /* INSERT CODE HERE */, will enable the class `Jungle` to determine whether the reference variable `animal` refers to an object of the class `Lion` and print 1? (Select 1 option.)

```
class Animal{ float age; }
class Lion extends Animal { int claws;}
class Jungle {
    public static void main(String args[]) {
        Animal animal = new Lion();
        /* INSERT CODE HERE */
            System.out.println(1);
    }
}
```

    ◉ **a** `if (animal instanceof Lion)`
    ◉ **b** `if (animal instanceOf Lion)`
    ◉ **c** `if (animal == Lion)`
    ◉ **d** `if (animal = Lion)`

Answer: a

Explanation: Option (b) is incorrect because the correct operator name is `instanceof` and not `instanceOf` (note the capitalized O).

    Options (c) and (d) are incorrect. Neither of these lines of code will compile because they are trying to compare and assign a class name to a variable, which isn't allowed.

⊞ [6.4] Differentiate between default and user-defined constructors

ME-Q75. Given that the file Test.java, which defines the following code, fails to compile, select the reasons for the compilation failure (choose 2 options):

```
class Person {
    Person(String value) {}
}
class Employee extends Person {}
class Test {
    public static void main(String args[]) {
        Employee e = new Employee();
    }
}
```

☐ **a** The class `Person` fails to compile.

☑ **b** The class `Employee` fails to compile.

☑ **c** The default constructor can call only no-argument constructor of a base class.

☐ **d** Code that creates an object of class `Employee` in class `Test` didn't pass a `String` value to the constructor of class `Employee`.

Answer: b, c

Explanation: The class `Employee` doesn't compile, so class `Test` can't use a variable of type `Employee`, and it fails to compile.

While trying to compile the class `Employee`, the Java compiler generates a default constructor for it, which looks like the following:

```
Employee() {
    super();
}
```

Note that a derived class constructor must always call a base class constructor. When Java generates the previous default constructor for the class `Employee`, it fails to compile because the base class doesn't have a no-argument constructor. The default constructor that's generated by Java can only define a call to a no-argument constructor in the base class. It can't call any other base class constructor.

⊞ [8.1] Differentiate among checked exceptions, RuntimeExceptions, and Errors

ME-Q76. Select the correct statements. (Choose 4 options.)

☑ **a** Checked exceptions are subclasses of `java.lang.Throwable`.

☑ **b** Runtime exceptions are subclasses of `java.lang.Exception`.

☑ **c** Errors are subclasses of `java.lang.Throwable`.

☐ **d** `java.lang.Throwable` is a subclass of `java.lang.Exception`.

☐ **e** `java.lang.Exception` is a subclass of `java.lang.Error`.

☑ **f Errors aren't subclasses of `java.lang.Exception`.**

☐ **g** `java.lang.Throwable` is a subclass of `java.lang.Error`.

☐ **h** Checked exceptions are subclasses of `java.lang.CheckedException`.

Answer: a, b, c, f

Explanation: Option (d) is incorrect because `java.lang.Exception` is a subclass of `java.lang.Throwable`.

Option (e) is incorrect because the class `java.lang.Exception` isn't a subclass of `java.lang.Error`. Both of these classes subclass `java.lang.Throwable`.

Option (g) is incorrect because `java.lang.Error` is a subclass of `java.lang.Throwable`.

Option (h) is incorrect because the Java API doesn't define any class `CheckedException` in package `java.lang`.

 [6.5]   Create and overload constructors

ME-Q77. Examine the following code and select the correct statements (choose 2 options):

```
class Bottle {
    void Bottle() {}
    void Bottle(WaterBottle w) {}
}
class WaterBottle extends Bottle {}
```

☐ **a** A base class can't pass reference variables of its defined class, as method parameters in constructors.

☑ **b The class compiles successfully—a base class can use reference variables of its derived class as method parameters.**

☐ **c** The class `Bottle` defines two overloaded constructors.

☑ **d The class `Bottle` can access only one constructor.**

Answer: b, d

Explanation: A base class can use reference variables and objects of its derived classes. Note that the methods defined in the class `Bottle` aren't constructors but regular methods with the name `Bottle`. The return type of a constructor isn't `void`.

[7.5]   Use super and this to access objects and constructors

ME-Q78. Given the following code, which option, if used to replace /* INSERT CODE HERE */, will cause the code to print 110? (Select 1 option.)

```
class Book {
    private int pages = 100;
}
```

```
class Magazine extends Book {
    private int interviews = 2;
    private int totalPages() { /* INSERT CODE HERE */ }

    public static void main(String[] args) {
        System.out.println(new Magazine().totalPages());
    }

}
```

- ○ **a** `return super.pages + this.interviews*5;`
- ○ **b** `return this.pages + this.interviews*5;`
- ○ **c** `return super.pages + interviews*5;`
- ○ **d** `return pages + this.interviews*5;`
- ● **e** **None of the above**

Answer: e

Explanation: The variable pages has private access in the class Book, and it can't be accessed from outside this class.

[8.4]   Invoke a method that throws an exception

ME-Q79. Given that the method write has been defined as follows,

```
class NoInkException extends Exception {}
class Pen{
    void write(String val) throws NoInkException {
        //.. some code
    }
    void article() {
        //INSERT CODE HERE
    }
}
```

which of the following options, when inserted at //INSERT CODE HERE, will define valid use of the method write in the method article? (Select 2 options.)

- ☑ **a**
```
try {
        new Pen().write("story");
    }
    catch (NoInkException e) {}
```
- ☐ **b**
```
try {
        new Pen().write("story");
    }
    finally {}
```
- ☑ **c**
```
try {
        write("story");
    }
    catch (Exception e) {}
```

```
  d try {
        new Pen().write("story");
    }
    catch (RuntimeException e) {}
```

Answer: a, c

Explanation: Because NoInkException extends the class Exception and not Runtime-Exception, NoInkException is a checked exception. When you call a method that throws a checked exception, you can either handle it using a try-catch block or declare it to be thrown in your method signature.

Option (a) is correct because a call to the method write is enclosed within a try block. The try block is followed by a catch block, which defines a handler for the exception NoInkException.

Option (b) is incorrect. The call to the method write is enclosed within a try block, followed by a finally block. The finally block is not used to handle an exception.

Option (c) is correct. Because NoInkException is a subclass of Exception, an exception handler for the class Exception can handle the exception NoInkException as well.

Option (d) is incorrect. This option defines an exception handler for the class RuntimeException. Because NoInkException is not a subclass of RuntimeException, this code won't handle NoInkException.

[1.1]   Define the scope of variables

ME-Q80. What is the output of the following code? (Select 1 option.)

```
class EMyMethods {
    static String name = "m1";
    void riverRafting() {
        String name = "m2";
        if (8 > 2) {
            String name = "m3";
            System.out.println(name);
        }
    }
    public static void main(String[] args) {
        EMyMethods m1 = new EMyMethods();
        m1.riverRafting();
    }
}
```

- a m1
- b m2
- c m3
- d **Code fails to compile.**

Answer: d

Explanation: The class EMyMethods defines three variables with the name name:

- The static variable name with the value "m1".
- The local variable name in method riverRafting with the value "m2".
- The variable name, local to the if block in the method riverRafting, with the value "m3".

The code fails to compile due to the definition of two local variables with the same name (name) in the method riverRafting. If this code were allowed to compile, the scope of both these local variables would overlap—the variable name defined outside the if block would be accessible to the complete method riverRafting. The scope of the local variable name, defined within the if block, would be limited to the if block.

Within the if block, how do you think the code would differentiate between these local variables? Because there is no way to do so, the code fails to compile.

 [2.7]   Create and manipulate strings

ME-Q81. What is the output of the following code? (Select 1 option.)

```
class EBowl {
    public static void main(String args[]) {
        String eFood = "Corn";
        System.out.println(eFood);
        mix(eFood);
        System.out.println(eFood);
    }
    static void mix(String foodIn) {
        foodIn.concat("A");
        foodIn.replace('C', 'B');
    }
}
```

- a Corn
   BornA
- b Corn
   CornA
- c Corn
   Born
- **d Corn**
   Corn

Answer: d

Explanation: String objects are immutable. This implies that using any method can't change the value of a String variable. In this case, the String object is passed to a method, which seems to, but doesn't, change the contents of String.

[3.5] Use a switch statement

ME-Q82. Which statement is true for the following code? (Select 1 option.)

```
class SwJava {
    public static void main(String args[]) {
        String[] shapes = {"Circle", "Square", "Triangle"};
        switch (shapes) {
            case "Square": System.out.println("Circle"); break;
            case "Triangle": System.out.println("Square"); break;
            case "Circle": System.out.println("Triangle"); break;
        }
    }
}
```

- ○ **a** The code prints `Circle`.
- ○ **b** The code prints `Square`.
- ○ **c** The code prints `Triangle`.
- ○ **d** The code prints

    ```
    Circle
    Square
    Triangle
    ```

- ○ **e** The code prints

    ```
    Triangle
    Circle
    Square
    ```

- ⦿ **f The code fails to compile.**

Answer: f

Explanation: The question tries to trick you; it passes a `String` value to a `switch` construct by passing it an array of `String` objects. The code fails to compile because an array isn't a valid argument to a `switch` construct. The code would have compiled if it passed an element from the array shapes (`shapes[0]`, `shapes[1]`, and `shapes[2]`).

 [5.3] Create and use do-while loops

ME-Q83. Which of the following options include the ideal conditions for choosing to use a do-while loop over a while loop? (Select 2 options.)

- ☑ **a Repeatedly display a menu to a user and accept input until the user chooses to exit the application.**
- ☐ **b** Repeatedly allow a student to sit in the exam only if she carries her identity card.
- ☑ **c Repeatedly serve food to a person until he wants no more.**
- ☐ **d** Repeatedly allow each passenger to board an airplane if the passengers have their boarding passes.

Answer: a, c

Explanation: Option (a) is correct. A menu should be displayed to a user at least once so that she can select whether she wants to exit an application.

Option (b) is incorrect. Because the condition of possession of an identity card should be checked *before* a student is allowed to sit an exam, this condition is best implemented using a while loop.

Option (c) is correct. Because a person should be served the food at least once *before* asking whether he needs more, this condition is best implemented using a do-while loop.

Option (d) is incorrect. Because none of the passengers would be allowed to board without a boarding pass, this condition is best implemented using a while loop.

[8.4]   Invoke a method that throws an exception

ME-Q84. Given the following definition of the classes Person, Father, and Home, which option, if used to replace /* INSERT CODE HERE */, will cause the code to compile successfully (select 3 options):

```
class Person {}
class Father extends Person {
    public void dance() throws ClassCastException {}
}
class Home {
    public static void main(String args[]) {
        Person p = new Person();
        try {
            ((Father)p).dance();
        }
        //INSERT CODE HERE
    }
}
```

☑ a catch (NullPointerException e) {}
    catch (ClassCastException e) {}
    catch (Exception e) {}
    catch (Throwable t) {}

☑ b catch (ClassCastException e) {}
    catch (NullPointerException e) {}
    catch (Exception e) {}
    catch (Throwable t) {}

☐ c catch (ClassCastException e) {}
    catch (Exception e) {}
    catch (NullPointerException e) {}
    catch (Throwable t) {}

☐ d catch (Throwable t) {}
    catch (Exception e) {}
    catch (ClassCastException e) {}
    catch (NullPointerException e) {}

☑ e finally {}

Answer: a, b, e

Explanation: Because `NullPointerException` and `ClassCastException` don't share a base class–derived class relationship, these can be placed before or after each other.

The class `Throwable` is the base class of `Exception`. Hence, the exception handler for the class `Throwable` can't be placed before the exception handler of the class `Exception`. Similarly, `Exception` is a base class for `NullPointerException` and `ClassCastException`. Hence, the exception handler for the class `Exception` can't be placed before the exception handlers of either the class `ClassCastException` or `NullPointerException`.

Option (e) is okay because no checked exceptions are defined to be thrown.

[5.1] Create and use while loops

ME-Q85. What is the output of the following code? (Select 1 option.)

```java
class Camera {
    public static void main(String args[]) {
        String settings;
        while (false) {
            settings = "Adjust settings manually";
        }
        System.out.println("Camera:" + settings);
    }
}
```

- ○ a The code prints `Camera:null`.
- ○ b The code prints `Camera:Adjust settings manually`.
- ○ c The code will print `Camera:`.
- ◉ **d The code will fail to compile.**

Answer: d

Explanation: The key to answering this question is to remember that if the compiler finds unreachable code at compilation time, the code won't compile. Use of the literal value `false` in the `while` loop will ensure that the code in the loop's body won't execute, and this can be determined by the compiler at compilation time.

[6.2] Apply the static keyword to methods and fields

ME-Q86. The output of the class `TestEJavaCourse`, defined as follows, is `300`:

```java
class Course {
    int enrollments;
}
class TestEJavaCourse {
    public static void main(String args[]) {
```

```
        Course c1 = new Course();
        Course c2 = new Course();
        c1.enrollments = 100;
        c2.enrollments = 200;
        System.out.println(c1.enrollments + c2.enrollments);
    }
}
```

What will happen if the variable `enrollments` is defined as a `static` variable? (Select 1 option.)

- ⚪ **a** No change in output. `TestEJavaCourse` prints 300.
- ⚪ **b** Change in output. `TestEJavaCourse` prints 200.
- ⦿ **c Change in output. `TestEJavaCourse` prints 400.**
- ⚪ **d** The class `TestEJavaCourse` fails to compile.

Answer: c

Explanation: The code doesn't fail compilation after the definition of the variable `enrollments` is changed to a `static` variable. A `static` variable can be accessed using a variable reference of the class in which it's defined. All the objects of a class share the same copy of the `static` variable. When the variable `enrollments` is modified using the reference variable `c2`, `c1.enrollments` is also equal to 200. Hence, the code prints 200+200, that is, 400.

[4.2]   Declare, instantiate, initialize, and use a multidimensional array

ME-Q87. What is the output of the following code? (Select 1 option.)

```
String ejgStr[] = new String[][]{{null},new String[]{"a","b","c"},{new
    String()}}[0]  ;
String ejgStr1[] = null;
String ejgStr2[] = {null};

System.out.println(ejgStr[0]);
System.out.println(ejgStr2[0]);
System.out.println(ejgStr1[0]);
```

- ⚪ **a** `null`
  `NullPointerException`

- ⦿ **b `null`**
  `null`
  `NullPointerException`

- ⚪ **c** `NullPointerException`

- ⚪ **d** `null`
  `null`
  `null`

Answer: b

Explanation: The trickiest assignment in this code is the assignment of variable `ejgStr`. The following line of code may *seem* to (but doesn't) assign a two-dimensional `String` array to the variable `ejgStr`:

```
String ejgStr[] = new String[][]{{null},new String[]{"a","b","c"},{new
    String()}}[0] ;
```

The preceding code assigns the first element of a two-dimensional `String` array to the variable `ejgStr`. The following indented code will make the previous statement easier to understand:

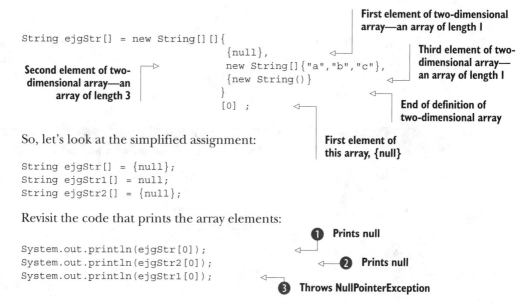

So, let's look at the simplified assignment:

```
String ejgStr[]  = {null};
String ejgStr1[] = null;
String ejgStr2[] = {null};
```

Revisit the code that prints the array elements:

```
System.out.println(ejgStr[0]);
System.out.println(ejgStr2[0]);
System.out.println(ejgStr1[0]);
```

① **Prints null**

② **Prints null**

③ **Throws NullPointerException**

Because `ejgStr` refers to an array of length 1 (`{null}`), `ejgStr[0]` prints `null`. `ejgStr2` also refers to an array of length 1 (`{null}`), so `ejgStr2[0]` also prints `null`. `ejgStr1` refers to `null`, not to an array. An attempt to access the first element of `ejgStr1` throws `NullPointerException`.

[4.3] Declare and use an ArrayList

ME-Q88. Examine the following code and select the correct statement (choose 1 option):

```java
import java.util.*;
class Person {}
class Emp extends Person {}

class TestArrayList {
    public static void main(String[] args) {
        ArrayList<Object> list = new ArrayList<>();
        list.add(new String("1234"));          //LINE1
        list.add(new Person());                 //LINE2
```

```
        list.add(new Emp());                    //LINE3
        list.add(new String[]{"abcd", "xyz"});  //LINE4
    }
}
```

      ○ **a** The code on line 1 won't compile.

      ○ **b** The code on line 2 won't compile.

      ○ **c** The code on line 3 won't compile.

      ○ **d** The code on line 4 won't compile.

      ◉ **e** **None of the above.**

Answer: e

Explanation: The type of an ArrayList determines the type of the objects that can be added to it. An ArrayList can add to it all the objects of its derived class. Because the class Object is the superclass of all Java classes, the ArrayList list as defined in this question will accept all types of objects, including arrays, because they are also objects.

[3.4]   Create if and if-else constructs

ME-Q89. What is the output of the following code? (Select 1 option.)

```
public class If2 {
    public static void main(String args[]) {
        int a = 10; int b = 20; boolean c = false;
        if (b > a) if (++a == 10) if (c!=true) System.out.println(1);
        else System.out.println(2); else System.out.println(3);
    }
}
```

      ○ **a** 1

      ○ **b** 2

      ◉ **c** 3

      ○ **d** No output

Answer: c

Explanation: The key to answering questions about unindented code is to indent it. Here's how:

```
if (b > a)
    if (++a == 10)
        if (c!=true)
            System.out.println(1);
        else
            System.out.println(2);
    else System.out.println(3);
```

Now the code becomes much simpler to look at and understand. Remember that the last else statement belongs to the inner if (++a == 10). As you can see, if (++a == 10) evaluates to false, and the code will print 3.

 **[5.4]** Compare loop constructs

ME-Q90. Select the incorrect statement (choose 1 option):

- ⊙ **a** An enhanced `for` loop can be used to iterate through the elements of an array and `ArrayList`.
- ⦿ **b** **The loop counter of an enhanced `for` loop can be used to modify the current element of the array being iterated over.**
- ⊙ **c** do-while and `while` loops can be used to iterate through the elements of an array and `ArrayList`.
- ⊙ **d** The loop counter of a regular `for` loop can be used to modify the current element of an `ArrayList` being iterated over.

Answer: b

Explanation: Note that this question asks you to select the incorrect statements.

All the looping constructs—a regular `for` loop, an enhanced `for` loop, and do-while and `while` loops—can be used to iterate through elements of an array and `ArrayList`. But the notion of a loop counter is available only for the `for` loop. A loop counter is a variable that's defined and accessible with the definition of the `for` loop. In the following quick example, the variable `ctr` is referred to as a loop counter:

```
for (int ctr=0; ctr< 10; ++ctr)
```

appendix
Answers to Twist
in the Tale exercises

Chapters 1 to 7 include multiple Twist in the Tale exercises. The answers to these exercises are given in this appendix, with comprehensive explanations. The answers to each exercise include the following elements:

- *Purpose:* The aim of the exercise (the *twist* to which each exercise is trying to draw your attention)
- *Answer:* The correct answer
- *Explanation:* A comprehensive explanation of the answer

Let's get started with the first chapter.

A.1   Chapter 1: Java basics

Chapter 1 includes four Twist in the Tale exercises.

A.1.1   Twist in the Tale 1.1

Purpose: This exercise encourages you to practice code with a combination of the correct contents (classes and interfaces) of a Java source code file.

Answer: c, d

Explanation: Options (a) and (b) are incorrect.
Option (c) is correct because a Java source code file can define multiple interfaces and classes.

Option (d) is correct because a `public` interface or class can be defined in a Java source code file with a matching name. The `public` interface `Printable` can't be defined in the Java source code file, Multiple.java. It should be defined in Printable.java.

A.1.2   *Twist in the Tale 1.2*

Purpose: Though similar to Twist in the Tale 1.1, this question is different in terms of its wording and intent. It asks you to select the options that are correct *individually.* Selecting an option that's correct individually means that an option should be correct on its own and not in combination with any other option. You may get to answer similar questions in the real exam.

Answer: a, c, d

Explanation: Option (a) is correct and (b) is incorrect because Multiple2.java won't compile. Multiple2.java can't define a `public` class `Car`.

Option (c) is correct because removal of the definition of the `public` class `Car` from Multiple2.java will leave only one `public` interface in Multiple2.java—`Multiple2`. Because the names of the `public` interface `Multiple2` and the source code file match, Multiple2.java will compile successfully.

Option (d) is correct. Changing `public` class `Car` to a non-public class will leave only one `public` interface in Multiple2.java—`Multiple2`. Because the names of the `public` interface `Multiple2` and source code file match, Multiple2.java will compile successfully.

Option (e) is incorrect. If you change the access modifier of the `public` interface `Multiple2` to non-public, Multiple2.java will contain a definition of a `public` class `Car`, which isn't allowed.

A.1.3   *Twist in the Tale 1.3*

Purpose: This exercise encourages you to execute the code in the options to understand the correct method signature of the method `main` together with the method parameters that are passed to it.

Answer: a, b

Explanation: All the options in this question are supposed to execute using the command `javaEJava java one one`. The purpose of each of these terms is as follows:

- Term 1: `java`—Used to execute a Java class
- Term 2: `EJava`—Name of class to execute
- Term 3: `java`—Passed as the first argument to the method `main`
- Term 4: one—Passed as the second argument to `main`
- Term 5: one—Passed as the third argument to `main`

To output "`java one`", the `main` method should output the first and either the second or third method parameters passed to it.

Options (a) and (b) are correct because they use the correct method signature of the method `main`. The name of the method parameter need not be `args`. It can be any other valid identifier. Option (a) outputs the values of the first and third terms passed to it. Option (b) outputs the values of the first and second terms passed to it.

Option (c) is incorrect because this `main` method accepts a two-dimensional array. Hence, it won't be treated as *the* main method.

Option (d) is incorrect because this code won't compile. The access modifier of a method (`public`) should be placed before its return type (`void`); otherwise, the code won't compile.

A.1.4   Twist in the Tale 1.4

Purpose: Apart from determining the right access modifier that can limit the visibility of a class within a package, this exercise wants you to try out different access modifiers that can be used to declare a class.

Answer: The code submitted by Harry.

Explanation: The code submitted by Paul is incorrect because when the class `Curtain` is defined with the `public` access modifier, it will be accessible outside the package `building`.

The code submitted by Shreya and Selvan is incorrect because the class `Curtain` is a top-level class (it's not defined within another class), so it can't be defined using the access modifiers `protected` and `private`.

A.2   Chapter 2—Working with Java data types

Chapter 2 includes four Twist in the Tale exercises. Twist in the Tale 2.1 has two parts.

A.2.1   Twist in the Tale 2.1 (part 1)

Purpose: By default, `System.out.println()` will print out a number in its decimal base. It does so regardless of the base number system that you use to initialize a number.

Answer: The code prints the following output:

```
534
534
```

Explanation: Often programmers are tricked by similar questions. If a variable is assigned a value using `0b100001011` (a number in the binary number system), a programmer might believe that `System.out.println()` will print out numbers in the binary number system, which is incorrect. By default, `System.out.println()` will print out a number in its decimal base. All four variables `baseDecimal`, `octVal`, `hexVal`, and `binVal` represent the decimal value `267` in the decimal, octal, hexadecimal, and binary number systems. The addition operation adds these values and prints `534` twice.

You can use a method from the class `Integer` to print out a value in the binary number system as follows:

```
System.out.println(Integer.toBinaryString(0b100001011));
```

Note that the class `Integer` isn't on this exam and you won't be asked any questions on it. This class is mentioned only for your reference.

A.2.2 *Twist in the Tale 2.1 (part 2)*

Purpose: A new Java 7 language feature is the use of the underscore in literal number values. If you haven't worked with underscores in literal number values, this exercise's purpose is to help you get familiar with this feature.

Answer: Only `var1`, `var6`, and `var7` correctly define a literal integer value.

Explanation: The literal value `0_x_4_13` defined by `var2` is incorrect because it uses underscores after the starting `0` and after the letter x, neither of which is allowed. The correct value is 0x4_13.

The literal value `0b_x10_BA_75` defined by `var3` is incorrect. You can't place an underscore right after the prefixes `0b` and `0B` that are used to define binary literal values. Also, a binary value can contain only the digits 1 and 0.

The literal value `0b_10000_10_11` defined by value `var4` is incorrect. You can't place an underscore right after the prefixes `0b` and `0B` used to define binary literal values. The correct value is `0b10000_10_11`.

The literal value `0xa10_AG_75` defined by `var5` is incorrect because it uses the letter `G`, which isn't allowed in a hexadecimal number system. A correct value is `0xa10_A_75`.

A.2.3 *Twist in the Tale 2.2*

Purpose: To reinforce the following concepts:

- Multiple variables of the *same type* can be defined on the same line of code.
- Variable assignment rule: if multiple variables of *similar types* are assigned values on the same line, assignment starts from right to left. Also, unlike other programming languages such as C, the literal value `0` can't be assigned to a variable of type `boolean`.
- Questions that ask you to select incorrect answers or code can be confusing. It's common to start by determining the incorrect options and then selecting the correct options. Make note of such questions.

Answer: a, b, c, e

Explanation: Options (a) and (b) are incorrect statements. You can define multiple variables of the same type on the same line. Also, you can assign values to variables of compatible types on the same line of code. Assignment starts from right to left. For proof, the following lines of code will compile:

```
int int1;
long long2;
long2 = int1 = 10;
```

But the following lines of code won't compile:

```
int i1;
long l2;
int1 = long2 = 10;
```

In the final line of the preceding code, a literal value 10 is assigned to the variable long2 of type long, which is acceptable. An attempt to assign the value of the variable long2 to int1 fails because it would need an explicit cast.

Option (c) is an incorrect statement because a literal value 0 can't be assigned to a variable of type boolean.

Option (d) is a correct statement.

Option (e) is an incorrect statement. The code doesn't define a variable with the name yes and thus seems to treat it like a literal value. Java doesn't define a literal value yes, so the code doesn't compile.

A.2.4   *Twist in the Tale 2.3*

Purpose: The exercise encourages you to

- Try code with increment and decrement postfix and prefix unary operators
- Get the hang of how variables are evaluated in an expression that has multiple occurrences of unary operators in postfix and prefix notation

Answer: 32

Explanation: The actual task is to evaluate the following expression:

```
int a = 10;
a = ++a + a + --a - --a + a++;
System.out.println(a);
```

This is the actual task because the question asks you to replace all occurrences of ++a with a++, --a with a--, and vice versa. This expression is depicted in figure A.1:

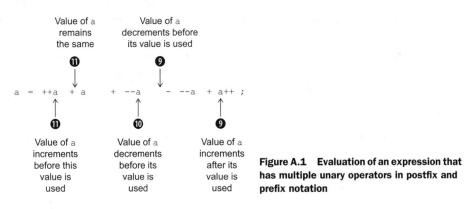

Figure A.1   **Evaluation of an expression that has multiple unary operators in postfix and prefix notation**

A.2.5   *Twist in the Tale 2.4*

Purpose: To determine whether the operands of an expression that uses the short-circuit operators && and || will evaluate.

Answer: The operands that will execute are circled and the ones that won't are enclosed in squares in figure A.2.

```
class TwistInTaleLogicalOperators {
  public static void main(String args[]){
    int a=10;
    int b=20;
    int c=40;

    System.out.println (a++>10) || (++b<30) ;          //line1
    System.out.println (a>90) && ++b<30 ;
    System.out.println (!(c>20)) && a==10 ;
    System.out.println (a>=99) || (a<=33) && (b==10) ;
    System.out.println (a>=99) && a<=33 ||(b==10) ;
  }
}
```

Figure A.2 In an expression that uses the short-circuit operators && and ||, the operands that are evaluated are circled and the ones that aren't evaluated are enclosed in rectangles.

Explanation: Both of the short-circuit operators, && and ||, will evaluate their first operand. For the short-circuit operator &&, if the first operand evaluates to false, it won't evaluate the second operator. For the short-circuit operator ||, if the first operand evaluates to true, it won't evaluate the second operator.

For the expression (a++ > 10 || ++b < 30), because a++ > 10 evaluates to false, both operands will evaluate.

For the expression (a > 90 && ++b < 30), because a > 90 evaluates to false, the second operand won't execute.

For expression (!(c > 20) && a == 10), because !(c > 20) evaluates to false, the second operand won't execute.

The expression (a >= 99 || a <= 33 && b == 10) has three operands together with the OR (||) and AND (&&) short-circuit operators. Because the short-circuit operator AND has higher operator precedence than the short-circuit operator OR, the expression is evaluated as follows:

```
(a >= 99 || (a <= 33 && b == 10))
```

Evaluation of the preceding expression starts with the evaluation of (a <= 33 && b == 10). Because a <= 33 evaluates to true, the operator && evaluates the second operand (b == 10) to determine whether (a <= 33 && b == 10) will return true or false. a <= 33 returns true and b == 10 returns false, so the expression (a <= 33 && b == 10) returns false.

The original expression—(a >= 99 || (a <= 33 && b == 10))—is now reduced to the following expression:

```
(a >= 99 || false)
```

The short-circuit operator OR (||) executes its first operand (even if the value of the second operand is known), evaluating a >= 99. So for this expression, all three operands are evaluated.

The expression (a >= 99 && a <= 33 || b == 10) also has three operands, together with OR and AND short-circuit operators. Because the short-circuit operator AND has a higher operator precedence than the short-circuit operator OR, this expression is evaluated as follows:

```
((a >= 99 && a <= 33) || b == 10 )
```

a >= 99 evaluates to `false`, so the next operand (a <= 33) isn't evaluated. Because the first operand to operator ||, a >= 99 && a <= 33), evaluates to `false`, b == 10 is evaluated.

A.3   *Chapter 3—Methods and encapsulation*

Chapter 3 includes three Twist in the Tale exercises.

A.3.1   *Twist in the Tale 3.1*

Purpose: In the same way that the class `TestPhone` in this exercise defines a local variable with the same name as its instance variable, I strongly recommend that you try out different combinations of defining variables with the same name in a class, but with different scope.

Answer: a

Explanation: The class `Phone` defines an instance variable with the name `phoneNumber`. The method `setNumber` also defines a local variable `phoneNumber` and assigns a value to its local variable. A local variable takes precedence over an instance variable defined in the class with the same names. Because there is no change in the value of the instance variable `phoneNumber`, `123456789` is printed to the console from the method `main`, defined in the class `TestPhone`.

A.3.2   *Twist in the Tale 3.2*

Purpose: To learn that *recursive* or *circular* calls to constructors aren't allowed.

Answer: The code fails to compile, with the following compilation error message:

```
Employee.java:4: error: recursive constructor invocation
    Employee() {
    ^
1 error
```

Explanation: A method calling itself is called *recursion*. Two or more methods calling each other, in a circular manner, is called *circular method calling*.

Starting in Java version 1.4.1, the Java compiler won't compile code with *recursive* or *circular* constructors. A constructor is used to initialize an object, so it doesn't make sense to allow recursive calls to a constructor. You can initialize an object once and then modify it. You can't initialize an object multiple times.

In case you're wondering whether you can call a constructor conditionally from another constructor: you can't. A call to a constructor must be the first statement:

```
class Employee {
    String name;
    int age;
    Employee() {
```

```
        if (7<2)
            this();
    }
    Employee(String newName, int newAge) {
        name = newName;
        age = newAge;
    }
}
```

> Won't compile—conditional execution of constructors isn't allowed. The call to this must be first statement in constructor.

Also, circular constructor calls aren't allowed:

```
class Employee {
    String name;
    int age;
    Employee() {
        this(null, 0);
    }
    Employee(String newName, int newAge) {
        this();
        name = newName;
        age = newAge;
    }
}
```

> Won't compile. This constructor calls back the no-argument constructor resulting in a circular constructor call.

The previous example doesn't compile, with the following compilation error message:

```
Employee.java:8: error: recursive constructor invocation
    Employee(String newName, int newAge) {
    ^
1 error
```

Note that similar recursive or circular calls defined in methods don't result in compilation errors.

A.3.3   Twist in the Tale 3.3

Purpose: A class with `public` instance variable(s) can never be designated as a well-encapsulated class.

Answer: e

Explanation: This question tries to trick you by defining options that play with multiple access modifiers for methods `getWeight` and `setWeight`. Because the instance variable `model` of the class `Phone` is defined using the `public` access modifier, it's accessible outside this class. So `Phone` isn't a well-encapsulated class.

A.4   Chapter 4—String, StringBuilder, Arrays, and ArrayList

Chapter 4 includes four Twist in the Tale exercises.

A.4.1   Twist in the Tale 4.1

Purpose: To remind you to be careful with the overloaded methods of class `String` that accept either `char` or `String` or both, the code in this exercise passes an invalid method argument—a `char`—to method `startsWith`.

Answer: e

Explanation: When it comes to the String class, it's easy to confuse the methods that accept char or String values as method arguments. For example, the overloaded method indexOf can accept both String and char values to search for a target value in a String. The methods startsWith and endsWith accept only arguments of type String. The method charAt accepts only method arguments of type int. Hence, this method can be passed char values, which are stored as unsigned integer values.

A.4.2   Twist in the Tale 4.2

Purpose: This exercise has multiple purposes:

- To confuse you with the use of method names, which are used in the Java API by other classes to create their objects.
- To encourage you to refer to the Java API documentation when you work with classes from the Java API. The Java API documentation is an extensive source of information and facts that are often not included in most books (because it's practically impossible to do so).

Answer: d

Explanation: The correct way to create an object of class StringBuilder with a default capacity of 16 characters is to call StringBuilder's no-argument constructor, as follows:

```
StringBuilder name = StringBuilder();
```

A.4.3   Twist in the Tale 4.3

Purpose: Identify the difference between an array element that isn't initialized and an array element that doesn't exist. A pictorial representation of a multidimensional array is quick to draw, and you can easily refer to its nonexistent or null array elements. This concept is shown in figure A.3.

Answer: b, d

Explanation: Option (a) is incorrect. Initializing a row of array multiStrArr with {"Jan","Feb",null} and {"Jan","Feb",null,null} isn't the same. The former option defines *three* array elements with the last array element assigned to null. The

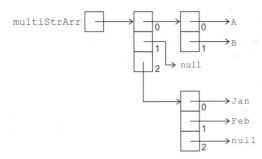

Figure A.3 Array multiStrArr and its elements

latter option defines *four* array elements with the last two array elements assigned to `null`.

Option (b) is correct. The array element at the position exists but isn't assigned any value. It's assigned to `null`.

Option (c) is incorrect. Because `multiStrArr[1]` refers to `null`, `multiStrArr[1][1]` doesn't exist.

Option (d) is correct. As shown in figure A.3, the array `multiStrArr` doesn't define an equal number of elements in each row, so it's asymmetric.

A.4.4   Twist in the Tale 4.4

Purpose: This exercise tries to trick you by using multiple objects of `ArrayList`, assigning the object reference of one `ArrayList` to another, and modifying the value of the `ArrayList` objects. `String` objects are immutable—you can't change their values.

Answer: a

Explanation: Option (a) is correct, and options (b), (c), and (d) are incorrect. The `ArrayLists myArrList` and `yourArrList` contain `String` objects. The value of `String` objects can't be modified once created.

A.5   Chapter 5—Flow control

Chapter 5 includes four *Twist in the Tale* exercises.

A.5.1   Twist in the Tale 5.1

Purpose: To emphasize multiple points:

- A variable of any type can be (re)assigned a value in an expression used in an `if` condition.
- `if-else-if` statements execute each `if` condition as control is passed to them, changing the value of any variable that's manipulated in the evaluation of the expression.
- An expression used in an `if` condition should evaluate to a `boolean` value.

Answer: f

Explanation: The flow of execution of code statements in this exercise is shown in figure A.4.

The arrows on the left in figure A.4 show the flow of execution of statements for this code snippet. The `if` conditions on the right show the actual values that are compared after the expression used in the `if` statements is evaluated. Following is a detailed description:

- The initial value of variable `score` is `10`. The first condition (`(score = score + 10) == 100`) reassigns the value of variable `score` to `20` and then compares it to the literal integer value `100`. The expression `20 == 100` returns a `boolean` value `false`. The control doesn't evaluate the *then* part of the `if` construct and moves on to the evaluation of the second `if` condition defined in the `else` part.

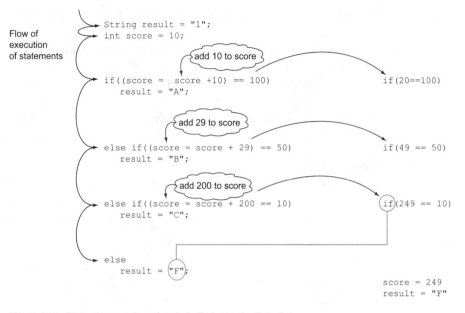

Figure A.4   Flow of execution of code in Twist In the Tale 5.1

- The second condition ((score = score + 29) == 50) adds 29 to the existing value 20 of variable score and then compares the new value 49 with 50. The expression 49 == 50 returns false again. The control doesn't evaluate the *then* part of the if construct and moves on to evaluation of the second if condition defined in the else part.

- The third condition ((score = score + 200) == 10) adds a value of 200 to the existing value 49 of variable score, making it 249, and compares that with the integer literal value 10. Because 249 == 10 evaluates to false, control moves to the else part. The else part assigns a literal value F to the variable result. At the end of execution of the if-else-if statement, the variable score is assigned a value of 249 and result is assigned a value of F. The code outputs F:249.

A.5.2   *Twist in the Tale 5.2*

Purpose: The switch construct uses the equals method to compare the value of its argument with the case values. It doesn't compare the variable references.

Answer: c

Explanation: You may have answered questions with code like the following, which print false:

```
String aDay = new String("SUN");
System.out.println(aDay == "SUN");
```

String objects, which are created using an assignment operator (=), are stored in a pool of Strings. String objects, which are created using the operator new, aren't stored in the pool of String objects.

When a String object is passed as an argument to a switch construct, it doesn't compare the object references; it compares the object values using the equals method. In the code snippet shown in the question, a match is found for the String literal value SUN, so the code prints Weekend!, executes the break statement, and exits the block.

A.5.3 *Twist in the Tale 5.3*

Purpose: Note the type of the variable that's passed as an argument to the switch construct. Among the primitive data types, you can pass on variables of types byte, short, char, and int to a switch construct. Other data types that you can pass to a switch construct are Byte, Short, Integer, Character, enum, and String.

This question tries to take your attention off this simple basic requirement and to move your focus to the logic of the question.

Answer: The submission by Harry.

Explanation: Paul's submission doesn't compile because a switch construct doesn't accept an argument of the long primitive data type.

A.5.4 *Twist in the Tale 5.4*

Purpose: When an unlabeled break statement is used within nested loops (for any combinations of for, do-while, or while loops), a break statement will end the execution of the *inner loop*, not all the nested loops. The *outer loop* will continue to execute, starting with its *next* iteration value.

Answer: a

Explanation: Let's start with the *outer loop*'s first iteration. In the first iteration, the value of the variable outer is Outer.

For the outer loop's first iteration, the inner loop should execute for the values Outer and Inner for the variable inner. For the first iteration of the inner loop, the value of the variable inner is Outer, so the condition inner.equals("Inner") evaluates to false and the break statement doesn't execute. The code prints the value of variable inner, which is Outer: and starts with the next iteration of the inner loop. In the second iteration of the inner loop, the value of the variable inner is Inner, so the condition inner.equals("Inner") evaluates to true and the break statement executes, ending the execution of the inner loop and skipping the code that prints out the value of the variable inner.

The outer loop starts its execution with the second iteration. In this iteration, the value of the variable outer is Outer. For the outer loop's iteration, the inner loop executes twice in the same manner as mentioned in the previous paragraph. This iteration of the outer loop again prints the value of the variable `inner` when it's equal to `Outer`.

The nested loops included in the question print out the value `Outer:` twice:

```
Outer:Outer:
```

A.6   *Chapter 6—Working with inheritance*

Chapter 6 includes four Twist in the Tale exercises.

A.6.1   *Twist in the Tale 6.1*

Purpose: This question is an example of a simple concept (`private` members are not accessible to a derived class) that is made to look complex by including code and options that try to divert your attention. Expect similar questions on the exam.

Answer: e

Explanation: The code fails to compile because the `private` members of a class can't be accessed outside a class—not even by its derived class. The compiler can detect such attempts; this code won't compile.

A.6.2   *Twist in the Tale 6.2*

Purpose: To help you to work with a combination of

- Arrays
- Assigning an object of a derived class to a reference variable of the base class
- Assigning an object of a class that implements an interface to a reference variable of the interface

Answer: a, c

Explanation: The rules you need to follow to assign a value to an array element are the same rules you follow when you assign an object to a reference variable. Because the type of array `interviewer` is `Interviewer`, you can assign objects of classes that implement this interface. The inheritance of classes `Employee`, `Manager`, and `HRExecutive`, and the interface `Interviewer` are shown in figure A.5.

As you can see in figure A.5, the classes `Manager` and `HRExecutive` implement the interface `Interviewer`. The class `Employee` doesn't implement the interface `Interviewer`; hence, an object of the class `Manager` can't be added to an array of type `Interviewer`.

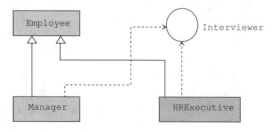

Figure A.5   **UML notation of inheritance hierarchy of the classes** `Employee`, `Manager`, **and** `HRExecutive`, **and the interface** `Interviewer`

From this explanation, it's apparent that options (a) and (c) are correct and option (b) is incorrect.

Option (d) is incorrect because you can't create objects of an interface. Option (d) tries to create an object of the interface `Interviewer`. Code that tries to create an instance of an interface won't compile.

A.6.3   *Twist in the Tale 6.3*

Purpose: If there is no collision with the name of a variable defined in the base class or derived class, the variable can be accessed using both `super` and `this` references from a derived class. If there is a collision, the base class variable can be accessed using the `super` reference.

Answer: b

Explanation: In a derived class, you'd normally use the implicit reference `super` to refer to a method or variable of a base class. Similarly, you'd normally use the implicit reference `this` to refer to a method or variable defined in the same class. A derived class contains within it an object of its base class and can access non-`private` members of its base class. A derived class can *also* refer to the members of its base class as its own members using the reference `this`. This approach is acceptable only if the same member isn't defined in the derived class; that is, if there are no name collisions.

The base class `Employee` defines two non-`private` variables, `name` and `address`, which are accessible in `Employee`'s derived class `Programmer`. The class `Programmer` also defines an instance variable `name`, so the variable `name` should be prefixed with the explicit references `super` and `this` to refer to the variable `name` defined in the classes `Employee` and `Programmer`. The variable `address` can be referred to using both `super` and `this` in the derived class `Programmer`.

Option (a) is incorrect. The derived class `Programmer` can refer to the variable `address` defined in the base class using `this.address`. This value won't print `null`.

Option (c) is incorrect. `this.address` won't print blank when accessed from the derived class `Programmer`.

Option (d) is incorrect. The code has no compilation issues.

A.6.4   *Twist in the Tale 6.4*

Purpose: Polymorphic methods should define a method's overriding rules.

Answer: a

Explanation: Polymorphic methods exist when classes or interfaces share an inheritance relationship. A polymorphic method can be defined by a derived class if

- The derived class implements an `abstract` method defined in a base class or interface
- The derived class overrides a non-`abstract` method defined in a base class

Options (b) and (d) are incorrect. A method can't be overridden if it defines a different parameter list.

Option (c) is incorrect. The return type of the overridden method must be the same in the base class and the derived class.

A.7   *Chapter 7—Exception handling*

Chapter 7 includes five Twist in the Tale exercises.

A.7.1   *Twist in the Tale 7.1*

Purpose: A `finally` block can't be placed before the `catch` blocks. A number of programmers have compared this question with placing the label `default` before label `case` in a `switch` construct. Though the latter approach works, the `finally` and `catch` blocks aren't so flexible.

Answer: d

Explanation: Options (a), (b), and (c) are incorrect because code that defines a `finally` block before `catch` blocks won't compile.

A.7.2   *Twist in the Tale 7.2*

Purpose: Unhandled exceptions thrown by an inner exception handler are passed on to the outer `try-catch` block to handle.

Answer: a

Explanation: Options (b), (c), and (d) are incorrect. The question assumes that a text file players.txt exists on your system so that the following code won't throw a `FileNotFoundException` exception:

```
players = new FileInputStream("players.txt");
```

The code defined for this question doesn't initialize the `static` variable `coach` before executing the following code, which is bound to throw `NullPointerException`:

```
coach.close();
```

The previous line of code is defined in the inner `try` block, which doesn't define an exception handler for the exception `NullPointerException`. This exception is propagated to the outer exception-handler block. The outer exception handler *catches* the `NullPointerException` thrown by the inner `try` block and executes the appropriate exception handler. Hence, the code prints the following:

```
players.txt found
NullPointerException
```

A.7.3 *Twist in the Tale 7.3*

Purpose: To determine whether exception-handling code for errors will execute.

Answer: b

Explanation: We know that typically errors shouldn't be handled programmatically and that they should be left for the JVM to take care of. Also, you can't be sure that error-handling code for all the errors will execute. For example, error-handling code for `StackOverFlowError` may execute but (as the name suggests) may not execute for `VirtualMachineError`.

A.7.4 *Twist in the Tale 7.4*

Purpose: `ClassCastException` is a runtime exception. As you know, a runtime exception can be thrown only by the JVM.

Answer: b, d

Explanation: Options (a) and (c) are incorrect because the code throws `ClassCast-Exception`, which is a runtime exception, for the following code:

```
printable = (Printable)blackInk;
```

Option (d) is correct because neither the class `BlackInk` nor any of its base classes implement the interface `Printable`. Thus, the code that assigns `blankInk` to `printable` without an explicit cast will fail to compile.

A.7.5 *Twist in the Tale 7.5*

Purpose: Trying to access a nonexistent position of an array throws `ArrayIndexOutOf-BoundsException`. Calling a member on a `null` value stored in an array throws `Null-PointerException`.

Answer: c

Explanation: Let's indent the assignment of the two-dimensional array `oldLaptops` so that it's easier to understand the values that are assigned to it:

```
String[][] oldLaptops = {
                         {"Dell", "Toshiba", "Vaio"},
                          null,
                         {"IBM"},
                          new String[10]
                        };
```

The preceding code results in the following assignments:

```
oldLaptops[0] = {"Dell", "Toshiba", "Vaio"};
oldLaptops[1] = null;
oldLaptops[2] = {"IBM"};
oldLaptops[3] = new String[10];
```

A pictorial representation of the two-dimensional `String` array `oldLaptops` is shown in figure A.6.

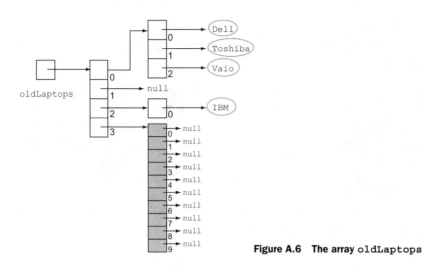

Figure A.6 The array oldLaptops

As you can see, oldLaptops[3] is an array of ten uninitialized String objects. All the members (from index position 0 to 9) of the array oldLaptops[3] are assigned a null value. The code on line 4 tries to call the method length on the first element of array oldLaptops[0], which is null, throwing a NullPointerException.

index

Symbols

– (unary decrement)
      operator 90–92
; character 261, 273
: character 265
!= operator 93, 189
{} characters 19, 249
@ sign 193
* character 18, 35
&& operator 94–96
+ operator 186–187, 242
++ (unary increment)
      operator 90–92
+= operator 186–187
< operator 92
<= operator 92
= operator 87, 93–94, 176, 252
== operator 93, 176, 188–189,
      252
<> character 208
> operator 92
>= operator 92
|| operator 94–96

A

abstract base class, vs. concrete
      base class 304
abstract method 302, 324, 327–
      328, 334
abstract modifier
   abstract classes 48
   abstract interfaces 49
   abstract methods 49
   abstract variables 49

AbstractStringBuilder class 190,
      193
Access method 122
access modifiers 37–47, 125,
      138, 327, 336
   default access 42–45
   for overloaded methods 135
   overview 38
   private access modifier 45–47
   protected access modifier 40
   public access modifier 39
   where to use 38
accessing elements, in ArrayList
      class 211–212, 217–219
addAll() method, ArrayList
      class 215–216
addition operators 97
allocation, for arrays 200–201
AND operator 94
angle brackets 208
Animal() method 405–406, 409,
      423, 440, 446, 472
AnnualExam class 16–17, 34–37
answers
   to mock exam 439
   to Twist in Tale exercise 502–
      518
append() method, String-
      Builder class 192–194
argument list, for overloaded
      methods 133–135
arguments, passed to switch
      statement 257
arithmetic operators 89–92
   – (unary decrement)
      operator 90–92

++ (unary increment)
      operator 90–92
arithmetic operators,
      overview 100
array type 199, 229
array variable 199
ArrayAccess class 349–350
ArrayIndexOutOfBounds-
      Exception 353–354, 371–
      372, 374–376, 399
ArrayList class 206–221
   addAll() method 215–216
   clear() method 217
   clone() method 219
   creating objects 209
   elements in
      accessing 211–212, 217–
         219
      adding 209–211
      deleting 213–215
      modifying 212–213
   toArray() method 220
arrays 197–225
   abstract class type 205
   allocation for 200–201
   ArrayList class 206–221
      accessing elements of 211–
         212, 217–219
      addAll() method 215
      adding elements to 209–
         211
      clear() method 217
      clone() method 219
      creating objects 209
      deleting elements of 213–
         215

arrays *(continued)*
    modifying elements
        of 212–213
    toArray() method 220
    declaring 199, 203–204
    defined 197–199
    initializing 201–204
    interface type 205
    members of 206
    multidimensional 204
    object 205–206
article() method 434, 492
Artist() method 422, 470
assignedArrList variable 220
AssignedArrVal variable 220
assignment operator 176, 179,
    201, 226–227, 252
asterisk character 18, 35
asymmetrical array 204
attendTraining method 305
average variable 77
avg variable 112–113

B

BankAccount class 221
base class 301, 303, 312
BaseInterface1 309
BaseInterface2 309
binary number system 74–75,
    99
binding, of variables 329
BlackInk class 376–377
Book class 38, 476
boolean data type 72, 98, 245
boolean values 79, 88, 93–96,
    101, 108
Boolean wrapper class 245
Bottle() method 434, 491
(braces), in if-else
    constructs 249–251
break statements 276–277
  in switch statement 259–260
  labeled break statements 279
bunAvailable variable 271
byte data type 73–76

C

Cabin class 33
calc() method 413, 454
calcAverage method 134
call() method 419, 428, 465,
    481
case keyword 254

casting 79, 88, 105, 316–318
catch block 362–366, 389–390,
    399
catch blocks
    both finally block and catch
      block return 362–363
    finally block modifies return
      value from 363–364
    order of exceptions caught
      by 364
    using multiple 359–361
certification package 31
chained methods 185
char data type 78–79, 99, 105–
    106
charAt() method 175, 182,
    226
checked exceptions 348–350,
    369–371, 398–399
child class 304
class variables, scope of 116–117
ClassCastException 371, 374,
    376–377, 392
classes 15–21
    abstract 48
    comments in 17–19
    constructors for 21
    declaring 19
    defined 20–21
    defining in packages 30–31
    final 49
    import statement 16–17
    importing from default
      package 36
    inheritance with 296–304
      abstract base class vs. con-
        crete base class 304
      base class members
        inherited 301
      base class members not
        inherited 301
      concentrating on special-
        ized behavior of
        classes 300
      derived class contains object
        of base class 300–301
      derived classes can define
        additional
        properties 301–302
      ease of modification 298
      extensibility 298–300
      logical structures and
        grouping 300
      smaller derived class
        definitions 298

instance attributes 21
instance methods 21
    multiple in source code
      files 22–23
    package statement 16
    polymorphism with 324–328
ClassLoader 387
classVariable 117
cleanup code 359
clear() method, ArrayList
    class 217
clone() method 206, 220, 233,
    237–238
clonedArrVal variable 220
close() method 368, 516
code exhibit button 12
code files
    classes in 15–21
      comments in 17–19
      constructors for 21
      declaring 19
      defined 20–21
      import statement 16–17
      instance attributes 21
      instance methods 21
      package statement 16
    interface in 21–22
    multiple classes in 22–23
    package statement in 24–25
colon character 265
ColorInk class 376–377
ColorPack() method 420, 467
ColorPencil() method 407,
    443
com.mobile package 117
com.oracle.javacert package 35
com.oracle.javacert.associate
    package 31
command-line parameters 29
comments, in classes 17–19
comparing objects, for
    equality 221–225
    equals() method 221, 223–
      225
    of String class 189
    user-defined classes 221–
      223
concatenation operators 186,
    228
concrete base class, vs. abstract
    base class 304
condition1 variable 245
condition2 variable 245
conductInterview method 318
ConferenceHall class 33

constructors 136–145
  default 140–142
  for classes 21
  overloaded 142–145
    invoking from another
      constructor 144
    overview 144–145
  super object reference
    for 322
  this object reference for 320
  user-defined 137–140
contains method 217, 223
continue statements, labeled
  continue statements 279–
  294
controls 244–294
  break statements 276–277
  continue statements, labeled
    continue statements 279–
    294
  do-while loops 272–274
  enhanced for loops 265–270
    limitations of 268–269
    nesting 269–270
  for loops 260–265
    initialization block 262–263
    nesting 264–265
    termination condition 263
    update clause 263–264
    vs. enhanced for loops 275
    vs. while loops 276
  if-else constructs 245–253
    (braces) in 249–251
    expressions for 251–252
    missing else blocks 248
    nesting 252–253
    overview 245–247
  switch statement 254–260
    arguments passed to 257
    break statements in 259–
    260
    overview 254–256
    values passed to label case
      of 258–259
  while loops 271–272
counting objects, in String
  class 178–179
countPages method 45–46
coupon for exam 11
Course() method 165, 171, 393,
  397–398, 438, 498
CourseBook class 38–40, 42, 44,
  46
create() method 379
CreateArrayList class 208

crossRapid method 357–358
ctr parameter 114
curly braces 16, 19

D

dance() method 437, 496
data types 69–109
  identifiers for 80–82
  object reference variables
    82–85
    defined 82–83
    vs. primitive variables 84–85
  primitive 70–80
    boolean 72
    byte 73–76
    char 78–79
    confusion with names
      of 79–80
    double 76–77
    float 76–77
    int 73–76
    long 73–76
    short 73–76
day variable 255
daysOffWork method 128, 149
decimal literal value 99
decimal number system 74
decimal numbers, storing 71
decimal type, primitive 257
declaring arrays 199, 203–204
default access 42–45
default accessibility 42, 57, 62,
  68
default constructors 140–142
default label 254
default members 301
default modifier 138
default package 16, 36, 57
delete() method, StringBuilder
  class 195
deletecharAt() method, String-
  Builder class 195
deleting, elements in ArrayList
  class 213–215
deliverMobileApp method 330,
  332
derived class, variable of 311–
  312
Diary() method 430, 483
dog leash analogy 84
dot notation 148
double data type 76–77
double quotes 78, 99, 176–177,
  179, 227

double value 99
do-while loops 80, 91, 260
  overview 272–274
  vs. while loops 275
DropOarException class 357–
  358

E

EJava() method 395, 400, 413,
  454
EJavaCourse() method 418, 463
EJavaDerived() method 396,
  402
EJavaTestMethods class 126
elementData variable 208, 211
elements, in ArrayList class
  accessing 211–212, 217–219
  adding 209–211
  deleting 213–215
  modifying 212–213
ellipses 129
else
  missing 248
  statement 247, 250, 253
Emp class 51, 455
emp variable 312
Emp() method 413, 439, 455,
  500
Employee class 137, 309, 320,
  324, 332
Employee() method 137–144,
  490, 508–509
EMyMethods() method 435,
  493
encapsulation 150–153
  applying 151–153
  need for 150–151
end-of-line comments 18, 56
endsWith() method, String
  class 185
enhanced for loops 265–270
  limitations of 268–269
  nesting 269–270
  vs. for loops 275
ensureCapacity method 211
equality operators 93, 186, 252
equality, comparing objects
  for 221–225
  equals() method 221, 223–
  225
  of String class 189
  user-defined classes 221–223
equals() method 187, 221, 223–
  225, 512–513

exam
    changes to 8–9
    comparison of versions 3–4
    completing before allotted
        time 11
    coupon for 11
    marking questions during 11
    preparing for 9
    retaking 11
    taking mock tests before 9
    testing engine used in 12
    using notes during 11
    where to take 10
Exam class 6, 69, 122
ExamQuestion class 16–17, 30–
    32, 34–36
Exception class 370, 390
exception handling
    exception classes 374–388
        ArrayIndexOutOfBounds-
            Exception 375–376
        ClassCastException 376–
            377
        ExceptionInInitializerError
            384–386
        IllegalArgumentException
            378
        IllegalStateException 378–
            379
        IndexOutOfBounds-
            Exception 375–376
        NoClassDefFoundError
            386–387
        NullPointerException 379–
            382
        NumberFormatException
            382–384
        OutOfMemoryError 387–
            388
        StackOverflowError 386
    importance of 352–354
    overview 349–351, 388–393
    rethrowing exceptions 366–
        367
    throwing exceptions instead
        of handling 367
    try-catch-finally blocks
        both catch and finally
            blocks have return 362–
            363
        finally block modifies
            return from catch
            block 363–364
        finally blocks in 361–362
        nesting 367–368

    order of exceptions caught
        by 364
    overview 356–359
    using multiple catch
        blocks 359–361
    types of exceptions
        checked exceptions 370–
            371
        errors 372–373
        hierarchy of
            categories 369–370
        runtime exceptions 371–
            372
ExceptionInInitializerError 374,
    384–386, 392–393, 402–403
executable applications 25–28
    executable classes vs. nonexe-
        cutable classes 25
    main method for 26–28
Execute method 155
exiting loops 276
experience, and preparation 9
expert1 variable 333
expressions, for if-else
    constructs 251–252
extended class 303
extends keyword 297, 304
extensibility, inheritance with
    classes 298–300

F

facebookId property 298–299
FallInRiverException class 357–
    358
fatal errors 362
fields, object
    defined 145
    reading and writing 145–148
FileInputStream class 350–351,
    359, 366–368, 371
FileNotFoundException
    class 350–351, 359, 361,
    370–371, 390, 402
FileOutputStream class 351
files, source code
    classes in 15–21
        comments in 17–19
        constructors for 21
        declaring 19
        defined 20–21
        import statement 16–17
        instance attributes 21
        instance methods 21
        package statement 16

    interface in 21–22
    multiple classes in 22–23
    package statement in 24–25
final modifier 49–51
    final classes 49
    final interfaces 50
    final methods 50–51
    final variables 50, 179, 181, 258
finalize method 120
finally blocks
    both finally block and catch
        block return 362–363
    modifies return value from
        catch block 363–364
    overview 361–362
float data type 76–77
flow control 244–294
    break statements 276–277
    continue statements 278
    do-while loops 272–274
    enhanced for loops 265–270
        limitations of 268–269
        nesting 269–270
    for loops 260–265
        initialization block 262–263
        nesting 264–265
        termination condition 263
        update clause 263–264
        vs. enhanced for loops 275
        vs. while loops 276
    if-else constructs 245–253
        (braces) in 249–251
        expressions for 251–252
        missing else blocks 248
        nesting 252–253
        overview 245–247
    switch statement 254–260
        arguments passed to 257
        break statements in 259–260
        overview 254–256
        values passed to label case
            of 258–259
    while loops 271–272, 275
foo() method 397, 403–404
for loops 91, 201, 251, 260–265
    enhanced for loops 265–270
        limitations of 268–269
        nesting 269–270
    initialization block 262–263
    nesting 264–265
    termination condition 263
    update clause 263–264
    vs. enhanced for loops 275
    vs. while loops 276
fully qualified names 32–33, 54

functions
  overloaded 132–135
    access modifiers for 135
    argument list for 133–135
    overview 133
    return type for 135
    trick to remembering rules
      for 135
  parameters for 129
  return statement for,
    overview 131–132
  return type of 125–127

G

garbage collector 120
get method 217
getAge() method 145, 407, 443
getAverage() method 112–113
getInt() method 362–363
getModel() method 427–428,
  480
getName() method 150, 155,
  157, 385, 420, 466
getPageCount() method 429–
  430, 483
getScreenSize() method 418,
  464
getShadeCount() method 420,
  467
getSpecialization()
  method 407–408, 443–444
getStringBuilder() method 364
Getter method 145
getWeight() method 126–127,
  152
Gray, John 84
guru() method 395, 400

H

hashCode() method 225
hasNext() method 212
hexadecimal number
  system 74–75, 99
Home() method 415, 459
House class 38
HRExecutive class 310, 312

I

identifiers, for data types 80–82
if-else constructs 91, 112, 118,
  245–253
  (braces) in 249–251

expressions for 251–252
missing else blocks 248
nesting 252–253
overview 245–247
IllegalArgumentException 374,
  378, 388, 392
IllegalStateException 374, 378–
  379, 392, 396, 403
immutable strings 182
implemented interface, variable
  of 312–313
implements keyword 304–305
implicit object references 319
import statement 24, 34
  in classes 16–17
  in source code files 24–25
  using packaged classes
    without 34
  using simple names with 32–
    34
importance of certification 2,
  10
importing
  classes from default
    package 36
  subpackages 35–36
indented code 254
indexOf() method 175, 182–
  183, 226
IndexOutOfBoundsException
  375–376
information hiding 152
inheritance 295–347
  casting 316–318
    need for using 318
    overview 317–318
  interfaces 304–310
    class cannot extend multi-
      ple classes 308
    implementing
      multiple 308–310
    properties of members
      of 307–308
  polymorphism 324–347
    and binding of
      variables 329
    with classes 324–328
    with interfaces 330–347
  reference variables 310–
    315
    need for using 315
    using variable of base
      class 312
    using variable of derived
      class 311–312

    using variable of imple-
      mented interface 312–
      313
  super object reference 321–
    323
    accessing constructors 322
    accessing variables and
      methods 321–322
    in static methods 323
  this object reference 319
    accessing constructors 320
    accessing variables and
      methods 319–320
    in static methods 323
  with classes 296–304
    abstract base class vs. con-
      crete base class 304
    base class members
      inherited 301
    base class members not
      inherited 301
    concentrating on special-
      ized behavior of
      classes 300
    derived class contains object
      of base class 300–301
    derived classes can define
      additional
      properties 301–302
    ease of modification 298
    extensibility 298–300
    logical structures and
      grouping 300
    smaller derived class
      definitions 298
initialization
  arrays 201–204
  block, of for loops 262–263
  blocks, vs. user-defined
    constructors 139–140
  of objects 120–122
  statements 261, 281
inner class 37
inner loops 264–265, 269, 277–
  278, 283
insert() method, StringBuilder
  class 194
instance attributes 21
instance methods 21
instance variables 115–116
instanceof operator 377
int data type 73–76
intArray 198
integer literal values 98
integer values 71

interfaceArray 205
interfaces 304–310
  abstract 49
  class cannot extend multiple
    classes 308
  final 50
  implementing multiple 308–
    310
  overview 21–22
  polymorphism with 330–347
  properties of members
    of 307–308
invalid identifiers 81
Invalid method 149
IOException class 351
ISBN object 476
isPrime method 114
issueCount variable 42
issueHistory method 42–44
isTested() method 114–115
iterators 268

J

Java Development Kit. *See* JDK
Java Runtime Environment. *See*
  JRE
Java Virtual Machine. *See* JVM
java.io.File class 351
java.io.FileInputStream
  class 351
java.io.FileOutputStream
  class 351
java.io.IOException class 351
java.lang.Error class 370, 373,
  388, 390–391, 393
java.lang.Exception class 369–
  370, 388, 390, 395, 401
java.lang.IndexOutOfBounds-
  Exception error 218
java.lang.Object class 120
java.lang.RuntimeException
  class 370–371, 388, 390,
  401
java.lang.Throwable class 354,
  370, 388–390, 395, 401
java.sql package 34
java.util package 34
java.util.Date class 125
JavaBean 146
JDK (Java Development Kit) 180
JRE (Java Runtime
  Environment) 32, 182
Jump() method 423, 432, 472,
  488

Jumpable() method 405, 440
JVM (Java Virtual Machine) 20

K

key-value pairs 225
keyword class 14–15, 19–20
keywords 81

L

L suffix 75
labeled break statements 279
labeled continue
  statements 279–294
labeled declarations 279
Laptop() method 421, 430–431,
  468, 485
LaserPrinter() method 411, 450
lastIndexOf method 217
LaunchApplication class 25
length() method 403–404, 406,
  441–442, 518
letters variable 184
Librarian class 38–39, 42, 44, 46
life cycle, of objects 120–124
  initialization 120–122
  when accessible 122–123
  when inaccessible 123–124
limitations, of enhanced for
  loops 268–269
Lion() method 406, 433, 440,
  489
List interface 207
literal value 72
local variables, scope of 112–114
localVariableInLoop()
  method 113
logical error 252
logical negation 95
logical operators 94–96
  && operator 95–96
  || operator 95–96
long data type 73–76
looping constructs 112

M

Magazine() method 434, 492
main method, for executable
  applications 26–28
Manager class 296–298, 300,
  324, 326, 330–332
marking questions 11
marks variable 254

McDonald's example 44
members of arrays 206
MethodAccess class 349–350
methods
  abstract 49
  arguments 127–128, 161–163,
    167–168
  calling on objects 148–150
  chaining, for String class 185–
    186
  final 50–51
  overloaded 132–135
    access modifiers for 135
    argument list for 133–135
    overview 133
    return type for 135
    trick to remembering rules
      for 135
  parameters for 129
  parameters, scope of 114–115
  passing object references to
    changing state of passed
      object 156
    keeping passed object
      unchanged 155–156
  passing primitive data types
    to 153–154
  return statement for,
    overview 131–132
  return type of 125–127
  signatures 367, 370–373, 401
  static 52–53
  super object reference
    for 321–322
  this object reference for 319–
    320
MiscMethodsArrayList4
  class 219
MobileAppExpert
  interface 330, 332
mock exam 405–439
mock exams 9–10
mock tests
  before exam 9
  preparing for exam using 10
modifiers 37–53
  abstract modifier 48–49
    abstract classes 48
    abstract interfaces 49
    abstract methods 49
    abstract variables 49
  default access 42–45
  final modifier 49–51
    final classes 49
    final interfaces 50

modifiers *(continued)*
final methods 50–51
final variables 50
overview 38
private access modifier 45–47
protected access modifier 40
public access modifier 39
static modifier 51–53
static methods 52–53
static variables 51–52
where to use 38
modify() method 379
modifying, elements in ArrayList
class 212–213
modifyTemplate() method 40–
41, 45
modifyVal method 154
msg variable 127
multidimensional array 198,
200–201, 203–204, 226,
229–230
multiline comments 17–18, 56
Multiple.java file 24
MultipleChoice interface 30
MultipleExceptions class 359
MultipleReturn() method 363–
364
multiplication operators 97
mutable, StringBuilder class 190

N

native method 48
nestedArrayList 266
nesting
arrays 266
class 37
collections 266, 269
enhanced for loops 269–270
for loops 264–265
if-else constructs 252–253
loops 264, 269, 277–278,
283
try-catch-finally blocks 367–
368
new keyword 200
new operator 82, 121, 177
no-arg constructor 322
NoClassDefFoundError 373–
374, 386–387, 391, 393
non-abstract methods 328
nonaccess modifiers 47–53, 125
abstract modifier 48–49
abstract classes 48
abstract interfaces 49

abstract methods 49
abstract variables 49
final modifier 49–51
final classes 49
final interfaces 50
final methods 50–51
final variables 50
static modifier 51–53
static methods 52–53
static variables 51–52
no-name package 36
nondecimal numbers 73–74, 98
nonexecutable classes, vs. executable classes 25
non-nested arrays 266
Nonprivate object 148
nonstatic methods 111, 115, 132
NOT operator 95
NullPointerException 379–382,
403–404
num parameter 114
number systems 74
NumberFormatException 374,
382–384, 392, 397, 403
Numeric data types, overview 98
numeric values 99

O

object reference variables 82–
85, 310
defined 82–83
vs. primitive variables 84–85
object references, passing to
methods
changing state of passed
object 156
keeping passed object
unchanged 155–156
objects
calling methods on 148–150
fields in
defined 145
reading and writing 145–148
life cycle of 120–124
initialization 120–122
when accessible 122–123
when inaccessible 123–124
OCA (Oracle Certified
Associate) 2–8
comparison of exam
versions 3–4
FAQ 8–11
importance of certification 2,
10

OCA vs. OCP exams 4
readiness checklist 4–8
OCP (Oracle Certified
Professional) 4
octal number system 74, 99
Office class 137
oldLaptops variable 381–382
one-dimensional array 174, 198,
203, 226, 229
OpenFile class 349–350, 371
operating system. *See* OS
Operator type 87
operators 85–97
and String class 186–187
arithmetic 89–92
– (unary decrement)
operator 90–92
++ (unary increment)
operator 90–92
assignment 87–89
logical 94–96
&& operator 95–96
|| operator 95–96
precedence of 96–97
relational 92–94
!= operator 93
= operator 93–94
== operator 93
OR operator 94
Oracle Certification Candidate
Agreement 12
Oracle Certified Associate. *See*
OCA
Oracle Certified Professional.
See OCP
orbit variable 77
OS (operating system) 354
outer loops 264, 269–270, 279–
280, 283
OutOfMemoryError 374, 387–
388, 391, 393
overloaded constructors 142–
145
invoking from another
constructor 144
overview 144–145
overloaded methods 132–135
access modifiers for 135
argument list for 133–135
overview 133
return type for 135
trick to remembering rules
for 135
overridden method 302, 327,
336, 341

P

package accessibility 42, 57
package statement
  in classes 16
  in source code files 24–25
packages 29–37
  defining classes in 30–31
  importing classes from default
    package 36
  importing single member
    of 35
  importing subpackages 35–36
  need for 29–30
  static imports 36–37
  using packaged classes with-
    out using import
    statement 34
  using simple names with
    import statements 32–34
Paper() method 431, 487
parameters, for methods 129
parent class 303
parseInt method 76, 383
Passing object 155, 161
Pen() method 435, 492–493
Person object 83
Person.class file 14
Person.java file 14
Person() method 84, 121, 163,
    168, 410, 496, 499
phNum variable 127
Phone class 115, 152, 431, 486
Phone() method 116, 126–127,
    151–152, 419, 481, 486
phoneNumber variable 119
polymorphism 324–347
  and binding of variables 329
  with classes 324–328
  with interfaces 330–347
positive integer 78
postfix notation 90–92, 96, 100
PostIt() method 432, 487
precedence, of operators 96–97
prefix notation 90, 92, 100
preparing for exam
  and experience 9
  time required for 9
  using mock tests 10
primitive data types 70–80
  boolean 72
  byte 73–76
  char 78–79
  confusion with names of 79–
    80

double 76–77
float 76–77
int 73–76
long 73–76
overview 98
passing to methods 153–154
short 73–76
primitive decimal type 257
primitive variables, vs. object ref-
    erence variables 84–85
printEmp() method 146–148
printHello() method 128
printKing() method 409, 446
println method 132, 362
println() method 132, 251,
    284, 287–288, 292–293,
    372
printlnBool method 133
printlnInt method 133
printlnString method 133
printName method 330
printVal method 125
private access modifier 45–47
private members 301
private modifier 138
Programmer class 296–297, 331
properties, of members of
    interfaces 307–308
protected access modifier 40
protected members 301
protected modifier 138
public access modifier 39
public class 23
public members 301
public modifier 138

Q

question() method 419, 466
questions, displaying 12

R

reachOffice method 324
read() method 359, 415, 458
readiness checklist 4–9
reading object fields 145–148
receiveCall() method 151
receiveSalary() method 308
recursion() method 386
reference variables, using
    inheritance 310–315
  need for using 315
  using variable of base
    class 312

using variable of derived
    class 311–312
using variable of implemented
    interface 312–313
relational operators 92–94
  != operator 93
  = operator 93–94
  == operator 93
remove() method 213, 268
replace class 181
replace() method 175, 182, 184,
    226
  String class 184
  StringBuilder class 196
reserved words 81
resetValueOfMemberVariable
    method 157
result variable 80, 114
retaking exam 11
rethrowing exceptions 366–367
return keyword 132
return statements 243, 279, 283
  for methods 130–132
  for overloaded methods 135
Return type 135
ReturnFromCatchBlock
    class 361
returnVal variable 363–364
reverse() method, StringBuilder
    class 195
rideWave() method 426, 477
RiverRafting class 357–358
rowRaft method 357–359
RuntimeException 370–372,
    380–381, 390–392

S

scope, of variables 112–120
  and variables with same
    name 118–120
  class variables 116–117
  instance variables 115–116
  local variables 112–114
  method parameters 114–115
  overlapping scopes 117–120
  overview 117–118
score, received immediately 11
scrollable middle section,
    engine UI 12
Season() method 416, 460–461
semicolon character 261, 273
sendInvitation method 299–
    300
sendMsg method 128

separate packages 24, 29, 32–33, 54, 56–57
ServerConnection class 25
setAverage method 112
setModel method 125
setName() method 122, 150
setNumber() method 508
Setter method 145
setTested method 114
setWeight mehtod 125
shallow copies 219
short data type 73–76
short int data type 79
short-circuit operators 95–96, 101, 108
single quotes 99
SingleClass.java file 22
size() method 217
SmartPhone() method 419, 428, 465, 481
SMS() method 379
softKeyboard variable 116
source code files
    classes in 15–21
        comments in 17–19
        constructors for 21
        declaring 19
        defined 20–21
        import statement 16–17
        instance attributes 21
        instance methods 21
        package statement 16
    import statement in 24–25
    interface in 21–22
    multiple classes in 22–23
    package statement in 24–25
specialization variable 317
square brackets 199, 229
StackOverflowError() method 395, 400
starAge variable 145
startProjectWork method 324
startProjectWork() method 326
startsWith() method, String class 185
static bottom section, engine UI 12
static imports 36–37
static initializer block 384–386, 393
static keyword 116, 384
static method 132, 380, 384–385, 392

static modifier 51–53
    static methods 52–53
    static variables 51–52
static upper section, engine UI 12
static variables 51–52, 119, 271, 273
StoryBook class 38–42, 44–46
strictfp modifier 48
String class 121, 171, 175–189, 510
    and operators 186–187
    charAt() method 182
    counting objects 178–179
    creating objects 176–179
    determining equality of 189
    endsWith() method 185
    indexOf() method 183
    length() method 185
    method chaining 185–186
    methods don't modify char array 181
    replace() method 184
    startsWith() method 185
    substring() method 183
    trim() method 184
    uses char array to store value 180–181
String value 76
String() method 430, 438, 485, 498–499
StringBuffer class 197
StringBuilder class 6, 189, 364, 472
    append() method 192–194
    creating objects 190–191
    delete() method 195
    deletecharAt() method 195
    insert() method 194
    is mutable 190
    replace() method 196
    reverse() method 195
    subsequence() method 196–197
    trim() method 195
StringBuilder() method 423, 471, 510
strings
    String class 175–189
        and operators 186–187
        charAt() method 182
        counting objects 178–179
        creating objects 176–179
        determining equality of 189

endsWith() method 185
indexOf() method 183
length() method 185
method chaining 185–186
methods don't modify char array 181
replace() method 184
startsWith() method 185
substring() method 183
trim() method 184
uses char array to store value 180–181
StringBuilder class 189
    append() method 192–194
    creating objects 190–191
    delete() method 195
    deletecharAt() method 195
    insert() method 194
    is mutable 190
    replace() method 196
    reverse() method 195
    subsequence() method 196–197
    trim() method 195
Student() method 407, 442
subclassing 298, 303, 333–334
subpackages 29–30
subsequence() method, StringBuilder class 196–197
substring() method 175, 182–183, 226
super keyword 319
super object reference 321–323
    accessing constructors 322
    accessing variables and methods 321–322
    in static methods 323
super() method 322, 490
swap method 156
switch statement 112, 254–260
    arguments passed to 257
    break statements in 259–260
    overview 254–256
    values passed to label case of 258–259
synchronized methods 48, 197
syntactical errors 252

T

Tablet() method 418, 429, 464, 482
termination condition, of for loops 263
tested variable 115

TestEmp class 140
testing engine, used in exam 12
this object reference 143–144
    accessing constructors 320
    accessing variables and
        methods 319–320
    in static methods 323
three-dimensional array 198,
    226, 229
ThrowIllegalStateException
    class 379
throwing exceptions, instead of
    handling 367
ThrowNullPointerException()
    method 380
throws statements 279, 283
time, remaining 12
toArray() method, ArrayList
    class 220
todaysDate method 125
toLowerCase method 181
totalPages() method 434, 492
toUpperCase method 181
Trace class 356
transient variable 48
transmit() method 379
trim() method
    String class 184
    StringBuilder class 195
try blocks 279, 283
tryAgain() method 395–396,
    401–402
try-catch-finally blocks 118, 158
    both catch and finally blocks
        have return 362–363
    finally block modifies return
        from catch block 363–
        364
    finally blocks in 361–362
    nesting 367–368

order of exceptions caught
    by 364
overview 356–359
using multiple catch
    blocks 359–361
TryFinally() method 396, 402
Twist in Tale exercise
    answers 502–518
two-dimensional array 198, 201–
    202, 204, 226, 229–230, 237

U

UML (Unified Modeling
    Language) 16
unary decrement (–)
    operator 90–92
unary increment (++)
    operator 90–92
unary operators 97, 100
unchecked exceptions. *See* run-
    time exceptions
underscores 99, 383
Unified Modeling Language. *See*
    UML
unscored questions 9–10
update clause, of for loops 263–
    264
UserData class 25
user-defined classes, comparing
    for equality 221–223
user-defined constructors, vs. ini-
    tializer blocks 137–140
UserPreferences class 25
utility methods 52

V

val variable 267
valid identifiers 81, 100

variables
    abstract 49
    as arguments 128
    binding of 329
    final 50
    of base class 312
    of derived class 311–312
    of implemented
        interface 312–313
    scope of 112–120
        and variables with same
            name 118–120
        class variables 116–117
        instance variables 115–
            116
        local variables 112–114
        method parameters 114–
            115
        overlapping scopes 117–
            120
        overview 117–118
    static 51–52
    super object reference
        for 321–322
    this object reference for 319–
        320
void keyword 128
volatile variable 48

W

while loops 91, 260
    overview 271–272
    vs. do-while loops 275
    vs. for loops 276
white spaces 184, 228
wildcard character 35
Window class 25
writing, object fields 145–
    148